BURNING WOMEN

Burning Women

A Global History of Widow Sacrifice from Ancient Times to the Present

JOERG FISCH

Translated from the German by
REKHA KAMATH RAJAN

london new york calcutta

Seagull Books
Editorial Offices
1st Floor, Angel Court, 81 St Clements Street
Oxford OX4 1AW, UK

1 Washington Square Village, Apt 1U
New York, NY 100012, USA

26 Circus Avenue, Calcutta 700017, India

Seagull Books 2006

ISBN 1 9054 2 203 2

British Library Cataloguing-in-Publication Data
A catalogue of this book is available from the British Library

This book was first published in German as
TÖDLICHE RITUALE: DIE INDISCHE WITWENVER BRENNUNG
UND ANDERE FORMEN DER TOTENFOLGE

Typeset by Guru Typograph Technology, Dwarka, New Delhi 110045
Printed and bound by Biddles Ltd, King's Lynn, UK

Contents

List of Tables and Maps

List of Illustrations

(pp. 489–511)

Abbreviations

EPW	*Economic and Political Weekly*
IOL	India Office Library
IOR	India Office Records
NS	New Series
PP	Parliamentary Papers
RE	*Real-Encyclopädie der classischen Altertumswissenschaft*

Introduction

On 29 November 1895 Richard Hartley Kennedy, a British medical officer in the Indian city of Baroda, witnessed an incident which shocked him to the core. That morning a Brahmin had died. His widow—a woman of about thirty—had decided to accompany him into death. The British Resident, who represented the interests of the colonial power in the nominally independent princely state of Baroda, tried in vain to stop the woman from carrying out her plan. 'The poor widow walked steadily and unassisted to the scene of her sufferings, and seemed in no way shaken from her steadfastness of purpose, though of necessity she had fasted the whole day, and must have been severely tried by previous vigils, in attendance on the dying man, so that she had everything against her, and nothing but an iron superstition to support her.' He continued:

> She displayed a calm dignity. [. . .] Her manner was wonderfully collected, and even graceful. I knew how matters stood a great deal too well to annoy her by any expostulation, but I took one quiet opportunity, unobserved by her people, to whisper in her ear, that if she felt any misgiving, my presence would prevent it from being too late, even at the supposed last moment. But her look of reply was quite sufficient; she had not come without counting the cost. Her belief in the Pythagorean doctrine of transmigration was firm and fixed; and she looked forward, without a doubt, to secure for herself and her husband, by this sacrifice, a new life of happier existence, and more refined enjoyments than the sordid realities which the world now offered; and her nearest relations about her were evidently of the same opinion, and as perfectly satisfied on the subject as herself.

Kennedy was distressed at 'the apparent sang froid and apathy of all concerned.' Only a small girl, the daughter-in-law of the widow, clung to her with an expression of horror. The latter remained unmoved. 'There was a kind of loftiness of manner in the victim herself, a gracefulness of speech and attitude, approaching to my conception of the sublime, or the inspiration of a Pythoness at the delivery of an oracle.'

The widow then distributed fruit and sweets to all those gathered and said a friendly word to all of them. The people acted as if 'she stood before them a representation of Divinity, or rather as an incarnation of Divinity, herself a present goddess, capable of conferring blessings, and warding off future evils. [. . .] her countenance all the time indicating rather the smiling joyousness of a festival, or elation of a triumph, than the gloom and sorrow of her husband's funeral, or the horror and alarm natural to the thrilling moment antecedent to her own death by fiery torture.'

Three or four middle-aged women now also promised to immolate themselves on their husband's pyre if he happened to die before them. The present victim had made a similar promise on an earlier occasion. 'She, however, exhibited no sign of reluctance, but conducted herself as one who met her fate with as much inward feeling of alacrity and readiness, as she undoubtedly did with all outward show of super-human fortitude.'

The funeral pyre was then erected and the dead body placed on it. A hut of sorts was built above the body. When everything was ready, the widow stood up 'with the most calm serenity; and, though she was to join them no more, she left them with the most tranquil quietude. No alarm on her part, no sorrow on theirs, was expressed or apparent; no parting tears were seen, no farewell sighs heard. They stood silent, and she went unmoved.'

First, various ceremonies were carried out, during which the priests received many gifts. Then 'she walked calmly and deliberately, without receiving or needing assistance, to the pile.' When she saw the pyre, however, 'she betrayed a startled agitation.' In order to distract her, the priests started reciting prayers loudly. 'But their distrust of the poor victim's self-command was altogether unnecessary; her feelings were again under control in a moment, and she resumed the calm composure and self-possession she had hitherto displayed.' She walked around the pyre thrice. 'The rest of her family continued standing where she had left them, looking on with a stupid stare, which, whether it were apathy and indifference, or profound admiration and astonishment, I know not. No expressions of grief were heard, nor a tear, that I could see, was shed, except by the poor child, her daughter-in-law.' Suddenly the crowd erupted in a 'loud frenzied burst of adoration'.

The widow looked into a mirror and said she was now burning herself for the fourth time. In order to achieve salvation she would have to do it a fifth time (in another life). This would happen in Benares.

In order to minimise her suffering a kind of neckband made of inflammable material was placed around the widow's neck. 'She now stepped forward; and, without any alteration of appearance or manner entered the pile.' According to the prescribed ritual she had to call out 'Ram! Bhaie! Ram!, but her cries were in a deep sepulchral, hollow tone, the sounds breaking forth in the most distressingly unnatural resemblance of the human voice I ever heard.' The priests were again alarmed and began to shout. The widow however had quickly regained control and 'bent forward to take leave of them with smiles, and the most perfect composure.' She then lay down on the pyre, in the 'hut'. This was then barricaded with blocks of wood, rendering any attempt to escape impossible. A priest still spoke to the woman. Her voice betrayed the same agitation as before, 'as if she were at last entirely overcome, and struggling in vain with the horrors of her mental agony, and quite conscious of the misery of her situation.'

Finally the widow's twelve-year-old son lit the pyre with 'trembling hand'. At once, about fifty more small fires were kindled, so that the whole pyre was aflame in less than two minutes. Kennedy remained as close to the pyre as the heat allowed. 'I think I should have heard any unrestrainable shriek of the extreme agony had it been uttered; and observed any convulsive movement, or desperate attempt to break forth, had it been made. I do not think that either took place. I saw her last lying down, and embracing the corpse, and I heard her voice to the last, as if she had never changed her position; and I confidently believe she did not change it.' Kennedy assumed that the widow had died almost immediately from asphyxiation.

The approximately 500 onlookers gathered there dispersed quickly, 'no doubt highly edified and gratified. [. . .] The entertainment was over.' The female relatives 'of the poor victim' were 'in a state of bewilderment and sorrow, but no voices were heard'.

Kennedy was so impressed with what he had seen that he prefaced his report with the following lines:

Of woman's
Worth supreme, her nobleness,
Of what she can achieve, and what endure,
Her loftiness of soul, with all her gentleness.[1]

[1] Kennedy. The report first appeared in 1843 in a journal, and in 1855 in independent form, without details of its first printing.

In 1803 the Frenchman Pierre Labarthe published an account of a journey to the West African coast in Guinea, in which he described the funeral customs of the kings of Dahomey.

There can be nothing more barbaric than the ceremonies that follow the death of a king of Dahomey; one cannot imagine customs more horrible than these; just writing it down makes one shudder.

As soon as the death of a king is announced, eight men dig a grave roughly 12 feet deep and 7 feet long, which is called the grave of the Water God. A bed is laid out in this grave, which is decorated with all the valuables that the dead man has left behind. On top of this a doll is laid out, wrapped in different kinds of materials. The eight men who have dug the grave then climb onto this structure, and as they climb up, their heads are chopped off, one after the other, and their bodies are thrown out onto the fields as prey for the wild beasts. Then the wives of the dead king arrive in large numbers and vie with each other for the honour of being buried with the dead king, in order to serve him in the next world. Only 24 wives are chosen for this honour and the rest wail and scream against the injustice meted out to them.

In order to maintain the delusion of the unlucky victims, the grave of the dead king is supplied with a large quantity of corals, with brandy, tobacco, pipes, with trimmed hats, gold and silver tobacco boxes, and with three gold-studded and three silver-studded canes.

The wives are enjoined to take great care of the king, to sprinkle him with brandy, to cover him with aromatic herbs, to see that he has enough to drink and smoke and to purify his body every day with incense. As soon as this speech comes to an end the women throng to the graveside and each wants to be the first to climb down into the grave. First however, in accordance with a barbaric custom, their legs are broken with a club. As soon as all of them are in the grave, it is closed and covered up with earth. For five days after that cannons are fired.

After a certain period of time has elapsed the great mourning cere-mony is held, and the commandants of the European colonies, the tributary princes and all the big and small chiefs are expected to at-tend. The Europeans are expected to bring presents of brandy, silk, hats and cowries, which are the coins of this country. The tributary princes have to each give four slaves of each sex, an ox, a ram, a pigeon, two ducks, a Pintado cock and 24 bottles of palm oil. Each big and small chief gives two slaves of each sex, a horse, an ox, a ram, two pigeons, 12 Pintado cocks, 12 ducks, 200 calabashes of cowries, each of which is equal to ten French livres, a piece of red silk and eight pieces of Silesian linen.

Soon afterwards the slaves, horses, oxen, rams, etc. are sacrificed to the spirits of the dead king; the corpses are then thrown out into the fields for the beasts of prey.[2]

The contrast between the two accounts could hardly be starker. The widow of Baroda stands self-assured in the midst of unfolding events. With stoic calm, unflinching, with enormous self-control and an iron will she goes to her death. She dictates the course of the ceremony, and the foreign observer, who makes no secret of his aversion to the custom of widow-immolation, cannot deny a feeling of admiration for the victim.

In Dahomey too it is said that some of the victims go voluntarily to their death. Yet doubts in the matter are justified, and the overall impression is one of innocent and uninvolved people being led to the slaughter.

However, if one disregards the spectacular aspects of both scenes and concentrates instead on their inner substance, the similarities become evident. The occasion in both cases is the death of a person. Other people follow this person into death, in one case apparently voluntarily, in the other probably under a lesser or greater degree of coercion. The killing or the self-killing takes place in a ritualised manner, within the framework of a larger, public ceremony. The circumstances clearly show that the intended goal is to reunite the deceased with his attendants in the next world.

The event described above is called 'following into death' (Totenfolge) and is defined as follows: 'After the death of a person one or more persons follow him or her into death in a ritualised and public act, voluntarily or involuntarily.'

Leaving aside possible differences in the more specialized uses of these words, the term following into death is also referred to as—as the case may be—'custom', 'practice', 'ritual', 'ceremony' or 'institution'.

The requirement of ritualisation means that the custom is not an isolated, solitary incident, but one that repeats itself, not necessarily in all, but, at least, in some similar cases.

The public nature of the event is decisive, although the size of the gathering can be restricted to a certain extent. The ceremony need

---

[2] Labarthe, French edition 123–6.

not be open to all. However it presupposes an audience. It is not a private matter concerning only the person going to his/her own death, or, in the case of death being brought about by a third person, of the victim and the killer alone. Rather, it unites the living with the dead through the person of the victim. The public witnesses and ratifies the event and it is only through this that it gains legitimacy in the community concerned.

Ordinary suicide cannot, therefore, be categorized as a following into death. It often occurs after a person has died. Someone who feels particularly close to the deceased, or is dependent on him, commits suicide out of a sense of grief or despair, or also in the hope of meeting the deceased in the next world.

This presents us with a certain conceptual inconsistency. The desire to be reunited with the deceased, to follow him into death, does not require either a ritual or spectators in order to be validated. A person committing suicide may well believe that he is following the deceased into death. It would, therefore, be necessary to distinguish between a narrower and a wider concept of following into death, where the narrower concept includes only the public, while the wider one takes into account the private following into death. Here, as a rule, only the narrower concept is taken into consideration. The resulting limitation of the study cannot be justified on the sole grounds that the topic would otherwise take on far too great an area as its province. Further justification is sought in the fact that the ritualized, public following into death is a clearer indicator and, at the same time, a more recognizable product of social conditions than is the private act.

The death of an important person and, particularly, of a ruler can spark off a power struggle, in which members of a rival party kill the followers of the deceased, whose camp has become weak as a result of his death. So long as the killing doesn't take place publicly and in a ritualized manner, this cannot be considered a following into death. The same holds good for acts of revenge of all kinds, in which private or political opponents are killed following the death of the ruler. This does not mean, however, that the custom cannot also occasion a change of power. Indeed, it is distinctly characterized by such aspects. These, however, must occur in the framework of particular forms that both create and ensure the legitimacy of the event.

What is decisive is the inner substance and not the external procedure. Burnings and self-burnings as well as other forms of killing and self-killing occur in various other contexts which have nothing to do with following into death. The burning of witches and heretics is just such an example. These are not part of our study.

A terminological problem arises while making a distinction between the person who gives cause for following the dead, and the person who accompanies the deceased. A clear linguistic differentiation is missing. In this study the former is generally referred to as *the deceased* or *the dead person*. Occasionally the more unwieldy term *the one to be accompanied* or *the accompanied* is used. The person who kills himself/ herself is sometimes called *the attendant*, more often however simply *the victim*.

Following into death is a very widespread, yet at the same time an extremely rare, phenomenon. Written accounts of such events are available from all parts of the world. These accounts are supported by archaeological evidence. Within a society, however, the custom is always an exception. Historically, only very few people have been accompanied into death by others.

For the first time, this book places the custom of following into death in a larger context. It goes into the origins, the prerequisites and the causes, the different forms, the functions and the frequency of this custom. What makes people voluntarily accompany others in death, or what makes them force other people to accompany the dead? What are the social conditions that give rise to such customs and what effect do these customs, in turn, have on society?

Today the custom is a thing of the past. The last known widow burning in India, however, occurred as recently as 4 September 1987.

The disappearance of the custom (or its suppression) in modern times, and particularly in the nineteenth and twentieth centuries, is mainly a result of the Europeanization of the world, of the worldwide spread of European power and, simultaneously, of European values, partly in the form of Christianity and partly in the form of a secularized moral code, emphasizing questions of equality and human rights. Had the suppression of the custom only been a result of external forces, it would not have been so complete, and, moreover, it would have resurfaced after the end of colonial rule. With the exception of India, this did not happen anywhere else, and even in India it occurred only a long time after independence and in a much weaker form. The success with which this custom was abolished, the unfolding and history of this success, can be seen as reflecting both the physical and intellectual power of Europe.

The gradual suppression of the custom is also taken into consideration here, although the sources allow an extensive treatment of only India. Following the dead as an independent phenomenon is not the focal point of interest in this context. Rather, what commands our attention is the custom as a catalyst for issues that characterize modernity and even more present times. The central question here is: How does one construct the relationship between the respect for cultural individuality and the universal claim of moral norms? The clash between the two views is particularly strong in this case. Is following into death a custom that has cultural and, more importantly, religious sanction, or is it simply a crime? A distant observer would simply say that it is a matter of perspective. This reply however does not suffice in practice, where the viewpoints are mutually exclusive and where a clear distinction between tolerance and suppression is demanded. Attempts to reconcile these contradictory aspects are doomed to failure. The British law of 4 December 1829, which made widow burning in India a punishable crime, condemned this practice as 'revolting to the feelings of human nature. It is nowhere enjoined by the religion of the Hindus as an imperative duty.'[3] However a custom, even a religious one, is, as a rule, not prescribed in conclusive terms. The British tried to avoid a decision by referring to the religion of the people involved, whereas, in the final instance, it was only the universal claim of European norms, introduced with reference to 'human nature', which was decisive. The practice itself was at least consistent with Hinduism, even if the religion did not prescribe it.

Structure and Methodology

The treatment of the phenomenon of following into death is marked by two factors.

1. The custom is a historically universal phenomenon, but it cannot be portrayed in the form of a universal history. The assumption that it arose somewhere and then gradually spread can be neither proven nor refuted. It appears time and again in history. The interconnections between its different forms, however, cannot be determined.

---

[3] Bentinck 1, 360. The formulation has been taken over in the more stringent law of 1987. Instead of Hinduism, however, the new law uses the more general term 'Indian religions'. *The Commission of Sati (Prevention) Act, 1987,* Preamble.

2. The origins of the custom cannot be reconstructed. Wherever it appears in written documents, it is already a fully developed institution, and must, therefore, have developed earlier. There are no documents that explain when and how this happened. Archaeological evidence, which dates back to earlier times, also does not throw any light on this question.

This has implications for the structure and methodology of our study. The description is primarily typological and systematic in its approach: what forms of the custom are found in the course of history? What are their causes, conditions and functions and how widespread are the different forms? The basic division is a geographical one, in which the different regions of the world are looked at one after the other. Since widow burning in India is better known and better documented than all other forms of following into death, the space devoted to India is larger than for all the other regions taken together. These regions are discussed in the first part. The second part is about India, and develops the insights gained in the first part, but it is also complete in itself and can therefore be read independently.

The typological-systematic approach dominates the study of individual regions as well. The sources allow a description of historical developments only in exceptional cases. To some extent, this is possible in the case of widow burning in India; the description of the suppression of this custom however allows for a more complete historical analysis.

The internal coherence of the study is, therefore, not a result of the coherence of a story, but the unity of the phenomenon under study, which is followed through in its diverse constellations. On the one hand, it becomes a reflection and an indicator of, and on the other, a factor in the interplay between aspects of this world and the next. What is interesting are the effects that views of the hereafter have on this world under concrete political and social conditions and how, vice versa, these conditions also affect those views.

Origins and Causes: Belief in the Hereafter and Inequality

Since the origins of following into death cannot be determined historically, the question will have to be formulated differently. How, and under what general conditions, could the custom have developed?

What conditions made such a custom possible and what triggered it off?

At this stage only two necessary conditions for following of the dead will be mentioned. Partly they can be derived empirically from the available material and partly they are the result of systematic analysis.

1. The sources indicate very clearly that the decisive precondition for following into death is a particular form of belief in the hereafter.[4] This is not to suggest by any means that the custom cannot have, and that in fact it does have, different kinds of material functions in this world. These include ensuring the power of ruling groups, enabling the appropriation of the victim's property by family members and a strengthening and deepening of inequality between the sexes. But wherever there is a more or less detailed description of the custom, the next world also comes into play. The term 'following into death' takes this into account. Systematic analysis also supports such a connection. If all belief in the hereafter were missing, then the persons concerned—the victim and the onlookers—would not be able to understand why someone should choose to die on the occasion of the death of another person. If the deceased has dissolved into nothingness, a reference to this person is no longer possible. The custom then degenerates into a mere (self) killing, even into a suicide, and is unable to maintain itself in the long run as a public ritual, legitimized by society. A marked belief in the hereafter on the other hand provides an unambiguous justification for society. The annihilation of a life is partly compensated for by the belief that the person killed has not been destroyed, but has merely been sent to another world, where his/her position cannot be any worse, and indeed may be better than in this world. More importantly, the person accompanying the dead will be at the service of the deceased even in the next world and will be able to lighten his burden or improve his life. The loss suffered by this world constitutes a gain in the hereafter.

This means that not all forms of belief in the hereafter can become the basis for following into death. Christianity and Islam do have very definite conceptions of the hereafter. Yet the custom has never

[4] The latest comprehensive overview of this is in Braun. Addison gives a useful overview. For more general aspects, see Lang/McDannell and Klimkeit.

been a part of these religions, and, in fact, they often opposed it very strongly. The decisive factor is the analogy drawn between this world and the next. The next world is, in effect, a continuation or a copy of this world and not its contrasting image. In particular, the social order of this life is considered to be a part of the hereafter too. This possibility is negated when conceptions of the hereafter are placed within a moral framework of any form of judgement after death.[5] This implies that one's social position in the hereafter is not linked with one's position in this life, but with the person's conduct in this life. If an individual can have a completely different position in the other world, if, for example, the rulers in this are the damned in the other, while the inferiors in this are the blessed in the other, then there is no justification for accompanying someone into death. If, on the other hand, rulers remain rulers and servants remain servants, then the custom merely re-creates the order of this life in the next. If the persons accompanying the dead are offered the promise of a better status, a further incentive is created for them.

2. If one takes the form of belief in the hereafter described above seriously, the consequences are problematic. The ultimate aim is to transfer the surroundings with which the deceased was familiar as completely as possible to the next world. Therefore, he has to be accompanied not only by all the objects with which he was surrounded, but by all the living beings as well, especially all the people with whom he lived. This applies to all those who die. If this were to be carried out to the letter, all human life in this world would soon be wiped out. Consistently applied, the custom would lead to its own end by destroying its own preconditions. If life is destroyed, death cannot occur.

There are two possible ways out of this dilemma.

(a) The claim remains valid in principle, but it is not carried out. Everyone has the right to be accompanied by others. But this possibility seldom materializes. This limitation helps prevent the self-destruction of society and at the same time ensures that the custom retains its egalitarian character.

(b) The above possibility does not exist in practice. The custom is never socially neutral, neither in theory nor in practice. Everywhere,

---

[5] On judgement after death, see Brandon.

it is built into very clear structures of inequality. If a general right to be followed in death can potentially destroy society, then it has to be limited. Only certain categories of people have the right to be accompanied in death. Therefore *social inequality* becomes the second necessary precondition of the custom.

Following into death thus combines material and spiritual aspects, this life and the hereafter, in an exemplary fashion. It blends serious social conflicts with sublime spiritual aspirations. Any attempt to reduce the phenomenon to any one of the two aspects leads to a distortion and makes it impossible to understand it adequately. The reasons behind the burning of a widow could be the intention of relatives to get rid of her, to appropriate her wealth and save the cost of her upkeep. This does not mean that the victim cannot go to her death the way the widow of Baroda did. One aspect cannot be refuted by means of the other.

At the same time, it becomes evident that following into death is not an anthropological constant, but that it presupposes certain social conditions, especially developed structures of inequality. These however form a necessary but not sufficient condition. Neither modern European societies nor colonial societies in which the custom was suppressed distinguished themselves by particularly egalitarian conditions.

Institutional and Individual Following into Death

The death of the ruler is the occasion for carrying out following into death in Dahomey. The social status of the deceased leads to a following into death. If the deceased had been of lower status, then he would have had either no one accompanying him, or just a small following.

Kennedy does not tell us anything about the social, political or professional status of the husband of the widow of Baroda. This is not a coincidence. The woman's decision to burn herself to death had nothing to do with status. She did not burn herself as the widow of a ruler, a high official, or of any other important personality, but as the widow of her husband.

Depending on the social position of the people involved, the custom takes on different forms. To understand this, two types are distinguished here, with the help of which actual cases can be classified and analysed. The distinguishing criterion is the question as to whether the circle of people in a particular society who have the right to be accompanied in death by others gain this right by virtue of their class or their status.

1. If class is the decisive factor, only highly placed people are entitled to be followed into death. This group could include only the ruler, or also the family of the ruler, or the nobility, or all top military commanders, or all those in high office, or all who possess a certain amount of wealth, etc.

Determining the circle of those entitled to be followed into death does not, however, help in ascertaining the circle of those bound to accompany them. Normally, these would come from the lower classes. However, not everyone who does not have the right to be followed into death is, necessarily, obliged to accompany someone else. The persons who are made to accompany the dead could also be taken from another society, either as prisoners of war or as slaves bought expressly for this purpose. A certain amount of overlapping is also possible: when highly placed persons, who are entitled to be accompanied themselves, have to accompany a ruler into death. This type is called *institutional following into death*.

2. Distinctions on the basis of status are to be found at all levels of society. In our case, the most important distinction is that of gender. Status distinctions also include age, relationship, citizenship, etc. Those entitled to be followed into death are members of a particular sex (in actual terms it is always the men), or the aged, or the fathers or the parents-in-law, etc. What is important here is the fact that these conditions are not specific to a particular class. Even the poorest and most insignificant husband can insist upon his right to be accompanied (by his wife).

In contrast to institutional following into death, the circle of those obliged to accompany the dead is determined by a specific intra-societal division. It is always the other part of a given society: husbands have to be accompanied by their wives, the old by the young, children by their parents, etc. This type is called *individual following into death*.

Institutional and individual following into death[6] are mutually exclusive on the basis of their underlying principles. If membership of the nobility or the ruling family determines the right to be

---

[6] This distinction is not to be confused with the distinction sometimes to be found in the literature on suicide between institutionalized (not institutional)

accompanied in death, then gender cannot play a role, and women also have to be accompanied, insofar as they have acquired the required social position, i.e. are allowed to become rulers. If, conversely, the status as husband confers such a right, then no man can be excluded from this on the basis of poverty, bondage, etc. These examples show that, in practice, combinations and mixings do take place, and that, in the first case, women and, in the second case, poor or socially inferior men are probably excluded, or that men are accompanied both by their wives and by their male servants or slaves. It is, therefore, important to ask in each case the extent to which a concrete example of the custom has an institutional or an individual character.

In the course of this study the specific differences between both forms of following into death will be elaborated progressively on the basis of numerous examples. However, some of the guiding aspects and categories can be presented here.

The point of departure is the personal relationship between the accompanied person and the person accompanying the dead. It can cover the entire scale from complete anonymity to complete intimacy, from the slaughter of people chosen indiscriminately from a crowd to the self-killing of a spouse after decades of marriage. Initially it is not important whether the personal relationship is characterized by affection or aversion, love or hatred.

In individual following into death there is, normally, a more or less close personal relationship between the accompanied person and the attendant. The institutional form, on the other hand, tends to be characterized by anonymity, although personal relationships are by no means excluded, as, for example, when a ruler is accompanied by his wives, concubines, servants, officials and other subordinates. Apart from these, however, any number of categories of attendants, having little or nothing to do with the deceased, can be used. In all probability, this constitutes a relatively late development. If one proceeds from the viewpoint that following into death is linked with a belief in the hereafter, then one can assume that originally the deceased were

---

and individual suicide. The latter occurs out of personal motives, while the former is a social affair. Following into death, insofar as it occurs through self-killing is, by its very nature as a public act, always institutionalized suicide. See Cavan 66–74; Fedden 17–19. Durkheim's distinction between egoistic (=individual) and altruistic (=institutionalized) suicide is also part of this: Durkheim, chaps 2–4.

accompanied by people who had a close personal relationship with them, since the idea was to be surrounded by familiar people in the next world. Taking along strangers (and particularly enemies) presupposes a view that could hardly have existed in the beginning: that the attendants would behave like familiar people in the next world, that enmity would not continue there.

The closer the bond, the greater the possibility that the persons accompanying the dead would go to their death voluntarily. If uninvolved persons are slain, for example, it is not possible to get the consent of the victims in advance. The probability of agreement and therefore of self-killing (as opposed to killing by others) is greater in individual than in institutional following into death.

In the case of institutional following into death, the number of victims is, in principle, unlimited. The smaller the circle of those entitled to be followed into death, and the higher the position of the entitled individual, the greater the possibility of a large number of victims. On the contrary the number of victims in the case of individual following into death is generally limited: the husband is accompanied by the wife, and, in cases of polygamy, by the wives. But the number of those entitled is larger, making it difficult to say in which case the total number of victims is greater.

A particularly important distinction between both these types concerns their functions in this world. Both types serve to emphasize and strengthen the position of those who have the right to be followed in death. The divisions within a society, however, determine the nature of the position. Institutional following into death has to do with the political system, with the position of the ruler or the ruling class. The individual form falls within the realm of social conditions, particularly the matrix of gender relations, in which the dominance of one sex over the other (concretely, of men over women), or of the old over the young, or a hierarchy among relatives, is endorsed. Both these functions are mutually exclusive. The king cannot demonstrate his power over the beggar with the help of the custom if the beggar is also entitled to it, and the power of men over women cannot be maintained if men also accompany women into death.

Free Choice and Coercion

Labarthe says that women fought for the honour of being killed at the grave of the ruler. This may have happened in some cases. The surrounding circumstances, however, lead one to the conclusion that normally there was no question of a free choice to die. The mass killing, indeed the slaughter of the victims, of those linked with the deceased as well as of strangers, supports this conjecture.

The burning of the widow in Baroda is a completely different case. Kennedy was watching closely for any signs of weakness, and, more than that, for any indications of unwillingness, coercion or the use of force. There could have been pressure from the relatives, but such pressure would certainly have been evident in the widow's behaviour. Also, on the occasion of an earlier widow burning, she had already announced her intention to burn herself to death with her husband. She was not unprepared at the moment of decision.[7]

Yet, even an Indian widow, who—as seen from the outside—burnt herself to death willingly, was a victim of various compulsions. Often what was in store for her was a life of poverty, devoid of all social contact, and of being regarded as a lesser being. Her decision to burn herself to death was taken immediately after the death of her husband—taken therefore in a state of shock. Often family members and priests would urge her to it. She had grown up in a society in which socialization was based on the subordination of women to men.

Can one, or should one, speak of an act of free choice under these circumstances? Wasn't the widow the victim of constraints, of structures that in the final analysis left her with no choice, or, in other words, wasn't she the victim of structural violence?[8]

It is, indeed, very important to point out the conditions leading up to an act, conditions that in one way or another influence the decision to embark upon an action, and that can, therefore, be interpreted as pressure being brought to bear on the person acting. In this

[7] Contradicting this is the fact that the entrance to the 'hut' was barricaded with stumps of wood, thus preventing the widow from escaping. This procedure points to problems that are discussed extensively in chap. 12. One can proceed from the fact that from the point of view of the widow the barricading of the entrance was part of the normal course of events and that she did not object to it. Seen objectively, escape was made impossible. Subjectively, however, her behaviour continued to demonstrate free choice. She knew the course of events. Before mounting the funeral pyre she could have refused to carry on.

[8] For the concept of structural violence see Galtung, and for a critique, Faber *et al.* For a general overview cf. Posern.

perspective, an act of free choice would be one in which no external force is applied. Seen from a social perspective this would mean a point in time when all inequality disappears, and a perfect egalitarian society free of all domination is established. This may be an important and significant perspective for the future, perhaps also a regulator for action in the present. With reference to the past, however, one can only state that there has never been a socially relevant act of free choice under such premises.

The argument also obscures important distinctions. We are concerned here with the difference between the structural conditions for a decision and the decision itself, i.e. the action resulting from it. The conditions are an expression of existing inequalities and structures of power which influence actions to a lesser or greater degree. Nevertheless, the action itself can be carried out willingly or unwillingly. What cannot be ignored in the case of following into death is the question of free choice. At the most, one in a thousand widows in India burnt herself to death. If one tries to deduce from the undoubtedly unfavourable structural conditions obtaining in India that one widow had no other option, that she was in fact forced to burn to death, then it isn't possible to explain why the other 999 widows didn't act in the same manner. Certainly, as with other forms of following the dead, one has to talk about the victims of a system, or, more precisely, of structures of inequality that are expressed in this custom. But in the concrete manner in which someone becomes a victim we have to distinguish between free choice and coercion. One cannot equate the manner in which the widow of Baroda went to her death with the burning of a widow who is dragged to the funeral pyre and tied down to it, or with the indiscriminate slaughter of those gathered at the funeral of a ruler. If such differences are sacrificed for an undifferentiated concept of force and violence, important aspects of the problem cannot be understood, and, in the end, no justice is done to the victims either. Therefore, the question of free choice and coercion is tackled here in two steps. Firstly, it must be established whether the action itself was voluntary or forced. The criterion for that is to ask whether the victim could have survived had he/she acted differently. This obviously does not apply only in cases where open force is used, quelling any resistance, but also when there is a clear threat of violence, and the victim knows that she will be killed if she doesn't kill herself first. In other cases, one would have to initially assume free choice, since the victim could have survived if she had acted differently. Secondly, one would then have to go into the degree of freedom inherent in the choice. This would entail a study of the conditions that favour a decision or impede it.

Following into Death and Human Sacrifice

Following into death is often studied in connection with human sacrifice and it isn't unusual to find the two customs being equated with one another, especially since till now there has been no consistent and comprehensive description of the phenomenon of following the dead.[9] Indeed, there are numerous correspondences in the external aspects of the process, especially when others kill the victim. Yet, even in human sacrifice a self-killing cannot be ruled out.

What is decisive is the inner substance, which is basically different. Sacrifice[10] is underpinned by the principle of human service and a hoped-for, expected, or received return from the god, or gods, in whose honour it is carried out. The higher the expected or received return, or the greater the threat to be averted, the greater must be the value of the sacrifice. The most valuable thing that can be sacrificed is man, whereby, especially when the gods demand it, even the person in the highest position is not excluded. The sacrifice of a ruler is a widespread phenomenon.[11] In contrast to following into death, human sacrifice is compatible with all forms of belief in the hereafter.

The practice of following the dead exists in a completely different context. It is not addressed to any god; it is carried out for the sake of a dead person. In its original form, at least, the living who organized the custom did not expect any returns from the deceased. They merely wanted to ensure that he would get what was due to him: company in the other world. Only in this way could they ensure their own chances of being accompanied in death.

Paradoxically, it is this link with the life hereafter that gives following into death its specific political significance in this world. Human

[9] Particularly evident in Maringer who in the title speaks only of human sacrifice, although he is primarily studying following into death. Davies in his book on human sacrifice published in 1981 also deals with following the dead without drawing a conceptual distinction between the two.

[10] For an overview of the latest discussions, cf. Van Baal and Henninger.

[11] This is one of the central themes in Frazer, *The Golden Bough*.

sacrifice *can* have positive repercussions for the entire community. The positive effects of following the dead, however, are limited to the circle of those who are also entitled to being accompanied. The custom serves to demonstrate and strengthen their power at the cost of those who are obliged to accompany the dead. It is, therefore, linked in a completely different way to structures of inequality than is human sacrifice. The ruler, at least, cannot become the person who accompanies another.

Despite this, following into death can contain certain elements that are comparable to those of human sacrifice: when the dead are imagined to be gods who can influence events in this life. Providing persons to accompany the dead then *also* serves to attain the help and protection of these gods or to deflect their attacks and infringements. In this way the custom assumes the character of a sacrifice without, however, becoming identical to it.

When the term 'victim' that is used in the context of following into death, it is used as one would normally use it, for example, when speaking of the victims of an accident. It is used here because the persons accompanying the dead are often called 'victims'. This does not mean that the process is considered a sacrifice. The victims of following into death fall prey to the custom, they are not offered up as sacrifice to anyone.

PART I
Following into Death Outside India

CHAPTER 1

Egypt and
the Ancient Near East

Egypt

In Upper Egypt a large number of tombs of the pre-dynastic era were found (*c.* 2900 BC), in which several dead people were interred.[1] In each of these the corpse of a man occupies a central position. Around it, as a rule, between one and four women are interred, sometimes with a child and/or another man.

It is not possible to prove beyond doubt that the inmates of the tomb were interred at the same time, and that they therefore died more or less at the same time. Nevertheless, various circumstances speak in favour of this theory. The hierarchical arrangement of the corpses, in particular, leads one to think of a following into death. However, the simultaneous deaths could also have had other causes.

The findings from the period of the First and Second Dynasty are more revelatory (*c.* 2900–2640 BC).[2] Big burial grounds—which were therefore called *royal tombs*—were found throughout the country. These have a burial chamber in the centre, in which presumably the main person is interred. Around it there are more chambers, most of which contain several interred persons, who are clearly of a lower status as seen from the funerary objects. Everything is oriented towards the main person, i.e. towards his chamber. Each burial ground contains up to 590 skeletons. Obviously the symbolism and the hierarchy of the court had to be kept intact in death. However, it is possible that the laying of the grounds and the burials took place over a long period of time so that the order of the living was only gradually carried over into a corresponding order of the dead. Nevertheless there is

[1] Green 112–18; Reisner, *Kerma* 67; 73–4.
[2] Green 112–18; Reisner, *Kerma* 67; 74; Reisner, *Egyptian tomb* 108; 118–21; 350–1; Emery, *Archaic Egypt* 62–90; 135; 152; 158; Murray 87; Gadd 52–3.

evidence that in some cases the burials occurred at the same time. This indicates the possibility that at least part of the court accompanied the ruler into the grave.

Tombs such as these disappear with the Second Dynasty, first in the north, then in the south. Similar findings are then missing for the period up till the Middle Kingdom (*c.* 2040–1650 BC). For the period in question George A. Reisner found, not in Egypt itself, but in Nubia, in Kerma, hundreds of multiple burials in a single field of tombs above the third cataract.[3] Arranged around a central corpse, prominent due to its position and outfitting, there are between one and twelve other corpses, mostly of women, predominantly young, but also of children and babies. There are also many bigger tombs, some of which have several chambers. Reisner found up to 322 human skeletons in them. Since most of the tombs had already been plundered much earlier, he estimated that the original number of persons interred must have been between 50 and 400. On the basis of different kinds of evidence he believed he was justified in drawing the conclusion that all of them had been interred at the same time. If this is true, one can state with almost absolute certainty that one is dealing here with following into death. Reisner, at any rate, was convinced that this was the case. In fact, he wrote of 'Sati-burials' (*sati* being the term used for widow burning in India). Reisner assumed that the big tombs contained the remains of the Egyptian governors of the Sudan, their wives and children, but also members of the court. This assumption is supported by further evidence. The arrangement and position of the dead show that they were interred alive. Some women, for example, tried to save themselves by creeping under the resting place of their master or mistress. The positions of other skeletons also point to the fact that there was a struggle for survival in the grave.[4] However, it is difficult for a lay person to arrive at any definite conclusions based on the arrangement of the skeletons in graves that had been plundered earlier.[5]

[3] Reisner, *Kerma* 65–79 and *passim*; Green 118–22. Kerma is situated about 1300 km south of the Nile delta as the crow flies, in what is today North Sudan.

[4] Reisner, *Kerma* 70.

[5] Even authors of more recent excavation reports on Kerma are certain that the custom was practised there to a great extent. Bonnet, *Excavations* 621–3; Bonnet as well as Simon *et al.*, in Bonnet (ed.), *Kerma* (1990) 71–3; 83; 106–7.

What, then, are the possible assertions that can be made with regard to following into death in Egypt? One cannot talk of a commonly practised custom. Nevertheless, the custom of kings and rulers being accompanied in death by members of their family and servants could have occurred for a while in pre-dynastic times in the south and, then, mainly during the First and Second Dynasty. After that, however, every trace of the custom disappears for several centuries, till it reappears again for a period of about 400 years in the Middle Kingdom, concentrated this time however in a single region, i.e. in Upper Nubia. Of course, the reliability of the sources, i.e., of the finds, has to be taken into account.

The question of motives is even more speculative. Reisner is convinced that death was, as a rule, voluntary. His conclusion is based on the belief in the hereafter. 'Thus self-sacrifice as practised in the sati-burials at Kerma was not a cruel inhuman thing, but rather a kindly custom, an act of loyalty which provided both him who had died and those who offered themselves to a living death, with the assurance of the continuation of the long-accustomed family life in the other world.'[6] Probably twentieth century ideals of a happy family life are responsible for this idea, rather than any interpretation of realities. The large number of victims, and the fact that they were interred alive, allows for reasonable doubt: that 400 people willingly accompanied another person into death, out of sheer devotion and in the hope of a better life in the other world, is hardly possible.

However, Reisner's indication of a belief in the hereafter is of great significance. The arrangement of the graves and the funerary objects indicates that the custom was to be seen in the context of notions about life in the hereafter. Such notions generally played an extraordinarily important role in Egypt.[7] The idea was to take as many of one's possessions as possible to the next world. In the light of such strong notions of the hereafter one wonders why following into death wasn't more widespread and why it is never mentioned in written documents. Whether this was a result of an early humanization, or whether it meant that the rulers and the aristocracy were not able to prevail, remains a matter of speculation.

Along with human skeletons, many of the tombs in Kerma contain the skeletons of rams, and in some these skeletons were in fact

---

[6] Reisner, *Kerma* 77 and *passim*; Reisner, *Egyptian tomb*, *passim*.
[7] Cf. Kees, Morenz and Brandon, chap. 1.

more numerous than others.[8] However, it is not clear whether these were also the later tombs. At any rate, one can suppose that humans as funerary objects were gradually replaced by animals. The evidence is by no means conclusive, especially if one does not consider the custom as sacrifice (in which humans can be replaced by animals), but as a following into death: animals can take over the work of humans— as servants, ministers or spouses—only in a very limited way.

What is more plausible, even though not proven historically, is the explanation for another phenomenon. An extraordinarily large number of graves contain clay figures (*ushabti*). They portray human beings carrying out different kinds of jobs—including that of guards. Scholars agree that these figures were meant to relieve the dead person of all the tasks he would be obliged to carry out in the other world.[9] The same holds true for the human figures painted on the walls of the burial chambers. In both the cases, we are dealing with functional equivalents of following into death that spare the living. This function is hardly a matter of dispute. The question that remains unresolved is whether a causal connection can be established. There are no reports that the clay figures first appeared in places where following the dead can be supposed to have existed. Later statements could simply be rationalizations: the custom of placing clay figures in the tombs, the origins of which are not known, are explained through the obvious, but by no means convincing, assumption of a humanization of following into death through substitution.

Despite the existence of a very strong belief in the hereafter, the custom of following the dead could not gain predominance in Egypt. This could be due largely to the idea of a Judgement of the dead, which gained ground around the middle of the third millennium.[10] If one's position in the other world is decided only after death, then taking along earthly possessions cannot secure it.

After the Middle Kingdom, there is no reference to the custom for about 2000 years. It is surprising to find traces of it again after the Roman period. Many tombs from the period between the fourth and the sixth century AD were discovered in Nubia, in which skeletons of

---

[8] Reisner, *Kerma* 71; 98 and *passim*; Bonnet, in Bonnet (ed.), *Kerma* (1990), 73–7.

[9] See Speleers; cf. also Green 147–8; Kees 129–30; Černý 91–4.

[10] Brandon, chap. 1.

horses, donkeys, camels, sheep and dogs were found. Near them lay the remains of the servants who had tended these animals, as well as those of other people charged with menial tasks, and especially those of women. It seems obvious that a part of the royal court had to accompany the ruler, or an important person, into death. The victims' bodies show no trace of violence, leading one to assume that they were first drugged.[11]

Sumer

During excavations in a large complex of tombs in Sumerian Ur in southern Mesopotamia in 1927/28 the British archaeologist Leonard Woolley found sixteen tombs which have become famous as the *Royal Tombs*, although today it is no longer believed that only kings were interred there.[12] Far greater care seems to have been taken on these tombs in comparison with the others. In contrast to the thousands of other tombs, these contained between six and eighty skeletons, indicating multiple burials. The corpses in each tomb seem to have been interred at the same time. The smaller tombs consist of only one chamber. The corpses are arranged around a central figure, a man or a woman, with the jewellery, the other funerary objects, and the posture distinguishing this central figure. The other deceased are arranged around it in positions that clearly indicate a menial status. In the bigger tombs the central chamber contains only the main figure and two or three female servants. The rest of the dead lie in a large entrance hall. Most of the skeletons here are of women arranged in proper order. Expensive jewellery indicates persons of high rank. Some have musical instruments next to them. There are also skeletons of armed men and animal drovers. In addition, the remains of war chariots and the skeletons of oxen and chariot drivers were found. Everything that one imagines as being part of a personal retinue is gathered here. However, only a few tombs display this kind of extravagance.

In contrast to Kerma, the skeletons in Ur did not bear the marks of a death struggle or of physical violence. On the contrary, they lay in normal positions and in a proper order, provided that robbers had

---

[11] Emery, *Nubia* 64–87.

[12] A detailed description is in Woolley, *Ur Excavations*, vol. 2. The revisions which have occurred since then have been incorporated in Woolley, *Ur 'of the Chaldees'* (1982) 51–103. Cf. Green 45–58.

not disturbed the tomb. From this we can conclude that the inmates of the tombs were either already dead or at least unconscious when the tombs were closed. Near each of the deceased Woolley found small bowls, which, he assumed, were drinking bowls, containing a poisonous or narcotic fluid. The victims, according to him, went into the tombs voluntarily, perhaps they sang and played music before drinking the poison and then lying or sitting down to die.

Woolley's interpretation has never been seriously questioned. What remains controversial however is another point that is significant for the present study: Are we dealing here with following into death or with human sacrifice? From the beginning Woolley vehemently argued in favour of the former. He assumed that rulers had been interred here with their court which would serve them in the other world too. Already at the time of excavation an alternative interpretation appeared, which was based on a kind of fertility cult and sacrifice.[13] In the framework of an annual ceremony to guarantee the fertility of the soil a symbolic marriage was said to have taken place between a priestess and the god of fertility, or a priest in the role of the god. Both were then killed along with their retinue.

For non-specialists this controversial question is difficult to resolve. Research today generally accepts Woolley's interpretation, since most of the evidence matches it. A comparison also favours this interpretation: Finds such as these occur in other places more often in connection with following into death than with human sacrifice. Time and again, one finds an entire court accompanying an important figure or a king into death, while human sacrifice on this scale and of so many persons of high rank—and that too apparently of a voluntary nature—has not been proven anywhere, neither archaeologically nor in written documents.

Although this evidence of following into death is convincing, it remains an isolated phenomenon in the history of the Ancient Near East. Woolley first dated the tombs between 3500 and 3200 BC.[14] Today they are generally placed between 2600 and 2450 BC.[15] Although the complex of tombs at Ur spans a much longer period of

[13] According to S. Smith (1928) 863–8 and Böhl (1930). Cf. for the controversy along with Woolley's writings Green 48–53.

[14] Woolley, *Excavations at Ur* (1928) 418.

[15] Woolley, *Ur 'of the Chaldees'* (1982) 51; Green 237.

time, even here we do not find anything relating to the custom from other periods.[16] Written sources with reference to following into death are absent not only in Egypt but in the entire Middle East—with one exception. One of the Sumerian Gilgamesh tales from the period around 2000 BC tells the story of Gilgamesh's journey to the underworld. His wife, his son, his concubine, his musicians and other servants are also mentioned. The possibility that these people represent his retinue for the underworld cannot be discounted. But it is by no means an indisputable fact, and what is even more uncertain is whether they died at the same time as he did.[17]

The link with the belief in the hereafter remains unresolved. In contrast with Egypt, Ancient Near Eastern notions of life in the hereafter proceeded on the assumption that all, both high and low, would lead a miserable existence after death in which individual differences in rank would no longer play a role. Therefore the question of being served in the other world did not arise.[18] Yet, it is possible that by taking one's retinue one hoped to be able to avoid such an outcome.

[16] Cf. Woolley, *Ur 'of the Chaldees'* 88; 131–2; 173–4; Green 53–6.

[17] Kramer, Gilgamesh 4, 6, 10; Kramer, *Sumerians* 129–35; on this Woolley, *Ur 'of the Chaldees'* 91–2 and, less sceptical, Green 85–6. Translation also in Pritchard 50–1.

[18] Cf. Brandon, ch. 2.

CHAPTER 2

Europe

Preliminary Remarks

In Europe, especially in the Christian tradition, following into death has, for centuries, been regarded as a barbaric, bloodthirsty custom, often even a crime. From this one could assume that European historical research has, as far as possible, tried to play down or even deny the existence of this custom, attempting to attribute such cruelty to the 'Other' rather than 'fouling up one's own nest'.

This assumption has been proven wrong. Since the nineteenth century various theories and speculations have existed about the supposedly extraordinarily important role of the custom in European history. In particular, the killing of widows is repeatedly characterized as a 'common Germanic', 'common European' or an 'ancient Indo-Germanic' custom. Maringer considers 'the occurrence of widow-sacrifice in early pre-historic Europe [. . .] to be an established fact.'[1] In conjunction with this the widespread occurrence of the custom on the death of rulers is regarded as self-evident. Following into death is supposed to have been gradually suppressed only in the Christian period.[2]

Such theories are based on speculation. There are very few sources and they usually deal with unverified findings. The method commonly used is to compare written documents and archaeological evidence and allow the two to corroborate each other. A dubious find is elevated to the status of a concrete piece of evidence on the basis of a written document that is no less dubious, and vice versa.[3] In order to

---

[1] Maringer 55.

[2] A comprehensive compilation of material of varying quality already existed in 1702 in Arnkiel, book 1, chaps 15–18. The hypotheses sketched above are mainly in Maringer; cf. in addition Ranke, Schetelig, Schreuer, Grimm, Dieck, Gaerte, Hirt, Hirzel and also M.W. Williams 419.

[3] For example Maringer 12–16; Schetelig 194–6; Gaerte 118–19. Substantially stricter standards are used for example by Engster and Preidel.

avoid these pitfalls, archaeological evidence and written documents will be considered separately.

These sceptical remarks could be criticized ideologically as an attempt to give Europe a special place in the history of the custom by proving that it has always been less prevalent in Europe than anywhere else. Such misgivings cannot be dismissed simply by the assertion of disinterested motives. Rather they are to be refuted on the basis that the same critical standard is applied to sources from all parts of the world. For the record, the custom is also absent in the Islamic world.

The Archaeological Evidence

As a result of extensive excavations all over Europe in the nineteenth century a large number of graves were discovered that could be connected with following into death.[4] The graves date from the third millennium BC to the first millennium AD. Johannes Maringer, in particular, has collated and evaluated these finds with respect to the questions that are of interest here. On the basis of hundreds of proofs Maringer came to the conclusion that these were cases of the killing or self-killing of widows. Along with this he saw cases of following into death by concubines, female servants and slaves, as also of male servants and slaves. Occasionally he even found a female ruler being followed into death by a male or female retinue.[5]

Most of the cases are double burials. The simplest thing to prove is that the corpses are of different sexes. The proof of simultaneous burial is plausible in many cases. It rests on the design of the tomb which excluded a later opening, or on the arrangement of the skeletons that are found, for example, in a position of embrace.

What is decisive, however, is the cause of death and the relationship of the deceased to each other. It is possible that both were victims of a crime, of war, a natural catastrophe, an illness or an epidemic. This assumption follows quite naturally when double burials are found to occur more rarely than single burials. In some periods however they occur quite often. In Thuizy near Reims (France), for example, there are twenty-eight double burials in a total of sixty-four

[4] For a broad overview over the older excavations see Ebert, *Reallexikon der Vorgeschichte*.

[5] For the different types cf. Maringer's Table of Contents.

graves.[6] But here, too, it is hardly possible to reach any definite conclusion. If one were to assume that they are all cases of following into death, then it would mean that the custom was very widespread. In fact, in specific situations, especially when the husband died, it would have been the rule. In the light of other evidence, and particularly on the basis of written sources, this appears highly improbable. At the most only one in a thousand widows in India burnt herself to death; in extreme cases, for a short period and in specific areas, it could have been one out of every fifty. Had burials been the common practice in India, the archaeological evidence would be very sparse.

At times, however, there are additional indications. The simultaneous burial of animals, particularly of horses, could be an indication of bloody burial rituals. In other cases, the corpse of the master shows no traces of violence, whereas those of the male and female attendants indicate a violent death. Yet indications such as these and others are by no means conclusive. If one applies a strict standard, the axiom must be that double burials are not sufficient proof of following into death.[7]

What remains to be considered is the proportionately small number of multiple burials.[8] In the case of three people being buried together the funerary objects often point out to the low status of the third person. This could therefore be a servant who was killed. In Gadebusch in Mecklenburg (Germany) two persons were discovered 'buried on a square stone slab as if on display and around them there were eight skeletons.'[9] In 1857 a female corpse was found in a cave near Granada. Twelve further skeletons, as well as an additional group of three, were arranged in a semicircle around her. Only a single corpse had a gold diadem. Although the details are not very precise,[10] the

---

[6] Maringer 31.

[7] Hughes 45–6 applies a less stringent standard. He considers double burials, in principle, to be archaeological proof of following into death, if the killing of the subordinate person can be proven, if indications of the ritual nature of the burial are present, and if there is enough corresponding archaeological evidence. Cf. also Jesch 25. Such conditions and similar ones can increase the probability of the custom, but they cannot be regarded as conclusive.

[8] Maringer 91–107.

[9] Maringer 15.

[10] Maringer 99.

theory of a mass burial can be advanced suggesting the improbability of the natural simultaneous deaths of all the victims.

In the 1920s a mound with fifteen skeletons from the Early Bronze period was found near Jois in the Burgenland in Austria. 'All except one had crushed skulls.' In the middle lay the skeleton of a man whose skull was intact. Next to him lay the skeleton of a six- to eight-year-old child. 'Lying across the male skeleton, near his knees, was the skeleton of a woman.' The other skeletons lay around this group of three.[11] It is possible to treat this as a case of following into death in which the woman, the children and the friends of the dead man were killed. It is equally possible, however, to picture a crime or the consequences of war. To talk of a common European custom of following the dead on the basis of such evidence would be erroneous.[12]

The Scythes are an exception in the European framework. Archaeological evidence concerning them has been found in the Ukraine and in Southern Russia, and they are far more numerous and present far stronger evidence than in any other region of Europe. These finds date back to the eighth century BC, but most of them are from the sixth to the fourth century BC.[13] Huge mounds, so-called *Kurgans*, measuring up to 21 metres in height and possessing a circumference of up to 130 metres, were found here.[14] Rulers, and possibly other important men, were buried in them. They have often been used for separate burials at different times. In addition, most have been plundered once or several times. This makes it difficult to determine the facts regarding following into death.

Most of the Kurgans contain several human skeletons along with numerous skeletons of horses. Both the arrangement as well as the furnishing of funerary objects are clearly hierarchical. The main figure

[11] Maringer 47; 97–8.

[12] Where Greece is concerned, archaeological evidence too has not been able to produce more than somewhat plausible results. Cf. Hughes 37–42; Karageorghis, *Salamis in Cyprus* 30–1; Karageorghis, *Salamis* 3, 9; 121.

[13] For overviews cf. Rolle, *Welt der Skythen*; Rolle, *Totenkult* 1, 1, 80–96; Grakow 57–66; 104–9; 119–20; 128–30; Ryce, chap. 3; Ebert, *Südrußland*, chap. 5; Ebert, Article 'Südrußland' in: Ebert, *Reallexikon* 13 (1928), 32–114; Potratz 36.

[14] Grakow 60–1. According to Grakow 58, thirty Kurgans were found by 1978.

is in the centre, and around it considerable wealth is put on display. Either few or no funerary objects surround the other dead people and they are found lying at the entrances or in adjoining rooms, often alongside the skeletons of horses. That the burials could have taken place at different times is a possibility that cannot safely be discounted with absolute certainty. At least in the (many) cases in which the corpses are all in the same burial chamber, a collective burial seems possible. The largest number of skeletons found in the same Kurgan, and probably buried at the same time, is thirteen.[15] Till now it has been proven that up to four persons accompanied the same dead person.[16] On the basis of the funerary objects, Rolle assumes that the high status of a dead man could be seen rather in status than in the number of those accompanying him.[17]

On the basis of this evidence archaeologists unanimously infer that the practice of following into death did indeed exist. The probability is strengthened by the fact that Herodotus gives a credible account of the custom among the Scythes, which corresponds to a great extent to the archaeological evidence.[18]

The custom of following the dead among the Scythes has a pronounced institutional character, since it can only be proven on the basis of the Kurgans, which were, obviously, reserved only for a small ruling group. This character is underlined by the fact that even women were among the privileged: more than once the main person in the grave is a woman.[19] Nothing definite can be said about the details of the killing. It cannot be proved that most of the victims went willingly to their death, as has been stated,[20] and, in fact, it seems rather improbable, since many corpses show traces of a violent death.

[15] Ebert, *Südrußland* 137–9 and Ebert, Article: Kostromskaja Mogila in: Ebert, *Reallexikon* 7 (1926), 55. Also see Grakow 104–9.

[16] Rolle, *Totenkult*, 1, 1, 144. The sources do not provide us with unequivocal statements as to the number of persons accompanying the dead which could be the result of the often inadequate quality of older excavation reports. It is absolutely certain, on the other hand, that the burial chambers contained several dead persons of differing status.

[17] Rolle, *Totenkult*, 1, 1, 96.

[18] Herodotus 4, 71–2. Cf. below, pp. 39–41.

[19] For example Rolle, *Totenkult* 1, 1, 90–2; Grakow 61–2.

[20] Rolle, *Welt der Skythen* 29; Rolle, *Totenkult* 1, 1, 90; Lincoln 195.

The Written Sources

Greece[21]

In accounts of Greek history there is not a single well-attested report about an event in Greece that could be interpreted unequivocally as a following into death. This is all the more remarkable since the earliest reports about widow burning in India came from Greek authors who would certainly have shown an interest in such practices. This suggests that similar practices did not occur in Greece during the period for which historical records have been found.

Literary sources, on the other hand, contain quite a few passages that fit into the context. The most famous one is perhaps the twenty-third song of the *Iliad*. After the death of Patroclus, Achilles takes twelve Trojans prisoners, deviating from his practice of slaughtering his opponents in his thirst for revenge. In order to burn the body of Patroclus he builds a massive pyre. He also slaughters numerous animals and throws them on the funeral pyre,

> And twelve valiant sons of the great-souled Trojans slew he with the
> bronze
> and grim was the work he purposed in his heart
> and thereto he set the iron might of fire, to range at large.[22]

On the basis of the external procedure this scene has to be interpreted as a following into death. On the occasion of the funeral of Patroclus other people are killed publicly, and in a more or less ritualized manner. On the basis of its inner substance, however, the event can scarcely be said to represent the custom. That the twelve victims were meant to be Patroclus' retinue, his servants for the other world, cannot be ruled out, although it is not mentioned anywhere in the text. It does not seem very probable either. Achilles' motives seem to be mainly anger, rage and a thirst for revenge. In the case of a following into death in the real sense the victims are killed primarily so that they may fulfil a function in the other world, not because of their deeds in this world. This holds true even for criminals sentenced to

---

[21] For an overview see especially Hughes; also Schwenn, Kurtz/Boardman, and for a more specialised account Heinrichs.

[22] Homer, *The Iliad* 23, 175–7, 507.

death. Their crime is merely the criterion for selection. If it were only a matter of *their* death, they could be executed in a more routine manner.

The event described by Homer does not resemble a following into death so much as a widespread killing of prisoners of war. This was done to exact revenge or to prevent their escape and not in order to provide servants for one's own killed.

If one treats the scene as a killing of prisoners, it is quite realistic. At least two similar cases have been recorded. In 183/182 BC the captive Achaean general Philopoemen was forced by the Messenians to drink poison. An Achean army then conquered the Messenian capital, took Philopoemen's ashes with them and buried them in their own capital. Captured Messenians were then stoned to death at the tomb.[23]

Here, the role of revenge is more obvious and the following the dead element is not as distinct as in the Homerian example. In any case, the special connection between Philopoemen and the victims isn't mentioned anywhere.

Revenge could also take the form of a punishment that maintained the outward trappings of a following into death. One author—not very reliable in all respects—reports that Alexander the Great had the murderers of his father, Philip II of Macedonia, executed at his grave.[24]

In literary sources, however, one can find evidence for, as it were, a classical following into death. In the tragedy *Supplices* by Euripides, Capaneus, one of the Seven against Thebes, dies, having been struck by Zeus' thunderbolt. His wife Euadne resolves to jump down from a rock onto the burning pyre. She regards her death as a proud, glorious, heroic act, the focal point of which is the belief in a reunion with her husband:

> From this cliff's brow
> For wifehood's glory,
> With spurning feet I dart
> Down into yon fire's heart
> To meet him, ne'er to part,—
> Flames reddening o'er me,—
> To nestle to his side,

[23] Plutarch, *Philopoemen* 18–21. Cf. Hughes 58; Schwenn 65.
[24] Justinus, *Epitome* 11, 2, 1. Cf. Hughes 57. Further examples ibid., 57–60.

In Cora's bowers a bride!
O love, though thou hast died,
I'll not forsake thee.[25]

A crowd is watching the events and does not intervene. Euadne's father Iphis then appears and urges his daughter not to carry out her intentions. She will not allow herself to be deterred and instead of one that mourns takes pride in her deed:

Euadne	Thou wouldst be no wise judge of my resolve.
Iphis	And why in this attire array thy form?
Euadne	Father, this vesture glorious meaning hath.
Iphis	Thou seemest not as one that mourns her lord.
Euadne	For deed unheard-of have I decked me thus.
Iphis	By tomb and pyre appear'st thou in such guise?
Euadne	Yea, I for victory's triumph hither come.
Iphis	What victory this? Fain would I learn of thee.
Euadne	Over all wives on whom the sun looks down.
Iphis	In works by Pallas taught, or prudent wit?
Euadne	In courage. With my lord will I lie dead.
Iphis	How sayest thou?—what sorry riddle this?
Euadne	I plunge to yon pyre dead Capaneus.
Iphis	O daughter, speak not so before a throng!
Euadne	Even this would I, that all the Argives hear.
Iphis	Nay, surely will I let thee from this deed.
Euadne	Let or let not—thou canst not reach nor seize me.
	Lo, hurled my body falls, for grief to thee,
	For joy to me and him with me consumed.[26]

To what extent is this dramatic scene true to life? At that time, in the late fifth century BC, it was probably an outcome of poetic fantasy. At any rate, no similar events have been recorded in Greek history. This suggests that conditions obtaining earlier are depicted in this scene. However there is no proof of this. While the story of Euadne and Capaneus is older, it is only Euripides who included or 'invented' the scene of Euadne burning herself to death.[27] This speaks against a corresponding Greek tradition.

[25] Euripides, *Supplices* 1015–24; cf. also Hughes 60–1; Schwenn 64; Escher, Article: *Euadne* 2, in: RE 6, 1 (1907), 818.
[26] Euripides, *Supplices* 1053–71.
[27] Hughes 60.

Hughes and Schwenn try to suggest that the episode exists entirely in the realm of poetic fantasy.[28] The passage cited, however, bears many similarities to detailed eyewitness accounts of widow burning in India. This always takes place in front of a large audience, which approves of the deed and often incites the widow to take the final step. The family members sometimes try to stop her. With heroic resolve she overcomes all opposition and regards her deed first and foremost as an act of loyalty to her husband. Fame in this world and reunion in the next are her primary goals.

The first Greek report about widow burning in India can be traced back to the first century BC, whereas its original sources, which have not been preserved, date back to the third century BC. The episode described in the report occurred in 316 BC, about a century after Euripides had written his tragedy (see pp. 217–18). If the similarity is merely coincidental, did Euripides then simply imagine something that came close to widow burning in India? Did he have documents at his disposal that have since been lost? Did he base himself on oral traditions? The sources do not provide an answer to these questions.

The same holds true for other scenes in literature, which are often to be seen in the framework of death out of love.[29] Generally, there is a tendency in Greece to attribute a number of customs that have died out, and that are considered to be barbaric, to one's own dark past. In this way an inversion can easily take place: the myths are no longer a mirror of actual conditions obtaining in the past, but project instead notions of the present about the past onto this past.[30]

The Greeks' knowledge about the custom of following the dead came not just from accounts of widow burning in India, as is seen from Lucian in the second century AD. He pours scorn on funeral customs of the Greeks and then says: 'But that is nothing. Have not many sacrificed horses, concubines, sometimes even cupbearers?' There were some, he says, who had also buried clothes and other objects with the dead person, as if they could use these in the other world.[31] From this

---

[28] Hughes 60–1; Schwenn 64.

[29] The well-known story of the dead Achilles appearing before his son Neoptolemus, and demanding that he sacrifice Polyxena on his grave, is not proven to have any correspondence in reality. Cf. Wüst, *Polyxena* 1841–3; Hughes 61–2; Schwenn 62–4.

[30] For this see Heinrichs 195–7; 204; 232–4; also Hughes 186–90.

[31] Lucian, *De Luctu* 14; Cf. Hughes 62–5; Kurtz/Boardman 215.

passage one cannot infer that such things happened in Greece, but only that accounts of such customs of other peoples were in circulation.

Rome[32]

Historical evidence for following into death in Roman history is lacking—with one possible exception. When Octavianus captured Perusia (Perugia) in the year 40 BC, according to Suetonius the following happened: 'Some write that three hundred men of both orders were selected from the prisoners of war and sacrificed on the Ides of March like so many victims at the altar raised to the Deified Julius [Caesar].'[33]

The focal point here is that of sacrifice as a form of pacification of Caesar, not that of following the dead. We are not told whether or how those killed are to be used in the other world, and what relationship would exist there between Caesar and them. This points to an act of delayed revenge. In addition, doubts about the story are in order. It is not handed down by any other source. Suetonius too distances himself with the words 'some write'.[34]

When we now go on to deal with the rest of Europe we must make allowances for the fact that the accounts refer to peoples who, for the period in question, did not leave behind their own written documents. Such peoples were portrayed as backward, barbaric and even inhuman, leading the authors to attribute the practice of following into death to them rather than to their own people.

The Scythians

In the fifth century BC Herodotus described in precise detail the funeral of a ruler among the Scythians who lived north of the Black Sea. The

---

[32] Overview in Schwenn 140–96.

[33] Suetonius, *Augustus* 15, trans. by J.C. Rolfe 141; cf. Schwenn 173. A similar event in a Near Eastern context can be found in the annals of Assurbanipal, who states that he 'massacred' enemy survivors as a 'sacrifice' to his grandfather. Streck 39.

[34] A possible connection to following the dead exists in the gladiator games, which are generally supposed to have originated from funeral games. The gladiators killed would then originally have represented something like the retinue for the dead person. However the sources do not furnish any precise indications, and certainly in the historical period concerned no one thought in terms of the custom. See K. Schneider 760–1.

embalmed body of the king is first taken throughout the country till it reaches the grave prepared for it. 'In the open space which is left in the tomb they bury, after strangling, one of the king's concubines, his cup-bearer, his cook, his groom, his squire and his messenger, besides horses, and first-fruits of all else, and golden cups. Having done this they all build a great barrow of earth, vying zealously with one another to make this as great as may be.'

After one year there is another death ceremony. The fifty best servants of the king and fifty of his best horses are strangled to death. The corpses of the servants are placed on the carcasses of the horses. 'So having set horsemen of this fashion round about the tomb they ride away.'[35]

What Herodotus describes here is a highly elaborate form of institutional following into death. This complex and destructive form must have been a ritual reserved for the ruler, in order to extol his power. At any rate Herodotus does not mention any ceremonies in connection with the death of ordinary people which could be interpreted as a following of the dead.[36]

Herodotus also does not supply any information about the background of this ritual. Yet one can detect links with notions of the hereafter.[37] The ruler is meant to go to the other world accompanied by surroundings familiar to him. This includes objects as well as living beings, humans as well as animals. The selection is carried out on the basis of proximity to the ruler in this world. However, this interpretation is only valid for the actual burial ceremony. If the slaughter of fifty servants and fifty horses at a later stage were a case of following into death, then these would probably be buried in the same mound as the ruler, or at least close to it. Instead the visible arrangement of horses and riders around the tomb leads one to assume that another aspect, later very widespread in Africa, played a role here: The people and horses killed were supposed to maintain the connection between this world and the next.

[35] Herodotus 4, 71–2.
[36] Herodotus 4, 73.
[37] Lincoln 191–5 emphatically rejects an interpretation in the sense of a following into death, since there are no indications of a belief in the hereafter among the Scythians. Instead he proceeds on the assumption of a simple suicide by the closest of the retinue because of a loss of their life-centre.

Are the assertions credible at all? Herodotus narrates all kinds of astonishing tales about distant peoples.[38] There are three reasons for these not to be considered as pure fiction. Firstly, despite the author's fascination for the subject, the description is precise and objective. Herodotus refrains from all moralizing commentary. What he narrates is at least not impossible. Secondly, the event described fits in the framework of what is known about the custom from other periods and other regions. Particularly, additional sacrifices on the death anniversary are common in Africa. Thirdly, the archaeological evidence that has already been mentioned. It corresponds to a great degree with Herodotus' description. Only the fifty riders arranged in the open are, naturally, not part of the archaeological finds. [39]

The Thracians

While Herodotus refers to institutional following into death in his account of the Scythians, he ascribes a particularly pronounced individual form to certain tribes living north of the Crestonaeans, in Thrace. Here

> each man having many wives, at his death there is a great rivalry among his wives, and eager contention on their friends' part, to prove which wife was best loved by her husband; and she to whom the honour is adjudged is praised by men and women, and then slain over the tomb by her nearest of kin, and after slaying she is buried with the husband. The rest of the wives take this sorely to heart, deeming themselves deeply dishonoured. [40]

A classic and stereotypical following into death by a widow is portrayed here. A certain artistic simplification is also evident. The statement that all men have many wives is either relevant for only a small group, making it an upper-class phenomenon, or else it cannot hold true. This idea that all women are eager to be killed when their husbands die is more male fantasy than reality. From this passage one can at best deduce that sometimes at the funeral of a leading personality one of his widows was killed, or that she allowed herself to be killed. Even

[38] For Herodotus' ethnographic methods cf. Nippel 13ff. and Lateiner 145–62.
[39] Similarly Lincoln 190–1.
[40] Herodotus 5, 5.

a statement such as this, however, needs to be considered carefully. Herodotus ascribes many strange, and sometimes perverse, customs to the Thracians. They form a kind of counter-world to the Greeks.[41] As the story of Euadne demonstrated, the topos of widow suicide was obviously already available in the fifth century BC. It is therefore possible that Herodotus merely took an element from another context and transferred it onto the Thracians.[42]

The Gauls

The function of a text to show the Other in a bad light becomes more prominent with Caesar. He writes of the Gauls: 'They cast into the fire everything, even living creatures, which they believe to have been dear to the departed during life, and but a short time before the present age, only a generation since, slaves and dependents known to have been beloved by their lords used to be burnt with them on the conclusion of the funeral formalities.'[43]

Caesar is cautious. He doesn't claim to be an eyewitness and he deliberately excludes the present. His account allows us only to draw one somewhat definite conclusion: Following into death was a known fact. Caesar certainly did not invent it. Maybe it occurred sporadically in Gaul. It could also have been a matter of rumours, or perhaps Caesar transferred something known from another context onto the Gauls. At any rate, it would be wrong to conclude from his account that this custom was practised regularly by the Gauls in earlier times, especially when one takes into account the fact that he was trying to justify his actions against them.

Late Antiquity

In the middle of the sixth century the Byzantine historian Procopius wrote the following about the North Germanic Eruli, settled between Morava and Tisza:

> And when a man of the Eruli died, it was necessary for his wife, if she laid claim to virtue and wished to leave a fair name behind her, to die

[41] Herodotus 5, 3–10.

[42] Herodotus' story was later taken over by Pomponius Mela 2, 2, 19 (middle of the first century AD) and Solinus 10, 3 (middle of the third century AD). Neither added anything new.

[43] Caesar, *The Gallic War*, 6, 19, 4.

not long afterward beside the tomb of her husband by hanging herself with a rope. And if she did not do this, the result was that she was in ill repute thereafter and an offence to the relatives of her husband. Such were the customs observed by the Eruli in ancient times.[44]

This account seems somewhat more realistic than the ones written by Caesar and Herodotus. Procopius does not say that all widows hanged themselves. Both the infamy of the widow as well as the marked interests of the husband's family are sufficiently well known from the Indian context. And yet the passage poses certain problems. Procopius, too, is careful to speak only of the past. Apparently he did not have access to eyewitness accounts. The passage is part of an extended description, in which many kinds of deviant and especially repugnant customs of the Eruli are discussed; the author evidently wished to harm the reputation of the people he described. Therefore, one has to take into account the fact that he might have inserted an element known to him from other contexts, even though one cannot negate the possibility that this form of killing widows did indeed occur from time to time. Had it been more widespread, Procopius would certainly have written about it in greater detail.[45]

The stereotypical way in which such details are inserted over the years is seen at the turn of the seventh century in the *Strategikon* of Maurikios. Although it is a military handbook it also contains an extended description of the Slavs and the Antae. Their 'wives are virtuous beyond the call of human nature, so that many of them regard the death of a husband as their own death and strangle themselves of their own free will, because they do not consider the life of a widow to be any life at all.'[46]

Around the middle of the sixth century, Jordanes writes far more concretely about two spectacular funerals. When Alaric died in the year 410 a river was diverted. The corpse was then buried in the riverbed and the river was diverted back to its original course. 'In order that the place remain undiscovered all the people who had done the digging were killed.'[47] At the funeral of Attila in the year 453 all the workers were killed too 'so that human curiosity could be kept away

[44] Procopius, 2, 14, 6–8.
[45] A detailed critical interpretation in Engster 33–52. See also Preidel 278–9. This passage is often taken over uncritically.
[46] Maurikios 11, 4.
[47] Jordanes, *Getica* 30, 158.

from such great wealth.'[48] If one believes Jordanes' commentary, the killings were not meant as a following of the dead, but as measures to prevent the plundering of the graves. Whether this was the only reason or whether it was also linked to the idea of sending a retinue to the next world is a question that remains unanswered.

The Middle Ages

After Caesar's—very dubious—account of the Gauls there is not a single text about Western and Central Europe that can be regarded as historically authentic and that contains indications of following into death. Although Christianity later contributed to the suppression of such customs in many parts of the world, their absence in this case cannot be attributed to the influence of Christianity. Other kinds of reports from pre-Christian days would otherwise have been available. The same holds true for Roman influence. Pre-Christian Roman sources, too, do not mention anywhere that Roman conquerors took steps against such practices.

It is different in the case of Eastern Europe, especially in the regions of the Slavs, the peoples from the Baltic and the (originally not Slavic but Scandinavian) Russians (Rus) as well as the Turks. Although not plentiful, one does come across statements about institutional as well as individual following into death in the Middle Ages. Foreign observers and compilers have written these accounts, but at least one seems to contain something more than just imputations and inventions. The Arabian diplomat Ibn Faḍlān visited the king of the Volga–Bulgarians, a Turkic people, in the year 921/22 as a secretary of a legation sent by the Caliph of Baghdad.[49] On this travel he also met Russian (Rus) merchants. When a distinguished man among them died, his relatives asked his concubines which of them wanted to die with him. One of them volunteered. She was then guarded closely, but also treated excep-tionally well. 'The girl then drinks all day and sings cheerfully in pleas-ant anticipation.' After about ten days an elaborate ceremony was carried out. The corpse of the dead man was placed in a tent, which stood on a ship pulled on land. First various animals were killed. Dur-ing the course of events the victim had a vision: 'I see my lord sitting

---

[48] Jordanes, *Getica* 49, 258.
[49] For the background, Togan, in Ibn Faḍlān (1939) xiiiff.; 119–23; Kowalska; Miquel 338–42; Jesch 119–23.

in Paradise, and Paradise is beautiful and green, and with him there are men and young boys (servants); he calls me, bring me to him.' In the last phase of the ceremony 'the men began to beat their shields with sticks to drown out her cries, so that the other girls would not be frightened'. Finally she was stabbed with daggers and strangled in the tent by several men and an old woman, whom they called angel of death. Wood was piled up around the ship and all of it was burnt.[50]

Even though the text poses some problems, it is characterized by its vividness, a richness of detail, and a directness that a mere invention would not have been able to convey. Everything points to the fact that the author was an eyewitness, including his own statement to this effect.[51] What strikes us here is that the custom is limited to one person. Servants are not included, nor—and that is even more remarkable—are other women, as if polygamy were forbidden in the hereafter. Apparently, the intention is not to carry this world as completely as possible over into the next, but to provide a companion for the other world who would at the same time maintain the link with this world. A further indication of this is the fact that in the course of the ceremony a number of men cohabit with the victim and each one instructs her to 'tell your master that I did this out of love for you'.[52] The statement made by Ibn Faḍlān in another context also supports this interpretation. He says that on the death of an important man it is not only his concubines or female slaves that are asked who among them would like to accompany him, but also his other (male) servants. If one of these came forward then a woman would not be killed. A clear gender-specific division of roles (in favour of men) is only present in the case of the person to be accompanied, not in the case of those who accompany him. However, men seldom seem to have fulfilled the function of accompanying the dead. 'Mostly it is women who do this (the self-sacrifice).'[53]

Ibn Faḍlān's description is a special case in European history. Apart from it—with only one exception that is discussed at the end of the

[50] Ibn Faḍlān (1939) 88–96; an older German translation in Frähn 13–19. See also the French translation by Canard 124–34, with a commentary (Ibn Faḍlān 1958).

[51] Ibn Faḍlān (1939) 90; Kowalska 227–8; Miquel 340.

[52] Ibn Faḍlān (1939) 92; 94. This aspect of the link is emphasized by Miquel 342.

[53] Ibn Faḍlān (1939) 89.

section—one only finds more or less stereotyped general statements, which do not appertain directly to actual experiences and initially only indicate that following into death was present in the general consciousness of the particular period.

This also holds true for the accounts of other Arabic-speaking travellers in Eastern Europe, particularly Russia. They refer partly to the Slavs, partly to the Rus. The oldest available account by the Persian Ibn Rusta (between 903 and 913) says of the Slavs that if a dead man had three wives, 'and one of them said she loved him the most', then she would hang herself on his death. After that 'she would be thrown into the fire to burn.'[54]

It is difficult to believe that something like this happened only when a dead man had three wives, and, moreover, this passage seems to be an amalgamation of different traditions. In Arabic sources one finds variations of this story, which leads us to believe that all texts can be traced to a common source, which is now lost.[55]

In Ibn Rusta's reports about the Rus he notes that on the death of an important man his favourite wife was buried alive with him; other authors state that she was burnt alive.[56]

With regard to the central role played later by Christianity and Europeans in suppressing and eliminating the custom, early Central European sources are, in many ways, more interesting.

Around 746/47 Boniface wrote an admonishing letter to King Aethelbald of Mercia (in England): 'Even the Wends [i.e. the Slavs], the ugliest and lowest race of men, carry reciprocal love in marriage to such an extent that a wife does not want to continue living after the death of her husband. They praise a woman when she kills herself and burns on the same pyre as her husband.'[57]

This passage is not meant to provide ethnographic information, but to hold up a mirror to Aethelbald and to urge him to 'improve' his ways. From this we can only infer that rumours of this kind were in circulation. Different authors, however, regarded the matter differently and held clearly dissimilar views. This was particularly marked

---

[54] Preidel 280–1; cf. for the following also Jesch 118–19.

[55] Preidel 280–7.

[56] Preidel 288–90.

[57] Boniface 220/221 (Letter 73). For an interpretation cf. Preidel 275–6.

with the passage of time. Whereas Boniface interprets the custom as a sign of strong love and loyalty, Thietmar von Merseburg (eleventh century) regards it more or less neutrally in moral terms, when he narrates that in earlier times among the Poles 'every woman was beheaded after her husband had been cremated, and she accompanied him in death'.[58] Although it was clear to Boniface that such customs did not occur among Christians, or, at least, that they should not occur, he did not condemn them. Thietmar limits the validity of his statement to the pre-Christian era in Poland. Three hundred years later, around 1324/26, Peter von Dusburg wrote that the Prussians had a false notion of the hereafter when they believed that the other world simply represented a continuation of this world. 'Therefore the dead nobleman was cremated with weapons, horses, servants and maids, clothes, hunting hounds, pickled birds and other things that were part of a nobleman's life.'[59] Here, too, there is no moral condemnation. One would, therefore, have to assume that in the Middle Ages Christians did not regard following into death as unacceptable in itself, and inhuman, even though it could not be reconciled with their beliefs.

This becomes evident in the Christburg Treaty, which the Teutonic Order signed under papal mediation with the renegade Prussians on 7 February 1249. According to the treaty the Prussians had to pledge 'that they and their descendants would not cremate or bury their dead any longer with horses, people (hominibus), weapons, clothes and other precious objects, [. . .] but that they would bury their dead according to Christian custom in sanctified ground.'[60] Christianity excludes the possibility of a following of the dead.

In view of the general nature of their statements, the passages from Boniface, Thietmar and Peter von Dusburg hardly allow us to draw any conclusions about the actual conditions among the Slavs (for example, the statement that every widow in Poland is beheaded is certainly false). The Christburg Treaty, on the other hand, is clear proof of the fact that following into death wasn't a fabrication by Christian authors. One cannot imagine that the Teutonic Order inserted the conditions of the treaty merely for purposes of propaganda and in

[58] Thietmar von Merseburg 8, 3 (p. 442). For an interpretation cf. Preidel 277–8.
[59] Peter von Dusburg 3, 5 (p. 102/103). For Prussia cf. also Gaerte.
[60] *Preußisches Urkundenbuch* 161.

order to harm the reputation of the Prussians. The custom, therefore, did exist. Its extent, however, cannot be gathered either from the treaty or from other sources.

Two more accounts from the same period indicate that following into death was a reality. In 1271 the Lithuanian Grand-Prince Swintorog is supposed to have been cremated along with his favourite slaves.[61] Around 1341 Grand-Prince Gedimin was cremated along with his 'favourite and most loyal servants' as well as with 'three captive Teutonic knights'.[62]

On the whole, medieval European sources give the impression that the custom of following into death occurred in the Slavic–Baltic region. Christianity did not conduct a crusade against such customs, but simply suppressed them in the course of its expansion. In the case of following into death, the fact of its existence is not used, at least in any major way, for the moral condemnation of a people. This increases the credibility of the statements, not in their details, but in the general sense that they are not merely fictitious accounts.

In the sixteenth century, statements relating to following into death only exist in the form of historical reminiscences, for example when Caspar Henneberger writes: 'In earlier times in Prussia when a prince died, his dearest and most faithful wife, his attendants and farmhands, his horse, clothes and other things would be burnt (willingly) with him. They believed that they would enjoy themselves in the other world and each one would have the same position there as they did here.'[63]

There was thus an East–West divide in Europe with regard to following the dead. This is confirmed by the only accurate account known to me of a ceremony of following the dead in a source from the Christian Middle Ages. Although it is not an eyewitness account, like that of Ibn Faḍlān, the informant is at least named. In 1251/52 the French historian of the Crusades, Jean de Joinville, met Philippe de Toucy, a French nobleman, at Caesarea. The latter had spent time with the Cumans, Turkic-speaking mounted nomads, who came from Central Asia and had by this time settled northwest of the Black Sea and soon after that in Hungary. A rich man died. Along with him they

---

[61] Janssen 193, without mentioning the original source.
[62] Hehn 521. The sources here however are not completely reliable.
[63] Cited in Gaerte 127.

buried alive his best horse and his best sergeant. Before the sergeant was laid in the grave,

> he went to the king of the Cumans and to the other rich men and while bidding him farewell they placed a large quantity of gold and silver in a cloth and each one said to him, 'When I come to the other world you will return what I have given you.' And he replied, 'I will gladly do that.' The great king of the Cumans also handed him a letter to their first king, in which he had written that the man had lived an exemplary life and had served him faithfully. He requested the king to reward him for his services. Then they laid him with his master and the horse into the grave, which they covered with planks fitted together. The whole army then fetched stones and earth and even before they lay down to rest they had heaped up a whole mountain as a monument to the buried.[64]

We will never know whether Philippe de Toucy was an eyewitness. The fundamental facts of the case however can hardly be disputed. The lack of exaggeration, particularly with regard to the number of victims, increases the credibility of the text. The account emphasizes the significance of belief in the hereafter as the victim is used as a bearer of news. Such examples can also be found on other continents. What is unique here is the function of the victim as a kind of bank. One can also assume that the victim has not been coerced; otherwise he would not have been given such messages to carry and would not have been commended to the king.

Literary Sources

In literature, one often comes across the theme of following into death, especially of spouses, mainly widows.[65] The central theme, however, is of non-ritualized death out of love.[66]

These sources have not been taken into account here, because it is impossible to draw any conclusions about an underlying reality from

[64] Jean de Joinville, chap. 97. Translated on the basis of the Middle French text in the 'Histoire' (1868), 177–8 and the New French translation by Wailly in the 'Histoire' (1865), 222–3. Cf. Gadd 56–8.

[65] Overviews in Gerhards, chap. 5 and especially in Engster. For the further Nordic background, Jesch.

[66] Cf. Engster 91–115.

them. The assumption that literature is a mirror of contemporary conditions does not hold true in such cases. It is again an unfounded assumption that customs of earlier times can be gleaned from the literature of the period. Instead of an echo of the past it is equally possible to find a continuous fabrication of new aspects. Engster proves that the themes which are of interest to us in this study are missing in the oldest manuscripts of Nordic literature. They only gradually begin to appear at a time when, as all other sources indicate, such things did not happen in reality.[67] The only definite conclusion that can be drawn from literature is that at least the motif of following into death was widespread. This is important for judging the different kinds of European accounts about regions outside Europe, accounts that began with the great discoveries. The starting point for a large number of authors may well have been in the literary, rather than in the historical, field. This has to be taken into consideration while questioning the degree of reality within these modern accounts.

[67] Engster 76; 109; 116–53.

CHAPTER 3

America

The ethnographic and historical sources on America contain different kinds of information about following into death for the period between the sixteenth and the nineteenth centuries. However, descriptions based on precise observations, and much less still eyewitness accounts, are very rare.

There were considerable differences in the circumstances surrounding the observation of the practice. The Spaniards tried to subjugate and Christianize large areas quickly and comprehensively. They suppressed heathen practices with such energy that these disappeared quickly, or else were only carried out secretly, so that European authors could only report them on the basis of hearsay. The other colonial powers generally proceeded more slowly (the same is true of the Spaniards in the border areas). Because of this, Europeans could frequently observe and record Indian customs.

Central America

Many early Spanish works on Mexico (which is taken here to be a part of Central America, as is the Caribbean) give detailed accounts of following the dead on the death of rulers and important men.[1] However, the number of texts that are independent of each other is small. Later authors very often took over statements made by their predecessors with inconsequential changes.

A very early account, presumably from the 1520s or the 1530s, describes the funeral rites for the rulers of Michoacán in Western Mexico. The son, and successor, determines the retinue for the dead ruler: firstly, seven female servants to attend on him, and along with them, an unknown number of other women; then, over forty male

---

[1] Following into death in Mexico has not been critically studied till now. For some references cf. González Torres 297–300.

servants, whose duties are laid down very clearly, as well as some of the doctors who were unsuccessful in their treatment of the dead man. All of them take the tools of their trade with them. Many other servants try to join the retinue out of fear that the successor will not treat them well, but are prevented from doing so. While the corpse of the ruler is burned, the persons who will accompany the dead are first rendered insensible with intoxicating drinks, then killed with clubs and buried separately.[2]

A few years later Motolinia adds a chapter to this account, in which he deals with the funeral ceremonies of other rulers in Mexico. In accordance with the importance of the dead ruler and the power wielded by him, between 100 and 200 female and male slaves are killed. Some are taken from the household of the dead ruler, and the leading men of the realm provide some. In addition to this, wives and concubines are killed. On the fourth, tenth, twentieth, fortieth, sixtieth and eightieth day after the ceremony a total of between 27 and 35 more people are killed. They are meant to help the dead person's soul on its way to the next world.[3]

Further descriptions by other authors can also be found.[4] These agree on the central points. From time to time, the killing of hunchbacks, dwarfs and priests is mentioned.[5] The numbers given go up to about 300 victims.

Along with these general descriptions there are scattered accounts of concrete events from the fifteenth and early sixteenth centuries,

[2] *Relacion . . . Mechuacan* 55–9. The anonymous account is not dated. Since Motolinia, who wrote between 1536 and 1543, has taken it over with minor changes, it must have been written earlier. Motolinia, *Memoriales* (*c.* 1536–43) 128–30 (book 2, chap. 1); López de Gómara, *México* (*c.* 1552) 333–4 (chap. 217); Torquemada (1615) 2, 523–6 (vol.2, book 13, chap. 46).

[3] Motolinia, *Memoriales* 130–2 (book 2, chap. 2). Taken over with minor changes by López de Gómara, *México* 331–2 (chap. 216); Torquemada 2, 521–3 (vol. 2, book 13, chap. 45).

[4] The most important short summary in Durán (1570) 1, 55–6 (*Libro de los ritos y ceremonias en las fiestas de los dioses y celebración de ellos*, chap. 5, no. 46–9). See also Sahagún (1570s) 207 (book 3, apéndice, chap. 1, § 29); Pomar (1582) 37–8 (for Tezcoco); Acosta (1590) 148 (book 5, chap. 8).

[5] Durán 1, 56 (*Historia de las Indias de Nueva España e islas de la tierra firme*, tomo 1, chap. 5, no. 48); Durán 2, 299; 474 (*Historia*, chap. 39; 54); Acosta 148 (book 5, chap. 8).

especially in Durán.[6] These mention that the persons accompanying the dead were exhorted to serve their master faithfully in the next world. They believed that in the other world they too would become important men, which is why they went cheerfully to their death.[7] In all these accounts an elaborate institutional form of the custom is described whose function is, on the one hand, to ensure that the dead person has a retinue appropriate to his rank in the next world; on the other hand, it served to consolidate the position of the ruler in this world.[8] Relevant reports are also available for other regions of Central America. In the early sixteenth century, Peter Martyr writes, in Española the favourite wives as well as female servants were buried alive with dead chiefs.[9] From two other passages by the same author we can infer that a belief in the hereafter played an important role. He heard that in the Panama region the belief was prevalent that 'only chiefs and important men had an immortal soul; the souls of other people were destroyed with their bodies. The only exceptions were the faithful servants of the chiefs and those who allowed themselves to be buried alive with their master at his funeral.'[10] He also writes about the Indians in the Gulf of Uraba (Colombia/Panama): 'When a mother with an infant has to die, they lay the child at her breast and bury it alive with her',[11] apparently because they believe that mother and child belong together even in the next world.

Around the middle of the sixteenth century Fernández de Oviedo writes that in Castilla del Oro, in the region of Panama, the family members, the servants, and the wives of an important man would poison themselves of their own free will when the man died. In each case the number of victims is supposed to be between forty and fifty. In other places, some of the wives of the dead man would let themselves be buried alive. They went to their death entirely of their own free

---

[6] Durán 2, 295–300; 391–5; 474 (*Historia*, chap. 39; 51; 54).

[7] Durán 2, 394; 474 (*Historia*, chap. 51, no.16; chap. 54, no. 7).

[8] A detailed review of further sources in Bancroft 2, 603–22. See also Bastian, *America* 2, 759–61.

[9] Petrus Martyr 137 (decade 3, book 9, chap. 53). Similarly Fernández de Oviedo 1, 119 (book 5, chap. 3).

[10] Petrus Martyr 238 (decade 7, book 10, chap. 44).

[11] Petrus Martyr 238 (decade 7, book 10, chap. 43). Cf. also Bancroft 1, 590; 781.

choice and in cheerful spirits, convinced that they would enter heaven with their husband. Before the grave was closed they would be anaesthetised with strong drinks.[12] The sources cited here are not the only ones for Central America.[13] However, in other cases the references to the custom are, as a rule, shorter and less precise, or have been taken from earlier authors; at times, later versions found in the literature are incorrect.[14]

How reliable are the sources mentioned here? The accounts about Mexico suggest parallels with the well-known human sacrifices of the Aztecs, especially since the authors analysed here also report extensively about these. Lately, however, important arguments have been put forward questioning the existence of human sacrifice in Mexico.[15] The arguments are based on the fact that there are no verified eyewitness accounts. This statement also holds true for texts about following into death. No author was an eyewitness to the ceremonies he describes. Nothing definite can be said about their Indian informants either. Should one therefore assume that the accounts are fictitious? One would be going too far in drawing such a conclusion. The two phenomena cannot be equated without examination. Whereas the accounts of human sacrifice are clearly concentrated in Mexico, accounts of following into death are spread evenly over all parts of America. The description of the manner of killing is sometimes similar to the descriptions of human sacrifice. Different authors state that at the ruler's grave the hearts of slaves were torn out of their bodies.[16] But these statements can probably be traced back to a common source and, in addition, we must take into account that descriptions of both phenomena were freely blended with each other. In the case of following into death, at any rate, other forms of killing are mentioned far more often, especially strangulation, but also stabbing, burying alive and killing

[12] Fernández de Oviedo 3, 337–9 (book 29, chap. 31).

[13] Cf. for example the compilations in Bancroft 1, 744; 781–3; 2, 799; *Handbook of South American Indians*, vol. 4; Krickeberg 59–60; 76; 79–80; 102–18.

[14] Further references, partly diffuse and difficult to verify, in Preuss, *Menschenopfer* 199–207; Wilkerson 108; Dorman 212–13.

[15] Hassler, *Menschenopfer bei den Azteken?* (1992).

[16] Motolinia, *Memoriales* 131 (book 2, chap. 2); López de Gómara, *México* 332 (chap. 216); Durán 2, 300; 395 (*Historia*, chap. 39, no. 25; chap. 51, no. 19); Torquemada 2, 522 (vol. 2, book 13, chap. 45).

with clubs. Such forms are also mentioned in other parts of the world in the context of this custom. Occasionally, it is said that the victims were rendered unconscious before the killing with the help of intoxicating drinks, for which parallels exist in other regions.[17] In the sources the custom is also ideologically less charged than human sacrifice. Moralizing condemnations are missing in the earliest texts and they appear only gradually at a later stage, when Durán for example says in 1570: 'In reality they went to enjoy the flames of hell eternally with their master!'[18] A categorical rejection of the custom can only be found in 1615 in Torquemada who, however, continues to emphasize the voluntary nature of the act.[19] The Indians are deluded, not immoral. The authors did not invent stories on which to base their negative opinions of the Indians, but they commented on the stories they heard, and even this they did very hesitantly.

Corresponding to this is the fact that all accounts emphasize the voluntary nature of the act, even mentioning servants who wanted to accompany their master but were prevented from doing so. There is no mention of compulsion or indeed of overt force. Sometimes self-killing is expressly mentioned.[20] If the European authors had been concerned mainly with condemning the old practices, they would probably have denounced the cruelty and violence in stronger terms, and would have invented the events in order to justify the Spanish conquest. Even an author like Las Casas, whose opinions about reports on human sacrifice ranged from scepticism to outright rejection, writes that on the death of an important person in the region around Vera Paz male and female slaves would be killed in order to serve their master in the other world.[21]

The repeated assurances that the victims went to their death willingly should not lead to the simple conclusion that it was, in fact, a voluntary act. The authors took over these versions directly from their informants. Sometimes they adapted the information to their own

[17] A compilation of the sources on America is in Bancroft 2, 603–22.

[18] Durán 2, 395 (*Historia*, chap. 51, no. 19).

[19] Torquemada 2, 521–6 (vol. 2, book 13, chap. 45–6).

[20] For example Bancroft 1, 781.

[21] Las Casas 4, 362 (*Apologética historia*, chap. 240). In the *Historia de las Indias* (book 3, chap. 117) Las Casas denies, in opposition to Cortés, the existence of human sacrifice in Yucatán (Las Casas 2, 455–6). Cf. Hassler 107–9.

background, which was characterized by the theme set out by Herodotus of the competition among the widows. It is hardly possible that slaves provided by subordinate leaders or neighbouring masters went to their death willingly. The Indian informants, however, were interested in portraying their earlier customs in a favourable light, so as not to discredit themselves in the eyes of the Spaniards.

One can, therefore, proceed with the assumption that the custom occurred in Central America. As a rule, it appeared in a marked institutional form to consolidate the position of the ruler and other important persons. Durán also gives a brief indication of the beginnings of individual following into death: each of the men who were killed in a war in Mexico received a slave from their people to accompany them into the next world.[22]

Finally, archaeology provides further clues. Evidence of multiple burials was found in different places with one high-ranking dead person in the centre.[23] On the other hand, these finds suggest the need for greater scepticism with regard to the large number of persons mentioned in the sources who accompany the dead.

South America

Accounts of following into death in South America are rather sparse.[24] In these Peru is clearly a focal point. As in the case of Mexico, the authors state that important persons were accompanied into death by others. It is therefore not possible to establish a correlation between following into death and human sacrifice, since the latter is mentioned far less in the context of Peru than in that of Mexico.

Pedro Cieza de León frequently mentions pertinent customs in a book published in 1553. However, the references are always very general. Accounts of concrete cases are missing. If an important man among the Quillacinga Indians dies, some of his wives and female servants are buried with him. The neighbours provide additional victims,

---

[22] Durán 2, 154 (*Historia*, chap. 17, no. 6).

[23] Helfrich 46–8; Krickeberg 59–60; Wilkerson 108–9; Borhegyi 14; 16–18; 22 (Guatemala); *Handbook of South American Indians* 4, 28; 147–8. A critical account exists in Hassler 110–22.

[24] For a compilation of the references see mainly *Handbook of South American Indians*, vols 1, 2, 4 and 5. See also Krickeberg 102–18. For the background of the belief in the hereafter see Cipolletti.

probably slaves. The victims are rendered senseless with the help of intoxicating drinks and are buried alive. On the whole twenty people are chosen. The dead man needs them in order to enter the other world 'with greater authority'.[25] Cieza de León reports on similar incidents among a number of other peoples.[26] Along with women, children were often also buried with the dead. The Spaniards suppressed 'this accursed custom'.[27]

Cieza de León's assertions are almost certainly based on hearsay alone. However, he does not use them to discredit the Indians. Although he does not speak of the voluntary nature of the act, he does not mention coercion or violence. Some women are supposed to have killed themselves before the burial ceremony.[28]

The information given by Acosta is more detailed, but it is also written later (1590). The leading men of the Incas, especially the rulers, had to be accompanied by a significant number of 'servants and women to serve them in the other world', and also by officials. On the death of Huayna Capac, the father of Huascar and Atahualpa, in 1527, over a thousand people are said to have been killed after a big feast had been given in their honour. Acosta emphasizes the voluntary nature of the act: 'They considered themselves favoured by fortune', they died 'willingly'. Many more offered themselves of their own free choice but could not be accommodated.[29]

Other authors also stress the voluntary nature, even in contexts that detract from its plausibility. According to Herrera a large number of beautiful women wanted to be buried alive with Atahualpa when he died in 1533. Since they were denied this, many hanged themselves. The basis for this, says Herrera, is 'the erroneous belief that they would serve the soul of their great master in heaven.'[30] At the beginning of the seventeenth century Garcilaso de la Vega writes that sometimes such frenzy breaks out among the favourite servants and wives of the dead

---

[25] Cieza de León 385 (chap. 33). Similarly Herrera 5, 1, 1 (p. 3) for the district San Miguel, whereby the author emphasizes that the custom was prevalent all over America.

[26] Cieza de León 394 (chap. 41); 404–5 (chap. 51); 414–16 (chap. 62–3).

[27] Cieza de León 414 (chap. 62); 416 (chap. 63).

[28] Cieza de León 415 (chap. 63).

[29] Acosta 147; 202 (book 5, chap. 7; book 6, chap. 22).

[30] Herrera 5, 3, 5 (p. 58).

man to kill themselves or to let themselves be buried alive that the authorities have to intervene.[31] Zárate writes in 1555 that such problems were sometimes resolved by the deceased during his lifetime by giving only certain people the right to accompany him.[32] Cobo is somewhat more realistic when he emphasizes, at the end of the sixteenth century, that it all happens voluntarily, but adds that those who refuse are regarded as infamous and considered traitors. Women, in such cases, are treated as adulteresses.[33]

In the case of Peru too, we can presume that the Spanish authors, who had never witnessed such events, were primarily reproducing the views of their Indian informants, who tended to exaggerate the number of victims and who attached great importance to the voluntary nature of the act. They did this also to protect themselves from being accused of aiding a crime.[34]

Relatively plausible accounts of customs relating to following into death are otherwise most easily found for Paraguay, especially for the Guaraní. Important persons among them are supposed to have been accompanied into the next world by servants and family members, and all the authors emphasize that this happened willingly. Charlevoix writes about the Guaycuru: 'There was never any trouble finding them [victims]; there were always enough people to volunteer for this honour.'[35] They are either strangulated or buried alive.

There are also brief, occasional references to other peoples.[36]

As in the case of Central America, one could assume with a similar degree of probability that institutional following into death was practised upon the death of rulers and other important men. However, it is not possible to give more precise details about the spread of the custom. Apart from persons who were not related to the deceased, members of the court, concubines and wives probably accompanied the dead.

[31] Garcilaso de La Vega 2, 18–19 (vol. 2, book 6, chap. 5).

[32] Zárate 1, 65 (book 1, chap. 12).

[33] Cobo 2, 274 (book 14, chap. 19).

[34] For Peru for example cf. Apollonius 34r and Santa Cruz 100 as well as Bastian, *America* 3, 37–8.

[35] Charlevoix, *Paraguay* 1, 119. Similarly Alvear 15 (Guaraní); Guevara 30–1 (Guaraní). Further references in *Handbook of South American Indians*, 1, 183.

[36] General, only partly verifiable details in Dorman 211–14; *Handbook of South American Indians*, vols 1, 2, 4 and 5; Preuss, *Menschenopfer* 198–203.

In the middle of the sixteenth century, however, López de Gómara stresses that persons accompanying the dead who were laid into the grave were 'not of flesh, but of wood'.[37] There is no proof for this. For all of America there is never any mention of such substitutions. In view of all the other statements, and the fact that Gómara was never in America, scepticism is justified. Moreover, he writes about human sacrifice in Mexico without expressing any doubt about its existence.

North America

Whereas the statements about Central and South America should be treated carefully since there are no absolute proofs, the extensive and varied sources from the sixteenth to the eighteenth centuries for North America leave no room for doubt—at least with regard to the important points.

Do the number and quality of sources simply reflect the fact that the custom played a more important role in North America? Or were the conditions on the entire continent similar, and the sources for the North only better because of more favourable conditions for observation? Both aspects probably play a role. Accounts like those about the Natchez could hardly have been written in the regions controlled by Spain, since the Spaniards would probably have taken strong repressive measures against such ceremonies. On the other hand, there are indications of very peculiar customs in the North. One cannot immediately assume that these customs were prevalent elsewhere.

The sources for North America are not only extensive, but also unusually varied. They provide information about an entire spectrum of customs related to following into death. In this context we have to ask whether these are the preliminary or the final stages of the custom, or whether they are completely independent phenomena. Do certain incidents, when they occur repeatedly, lead at some point to following into death? Or, on the contrary, does a following of the dead end over a period of time in certain reduced forms, in which human life is not destroyed? Or are all theories of a development following a set pattern inappropriate, since the custom can appear suddenly and just as suddenly disappear?

In order to analyse these aspects the events described in the sources are divided into different categories. Even those events that do not have

---

[37] López de Gómara, *Historia general* 1, 219 (book 1, chap. 125).

all the characteristics of following into death are taken into consideration.

Non-ritualized Self-killings
(private following into death)

In the 1760s Jonathan Carver lived with the Naudowessies (Sioux) near the tent of a couple, whose four-year-old son died. As a sign of their sorrow and mourning the parents inflicted severe injuries on themselves, and the father died a few days later of his injuries. His wife, who had been inconsolable till then, 'dried up her tears, and appeared cheerful and resigned'. Asked about the reason for her newly found peace of mind she replied that, being so young, her child would not have been able to take care of itself in the other world. Now however the father could take care of it.[38]

The aim of accompanying someone to the other world, the anxiety about the well-being of the dead person, is evident. However, the manner of death is not ritualistic. One cannot, therefore, speak of following into death in the way it is defined here. It is, rather, a case of a private following into death.

The sources mention a number of similar cases. George Catlin hands down the account, written by a trader, of a smallpox epidemic in 1858 that almost completely destroyed the Mandan people in the Upper Missouri valley. A man who had lost his entire family starved himself to death and died lying down next to his dead family.[39] In the early nineteenth century, John West wrote about the Indians of the Red River Colony near Lake Winnipeg where, sometimes, when a child died the mother would commit suicide in order to accompany it to the next world.[40] In the middle of the nineteenth century all the sons of a chief of the Walla-Walla people died in quick succession. The chief had himself buried alive with the corpse of the last, the youngest son.[41]

Such incidents and similar ones are not limited to North America, especially if one also takes the suicide of the surviving spouse into account. This practice is supposed to have been widespread among both sexes of the Apache Indians.[42] What is striking, however, is the close

---

[38] Carver 378.
[39] Catlin 2, 258.
[40] West 141.
[41] Kane, 285. Further details in Bancroft 1, 288.
[42] Hrdlička 171.

connection that the sources usually establish with following into death. The suicide makes it possible to meet the dead person again in the other world.

This connection becomes very clear when Lahontan reports that it is customary among the Indians for a widow or widower, who dreams of his/her dead partner on two consecutive nights during the mourning period of six months, to 'poison himself/herself cold-bloodedly with a cheerful countenance, singing all the while in a heartfelt manner'.[43] In its generality this statement is undoubtedly exaggerated, maybe even completely fictitious. The link with dreams, however, underlines the connection with the other world, which is explicitly mentioned by the author.

All these are cases of self-killing. It is difficult to imagine a non-ritualized killing by another person in the context of following into death, as that would be murder even according to the standard of the society in which it happened. The difference between a legitimate killing and a crime lies in the ritualized manner of the killing, which presupposes the co-operation, or at least the presence, of the public as a guarantee of its legitimacy. A case in 1734 shows the possible connection, as also the difference, between a killing and following into death. During the course of a rebellion in California a missionary was murdered. He left behind 'an innocent young Californian boy, who used to wait on the priest at table.' The boy wept for his guardian, until one of the rebels killed him, saying: 'He shall continue to serve him, whom he mourns, and be his companion in the other world.'[44] From the killer's perspective the allusion to the custom is perhaps not completely misleading. But his action remains a crime in the absence of the framework necessary for following into death.

In the case sketched above, and in similar cases, the relationship of the persons involved with each other is comparatively open. Parents accompany their children, friends and spouses accompany each other, fathers accompany their families, etc.[45] The relationship between the sexes is particularly remarkable. Both can assume the role of the person being accompanied or of the person accompanying the dead. The passage from Lahontan cited earlier is typical in this regard, for it does not differentiate between the sexes at all. In the absence of ritualized

---

[43] Lahontan 2, 139.

[44] Begert 274.

[45] Further situations in Yarrow 109 (suicide of the mother on the death of her child) and in Schoolcraft 2, 134 (a Comanche widow).

forms there is no fixed allocation of roles, and therefore the structures of inequality, which are linked with a following of the dead, do not appear either.

Do the forms described above represent the early forms or the last phases of a (public) following into death? It is possible to propound the thesis that the act itself, the killing, was already happening before a definite ritualized framework came into being. One could also argue, however, that this framework was no longer available after it had been given up by the society concerned. A person who still wanted to carry out the act would have to go about it differently and would not be propped up by a ritual. The arguments in both directions are plausible but not conclusive. This state of affairs highlights the problems of an evolutionary interpretation. One can speak of early forms or late phases only in a systematic and not in a chronological sense.

Ritualized Non-killings

In 1831 MacGillivray described a custom that he had observed among the Talkotins (Carriers) in the northwest of what is today the United States. When a man died, he was cremated on the tenth day. Regardless of the weather, his widow had to sleep beside the corpse for nine nights. After that the corpse was placed on a pyre and the widow was also made to lie down on it. The wood was then kindled. The woman had to remain on the pyre till the medicine man allowed her to be carried off,

> which, however, is never done until her body is completely covered with blisters. After being placed on her legs, she is obliged to pass her hands gently through the flames, and collect some of the liquid fat which issues from the corpse, with which she is permitted to rub her face and body! When the friends of the deceased observe the sinews of the legs and arms beginning to contract, they compel the unfortunate widow to go again on the pile, and by dint of hard pressing to straighten those members.

If the widow had cheated on her husband during his lifetime, or had not pampered him sufficiently, the relatives of the dead man now take their revenge. They 'frequently fling her on the funeral pile, from which she is dragged by her friends; and thus, between alternate scorching and cooling she is dragged backwards and forwards until she falls into a state of insensibility.'

After this the widow has to collect the larger bones and carry them for several years in a bag on her back. During this time the whole community treats her like a slave. She has to tend her husband's grave with great care and pluck out the weeds with her bare hands, otherwise she is beaten by the family members. 'The wretched widows, to avoid this complicated cruelty, frequently commit suicide.' If they survive the three to four years' mourning period, a big feast is arranged in their honour. They are now allowed to remarry, 'but few of them I believe wish to encounter the risk attending a second widowhood'.[46]

Several authors, partly independent of each other, have described the above events.[47] Similar customs are also found among other peoples in this region.[48]

The above description gives the impression of an unfinished widow burning. The indisputable similarity in the outward appearance is then fitted into a general model of evolution and declared to be an early form of widow burning, an 'incipient suttee'.[49] This interpretation, however, is not convincing. It is possible that if the ritual was performed frequently it dulled the emotions or else raised the expectations of the audience to such an extent that the widow was finally no longer scorched but burnt. However it is difficult to imagine that following into death originated in this manner. If it were a matter of sending the widow to the other world as a companion for her husband, there would be no reason to subject her to torture of this kind. What we have here is rather a different kind of ritual, whose point becomes clearer in other examples. The Se-nél in California burnt the dead body of a chief. The women threw all their possessions on the funeral pyre. They shouted, lamented and beat themselves and 'some of them would have cast themselves bodily into the flaming ruins and perished with the chief had they not been restrained by their companions.'[50] Even in the

---

[46] MacGillivray in Cox 2, 389–92; also in Yarrow 144–6. Cf. MacLeod, *Northwest Coast culture* 122–6 with references to further sources that were not accessible.

[47] Kane 243–5; Smet 268. Further details in MacLeod, *Suttee: antecedents* 114; MacLeod, *Northwest Coast culture* 122–6; Bancroft 1, 125–6.

[48] Kane 243–5; Harmon 180 (Sikanni; eyewitness account of 1812, also in Morse 339–40), 232 (Carriers); MacLean 154–5 (New Caledonia District); Bancroft 1, 126 (Tacully); MacLeod, *Northwest Coast culture* 122–6; MacLeod, *Suttee: antecedents* 109–18.

[49] MacLeod, *Northwest Coast culture* 122.

[50] Stephen Powers (1877), in Yarrow 147.

twentieth century Devereux observed cases among the Mohave of attempted suicide by widows and widowers at the cremation of their spouse. The surviving spouse tried to jump into the fire but was prevented from doing so. The statements of the people concerned established the connection with following into death. They believed that if a person did not die soon after the death of the spouse, he/she would never be able to meet the other in the next world. Nevertheless, the attempt to jump onto the pyre was, according to these people, a kind of ritual in its own right.[51] By this they demonstrated, on the one hand, the firm will to follow the dead person. On the other hand, however, the onlookers were also expected to intervene. The rules of the game therefore included the unspoken agreement that the proceedings would not end in death. One could speak here of a symbolic following of the dead. The ritual of the Talkotin described by MacGillivray can only partially be compared with this, because the widow is not expected to demonstrate the will to kill herself. Yet she is forced to behave in a way that expresses this very intention. Here, too, it is the duty of the spectators to save her from death. They, therefore, play a dual role: of ostensibly forcing her to die and then of saving her, whereas among the Se-nél and the Mohave the former role is taken on by the widow herself.

Just as it is possible to interpret this custom as an early form of widow burning, it can also be regarded as a last phase. After burning widows mercilessly in the beginning, they were later at least allowed to live. This view is not convincing either. The systematic connections cannot be interpreted as chronological or evolutionary processes. The same holds true for many other mourning rites which are frequently linked to following of the dead, like the self-infliction of injuries, self-mutilation, cutting of hair and other such practices.[52]

MacGillivray's description gives the impression that the ritual is directed mainly against the widow and is an instrument of oppression in the hands of the dead husband's relatives. This would also make it a means to maintain and strengthen the inequality of the sexes. But the author adds at the end of his account: 'The men are condemned to a similar torture. But they cannot withstand it with the same fortitude

[51] Devereux 431–42; 453–9.

[52] For these questions, which are often mentioned in the literature cf. for example MacLeod, *Suttee: antecedents*; Wilken, *Haaropfer*; W. Ellis, *Hawaii* 164–71; Steinmetz, *Strafe*.

and they flee in great numbers to distant regions in order to escape the brutal treatment which custom has introduced as a religious ritual.'[53]

In the ritualized customs that cannot be considered as following into death in a strict sense, the difference between the sexes does not seem to play an important role. This applies both to voluntary and non-voluntary acts. The circumstances are to a large extent egalitarian, so that one cannot speak of either institutional or individual following into death. The brutal ritual among the Talkotins gives us an insight into possible reasons for change. Although both men and women are required to subject themselves to a situation in which they are almost burnt to death, men can evidently avoid it more easily. What is at first simply a factual case could in the course of time be made a norm, which applies only to women. Increasing ritualization probably favours such a development.[54]

Following into Death as the Central Component of a Social Order: The Natchez

In their advance through the southern part of the Mississippi Valley the French encountered the Natchez people, with whom they developed good trade relations. From time to time Frenchmen lived among them or near them in small bases. They thus had the opportunity to observe Indian customs without however being able to influence them in any significant way.[55] In 1704 the trader Pénicaut described a particularly striking burial ceremony which the French traders had witnessed many times:

> It happened in our time that the grand chieftainess Noble being dead, we saw the burial ceremony, which is indeed the most horrible tragedy that one can witness. It made myself and all my comrades tremble with

[53] Cox 2, 392. Cf. Devereux 454–9.

[54] More far-reaching hypotheses in MacLeod, *Suttee: antecedents* 108; 115–17; MacLeod, *Distribution* 212.

[55] A compilation of the most important sources about the Natchez in an English translation, along with an analysis of their social conditions, can be found in Swanton 45–257, particularly 100–8 and 138–57. Ethnologists have displayed great interest in the social organization of the Natchez. For an overview of the sources cf. Swanton 2–3 and White *et al.* 383–6; for an overview of the literature White *et al.* 387–8. Important contributions to the discussion are Brain; Hart; MacLeod, *Natchez cultural origins*; MacLeod, *Natchez political evolution*; MacLeod, *Origin of the state*; Mason and Tooker.

horror. She was a chieftainess Noble in her own right. Her husband, who was not at all noble, was immediately strangled by the first boy she had had by him, to accompany his wife into the great village, where they believe that they go. After such a fine beginning they put outside of the cabin of the great chief all that was there. As is customary they made a kind of triumphal car in the cabin, where they placed the dead woman and her strangled husband. A moment later, they brought 12 little dead infants, who had been strangled, and whom they placed around the dead woman. It was their fathers and mothers who brought them there, by order of the eldest of the dead chieftainess's children, and who then, as grand chief, commands to have die to honor the funeral rites of his mother as many persons as he wishes. They had scaffolds prepared in the public square, which they ornamented with branches of trees and with cloth covered with pictures. On each scaffold a man placed himself who was going to accompany the defunct to the other world. They stood on these scaffolds surrounded by their nearest relatives; they are sometimes warned more than ten years before their death. It is an honor for their relatives. Ordinarily they have offered to die during the life of the defunct, for the good will which they bear him, and they themselves have tied the cord with which they are strangled. They are dressed in their finest clothing, with a large shell in the right hand, and the nearest relative—for example, if it is the father of a family who dies, his eldest son—walks behind him bearing the cord under his arm and a war club in his right hand. He makes a frightful cry which they call the death cry. Then all these unfortunate victims every quarter of an hour descend from their scaffolds and unite in the middle of the square, where they dance together before the temple and before the house of the dead female chief, when they remount their scaffolds to resume their places. They are very much respected that day, and each one has five servants. Their faces are all reddened with vermilion. For my part I have thought that it was in order not to let the fear that they might have of their approaching death be apparent.

At the end of four days they begin the ceremony of 'the march of the bodies'.

The fathers and the mothers who had brought their dead children took them and held them in their hands; the oldest of these children did not appear to be more than three years old. They placed them to right and left of the entrance to the cabin of the dead female chief. The fourteen victims destined to be strangled repaired there in the same order; the chiefs and the relatives of the dead woman appeared there all in mourning—that is to say with their hair cut. They then made such frightful cries that we thought the devils were come out of the hells to come and howl in this place. The unfortunate persons destined to death danced and the relatives of the dead woman sang. When the march of this fine convoy was begun by two and two, the dead woman was brought out of her cabin on the shoulders of four savages as on a stretcher. As soon as she had been taken out, they set fire to the cabin (it is the usual custom with the Nobles). The fathers, who carried their dead children in their hands, marched in front, four paces distant from each other, and after marching ten steps they let them fall to the ground. Those who bore the dead woman passed over and went around these children three times. The fathers then gathered them up and resumed their places in the ranks, and at every ten paces they re-commenced this frightful ceremony, until they reached the temple, so that these children were in pieces when this fine convoy arrived. While they interred the female Noble in the temple the victims were stripped before the door, and, after they had been made to sit on the ground, a savage seated himself on the knees of each of them while another behind held his arms. They then passed a cord around his neck and put the skin of a deer over his head; they made each of these poor un-fortunates swallow three pills of tobacco, and gave him a draught of water to drink, in order that the pills should dissolve in his stomach, which made him lose consciousness; then the relatives of the deceased ranged themselves at their sides, to right and left, and each, as he sang, drew an end of a cord, which was passed around the neck with a run-ning knot, until they were dead, after which they buried them.

If a chief dies and still has his nurse, she must die with him.

This nation still follows this execrable custom, in spite of all that has been done to turn them from it. Our missionaries have never been able to succeed in that; all that they were able to do was to succeed some-times in baptizing those poor little infants before their fathers strangled them.[56]

Pénicaut asserts that he was an eyewitness.[57] Besides there is a second precise account of the same incident, although it is possible that the second account was derived to a greater or lesser degree from the original one.[58] What is more important is the fact that three authors

[56] Pénicaut, in Margry 452–5. English translation in Swanton 140–1.

[57] White *et al.* 384 also proceed on this assumption.

[58] Charlevoix, *Nouvelle France* 3, 421–3. English translation in Swanton 141–2.

have described a similar event, which took place in 1725.[59] In other accounts of the Natchez the custom is at least mentioned.[60]

The form of following into death described here was a constitutive element of the social order of the Natchez.[61] The most important distinction in their society was the one between nobles and commoners. The nobility for its part was divided into three groups, or, according to some, into two groups. The rulers and the other chiefs had to descend from the highest category of the so-called *suns*. The position was handed down through the female line. *Suns* of both sexes could only marry commoners. The children of male *suns* were relegated to a lower category of nobility, in later generations they even became commoners. The spouses of the *suns* received the privileges of nobility. But they had to accompany their spouses in death, which the *suns* were not obliged to do.[62] There was no distinction between the sexes in this regard. This is the only known and attested case in which the obligation of the husbands to accompany their wives in death is no less than the corresponding obligation of the wives.

This consistent subordination of the gender difference to that of social status shows how well following into death was integrated in the social organization of the Natchez—better than in all other known cases. It had a marked functional character. This impression is strengthened by other circumstances. Apart from the spouse a large number of persons accompanied the dead. The criteria for selecting these victims are not stated clearly in the sources. Yet definite rules obviously existed since it was, normally, not a spontaneous decision on the part of the accompanying person that determined the matter. The possibility of a rise in social status in connection with a following of the dead was a crucial point. Commoners could rise to the lowest ranks of nobility in different ways: by proving martial valour, by providing a family

[59] Le Page du Pratz 3, 36–59 (English trans. in Swanton 143–9); Dumont de Montigny 1, 208–39 (Swanton 149–57); Bossu: English trans. in Yarrow 187–9.

[60] Gravier 142–4 (Swanton 139–40); Le Petit 130–2 (Swanton 142–3).

[61] Details of the structure and function of Natchez society are a matter of dispute in research, especially since the sources mentioned are not consistent in all respects. For the questions which are of interest here, however, these differences are not of prime importance. For a compilation of the sources see Swanton 100–8. For the literature see footnote 55.

[62] Cf. MacLeod, *Distribution* 211–12.

member—either adults or children—to accompany a dead *sun*, and finally by participating in the strangulation of an adult victim.[63] The popularity of such participation is evident from the fact that the number of helpers, i.e. executioners, per victim, had to be limited to eight.[64] According to some sources, the fate of the adult commoners who were obliged to accompany a dead person had been decided in their infancy, when a future ruler was born.[65] During the ruler's lifetime they constituted a particularly faithful and privileged band of followers. According to others the nomination of these victims took place later in the form of a self-pledge.[66] At any rate, it was not the random product of a situation caused by the death of the person to be accompanied.

The custom among the Natchez thus had a very marked institutional character. The relationship between the dead person and the accompanying person was determined by social position and not by a close personal relationship. Only members of the nobility had greater latitude in this matter. They were not obliged to accompany the dead. Nevertheless, at times some of them would have themselves killed.[67]

The fact that functions in this world were apparently more important than those in the other corresponds to the institutional character of the custom. The idea of providing a retinue for the other world is occasionally mentioned in the sources. The special character of the custom however seems to be a result of the needs of this world: it served to maintain and strengthen the social order.

The strong institutional character is also evident when the question of free choice and coercion is raised. Posing the question itself in this context is misleading because it is directed to the moment of decision after the death of the person to be accompanied. The Natchez consistently avoided this situation—at least in the case of those who did not belong to the nobility. Those who married a *sun* ran the risk of having to follow their spouse into death, if the spouse died first. When this happened, there was nothing left to decide, even though in

---

[63] Dumont de Montigny 1, 179–80 (Swanton 104–5). Cf. Mason 124, Brain 215–16; White 370.

[64] Le Page du Pratz 3, 45 (Swanton 146).

[65] Le Petit 130–2 (Swanton 142–3).

[66] Charlevoix, *Nouvelle France* 3, 422 (Swanton 142); Pénicaut, in Margry 453 (Swanton 140).

[67] Cf. MacLeod, *Evolution* 221–2.

practice some may have gone more readily to their death than others. This was also valid for the other adult victims. If they had been intended for this as infants, they would have had no say in the matter. If they had committed themselves as adults, they had done so long before the death of the person to be accompanied, at a point of time when the question of having to redeem the pledge was not relevant, and when the possibility existed that the ruler would survive them.

Yet, in practice, free choice in the sense of determined and conscious consent seems to have played a role. This was generally the case with members of the nobility who were not obliged to accompany the dead. But even among those who were under this obligation, there was often a firm resolution to accompany the dead even in the face of opposition. This became very evident in one situation. Women nursing infants were not killed. Yet 'we often see many who endeavor to find nurses, or who themselves strangle their infants, so that they shall not lose the right of sacrificing themselves in the public square.'[68] What remains unanswered is the question about the fate of a mother who survived because of her infant. Was it fear of an existence in disgrace and contempt or a kind of heroism which led them to murder and suicide?

Even though social pressure on the victim was probably strong, direct force does not seem to have been used, as we can see from a case which also shows that not all the victims acquiesced in their fate. Living for years with the knowledge of the obligation to die does not mean automatic protection against the fear that sets in when the time to redeem the promise arrives. A noblewoman had married a commoner named Ette-actal or Taotal. She died and he fled to the French, who gave him protection. In 1725 he returned to his country, where he was arrested. In connection with a new funeral he was expected to redeem his promise at this later date. However he displayed a most pitiful fear of death, and so he was allowed to run away again. A short while later three old women, two of whom were related to him, presented themselves of their own free will as substitute victims. The offer was accepted, and the man who had escaped death now participated

---

[68] Le Petit 132 (Swanton 143). For indications of free choice among the 'normal' victims see Gravier 142 (Swanton 139): 'These wretched victims deeming themselves greatly honored to accompany their chief by a violent death'; Le Petit 132 (Swanton 143): 'All these servants sacrifice themselves, with joy, to follow their dear master'; Charlevoix, *Nouvelle France* 3, 421–2 (Swanton 142).

in the strangling of these women, and it seemed 'that he appeared to draw with great pleasure' on the rope with which these women were strangled.[69] The role of the executioner was coveted because it led to a rise in status.

This example of a deviation once again confirms the strictly functional character of following into death among the Natchez. A person is not regarded as an individual, but only on the basis of his role in the social system. If this role is taken over by another person, then the original bearer of the role is free to take on a new one. Following the dead is a component of the social order of this and the other world, not an outflow of individual relationships or even of feelings—which does not mean that these could not have played a role in the concrete act.

These accounts of the Natchez seem to constitute an exception. No analogous ceremonies are known from other continents and nothing similar is reported about any other people in North America. This exceptional character could hardly be a coincidence. The consistent link between following into death and significant social constellations, which recur frequently, endangers the existence of the concerned society, both on account of the conflicts between potential victims and those to be accompanied, as well as on account of the number of victims. Such a system functions best within a small, well-balanced society.

Other Cases of Following into Death

Around 1860, the French traveller Jules Remy witnessed the funeral of a small chief of the Shoshone in the region of what is today the state of Utah. He found it 'moving and horrible alike. [. . .] According to the custom one of his wives and two horses were sacrificed at his grave' to keep him company in the other world.

The dead man had chosen his prettiest wife to accompany him on his last journey. After both the horses had been sacrificed, the young woman stepped up to her husband's grave without any sign of fear. Her husband's brother first cut her hair and then drove a bullet through her

---

[69] Le Page du Pratz 3, 46–50 (Swanton 146–7); Dumont de Montigny 1, 216–17; 226–28 (Swanton 151–2; 154); Bossu, in Yarrow 187–8. Quote: Swanton 154.

heart. [. . .] Both corpses were then covered with earth and the horses were buried next to them. The hair of the victim was buried at some distance and everything was over.[70]

The widow goes to her death with amazing self-control. One gets the impression of a complete exercise of free choice. This is not true for the selection of the victim, which actually shows the extreme subordination of the woman to the man. His authority over her extends beyond his death since it is the woman he chooses who has to die with him. This is a case of direct coercion. The victim would not have been allowed to live had she wanted to.

Similar forms, in which following into death is limited to a single close relative of the dead person, are known only with regard to a few of the North American peoples. Mackenzie writes about the Knistenaux in the northwest: 'I have been informed that women, as in the East, have been known to sacrifice themselves to the manes of their husbands.'[71] Among the Carriers the widow is sometimes said to have been burnt to death.[72]

The relative scarcity of such accounts cannot be blamed on the contingencies of transmission alone. The sources give the impression that, seen as a whole, the institutional character of the custom prevailed. This is underlined by the use of slaves as victims, either exclusively or in addition to the killing of widows.[73] In principle, the possibility of using slaves was open to all free people—in practice, however, it was naturally limited to those who could afford slaves.

The important role of the slaves indicates that following into death had a marked functional and instrumental character, not only among the Natchez, but in the whole of North America. The deceased requires a retinue and this has to be obtained by any means possible. The retinue

---

[70] Remy 1, 115.

[71] A. Mackenzie XCVIII. It is not clear from the text whether this is a case of killing or self-killing. Similarly in Dunn 94.

[72] West 141. According to Wells 602, it had earlier (with reference to 1856) been customary among the Coos in Oregon to kill the widow and bury her with her husband's body. For further, less reliable information about the Ute, Comanche and Chickasaw, see MacLeod, *Distribution* 209–10. Cf. Bancroft 1, 439; Steinmetz, *Strafe* 154.

[73] See for example Dunn 120 (peoples at the mouth of the Columbia River); Gibbs 189; 204 (Washington); West 141–2; Schoolcraft 5, 654 (Oregon). See Bancroft 1, 86; 93; Steinmetz, *Strafe* 155–6.

relationship only arises through death; the relationship of the participants to each other during their lifetime does not play a role here, or at least not a decisive one. When the daughter of a chief of the Chinook on the northwestern coast died, a slave was tied to the corpse. Both were then placed in a canoe, which was dragged to a high rock. The slave was left alive for another three days, after which he was strangled by another slave.[74] The killing of the persons accompanying the dead often occurred a long time after the death of the person to be accompanied.[75]

A story from the sixteenth century demonstrates the objective and functional understanding of the custom that formed the basis of such rituals. The Spanish discoverer and conqueror Hernando de Soto died in 1542 in the region of the Lower Mississippi. The Indians living in the area offered the Spaniards two men who could be killed to accompany the dead man. The Spaniards sent them back.[76]

These aspects become even clearer in another custom, which, however, has rarely been attested to. In 1840, McCoy writes that the Osage bury the corpse in the ground and pile stones on top of it. Sometimes they stuck a pole into these stones, on which an enemy scalp had been fixed. They believe that 'the spirit of the former [slain enemy] became subjected as a slave to the spirit of the latter [the slayer], in the world of spirits. Hence the last and best service that can be performed for a deceased relative is to take the life of an enemy.'[77]

Such customs are otherwise rarely mentioned in the sources. In view of the significance of scalping in different regions of North America, one can presume that it occurred more often, even if sometimes essentially different functions are ascribed to the scalp.[78]

In this case, all personal components are missing in the relationship between the attendant and the person being accompanied, otherwise it would be impossible to chain sworn enemies together as master and slave. In the other world everything personal is eliminated and only the outwardly ascribed function remains.

Corresponding to this is the fact that free choice does not play a role

[74] Schoolcraft 2, 71, without mentioning the sex of the slave.
[75] Schoolcraft 5, 654: Lower Oregon: A slave would be killed one or two years after the death of his master.
[76] Elvas 128 (chap. 30).
[77] McCoy 360.
[78] On scalping see Friederici, here mainly 114–16.

here. It is of no concern to the participants. The victim is not expected to go to his death of his own free choice. Therefore the Indian informants also do not seem to have stressed this aspect. Although the authors point out from time to time that the victims go willingly to their death, there is no specific information with regard to this that either rests on eyewitness accounts or that mentions plausible details. In addition, there is no clear mention of the self-killing of a victim.

On the whole, the voluntary nature of the act is emphasized more often for Central and South America than for North America. There is enough evidence to support the view that this situation is not the result of differences in the act itself, but of differences in the conditions that generated the sources. The informants of the Spaniards, especially in the early period, were probably under greater pressure to justify themselves than the informants of the French or the British.

The number of victims in each case was, as a rule, apparently relatively small and amounted to between one and maybe ten. The funerals of the Natchez, at which between two or three dozen people might be killed, seem to be a distinct exception. An account of 1682 speaking of a hundred people being killed on the death of a chief of the Taensa in the Lower Mississippi region would have to be an exaggeration, especially since the account is extremely short and stereotyped.[79]

The Suppression

In North America, too, following into death disappeared with the onset of European influence, although in remote regions this happened slowly. With the increase of settlers in the nineteenth century, this influence made itself felt to a greater extent. John Dunn reports in 1844 that 'this barbarous superstition' of killing slaves at the grave of the chief had been given up among the peoples at the mouth of the Columbia River in the region of the Hudson's Bay Company.[80] George Gibbs writes in 1877 about two relevant cases from the region of the future state of Washington. In 1850, someone from among the Tsinuk tried to make a young female slave starve to death to accompany a dead child, 'and her life was only saved by the intervention of the citizens, who offered to pay her price, representing that it would be as good to destroy the value in merchandise, and adding the weight of a threat in

[79] Tonti, in Swanton 260.
[80] Dunn 120.

case of refusal.'[81] The threat must have had a greater effect than the peculiar reason that was provided along with it, which obviously very consciously ignored the idea of following the dead and, instead, referred to the custom of placing the dead person's possessions in the grave, or of burning them on the grave. In the same region in 1853 a chief 'undertook to kill a slave girl belonging to his daughter, who, in dying, had requested that this might be done. The woman fled and was found by some citizens in the woods half starved. Her master attempted to reclaim her, but was soundly thrashed, and warned against another attempt.'[82]

[81] Gibbs 189.
[82] Gibbs 204.

CHAPTER 4

Africa

For Africa south of the Sahara there are many more and also far more substantial accounts about following into death than there are for America or even for Europe. This may be a result of the favourable conditions for observation, or it may well be an indication of the spread of corresponding customs. Islamic travellers had already visited the region in mediaeval times.[1] From the fifteenth century onwards Europeans came increasingly into contact with African states, but apart from a few small points they did not rule over any areas. This situation continued till the late nineteenth century, although European penetration of the continent increased during this time. Thus, for centuries, Europeans were witness to events, but were not in a position to intervene.

The unequal spatial distribution of recorded cases also indicates that the frequent mention of following into death in the sources corresponds to actual practice. There is no information about following into death in the Islamic regions, neither in pre-European nor in European times. Europeans seldom ventured into Islamic regions, most of which were inland. However, had the custom been widespread, they would still have heard and certainly have written about it, since that would have harmed the reputation of their greatest enemies. Relevant accounts are also missing from areas converted to Christianity. From time to time, cases of a 'relapse' are mentioned for the border regions, which had only just converted to Christianity or Islam, and the authors judge this to be a sign of an incomplete conversion.[2]

---

[1] A compilation of the sources since the tenth century exists in Levtzion/ Hopkins.

[2] For the Christians in the kingdom of Congo see for example Cavazzi 94 (book 1, chap. 262) and Merolla 397 (1692). In the fourteenth century Ibn Baṭṭūṭa describes how a highly placed Muslim had to pay money to free his son, who had been chosen as an attendant in death. Levtzion/Hopkins 281.

Although the sources are abundant, their quality leaves much to be desired. The actual number of eyewitness accounts is very small. They begin only in the eighteenth century, and their authors often tend to exaggerate. Old themes going back to Herodotus are often repeated. In the late nineteenth and twentieth century the accounts become increasingly more matter of fact. Scientific standards were gradually established. The later the scientific inquiry took place, the further back in time were cases of following the dead pushed, as the colonial powers had forbidden the practice everywhere. As a rule, therefore, the authors could only record what they had heard from Africans and not what they had actually seen.[3]

A further reason for scepticism is the fact that many Europeans were interested in portraying Africans as bloodthirsty barbarians, in order to justify the slave trade and, later, the conquest, or also to emphasize the necessity of missionary activity.[4]

A critical evaluation of the sources, though necessary, does not mean that one has to seriously doubt the existence of following into death in Africa. In contrast to Latin America, all the events described did not take place only before the Europeans arrived.[5] Until well into the nineteenth century the Africans, as a rule, never thought of keeping their actions secret. On the contrary they often invited European diplomats, traders and missionaries to their ceremonies.[6] Quite often they more or less forced them to participate.[7] Sometimes they even

---

[3] Cf. Rathbone.

[4] Isichei, *Social reform* 470; Coquery-Vidrovitch 702. Cf. 1861 *Journal des missions évangéliques* 148: 'Those who write about such events speak more strongly for the concerns of the Protestant mission than had they employed arguments based on reason alone.' Similarly 1844 T.B. Freeman 25; 128.

[5] To name only a few of the detailed descriptions: Burton, *Gelele* 1, 343–86; 2, 1–62 (1864) and Skertchly (1874); also the short but precise descriptions by Lartigue (1860), in Brunschwig 126–30 and by Coquilhat 168–74 (for 1883). A compilation of the sources for Dahomey since the eighteenth century, which has been best documented in this regard, can be found in Coquery-Vidrovitch 715–16. For the problem of the relative lack of reliable eyewitness accounts see C. Williams 434–5. Wilhelm Johann Müller 96 claimed in his travelogue of 1676 to have been an eyewitness to the killing of eighty-five people. Cavazzi 97 (book 1, chap. 67); 166 (book 2, chap. 38) claims to have frequently been an eyewitness.

[6] For example Omboni 313–14; Brunschwig 125–6.

[7] Forbes 2, 50–3; Skertchly VIII; 183; Pommegorge 178; *Le tour du Monde*

tried to make the Europeans provide victims. In 1846 the King of
Dahomey invited the British traveller John Duncan to execute four
criminals with his own hands. The man thus honoured thanked him,
but refused.[8]
Finally, there is also isolated archaeological evidence. A mass grave
with the skeletons of forty-one young women was found in Benin.
Although the cause of death could not be determined, the excavators
presumed a connection with following into death.[9]

The custom is mentioned frequently for West Africa, much less
often for Central and East Africa, and even more rarely for Southern
Africa.[10] Taken as a whole, from the fifteenth to the nineteenth centuries there were far more European travellers, traders, and missionaries in West Africa than in other regions (the southern point of Africa
as a European colony of settlement is a special case). The greater
frequency could therefore simply be a result of the greater opportunities for observation. In some of the larger kingdoms of West Africa,
notably in Dahomey, Asante and Benin, there is some evidence to support the view that following into death had a special political significance and, therefore, also a greater range than elsewhere.

It is even less possible to make reliable statements about changes in
frequency over a period of time, although such attempts have been
made from time to time, not least in order to assign historical guilt. The
starting point is the assumption that in pre-European times following
into death already existed, but that the number of victims in each case
was small. This is supposed to have changed gradually as a result of the
general brutalization caused by the Atlantic slave trade. Paradoxically,
the prohibition of the slave trade in the nineteenth century is said to
have brought about a further rise in the number of victims and the climax of the custom, since there was no other use for the prisoners of war,
who had till then been sold into slavery.[11]

108; Campion-Vincent 33; Herskovits 2, 56; Ellis, *Ewe* 129; Schneider, *Reli-*
gion 120–1.
[8] Duncan 1, 247–52.
[9] Connah (1975) 62–7; 209–18. See Law, *Human sacrifice* 62; Ryder
188.
[10] See the map in Irstam 163, in which however West Africa is not sufficiently taken into account.
[11] Davidson 196–7; 207–8; Isichei, *Ibo* 56–8; Isichei, *Social reform* 469–
70; Graham 318 (quoting J.D. Fage, *An Introduction to the History of West*

This theory is plausible to some extent, though its weakness lies in the fact that it regards both the introduction as well as the abolition of the slave trade as factors that increased the significance of following into death. One could just as well assert that the slave trade led to a decrease of this significance, because potential victims could now be sold for a profit.[12] The important point here is that we are dealing with a hypothesis that cannot be verified on the basis of the sources. It is true that the number of relevant accounts increases in the nineteenth century, and that often a very high number of victims is mentioned. However, the number of Europeans writing about Africa also increased during this time. Apart from that, many authors deliberately supplied exaggerated figures in order to justify European intervention.[13]

Such debates are problematic for yet another reason. In the final analysis, they accept the premises of the contemporary arguments, even if they draw different conclusions from them. Using value-judgements based on Christian–European beliefs, the missionary-philanthropic movement of the nineteenth century abhorred the rituals, which it generally labelled as human sacrifice. The attempt to show that matters had not been so bad in Africa, as well as the attempt to provide evidence of a strong European influence, serves to exonerate Africans.[14] In this manner, however, Africa continues to remain in the dock, since the basic facts of the matter have not changed, there being only a question of extenuating circumstances. A conclusion such as

---

Africa, 1961), and Wilks, *Human sacrifice* 451–2 argue in this manner. The statements in Coquery-Vidrovitch are partly false and partly contradictory. She states on p.699 that such events are not mentioned in the older Portuguese sources. That is not the case. On the contrary, such information is even older; it is found in authors writing in Arabic since the tenth century (Levtzion/ Hopkins 52). While on p. 699 the author explains that the killings only began in the sixteenth century, on p. 708 she proceeds on the assumption that they had always been carried out. Law, *Human sacrifice* 64–77 is considerably more cautious. In some cases he is able to render an increase in the nineteenth century plausible; real proof is, however, not possible. See also Home 1, 103, and on the sources in general A. Jones, *Quellenproblematik* 72–6; 79–80.

[12] For example Dalzel 25; 230; Roth, *Benin* 103 (Beauvais).

[13] Ryder 247–9. Cf. Forbes 2, 53.

[14] Cf. along with the authors mentioned in footnote 11 also Brunschwig 131–2; Rattray 104ff.

this can only be avoided if one ceases to make all moralizing statements and looks at the custom as an institution. Only then can one engage with the perspective of Africans, who at first did not understand the moral reservations of Europeans. In 1883, when nine people were killed to accompany a chief in the Congo, certain Africans remarked, without a trace of irony, to French soldiers: 'You must be killing many more slaves, since your chiefs are much richer than ours.'[15] The deep-rootedness of such customs outlived even the long period of contact with Europeans. In the 1820s the British gave protection, in their fort at Cape Coast, to Cheboe, the King of Dinkera, against the army of Asante. While he was at the fort his sister died, and he wanted a female servant to accompany her. African soldiers in British pay prevented him at the last minute from carrying out his plan.[16] He could scarcely have been unaware of his hosts' aversion to following into death, and he could hardly have wanted to incur their displeasure. If, despite this, he tried to carry out the practice, it shows that European arguments had failed to influence him.

Individual Following into Death

The individual form of the custom is not very important in Africa. In the sources evaluated here one does not see the predominance of this aspect in a single, well-testified case. The manner in which the institutional aspect eclipses the individual aspect can be seen very clearly in an institution known to have existed in West Africa. Nothing definite is known, however, about the spread of this institution. Men and women of high rank had an 'intimate [male] friend (Okra)' and an 'intimate [female] friend (Okrara)', respectively, who, as a rule, killed themselves on the death of their master or mistress 'like the members of a brotherhood among us earlier'.[17] The personal relationship may have been a close one, but at its base was a division of society along class lines and not according to status. In the final analysis it is the servant who accompanied the master, not the friend who accompanied the friend.

This conclusion is strengthened when one considers that even those impersonal forms that can at least partly be regarded as individual

[15] Coquilhat 169.
[16] Ricketts 107–8.
[17] Monrad 253–4.

following into death, namely head-hunting and scalping, are not mentioned, and, therefore, in all probability also hardly occurred.[18]

Institutional Following into Death

In Africa following into death thus has a predominantly institutional character. The personal relationship is subordinated to the institutional context, as for example when the wife of a ruler has to accompany him into death. This happens independently of her feelings for him. She has to die because he is the ruler, and not because he is her husband.

Accordingly, the custom always has an eminently political character in Africa (this does not rule out, but, on the contrary, presupposes the religious basis, as will be shown). It is functional with regard to the political and social position of the dead person, and therefore also serves to emphasize and strengthen this position. It is both an expression of power and a means to concentrate power. It creates, maintains, and strengthens political and social hierarchies. This conclusion is important in view of the tendency apparent till recently to view Africa within the framework of an extreme political decentralization, even anarchy.

The Accompanied

If one goes by the sources, generally only members of the ruling class were accompanied in death in Africa. The logical consequence of this restriction of the right to be accompanied was its monopolization by the ruler. In Dahomey, for example, since around 1845 this right was indeed reserved solely for the ruler who jealously guarded his privilege.[19] In Benin and in Asante it was available to a larger circle of people, but only with the express permission of the ruler.[20] If a ruler

[18] An exception is Tremearne 178–80, about head-hunting among the Kagoro in Nigeria. For a general account see Law, *Head*. For more details on both these forms cf. pp. 73 and 171–8.

[19] Duncan 1, 258; 2, 305; Law, *Human sacrifice* 74. Cf. Coquery-Vidrovitch 710; Campion-Vincent 31; Herskovits 2, 54–6. Ellis, *Ewe* 128 states that in Dahomey following into death earlier also existed for other important men. See also Kalous 373.

[20] C.Williams 438; McCaskie, *State* 201 (Asante); Law, *Human sacrifice* 74 (Benin).

was unable to establish his monopoly over the custom, it was seen as a sign of the erosion of his power. These conditions were known even to observers in the nineteenth century, for example when Allen and Thomson wrote about Whydah in West Africa in 1848: 'Human sacrifices always take place on the death of the King; on which occasion, one or more wives, and several eunuchs of his establishment, are killed, to accompany the great man in the new world he has entered upon. Every sovereign, on coming to the throne, does this also, to exemplify the control which his position gives him over the lives of his people.'[21]

The states in which the custom was the ruler's prerogative are, however, an exception. As a rule, the circle of people who were allowed to practise the custom was larger. The accounts do not give exact details about its extent. Often, the authors were probably not well informed. Yet it is also important to note that the boundaries were flexible. In the final analysis, it was a question of which group, family or clan was in a position to gain entry into the privileged circle. For upwardly mobile classes, gaining the right to be followed in death could become proof of their new position. African traders who had become rich through their dealings with Europeans occasionally maintained the relevant rituals, although this gave rise to aversion and disgust among their trading partners.[22]

The institutional character of the custom in Africa is also evident in the fact that women were generally excluded from the circle of entitled persons. For reasons that are not connected with the custom, they could seldom become rulers or rise to the position of important persons. Whenever possible, and if for example they were members of important families, they were given the right to be accompanied in death.[23] In one region there is even a report of the reversal of the conditions of subordination between the sexes on the basis of social position.

[21] Allen/Thomson 1, 328.

[22] Adams 24–7.

[23] Bowdich 283 (Asante); François 59 (Ibengo on the Lulongo, sister of the chief); T.B. Freeman 151 (Asante, daughter of the King); William Allen, in T.B. Freeman 193–4 (mother of the King of Apollonia, Gold Coast, around 1842); Ricketts 107–8 (sister of the King of Dinkera, Cape Coast); Gyamfi 30; Roscoe, *Baganda* 114–16 (Queen and Queen Mother in Buganda); Wissmann *et al.*, *Im Innern Afrikas* 101–2 (Queen Mother in the kingdom of Lunda); Dapper (1668) 1,498 (Benin); Cardi, in Kingsley 452–3 (Benin); Kranz 57; Kidd 246; Bryant 609–11; Shooter 243–5 and Hartmann 191

In Asante, when the sisters of the ruler married men who were not of high birth, these men had to die with their wives, without the women having to take on a similar obligation on the death of their husbands.[24]

Persons Accompanying the Dead

The consequence of the pronounced institutional and political character of the custom in Africa was its tendency to intensification. If following into death served to demonstrate the power of the person being accompanied and that of his successors, then this power was more evident if the ritual was grand and the number of victims large. It is very seldom mentioned that just one person accompanied the dead to the next world. It is, as a rule, a woman or a slave.[25] These accounts are, however, so imprecise that the question concerning the number of victims remains unanswered. Normally, what clearly emerges from the sources is that several persons, often a large number, accompanied the dead. The numbers given extend to several thousand people.[26] In most cases, this is probably an exaggeration. Yet there can be no doubt that following into death was very often a collective and even a mass affair.[27]

(all: Shaka's mother, whereby considerable doubts about the handing down of the text are in order).

[24] Bowdich 291; Ellis, *Tshi* 287.

[25] For example Burton, *Lake regions* 25–6 (Chiefs of Wanyamwezi); Des Marchais 1, 153–9 (Rio Sexto); Talbot 140 (Ibibio, Nigeria: killing of a slave).

[26] Bowdich 289 (over 3,500); Burton, *Gelele* 2, 234 (over 2,000); Ellis, *Tshi* 164 (over 3,000 in the year 1816); Grandidier (about 3,000; account from the year 1620); Hutton 86; Mackay 185 (over 2,000 in Uganda 1881); Meyerowitz 64 (over 4,000); Ramseyer/Kühne, second German edition 287 (over 1,000 in Asante). Barbot 2,595 (2,000); McCaskie, *Death* 431–7 (upto 3,600); Macdonald 74 (upto 2,000 in East Africa). C. Williams 439 mentions only figures upto 2,000, Campion-Vincent 48 on the other hand upto 5,000 (Dahomey). Fynn 134, apparently an eyewitness, speaks of 7,000 victims on the death of Shaka's mother (1827). (Cf. Shooter 243–4; Bryant 609; Kidd 246; Kranz 57–8.) R.A. Freeman 473 in 1898 already termed most of the figures given as gross exaggerations. For an extreme form of general and unverified statements about the alleged limitless bloodthirstiness, cf. Bacon 86–93 and Home for Benin. Cf. also footnote 5.

[27] Herskovits 2, 53 points out in 1938 that his informants in Dahomey named even larger numbers of victims than are mentioned in the accounts of

If one proceeds from a hypothetical number of total cases, then killings in large numbers would have been the exception, even in Africa.
Normally the retinues for the other world would have consisted of a
few, perhaps even only of one or two people. The sources understandably mention the spectacular events more frequently than the less
remarkable ones.

The persons accompanying the dead can be divided into two categories, depending on whether there was a close personal relationship
between them and the person being accompanied. Accordingly, we can
speak of personal and anonymous attendants in death.

1. In practically all the cases of following into death there are some
personal attendants who, as a rule, represented different groups and
occupied different positions. Wives and concubines are mentioned
most frequently. Then come the female and male slaves, but also female
and male servants, dignitaries and officials of all kinds, as well as members of the royal court in the broadest sense. What they had in common
was close personal relationship with the dead man, even if there were
enormous differences in the intensity of this relationship, ranging
from the favourite wife to the kitchen slave, from the minister to the
house servant. According to Roscoe the following persons were stabbed to death at the funeral of a ruler of the Baganda: the first cook, the
first brewer, the principal shepherd, the first guardian of the holy fire,
the man who supervised the king's well, a female cook and a female
beer-brewer, as well as the respective female heads of the royal sleeping-
chambers, water, clothes, milk-pots and milk.[28]

2. In a considerable number of cases, especially at the funeral of
rulers of large kingdoms, when the number of attendants in death was
particularly large, these groups were enhanced by the category of
anonymous attendants. No personal relationship existed, till then,
between them and the person being accompanied. The deceased
generally did not know these victims; they may have seen them at best
from afar. They were chosen arbitrarily and were therefore interchangeable.

Burton and Skertchly. The most considered reflections are in McCaskie, *Death*
431–7 with estimates for Asante for 1867/68 ranging between 1,853 and
3,600 victims.

[28] Roscoe, *Baganda* 106–7. Similarly Roscoe, *Bantu* 52 (Banyoro).
Cf. Irstam 35. Similar lists are to be found in Spanish works of the sixteenth
century on Mexico. See above pp. 51–2.

These anonymous victims can again be divided into different groups.

a) The numerically most important group was probably that of *prisoners of war*, although they were used only by a minority of the states that practised the custom. Those that did, employed them in large numbers. It is repeatedly maintained that even during a war, or soon after, prisoners would be slaughtered in the hundreds or even thousands in honour of important military persons from the victor's camp who had lost their lives in battle.[29]

The killing of prisoners, however, would originally have had little to do with following into death. The starting point for this was probably the difficulties encountered in guarding large numbers of prisoners. Not least in order to make the killings appear legitimate, they may have been ritualized by linking them with the funeral ceremonies of one's own dead. The killings would have taken on the character of following into death if a certain amount of time had elapsed between being taken prisoner and being killed on the occasion of a funeral ceremony, and if the person being accompanied had not been killed in war. This would establish that the prisoners had not been killed primarily for reasons of security. In 1727, when Snelgrave asked in Dahomey why so many strong young men were being killed, when they could be sold as slaves to the Europeans, he was told that 'these young people had been destined to serve the wives of the King in the other world whom those of Tuffoe, their country, had killed.'[30]

The important function of prisoners of war as victims makes us wonder whether at times, when attendants in death were required, wars were fought in order to get them. This appears actually to have happened. However, the statements in this regard are fairly vague.[31] At

---

[29] Bayol 19–20 (Dahomey); Beecham 224; 232; 237 (over 4,000 victims in Asante); Dalzel 158; 226; Buchholz 25 (Duala); Hecquard 47 (Great-Bassam); for general information see Ellis, *Tshi* 164–6; Coquery-Vidrovitch 706; Wilks, *Human sacrifice* 443–52; Law, *Human sacrifice* 60; Campion-Vincent 30; Kalous 373.

[30] Snelgrave 55. Cf. Ellis, *Tshi* 163–4; Ramseyer/Kühne, English edition 254–5; Skertchly 193; Valdez 1, 333.

[31] For example Buchholz 34; Bayol 20 (Dahomey); Le Hérissé 189 (Dahomey); Dalzel 226 (Dahomey); Lartigue, in Brunschwig 130. Cf. Coquery-Vidrovitch 706. In what is no doubt a fictitious speech, which Dalzel 218 ascribes to an African king, this aspect is denied.

best we can presume that it played a certain role in smaller contexts. On the death of the ruler of the Toma in Liberia his successor was made to carry out a military expedition, from which he was only allowed to return when he had two male prisoners who were then killed and buried with the corpse of the ruler.[32] Larger military expeditions, however, were mainly carried out for the capture of prisoners to be sold as slaves.

This leads us to ask why the prisoners were killed to accompany the dead and not sold off. All the sources agree that most of the people killed were not unfit for work.[33]

What was the relationship between following into death and the Atlantic slave trade, and how did material and non-material motives relate to each other? A strictly materialist view would have to stem from the fact that there was a clear connection between the extent of the custom and the amount paid for slaves. When the demand for slaves was low, the number of persons accompanying the dead increased; if the demand went up, only a few persons who could not be sold would have been killed.

Various statements in the sources point in this direction. A sudden rise in the price of slaves in 1791, for example, saved the lives of a number of prisoners.[34] Yet even when the prices were at their highest, prisoners who could otherwise have been sold as slaves were killed to accompany the dead.

This relative independence of the economy of the slave trade shows very clearly that the events being examined here actually had the character of following into death. If it were only a matter of getting rid of the prisoners, one could just as easily have sold them to the Europeans, making a big profit in the bargain. If, on the other hand, it was a question of the link with the other world, of needing to satisfy the dead person, and also to prevent his infringements on this world, then one could not forgo it, even for favourable material prospects.[35]

b) This impression that allowances were made for material disadvantages is strengthened through the second category of anonymous

[32] Néel 472.

[33] Isichei, *Social reform* 469 maintains, on the other hand, that among the prisoners killed those unfit for work were in the majority. Similarly Beauvais, in Roth, *Benin* 103.

[34] Burton, *Gelele* 1, 344; cf. Wilks, *Human sacrifice* 451–2.

[35] This is reiterated in the fictitious speech mentioned in Dalzel 218–21. See footnote 31.

attendants. Instead of creating opportunities for war in order to capture prisoners, in many places slaves were bought on the death of an important person for the express purpose of accompanying him.[36] This transaction normally took place outside one's own state, one of the reasons definitely being the desire not to place too heavy a load on one's own society. Often, the slaves were bought before the person to be accompanied had died, and kept as a reserve supply.[37] Sometimes, these candidates for death lived in their own villages.[38] In this way, the slaves often blended in with the personal attendants, especially when there were only a few of them and they lived in direct contact with the person to be accompanied.

c) In some countries criminals condemned to death played an important role in the custom.[39] Their execution was stayed till the next opportunity for their ritual killing presented itself. These killings seldom occurred, and only on the unforeseeable death of an important person. Many years could elapse before the next ceremony. This was too long to wait for the executions. Hence the use of criminals was customary in those places where the system of sacrifice had, to some extent, become a continual process. This happened mainly at the annual memorial ceremonies, when the dead person would be provided with additional attendants.[40]

This method of integrating executions into following into death clearly demonstrates the political character of the custom. European observers compared the events with public executions in Europe, as Skertchly did in 1874, while writing about Dahomey. In this way he

[36] For example Bosman 2, 13; Leonard 160; 444–6; Lewin 65 (Asante); Kalous 373; Wissmann, *Durchquerung* 115; Wilks, *Human sacrifice* 449 (Asante). According to Wilks these are prisoners condemned to death and sold by the state, to be executed during the relevant ceremony. However this does not hold true in a general fashion for all regions. The slaves who were bought could for their part be former prisoners of war of those who were selling them.

[37] Buchholz 26; François 68; Herskovits 1, 100; Ramseyer/Kühne, second German edition 284; Weeks 319–20.

[38] Rattray 106; Mc Caskie, *State* 98–9; 297 (Asante).

[39] Dapper (1668) 1, 503; Bradbury 55 (both Benin); Ramseyer/Kühne, English edition 235; Rattray 106; Freeman 475; McCaskie, *State* 297 (all Asante); Skertchly 193 and *passim;* Ellis, *Ewe* 129; Omboni 313–14 (Dahomey).

[40] Apart from the sources mentioned in the preceding footnote, cf. especially Burton, *Gelele*, chap. 14.

defends and exonerates the custom to some extent, but in the process ignores its specific character: 'Much of the horror of this barbarous practice is therefore taken off when we consider that nearly all the capital punishments inflicted in a year are carried out during the Customs; and I doubt not that if we were to hang all our murderers at one period of the year—say at Christmas—the list would be as long as that of Dahomey.'[41]

The execution of criminals has played a special role in the academic debate on following into death in Africa. It has repeatedly been stated that in Africa the victims of the custom were predominantly, if not exclusively, criminals condemned to death.[42] However, there is no empirical proof for this assertion.[43] As mentioned earlier, executions could be replaced by ritualized killings only where the form of the custom was repeated at fairly regular intervals. Apart from this, there were other forms. Even when delinquents were used, in the understanding of all concerned (the killers, the victims and the onlookers) it was a matter primarily of following into death and not of an execution. The victims were not sent to the other world as criminals, as innocent people, or as volunteers for death, but simply as persons accompanying the dead. Following into death is not an execution; rather, executions are also used to obtain a retinue for the dead person. Otherwise the deceased would decline the offer to let criminals, who would be a potential source of danger, accompany him. Through the act of following the dead, the criminal is no longer a criminal but becomes a loyal attendant in death.

One also has to ask whether such attendants in death were persons who were condemned to death by due process of law for a crime that merited capital punishment according to the law of the land, or whether, when required, additional death sentences were passed that did not conform to the law. The sources justify an element of doubt. Among the Bakuba, for example, people who were guilty of small transgressions against the person or the property of the ruler would be earmarked as victims. Till they were required for this purpose they were

[41] Skertchly 193.
[42] Collins 121–2 (Asante); Graham 330 (Benin); Lewin 63–4 (Asante); Wilks, *Nineteenth century* 592–3; Wilks, *Human sacrifice*, and also Skertchly 193 (Dahomey).
[43] For a critique especially C. Williams 433–5; in addition Law, *Human sacrifice* 59–60. Similarly earlier Forbes 1, 53 (Dahomey).

allowed to move around freely. It would appear, therefore, that they were not regarded as criminals who deserved to die.[44]

d) This last point brings us to the fourth category of anonymous victims—the innocent and the uninvolved. The sources repeatedly mention that in some countries the death of a ruler led to a—shorter or longer—period of anarchy.[45] During this time armed men would often swarm into the streets and indiscriminately either directly kill people[46]—as attendants for the dead—or seize them as victims for later rituals.[47] In 1875 such a situation in Asante was described:

Kwaku Dua died on Saturday, 27 April 1867. The princes, who had looked after the king in his last days, kept his passing away a secret for a few hours, during which as many people as possible were lured into the palace. Suddenly the gates were closed and the princes with their men threw themselves onto these unlucky people, who soon lay in their own blood. The news travels through the city with the speed of lightning, in no time at all the streets are empty, trembling, each one tries to hide in the furthest room. Woe to them who return unsuspectingly from their fields! The princes spread out in all directions and kill everyone they can reach with a knife or a musket; whether slave or chieftain does not matter in the least on this day. The heads are carried into the palace, the bloodthirsty villains however find the number too small, and they force their way into the houses also and continue their murdering spree. They even stormed into the mission yard and seized the two female slaves of the native catechist, but he saved their lives by declaring that the men would have to kill him first.

There was now complete anarchy. Every chieftain stood armed in front of his house, around him all his people with weapons in their hands. This readiness to strike back had to continue day and night. All those who were alone were hounded to death, but when the princes came upon such an armed band of men they greeted them politely

---

[44] Wolf, in Wissmann *et al*. 244. Cf. Ellis, *Tshi* 166 and particularly C.Williams 439–40 (for Asante).

[45] For example Lander, *Journal* 96. A broad overview in Irstam 152–3.

[46] For example Johnston 2, 716 (Uganda); Landolphe 55 (Benin); Rattray 109–10 (Asante); Waddell 336; Dapper (1668) 1, 503 (Benin).

[47] For example Ellis, *Tshi* 161 (Asante); Ramseyer/Kühne, English edition 234–6 (Asante); Roscoe, *Baganda* 114; Baker 202; Cunningham 30 (both Unyoro); Macdonald 75 (Lubare); denied by Skertchly 193 (for Dahomey).

(because defending one's people is a sacred right of the Asante) and continued on their way. The executioners also hurried into the plantation villages and brought back baskets full of human heads from there.

After the massacre had continued for eight days, the newly chosen king, Kofi Karakari, had the gongs beaten and proclaimed that from now on only slaves could be 'put down'.[48]

The description (not an eyewitness account) is perhaps exaggerated, but could hardly be completely fictitious.[49]

Naturally, it would be difficult to speak of completely arbitrary acts since such occasions were used to settle personal accounts, and corruption too came into play, so that the rich for example could buy their freedom. The sources do not provide any information with regard to these questions.[50] It seems, however, that the victims were innocent according to the laws of even the concerned states. This was even truer in the frequent cases where people, who encountered the funeral procession by chance, were killed purely for the purpose of accompanying the dead.[51]

What is the relationship between the personal and the anonymous attendants in death? More importantly: what is the historical sequence of events; which form came earlier? At least two processes are conceivable. Following into death could have begun with anonymous victims. Gradually, however, a certain personal relationship would have been established between the person to be accompanied and his attendant in death. Another explanation could be that in the beginning there were only personal attendants, but that the number of persons required to accompany the dead was constantly increased, which made it necessary to fall back on other anonymous categories of victims.

There are several, more plausible, arguments in favour of the second

---

[48] Ramseyer/Kühne, second German edition 285. Not in the English edition, which is translated from the first German edition. On the complicated problems of this work with regard to an evaluation of its sources, see Arhin and especially Jones, *Four years*.

[49] An exact description on the basis of more detailed sources is in McCaskie, *Death* 431–7.

[50] Conjectures for Benin in Dapper (1668) 1, 503. For Asante cf. Lloyd 52–3.

[51] Dalzel 224 (Dahomey, killing of forty-eight men); Magyar 353 (Kimbundu); Rattray 114 (Asante); cf. also Roscoe, *Baganda* 284.

hypothesis. It is seen that in all surviving records of following into death in Africa, the presence of personal attendants is a constant. Very often they form the only category.[52] On the whole, anonymous attendants were without doubt more numerous than personal ones. But they were to be found on fewer occasions, mainly in particularly spectacular mass-slaughters and hardly ever when the deceased had only one or a few attendants in death. This indicates that the anonymous victims were a later addition to the practice. The number of people accompanying the dead from the circle of personal attendants could not be increased continuously without endangering the entire system. The ruling class would otherwise risk decimation and, consequently, a loss of power. While the number of victims was sought to be increased in order to demonstrate and concentrate power, it had to be kept within certain limits in order to preserve this power. This restriction did not apply in the same way to anonymous attendants, especially when they were recruited from among other nations.

It is also difficult to imagine following into death emerging from the killing of anonymous victims. If one proceeds from the fact that the custom was engendered by a marked belief in the hereafter, then one can assume that the persons accompanied would want familiar and dependable people, in many cases even loved ones, around them. The idea of being surrounded instead by enemies and criminals, or at best by completely unknown people, was hardly likely to make the custom popular amongst those who were to acquire this privilege. Everything points to the fact that the use of anonymous victims only began later for reasons of state and with the help of the barely plausible contention that enemies and criminals would change their character in the other world and would become dependable attendants. However, this proposition could not have become very popular, particularly in spheres where personal bonds were of prime importance. At any rate, we do not know of a case where powerful rulers would allow female criminals or female personal enemies to accompany them as concubines into the other world.

Nevertheless, in certain parts of Africa, views of the hereafter connected with anonymous victims seem to have extended their influence beyond the political sphere to the field of law, and the custom came to be regarded as a kind of mechanical following. In 1893 Macdonald wrote about the Wayao in the region of the Great Lakes:

[52] For example Lander, in Clapperton 323; Junker 1, 366–7; Johnston 2, 610.

If a Wayao murderer is caught he may make compensation by giving a few slaves to be put to death, so that they may accompany the murdered man, taking his place to attend upon him. Should the murderer escape, one of his relatives is caught and treated as if he were the murderer. The object here is not so much the punishment of crime as an offering to the deceased, whose spirit would naturally be enraged at his own relatives were they not to pay due honour to it by sending, either the murderer to be his slave, or such of his relatives or slaves as make amends for his absence.[53]

Women were seldom among the persons to be accompanied, but played a far more important role among the attendants. However, the burden of accompanying the dead was by no means placed mainly, or, as in the case of widow burning in India, entirely on the women. On the whole, men could have constituted the majority of the victims. This can be traced back to their numbers among the anonymous victims, mainly among prisoners of war and criminals, but also, to a considerable extent, among those who were arbitrarily seized. Among the personal attendants, the ratio of the sexes was probably approximately equal. Women were no doubt in the majority among those who were meant for the personal care of the deceased, while only men were considered for the official and political functions. In this way, the custom reflected the relationship of the sexes in this world; as an institution, however, it was not an instrument that would have tipped the existing balance of power in favour of, or against, either of the sexes.[54] This was a consequence of the institutional character of the custom. Since it served to guarantee the hierarchical structure of society, it could not be used, simultaneously, to create a division between the sexes.

The Time of Killing or Self-killing

Almost all authors stress that the idea of transporting personal and institutional relationships of this world into the next forms the indispensable precondition for following into death. In the dispassionate language of an observer from the nineteenth century:

[53] MacDonald 70.

[54] According to Ryder 249 women were used in Benin to accompany the dead only from the middle of the nineteenth century; according to Skertchly 415–17 women were never used in Dahomey. In contrast Burton, *Gelele* 2, 22 states that in Dahomey about half the victims were women. According to François 68, on the Congo old men were specially bought as victims.

From this belief in a continuance of the former life in the next world naturally and deductively follows the custom of putting persons to death at the decease of a man of rank, to enable those sacrificed to continue a ghostly attendance. A chief who has been accustomed to be waited upon by a number of attendants during life, will, the natives argue, require and expect a similar attendance in Srahmanadzi. Therefore they put to death the wives and slaves of a deceased chief, in order that their ghosts, being released from their bodies, may be enabled to enter upon a ghostly servitude.[55]

From this we gather that the persons accompanying the deceased have to follow him as quickly as possible. On the other hand, a ritualized public ceremony is necessary. This is fulfilled only when the obsequies are performed. Since these generally take place shortly after death, they constitute the occasion and the framework for the custom. In Africa too the funeral of the person to be accompanied and the killing or self-killing of the attendants occur, as a rule, at the same time.

The importance of the custom in Africa is also expressed in the fact that in the particularly important and spectacular cases involving a large number of victims, the main ceremony is transformed into a whole system of occasions staggered in time, which are more or less connected with following into death. A one-time act becomes almost a permanent state of affairs, or at least a protracted process.[56]

Firstly, the final funeral ceremony is often postponed to a later point in time in order that it may be organized on a grander scale. One waits till the flesh drops off the bones,[57] or one carries out a provisional burial till the mausoleum is ready.[58] In the intervening period repeated opportunities for following into death are availed of. At the time of death of the person to be accompanied victims are arbitrarily caught and killed.[59] Or else women or members of the court are killed.[60] After this,

[55] Ellis, *Tshi* 158.

[56] McCaskie, *Death* 431–7 gives the most precise description of such a sequence of different ceremonies and the following of the dead connected with each of them for a case in Asante in 1867/68. Cf. also Valdez 1, 333–5 for Dahomey.

[57] Rattray 114–15; Doke 186–9; Hofmayr 179; Westermann, *Shilluk* 136.

[58] Rattray 109–15; Valdez 1, 335; 2, 332.

[59] See footnotes 46 and 47.

[60] For example Rattray 108–12; Ray 56 (Buganda); Waddell 295; 336; Baden-Powell 25.

and till the main ceremony takes place, many preparatory rituals are conducted, which also involve the killing of people.[61]

The most important, the most extensive and the longest-lasting ceremony which, as a rule, also requires the most victims, is the final interment. In the West African states, in which the system of accompanying the dead was the most elaborate, one spoke of the *grande coutume* or the *grand custom*.[62] Memorial services were also conducted, mainly for the ruler who had died most recently, usually in the form of anniversary ceremonies that often involved a considerable number of victims.[63] These were large popular festivals with a variety of attractions that continued for days. According to the descriptions of European observers, the killings were the focal point of the festivals—however, this may not have been the view of the Africans.

Even outside the framework of such annual ceremonies people continued to be sent to accompany the dead after the great burial ceremony.[64]

On the occasions that followed the main ceremony, anonymous victims played a particularly important role. This is easy to understand: the longer the gap between the death of the person to be

[61] For example Beecham 230; Le Hérissé 180; Roth, *Benin* 101 (account by C.Punch); Waddell 294–5.

[62] Skertchly's work is particularly important. Cf. also Lartigue, in Brunschwig 126–30; Ramseyer/Kühne, English edition, 117ff.; Burton, *Gelele* I, chap. 13; Forbes and the popular account of 1861: *Die große Ada (Sitte) in Abomey.* For the background see especially Coquery-Vidrovitch 708.

[63] Most detailed in Burton, *Gelele* I, chap. 14. Further accounts in: Bradbury 55; Bayol 17–20; Coquery-Vidrovitch 703–10; Ellis, *Tshi* 168; Forbes 2, 152–73; Isert 148–9; Merolla 400 (Benin); M'Leod 53–65 (Dahomey); Rattray 127–43; Roth, *Benin* 71–2; Skertchly 179ff. Campion-Vincent 30 distinguishes two types of annual ceremonies. The number of victims mentioned ranges from a few to several hundred. Coquery-Vidrovitch 705 estimates the average number of victims for the *grande coutume* in Dahomey to be 500, for the *coutume annuelle* 50 (ibid., 710, 60–70). Campion-Vincent 31: over 500 and 30–40 respectively. Skertchly 239: at large ceremonies at least 600. For Asante Ellis, *Ewe* 129, speaks of 70–80 annually, Fuller 173 of around 50, and Baden-Powell 25 of 20 victims every three months. Dapper (1668) 1, 503 places the number of annual victims in Benin at 400–500. The changes that occurred from year to year and from ruler to ruler were probably considerable.

[64] Cf. for example Ellis, *Tshi* 159 and especially Herskovits II: 49–55.

accompanied and the following into death ceremony, the more difficult it was to invoke a close personal bond between the former and the latter.

Finally there was a third form of extension, which had less to do with the time factor than with the connection between this world and the next. The deceased was kept in touch with events in this world through messengers.[65] The messages could concern important acts of state like war and peace, the quality of the harvest, but also relatively trivial events like the arrival of a white man, the marriage of a princess or the invention of a new dance.[66] The messenger was entrusted with the news and enjoined to transmit it accurately to the addressee—as a rule, the last king. Skertchly described such a scene. The victims had to kneel down.

A bottle of rum, a head of cowries, and a pellet of cankie were placed before each, and one of the court jesters sat grinning in the opposite corner, carrying on his buffoonery in the very presence of death itself. [. . .]

The king's strong names were then called out, the recital occupying nearly an hour. The victims were then placed with their heads bowed to the earth, while the message was delivered. The purport of it was as follows: 'Gelelé [the ruler of Dahomey] sends his compliments to his father, and declares that he would do all things as he had wished his son to do. He has made one Custom for him and now makes another, so that Gézu shall know that his son Gelelé does not forget Him.' With a long ting-tang on the gong-gong the message was concluded, and the preparations for the fearful consummation commenced. The rum bottle was opened, part poured on the ground, and the remainder on the heads of the victims. The bunches of cowries were then laid on their heads for an instant, and afterwards placed before them. The cankie was placed in the waist cloths of the poor wretches, and then the executioner made his appearance.[67]

[65] The most detailed descriptions are to be found in Skertchly 193; 238–9; 338–61 and *passim,* which have been taken over in parts by Oberländer, *Westafrika* 234–6. In addition Herskovits 1: 100; Bayol 19; Burton, *Gelele* 2, 24–5; 331–2; Coquery-Vidrovitch 708–9; Ellis, *Ewe* 118; 137; M'Leod 64–5; Ramseyer/Kühne, second German edition, 287; Roth, *Benin* 74; Macdonald 75 and earlier Cavazzi 166 (book 2, chap. 38). Campion-Vincent 31: even women.

[66] Skertchly 239.

[67] Skertchly 339–40. On p. 361 there is another message.

One victim after the other was beheaded. Such 'messengers' were killed in considerable numbers especially in Dahomey; every year there are supposed to have been several hundred of them.[68] However, it was particularly easy to exaggerate in this case, because even eyewitnesses could observe only individual cases.

What happened to the messengers once they had carried out their tasks is not mentioned. One can assume that they joined the retinue of the dead king. But this was definitely not the main purpose of their death. Rather, it was a question of establishing and maintaining the connection between this world and the next. We will return to this in the context of the functions of the custom in the other world.

The Manner of Killing

Self-killing is mentioned relatively often in the sources, but never in the verifiable eyewitness accounts.[69] One can assume that, normally, the victims, especially the anonymous ones, were killed.

Seen in the context of the function of the custom, the killing was merely meant to effect the passage to the other world. There was no reason to make this passage more difficult. Therefore it would have been natural to carry out the killing as quickly and as painlessly as possible, which is why it was also considered advisable to anaesthetize the victims first. The only exception was the execution of criminals, since here the factor of punishment came into play.

The reality was quite different. The victims were seldom treated with much consideration.[70] At the most, they were allowed to take poison; a refusal to do so could lead to more cruel forms of killing.[71] The forms of killing that were widespread corresponded roughly to

---

[68] Burton, *Gelele* 2, 24: around 500 per year; Ellis, *Ewe* 137: 500 (possibly taken over from Burton); Skertchly 239: at least 200.

[69] Allier 91–2; 100; Ashe 342; Ellis, *Ewe* 128; Ellis, *Yoruba* 104–5; Forbes 2, 200; Haarhoff 87; Hartmann 190; Johnston 2, 610; Lander, in Clapperton 323; Lartigue, in Brunschwig 130; Roscoe, *Banyankale* 61–2; Roscoe, *Bantu* 52; Steinmetz, *Selbstmord* 361–2; Theal 88; Johnson 55; Schebesta, *Zimbabwe* 498. Cf. also the collection of evidence in Irstam 153–5.

[70] For example Oldendorp 317: Among the Ibo, the wife, and the highest servant could choose their manner of death. Similarly Rattray 109.

[71] Cf. for example Lander, *Journal* 92–8; Lander, in Clapperton 323; Brun, in Jones, *German sources* 57; Ellis, *Yoruba* 104–5; Lartigue, in Brunschwig 130; Theal 88; Roscoe, *Bantu* 52; Clapperton 49; Johnson 56–7.

those used in Europe for normal executions. On the whole, the most common method would have been beheading, especially in Dahomey.[72]

Other forms that are mentioned are hanging,[73] strangling,[74] choking[75] and breaking of the neck,[76] and killing with daggers, spears or sabres.[77] Drowning is also mentioned; the victims are tied down in a boat punctured with holes.[78] Apart from this, the sources speak of burning alive, either together with the body of the person to be accompanied[79] or separately.[80] Very often the killing was a painful process, with a long period of suffering in which death was delayed, partly on purpose,[81] partly through incompetence. Sometimes lynching is mentioned.[82] Bosman asserts that at the beginning of the eighteenth century he witnessed a six-year-old boy cutting off a man's head, a task that took him almost an hour.[83] Among the Ibibio in Nigeria a slave was sacrificed, 'who was tied to a tree by throat, waist, arms and ankles, and there left to starve'.[84] In 1871 Skertchly saw how four victims were thrown down from a platform in Dahomey. The executioners were waiting below.

> The first three were not put to any extra torture, but the fourth must have suffered excruciating agony. Four blows were given without severing the vertebral column, the back of the head presenting a fearful sight. The butcher then put the bloody knife in his mouth, and seizing

[72] Cf. for example Burton, *Gelele* and Skertchly. In addition Hutton 85; Leonard 444–6.

[73] For example Clapperton 49; Johnson 56–7.

[74] For example Dapper (1668) 1, 403; Meek, *Nigeria* 493; Meek, *Kingdom* 176; Krafft 25; Roscoe, *Bakitara* 126–7.

[75] For example Dapper (1668) 1, 493.

[76] For example Meek, *Kingdom* 174–5.

[77] For example Pommegorge 194; Roscoe, *Bantu* 52; Doke 189.

[78] Westermann, *Shilluk* 136; Hofmayr 180 (source uncertain).

[79] Dapper (1668) 1, 649 (Hottentots).

[80] Kidd 246 (Swazi).

[81] For example Baden-Powell 28: Only when an order was given to this effect.

[82] Pommegorge 193–4; Campion-Vincent 37–8; Norris, *Memoirs* 126.

[83] Bosman 13.

[84] Talbot 140. Cf. also Bowdich, 287–8; Callaway 213; Huntley 14; Hutton 85; Ulsheimer, in Jones, *German sources* 348.

the ears of the wretched being, wrenched it from side to side in the endeavour to screw it off, and finally, having dislocated the atlas, cut the flesh that still connected the head with the trunk. A more horrible sight I never witnessed.[85]

In most of the sources such a description could be dismissed as an exaggeration or an invention. However, Skertchly elsewhere defended the Africans against any unjustified accusations by denying all claims of cruelty and torture. The killings are to be deplored, 'nevertheless they are not the mere vents of a cruel, bloodthirsty mind. [. . .] In every case the victim's passage to the other world is as speedy as that by hanging or other orthodox modes of capital punishment.' He even maintained that the killings 'are not one whit more barbarous than the suttee of the Hindoo, and far less so than the incarceration of an unwilling maiden within the loathsome walls of a Popish nunnery'.[86] In view of this obvious tendency to minimize the more cruel aspects, it is difficult to imagine that Skertchly could have invented the horrible scene. Rather we would have to assume that while writing under the pressure of this reality he forgot his own attempts at justification.[87]

The corpses were sometimes mutilated and placed, either whole or in parts on public display, or else thrown to the animals. This was done not only in the case of criminals.[88] According to some sources even the corpses of women were treated in this manner.[89] The practice of impaling the heads around the grave[90] or at the royal palace[91] was also widespread. In 1842 a missionary wrote that twenty men, women and

[85] Skertchly 368. Similarly ibid., 416.

[86] Skertchly 235–7.

[87] The same is true for Burton, *Gelele*, who in 2, 18–21 defends Dahomey but at other places serves up detailed, bloodthirsty descriptions.

[88] For example M'Leod 59–60; Denis 826 (description of a scene of 1917); Forbes 1, 52; T.B. Freeman 24–5; 52–4; 128; Labarthe (French edition) 123–5, 151–2; Lartigue, in Brunschwig 126–30; McCaskie, *Death* 432–7; McCaskie, *State* 213; Norris, *Memoirs* 110; Roscoe, *Baganda* 107; Ramseyer/ Kühne, English edition 130.

[89] Doke 189 (North Rhodesia).

[90] For example Bastian, Loangoküste 1, 232; T.B. Freeman 53; Isert 149; Coquilhat 172.

[91] For example T.B. Freeman 53; Labarthe (French edition) 151–2; Norris, *Memoirs* 93; 106; 111; Coquery-Vidrovitch 709; Lartigue, in Brunschwig 126–30; Schynse 90; Tremearne 178; 180.

young girls had recently been killed on the death of the mother of the ruler of Apollonia on the Gold Coast. 'They partly cut the throats of the men, and then tied ropes to their legs, and drew them round the town, their throats still bleeding, and men following them with clubs, striking them on their stomachs; and when they were brought back to the place from whence they started, they cut off the heads of those who were still living. The bodies of both male and female were thrown into a hole in the bush, to be food for beasts of prey.'[92]

What was the reason for this cruelty, which was not part of the framework of following into death? We have to take into account that on such occasions baser instincts tended to surface. As an explanation however this is as insufficient as the indication of acts of revenge in the context of altercations between different factions of the royal household. Both aspects are more in the nature of concomitant symptoms than of causes. The specific circumstances of following into death were more important.

A first condition was the public nature of the killing. It had to be clearly visible to the public and it had to happen in a ritualized form. Victims who were unconscious from the beginning were hardly suited for this. In addition, the temptation to satisfy a frenzied crowd with a bloodthirsty spectacle would have been difficult to resist. In some cases however the killings appear not to have been carried out in front of the crowd, but inside the palace, especially in the case of the wives of the king of Dahomey.[93] No details about the manner of their killing are therefore available.

There were also specific ideas at work about the relationship in the other world between the person being accompanied and the persons accompanying him, as well as the connection that had to be maintained between this world and the other. The latter aspect would have contributed to the special significance of a manner of killing that has not been mentioned till now. If one ignores the spectacular events with a large number of victims, and only looks at the cases with one or a few attendants in death, then being buried alive is mentioned most often. As a rule it took place by filling up and closing the grave,[94] leading to

[92] William Allen, letter dated 2 February 1842, in T.B. Freeman 193–4.

[93] Burton, *Gelele* 2, 22; 334. Skertchly 355; cf. Coquery-Vidrovitch 709–10 and Campion-Vincent 32ff.

[94] Ankermann 31–3; Baker 2, 201–2; Baumann 188; Lartigue in Brunschwig 130; Beecham 230; Bösch 487–8; 232; Buchholz 26; Burton,

quick suffocation. When the chief of the Konde in the region of Lake Nyasa died, his councillors dug a grave and carried the dead body to it. 'Six or eight slaves, who did not return, went with them. Four went down into the grave to receive the body of their dead master, two at the head and two at the feet, and, in sitting position, held him in their arms. The remaining slaves being placed on the top, the soil was filled in on living and dead.'[95]

Sometimes, however, the persons accompanying the dead were locked into tombs, in which they remained alive for days.[96] An account written between 1535 and 1550 says:

> In the Kingdom of Benin there exists this old custom, which is practised till today: when the King dies the people gather in a large field. In the centre of this field they dig a very deep grave, which is wide at the bottom and tapers off at the top. They lower the body of the King into this. Now all the friends and servants of the King step forward, as well as those who were considered to be his favourites. This leads to many a squabble, since everyone wants to have this honour. They are allowed to accompany the King voluntarily. As soon as they climb down into the grave a large stone is rolled over the top of the grave and the people stay there day and night. On the second day those deputed with the task come and roll back the stone, and they ask the people inside the grave what they are doing and whether one of them has already gone to serve the King. They answer: No. On the third day they repeat the same question and the answer comes back: such and such, whereby they give the name, was the first to go, and such and such was

---

Lake regions 2, 25–6; Cavazzi 94–5 (book 1, chap. 262); 97 (Book 1, chap. 267); Dalzel 150–1; Des Marchais 2, 92; Durand 373; Ellis, *Yoruba* 105; Fernandes 76; 87; Field 204; Frobenius 1, 184; 3, 85; Fülleborn 32–3; Fynn 136; Grandidier 39; Ihle 172–3; Johnston 2, 694; Junker 1, 366–7; Kranz 57–8; Leonard 160; Levtzion/Hopkins 80–1; 213; 281; 406 (accounts from the eleventh to the fourteenth century); Marquardsen 18; Meek, *Nigeria* 493; Merolla 396; M'Leod 132; Mockler-Ferryman 235; Nachtigal 2,687; Oberländer, *Westafrika* 236; Roscoe, *Bakitara* 126; Roscoe, *Negro* 153; Seligman/Seligman 338; 539; Shooter 245; Talbot 142; 153–4; 333–4; J. Thomson 1, 320; 2, 258; Tönjes 150; Waddell 336; Ward 204–7; Wing 283.
[95] D.R. Mackenzie 70.
[96] For example Omboni 306; Schütt 113; Mueller, in Wissmann *et al.*, 102; Schebesta, *Vollblutneger* 238.

the second. It is regarded as being particularly praiseworthy to have been the first, and all the assembled people speak of the dead person with the greatest admiration. He is considered to be lucky and blessed. After four or five days all those poor people die.[97]

Among the Shilluk the dead body of the king was placed in a hut. One or several persons were locked into the hut, which was then bricked up.[98] The practice of burying alive the attendants in death confined the person being accompanied and his attendants in close quarters, which was emphasized by the slow death of the persons buried alive. This gradual passage from this world into the next expressed in an eloquent and drastic manner the close connection between the living and the dead.[99]

In other cases, the victim had to occupy a definite position in relation to the deceased, a position also evident in this world. The manner of killing resulted from this as, for example, when the victims had to form a resting place for the person to be accompanied. In May 1875 in the Central African kingdom of Kasango the British traveller Cameron, who seems not to have been an eyewitness, was

> acquainted with the ceremonies observed at the burial of a chief of Urua, which are probably unequalled in their savagery.
>
> The first proceeding is to divert the course of a stream and in its bed to dig an enormous pit, the bottom of which is then covered with living women. At one end a woman is placed on her hands and knees, and upon her back the dead chief, covered with his beads and other

---

[97] *Navigazione da Lisbona all'isola di San Tomé...*, in Ramusio 1, 572. Similarly Dapper (1668) 1, 502–3; Cardi, in Kingsley 452; Landolphe 54–5; Oldendorp 316. Cf. also Macdonald 156 and Kalous 366.

[98] For example Seligman 90; Westermann, *Shilluk* 136; Hofmayr 179. Similarly Meek, *Kingdom* 176. Cf. Dapper (1668) 1, 480 and Cunningham 29–31.

[99] The idea underlying the connection between this world and the other becomes particularly clear in Frässle 52, even if the factual details, especially the reference to cannibalism, are not correct. He states that in earlier times in the Congo region the 'favourite wives and best warriors' offered themselves up 'willingly and courageously to be sacrificed, to be half-buried and half-eaten, in order to reach their master soon in the other world and yet to leave their strength behind for their people.'

treasures, is seated, being supported on either side by one of his wives, while his second wife sits at his feet.

The earth is then shovelled in on them, and all the women are buried alive with the exception of the second wife. To her custom is more merciful than to her companions, and grants her the privilege of being killed before the huge grave is filled in.

This being completed, a number of male slaves—sometimes forty or fifty—are slaughtered and their blood poured over the grave; after which the river is allowed to resume its course.

Stories were rife that no fewer than a hundred women were buried alive with Bambarré, Kasongo's father; but let us hope that this may be an exaggeration.

Smaller chiefs are buried with two or three wives, and a few slaves only are killed that their blood may be shed on the grave; whilst one of the common herd has to be content with solitary burial, being placed in a sitting posture with the right forefinger pointing heavenwards, just level with the top of the mound over his grave.[100]

The manner of killing could also result directly from certain religious convictions with reference to the hereafter. In southwest Africa 'it is customary among the Ovakuanjama to bury the chief with many of his wives, so that they keep the fires burning for him in the new world, fetch water and take care of all his comforts. Superstition demands that these women are not killed with weapons, but strangled, in order to be without any mutilations—i.e. healthy—in the next world.'[101] Instead of reasons relating to the other world, privileges of rank in this world could lead to the same result: 'Strangling in Ashanti is considered the aristocratic method of killing, because blood is not shed and there is not any mutilation.'[102]

The fact that the custom also served to demonstrate the power of the new ruler meant that he would often kill victims with his own hands. Since European observers generally did not notice the new king expressing sadistic pleasure at such occasions, but rather aversion and

[100] Cameron 2, 110–11. Similarly Ankermann 33; Baikie 315–16; Baker 2, 201–2; Coquilhat 172; Dapper (1668) 1, 403; Grandidier 36–7; Ihle 173; D.R. Mackenzie 70; Seligman 539; Sibree 226; Talbot 142; Theal 88; Weeks 319–20; Wolf, in Wissmann *et al.* 243–4.
[101] Krafft 25
[102] Rattray 109.

reluctance, we can assume that it was less a matter of unbridled cruelty than part of a ritual aimed at political effect.[103]

The treatment of the corpses would also have to be matched more closely with the notions of the people concerned, although the sources provide very few relevant indications for this. In many regions, even outside the context of following into death, only highly placed persons had the privilege of being buried, while the corpses of common people were left out in the open.[104] Cannibalism would not have played much of a role, or, indeed, no role at all. It is mentioned repeatedly, but never by eyewitnesses, and the statements are very vague.[105]

Contemporary authors, too, sometimes tried to prove that cruelty was by no means the basis of the custom. Burton called it in fact 'a touching instance of the King's filial piety' and reminded readers of public executions in England.[106] Such an attitude could easily relegate the actual events to the background. Ellis' explanation of 1887 almost seems to be a glorification:

> The practice of sacrificing human beings at funerals, therefore [in view of the specific belief in the hereafter] arises from a feeling of affection, respect, and awe for the dead. It is done so that the departed may suffer no discomfort in his new abode, but find himself surrounded by those attentions and ministrations to which he has been accustomed. So far from being due to any inherent bloodthirstiness in the Tshi-speaking peoples, it is really due to an exaggerated regard for the dead.[107]

There is no talk of regard for the living.

[103] Ellis, *Ewe* 129; Lartigue, in Brunschwig 128; M'Leod 64–5; Ramseyer/ Kühne, English edition 237; Skertchly 238; Mayer 175; Oldendorp 317.
[104] Cf. Rattray 108–9; Bösch 482; Kidd 245.
[105] Cavazzi 161–2 (book 2, chap. 29); Ellis, *Ewe* 121; 134; Partridge 59; Leonard 161; 446; Baumann 198; Bouche 370; Frässle 52; Valdez 2, 332; Norris, *Memoirs* 126. Such details are mentioned very often in uncritical compilations, for example Volhard 417–20; K. Schneider 119–20; 135. See Coquery-Vidrovitch 709; Law, *Human sacrifice* 58. While Coquilhat 172, who was an eyewitness, regards cannibalism as improbable, Schebesta, *Vollblutneger* 239, who probably relies on Coquilhat, portrays it as an undisputed fact.
[106] Burton, *Gelele* 2, 19–22, quote: 19. Cf. also Skertchly 235–7.
[107] Ellis, *Tshi* 159.

Functions in the Other World

The main function of following into death was to provide the deceased with company in the other world.[108] Skertchly stated that 'whatever may be the social condition of the person at the moment of his death, so will he remain for all eternity.'[109] In addition, the custom establishes a close link between this world and the other, which is to be seen mainly in the context of ancestor-worship. The point of departure for this is the power ascribed to the dead person to influence events in this world.[110] He has to be prevented from harming the living and, as far as possible, be made to intervene on their behalf. In Skertchly's view, 'the continual sending of messengers to them [the dead rulers] by their successors in this world, keeps the departed sovereigns in a happy state of mind, as to whether their greatness is forgotten on earth, and they are induced to give the living monarch the benefit of their ghostly advice.'[111] In 1793, Dalzel made an African ruler express this even more clearly in what is no doubt a fictitious speech:

> Besides, if I should neglect this indispensable duty, would my ancestors suffer me to live? Would they not trouble me day and night, and say, that I sent nobody to serve them; that I was only solicitous about my own name, and forgetful of my ancestors? White men are not acquainted with these circumstances; but I now tell you, that you may hear, and know, and inform your countrymen, why Customs are made, and will be made, as long as black men continue to possess their own country.[112]

This aspect is found especially in the periodic staggering of the rituals of following into death. The survivors constantly solicit the attention of the deceased with the help of ceremonies. This becomes even more evident when messengers are sent, a practice that only makes sense if the deceased is thought to possess a lively interest in the events of this world and is capable of influencing them. By satisfying his needs, in the case of information, one can also hope to influence his actions. The custom therefore helped in strengthening those who

---

[108] This is emphasized in almost all the sources.
[109] Skertchly 461.
[110] References to this for example in Weeks 97.
[111] Skertchly 181. Cf. also ibid. 462
[112] Dalzel 220–1.

organized it, i.e. chiefly the living ruler.[113] It was always the direct predecessor on whom all efforts were concentrated. Sometimes, however, all past generations were together considered the object of the rituals, especially during ceremonies at the graves of dead rulers.[114]

An inconsistency in the logic of the model has to be pointed out here, which, however, did not affect its functioning in practice. The power of the deceased in the other world accrued to him apparently automatically, so that one would have to deal with it in any case. The model of following into death, on the contrary, leads one to believe that the deceased acquired his power only when he was provided with a retinue for the other world, and one could deny him this. Therefore, the people who followed him were a necessary attribute, but not the actual source of power of the dead ruler.

In this way many forms of following the dead took on the character of a sacrifice, and more so when the death of the person to be accompanied had taken place far back in time. Thus, one can speak of a gradual change in the function of the custom in the course of time. One can proceed on the assumption that even when the killings occurred long after the funeral of the person to be accompanied, the people killed were meant for the retinue of the deceased. However, that was hardly emphasized. On the face of it, other aspects were central. In many places, the annual ceremonies were conducted in order to 'water the grave'.[115] This had to be sprinkled with the blood of the victims, or the bones of the dead ruler would be washed with it. Ramseyer, a missionary of the Basel Mission, described how the king of Asante visited the skeletons of about twenty predecessors on 5 February 1871.

> On this occasion every skeleton was placed on a chair in his cell to receive the royal visitor; who, on entering, offered it food; after which a band played the favourite melodies of the departed. The poor victim selected as a sacrifice, with a knife thrust through his cheeks, was then

[113] Cf. Roscoe, *Baganda* 209–10. On the connection between ancestor-worship and following the dead cf. also Herskovits 2, 49; Law, *Human sacrifice* 75; Ramseyer/Kühne, second German edition 287; Rattray 104; Skertchly 181 and especially McCaskie, *Death* 427–9.

[114] Cf. footnotes 62–3 and 115–16.

[115] This euphemistic expression is used often, for example in Forbes 2, 128; 152; Hutton 85; M'Leod 57; Cameron 2, 95; Bowdich 289; Dalzel 158; Hartmann 190; cf. Coquery-Vidrovitch 704.

dragged forward and slain, the king washing the skeleton with his blood. Thus was each cell visited in turn, sacrifice after sacrifice being offered, till evening closed ere the dreadful round was completed.[116]

The sacrificial aspect is linked with the belief in the power of the deceased, who has to be prejudiced in favour of the living. This aspect became very evident when, in the face of an impending drought, the Jukun in Nigeria sacrificed two slaves provided by the ruler to his predecessor, since it was assumed that he was holding back the rain.[117] Here, the dead ruler is addressed and treated not as the dead but as a divine being.

The consequences and functions of the custom in the other world were undoubtedly considered to be more important for those accompanied and for the present rulers than for the attendants in death. Yet it is not possible to separate the attendants from these functions. The hope of a continuation of this life and possibly of an improved social position would have influenced the attitude of the victims in many cases. Although this was only a matter of conjecture on the part of European observers and commentators, the sources repeatedly speak of the victims' belief and hope in the hereafter. In 1730 Des Marchais described the funeral of a king on the Gold Coast. Four slaves bury the corpse in a forest. They then return to the palace, 'kneel down at the entrance without saying a word, and proffer their necks, in order that they might be killed, so that they can go and serve their master in the other world. They are convinced that he will reward them for their loyalty by giving them the best posts in his government.'[118] The account is definitely not authentic, but it is by no means untypical. Samuel Johnson, who was better informed, wrote about the Yoruba in Nigeria that some slaves, who one does not expect to go to their deaths, 'often commit suicide in order to serve their master in the other world, expecting to be handsomely rewarded like it is done in this world.'[119]

If one considers the other-world aspects as religious ones, then following into death in Africa shows a marked religious character.

[116] Ramseyer/Kühne, English edition 117. However the missionaries weren't eyewitnesses. Similarly Omboni 306; Brunschwig 126–7; Landolphe 55. Denied by Rattray 113.
[117] Meek, *Kingdom* 175.
[118] Des Marchais 1, 359. Cf. Bowdich 262.
[119] Johnson 57.

The main aspects of this are elements of ancestor-worship and sacrifice.[120]

Functions in This World

If the connection with the other world serves as a guarantee of general prosperity, and to ward off danger for the whole community in this world, then the functions directly connected with this world are mainly those of maintaining differences within a society, of creating, preserving and consolidating structures of power. The difference between rulers and subjects is emphasized in two different ways that partly complement and partly contradict each other.

1. The personal attendants in death seldom come from the family of the deceased,[121] but from the larger circle of the privileged. Although there is a marked social difference between the person being accompanied and the persons accompanying him, the social difference between these two groups, on the one hand, and the masses, on the other, is even greater. The latter are completely excluded from these practices. In this way, the difference in status between the rulers and the subjects, between the upper and the lower classes, is emphasized.

2. A division along the same lines occurs in another more distinct way, when anonymous victims, who are mainly from among the masses, are killed. A section of the personal attendants can also be counted among these, especially the slaves. The difference between the accompanied persons and the attendants now marks the difference between the rulers and the subjects. The ruling order finds confirmation in an act which is not only symbolic in nature, but, in physical terms, represents an unsurpassable extreme: the complete subjugation of the subjects through their death for the rulers. The unequal values accorded to individual lives manifest themselves in death. Since it can befall everyone, the death of a few, more or less arbitrarily selected persons, expresses the general claim to power of the ruling order.

[120] The following authors emphasize the religious aspect: Burton, *Gelele* 2, 18–21; Skertchly 181; 461–2; Campion-Vincent 28.

[121] This does not hold true for widows, who are killed very often. Other family members are however mentioned only in isolated cases. Cf. for example Haarhoff 87; Lander, in Clapperton 323; Tremearne 187. More plausible in Lewin 65 (Asante), who at the same time emphasizes that normally members of the royal family were spared.

However, a further intensification occurs, which carries within it the nucleus for the destruction of the system. If it were only a matter of the exemplary meaning of the act of following the dead, then a single victim would suffice. But beyond that, it is also a direct demonstration of power, in which the number of victims plays an important role; every additional attendant in death is further proof of the power of the person being accompanied. This extension can, if it is carried too far, lead to resistance among the people affected, or, if the victims come from the ruling class, it could endanger the existence of this class. Indeed, at times there seem to have been disputes within the ruling class, not, it is true, about the principle of the custom, but certainly about its extent.[122] Similarly, from time to time, as will be shown in the next section, the resistance of potential victims came to the fore. Both these factors however were not able to endanger the custom as an institution. Where did this persistent strength come from?

Following into death not only served to emphasize the difference between the rulers and the ruled, it also joined these two groups together without eliminating the basic differences. First, it bound ruler and ruled with one another in death, although as unequals. Then, by virtue of its public nature, as it was linked with large, elaborate feasts, which served to underscore the unity of the country and, thereby, prevented inner conflicts.[123] The people too benefited from it. They cried out for victims, even though these were taken from their own ranks.[124] 'Ideally', therefore, the people demanded exactly what symbolized and sealed their subordination and subjugation. The rulers, however, gave in only to a limited extent to the demands that the crowd be allowed to kill the victims. As a rule, they reserved the right to kill for themselves. Only rarely were those destined to die thrown alive to the crowd to be lynched.[125] Instead, the corpses were often handed

[122] Law, *Human sacrifice* 81–2 (seventeenth and eighteenth centuries); McCaskie, *Death* 433–7 (Asante 1867).

[123] This holds true particularly for the annual ceremonies and even more for the *grandes coutumes*. For references see footnotes 62–3. Even at other ceremonies mass gatherings are often mentioned.

[124] For example M'Leod 58; Reade 54; Bowdich 284–5; Forbes 1, 44ff.; Adams 24–7. The assertion made by Ellis, *Yoruba* 104, that the masses were always against such killings, is not proven.

[125] Cf. Campion-Vincent 37–8; Pommegorge 193–4; Norris, *Memoirs* 126.

over to the crowd for mutilation or for public display. In these public displays one could frequently see people who had been hanged or crucified. It was customary to see heads on stakes, while the bodies were left to the animals.[126]

The socially binding force of the custom becomes truly comprehensible only if its other-world component is taken into account. As a rule, the burden of carrying it out fell to the subjects, who had to provide the victims. The consequences of neglecting the custom, on the other hand, affected—that was the belief at any rate—not only the rulers or the subjects, but the entire community: the neglected dead would punish the community or leave it to its downfall. The subjects were, thus, completely bound to the system, so long as they shared this belief. They had at least as vital an interest in maintaining the custom as the rulers. One could, at most, try individually to escape the fate of a victim or to shift the responsibility onto others, but one could hardly demand the abolition of the custom as long as one believed that it would lead to the ruin of the whole community.

This was the reason why potential victims defended the custom with as much determination as the privileged, i.e. the rulers. According to Skertchly the people in Dahomey believed that if one were to stop the custom, 'the glory of the kingdom would depart'.[127]

Following into death was, therefore, and especially in some of the larger centralized states, a very significant political factor, which guaranteed, or at least strengthened, the unity of the state. Burton even felt that 'to abolish human sacrifice here is to abolish Dahome.'[128]

At times the people defended the custom even against attempts from above to curb or to abolish it. Some rulers remarked to European visitors in the nineteenth century that they would love to abolish the bloody rituals. However, they could not afford to do so for fear that the people would react angrily and would interpret the step as a sign of weakness on the part of the ruler, quite apart from the sacredness of tradition.[129] These were undoubtedly chiefly defensive statements

[126] For example Forbes 1, 44ff.; M'Leod 60; Norris 125–6; Doke 189; Coquilhat 172. Cf. also footnotes 88–91.

[127] Skertchly 181.

[128] Burton, *Gelele* 2, 26. Similarly Coquery-Vidrovitch 702–3; Law, *Human sacrifice* 86.

[129] Cf. for example T.B. Freeman 29; Waddell 294; Skertchly 180–1; 235; 237; 462; Law, *Human sacrifice* 85.

through which the rulers tried to gain the goodwill of Europeans and, simultaneously, justify their own inaction. Yet European witnesses were prone to take their arguments seriously. Reade wrote in 1864: 'Vox populi, vox diaboli. The mob of Dahomey are man-eaters; they have cannibal minds; they have been accustomed to feed on murder; were the King, whom we supplicate, to attempt compliance with our requests [for abolition], the graves of his ancestors would be watered with his own blood.'[130] Skertchly stated, in 1874, that King Glele of Dahomey would love to stop the killings since he knew that the Europeans were against it, but was afraid of being overthrown if he attempted it. Skertchly did not say whether the king was thinking of resistance from the people or from rival factions within the ruling class.[131] He regarded the religious convictions of the people as 'the one great stumbling block' for abolishing the custom. 'The suppression of these [customs] would be looked upon by the popular eye as a direct insult to the protecting spirits of the country, and a general revolt would be the inevitable consequence.'[132] Bouche stated, in 1885, that King Gezo of Dahomey was poisoned because he was against the killings and had tried to curb them. His successor Glele had only been chosen after he had promised to continue the custom.[133]

Besides these functions which concerned the whole community, the custom also had more specific political functions. The obligation of the closest companions to follow the ruler in death contributed to his safety, as Johnson formulates very clearly for Nigeria in 1921. The companions named as attendants in death are 'those who by virtue of their office are nearest to the King at all times, and have the easiest access to his person; to make their life dependent on his, therefore, is to ensure safety for him against the risk of poisoning, or the dagger of the assassin.'[134]

The custom could also serve to tie the smaller chiefs, the important men of the kingdom and sundry local powers, to the ruler. Often, they were obliged to provide a certain number of victims for larger ceremonies in the framework of following into death.[135] Some rulers

---

[130] Reade 54.
[131] Skertchly 237.
[132] Skertchly 462.
[133] Bouche 368–9.
[134] Johnson 56. Similarly for Asante Ellis, *Tshi* 165.
[135] Lartigue, in Brunschwig 126; Labarthe, French edition 125; Ramseyer/

even tried to extend the scope of this obligation to include Europeans.[136]

Finally, the custom also constituted a demonstration of power to the external world. In the previously quoted fictitious speech in Dalzel, the king says: 'This [the killings] gives a grandeur to my customs, far beyond the display of fine things which I buy. This makes my enemies fear me, and gives me such a name in the bush.'[137]

Free Choice and Coercion

In Africa the act of following into death did not primarily depend on whether people who were willing to accompany the dead could be found, but on whether the successor of the deceased or his nearest relatives could assert his right to the custom. If they were successful in this, then they generally also knew how to find persons to accompany him.

The structural conditions for following into death were, therefore, characterized by force. Although free choice was not ruled out, it was by no means the principal element. The determining factor was the will of the powerful, not the readiness of the subjects to make sacrifices.

This violent nature is particularly evident in the case of anonymous victims. The question of free choice on the part of the victim is in this case meaningless. There was no question of their being asked first, and the decision about their killing was made regardless of their own attitude.

Yet one cannot simply exclude the element of free choice from following into death in Africa. That would have focused more on the personal attendants. The sources repeatedly report that the attendants in death killed themselves of their own free choice, or willingly allowed themselves to be killed. Often they are said to have insisted on it, or to have vied with each other for the honour of being allowed to accompany the dead. This refers to wives and concubines, servants, slaves and officials.[138]

Kühne, English edition 174–5, 235–7; Lewin 65; Rattray 112; Valdez 2, 332; Baden-Powell 27.

[136] Cf. footnotes 159–60.

[137] Dalzel 220.

[138] Allen/Thomson 1,328–9; Des Marchais 2, 93; Forbes 1, 171; Lartigue, in Brunschwig 130; Junker (1889) 367; Meyerowitz 63–4; Oberländer, *Westafrika* 236; Omboni 306; Rattray 106–9; Theal 88; McCaskie, *Death*

If one looks at the structural conditions, then these repeated assertions of the voluntary nature of the act generate a certain amount of
doubt. The relatively large number of victims per person did not
favour an independent decision on the part of the victims. The occasionally very painful method of killing would also have had a deterring
effect. Sometimes a victim who refused to die would be killed despite
his desire to live.[139] Several of the statements in the sources cannot be
taken at face value. This is particularly true of older accounts, which
are influenced by the theme, dating back to Herodotus, of the competition among the Thracian widows for the honour of following the
deceased into his grave. Dapper, for example, writes in 1668 about the
kingdom of Congo: when the ruler dies,

> he is buried in a sitting position in a deep grave. In earlier times twelve
> young maidens would jump, according to the old custom, of their own
> free will into the grave, to serve him in the other life. They believed that
> the King did not remain dead, but that he went into another world,
> where he would live and receive their services. Indeed, these maidens
> were so covetous of being buried alive with the King, that they are said
> to have killed each other for this, since each always wanted to be the
> first.[140]

While Dapper is at least careful to speak of the past, such qualifications do not appear in Labarthe's account at the beginning of the
nineteenth century. In Dahomey 'the wives of the dead King come in
large numbers and vie for the honour of being buried with him, in
order to be able to serve him in the other life. Only 24 of them are
chosen to receive this honour and the rest wail and scream against the
injustice, which excludes them from it.'[141]

This reading of the sources is particularly important in the case of
Africa. One hypothesis that has been put forward repeatedly is that till

---

433; Wilks, *Human sacrifice* 443; Wilks, *Nineteenth century* 593; C. Williams
439; Hartmann 190; Le Hérissé 180; Ankermann 33; Frässle 52; Johnson
57; Valdez 1, 333; Cardi, in Kingsley 452.

[139] Lander, *Journal* 1, 92; M'Leod 65; Theal 88 (only a very general and
vague assertion).

[140] Dapper (1670) 1, 563; (1668) 1, 581–2. Elsewhere Dapper speaks,
on the contrary, of force being used in the custom, for example (1668) 1,
403; 498, and even denies the belief in the hereafter among the people concerned: ibid., 480; 493.

[141] Labarthe, German edition 355 (French edition 124). Further passages

the intensification of European influence, which made itself felt mainly through the slave trade, following into death, while certainly extant in Africa, seldom occurred and involved only a small number of victims who were mostly volunteers. 'Acceptance of death by royal wives and relatives and servants was a question of moral integrity and of quick passage to an honourable place among "the other half of humanity"—those who lived as spirits.'[142] This may actually have been the case. But the sources from the sixteenth and seventeenth centuries, with their stereotyped statements, do not prove it. It is equally possible to assume that the increase in the number of victims through the inclusion of anonymous attendants happened much earlier. This would seem even more probable if one takes into account that such customs normally develop very slowly.

The relative scarcity of a truly voluntary following into death is also evident in the fact that the persons accompanying the dead did not kill themselves, but were, as a rule, killed. Different authors, however, emphasize that no general rules can be observed, that some victims were coerced while others went to their death in the face of opposition. Thus, rather than being able to draw conclusions about concrete cases of voluntary death, one can only speak about the uncertainty of European judgement.[143]

At least in one of the given scenarios, however, accounts of voluntary deaths appear completely plausible. If the deceased had had favourite wives, servants or slaves who had achieved this position at the cost of rivals, then they were now faced with the prospect of revenge, and death combined with expectations of the other world would appear to be a welcome alternative.[144] During the lifetime of the deceased these favourites sometimes pledged to accompany him in death.[145]

The extent of free choice would have depended on the kind of ceremony as well as the time frame in which it took place (which in turn determined the kind of attendants). The right to choose was

in Cavazzi 94–5 (book 1, chap. 262); 97–8 (book 1, chap. 267); Leo Africanus and Ramusio, quoted in Graham 327; Ihle 173; Le Hérissé 180; Cardi, in Kingsley 452; Roth, *Benin* 43; Schneider, *Religion* 133.

[142] Davidson 196; cf. Coquery-Vidrovitch 697-702; Isichei, *Ibo* 57–8 and pp. 78–9 above.

[143] Stated already in Cavazzi 161 (book 2, chap. 29) and 166 (book 2, chap. 38) and Oldendorp 316–17.

[144] Cf. Meek, *Kingdom* 174.

[145] For example Johnson 55–6. Cf. also p. 80 above, about the *okra*.

undoubtedly greatest at the actual funeral ceremony, when most of the personal attendants went to their death. The messengers were an exception. Some authors state that only volunteers were used as messengers.[146] This makes sense. If the messenger was coerced to go, there was the risk that he would not carry out his task or that he would act with malicious intent. He could, for example, convey a false message, which would provoke the recipient to act against the people left behind in this world. On the other hand, the messengers did not belong to those groups of attendants who had had a particularly intimate bond with the deceased. The sources do not say how this problem was solved. We can assume that the promise of reward in the other world played an important role. Yet it is only in the rarest of cases that one can speak of a truly voluntary act. Those who refused to act as messengers were, as a rule, not set free, but were killed in some other connection, at which point of time there were no rewards beckoning in the other world.[147]

Resistance

Despite the pronounced violent character of the rituals, the sources do not mention any noteworthy resistance on the part of the victims once they were in the power of the relatives of the deceased, or of the organs of state. This was obviously on account of their inability to change the situation.

It was a different matter in the early stage, so long as real alternatives still existed. This is especially true of groups who regularly had to provide numerous persons to accompany the dead, like the servants and slaves of highly-placed persons. The most common reaction among them was to escape, either directly after the death of the person to be accompanied, or, as often happened, when the person was on the verge of dying.[148] They went into hiding and only returned when the most

---

[146] For example Roth, *Benin* 74. Skertchly 193 however also mentions prisoners.

[147] M'Leod 65 gives an account about a messenger in Dahomey who refused to go to his death and was subsequently beheaded personally by the ruler.

[148] Beecham 232; Bowdich 376–7; Dapper (1668) 1, 403; Des Marchais 1, 153–4; 2, 93; Ellis, *Tshi* 162; 242; Lander, *Journal* 1, 92; McCaskie, *Death* 432–3; Mockler-Ferryman 235; Oldendorp 316–17; Thomas 284–5; Waddell 295; 336; 642–3; Kidd 246–7; Meek, *Kingdom* 174.

important ceremonies had been concluded. 'The decease of a person is announced by a discharge of musketry, proportionate to his rank, or the wealth of his family. In an instant you see a crowd of slaves burst from the house, and run towards the bush, flattering themselves that the hindmost, or those surprised in the house, will furnish the human victims for sacrifice, if they can but secrete themselves until the custom is over.'[149]

When potential victims ran away the ritual was not cancelled, but merely conducted using other victims,[150] although their numbers were possibly smaller than originally planned. Sometimes escape was sought to be prevented by confinement.[151]

Resistance, however, could also take more far-reaching forms. In the 1850s, in Calabar, in South Nigeria, slaves who had fled the ritual often co-operated. The condition they imposed for their return was that in future victims would not be taken from their ranks.[152] The demonstration of power through the custom had reached its limits. It had turned into a risk for the system, because the number of victims from within the country had become too high. The demands of the slaves were met each time and the rebels returned. We do not know to what extent the promises were kept. However, it is at least evident that the question of providing victims was an important one for the slaves, since they did not challenge slavery as an institution.

In 1867, citizens and slaves in Asante took up arms to defend themselves against a massacre that had continued for many days.[153]

We do not know whether similar uprisings had occurred in earlier times. The frequent escapes indicate such a possibility.

These events again throw light on the voluntary nature of the act. After all, according to the criteria used here, slaves and servants belonged partly to the group of personal attendants. Despite this, most of them did not seem to feel the need to voluntarily accompany their masters into death. This speaks for the efficiency of the entire system. Only a functioning state could kill people in large numbers against

---

[149] Bowdich 282.

[150] Ellis, *Tshi* 162; 242; Ramseyer/Kühne, English edition 235–7; Waddell 336–7; C. Williams 436–7.

[151] For example Doke 186.

[152] Davidson 196–7; Isichei, *West Africa* 11; 117; Law, *Human sacrifice* 80–1; Waddell 642–4.

[153] McCaskie, *Death* 433–4.

their will. And only a stable political system could carry this out without causing major political and social upheavals.

The End

Following into death therefore did provoke resistance. However, we cannot derive a natural progression towards the abolition of the custom from this one fact. The resistance was concerned with the distribution of the costs and not with the question of whether it was right for the deceased to have people accompanying him to the other world. The fact that power struggles took place within the framework of the custom is a consequence of the nature of the custom itself, since it was after all characterized by marked inequality.

The fight against the custom and its ultimate suppression was the work of external forces, even where these forces, for tactical reasons, sometimes allied themselves with the Africans, especially with potential victims, while other Africans joined the fight out of conviction.[154] Islam first tipped the scales, and in the final phase it was predominantly the European–Christian influence at work. The process began very slowly. It gathered momentum only in the nineteenth century, and, finally, in the late nineteenth century it intensified with almost breathtaking rapidity.

The role of Islam was limited to the north. With the slow expansion of this religion the custom was pushed back—probably at the same speed—since it was not compatible with Islamic conceptions of the hereafter.[155] Complete suppression, however, would not have occurred with superficial contact, but only with a longer and more enduring Islamic influence.

The European–Christian influence played the decisive role in this suppression. Europeans, no doubt, tried from the beginning to prevent such ceremonies in the places and regions under their control,[156] and formal prohibitions are known to have been issued from the seventeenth century.[157] The same holds true for regions converted

[154] Isichei, *Social reform* 470–2.

[155] Law, *Human sacrifice* 62; 78; J. Thomson 2, 258; Junker 3, 292. According to Lewin 65, Muslims were not chosen as victims in Asante.

[156] Bosman, with reference to the Dutch territories. Cf. Cruickshank 221; 262. For Britain: Adams 26–7; Ricketts 107–8.

[157] Law, *Human sacrifice* 78; Ricketts 108.

to Christianity in which, however, relapses did take place.[158] Europeans living in Africa showed practically no interest in the other regions. Conflicts were sought to be avoided in the interest of (slave) trade. Combined with a certain adjustment to African conditions, this attitude apparently implicated Europeans in places. It is reported, for example, that in 1860 the Portuguese, like the neighbouring African chiefs, provided twenty victims for an annual ceremony. The other Europeans, on the contrary, are said to have refused to provide victims and to have offered only other gifts.[159] We cannot say how often such things happened. If Europeans or European-educated persons became dignitaries in African kingdoms, then they could, on the basis of their position, in certain cases be accompanied in death. In 1849 King Gezo of Dahomey had a boy, a girl, and three men killed as attendants in death at the grave of his white Brazilian adviser, Francisco Felix da Souza.[160] On the other hand, Europeans seem to have never, or only extremely seldom, figured as victims. Such a case has only been handed down in the context of early-seventeenth-century Madagascar, in an account that is not very credible.[161] The cultural dividing line remained clear, and the desire to avoid conflicts was strong. If such things had happened more often, they would no doubt have been mentioned frequently in European sources.

In the nineteenth century, European opposition to the custom intensified.[162] This was probably due to the influence of missionary movements, which were rapidly gaining ground, as well as to the spread of views and theories regarding the civilizing mission of Europeans. Missionaries as well as traders, travellers and other secular Europeans frequently tried to save victims from ceremonies of following into death. They were often successful in this, either by being able to buy the freedom of some of the persons who were meant to die, or by procuring a reprieve for them.[163] However, they were not successful in their main aim of eliminating the institution. They were never able to

---

[158] Merolla 397 (1709); Cavazzi 94 (book 1, chap. 94).

[159] Burton, *Gelele* 2, 332. Similarly *Le Tour du Monde* 106; Lartigue, in Brunschwig 129: 13 victims.

[160] Forbes 1, 32–3; cf. Law, *Human sacrifice* 85.

[161] Grandidier 533 (account of 1620 where the number of victims is clearly exaggerated).

[162] For early efforts see for example Cruickshank 84–5; 221; 262.

[163] Missionaries: Cavazzi 97–9 (book 1, chap. 268); François 191; Waddell

make the custom disappear permanently on a larger scale. Apart from its religious moorings the custom was, in the final analysis, securely bound to important political issues of power.

European states and their agencies in Africa, which had increasingly, albeit reluctantly, to deal with the matter, initially had the same experiences as private individuals. They also came under pressure from public opinion in Europe. One of the main objects of criticism—apart from slave trade and slavery—were the so-called human sacrifices, which were first and foremost a kind of following into death.[164] Under this pressure attempts were made with the help of treaties to motivate the states neighbouring colonial territories to ban the custom. From the middle of the nineteenth century such commitments were regularly signed.[165] Wherever this could not be accomplished, diplomatic, political and economic pressure was exerted when concrete occasions came up.[166] But government officials were hardly more successful than private persons. The agreements were repeatedly violated.[167] This sometimes gave Europeans a good excuse to carry out so-called punitive expeditions against a state, where in any case they had accounts to settle.[168] But for the most part the colonial powers did not want to be dragged into conflicts and preferred to ignore matters.

Sometimes the position of Europeans would be weakened by conflicts between missionaries and traders or between other interest groups. When an alleged ban was violated in 1855 in South Nigeria, the missionaries wanted the guilty to be punished, but the traders prevailed with a bombardment from ships, which was completely ineffective. The action was clearly illegal, since the persons to be

---

293–4 (without success). Others: Forbes 1, 49–50 (freedom bought); Freeman 24 (giving up the claim to a larger number of victims out of consideration for the Europeans); Burton, *Gelele* 2, 7 (reprieve); Skertchly 368; 376 (reprieve); Forbes 2, 49–51; Hutton 85; Adams 27; M'Leod 133; Talbot 148 (effect of the mere presence of a white person). Without success: *Eine portugiesische Expedition* 262; Adams 26.

[164] An important case study in this context is Campion-Vincent.

[165] For example Allen/Thomson 2, 244; Ellis, *Yoruba* 105; Waddell 421–2; Baden-Powell 28; Law, *Human sacrifice* 78–9; 83–4.

[166] For example Metcalfe 142–3; 206; Law, *Human sacrifice* 71.

[167] Ellis, *Yoruba* 105; Waddell 551; Baden-Powell 28; Law, *Human sacrifice* 78–84; Davidson 196–7.

[168] Cf. the detailed descriptions in Waddell 421–2; 444–8; 553–4.

punished had not given any binding commitment to do away with the custom.[169]

With this it finally became clear that the custom was deeply entrenched. The Europeans were not in a position to suppress it in spite of employing all the means at their disposal, short of using state force. The increasingly uncompromising stance of rejection and abhorrence on the part of Europeans gave to the custom an additional symbolic value in the eyes of Africans and thereby provoked resistance. However, European pressure also led to debates within the African states. Traditionalists wanted to hold on to the old customs, while their opponents demanded that they conform to European conditions. The reformers were not able to prevail anywhere.[170]

Real success came only, but then quickly and effectively, with the establishment of colonial rule.[171] It was clear from the beginning that the custom could not exist alongside European colonialism. No state could have afforded to tolerate it for fear of invoking the wrath of a strong philanthropic lobby.

Indeed, the custom then disappeared remarkably quickly. The new rulers issued bans everywhere, and whenever necessary they intervened directly with armed forces.[172] Offenders were severely punished.[173] Such rigorous methods were, however, only used after colonial rule had been consolidated. In October 1883, a few months after establishing a military post in the Congo, the French were invited to a ceremony of following into death with nine victims. Although they had fifty rapid fire guns, they thought it more prudent to make a virtue out of a necessity. 'However horrible the barbaric custom of human sacrifice is for us, we do not believe that we have the right to endanger the future of our work through ill-timed force.'[174]

The process of abolition was accompanied by different acts of substitution, in which the victims were replaced by other living things, by objects or by symbolic actions. For this, one could partly fall back on

---

[169] Waddell 550–5.

[170] Law, *Human sacrifice* 82–6. Bieber 2, 149 mentions a possible exception: Supposedly the Kaffa empire (Ethiopia) suppressed the custom between 1870 and 1890 on its own strength and initiative.

[171] Cf. Coquery-Vidrovitch 714–15.

[172] For example Velde 390–1 (Congo).

[173] For example Mockler-Ferryman 234 (Nigeria).

[174] Coquilhat 169.

indigenous traditions. Among the Mundang in Ethiopia a boy and a girl would be interred with the king. 'If however the king who thus journeyed to the other world has been a very small one, a poor wretch, in whose estate there were no such slave girls and boys, then one only carves two pieces of wood nicely, colours them black and throws them into the pit instead of the human victims.'[175] Among the Yoruba, human victims were replaced with a horse and an ox.[176] In Swaziland the women who would earlier be killed had to run away for some time into the bush or to the mountains and burn all their clothes there.[177]

The quick success of the measures taken for the suppression of the custom is surprising, given that the earlier opposition had lasted for so long and had to a great extent held out successfully. The explanation could arise primarily from the political and institutional character of the custom. With the end, or at least with the extreme weakening of African states brought about by colonial rule, the custom had little support. Had it possessed a more individual character, it would have been more difficult to suppress.

Given the fact that European rule was initially extremely slack, we cannot dismiss the possibility that, in the beginning, the success was confined to administrative reports, and that ceremonies continued secretly.[178] On the other hand, however, its public nature was of central importance, and an event of this kind hardly lent itself to secrecy. In 1927, an author mentions that among the Baya in Cameroon, when an important person died, 'some slaves would be slaughtered for the dead man.'[179] The oral tradition also tells of isolated cases. Thus a student in Zurich wrote in 1994: 'After the death of my great-grandfather, a respected chief in Asaba [Nigeria], in the 1920s [between 1922 and

[175] Frobenius 3, 147. Similarly Krafft 25.

[176] Johnson 55. Similarly Meek, *Kingdom* 174. Cf. Oldendorp 315: Hens, goats and cows for less important persons; Schebesta, *Vollblutneger* 239: Goats as substitutes for humans.

[177] Kidd 246. The British distributed liquor and gunpowder as compensation for two children who were meant as victims, and who they had given shelter to in their fort; this cannot, however, be taken as a case of real substitution. Adams 27 (before 1823).

[178] Conjectures of this nature in Frässle 52. Freeman 473–5 emphasizes in 1898 that British intervention in Asante had not been able to suppress the custom—a certain momentum was obviously required.

[179] Hartmann 15.

1927], his favourite slave was buried alive with him.'[180] We cannot suppose that such family traditions were invented at a time in which the custom was increasingly regarded as barbaric. An event which took place in Ghana, in 1944, and became very famous—in which three people were sentenced to death—has however not been elucidated till today.[181]

The success was not just superficial. The people concerned internalized the ban. In course of time they gave up the custom out of conviction, and external pressure was no longer required. The continuing spread of Christianity and Islam must have played a role in this. At any rate, even after the end of colonial rule, there does not seem to have been any major attempt to revive the custom, and certainly no successful attempts at carrying it out publicly. European influence, initially based only on superior strength, had also led to a change in the inner preconditions.

The end of the custom was preceded by the end of the traditional African states. As a result, the question of their surviving without the custom cannot be answered.

---

[180] Nadler 22. I am grateful to Albert Leemann for this reference.
[181] For this see the monograph by Rathbone (1993).

CHAPTER 5

Oceania

The name 'Oceania' refers here to the Pacific islands, including New Zealand and New Guinea, and excluding the rest of Indonesia and the Philippines. Since none of the sources consulted mention following into death in Australia, it is not included here. The custom has been recorded for most of the larger groups of islands of Oceania. Two different types of relevant events can be distinguished which are dealt with separately here, although, in actual practice they coincide. On several groups of islands one finds evidence of a regular following of the dead, in which widows accompanying their husbands were the focal point of the custom. In New Zealand and New Guinea, on the other hand, non-ritualized self-killings following the death of a closely related person seem to have been widespread.

Non-ritualized Self-killings: Precursors of Following into Death?

A German author wrote at the beginning of the twentieth century about New Guinea:

> If a man or a woman hangs or poisons him-/herself after a marital dispute, which occurs quite often in Sissanu, then it is a matter of honour for the surviving partner to accompany the dead one. If however through constant vigilance the relatives are able to prevent the survivor from killing him-/herself before the dead person is buried—this happens in Sissanu on the second day after death—then the suicide does not take place, because the attendant can then no longer catch up with the deceased. The couple can go together to the other world only if they are laid into the same grave.[1]

This is not following into death at it has been defined here. The ritual and the public elements are missing. On the contrary, the public tries to prevent the suicide.

[1] Neuhauss 1, 171 (1911). Cf. F.E. Williams 213.

Yet one cannot simply equate these acts with suicides committed out of despair on the death of a spouse. One gets the impression that society approves of, and, indeed, expects these acts, even if it formally tries to prevent them. Otherwise, it would not be a 'matter of honour' for the surviving spouse. The basic precondition of the custom, the belief that life in this world is continued in the next, is found here. The question that remains unanswered, however, is why this kind of suicide was customary only after 'marital disputes', since the belief in the hereafter would suggest that the spouse be accompanied even without such special conditions. The absence of any differentiation between the sexes is conspicuous.

The precursors of following into death can be seen in the conditions described above. The private, indeed, the secret event would, in course of time, have been ritualized and legitimized by the public. In this way, the event would have gained social and, later, perhaps political functions. Simultaneously, the neutrality of the act with regard to the sexes would have been converted into male domination, in that only women would have killed themselves. Finally, being killed by others would have replaced suicide. This would have also enhanced the role of the public, transforming it from one of mere observation to one demanding active participation.

At least for the Maori in New Zealand there are several indications of such a development. A chronology, however, cannot be established; rather, the different elements existed alongside each other.

In 1863 Maning stated that in earlier times suicides were a very frequent phenomenon. He heard about them almost every day. 'When a man died it was almost a matter of course that his wife, or wives, hanged themselves. When the wife died, the man very commonly shot himself.'[2]

A direct connection with the belief in the hereafter has not been established here. The frequency of the incidents, however, seems unusual. Both sexes behave in a similar fashion, the only difference being the manner of suicide.

Along with this non-ritualized suicide, other forms also existed which mark the transition to an actual following of the dead. Even prior to being ritualized, the differentiation between the sexes is evident. Most of the accounts only speak of women killing themselves,

[2] Maning 186. Similarly Dieffenbach 2, 111, who also mentions the suicide of parents on the death of their children.

most frequently on the death of the husband, but sometimes also to accompany a child or a brother.[3]

A statement of 1824 is more limited: 'In the event of the premature or violent death of the husband, it is the custom of the country for the head wife to hang herself.'[4] Along with the inequality of gender roles, the concentration in the upper class becomes apparent here, since practically only members of this class would have several wives and, therefore, a head wife. At this point, one can also assume that a certain ritualization had already occurred; the head wife would hardly be able to kill herself unnoticed.

This phenomenon leads us to another hypothesis. The tendency towards ritualization is to be found mainly among the upper class. For them the custom becomes a means of claiming and maintaining a social and political position. More than the other groups this class is in a position to stage an elaborate public ceremony aimed at establishing social boundaries.

One-sidedness and ritualization are linked to the enlargement of the circle of persons accompanying the dead beyond the immediate family. Taylor writes in 1855: 'In former times, one or more of the chief's wives would strangle themselves to accompany and wait upon their lord in the other world; for this purpose, also, several slaves were killed, that the chief might not be without attendants.'[5]

Those victims who are linked by a less personal bond with the person to be accompanied, for example, slaves, do not kill themselves, but are killed by the public. The public's importance increases with ritualization, in that it no longer simply looks on but actually executes the act. In the next step, the widows no longer kill themselves but are strangulated, although this has only been recorded in the case of New Guinea.[6]

This suggests that the rise of following into death was linked here with the emergence, or the intensification, of a division of roles and the inequality between the sexes. The reactions of members of both the sexes on the death of a spouse would originally not have differed fundamentally. Unaffected emotion was replaced, in the framework of the custom, by an outward display of sentiment governed by prevailing

---

[3] Colenso 57. Similarly Dieffenbach 2, 40.

[4] Cruise 278.

[5] Taylor 99. Similarly Tregear 389–90; Polack 1, 66; 78–9; 116; 156–8.

[6] Keysser, in Neuhauss 3, 83–4. Cf. Krieger 174; Schellong 21–4; Steinmetz, *Strafe* 223.

social mores. This led to gender-specific expectations and finally to corresponding actions. The institution of following into death transformed an individual act into a socially determined one.

Ritualized Killings and Self-killings

While non-ritualized self-killings have only been mentioned in the case of New Guinea and New Zealand, ritualized killings and self-killings have also been recorded for many other islands. The US-American Charles Wilkes, who travelled the Pacific between 1838 and 1842, described the events on the death of a chief on the Fiji Islands, not as an eyewitness, but based on the accounts of different observers:

> If any of his wives wish to die and be buried with him, she runs to her brother or nearest relative and exclaims, 'I wish to die, that I may accompany my husband to the land where his spirit has gone! Love me and make haste to strangle me, that I may overtake him!' Her friends applaud her purpose, and being dressed and decorated in her best clothes, she seats herself on a mat, reclining her head on the lap of a woman; another holds her nostrils, that she may not breathe through them; a cord, made by twisting fine tapa (masi) [Polynesian rope], is then put around her neck, and drawn tight by four or five strong men, so that the struggle is soon over. [. . .] When the grave is finished, the principal workman [. . .] lines the pit or grave with fine mats, and lays two of the leaves at the head and two at the foot of the grave; on these the corpse of the chief is placed, with two of his wives, one on each side, having their right and left hands, respectively, laid on his breast; the bodies are then wrapped together in folds of native cloth; the grave is then filled in, and the sacred earth is laid on, and a stone over it.[7]

Events such as this are reported from most of the larger groups of islands in the Pacific, often by eyewitnesses. Fiji seems to have constituted a kind of centre for such events.[8] Apart from New Guinea and New Zealand, the places to be mentioned are the New Hebrides (today Vanuatu),[9] the Solomon Islands,[10] New Caledonia,[11] Tonga[12] and

[7] Wilkes 98–9. Similarly Hale 64–5.

[8] Dumont d'Urville 705; Erskine 228–33; Hale 63–5; Michelena y Rojas 170–1; B.Thomson 132; Williams/Calvert 1, 132–4; 187–206; 2, 244.

[9] Gill 302; Speiser, *Südsee* 94; Turner, *Polynesia* 93–4; 371–2.

[10] Eckardt 376; Hocart 86; Ivens 87; 223.

[11] Garnier 156; Legrand 118.

[12] Mariner 1, 341–4; 2, 220–2.

Hawaii.[13] The most important exceptions are Samoa and, most probably, the Society Islands with Tahiti. At least in the case of Tahiti this cannot be ascribed only to the contingencies of scientific tradition. The numerous Europeans who visited the islands, especially the missionaries, would definitely have written about such a remarkable custom, especially since human sacrifice in Tahiti is otherwise mentioned very often. On the other hand, following into death is mentioned only very vaguely in two different accounts of the same event.[14]

Persons Accompanying the Dead

Since there appear to be several common threads linking different versions of the process, one can indeed talk of a special form of the custom in Oceania. Let us first consider the persons accompanying the dead. Following into death in Oceania was, essentially, the accompanying of the husband by his widow or widows. Even if servants or slaves are killed, at least one widow is present among them. The only possible exception is Hawaii, which is, to a large extent, geographically isolated from the rest of Oceania. Various authors state that in earlier times, when rulers and important men died, one or more persons, mostly slaves or members of the lower classes, were killed[15]—wives or

---

[13] Schoch 18–19; Chamisso 503; Cook 3, 1, 270–1; 505; 597; 620–1; 1177; 1184 (different authors).

[14] The Spanish interpreter Máximo Rodríguez wrote in 1775 that the Papara had prepared a human sacrifice 'in memory of their chief' (Corney 3, 187). However Rodríguez was not an eyewitness, and he also does not say whether the sacrifice is to be understood in the sense of following into death. Gerónimo Clota and Narciso González speak in even more indefinite terms about it (ibid., 342–9).

In the relevant literature the passages mentioned above are sometimes interpreted as proof of the existence of following into death, as has been done by Ferdon 173 and by Oliver 1, 501. In the light of other abundant sources on the history of Tahiti, in which nothing comparable is mentioned, this interpretation goes too far.

Human sacrifices for gods were, on the other hand, common, for example to pray for victory in war. For the different references and eyewitness accounts see Cook 2, 233–4; 238; 3, 1, 198–204; 3, 2, 978–83; 1315–16, as well as Corney 2, 342–9; 3, 178; 187–9; Ferdon 65–70; 270–1; Henry 176–8; Oliver 1, 487–521; Schoch 55.

[15] Schoch 18–19; Chamisso 503; Cook 3,1, 270–1; 505; 597; 620–1;

concubines, however, are mentioned only once and in a very vague manner.[16]

Among married couples the one-sidedness was absolute. The sources never mention a widower accompanying his wife in a ritualized and public ceremony. If the dead man had many wives, his principal or his favourite wife followed him into the other world.[17] Often other wives joined her.[18] This tendency to expand continued with concubines, servants, slaves and members of the court. Then, however, it was no longer only women who were killed.[19] Yet, the killing of widows formed the core of the custom in Oceania. The indications of a close personal bond become stronger when mothers, aunts or grandmothers killed themselves, or allowed themselves to be killed, on the death of their children, nephews, nieces or grandchildren.[20] Once even the daughter of a dead man is named as his attendant in death.[21]

Women, therefore, provided the majority of attendants. This is also

---

1177; 1184; Obeyesekere 83; Stannard 61. According to Chamisso 503, certain families 'from the lowest caste' had to regularly provide the victims.

[16] Cook 3, 621: It is said here that a chief and his wife were buried in the same place—when and how the wife died is not mentioned. A further exception is the statement by Michelena y Rojas (1843) 170–1, that on Rotuma near the Fiji Islands till not very long ago, when a chief died, a twelve-year old boy would be killed and buried with him. On the death of the principal wife of the chief the same would be done with a girl. Widows are not mentioned in this context. This very specific form could hardly have been a widespread phenomenon. A case from the Solomon Islands mentioned in Guppy 37–8 is again of a different nature. A shark killed a chief's son. In order to appease the spirit of the shark, a human victim bought from neighbouring headhunters was killed. Here one can talk of following into death only in a very limited sense. In addition, it is not clear whether the dead man actually left behind a widow.

[17] For example Mariner 1, 330; 210 (Tonga); Polack 1, 158 (New Zealand).

[18] For example Eckardt 376 (Solomons); Erskine 228; 232 (Fiji); Garnier 156 (New Caledonia); Turner 93–4 (Aneityum: New Hebrides).

[19] For example Gill 302 (Aneityum); Hocart 86 (slaves on the Solomon Islands); Polack 1, 66; 78; 116; 156–8 (New Zealand); Schoch 18 (Hawaii); Taylor 99 (New Zealand); Tregear 389 (New Zealand); Wilkes 97 (Fiji); Williams/Calvert 1, 189; 197 (Fiji).

[20] See footnotes 24–6.

[21] Wilkes 96.

connected with the absence of the different categories of anonymous followers so widespread in Africa. From time to time the killing of prisoners of war is also mentioned, but only in the context of Hawaii.[22]

The Accompanied

In Oceania individual following into death clearly predominated. The accompanied were almost exclusively men. But there are exceptions. In isolated cases, the sources consulted mention that the favourite wife of a chief is accompanied into the other world.[23]

The issue, therefore, was not primarily of the political position of the person to be accompanied as a chief or as a ruler, but of his role as a husband. Status-based divisions were thus reflected in the distinctions between attendants and persons to be accompanied. This was even more evident in cases where, as is occasionally mentioned, women allowed themselves to be killed on the death of a small child,[24] an unmarried son,[25] a nephew, a niece or a grandchild.[26]

Alongside this, there are some institutional elements. In most places the custom was practised mainly by the upper classes. Yet, this does not seem to have been a consequence of legally binding limitations, but rather a question of customs that were fairly consistently observed. None of the sources mention that following into death was permitted only to the highly placed,[27] just as it is not said that it was made into a privilege of the rulers. On the basis of the circumstances therefore it more or less became a privilege of the upper class—a privilege that the lower classes could hardly afford.

Instead of an increasing concentration in the most powerful families, or, indeed, only among the rulers, there is a downward filtering process in Oceania. On certain islands the widows are generally said

---

[22] Schoch 18–19.

[23] Tregear 389; Michelena y Rojas 170–1 (see footnote 19).

[24] Codrington 289.

[25] Gill 302; Williams/Calvert 1, 134; 189.

[26] Turner 372.

[27] Here too Hawaii is most likely an exception, since it is always stated very clearly that following into death only takes place for important persons (see footnote 15). This would match the fact that wives and concubines are not mentioned as persons accompanying the dead and that the individual element is therefore much less pronounced.

to have killed themselves on the death of their husbands.[28] If these statements are taken as an indication, not of the actual observance of the practice, but rather of its availability to even the less privileged classes, then they need not be dismissed out of hand. Following into death was first and foremost a matter of the relationship between the sexes, in concrete terms between married couples. In this respect, its spread to the lower echelons did not endanger the prerogatives of the upper class.

Frequency

The number of victims could hardly ever have been higher than ten. In many cases only the widow was put to death. Sometimes several wives or concubines were killed as attendants. Servants and slaves were seldom killed. Considerably higher numbers are mentioned occasionally, but not in eyewitness accounts. Considering the possibility of inflated numbers, such cases would have constituted clear exceptions. When on Fiji, 'Ra Mbithi, the pride of Somosomo, was lost at sea, seventeen of his wives were destroyed. After the news of the massacre of the Namena people at Viwa in 1839, eighty women were strangled to accompany the spirits of their murdered husbands.'[29] This is the highest number mentioned in the sources. But the number of persons to be accompanied here—over 100—was also extraordinarily high.[30]

In some regions, however, the number of cases seems to have been large. Even if they were exaggerated, there are references which indicate that in some places the custom was more than just a curious fact and that it had notable demographic consequences, and could even become dangerous for the survival of a society. In 1924, Speiser writes about the New Hebrides: 'The number of women here is at the most one-fourth that of men, which explains the progressive extinction of the race. One of the causes of this lack of women is the custom of strangling all the wives of a chief when he dies, a custom which is all the more pernicious because the chiefs always have a number of young wives, while the young men can at the most buy themselves an old

---

[28] Codrington 289 (Maewo: New Hebrides); Eckardt 376 (Solomon Islands); Speiser, *Neue Hebriden* 43 (Aneityum); Wilkes 100–1 (Fiji); Williams/Calvert 1, 134 (Fiji).

[29] Williams/Calvert 1,200. Cf. also ibid., 1,189. Similarly Wilkes 158–9.

[30] Williams/Calvert 2, 244.

one.'[31] Some statements made by missionaries are less far-reaching, but somewhat more precise. Williams asserts in 1858 that death from natural causes seldom occurs among the heathen population of the Fiji Islands because of 'the prevalence of war and the various systems of murder which custom demands.' The number of orphans in the mission schools, he says, is very large. In one class alone, of fourteen possible parents only four are still living, and this, he maintains, is no exception. A considerable number of women have been murdered.[32]

However, there are no accounts of intra-societal conflicts provoked by such dangerous effects. The probability of rebellion among attendants in death, who are linked by a close personal bond with the person to be accompanied, is definitely less than among anonymous victims.[33]

The Time of Killing

In most cases, the killing or self-killing occurs directly after the death of the person to be accompanied, normally at the funeral, with the victim being buried together with the dead person in the same grave. Sometimes, the widow (or widows) is (are) strangled directly after the death of the husband, and the common funeral takes place a little later.[34] The tendency to turn following into death into a process carried out over a period of time cannot be found anywhere. The main purpose is to provide the deceased with attendants. In some places, a delay in following the dead is in fact ruled out with arguments based on references to the other world: if the attendant hesitates for too long, she cannot catch up with the deceased in the other world.[35]

Through a link with another custom, independent of following into death, the order was even reversed in some regions, and the attendants were killed first. The practice of killing old and sick people is common in many parts of the world. This is particularly widespread

---

[31] Speiser, *Südsee* 94.

[32] Williams/Calvert 1, 203–4; cf. Wilkes 158–9.

[33] Schoch 19 however speaks of the flight of the inhabitants of Hawaii in the face of the approaching death of the ruler. But the circumstances were different to those obtaining otherwise in Oceania, since the victims here were more or less anonymous.

[34] For example Mariner 1, 329 (Fiji); Williams/Calvert 1, 134 (Fiji).

[35] Neuhauss 1, 171 (New Guinea)

in the case of rulers.[36] From the justifications put forward in this context we need to look only at the connection with a belief in the hereafter, which was often explicitly established by the people concerned. The belief that the other world is identical to this one leads to the assumption that the infirmities of this world will continue to exist in the other world. This is why it was considered preferable to get there while still in full possession of one's strength. In August 1845, after it had been decided that King Tuithakau of Somosomo on the Fiji Islands should die, his wives were first strangled. After that he was placed alive in the common grave and the corpses of his wives served as a resting-place.[37] In the external course of events there is a reversal: the wives are the ones accompanied and the king accompanies them. That was obviously not the view of the people concerned, nor did it correspond to the inner substance of the ritual.

Killing and Self-killing

Killing by others was the rule in Oceania, self-killing the exception. This is surprising, given the individual character of the custom prevalent here, and given also the close personal bond that existed, in most cases, between the person to be accompanied and the person(s) accompanying him. Yet the accounts are often quite precise and they are not written exclusively by missionaries.[38] Only for New Zealand is suicide mentioned as the sole manner in which a widow would be killed. This could be because the custom there was ritualized to a lesser degree. It was more a matter concerning those directly affected than one concerning the public. Everywhere else, on the other hand, the public plays an important role by carrying out the killing.

Self-killing occurred in most places through hanging, especially when the event had, to some extent, become a ritual. Strangling, drowning and death by starvation are also mentioned.[39]

Strangling is mentioned most often when others carried out the killing. The reasons for favouring this method of killing are not clear.

[36] Hale 65; Oberländer, *Ozeanien* 176; Wilkes 96–7; 158. Frazer, *Golden Bough*, deals with this theme very extensively.
[37] Williams/Calvert 1, 193–7. Cf. Erskine 231–3; Oberländer, *Ozeanien* 176.
[38] For example Eckardt 376 (Solomon Islands); Hocart 86 (Solomon Islands); Ivens 87 (Saa: Solomon Islands); Legrand 118 (New Caledonia).
[39] Polack 1, 156.

It is possible that visible injuries or mutilations were sought to be avoided, since it was assumed that these would remain even in the other world. This view is supported by the fact that all the other methods of killing and self-killing that are mentioned also fulfil this requirement.

Strangling, at any rate, did not cause unnecessary suffering. The same is true of the other, more infrequently used, methods of killing, among which hanging was, most likely, the most important. Intentional brutality and cruelty are not evident anywhere in the sources, and the missionaries especially would definitely have written about it, had it been part of the custom. Sometimes, the victims would even be strangled in their sleep.[40]

An exception to this is, however, burying alive, which is mentioned relatively often.[41] Yet it probably did not have a sadistic background, but was, more conceivably, a direct outcome of notions connected with following the dead. When the living attendants followed the deceased into the grave, the aspect of accompanying, of caring for, and serving the deceased was expressed in an unambiguous manner, as was the link between the living and the dead.

Free Choice and Coercion

The infrequency of self-killing suggests the infrequency of voluntary death. Opposed to this is the fact, emphasized in many sources, that the victims went to their death of their own free will and that, in fact, some even insisted on being killed.[42] As a rule, these are not stereotypical formulations. Rather, such passages are found in eyewitness accounts and in accounts by authors whose antipathy to the custom is only too clear.

In the following account written by the missionary Thomas Williams, one can clearly feel how difficult it is for him to admit to the voluntary nature of the act:

> It has been said that most of the women thus destroyed are sacrificed at their own instance. There is truth in this statement; but, unless other

[40] Eckardt 376 (Solomon Islands).

[41] For example Codrington 289 (a woman on the death of her child in Maewo, New Hebrides); Gill 219 (Faté); Wilkes 96 (Fiji).

[42] For example Mariner 1, 330; Oberländer, *Ozeanien* 176; Polack 1, 158; Turner 93; Wilkes 176.

facts are taken into account, it produces an untruthful impression. Many are importunate to be killed, because they know that life would henceforth be to them prolonged insult, neglect, and want. Very often, too, their resolution is grounded upon knowing that their friends or children have determined that they shall die. [. . .] Generally such courage is forced, or the result of despair. Death offers an escape from the suffering and wrong which await the woman who survives her husband; and the dark grave is an asylum into which she hastens from 'the bitterness of sting of taunting tongues.'[43]

After all, the missionaries, among them also Williams, would have had some first-hand experience of the obstinacy of such women. 'When Mbati Namu was killed, the relatives of Sa Ndrungu, his chief wife, brought and offered her to his friends.' Williams managed to free her,

and sent the disappointed murderers about their business. [. . .] A short time after, in consequence of the dissatisfaction of her friends, the woman left the Christian village, crossed the river, and entered the house of the man who was most anxious to destroy her, taking her stand in the midst, so as to intimate that she gave herself up to his will. I followed, and got permission from the dead Chief's brother to take her back with me, and, by taking my proffered hand, she might have lived. She intimated her sense of my kind intention, but declined to accompany me. Next morning she was strangled.[44]

The fact that most of the persons accompanying the dead did not kill themselves does not automatically mean that coercion was involved. In at least some of the cases there was no fundamental difference between killing oneself and being strangled by others. The victim requested other people to carry out the killing after she had resolved to die. The fact that the persons accompanying the dead did not kill themselves would then have had less to do with a lack of will or courage than with the ritual nature of the process, which bound the survivors together by stronger ties in order to emphasize the fact that the attendants in death established a link between the living and the dead.

General considerations also support the fact that references to the voluntary nature of the act are to be taken more seriously than in the

[43] Williams/Calvert 1, 200–1.

[44] Williams/Calvert 1, 202 (cited passage); Erskine 228. Cf. also Wilkes
96.

case of Africa. The individual character of the custom was far more pronounced in Oceania than in Africa. The extent of free choice was apparently greater when the personal bond between the person to be accompanied and the attendants in death was closer. According to the sources, voluntary death was fairly common among widows, whereas in the case of servants and slaves it is not mentioned very often.[45]

Yet, how voluntary was this voluntary death? The criterion used here, that the victims could have avoided death by acting differently, is no doubt fulfilled in most of the cases. From time to time, an intended victim refused to die, and would then not be killed.[46] There are hardly any statements that throw light on the circumstances accompanying the decisions of the victims and on the substance of the different motives.[47] The situation undoubtedly fostered the decision, especially in the case of widows. It had to be taken immediately after the husband's death. The sources do not give any exact account of the position of a surviving widow, but they do indicate that it was not very good. General considerations also support this conclusion. If a society legitimizes the act of a widow accompanying her dead husband as a meritorious act, then it would hardly single out a surviving widow with special honours and material security. A statement contradicting this can only be found with reference to the Maori. Dieffenbach writes: 'Widows of *arikis*, or hereditary chiefs, hold for life the highest influence over the tribe, or convey this influence to the chief whom they may marry.'[48] Widow-remarriage is not mentioned anywhere else, and even Dieffenbach speaks of the suicide of widows.

Psychological pressure, as well as the offer of material incentives to family members, could increase the compulsion for the widows:

> If the friends of the woman are not the most clamorous for her death, their indifference is construed into disrespect either for her late husband or his friends, and would be accordingly resented. Thus the friends and children of the woman are prompted to urge her death, more by self-interest than affection for her, and by fear of the survivors rather than respect for the dead. Another motive is to secure landed

[45] Chamisso 503 (Hawaii). Polack 1,157 on the other hand emphasizes that in New Zealand the slaves were murdered, whereas the widows killed themselves voluntarily.

[46] Williams/Calvert 1, 132; 189. Contradictory statement in Wilkes 96.

[47] Cf. Williams/Calvert 1, 200–1.

[48] Dieffenbach 2, 40.

property belonging to the husband, to obtain which they are ready to sacrifice a daughter, a sister, or a mother. Many a poor widow has been urged by the force of such motives as these, more than by her own apparent ambition to become the favourite wife in the abode of spirits.[49]

This information about Fiji contrasts with an account on New Guinea: 'The women are strangled only if they actively express a desire for it. The survivors have no interest at all in the death of the woman, on the contrary, for she is then taken away from them. Even the family members of the dead man never want the widow to be killed, because they have to pay dearly to the relatives for her devotion to death.'[50]

It would not be correct to conclude from the quoted passages that there were basic differences between the two islands. Rather, the passages show how difficult it is to elicit the exact motives. In addition, both these authors have a different thrust. At any rate, the frequent mention of voluntary death does not imply that in Oceania following into death was always voluntary. This is not only true of the servants and slaves, but also of many of the widows. Not all of them who were saved by missionaries, other Europeans, or even by their own people, rushed back to their executioners.[51]

Functions in This World

The main aspect of the functions of following into death in this world lay in the personal and social spheres and not in the political sphere. The most important point was the legitimacy given to the inequality of the sexes, the subordination of the woman to the man. This central aspect seems to have been connected with the ritualization of the event. In the context of non-ritualized self-killings, on the other hand, there was largely a symmetry between the sexes.

In addition to this, the custom also strengthened other social power relations, especially between masters and their subordinates: servants, slaves, and members of the court. In the context of the Solomon Islands a strong status consciousness has been mentioned: 'It would be a disgrace for them [the widows] and for the memory of the dead man, if they were to remain alive and later perhaps marry men of a lower station.'[52] On the other hand, more far-reaching political aspects are

[49] Williams/Calvert 1, 201. Similarly Wilkes 96.
[50] Keysser, in Neuhauss 3, 83.
[51] Cf. for example Williams/Calvert 1, 202–3.
[52] Eckardt 376.

missing, as is, despite the concourse of the public, the aspect of a mass spectacle.

Functions in the Other World

Following into death was closely connected with a belief in the hereafter, which assumed that through death this world passes into the next. The plausibility of this belief, and the incentives linked with it, were sometimes reinforced by additional assumptions. This was done, for example, by saying that the persons accompanying the dead could only reach the other world with the guidance of the dead person, or that they would only be able to meet the person being accompanied, if they followed him quickly into death.[53] The persons accompanying the dead were mainly supposed to enable the accompanied person to continue in the other world the life he had had in this one. On the Fiji Islands 'the natives consider that the wife, in accompanying him to this residence, is merely doing her duty towards her companion, who, without her, would be living a lonely and cheerless existence.'[54] As a rule, it was not a matter of preventing the dead from encroaching onto this world. Only once, in the context of the New Hebrides, is it said that the women were unhappy with the suppression of the custom under the influence of missionaries and planters, 'and many wished to die, because otherwise they would be disturbed by the soul of their departed husband.'[55] Among the Kai in New Guinea, 'a woman, who wants to be strangled to death, is not held back for fear of the spirit of the dead man, who could harm them in all sorts of ways, if his wife is not allowed to accompany him.'[56]

It was, however, not important to create a lasting connection between the living and the dead in order to enable the dead man to continue influencing this world. The functions of the custom in this and in the other world were therefore more clearly separated than in Africa and America. This also means that its character as a sacrifice was less pronounced.

[53] For example Neuhauss 1, 171 (New Guinea); Wilkes 96 (Fiji); Schoch 19 (Hawaii).
[54] Hale 63.
[55] Speiser, *Südsee* 94.
[56] Keysser, in Neuhauss 3, 84.

The End

Following into death does not seem to have been curbed to a significant degree and much less to have been completely abolished with the arrival of Europeans. Because of its primarily individual character, the victims, too, did not protest. It is even more difficult to conceive of reform movements that questioned the meaning of the institution and its justification. Only isolated cases of resistance, in the form of escape, are mentioned.[57]

The impulses for the abolition of the custom were essentially external ones. Europeans rejected the custom altogether. Rejection, however, did not automatically lead to a fight against it. The missionaries were the most active in this regard. However, so long as they did not have the support of state power, their successes were modest. They admonished the persons concerned and tried to convince them of the folly of their beliefs. But they only succeeded in freeing individual victims from time to time.[58] This did not stifle the custom. It seems that under the influence of such events, there was a tendency to make following into death into a symbol of the will to self-assertion. The missionary Turner wrote, in 1861, that on Aneityum in the New Hebrides following into death had disappeared as a result of the spread of Christianity. To make up, however, it was now rife in neighbouring heathen Tanna, where hitherto it had been unknown.[59] Williams complained in 1858:

> The idea of a Chieftain going into the world of spirits unattended, is most repugnant to the native mind. So strong is the feeling in favour of the loloku [the strangling of widows], that Christianity is disliked because it rigorously discountenances the cherished custom. When the Christian chief of Dama fell by the concealed musketry of the Nawathans, a stray shot entered the forehead of a young man at some distance from him, and killed him. The event was regarded by many of the nominal Christians as most fortunate, since it provided a companion for the spirit of the slain Chief.[60]

[57] Cf. footnote 33.
[58] For this see mainly Williams/Calvert 1,189; 195–6; 202. Cf. also Turner 93–4; 371–2; Erskine 228–33; Speiser, *Südsee* 94.
[59] Turner 93–4.
[60] Williams/Calvert 1, 188–9.

With the increasing spread of Christianity the successes became more significant. Groups of local people were formed who fought against the custom and prevented it in some regions,[61] till the new attitude spread throughout the island, possibly even before European rule.[62]

Sometimes local people not converted to Christianity turned against the custom. In 1817 Mariner sets down the cry of a chief of Tonga: 'What, said he, is the use of destroying a young and beautiful woman? Who is there dares say that the gods are merciless and cruel? My daughter shall not be strangled!' The chief enforced this view.[63]

Traders, seafarers, adventurers and settlers did not engage with the custom as much as missionaries. But the settlers at least—on the basis of their numbers—had a noticeable effect. They began to suppress the custom when they were in the majority. When Chief Upokia of Wangani in New Zealand died, by way of exception no slaves were killed to serve him in the other world:

> Several Europeans residing in the vicinity, whose intercourse and re-monstrances with the defunct, had induced him to desire that such a barbarous crime should not be committed at his decease. This was effected by working on the superstitious feelings of the chief, who was told that the blood of the murdered slave would demand atonement from him in after life. His several wives and slave concubines desisted from hanging or drowning themselves on the same principle, much to the annoyance of the priesthood, who view these foreign innovations as a prelude to the gradual decadence of native religious feeling in New Zealand.[64]

According to Polack economic factors also played a role, at least in New Zealand. He stated in 1840 that the killing of slaves and wives on the death of a chief had stopped in the past years 'from the scarcity of slaves, or rather from the profits accruing from their employment [in the service of Europeans] in rearing pigs' and through other activities.[65]

[61] For example Gill 219; Erskine 228; Turner 93–4; Williams/Calvert 1, 201–3.
[62] For example in Aneityum (New Hebrides). Turner 93–4.
[63] Mariner 2, 210; cf. also ibid. 1, 330; Williams/Calvert 1, 201.
[64] Polack 1, 66.
[65] Polack 1, 78–9.

The results were the most far reaching when a European power intervened, especially when the weight of the settlers was added to it. In 1866, two wives of a local ruler in New Caledonia were strangled upon his death. The French governor heard of this and made the police investigate the case. Everyone asserted that the victims had killed themselves. 'The arrival of an armed detachment however was a lesson for the future', and after the death of the next important person no one was killed.[66]

The abolition of the custom was therefore essentially the work of external forces. Yet, what was at first reaction to force was soon internalized, particularly in the course of the spread of Christianity. This was evident in the participation of local Christians in the campaign against following into death. After the end of colonial rule there do not seem to have been any serious attempts at restoring the custom.

---

[66] Garnier 156; cf. also Oberländer, *Ozeanien* 100; Sarasin, *Ethnologie* 256; Legrand 118.

CHAPTER 6

China

Whereas the sources for all the regions discussed till now come from outsiders, following into death in China has been handed down to a large extent by Chinese sources. European and American accounts gain some importance only for the nineteenth and twentieth centuries. Chinese accounts in history, literature, and, for later times, in various official publications at the regional and local levels, are not only substantial, they also go further back than accounts for all other parts of the world.

In Chinese history the custom has two different forms. In earlier times, humans served as burial objects for highly-placed persons. In later times, we find a more or less ritualized self-killing after the death of a closely related person, especially widow-suicide.

Humans as Burial Objects

It is an undisputed fact that in ancient China people were buried along with dead rulers, members of the ruling house, and other highly-placed persons.[1] There is even a special character in the Chinese script for this.[2] The number of victims was roughly proportional to the position of the person to be accompanied,[3] and it could run into hundreds.[4] There were even rules, or at least recommendations, for the number of victims appropriate to the position of the deceased. It was said 'that the maximum number to be killed and buried in the case of

[1] See particularly De Groot 2, 400–1; 721–35. See also Ball, *Human sacrifice* 845–6; Bauer 26; Erkes 1–2; Franke 1, 75; Granet 217–25; Gray 1, 338; Matignon 130–1; 149; T. Chang 68; 74–8; Brinker/Goepper 28–31; 275; Falkenhausen 41–6; Kuhn, *Totenritual* 67.

[2] Erkes 2.

[3] Ball, *Human sacrifice* 846.

[4] Ball, *Human sacrifice* 846; De Groot 2, 400–1; 721–8; Franke 3, 51; T. Chang 74; Falkenhausen 41–6.

a Son of Heaven [the Emperor] must amount to several hundreds, and the minimum to several times ten, and that for a prince or a Great officer the number ought not to exceed several times ten, but may not be less than a certain cipher.'[5] Those who enjoyed this privilege were mainly men, but women were not excluded, either as rulers or as members of the ruling family.[6] The persons accompanying the dead were wives, concubines, servants, slaves, and members of the royal household. Apart from these, anonymous victims also played an important role. More than once it has been reported that persons not connected with the dead were lured with tricks in large numbers into the vault and locked up, with the number sometimes running into hundreds.[7] Criminals and prisoners of war are, however, not mentioned.[8]

Further details about the manner of killing are not given; we only know that most of the victims, particularly the anonymous ones, were buried alive. Often, the burial chamber was not filled in with earth, so that the people locked in died a slow and agonizing death.[9] This method of killing was probably motivated less by cruelty and sadism than by the desire to reproduce the imperial household faithfully and to effect a smooth and uninterrupted transition to the other world. The function of the custom with regard to the other world also becomes apparent through this.[10] An exalted position in this world was to be maintained in the other.

The function of the custom with regard to this world is no less pronounced. In practising it the ruling class demonstrates its power. From this results a tendency to increase the number of victims, which again allows us to draw conclusions about the voluntary nature of the act, although the sources hardly contain any information on this aspect.[11] As far as persons intimately linked with the dead are concerned, the

[5] De Groot 2, 669; 728.

[6] Cf. Granet 217–25 and also De Groot 2, 726; 730–1. For the archaeological evidence: Brinker/Goepper 30–1; K. Chang, *Art* 97–100.

[7] Granet 221–2; De Groot 2, 400–1; 726; 730; Ball, *Human sacrifice* 846.

[8] Yang 62 presumes that in early times many prisoners of war were used for this purpose, but does not provide any evidence for this statement.

[9] De Groot 2, 400–1; 724–31; Granet 220–3; Ball, *Human sacrifice* 846; Erkes 1; Kuhn, *Totenritual* 53.

[10] Ball, *Human sacrifice* 845–6. Cf. also Bauer 25–6; 45–6; 150–1; De Groot 2, 721–2; Falkenhausen 44–5.

[11] Cf. De Groot 2, 723–5.

decision to die may sometimes well have been a voluntary one. For the mass of attendants, however, this is improbable, and for those tricked into the chamber it is out of the question. At any rate, the idea of following into death ascribed only a subordinate role to voluntary death. If volunteers were not available, rather than waiving the ceremony victims were obtained through other means. This is elucidated in an anecdote—not a historical one—from a Confucian text:

> Khan Sze-kü having died in Wei, his wife and the principal officer of the family consulted together about burying some living persons (to follow him). When they had decided to do so, (his brother), Khan Sze-khang [a student of Confucius] arrived, and they informed him about their plan, saying, 'When the master was ill, (he was far away) and there was no provision for his nourishment in the lower world; let us bury some persons alive (to supply it).' Sze-khang said, 'To bury living persons (for the sake of the dead) is contrary to what is proper. Nevertheless, in the event of his being ill, and requiring to be nourished, who are so fit for that purpose as his wife and steward? If the thing can be done without, I wish it to be so. If it cannot be done without, I wish you two to be the parties for it.' On this the proposal was not carried into effect.

In Oceania and in India, in later times also in China, the widow would have killed herself, or allowed others to kill her. Here she looks for anonymous victims.[13]

Archaeological research proceeds on the assumption that the custom had been practised since the fourth millennium BC and was widespread in the second and first millennium BC.[14] At this point we shall refer only to a few results. In a royal tomb of the late thirteenth or early twelfth century BC, seventy-nine persons are buried in a hierarchical arrangement, but it cannot be proven with certainty that they were buried at the same time, or, indeed, that they died at the same

---

[12] *Lî kî (Liji)* 2, 2, 2, 15 (Trans. Legge 181–2). Cf. Erkes 2; Granet 223; De Groot 2, 227.

[13] There is an example from AD 926 from the Chinese–Mongolian border area for this kind of an active role of the widow in choosing the victims. See pp. 168 and 184 below.

[14] Brinker/Goepper 28–31; 34–7; Kuhn, *Status* 129–32; Kuhn, *Totenritual* 51–5; Yang 53–62; Falkenhausen 44–7; K. Chang, *Art* 97; 100; 110; K. Chang, *Archaeology* 255; T. Chang 74–8. Cf. Bauer 151.

time.[15] By far the largest pre-imperial tomb in China found thus far is from the kingdom of Qin. It dates back approximately to the middle of the first millennium BC. Along with the main body the skeletons of 182 people were found here.[16] A simultaneous burial seems very likely in this case. We also know of a tomb, which has not been plundered and is completely intact, dating back to the Shang period (second millennium BC), in which the wife of a ruler is buried with sixteen other persons.[17]

Written evidence is also available for early times. Oracular inscriptions on bones and tortoise shells from the second millennium BC are not very detailed, but we can gather from them that following into death in the manner described was widespread, and that young people particularly were used as victims.[18] The first precise details are given for the year 678 BC, when sixty-six people were buried alive with Duke Wu of Qin.[19] Many similar accounts are available for the following centuries, in which the number of victims mentioned ranges from a few to several hundreds.[20]

As far as the question of frequency is concerned, almost every tenth grave in a large complex of graves from the Shang period contains indications of a (mostly violent) following into death.[21] This would make it a unique phenomenon in the entire history of the custom, and would mean that far more than ten per cent of the deaths occurred in the framework of following into death (considering the fact that the deceased very often had more than one attendant).

The pronounced institutional character of following into death in China, with its ever-increasing number of anonymous victims, contained self-destructive elements which could easily lead to the formation of resistance. In China, this actually becomes evident earlier than in other places. We do not know to what extent the victims actively

---

[15] Kuhn, *Status* 129–31; Kuhn, *Totenritual* 51–3; Brinker/Goepper 28.

[16] Falkenhausen 41.

[17] Brinker/Goepper 30–1; K. Chang, *Art* 97–100.

[18] T. Chang 68; 75; Brinker/Goepper 28.

[19] De Groot 2, 721–2; Erkes 1; Granet 217–18; Matignon 149; Kuhn, *Totenritual* 67.

[20] Compiled in De Groot 2, 722–9. Apart from this Ball, *Human sacrifice* 846; Granet 217–20; Franke 3, 51; Matignon 149; T. Chang 74; Falkenhausen 41; Kuhn, *Totenritual* 51–5; 67.

[21] Kuhn, *Totenritual* 53.

resisted death, or whether they avoided it by running away. What has been handed down, however, is the opposition of the people[22] and of the intellectuals.[23] Confucius (551–479 BC) spoke out very clearly against the custom.[24] The opponents used pragmatic arguments with reference to this world, arguments that attacked the belief in the hereafter, or, at least, refused to acknowledge it. According to them a person's tasks lay in this world, and the custom did not allow these to be fulfilled in the next.[25]

This opposition must have begun earlier. The arguments, which had crystallized over a period of time, would later have been projected on to the figure of Confucius in order to give them greater authority. This seems to have had an effect, as an anecdote from a Confucian text leads us to believe: 'When Khan Kan-hsi was lying ill, he assembled his brethren, and charged his son Zun-ki saying, "When I am dead, you must make my coffin large, and make my two concubines lie in it with me, one on each side." When he had died, his son said, "To bury the living with the dead is contrary to propriety; how much more must it be so to bury them in the same coffin!" Accordingly he did not put the two ladies to death.'[26]

Yet the opposition did not meet with untrammelled success. The main problem, apart from the politically motivated desire of rulers to maintain the custom as a demonstration of power, would have been belief in the hereafter, which could not simply be disposed of with rational arguments. This can be seen in the manner in which the custom was gradually suppressed. Living persons were replaced by different kinds of dummies. In the beginning, complex wooden mechanical figures were made. They were imitations of human beings, which could be made to move with the help of springs. Along with this there were straw figures, later wooden, clay and bronze figures also, till one finally went over to paper models, which were used right up to the present.[27] Impressive archaeological evidence is available, particularly

[22] De Groot 2, 726–7; 730–1; Ball, *Human sacrifice* 846; Erkes 2.

[23] De Groot 2, 659–720; 727ff.

[24] Matignon 147–50; Granet 218–23; De Groot 2, 807–8; Erkes 2.

[25] Cf. for example Granet 218–23.

[26] *Lî kî* 2, 2, 2, 19 (Trans. Legge 183–4); see Erkes 2; De Groot 2, 227.

[27] De Groot 2, 717; 806–9; Ball, *Human sacrifice* 845–6; Bauer 151; Erkes 1; Matignon 131; Brinker/Goepper 275; Falkenhausen 46–7.

for clay figures.[28] The complex of graves of Qin Shihuangdi, the first Emperor of China (259–210 BC), discovered in 1974, is the most famous. It contains a whole army of soldiers, horses and chariots of war, amounting to a number greater than 7,000.[29]

The fact that substitutes were considered necessary showed that the basis of the custom, a particular form of a belief in the hereafter, had by no means disappeared. Therefore, the custom itself could easily be resuscitated. In any case, it could not be completely suppressed at first. The processes of substitution mentioned above are spoken of since the twelfth century BC.[30] However, their effect was limited, as can be seen from the numerous accounts of following of the dead in later centuries. The sources record a first definite ban for the year 384 BC from the northern state of Qin.[31] Further important cases of following into death are recorded in subsequent periods.[32] In 210 BC concubines followed the first emperor of China in 'very large numbers' into the grave.[33] In the case of the army, those claiming the right to be followed were obviously more easily satisfied with clay figures than where their female companions were concerned.[34]

From 209 BC, however, the suppression of the custom was apparently successful. After that, larger incidences of following into death are no longer mentioned; but it never seems to have died out completely.[35] The upper class, at least, appears to have dissociated itself from the custom. This can be gathered from the fact that the state ordered old graves to be opened up in order to determine how high the number of victims had been.[36]

---

[28] De Groot 2, 811–27; Ball, *Human sacrifice* 847; Erkes 1, and mainly Brinker/Goepper 131–3; 237–50; 275–86.

[29] Brinker/Goepper 101–16; Kuhn, *Status* 293–7, and especially Ledderose/Schlombs.

[30] Brinker/Goepper 275; Ball, *Human sacrifice* 845–6; T. Chang 74.

[31] T. Chang 74; Franke 3, 51; De Groot 2, 729 (dated for 383); Falkenhausen 46.

[32] Ball, *Human sacrifice* 846; De Groot 2, 729–31.

[33] Falkenhausen 46.

[34] Even in other graves human beings were found along with substitutes. Falkenhausen 46–7.

[35] Falkenhausen 46.

[36] De Groot 2, 728–9; Ball, *Human sacrifice* 846; Granet 220.

The situation changed again in the Song dynasty (960–1279), when people were killed, sometimes in large numbers, at the funerals of rulers and their family members.[37] This also occurred during the Yuan dynasty (1280–1368) and the Ming dynasty (1368–1644), as well as during the early Qing dynasty (1644–1911), the last case being recorded in 1662. [38] In 1660, thirty slaves are said to have been killed on the grave of the first Qing emperor, after which his successor, the Kangxi emperor, issued a decree prohibiting the custom.[39] In 1718, the same emperor had to prevent the suicide of four female servants after his mother's death.[40]

The reactivation of this custom under foreign dynasties has led Chinese and other authors to declare that following into death was imported into China by foreigners.[41] This may indeed be true for the later period, although it cannot be substantiated. But a revival was only possible because the required belief in the hereafter was still present in the country. Attempts to revive or to introduce the custom in medieval or modern Europe or in Islamic regions would definitely have met with greater resistance. The actual origin of following into death in China, however, can be traced back to much earlier times, where it is not possible to distinguish between foreign and indigenous influences.

The peculiarity of the Chinese opposition to following into death is that it apparently began much earlier than anywhere else, but it was not completely successful till the twentieth century, particularly not with regard to the more individual forms, as will be shown below.

Widow-suicide

Institutional following into death having been largely suppressed, a peculiar situation arose. The custom had lost its political function. As a result, the state, viz. the upper class, was no longer interested in preventing other groups from practising similar customs, since it no

[37] De Groot 2, 732; Ball, *Human sacrifice* 846; Erkes 2–3.

[38] De Groot 2, 733–5; Ball, *Human sacrifice* 846–7; Aston 58–9 (1662); De Guignes 2, 304; Ibn Baṭṭūṭa in Yule, *Cathay* 4, 142–4.

[39] Grosier 1, XLII.

[40] De Guignes 2, 304; De Groot 2, 734; Matignon 150.

[41] Erkes 2–3; cf. Granet 217 and already in 1777 Grosier 1, XLIII. De Groot 2, 723–4 and Ball, *Human sacrifice* 846 reject this hypothesis.

longer encroached on their privileges and their claim to power. The suppression of institutional following into death facilitated the spread of the individual form. Since the belief that this world is reproduced in the next still existed, individual following into death became popular, mainly in the form of the widow killing herself after the death of her husband. No social class was excluded from this.[42] Individual following into death has been documented since the Han period (206 BC–AD 220).[43] It cannot be established with certainty when it began to spread.[44] Some authors assume that it played a greater role only from the thirteenth/fourteenth centuries. At any rate, it is mentioned very often from the Ming period (1368–1644) onward.[45] On the other hand, there are isolated references to institutional following into death even in later times. For example, male and female servants are sometimes said to have killed themselves on the death of their master's wife.[46] Moreover, since the same written character is used for both forms of following into death,[47] there is more evidence in support of the view that there was a gradual change from one form to the other, than in support of a radical break.[48]

Widow-suicide is best documented in the nineteenth century. Numerous accounts now reached the West. There is hardly any doubt about the credibility of these accounts, since there is also a substantial amount of material for the same period in official Chinese publications, at the local and regional level. Most of this material has not yet been analysed.[49] In addition there are public inscriptions and honorary gates for the widows who killed themselves.[50]

[42] See Elvin 121–3; Doolittle 112.

[43] De Groot 2, 735; 739–41.

[44] Cf. Hsieh/Spence 45; Linck-Kesting 146–52; Linck 367–9; Elvin 112ff; 121ff.

[45] For example Gray 1, 338; De Groot 2, 735–69; Matignon 131–4; Ruhstrat 109; Elvin, *passim*.

[46] Elvin 127; cf. De Groot 2, 736. Concrete cases are however not mentioned for more recent times.

[47] De Groot 2, 735.

[48] The hypothesis of continuity exists also in Matignon 130, and especially in De Groot 2, 735–6.

[49] Used till now mainly by Elvin. See also De Groot 2, 746.

[50] De Groot 2, 746–50; 769–94; Prahl 678–9; Matignon 132–3; Doolittle 110–12; Elvin 134–5; 151.

In the *Hong-Kong Daily Press* dated 20 January 1861 there was the following typical account:

A few days since I met a Chinese procession passing through the foreign settlement, escorting a young person in scarlet and gold in a richly decorated chair—the object of which I found was to invite the public to come and see her hang herself; a step she had resolved to take in consequence of the death of her husband by which she had been left a childless widow. Both being orphans this event had severed her dearest earthly ties, and she hoped by this sacrifice to secure herself eternal happiness, and a meeting with her husband in the next world. Availing myself of the general invitation, I repaired on the day appointed to the indicated spot. We had scarcely arrived, when the same procession was seen advancing from the joss-house of the widow's native village towards a scaffold or gallows erected in an adjacent field, and surrounded by hundreds of natives of both sexes; the female portion attired in gayest holiday costume, was very numerous. I and a friend obtained a bench for a consideration, which being placed within a few yards of the scaffold gave us a good view of the performance. The procession having reached the foot of the scaffold, the lady was assisted to ascend by her male attendant, and, after having welcomed the crowd, partook with some female relatives of a repast prepared for her at a table on the scaffold, which she appeared to appreciate extremely. A child in arms was then placed upon the table, whom she caressed and adorned with a necklace which she had worn herself. She then took an ornamented basket containing rice, herbs and flowers, and whilst scattering them amongst the crowd, delivered a short address thanking them for their attendance, and upholding the motives which urged her to the step she was about to take. This done, a salute of bombards announced the arrival of the time for the performance of the last act of her existence, when a delay was occasioned by the discovery of the absence of a reluctant brother, pending whose arrival let me describe the means of extermination. The gallows was formed by an upright timber on each side of the scaffold, supporting a stout bamboo from the centre of which was suspended a loop of cord with a small wooden ring embracing both parts of it, which was covered by a red silk handkerchief; the whole being surrounded by an awning.

The missing brother having been induced to appear, the widow now proceeded to mount on a chair placed under the noose, and, to ascertain its fitness for her reception, deliberately placed her head in it; then withdrawing her head, she waved a final adieu to the admiring spectators and committed herself to its embraces for the last time, throwing the red handkerchief over her head. Her supports were now about to be withdrawn, when she was reminded by several voices from the crowd that she had omitted to draw down the ring which should tighten the cord round her neck; smiling an acknowledgement of the reminder, she adjusted the ring, and motioning away her supports was left hanging in mid air—a suicide. With extraordinary self-possession she now placed her hands before her, and continued to perform the manual chin-chins, until the convulsions of strangulation separated them, and she was dead. The body was left hanging about half an hour, and then taken down by her male attendants. [. . .] This is the third instance of suicide of this sort within as many weeks. The authorities are quite unable to prevent it, and a monument is invariably erected to the memory of the devoted widow.[51]

The greatest difference with regard to earlier institutional following into death concerned the persons who were accompanied in death. Widow-suicide, too, was primarily an upper-class phenomenon. The reasons for this were mainly material. Holding a ceremony like the one described was very expensive.[52] Those who considered themselves important tried to get high officials to take part in the ceremony. Their participation bestowed on the act the character of a solemn festivity, but it necessitated the distribution of a considerable amount of gifts. Obtaining public honours was also expensive.[53] On the other hand, there were no legal restrictions. The custom was generally open to all

[51] Gray 1, 338–9. A French translation appeared in the *Journal des missions évangéliques* 36 (1861), 194–6; a slightly abridged German one of 1881 is in Katscher 239–40. Another, somewhat more detailed eyewitness account, written in English and translated into German in the same year, most probably described the same event, dated 16 January 1861, without mentioning the English source: *Chinesische Wittwenopfer* 1051–3. Both stories probably originated independently of each other. While there are differences in the details, the central points correspond to each other. The second version mentions several hundred onlookers. The woman is said to have been about twenty-five years old. Ibid., 1052. Cf. Brandt 84–5.

[52] The author of the second account about the event described above presumes that the widow belonged to 'a lower class'. He does not say who paid for the ceremony. Afterwards however the woman is said to have been given 'a grand funeral at public expense'. *Chinesische Wittwenopfer* 1051–2. But we cannot assume that in the normal course of events such grand ceremonies were held by the poor or for them. The reference in the text to the widow's small feet alone rules out the possibility of her coming from the lower classes.

[53] De Groot 2, 748–53; Doolittle 109.

classes, and it also occurred at all levels of society, though less amongst the lower classes than amongst the upper.[54] By simplifying the ceremony it was possible to overcome the material hurdles to some extent. Hanging, for example, then did not take place in a public square, but was done in the widow's house in front of a smaller audience.[55] Even this formality could be dropped if the widow killed herself in front of a few witnesses, at times employing a less spectacular method to kill herself, such as drowning or poisoning.[56] If, despite this, the custom remained less widespread in the lower classes, then it must have been mainly because the widow's labour was required, and because there was less emphasis on the values underlying the custom.

There was usually a close personal bond between the person to be accompanied and the attendant in death. In most cases, they had been spouses. Sometimes women killed themselves on the death of their children, parents, siblings or other close relatives.[57] Occasionally, a woman would be accompanied in death, but this did not affect the fundamental bias of the custom in favour of men. At any rate, men never followed women into death,[58] and the attendants were always women.

There was, however, one exception to the rule of a close personal bond between those participating in a following into death. Women (or girls) often killed themselves after the death of their fiancé.[59] Generally, the victims hardly knew these men. Here it was not so much a question of a personal relationship as of the bonds between the families concerned.

The sources do not allow us to determine the frequency of the custom. However, one would have to proceed on the assumption that it was less widespread than in India, where, depending on the region, one

[54] Cf. Elvin 121–3; Doolittle 112. The official politics of recognition and reward did not formally recognise class distinctions, even if in practice the upper classes had better chances of official recognition. Cf. De Groot 2, 751–3.

[55] Doolittle 108; Gray 1, 338; Matignon 129.

[56] Doolittle 108; De Groot 2, 748.

[57] Elvin 127; Matignon 146; De Groot 2, 735–6; 741–2.

[58] Matignon 128; De Groot 2, 735.

[59] Doolittle 110; Elvin 127; Gray 1, 340; Katscher 241; Matignon 129–30; De Groot 2, 741; 745.

in several hundred or one in several thousand widows met her end on her husband's funeral pyre. It is equally difficult to determine variations in frequency over a period of time. The fact that the condition of Chinese widows grew worse in modern times allows us to presume that the number of widow-suicides increased.[60] The argument, however, is not conclusive as, on the other hand, official measures were taken to suppress the custom, measures whose effect can also not be estimated properly. What is certain is that these measures did not put an end to the custom.[61]

Often the ceremony only took place weeks, months, or even years after the husband's funeral.[62] Generally, such delays did not result from a lack of resolution. On the contrary, the widow might have decided for example to first bring up her children or to care for her parents or her in-laws till they died.[63] In other cases, pregnant women waited till their child was born. If it was a son, they stayed alive, and if it was a daughter, they killed themselves.[64] On the whole, the custom was hardly regulated. There were, for example, no laws against pregnant women or mothers of small children killing themselves, and such cases are reported to have occurred from time to time.[65] Some widows are even said to have killed their children first.[66]

The absence of fixed rules for the ceremony is also evident in the manner of self-killing. Hanging and poisoning (mainly with opium) were the most common methods. But strangling, drowning, and death by starvation are also mentioned.[67] It is strange that burning alive, which was used almost exclusively in India, never played a role in

---

[60] Cf. for example Linck-Kesting 146–52.

[61] Elvin 130 sees the peak in the first half of the nineteenth century on the basis of the number of public monuments. Although this is not conclusive, it is at least plausible.

[62] For this see especially Elvin 136–8; 144–6; De Groot 2, 736. In the account of 1861 cited above (Gray 1, 338–9), the husband is not mentioned at all.

[63] Elvin 136–8; 144–6; De Groot 2, 736.

[64] Elvin 144–6; see also ibid., 132.

[65] Elvin 144–6.

[66] De Groot 2, 736.

[67] Matignon 155–61; De Groot 2, 735–6; 748; Doolittle 108; Ruhstrat 109.

China. Some authors emphasize that widow burning never occurred in China.[68] However, isolated cases have been mentioned.[69]

This distinction signals other and more far-reaching differences between China and India. Of all the methods of killing, burning alive is the one that demands the greatest participation of the public, even though it is an unequivocal case of self-killing. This participation begins with the construction of the funeral pyre. The pyre also cannot be lit without the consent of the audience. They can prevent the death of the victim without touching her. If they were to stop her from hanging or drowning herself, however, they would have to use physical force. In the event of the victim poisoning or starving herself to death, the possibilities of intervention are even fewer.

In all this we must also take into consideration the fact that cremation seldom took place in China and that widow burning was almost ruled out for this reason alone.

These facts indicate that there was hardly any open use of force. This impression is further strengthened by the fact that the sources always speak of self-killing and never of killing by others. Since such statements are also found in accounts by Europeans, who were not at all well disposed towards the custom, one can assume that we are not dealing with fabrications.[70] The widow, or any other attendant in death, apparently never delegated the killing to others, in contrast especially to Oceania. One can speak even less of the slaughter of victims against their will. The only grey area concerns the following into death of servants and slaves, when the method of killing is not specified.[71] On the whole, however, one can say that individual following into death in China occurred through self-killing. This marks the contrast to the institutional form of the custom of earlier times. It seems possible that in a transitory phase, which cannot be determined exactly on the basis of the sources, both forms occurred simultaneously, that servants and slaves, too, often served as attendants, and that besides self-killing, killing by others also took place—sometimes of widows.

The predominance of self-killing leads us to assume that at least

[68] Doolittle 108; Ruhstrat 109.

[69] Elvin 146; De Groot 2, 736–40. Katscher 326 reports that four tribes of native peoples practised widow burning. He neither names them nor says where they live nor provides any evidence.

[70] Cf. Matignon 98; 132–5; Katscher 238; De Groot 2, 735ff.

[71] Elvin 127.

formally, death was voluntary. This is also emphasized in the relevant literature.[72] If a widow refused to die, she was allowed to live, even if it was perhaps under miserable conditions.[73] She could have been subjected to pressure, but not in the same way as in India. There the decision had to be taken within a few hours of the husband's death, whereas in China a long delay was not unusual, so that the widow could consider her step carefully.

This leads us to the question of motives and the determining factors behind the will to die. The position of widows worsened in the course of the second millennium AD, especially during the Ming period (1368–1644).[74] The inequality of the sexes became more pronounced, and widow remarriage was increasingly rejected. However, other interests worked against the adherence to the ban on widow remarriage. The widow was generally under the control of her husband's family. Often, they tried to get rid of her as soon as possible and demanded her consent to a new marriage.[75] The motives for such demands were stronger when the family could appropriate the widow's wealth.[76] This meant that the widow was torn between society's demand for loyalty to the husband beyond death and the remarriage forced on her by the family (a marriage, in which generally only the position of a concubine and no longer that of a chief wife was possible). Faced with this conflict, the only way out seemed to be suicide, which also served the purpose of the family.

The reference to these determining factors lends plausibility to the widow's actions. However, one risks drawing the wrong conclusion. The negative conditions were valid, if not for all, then at least for many widows. Despite this, only very few killed themselves. Therefore, one cannot say that those factors led inevitably to widow-suicide. Otherwise, we would have to explain why the overwhelming majority of

---

[72] Cf. De Groot 2, 736–40.

[73] Cf. Doolittle 109–10.

[74] Linck-Kesting 146–52; Linck 367–9; Doolittle 108; Matignon 131–3; Ruhstrat 109; De Groot 2, 754–69.

[75] Doolittle 109; Elvin 144–8; Hoang 170–1; Hsieh/Spence 30; Katscher 240–1; De Groot 2, 756–69. The pressure could also come from the widow's own family. On the other hand the official encouragement given to widow-chastity could also induce the family to support the widow in her decision to remain chaste, in order to receive an award. De Groot 2, 757.

[76] Elvin 132; 144–8; Linck-Kesting 148–9.

widows did not kill themselves. Here, the effects of other forces linked to the individual situation and the condition of the victim came into play. Material factors would have been an important, though not the only explanation. An anonymous European, who was eyewitness to a hanging in 1861, advocated the view that childless widows, who were orphans themselves, were the ones most likely to kill themselves. 'It is usually a suicide of the desperate, which is portrayed as a public and glorious act of piety.' The widow he saw was

> completely without means and without protection. Her small feet prevented her from earning her living through working in the fields or any other such occupation. Her face, which could not captivate any-one, [the author describes the face elsewhere as 'positively ugly'] held out no hopes of her being bought for the harem of a rich man. If this kind of a situation is bad enough in England, then how much worse in China, where the wounded stag is always either thrust out of the herd or tortured to death. The choice was between a miserable life as a household drudge and a victorious death as a saint—and the woman preferred the latter.[77]

The consequences of the negative factors mentioned here often became apparent only over a period of time. In this way, the delay, which frequently occurred in the self-killing, also becomes easier to understand.

In contrast to this, sorrow and desperation in the face of the husband's death seems to have played a subordinate role. This is, at any rate, indicated by the frequent suicides on the death of a fiancé, who the bride at best knew only slightly.[78] This impression is strengthened by the time chosen for the self-killing: the later it occurs, the smaller the role of personal bonds. Although these bonds were almost always a precondition for following into death, they were not the cause.

From this we can infer that aspects concerning the other world were not very important.[79] All the evidence suggests that it was not so much the attraction of the other world as the uninviting reality of this world which led to the decision to kill oneself. Suicide is not actually carried out to accompany the husband as soon as possible to the other world

[77] *Chinesische Wittwenopfer* 1051–3.
[78] See footnote 59.
[79] For aspects of the belief in the hereafter see Bauer 22ff.; 150ff.; Elvin 136ff.; Hsieh/Spence 30.

and to experience eternal happiness with him there. If that were the case, the suicide would have to take place immediately after the husband's death. One would also expect the husband's corpse to play an important role in the ceremony, in order to emphasize the link between the couple. And yet elements of the other world are by no means lacking. In particular, the substitution of humans as burial objects showed that the belief in the hereafter, which makes following into death possible, was apparently widespread even in the second millennium AD. The hope of catching up with the dead person in the other world is often mentioned in the sources as a motive.[80] Many widows killed themselves at their husband's grave, sometimes even next to his corpse, and insisted on being buried in the same coffin.[81] The self-killing was sometimes staged as a repetition of the wedding ceremony.[82]

As far as the aspects of this world are concerned,[83] we would have to proceed from the fact that following into death in China was always, or at least for a very long time, viewed positively by society.[84] It brought fame, honour and prestige not only to the victims, but also to their families. Had the view been negative, the custom would have died out very quickly. Society's attitude was taken over and ratified by the state and therefore strengthened. In view of the state's opposition to institutional following into death this appears to be a contradiction. Yet it was entirely possible to separate both these aspects. The expansion of institutional following into death jeopardized the monopoly of power of the ruling class, whereas the individual form contributed to the stability of the social order. At any rate it was included in the framework of a policy for the promotion of virtue.[85] This policy operated on the basis of a kind of secular canonization. On the one hand, it referred to general family virtues, mainly of the duties of children towards their parents, and, on the other hand, to specifically feminine virtues. Women who had embodied these virtues in an exemplary fashion received state honours. Among other things the chastity of a

---

[80] See for example *Chinesische Wittwenopfer* 1051.

[81] De Groot 2, 735.

[82] *Chinesische Wittwenopfer* 1051.

[83] Matignon 130; De Groot 2, 749–94.

[84] Cf. for example Doolittle 110; Ball, *Things Chinese* 435; De Groot 2, 745–6; 748.

[85] For this aspect see especially Elvin and De Groot 2, 746–94.

widow was honoured. Later, widow-suicide was also marked out for honours, with the dead widow being considered heroic.[86] After her case was duly examined, an inscription in her memory was consecrated in temples specially built for this purpose, or she was even given her own honorary gate. In addition, sacrifices were offered to her regularly.[87] The large number of such honorable distinctions testify to the success of this policy, although by no means all widows who killed themselves enjoyed such distinctions; a lesser form of honour was the mention in official publications at the local and regional level.[88] These were not casual honours. Rather, the widows received 'the greatest distinction that can be conferred on mortal man in China, viz. rewards and honours from the Son of Heaven himself. [. . .] Being qualified to such honours, the women [. . .] stand on a par with the divinities of the State.'[89] The effect seems to have been considerable. A German medical officer wrote in 1908 that such 'posthumous honours and distinctions' were 'often so sought after, that some women killed themselves for entirely selfish reasons.'[90]

The distinctions not only bestowed prestige, they also meant material advantages for the family: for example, exemptions from tax or from work. Thus, they constituted an incentive to actively support the widow in her decision.

The transition from institutional to individual following into death is linked with a marked shift of the person thus honoured. The former is concerned with the fame of the person accompanied; the attendants remain subordinate and are often anonymous. In the second form, which is at least formally voluntary, the attendant is the focus of attention. It is the widows who receive official honours, not the husbands, who for the most part do not play any role in the suicide ceremony.

The opponents of the old institutional form of following into death could hardly have found the individual form acceptable, though the element of free choice played a far greater role than earlier. Rationalist objections were valid even in this case. The opposition made itself felt

---

[86] Elvin 127.
[87] Matignon 132–3; Gray 1, 338–40; Doolittle 110–12; Elvin 134–5; *Chinesische Wittwenopfer* 1052; De Groot 2, 750; 769–94: Some widows even received both kinds of honours (792).
[88] Elvin 151; Doolittle 112.
[89] De Groot 2, 746; 750.
[90] Prahl 679.

from time to time, but it never gained complete acceptance. Evidently, it also never had a stable majority in higher state positions. Sometimes laws prohibiting the custom are mentioned, but they seem to have achieved very little. At any rate, even official sanction and the bestowing of honours did not stop, but was only partially reduced.[91] Of greater import was an order passed by the Yongzheng emperor in 1729, which prohibited the bestowing of official honours on widows who had killed themselves; in future, only widows who continued to live, and to live a chaste life, were to receive distinctions.[92] This cannot be considered a ban on the custom, and it indicates how deeply rooted the custom was. No one dared to attack it directly. Restrictions sometimes only had the pragmatic function of preventing an inflation of honours and conserving the state treasury.

The order of 1729 had little effect. Whether the number of widow-suicides decreased afterwards is debatable.[93] By the nineteenth century, the number, according to the evidence provided by Western observers, had again risen.[94] Doubts about the efficacy of the ban are also justified because it could not be implemented even within the state apparatus: official honours continued to be given after 1729.[95] This was not because there was fear of the people's anger. Rather, from the very beginning, the regulations did not correspond to the convictions of those who were supposed to enforce them.

This situation continued till the twentieth century. External reasons for a change were missing, since Western influence in these matters was limited. Cases therefore continued to occur:

> In February 1935, a woman of twenty-seven, secondary wife of Lu Ti-ping, Chairman of the Chêkiang Provincial government, in despair at her husband's death, threw herself from a high terrace with fatal result. She left a life that was full and sweet: not only had she a son and daughter but she was six months pregnant. More than a hundred leading officials urged the National Government to grant her posthumous honours in recognition of her loyalty to Lu Ti-ping. First Lady also

[91] Cf. Hsieh/Spence 45; Elvin 127–9.

[92] De Groot 2, 747; Matignon 132–3; Elvin 128–9 (law dated 1728).

[93] Matignon 132–5; 167; De Groot 2, 747–8; 754.

[94] See footnote 45.

[95] Matignon 132–5; Hoang 170–1; De Groot 2, 747–50; Katscher 242; Doolittle 109–11; Ball, *Things Chinese* 435; Elvin 124–9; 138; Gray 1, 338–40.

contemplated suicide but was prevented from carrying out her intention by members of the household who caught her by the feet, as she was about to take the fatal plunge.

The western reporter added: 'It would be interesting to know whether, feeling that the defunct chairman should have company in the Shadow World, the household acquiesced in the leap of Second Lady.'[96]

The custom was eliminated completely probably only after 1949. At any rate there are no more reports about it after that, which however does not exclude the possibility that it continued in remote places. It is particularly difficult in this case to determine the end exactly, because in China, more than in other places, the transition from ritualized to non-ritualized suicide is fluid.

---

[96] Ayscough 73–4.

CHAPTER 7

Japan

Till now no definite archaeological indications of following into death have been found in Japan.[1] Nor are there any Western accounts that mention the custom more than just in passing. However, relevant Japanese—and Chinese—sources are available. These allow us to distinguish between two different forms of the custom over a period of time. In early times, humans were used as burial objects at the death of rulers, while in later times the custom was concentrated on the self-killing of vassals of feudal lords.

Humans as Burial Objects

Different testimonies are proof of the fact that in older times in Japan wives, concubines, servants and members of the imperial household killed themselves (or were killed) at the funeral of an emperor or of a member of the dynasty.[2] The earliest verified case took place in AD 247.[3] However, the sources clearly indicate that at that time it was already a well-established custom. High-ranking women also enjoyed the privilege of being followed into death. This shows that the custom primarily had a political function, which helped to proclaim the power of the central authority. The incident of AD 247, at the death of Queen Himiko of Yamatai, is also the one for which the largest number of victims is mentioned: 'More than a hundred of her male and female attendants followed her into death.'[4] The most frequently mentioned method of killing is burying alive.[5] This allows us to assume that in the

---

[1] Bitō 84.
[2] References in Aston 56–8; Bitō 84; *Junshi* 78; Mamoru Iga/ Kichinosuke Totai, in Farberow 259; Pinguet 76–82.
[3] Aston 58 (Chinese source).
[4] Aston 58. Cf. *Junshi* 78; Bitō 84.
[5] *Nihongi* 1, 178; Aston 219; Bitō 84; Farberow 259; *Junshi* 78; Pinguet

normal course of events the killing was carried out by others and voluntary death had, at best, a subordinate role. This assumption is supported by the fact that resistance to the custom began very early, possibly on the part of the victims (for which, however, there is no proof), but definitely on the part of the educated, and apparently also on the part of those who enjoyed the privilege of this custom. According to an account from the year 720—which is definitely not authentic, but seems to give an accurate portrayal of the background—found in one of the most important sources of ancient Japanese history, a brother of the Mikado died in 2 BC. After his funeral

> his personal attendants were assembled, and were all buried alive upright in the precinct of the misasagi. For several days they died not, but wept and wailed day and night. At last they died and rotted. Dogs and crows gathered and ate them.
>
> The Emperor, hearing the sound of their weeping and wailing, was grieved in heart, and commanded his high officers, saying: 'It is a very painful thing to force those whom one has loved in life to follow him in death. Though it be an ancient custom, why follow it, if it is bad? From this time forward, take counsel so as to put a stop to the following of the dead.'[6]

Five years later the empress died, and the emperor forbade following her into death. A minister suggested that instead they should place clay figures in the grave. His suggestion found favour. It was carried out, and the minister was rewarded.[7]

The event has probably been dated too early in the official Japanese chronology.[8] The suppression of the custom seems to have been tackled more energetically only from the middle of the seventh century AD. A royal edict of AD 646 banned the custom,[9] which then apparently disappeared fairly quickly. At any rate, we do not know of any important cases from later times.[10]

The opposition to the custom, therefore, seems to have begun later

---

76–7. Pinguet also speaks of strangling. The ban of 646 in *Nihongi* 2, 220 in fact mentions only strangling.

[6] *Nihongi* 1, 178.

[7] *Nihongi* 1, 180–1. Cf. also Ball, *Human sacrifice* 846; *Junshi* 78.

[8] Aston 58; Bitō 84.

[9] *Nihongi* 2, 220; *Junshi* 78; Pinguet 82: AD 645; Farberow 259: AD 659.

[10] A case from AD 649 in *Nihongi* 2, 233–4.

than in China. The process, however, was similar. Burial objects were not forbidden, but replaced by inanimate figures, indicating that the underlying belief in the hereafter continued. It is difficult to say to what extent the ban was connected with the spread of Buddhism.[11] In China, at least, the resistance to the custom would have predated Buddhism.

Self-killing of the Vassals of Feudal Lords

Till this point developments in Japan were more or less parallel to those in China. The predominantly institutional form of following into death, which fulfilled essentially political functions, had been suppressed. However, since the underlying belief in the hereafter still existed, the custom could easily be resurrected. This also happened in Japan, but in a context different from that in China. The custom was not open to all classes, and only a small circle was entitled to being followed into death—including now, apart from the ruler and his family, the feudal nobility. Simultaneously, the circle of attendants was limited and defined more precisely. On the death of a feudal lord (*Daimyō*) one or several of his vassals (*Samurai*) killed themselves. This was also the case when the supreme military commander (*Shōgun*) or the emperor died.[12] A European book of 1586 about Japan says: 'This is why it happens, that even the servants kill themselves without any need, compulsion or cause, only so that they may demonstrate their great love and loyalty to their master and patron.'[13] A century later the German compiler Happel summarized the state of affairs more succinctly: 'When a king dies, his servants cut open their bellies and die, and they often quarrel with each other for this imagined honour.'[14]

Sometimes a chain reaction would be set in motion. If the samurai had killed themselves at their master's grave, vassals of these samurai for their part took their own lives at the graves of their masters.[15]

[11] Its influence is emphasised in *Junshi* 78.

[12] Bitō 84–5; *Junshi* 79; Pinguet 166.

[13] Gualtieri (1586), in Kapitza 1, 155. This passage can also be found in Alemán (1604), in Kapitza 1, 305 and, only slightly modified, in Linschoten (1596), in Kapitza 1, 250 and Francisci (1670), in Kapitza 1, 752. Somewhat more detailed Caron 77 (1663).

[14] Happel, in Kapitza 1, 889. Further passages in Kapitza 1, 381 (Saris, 1617); 1, 402 (Cocks); 1,421 (Romano, 1615); 2, 596 (Smollett, 1769).

[15] *Junshi* 79; Bitō 84.

Attendants other than military vassals were apparently not considered suitable. This led to a unique phenomenon in the history of following into death. It became a matter involving only men. The persons being accompanied as well as the attendants in death were exclusively men.

This custom was called *junshi*, meaning 'to follow into death'. Nothing definite can be said about its frequency. It seems to have been by no means unusual among the narrow circle that enjoyed this privilege. Frequently, quite a number of vassals killed themselves on such occasions. This must inevitably have given rise to a contest among those entitled to being followed into death, in which status was measured according to the number of attendants. A case is known from the year 1703, in which 47 followers of a Daimyō killed themselves.[16] But this was probably an exception.[17]

With this, following into death gained a far greater personal component than before, since a close liege relationship formed its main precondition. But it had remained an essentially institutional form of following into death, since it helped to consolidate and strengthen the position of the high nobility. In the process, a marked formalization and standardization took place. Killing by others was ruled out, and self-killing took place uniformly by *seppuku* (cutting open the belly, disembowelling, also known as *harakiri*). From this we have to infer that in principle we are dealing with voluntary death. No one was killed if he chose not to kill himself. It was an act of genuine liege loyalty.[18] This was also emphasized in European sources. In many cases there would of course have been strong pressure on the vassals, which would have been increased by the prospect of not only losing one's position in case of a refusal, but also one's social standing. The background for this was an unusually strict code of honour. The liege obligations also extended to the other world, and one had to prove loyalty in this world through death. Some apparently pledged themselves

---

[16] Bitō 85.

[17] Bitō 84 mentions cases in the seventeenth century with 5, 15 and 18 attendants. According to *Junshi* 79, as a rule more than ten people killed themselves on the death of a Daimyō. Caron 77 wrote in 1663 that when an important man died, 10, 20 or 30 of his most loyal followers would kill themselves. Similarly 1769 Smollett, in Kapitza 2, 596.

[18] Bitō 85 denies this, and is of the opinion that the act was not committed out of a sense of loyalty, but to save face.

while their lord was still alive.[19] However, such factors should not be given undue importance, since not *all* vassals followed their lord into death. If that were the case the system would have destroyed itself very quickly. Only those with a special position, or those who felt a particularly close bond to the dead lord, were likely to accompany him. The decision to kill oneself can hardly be considered a consequence of the general liege obligation.

These circumstances indicate that the functions and motives in this world were more important than any thought of the other world.[20] It would have been more a matter of preserving one's honour and proving one's loyalty, thus maintaining one's reputation with posterity and gaining fame, rather than the hope or the intention of meeting the deceased again in the other world. European accounts never mention this motive for the decision to die, although it is the standard European explanation for following into death. Yet in cases like this, clearly oriented to this world in its motives, we see that the custom cannot be dissociated from belief in the hereafter. The issue at hand was to prove the loyalty of a vassal to his lord beyond death. As long as loyalty is not given a purely abstract value, which can hardly be expected from a military liege relationship, it still requires an object. It has therefore to be linked in some way to the dead lord. Where, and in what form, he is imagined, is not important. The crucial point is the contrast to nothingness. If the deceased were to have dissolved in every respect into nothingness, then loyalty and devotion would lack an object and therefore not have any meaning either. As far as belief in the hereafter is concerned, one therefore has to distinguish between the direct cause of the custom and its general prerequisites. The second factor would always have to be present, not the first.

Why did following into death develop differently in Japan after the initial parallels with China? Is it connected with a different, or even a better, position of women in Japan? This conclusion would go too far. Where only widows, and not widowers, kill themselves, we would have to assume an unequal relationship between the sexes. However, neither in Japan, nor in Europe or the Islamic world does absence of such a custom indicate equality. The important point here is that the many possible functions and manifestations of following into death are at least partially mutually exclusive. This is especially true for the

[19] Caron 77; Saris, in Kapitza 1, 381–2.
[20] Especially emphasized by Aston 59–61.

individual and the institutional forms. In Japan, the military nobility played a far more important role than in China. That is why it managed to make the custom into its own instrument and withhold it from the classes below it. In this way it was able to strengthen its autonomy vis-à-vis the rulers above it, and ensure the subordination of the vassals under it.

The difference between the two forms of following into death was therefore smaller in Japan than in China. This suggests that no radical break occurred, that the later form did not arise as a new one, but gradually developed out of the old form by extending the circle of those entitled to being followed in death to include the high nobility, and by simultaneously limiting the circle of attendants to military vassals. The strict rule about self-killing is also a part of this.[21] This process probably ensured the continuance of the custom in the face of opposition. Instead of the mass killings of different people, which were generally associated with considerable use of physical force, the principally voluntary, strictly ritualized, self-killing of vassals arose.

This development, which diverged from that in China, had an effect on the final suppression of the custom. In China, the elimination of following into death was essentially a concern of society and was therefore a difficult task, whereas in Japan it was linked primarily to political issues. Following into death helped the military nobility to strengthen its position. When this position was attacked, the custom, too, had to be called into question. Such a situation arose in the middle of the seventeenth century alongside the centralizing efforts of the Shōguns, directed against the nobility. In 1663, there was a verbal ban, followed, in 1668, by a written prohibition, which more or less brought an end to the custom in the course of the eighteenth century— at any rate it was far more effective than similar attempts in China.[22]

The ban left the mental attitudes underlying the custom untouched, especially the belief in the hereafter and the concept of loyalty. This

[21] It is not possible however to give historical proof of this. According to *Junshi* 78, the later form has nothing to do with the earlier one. According to Bitō 84, the new custom arose only around the tenth century in the context of the rise of a warrior caste. In *Nihongi* 1, 331, however, a case has been recorded, dated AD 454, which marks a transition. Three followers of a royal prince cut their throats after his death. See also ibid., 2, 233–4 (AD 649).

[22] On the ban see Bitō 85; *Junshi* 79; Pinguet 166; Aston 59 mentions a case of 1868, without any proof.

became very clear in the twentieth century. When the Meiji emperor died in 1912, one of his most famous generals, Nogi Maresuke, killed his wife and himself in a traditional manner. This did not, however, take place publicly at the grave of the emperor, but privately, without witnesses. Yet, in view of his position, Nogi could count on the fact that the act would have an important public effect. For a section of the intellectuals the suicide was an anachronism or even a shock. The large majority of the people and the press, however, admired the deed. In this respect, there was no basic difference with China. The official reaction confirmed this impression. Although Nogi had committed an illegal act, the government treated him like a great hero after his death. He had acted according to values that were highly respected even among the representatives of state power.[23]

---

[23] Lifton *et al.* 29–66.

CHAPTER 8

Central Asia

The name 'Central Asia' refers here to a very roughly defined area. It encompasses the Asian regions of Russia, the former Soviet Central Asian Republics, Mongolia, as well as regions in north-west China, which at least in the past were not populated by Chinese. In addition, Afghanistan and parts of Iran are considered a part of the region. A clear demarcation is also not appropriate because the peoples of Central Asia often migrated on a large scale.

The situation concerning sources and research is highly unfavourable. A person who has not specialized on the region has to rely on random findings in source material and secondary works. Relevant passages are so rare that one is led to assume that following into death did not play a major role in Central Asia. Yet the references are so numerous that we would have to proceed from the fact that corresponding customs existed.

Archaeological Evidence

Till now archaeology has provided only very few clues for following into death. Yet one of the most spectacular Scythian finds was made in Central Asia.[1] In the Russian republic Tuva, about 500 km west of Lake Baikal, a flat complex of graves from the eighth to the sixth centuries BC, with a circumference of about 110m, was examined. Fifteen skeletons were found around two main burials, more than in any other Scythian grave. A simultaneous burial cannot be established with certainty, much less a simultaneous death. But human skeletons next to the skeletons of horses make us think of grooms being killed. If Scythian graves lead to the assumption of the existence of the custom

---

[1] Rolle, *Welt der Skythen* 38–44.

in Europe, the same would have to be supposed for this region. As a rule, research today assumes a Central Asian origin for the Scythians.

The Middle Ages

There is isolated evidence given by Islamic and Christian European authors in the Middle Ages. Procopius writes that among the Hunnish people of the Ephthalites, who in the late fifth century AD settled between Syr-Darja and Amu-Darja, the rich had a retinue of twenty or more men, who, according to custom, had to be buried alive on the death of their master.[2] The Kirghiz on the Yenisei are said to have burned alive female and male slaves along with the bodies of their leaders between the eighth and the tenth centuries.[3] According to the Armenian historian Kirakos, who wrote in the thirteenth century, the Tartars, in case of interment, placed 'male and female servants in the grave, so that they may continue to serve him [the dead man]'.[4] According to different authors, the Mongols gave their dignitaries male slaves for the other world. Only the rulers received the special privilege of being accompanied by female slaves,[5] the last one to enjoy this privilege being Great Khan Hulagu in 1256.[6] If this is true, we can draw certain conclusions about the relationship between institutional and individual following into death. A very pronounced institutional form would have marked the beginning. It was a political matter of a retinue that could apparently include only men. A close personal bond would only have been added as a second step, in which the private needs of the dead person were taken into consideration. This was apparently considered to be a marked privilege, which only the king enjoyed, and which disappeared again after Hulagu.

A passage in Marco Polo from the late thirteenth century is more detailed and gives us a more vivid picture. He writes that the Tartar kings were always buried in the Altai, even if they had died far away. 'Let me tell you a strange thing too. When they are carrying the body of any Emperor to be buried with the others, the convoy that goes with

---

[2] Procopius, *Bella* 1, 3, 6–7.
[3] Togan in Ibn Faḍlān (1939) 237.
[4] Altunian 60.
[5] Spuler 175–6.
[6] Barthold/Boyle 589.

the body doth put to the sword all whom they fall in with on the road, saying: Go and wait upon your Lord in the other world! [. . .] And I tell you as a certain truth, that when Mongou Kaan died, more than 20,000 persons, who chanced to meet the body on its way, were slain in the manner I have told.'[7]

Marco Polo was definitely not an eyewitness, and he could not have met any eyewitnesses. The figure mentioned is almost certainly an exaggeration. On the other hand, given Marco Polo's usual reliability, we do not need to assume that the entire description is fabricated. Can one talk of following into death here at all? Although Marco Polo emphasizes this aspect, it is by no means conclusive. In the nineteenth century D'Ohsson, for example, was of the view that the purpose was more a question of secrecy.[8] However, this would also have meant killing those who participated directly in the funeral, as has been reported about the funerals of Alarich (410) and Attila (453).[9]

Following into death is also mentioned for the region on the Mongolian–Chinese border, in the north of what is today China. According to a Chinese work of history, in 926, on the death of Abaoji Taizu, the founder of the Liao Empire, the following occurred: Abaoji's widow, the Empress Shulü, 'was a hard-hearted and cunning person.' She summoned 'all the officers' wives and said: "I am a widow now— why should you then have husbands?" She then had more than a hundred officers killed and said: "They can accompany their former ruler." Anyone, who had done anything wrong, was sent to the Muye mountain and killed at the grave of Abaoji. Each of them said: "I hope to meet the former king below the earth." '[10] The reliability of this source is by no means unquestionable. Foreigners were sought to be portrayed in a negative light, since institutional following into death was long considered barbaric in China. On the other hand, it had not died out here completely. If we assume that the essence of the passage

---

[7] Marco Polo, book.1, chap. 51 (Trans. H. Yule, vol. 1, 246).

[8] D'Ohsson 1, 381–2.

[9] Jordanes, *Getica* 30, 158; 49, 258. See above pp. 43–4.

[10] The New History of the Five Dynasties, chap.: Appendix about the four barbaric peoples. Cited in Yang Shushen, *Liao shi jiaubiau* [Introduction to the History of the Liao], Shenyang 1984, 40. I would like to thank Sabine Dabringhaus for the reference to this passage and for the translation. See also D'Ohsson 1, 385.

is true, then the contrast to individual following into death is particularly conspicuous. The widow determines who the attendants will be and apparently never thinks of joining them herself.

Finally, the account by Jean de Joinville from the middle of the thirteenth century refers indirectly to the custom of following the dead among the Cumans, who had reached Europe from Central Asia only a short while earlier.[11]

These scattered references do not allow the conclusion that the custom was a widespread phenomenon. It may well have been an exception. Following into death is not mentioned, for example, in relation to the funeral of Genghis Khan (1227).[12]

The Modern Age

There are far fewer, and less precise, sources for the Modern Age than for the medieval period. The most substantial piece of evidence is of an indirect nature. After institutional following into death had been more or less suppressed in China in the first millennium AD, it surfaced again, if only in the ruling houses, under the Song, the Yuan, the Ming and even the early Qing dynasties, although it remained a rare occurrence.[13] Most of these dynasties originally came from Central Asia. It is not likely that the accounts were fabricated, given that they contradicted the self-image of the Chinese. One would, therefore, have to assume that these foreign dynasties held on to customs they had brought with them from Central Asia, rather than to suppose that they adopted Chinese customs, which had long been suppressed and which in China itself were considered barbaric.

Along with this, there are testimonies that refer directly to Central Asia. The Jesuit Álvarez Semedo, who worked in China, wrote in the seventeenth century that it was a practice among the Tartars to burn alive women and servants on the funeral pyre of an important man.[14]

---

[11] Jean de Joinville, *Histoire* (1868) 177–8; Göckenjan 1568–9. See above pp. 48–9.

[12] D'Ohsson 1, 381–3.

[13] De Groot 2, 732–5; Ball, *Human sacrifice* 846–7; Erkes 2–3. See also above, p. 147.

[14] Cited in Aston 58 (without mentioning the source). Similarly, in 1782 Sonnerat 1, 97.

The French missionary E.R. Huc also wrote, in 1850, about the Tartars (whereby the term is generally used in the sense of an indefinite collective description) that they buried slaves as well as children of both sexes with a king. Beautiful children were chosen for this, who were made to swallow mercury in order to remain fresh. They were then placed in a standing position around the king, holding different objects for him.[15] This too is not an eyewitness account. One can only say that, well into the nineteenth century, reports about following into death among the 'Tartars' were in circulation.

[15] Huc 1, 115–16.

CHAPTER 9

Southeast Asia

S outheast Asia includes here the islands belonging to the Philippines and Indonesia, apart from New Guinea, as well as the
mainland from Burma to Malaysia and Vietnam. It also includes those regions of Northeast India whose population is neither
Hindu nor Muslim.

In Southeast Asia we find two very different forms of following into
death, neither of which, it is likely, had anything in common with the
other as far as their origin and development are concerned. On the one
hand, there is widow burning, and, on the other, there is head-hunting
and the killing of slaves. Widow burning would have reached Southeast Asia through Indian influence. At any rate, it was only prevalent
in regions converted to Hinduism. It will be discussed separately in
chapter 10, which focuses on Bali.

Whereas widow burning occurred mainly in cultural centres, head-
hunting and the killing of slaves were practised in remote and inaccessible regions, among communities with a low degree of political
organization which, as a rule, did not have a script. As a result, indigenous written sources are not available, except for Assam. Europeans
generally reached these regions very late, since they were not of any
great economic interest. It took even longer to bring them under
European rule. This occurred only in the course of the nineteenth or
even in the early twentieth century. The sources too originate mainly
from this period. The advantage of this is that many of them are of
relatively high academic standards.

Head-hunting

From no other region of the world are there so many accounts of head-
hunting as from Southeast Asia. Attention is focused primarily on

Borneo (Kalimantan). In addition many other Indonesian islands are mentioned, especially Sumatra and Celebes (Sulawesi), as are the Philippine islands and the mainland regions in Malaya, Burma (Myanmar) and Assam. The custom seems to have been more wide-spread on the islands than on the mainland.

The distribution of sources would probably be a rough reflection of actual conditions. Head-hunting belongs to that category of phenomena, in the regions outside Europe, which was among the most sensational in Europe. There is hardly any writer who failed to describe it, if he had observed it, or even just heard about it.

We can only speculate about the reasons for the particularly high frequency of head-hunting in Southeast Asia. The geographical conditions would probably have played a role in this. Head-hunting took place mainly in very remote and inaccessible regions, among peoples, whose numbers were small, and who had little contact with the outside world. With the exception of the densely populated islands of Java and Bali, this was especially true for the Indonesian islands, as well as for parts of the Philippines.

Head-hunting cannot be equated with following into death.[1] Its origins probably had nothing to do with the custom. It was mainly a means employed during violent exchanges between rival groups. In many regions, however, the procurement of attendants for the other world, sooner or later, became an additional and sometimes even the most important function.[2] At all events, the people involved often assured European observers that the person killed would become the servant in the other world of the person who had captured his head.[3]

---

[1] Cf. for example Heine-Geldern 7, 19; Schärer, *Totenkult* 16ff. In more recent literature on head-hunting, its possible function as following into death is either dealt with only briefly or not at all. Höllmann 120 denies it generally with reference to Schuster 69–70 who, however, argues in a more differentiated manner and is merely of the opinion that it was not the chief function (ibid., 62–70).

[2] Volmering gives the most detailed overview of the possible functions of head-hunting.

[3] Some examples: Haddon 394; Roth, *Sarawak* 2, 141; Dalrymple (1849) 556; Wilken, *Animisme* 93–6; Earl 266; Gohain vii; 22–3; 25; 36–7; Heine-Geldern 10; 14; 20; Cole 372–3; Grubauer 390; Kleiweg de Zwaan 34; Krohn 275; Lumholtz 2, 256; 361; Mjöberg 257; Modigliani 258–9; Nieuwenhuis 1, 92; Pleyte 924; 926; Rutter 182; Elbert 1, 264. Doubts expressed

According to the definition used here, however, this process is not a matter of following into death, since the killing of the attendant precedes the death of the person to be accompanied. If the latter were to die first, it would mean that he was killed by the enemy and would, therefore, himself have to take on the role of the attendant for the person he wanted to kill. Attendants are collected and kept in stock, and sometimes many years go by till the person to be accompanied dies. In addition, the killing is not a ritual, but an underhand act, and it is also not carried out publicly.

And yet it is difficult to deny all links with following into death, especially when it is emphasized by the people involved. The lack of ritual and audience at the time of killing is normally made up for by elaborate ceremonies on the return of the head-hunters to their village.[4] The central element of the custom, that of accompanying the dead, is always present. The fact that the killing takes place before the death of the person to be accompanied does not change this.

It could be argued here that the statements of the informants were merely the result of leading questions, or that they were attempts at self-justification.

Such an interpretation is in marked contrast to another form of head-hunting, which, not only according to the declarations of the people involved, but also according to outward appearance, is undoubtedly a following of the dead. Among many peoples, expeditions were sent out at the death of important persons in order to procure one or several heads.[5] Sometimes the persons to be accompanied

---

in Downs 40; Fries 87; Volmering 1332; Kruyt, *Koppensnellen* 197ff. This very author, who can support his claims on the basis of extensive fieldwork, assures us elsewhere that most of the informants had named following into death as the central function of head-hunting. Kruyt, *Toradjas* (1938) 3, 491. In general, and also with reference to the following, see Schuster 62–70, who gives us a large number of further references.

[4] For example Gohain 38: Lushai. Elbert 1, 268: Celebes. In general Schuster 14–54.

[5] There are numerous references to this in the sources. See for example Gohain 36–8; Heine-Geldern 7; 10; Haddon 395; Roth, *Sarawak* 1, 158; Stresemann 311; Wilken, *Animisme* 93–6; St. John 1, 63; Kruyt, *Toradjas* (1923) 260; Kruyt, *Toradjas* (1938) 3, 476ff.; Dalton 68; Parry 205–6; Furness 140; Adriani/Kruijt 1, 359; 2, 105; Blumentritt 25–6; 39; 49; Elshout 232; Fries 74ff.; Lumholtz 2, 256; Krohn 275; Modigliani 210; Pleyte 914;

demanded a certain number of attendants,[6] or the desired number was read from the number of outstretched fingers of the corpse.[7] The people killed were regarded as the attendants of the dead man.[8] The interest of the participants in these events was generated by the fact that the often very restrictive rules of mourning for the family members and the whole village were only lifted when the head was procured.[9]

As a rule, this custom was found in regions where 'normal' head-hunting was also carried out. In what follows this custom will be referred to as *head-hunting in favour of the dead*. It does not take place at a time convenient to the hunters, but results from the death of the person to be accompanied. At his funeral the public rituals, missing at the time of killing, are carried out. Sometimes the victim is also only killed at the grave of the person to be accompanied,[10] signifying a transition to the killing of slaves.

This brings us to the relationship between both forms of head-hunting as acts of following into death. The differences are pronounced, and they lead us to the possibility of a chronological sequence.

In 'normal' head-hunting the status of a person to be accompanied is open to all, more precisely, to all warriors. Women, children and men incapable of fighting are excluded. Often, head-hunting represented a kind of initiation rite: those who wished to be recognized as real men, i.e. as warriors, or who wished to marry, had to produce a head.[11] A man's reputation in society rose with the number of captured heads. Such a system presupposes that everyone has a chance to try his hand at head-hunting. One would therefore have to speak of a decidedly individual character of the custom.

The conditions of head-hunting in favour of the dead were different. It was in the nature of things that it did not happen very often—only at the death of highly-placed persons, which is also emphasized

---

923; Schröder 1, 296; Tauern 140; Volmering 1167–73; Worcester 927; Blair/Robertson 34, 377 (account of 1586); San Nicolas 140 (1664).

[6] Pleyte 914; Schröder 1, 296; Modigliani 282; Nieuwenhuisen/Rosenberg 43; Volmering 1174.

[7] Blumentritt 28–9; Cole 373. Often each son was supposed to contribute a head: Fries 76; Sarasin/Sarasin 1, 374.

[8] See footnote 3.

[9] This is emphasized in almost all the sources.

[10] Cf. for example Heine-Geldern 28; Adriani/Kruijt 2, 106.

[11] Earl 266; Schärer, *Totenkult* 6–7; Pleyte 910–11; Elbert 1, 264; Schuster 70.

in the sources.[12] Only the ruling group had the privilege of being followed into death. Accordingly, heads were also procured at the death of women belonging to this group.[13] The individual form of the custom had become institutional. Highly-placed persons safeguarded their privileges even across borders. The Torajas on Celebes, for example, did not offer resistance to expeditions from neighbouring peoples for the procurement of heads as long as no highly-placed members of their own group were killed.[14] Sometimes chiefs even sent victims to other chiefs with whom they were friendly.[15]

This suggests a sequence of events, which cannot be proved, but which appears plausible.[16] The sequence should not be construed unequivocally as a process of evolution, but should, nevertheless, be identified, in itself, as a possibility. In the beginning there would have been individual following into death, open to all warriors. With the gradual emergence of political and social distinctions it would have gained an institutional character and would have been used by the rulers to strengthen their position. The individual form, however, which consisted of procuring attendants during one's lifetime, would have continued to exist.

In both forms of head-hunting all members of a hostile community could theoretically be victims. Various accounts emphasize that not only warriors, but also women, children and old men were killed,[17] and sometimes there was even a preference for them.[18] At any rate, head-hunting seems to have been determined just as often by cunningly planned cold-blooded murder as it was by heroic deeds.[19] The

---

[12] Some authors state that heads were required for all cases of death. See for example Blumentritt 39; 49; Cole 286; Lumholtz 2, 256, and as early as 1680 Domingo Pérez 313–14. This would, however, have led to the quick extinction of the societies concerned.

[13] Cf. for example St. John 1,71; Adriani/Kruijt 2, 107; Kruyt, *Toradjas* (1938) 3, 476; Lumholtz 2, 256. Cf. Schuster 65–6.

[14] Kruyt, *Toradjas* (1938) 3, 476–9.

[15] Adriani/Kruijt 1, 359.

[16] Cf. Schärer, *Totenkult* 26–30.

[17] Heine-Geldern 22; Parry 207–8; Downs 44; Grubauer 149; Kruyt, *Timoreezen* 432; Pryer 233. See Boelaars 164.

[18] Heine-Geldern 22. According to Höllmann 117 the majority of victims generally consisted of non-combatants.

[19] Emphasized by Schuster 6–9; Grubauer 149; Jensen, *Ströme* 257; Rutter 187; Pryer 233.

victims obviously could not form a close personal bond with the one to be accompanied in death. The victims were not important as persons, but only as bearers of a specific role. As a result they could be arbitrarily exchanged. There are indications that there was an awareness of the problem. In some places, the people killed had to be transformed with the help of special ceremonies from enemies into followers. The killing alone was apparently not sufficient. Among the Lakhers in North East India for example

[. . .] the object of this ceremony [called *Ia*] is twofold: first, to render the spirit of the slain, which is called *saw*, harmless to his slayer, and secondly to ensure that the spirit of the slain shall be the slave of his slayer in the next world. It is believed that unless the *Ia* ceremony is performed over the heads of men killed in war, their *saw* will render their slayers blind, lame, or paralysed, and that if by any lucky chance a man who has omitted to perform the *Ia* ceremony escapes these evils, they will surely fall upon his children or his grand-children. Again, unless the *Ia* ceremony is performed, the spirits of those slain in war go to a special abode called *Sawvawkhi*, where dwell the spirits of all those who have suffered violent deaths, so it is only by performing the *Ia* ceremony that a man can ensure that the spirit of his dead enemy shall accompany him to *Athikhi* [the other world] as his slave.[20]

If the killing of enemies only served goals in this world, such concerns would have been unfounded. At the same time, the functions of the other world seem to have gained importance in the course of time. In head-hunting *before* the death of the person to be accompanied, aspects of this world were the primary concern. Those who killed enemies (or even persons not involved in war), definitely pursued interests of this world, for example, social recognition as a warrior, or gaining a wife. The other world still seemed far away. It was different in the case of head-hunting in favour of the dead. The needs of the dead person, and not of the living, became the point of departure of the actions. At the same time, both aspects would often have been closely linked to each other, if, for example, the fear that the dead man would

---

[20] Parry 213. Cf. also for example Heine-Geldern 10; 31; Gohain 38–9, and in general Schuster 40–54.

infringe on the living strengthened the willingness to satisfy his needs.[21]

Naturally, we cannot state the frequency of the custom.[22] Yet there are occasional indications of the serious consequences of the practices described. Some authors are of the opinion that, on account of the general feeling of insecurity that it engendered, the communication that it thwarted and the population growth that it prevented—causing even de-population—head-hunting was responsible for the low level of development of a region.[23] It is highly unlikely that such statements were entirely fabricated. Head-hunting, along with warfare for the purpose of procuring prisoners as victims, displayed an important difference to all other forms of following into death. While the former, to use a somewhat anachronistic expression, essentially had functions pertaining to international or foreign affairs, the latter were situated in the context of the internal politics of a state. Their victims, as a rule, were from their own society, and the relationship between the victims and the person being accompanied was a reflection of internal social and political power relations. Following into death for its part could become an instrument of domination. The rulers had the power to impose the custom on their subjects, and they were even in a position to order them to kill themselves. If they carried matters too far, resistance was sparked off. However, the rulers were generally not interested in endangering their own society through too great an increase in the number of victims. Things were most likely to become dangerous when there was an extreme expansion of individual following into death. Developments in this direction are to be seen only in Oceania.

Head-hunting is completely different in that the victims are not taken from one's own society, but from that of the external, independent enemy. If the enemy community is subjugated, the relationship becomes an internal one—one of dependence—such as that which exists between conquerors and the conquered where the latter are subsumed in the former. If the enemy, on the other hand, remains independent, then chances are that he will strike back. This results in

---

[21] Cf. footnote 61.

[22] This is also emphasized by Boelaars 144 in the context of New Guinea.

[23] For example in Earl 266 and Roth, *Sarawak* 2, 140 (St. John). Particularly emphasized in Fries 80 (Nias). Denied by Nieuwenhuis 1, 418 (Borneo).

escalation. Every action has a reaction, and enmity can finally lead to mutual annihilation. Along with the internal relations of subjugation, the mechanisms to control the immanent destructive potential of following into death are missing.

What has been derived here from the character of head-hunting is only a possibility and by no means an inescapable necessity. Head-hunting would often have hindered development, but there is no proof that it led to the depopulation of entire regions in any part of the world. In the normal course of events there were other mechanisms that prevented uncontrolled escalation. The arrangements between rulers mentioned above are part of this. The ritual character of the custom was also important. The accounts of head-hunting often give the impression of an everyday occurrence which, for logical reasons alone, was not possible. If every dead person had to be buried with at least one skull, if a wife could only be obtained with a head, and if initiation as a warrior required the capture of a head, then this would have meant that each man required several heads in the course of his life, something that would have soon led to social annihilation. Two authors remark quite rightly that this could only have been possible 'among a hydra-headed race'.[24] One would, therefore, always have to keep in mind that this phenomenon was an exception and not the rule. There were various provisions to guarantee this character, as, for example, the repeated use of the same (and therefore often very old) skull, or the use of a single skull for a ceremony, in which many people participated.[25] In some regions of Celebes one skull was offered collectively every year for all the ordinary people who had died.[26]

Someone who has captured heads can himself later become the victim of head-hunters. Will those killed by him still be his servants in the other world, while he for his part has to serve the person who killed him? In this way a whole series of attendant relationships can arise.

[24] Hose/Mc Dougall 1, 76. A critique exists also in Nieuwenhuis 1, 95. The Spanish Dominican priest Domingo Pérez, however, maintained in 1680 that among the Zambals in the Philippines almost each murder led to another, and that roughly three-fourths of all deaths were caused in this manner. Nevertheless, since he does not mention that the population shrank, his information is probably exaggerated. Pérez 313–14.

[25] For example Boelaars 134–5; Kruijt/Adriani 2, 105; second edition 2, 524; Mjöberg 323; Nieuwenhuis 1, 92; Hose/McDougall 1, 159.

[26] Elbert 1, 266.

These questions were probably not debated with any great intensity. At any rate it has been said of the Chin (in Burma) that they believed that the hierarchy of dependence would also be strictly adhered to in the other world, so that each one became the slave of his murderer.[27]

The Killing of Slaves

In many regions, where head-hunting in honour of the dead took place, there was another form of following into death which sometimes occurred independent of the former, and which had the same functions, especially that of bringing to a close the mourning period. At the death of a person—mostly an important individual—one or more slaves were killed.[28] Usually the occasion for this was the funeral, which often took place much later. Sometimes the slaves still had to be procured, for which the means were not always immediately available. Generally, a considerable time lag between the death of the person to be accompanied and the following into death was part of the plan. After about a year, or even later, a final big ceremony would be held for the dead.[29]

In some regions, following into death developed into a kind of process which lasted at least a year, but could also extend over several years. In this the political aspect of a demonstration of power and maintaining the right to rule would have played a far smaller role than in Africa. More important here were the links with ideas about the gradual passage of the dead person from this world into the other.[30] Among the

[27] Heine-Geldern 10.

[28] Wilken, *Animisme* 91–7; St. John 1, 35–6; Dalrymple (1849) 556; Perelaer 18; Gohain 38; Logan 359; Roth, *Sarawak* 1, 157–8; 2, 216; Jacquet 32; 39 (Spanish accounts from the sixteenth century about the Philippines); Hardeland; Adriani/Kruijt 1, 359–60; 2, 105–7; *Bijdragen* 180; Grubauer 289–90; Junghuhn 2, 333; Kleiweg de Zwaan 28–9; Kruyt, *Soembaneezen* 522; 540; Kruyt, *Timoreezen* 430–1; Kruyt, *Toradjas* (1938) 3, 476–92; Kruyt, *Koppensnellen* 225; Lumholtz 2, 361; Modigliani 281–2; Rutter 218; Volmering 1160–1; 1167–73; Wijngaarden 372–3. For the entire context the two analyses by Schärer are the most important. Although they are limited to a few groups in Borneo, they provide us with fundamental insights. For general questions see also Schuster 62–70.

[29] Cf. Kruyt, *Toradjas* (1938) 3, 485; 489.

[30] Cf. Wilken, *Animisme* 90; Schärer, *Totenkult* 7–8.

Dayak it was customary to behead one or more slaves over the coffin of the person to be accompanied, immediately after his death. A week after the funeral another slave (or several) would be killed. A year later, the funeral ceremony would take place on a large scale, where the numbers killed corresponded to the position of the deceased. Thereafter a slave was killed at two separate points in time—first, when a receptacle for the bones of the deceased was consecrated, and later, when a memorial post was erected for him.[31]

As far as the persons accompanied are concerned, in societies with very little material wealth the number of slave-owners was small, and it was rare to find people who could afford to lose a slave. Yet it is never stated that the custom was a privilege only of such circles. In principle, it seems to have been open to everyone. From time to time, several persons got together to buy a slave as an attendant in death.[32] Yet, these were exceptions. One would have to assume that, in theory, it was an individual, in practice, however, mainly an institutional following into death. The fact that women were also accompanied supports this assumption.[33]

The attendants were slaves, mainly men, but sometimes also women.[34] As a rule, there was hardly any personal link between them and the person being accompanied. In contrast to head-hunting though, the link was not always completely absent. At times, slaves were killed, who had been in the possession of the person to be accompanied for years.[35] Sometimes they had known for a long time what function they had to fulfil. Often, however, they were only bought at the death of the

---

[31] Detailed descriptions in Schärer, *Katinganer*, especially 549–55 and Schärer, *Totenkult*, especially 26–30. Cf. also Kruyt, *Toradjas* (1938) 3, 476–92; Adriani/Kruijt 2, 105–9.

[32] Roth, *Sarawak* 1, 158; Rutter 218. Pryer 234 speaks in fact of a subscription.

[33] For example Schärer, *Totenkult* 12, 17, 22; Kruyt, *Timoreezen* 430; Elbert 1, 266; Jacquet 39 (Spanish account from the sixteenth century about the Philippines, in which accompanied children are mentioned). Cf. Schuster 65–6.

[34] Cf. Roth, *Sarawak* 1, 145; 159–60; Schärer, *Totenkult* 10; 13; Schärer, *Katinganer* 554–5.

[35] For example Wilken, *Animisme* 90; Perelaer 161–2. Colin 80 even speaks of a favourite slave.

person to be accompanied.[36] At any rate it is never mentioned, for example, that favourite female slaves or concubines of the dead man were killed. The attendant was not important as a person, but only in his specific role.

The impression one has of the functional, impersonal character of the custom is strengthened by other factors. Self-killing is never mentioned. The victims are always killed by others, who employ different methods. Beheading the victim over the grave of the dead person is evidently within the framework of head-hunting, and the head is either placed inside the grave,[37] or on top of it.[38] At times, the slaves were killed with a spear or a similar weapon.[39] Strangling is mentioned once,[40] burying alive repeatedly.[41] Sometimes the grave was not filled up, so that the victims had to suffer for a long time before they died. The Sultan of Brunei is said to have written about the Bisayas on the river Kalias in North Borneo: 'A large hole was dug in the ground, in which was (*sic*) placed four slaves and the body of a dead chief. A small supply of provisions was added, when beams and boughs were thrown upon the grave, and earth heaped to a great height over the whole. A prepared bamboo was allowed to convey air to those confined, who were thus left to starve.'[42] Generally, the victim seems to have been killed first and then buried with the person to be accompanied, whose body was placed on the corpse of the slave.[43] There were other methods, too, that prolonged death. Among the Milanaus, between one and ten slaves are said to have been tied down at the grave of an important person, and they 'were left thus miserably to die, that their spirits might wait upon

[36] For example Perelaer 161–2; Roth, *Sarawak* 1, 157. In great detail Kruyt, *Toradjas* (1938) 3, 476–92.

[37] For example Heine-Geldern 10–11; Wilken, *Animisme* 96–7; Schärer, *Totenkult* 11; 26; Schärer, *Katinganer* 555; Grubauer 389; Kruyt, *Toradjas* (1938) 3, 480; Blumentritt 39.

[38] For example Gohain 36; Heine-Geldern 10; Parry 200; Hose/McDougall 2, 38; 46; Kruyt, *Timoreezen* 394, 431; Lumholtz 2, 258.

[39] Logan 359; Schärer, *Katinganer* 551; 555; Schärer, *Totenkult* 27.

[40] Wijngaarden 373.

[41] Roth, *Sarawak* 1, 157; Wilken, *Animisme* 96; Jacquet 39; cf. Parry 226.

[42] St. John 1, 36.

[43] Kruyt, *Timoreezen* 430–1; Kruyt, *Toradjas* (1938) 3, 484; *Bijdragen* 180; Lumholtz 2, 361.

their master.'[44] A reason for this manner of killing seems to have been the belief that people killed violently did not go into the usual other world, and therefore could not become servants.[45]

There is also another manner of killing involving exquisite cruelty, which is mentioned relatively often, especially in connection with Borneo. The victim was tied to a stake, and the entire village community gathered around. In an order laid down precisely, each one stabbed the victim lightly. There could be hundreds of people participating, and hours could pass before the victim died.[46] In a German missionary journal, published in order to collect donations, such a scene was described in the following manner:

> While I was there, they captured five people from the Malahoi river. All of them were killed and eaten in my presence, and despite my best efforts, I could not save them, even though I had offered 500 fl. for their lives. If I had not finally stopped in my efforts to rescue them, my own life would have been in danger. They were not killed all at once, and not immediately either, rather they were singly and slowly tortured to death. The first of these unlucky men was tied naked and with outstretched arms to a stake in an open field. A number of women danced a round dance around him for an hour. After this slow dance had come to an end, the men approached with their lances, which they handed over to the women. All the women then thrust the tips of their lances into the poor victim's fleshy parts, so that he was completely covered in blood in a matter of moments. The women now moved aside, and the men took their place. They also danced around the victim, but when they had ended their dance, they did not reach for the lance, but for the mandau. [. . .] The person of highest standing stepped up slowly to the victim, swung his mandau, and—a leg lay detached on the ground. A second man came up, raised his mandau, and both legs were off. A third and a fourth approached, now the arms too lay on the ground. The fifth man now stepped up, and with one blow he cut off

[44] Roth, *Sarawak* 1, 141. Similarly ibid., 157; 145 (a female slave); Hose/Mcdougall 2, 46.

[45] Schuster 63; 69–70; Hose/McDougall 2, 46; Kruyt, *Toradjas* (1938) 3, 491–2.

[46] The two articles by Schärer are very important for this. Apart from these there are Furness 140, who speaks of 600–700 stabs; Wilken, *Haaropfer* 479–80; Perelaer 162; Roth, *Sarawak* 1, 158–60; Grubauer 390; Hose/McDougall 1, 191–2; 2, 46; Rutter 218; 234; Sarasin/Sarasin 1, 45; Modigliani 281–2; Volmering 1169–70.

the drooping head. After this, the four other prisoners, who had had to watch this cruel procedure, were also killed in the same manner. When everything was over, when this terrible, hellish ceremony had come to an end, the crowd, which had gathered, rushed up wildly, quickly fell on the mutilated corpses, cut them up into small pieces, laid them on the fire and consumed them completely. The brain, which had been saved up till then, was now also fetched and mixed with chopped up hair from the victim's head. This was filled into bamboo-pipes, held over the fire for a few minutes and then eaten as the most splendid dish for desert. The Chief, mentioned above, stated that nothing in the world tasted as good as human flesh.

However, only some of the Paris, not the whole tribe, eats human flesh. The greater majority uses the prisoners only at sacrifices or kills them on the death of a chief, in the belief that they will serve as his slaves in the other world.[47]

Despite what this graphic description would have us believe, one cannot really talk of conscious sadism or, at least, of sadism as the ritual's principal objective. The process served mainly to increase the importance of the public. The killing became a collective act. With this the community was involved not just as a witness, but as a perpetrator, thus emphasizing to the greatest possible extent the link between the living and the dead. Cruelty, however, was considered a part of the process. Yet, before the killing began, another ritual took place in which, with the help of magic procedures, the soul was freed from the body of the victim.[48] With this the victim was considered to be dead and therefore no longer capable of suffering. 'The Dayak is convinced, that through this "mangang koeit" the victims are only soulless bodies, who he can now torture as much as he wants.'[49] Yet, it is hardly possible that such an abstract construct was really able to obscure the concrete evidence of what one saw, namely that the victim was still alive and indeed suffered. Even a subsequent, well-meaning interpretation

[47] Becker. This missionary bases himself on statements made by a German naturalist, Dr. Schwaner, who was in the service of the Dutch government. See also Hardeland. For cannibalism—either invented or exaggerated—see Boelaars 167 and Schuster 93–8. Rutter 203 disputes its existence. At any rate there are no reliable eyewitness accounts about cannibalism in connection with following into death.

[48] Perelaer 243–4; Schärer, *Katinganer* 543–4; Wilken, *Animisme* 91; Wilken, *Haaropfer* 480.

[49] Perelaer 244.

should not excuse obvious cruelty by referring to cultural differences.[50] In other places slaves were killed with just a few blows.[51] Whether the victims accepted their fate or not was of little importance. Since the number of victims was generally small, there was no question of resistance. The intended victims were prevented from escaping, sometimes being locked into cages;[52] but otherwise they were treated well.[53] Often they were spoilt and fattened, because it was considered a disgrace to arrive in the other world with skinny attendants.[54]

The difference between this extremely impersonal, functional form of the custom and self-killing, which was centred on the personal, though unequal, relationship, can be seen in the report of a missionary on the Kayan in Borneo, written in 1841: 'A widow kills one or several such slaves, in order that her dead husband may have servants in the shadow world.'[55] Here the widow is not the victim, but she arranges for one, and apparently kills him or her with her own hands.

Despite this objectified character of the custom, concerns about the other world seem to have played a greater role than those about this world.[56] At any rate, material losses were accepted. The killing of slaves destroyed objects of considerable value (in this world). Though the victims were usually chosen from among the old, the infirm, those

---

[50] Cf. Wilken, *Animisme* 91–2; Wilken, *Haaropfer* 480–1. Schärer writes in *Katinganer* 541, and in *Totenkult* 9–11; 24, that this manner of killing was used mainly for criminals and offenders. In some cases, he says, one could even speak of executions. However, he feels that it is not possible to reduce it to the aspect of punishment. After all, other innocent victims were also killed, only a little faster. According to Perelaer 162 the number of victims available also influenced the duration of the torture. The fewer the available victims, the longer drawn-out was the killing of each individual.

[51] Adriani/Kruijt 2, 106; Kruyt, *Toradjas* (1938) 3, 480; Nieuwenhuis 1, 95.

[52] Furness 140; Perelaer 161; Wilken, *Animisme* 91; Schärer, *Katinganer* 541; Schärer, *Totenkult* 10; Hose/McDougall 2, 46.

[53] Perelaer 161; Wilken, *Animisme* 91; Schärer, *Katinganer* 542–3; 555; Schärer, *Totenkult* 10–14; Adriani/Kruijt 2, 106.

[54] Perelaer 161–2; Schärer, *Katinganer* 555; Wilken, *Animisme* 91; Kruyt, *Soembaneezen* 430.

[55] Hupperts (letter dated 26 October 1841). For a parallel in the Chinese-Mongolian region see above, p. 142.

[56] For general aspects of the belief in the hereafter see Stöhr 42; Wilken, *Animisme* 90; Gohain 36–9. See also footnote 3.

accused of witchcraft, as well as persons who were generally disliked,[57] there is no way for us to be certain that the able-bodied were always, and without exception, spared. The fattening of the victims, which cannot be attributed to any earthly functions, shows us, on the other hand, the precise notions that prevailed concerning the other world. In a custom reported in 1570 from the Philippines, it becomes evident that even functional thinking was centred on the other world. If the deceased 'was a man of the sea and a chief, he is buried with his ship, and with many slaves to row it, so that he can reach the other world in it.'[58]

Both head-hunting in favour of the dead, as well as the killing of slaves, were based on the conviction that the dead could only obtain an appropriate place in the other world with the help of attendants.[59] In Nias they believed that a dead chief first went into the underworld meant for common people, and that he could reach the heaven meant specially for chiefs only with the help of attendants.[60]

Ancestor worship generally played a central role and was accompanied by the fear that if the dead were not satisfied, they could harm the living in many different ways.[61] This shows us that it is not really possible to separate the order of this world from the order of the other world. The close link between the two becomes evident in the fact that the victims often (although not, as in Africa, exclusively) served as messengers.[62]

The belief in the hereafter becomes even more evident when the victims are told to look after their master or their mistress well. Among the Dayak in Borneo the victims were exhorted in the following manner: 'You will have to accompany the dead person to *lewoe liau* [the other world]. There you will chop wood for him, fetch water from

---

[57] Perelaer 161; Kruyt, *Toradjas* (1938) 3, 478–82; Adriani/Kruijt 2, 107.

[58] Jacquet 32.

[59] For example Gohain 37 (Lakhers); Roth, *Sarawak* 1, 159; 2, 142; Earl 266; St. John 1, 71; Hose/McDougall 2, 41. Cf. Schuster 70, who states that this required the head of a man whom the dead man had killed personally.

[60] Fries 83.

[61] For example St. John 1, 71; Gohain 37; Pleyte 910; Volmering 1331–5; Nieuwenhuisen/Rosenberg 43; Krohn 274; Adriani/Kruijt 1, 107; Elbert 1, 266; 2, 16.

[62] For example Roth, *Sarawak* 1, 158–9; Volmering 1169–71. According to Rutter 218, hundreds of people who stabbed the victim sometimes each gave him their own message to carry. Similarly Pryer 234.

the river, feed the animals, go fishing and hunting and cook for him. Carry out your tasks well. Do not complain when your master is angry, be happy when he is friendly. Do not be reluctant to work, and be obedient.'[63]

In contrast to the 'international' character of head-hunting, the killing of slaves had an internal character.[64] Along with the high slave-price[65] this would have lessened its potential for destruction, since not every act of following into death resulted in a corresponding act of revenge.

While the number of cases is not known, one finds information in different places about the number of victims for the individual ceremonies. There were a considerable number of killings particularly at the big funerary ceremonies. The highest number mentioned was more than forty victims and is found in Schärer, who rarely exaggerates.[66] There are various accounts, in which between ten and forty people are said to have been killed.[67]

The Relationship Between Head-hunting and the Killing of Slaves

Head-hunting for the purpose of following into death, especially with the idea of procuring attendants for the dead, is often found alongside

[63] Schärer, *Katinganer* 542. Similarly Logan 359. Cf. Volmering 1171.

[64] This does not mean that the victims were chiefly taken from one's own community. Rather the attempt everywhere was to buy slaves from other regions. In some places slaves from one's own community were regarded as less valuable: Kruyt, *Toradjas* (1938) 3, 476–87. In this way one tried to limit the negative effects of the custom on one's own society. Among the Kayan in Borneo the use of one's own slaves was out of the question: Nieuwenhuis 1, 59. Cf. Adriani/Kruijt 2, 106–7; Elshout 232; Loarca 134. In Nias, on the other hand, this distinction does not appear to have been made: Modigliani 282.

[65] Adriani/Kruijt 2,106: 4 buffaloes; Kruyt, *Toradjas* (1938) 3,478: 3 buffaloes.

[66] Schärer, *Totenkult* 30; Colin 80 speaks in 1663 of seventy slaves killed with a leader. This would, however, be more in the nature of a symbolic number.

[67] Schärer, *Katinganer* 556: 40; Perelaer 160: 40 in eight days (Dayak); Wilken, *Animisme* 96: upto 30, in Sumba; Volmering 1172: upto 30; St. John 2, 27–8: 35; Roth, *Sarawak* 2, 216: 20; ibid., 1,158: 10–12; Hupperts: 20, in Borneo; Nieuwenhuisen/Rosenberg 43: upto 20, in Nias; Hardeland: 10, in Borneo; Wijngaarden 372: 10 and more.

the killing of slaves.[68] This raises the question as to whether both forms arose and existed independently of each other, or whether the one arose out of the other and superseded it in the course of time. The sources contain different indications. Sometimes head-hunting in favour of the dead appears to be the original form, which was valued more highly, but was only rarely carried out.[69] Sometimes, both forms appear to be perfectly interchangeable when, for example among the Torajas, neighbouring chiefs sent either a head or a slave on the death of a colleague.[70] Sometimes, too, when slaves were not available, or one desired to spare one's own slaves, recourse was had to head-hunting.[71]

These references show that we cannot follow the pattern of a unilinear historical development that was identical everywhere. However, in connection with the reflections on the transition from 'normal' head-hunting to head-hunting in favour of the dead (see pp. 174–5) we can construct a model, which can be regarded as describing the standard occurrence with a certain degree of plausibility. It comprises three stages, which correspond to levels of socio-economic development. In the beginning, there would have been normal head-hunting, which gradually acquires the function of following into death for those who had captured the heads. Along with growing social distinctions, this original form of a purely individual following of the dead takes on a strong institutional character, with heads being procured for highly-placed dead persons. Subsequent economic development, and the increasing exchange between neighbouring communities, lead to an overlap and, finally, to a replacement of head-hunting by the killing of slaves.

This model, with certain variations, is also constructed or accepted in the relevant literature.[72] However, it should not be unduly generalized. Killing of slaves is found in many other parts of the world, but there is nothing to suggest that it was preceded by head-hunting. One

---

[68] For example Wilken, *Animisme* 94–7; Schärer, *Totenkult* 4; Schärer, *Katinganer* 555; Roth, *Sarawak* 1, 158; 2, 140ff.; Grubauer 389; Adriani/ Kruijt 1, 359. Cf. Schuster 63–6.

[69] Furness 140; Heine-Geldern 28–9; Kleiweg de Zwaan 29; Rutter 164; Volmering 1171; Adriani/Kruijt 2, 107; Hose/McDougall 1, 159.

[70] Adriani/Kruijt 1, 359.

[71] Gohain 36; Heine-Geldern 7; Playfair 77–8; Parry 206; Schärer, *Katinganer* 555; Schärer, *Totenkult* 4; Wilken, *Animisme* 92–3; Volmering 1161; 1171; Hose/McDougall 1, 189.

[72] Heine-Geldern 28; 31; Schärer, *Totenkult* 3–4.

could also imagine a regressive model in which a society isolates itself increasingly and is pushed back further into barren regions, which necessitates changes in its economy, and it therefore also has to replace the killing of slaves with head-hunting.[73] In reality the development was seldom unilinear.

Other Forms of Following the Dead

In Assam one finds institutional following into death among the Ahom till the seventeenth century: on the death of a ruler or an important man, his wives, concubines, servants and slaves go to their death or are killed.[74] The Ahom of this period constituted a large, well-organized society.[75]

It is possible that similar customs existed in some of the other more important Southeast Asian kingdoms. However, till now only isolated and relatively unreliable sources have been found, which do not allow us to draw any definite conclusions. The Portuguese Tomé Pires, for example, writes laconically in the early sixteenth century about the kingdom of Champa in Indochina: 'In this country the lords burn themselves on the death of the king—as do the king's wives and the other women on the death of their husbands.'[76]

The End

Apart from the killing and self-killing of widows in China and, especially, in India, following into death probably did not survive in any other region of the world as long as it did in Southeast Asia. In view of the relatively static social conditions till the twentieth century, an internal opposition could not be expected. Assam is an exception, where the custom described was suppressed relatively early, possibly in the seventeenth century, under the influence of Hinduism and

---

[73] Such a model, although with completely different arguments, in Hose/McDougall 1, 189–90. In this model head-hunting appears as a later, less expensive stage in relation to the killing of slaves (for example, the cost of guarding the slaves is no longer a necessity).

[74] Gait, first edition 121; second edition 149; Gohain 21–2; Heine-Geldern 41.

[75] For this see especially Gait.

[76] Pires 112.

Islam.[77] On many islands, Islam seems to have had at least a moderating effect.[78] The elimination of the custom, however, was only due to European pressure, and the colonial powers advanced to these mostly remote areas very slowly. Although they issued bans very early, they were not able to enforce them at first.[79] One resorted to substitutions, whereby animals took the place of human victims, as did simulated ceremonies. In Borneo, for example, buffaloes were used for memorial ceremonies, which took place after a year.[80] New myths were invented as a justification, which explained why the gods now desired these forms of burial objects.[81] It is difficult to say how long the custom continued despite this, since state control did not penetrate these areas very deeply till independence—and beyond that. At least till 1918 such events are mentioned occasionally.[82]

[77] Gohain, 21–2, 30; Gait, first edition 121. Later Islamic rulers even had the graves opened and found evidence of following of the dead. The British did the same. Ibid.

[78] Elbert 2, 16; Kruyt, *Toradjas* (1938) 3, 486. Adriani/Kruijt 1, 360 are sceptical.

[79] Playfair 78; Perelaer 163–4; 244; Gohain 37; Roth, *Sarawak* 1, 159; 2, 142–3.

[80] Schärer, *Katinganer* 536–7; Schärer, *Totenkult* 24–5; other processes of substitution are described by Gohain 37–8 (Lakhers); Parry 207 (Lakhers); Perelaer 244 (Dayaks); Roth, *Sarawak* 1, 159 (pig as substitute); Heine-Geldern 14; 21; Rutter 219; Kruyt, *Toradjas* (1938) 3, 486; Lumholtz 2, 260; 363; 365; Nieuwenhuis 2, 127; Jensen, *Ströme* 160; 246 (porcelain); Elbert 2, 16 (symbolic head-hunting, offering of incense); Nieuwenhuisen/Rosenberg 43 and Modigliani 282–3 (simulated killing). At the same time we have to remember that in many regions animals were always *also* killed along with humans. In such a case one cannot really talk of substitution. Wilken, *Animisme* 101–8 and Schuster 52–3 go into this aspect in greater detail.

[81] Schärer, *Totenkult* 25.

[82] For example Kruyt, *Soembaneezen* 540 (1910); Fries 81; Krohn 271; Tauern 140 (not yet abolished in 1918); Volmering 1483 (cases till 1908); Elbert 1, 269–70.

The Indian Influence in Southeast Asia: Java and Bali

Java

In a detailed description of Java, a Chinese travel account of 1416 carries the remark:

> When rich people, chiefs, or men of rank die, their favourite concubines swear before their master's death, that in case he dies they will go with him. On the day the corpse is taken out of the house, a high wooden scaffolding is erected, at the foot of which wood is piled up in a large heap, and when the fire burns fiercely, two or three of his concubines, who have sworn before, their heads covered with flowers and their body decked with pieces of cloth of various colours, mount on the scaffolding and weeping dance a long time, after which they jump down into the fire and are burnt together with the corpse of their lord.[1]

Brief references to this custom in Java are also found in other Chinese works of this period.[2] They are confirmed by the earliest European accounts. Between 1512 and 1515, Tomé Pires writes that on the death of Hindu (not Islamic) kings and persons of high rank in Java, their wives and members of their retinue would burn, drown, or stab themselves to death. However, no one is forced to take this step.[3] Antonio Pigafetta, chronicler of the first circumnavigation of the world, wrote in 1521:

> We were told also that when one of the chief men of Java Major dies, his body is burned. His principal wife adorns herself with garlands of flowers and has herself carried on a chair through the entire village by

---

[1] Ma Huan: *Ying-yai Shêng-lan*; English translation in Groeneveldt 52.
[2] Groeneveldt 40; Schlegel 15; 26–7.
[3] Pires 413; 418–19; 436.

three or four men. Smiling and consoling her relatives who are weeping, she says: 'Do not weep, for I am going to sup with my dear husband this evening, and to sleep with him this night.' Then she is carried to the fire, where her husband is being burned. Turning toward her relatives, and again consoling them, she throws herself into the fire, where her husband is being burned. Did she not do that, she would not be considered an honorable woman or a true wife to her dear husband.[4]

What strikes us is that all the three authors emphasize the voluntary nature of the act. Pigafetta quite obviously idealizes the action of the widow, but points out at the same time to the pressure of society. In shorter Chinese accounts, on the other hand, the voluntary nature of the act is not mentioned. Rather, one of them remarks laconically: 'Their wives and concubines are often burned, so that they can keep the dead man company.'[5]

However, these early accounts are not written by eyewitnesses. Even for later times, when large numbers of Europeans, mainly the Dutch, established a constant presence in Java, ruled over part of the island and maintained close contact with the other parts, no eyewitness account is available.

Yet it would be wrong to completely deny the credibility of the older texts. Between the fifteenth and the seventeenth centuries Islam spread rapidly in Java. Hinduism, which does not forbid widow burning, was supplanted by a religion that rejects following into death in principle.[6] The assumption of a link between Hinduism and widow burning or killing is strengthened by the fact that widow burning occurred in Bali, the only island on which Hinduism continued to exist. Apart from this, there are some scattered references from later periods, which can be interpreted as indications of the gradual demise of the custom in Java. A Dutch seafarer, for example, wrote in 1605 that in Bantam (today Banten, West Java) the wife of a deceased man gets ready to jump into his grave, but is held back.[7] Five weeks later, the same author learns on the island of Sumbawa, which is much closer to Bali, that 'when the husband dies, the chief wife has to be buried with him. She allows

---

[4] Pigafetta 169. Cf. Boon, *Affinities* 56–60.

[5] Schlegel 15. Similarly Groeneveldt 40. In somewhat greater detail Schlegel 27: The favourite concubines were thrown into the fire.

[6] Cf. Boon, *Affinities* 59 and chapter 2.

[7] Diary of Hendrik Jansz Craen, in De Jonge 3, 180–1. Cf. Wilken, *Animisme* 98–9.

herself to be stabbed to death, or does it herself with the help of one of her female slaves, who will serve her in the other world.'[8] The kingdom of Blambangan at the eastern tip of Java, opposite Bali, constitutes a special case. Till the end of the seventeenth century it remained under Balinese influence. The Portuguese had already heard of the killing of widows here.[9] According to François Valentyn, the author of a monumental work on the Dutch in Asia, when one of the rulers of the kingdom died on 13 October 1691, 270 of his 400 wives were stabbed to death in accordance with his last wishes, 'in the belief that their souls [. . .] would soon be with the soul of the dead king.'[10]

Finally, early evidence based on literature and inscriptions is also available, going back to the sixth century AD. This shows us that widow burning under Indian influence was definitely present in Java.[11]

Bali

For Bali, as well as for the Balinese settled in Lombok, there can be no doubt about the fact that following into death was practised. There are five detailed descriptions by eyewitnesses of cases that occurred between 1633 and 1847.[12] In addition there are references made by people who seem to have been present, but who did not leave behind any exact descriptions.[13]

[8] Jonge 3, 184. Cf. Wilken, *Animisme* 100.

[9] Crawfurd, *History* 2, 253–4; Wilken, *Animisme* 98.

[10] Valentyn 4, 1, 207. The author cites a Dutch eyewitness as his authority. The number of victims is certainly exaggerated, but the description of the event corresponds largely to eyewitness accounts of Bali. Cf. Humboldt 91.

[11] Humboldt 87–90.

[12] The accounts have been reproduced in an English translation in van der Kraan 92–117. This edition, which is otherwise very commendable, does not, however, meet the requirements of textual criticism. This is especially true of the earliest account of 1633 in which two different versions are blended into one another (92–5; see below, footnote 71). Therefore the original editions or the manuscript (for Dubois) have also to be consulted: 1633: *Dagh-Register* 179–81. 1829: Dubois 1–25. 1846: Zollinger 345–9. 1847: Helms 57–66. 1847: Friederich, *Bali* (1850) 9–14; Friederich, *Gianjar* 421–9. Helms and Friederich write about the same event. For critical aspects with regard to the content see Boon, *Affinities* 42–4. For the custom in Bali in general see Weinberger-Thomas (1996) 13–25.

[13] Cf. van der Kraan 91. References based on hearsay can be found for

The five eyewitness accounts vary in their details, a fact that has less to do with unsatisfactory observation or imprecise description than with factual differences in the ceremonies. In the central aspects, however, there is a marked correspondence. Therefore, one particularly well-observed case is described here in detail.

Pierre Dubois, an official of the Dutch colonial administration, lived in Bali from 1827 to 1831, in order to recruit soldiers.[14] In 1829 he witnessed the funeral rites for the Raja of Badung (at this time there were several princely states on the island). The ceremony took place in the centre of the town, near the palace. A large pavilion stood in the middle of the square; seven smaller ones were arranged around it. After seven wives had preceded it on smaller pyramids the coffin with the remains of the king was brought there, carried on an elaborate bamboo pyramid eleven storeys high carried by several hundred men. Each of the wives made her way into a small house, from which a bridge led to one of the pavilions, in which a fire was going to be lit.

First the coffin with the remains of the king was committed to the fire. After that the fire was lit in the pavilion of the first widow:

> As soon as flames appear in the pavilion, the Bela [widow] who occupies the right-hand position in the row of pit-structures, comes out of her little house. She is dressed in white from the bosom to the knees, while her hair, curiously arranged, is decorated with flowers. Her relatives and the Manko [mangku, a priestess of the temple, who accompanies the widow] are squatting along the ramps of the small horizontal bridge. While she advances slowly they encourage her to sustain her part nobly. The Bela begins a trance-like dance (tandak); a profound silence reigns and one hears nothing but the sinister murmur of the blazing pits. After about ten minutes she arrives half-way across her bridge where there is a door. While the Bela is in the doorway a turtledove, which had been tied to it with a piece of string, is cut loose by the Manko and flies away up into the sky. At that moment the acclamations of a hundred thousand Stentors burst forth from all sides; it is the signal that the self-sacrifice has been approved by the Gods. [. . .]

---

example in Junghuhn 2, 340; Moor 92; Crawfurd, *History* 2, 241; Crawfurd, *Religion* 135–6; Raffles 2, CCXXXVIII; van Bloemen Waanders 146; Valentyn 3, 2, 256.

[14] For the background see van der Kraan 95–7.

When the bravos have ceased, the Bela continues her way. She now walks a plank which extends to the end of her bridge. . . . most of the audience intones funeral chants. . . . the Bela loosens her hair and lets it fall over her shoulders. . . . they tie her skirt [sarong] over her knees. . . . she resumes her trance-like dance. . . . her father hands her his kris [dagger] with which she wounds her arm and shoulder. . . . with the tip of the kris she draws blood from the wounds and she reddens her forehead. This act is intended to show her relatives, who are encouraging her to persevere, that she does not fear death. The Bela joins in the pious chants she hears around her. . . . she arrives at the fatal edge of her plank. . . . she returns the kris to her father and clasping her hands together over her chest, she falls straight, appears for one second in the air, and is engulfed in the pit of embers which awaited her. A dozen men, positioned around the pit, watching for this moment, armed with fagots and long bamboos full of oil, throw them over her. How the noisy acclamations of the multitude bless her happy destiny! How a great column of black smoke shoots up into the air!

During her journey on the bridge and over the plank one did not perceive any sign of fear or repugnance. On the contrary her face bore the mark of serenity and of ecstatic anticipation. Nevertheless, not all of them are endowed with such intrepid courage. There are those who, on arriving at the edge of eternity, feeling the hot air and seeing the fiery pit below, lose courage and hesitate to take their last step. But then their father or their brother, who has been holding the other end of the plank lifts it. . . . and. . . . the last step is taken.

This process was repeated five times. It changed with the seventh and last wife. She

had chosen to die by means of a kris-thrust to the heart and for her sacrifice a little house had been prepared on the ground with a pit to the side. When it is her turn she comes out of her little house; she is surrounded by her closest relatives, and receives the kris from her father with which she at once runs herself through straight down from the top of her left shoulder. She falls, whereupon her father and her brother lift her up and throw her all throbbing into the blazing fire. This scene was not the least hideous of the piece.

Dubois felt that the onlookers were satisfied:

They are convinced that the souls of the persons who have just been delivered to the flames are now settled in the abode of eternal delights. Every one returns home happily; and those most intoxicated with gaiety are the relatives of the unfortunate Belas. They believe themselves to be henceforth free from calamities, for a powerful arm, that of their respective Bela, will avert such misfortunes as might befall them.[15]

The Accompanied

The eyewitness accounts, as well as the other references to concrete cases, refer to funeral ceremonies for rulers, for highly-placed members of a ruling family, or for the nobility. It was therefore an upper-class phenomenon.[16] Its institutional character is confirmed by the fact that women were also accompanied. The earliest European account thus describes the funeral of a ruler's mother. In the nineteenth century, however, when most of the accounts were written, no women were accompanied.

Based on the evidence it would be incorrect to say that the upper classes, or even that the ruling families, monopolized the custom. Following into death does not seem to have been prohibited for the lower castes,[17] even though its practice was more or less prohibitive. A ceremony like the one described incurred expenses that only the richest could afford.[18] The procedure could, obviously, have been simplified, but there does not seem to have been any trend in this direction. In the sources the statements on widow burning among the lower castes are very vague.[19] Some authors emphasize that the custom did not occur among the priestly caste,[20] while others do mention occasional cases.[21] The conditions were obviously not very clear.[22]

[15] Van der Kraan 95–6; 104–7. French original in Dubois 18–23.

[16] Also emphasised by Van der Kraan 119 and earlier by Raffles 2, CCXXXVIII.

[17] Expressly stated by Crawfurd, *History* 2, 241; Raffles 2, ccxxxviii and Friederich, *Bali* (1850) 10, while the *Encyclopaedie van Nederlandsch-Indië* 1, 118 writes that the Shudras (lowest caste) were not allowed to practise the custom.

[18] Van Geuns 66; Friederich, *Bali* (1850) 5.

[19] Cf. for example Crawfurd, *History* 2, 243; van Bloemen Waanders 146; Purchas, in Boon, *Bali* 11.

[20] Zollinger 345 (for the Balinese in Lombok); Covarrubias 381–2; Crawfurd, *History* 2, 241.

[21] Van Bloemen Waanders 145; Friederich, *Gianjar* 424; Friederich, *Bali* (1850) 10. This author writes, like Humboldt 92, that the custom was common among members of the second and the third caste, but occurred only seldom among those of the first (Brahmins) and the fourth (Sudras) caste.

[22] According to a communication from I Dewa Gede Raka, Amlapuri/

The Attendants in Death

The limited institutional character becomes more evident in the case of the attendants, who comprised only women.[23] Normally, they were wives and concubines. Some women, however, also accompanied persons to whom they were linked in a different manner. In the case described by Dubois, for instance, the dead man's nurse killed herself along with the widows.[24] Another author writes that the ten-year-old daughter of an important man threw herself into the fire on his death.[25] From time to time, mothers killed themselves on the death of their sons.[26] In all these cases the personal relationship between the accompanied and the attendants is a very close one. The only exception here is an early account, of 1633, which talks about the killing of female slaves on the death of their mistress.[27]

The Time and Manner of Killing

The ceremonies connected with following into death were never conducted directly after the death of the person to be accompanied. Sometimes the burning seems to have taken place only eight days later. Generally, however, there was a time gap of at least a few weeks. On several occasions an interval of about forty days is mentioned.[28] Months or years could also elapse.[29] The killings or self-killings took place only during the large funeral ceremony.

Bali to Albert Leemann, Zurich, dated 3 January 1994, widow burning only occurred on the death of rulers (raja). Although it was not forbidden for members of the other castes, they never practised it.

[23] Also stressed by van der Kraan 120. Van Bloemen Waanders 146 states that according to the information given by the priest (*pandit*) of Buleleng, men could also offer themselves up as attendants. In actual practice, however, it is never mentioned. Forrest 170–1 writes in 1779 that in Bali 'men do burn in honour of their deceased masters.' They would announce their decision in advance and would gain a lot of respect for it. All indications suggest that Forrest, who writes on the basis of hearsay, projects on to men what was practised in reality only by women.

[24] Dubois 22–3; cf. also Moor 92.

[25] Van Bloemen Waanders 146.

[26] Ibid., 145.

[27] *Dagh-Register* 179–81. Cf. Friederich, *Gianjar* 424.

[28] Friederich, *Gianjar* 425; Crawfurd, *History* 2, 244.

[29] Friederich, *Gianjar* 426; Friederich, *Bali* (1850) 4; Zollinger 345; Crawfurd, *Religion* 136; Crawfurd, *History* 2, 255; Raffles 2, CCXXXVIII.

The manner of killing seems to have been more strictly standardized than in any other region, with the exception of India. Burning alive and death by stabbing were the only options allowed.[30] The burning occurred in the manner described, with the victim jumping into the fire.[31] Technically at least, one would have to speak of a self-killing. The stabbing was either carried out by the victim herself, as Dubois described it, or, on the victim's request, by another person, generally a close family member.[32]

The relationship between these two methods of killing cannot be established with any degree of certainty. This is probably the result of the lack of uniformity in practice. Dubois emphasizes that every woman had the right to choose.[33] In his work, death by stabbing appears to be an exception. According to Zollinger, burning alive

[30] There is considerable confusion, both in the sources and in modern research, with regard to the manner of killing. There is a general agreement on the point that two different terms were used for the victims in Bali: *satia* and *bela*. Crawfurd in *History* 2, 241 and in *Religion* 135, and, following him Humboldt 93 differentiated on the basis of social position: the wives among the victims were called *satia*, and the concubines or female slaves were called *bela*. This distinction was taken over in 1950 by Covarrubias 382. Friederich, in *Gianjar* 423–4 and in *Bali* (1850) 10, had already contradicted this in 1847: *bela*, according to him, is one who jumps into the fire; *satia* one who stabs herself to death independent of the status of wife or concubine. On the whole, this distinction found more followers. However the terms are often interchanged, and *satia* is then the one who jumps into the fire and *bela* the one who is stabbed to death (*Encyclopaedie van Nederlandsch-Indië* 1, 118). This usage corresponds to the fact that in India the term *sati* is used primarily for the widow who burns herself. The confusion, however, goes further: Dubois 11–12 calls all victims *bela*, while van Bloemen Waanders 145 uses both terms synonymously. Cf. also Humboldt 93–5 and Wilken, *Animisme* 99. For a discussion of the entire problem see Weinberger-Thomas (1996) 23–5. In view of this state of terminological confusion I have consistently avoided both terms.

[31] The eyewitness accounts always state that the widows jumped into a separate fire, not into the one in which their husband's body was being burnt. Some more general accounts talk of both burning in the same fire, as Covarrubias 382 does, limiting this however to members of the upper castes. See also Friederich, *Gianjar* 423–4; Friederich, *Bali* (1850) 10.

[32] Zollinger 348. Cf. also *Dagh-Register* 181; Friederich, *Bali* (1850) 10–11; Helms 63–5 and footnote 61 below.

[33] Dubois 12. Also Zollinger 345. According to Zollinger wives of rulers were only allowed the option of burning.

occurred less frequently because it was more expensive.[34] Others say that the wives always, or almost always, jumped into the fire, because their social position and their caste did not allow them to be touched by others. Concubines, on the other hand, were generally stabbed to death.[35] Some authors state that only wives were allowed to jump into the fire and only concubines could be stabbed to death.[36] These references indicate that the former method was considered more honourable than the latter. Even the logic internal to the system suggests that the more spectacular form was accorded greater prestige. If this is true, we can also assume that the stabbing was carried out mainly by family members and not by the victim herself. Those who did not have the courage to jump into the fire, which would also have given them more prestige, would hardly have stabbed themselves to death.[37]

Free Choice and Coercion

All European observers, and especially those who have left behind detailed descriptions, emphasize the point that the victims went to their death willingly, regardless of whether they jumped into the fire, stabbed themselves to death or allowed themselves to be stabbed.[38] Although, like Dubois, the authors admit that there are exceptions, that sometimes a hesitant victim is pushed into death, or is stabbed to death against her will, this does not, on the whole, influence their opinion.[39] At the same time all of them condemn this custom in no uncertain terms. Helms thus wrote in 1847: 'The whole surroundings bore an impress of plenty, peace, and happiness, and, in a measure, of

[34] Zollinger 349.

[35] *Dagh-Register* 181. This account subsequently states that on the death of a ruler all women, even the concubines, jumped into the fire.

[36] Junghuhn 2, 340; Geertz 214.

[37] Friederich, *Gianjar* 424 and Friederich, *Bali* (1850) 10–11 is of the opinion—without any proof—that in later times widows in Bali always stabbed themselves to death.

[38] *Dagh-Register* 180–1; Dubois 21; Zollinger 345; Helms 59; 62–3; Raffles 2, CCXXXVIII; Crawfurd, *History* 2, 242; Crawfurd, *Religion* 136. Reaffirmed by Covarrubias 382. Somewhat more sceptical: *Encyclopaedie van Nederlandsch-Indië* 1, 118 and especially van der Kraan 91; 120. Friederich, *Gianjar* 425 is very sceptical in 1847, whereas in 1850 (*Bali* 11) he articulates his doubts to a far lesser degree.

[39] Crawfurd, *History* 2, 242; Friederich, *Gianjar* 425; Friederich, *Bali* (1850) 11; Dubois 21.

civilisation. It was hard to believe that within a few miles of such a scene, three women, guiltless of any crime, were, for their affection's sake, and in the name of religion, to suffer the most horrible of deaths, while thousands of their countrymen looked on.'[40] Friederich spoke of an 'abominable degeneration of idol-worship',[41] and Dubois of an 'infernal procession'; the participants are, in his opinion, 'individuals, who could be mistaken for devils because of their wild appearance. [. . .] I only noticed preparations invented through trickery and superstition, which are supposed to allow fanatical murders to go unpunished.'[42]

In view of these opinions it is difficult to push aside the protestations of voluntary death.

The widow who killed herself, or allowed herself to be killed, had to announce her decision in advance.[43] This requirement seems to have been met most of the time; a statement supported by the fact that a widow, who had not agreed to be a victim when asked, was no longer allowed to be one if she changed her mind later.[44] The elaborate ceremonies could hardly have been carried out with unwilling victims. The decision also did not have to be taken within hours of the husband's death in a situation charged with sorrow and desperation. According to Friederich, the decision was taken eight days after the husband's death;[45] yet it must often have been later. Moor even reports that consent had to be given several times at different intervals.[46]

This procedure would have hampered the use of drugs. It would have been difficult to drug a victim over a long period of time to make her agree to something to which she would otherwise not have given her consent.[47] On the other hand, drugs could have played a role in the

---

[40] Helms 60.

[41] Friederich, *Gianjar* 429.

[42] Dubois 9. See also footnote 81.

[43] Friederich, *Gianjar* 425; Friederich, *Bali* (1850) 11.

[44] Friederich, *Gianjar* 425; Friederich, *Bali* (1850) 11; Covarrubias 383.

[45] Friederich, *Gianjar* 425; Friederich, *Bali* (1850) 11.

[46] Moor 92. Junghuhn 2, 341, on the other hand, writes that the victims had given their consent while the person to be accompanied was still alive. A corresponding statement was made already in 1416 in a Chinese account (see footnote 1). Similarly (1779) Forrest 170–1. The eyewitness accounts, however, do not mention this at all.

[47] Moor 92 states on the contrary that the consent was obtained more or less by force with the use of drugs.

actual ceremony as a means to guarantee that the victim remained calm and steadfast.[48] At this point there was an end to the freedom of choice. Theoretically the decision could have been revoked even at the last moment, even if it had enormous disadvantages for the intended victim.[49] This, however, was not accepted in practice. Once the ceremony was under way the victim was thrown into the fire by force if necessary, or stabbed to death against her will.[50]

We should not attach too much importance to the fact that in some cases the killing was carried out by others. The victim merely delegated the execution of the deed. This suggests a parallel to the strangling of widows in Oceania.

While considering the question of free choice and coercion it is important to take the time lapse into account. A widow who from the very beginning steadfastly refused to kill herself was most probably not pestered later. Even if she initially announced her decision to die, she still had time till the beginning of the ceremony to revoke her decision, although this would have been far more difficult than to have refused at the beginning. After the commencement of the ceremony, freedom of choice existed only in theory.

However, a further differentiation is necessary here. On the death of a ruler, it was imperative for at least one or, if possible, several of his wives or concubines to accompany him.[51] Relinquishing all claims to attendants would have meant an intolerable loss of status. It did not have to be *all* the wives and the widows were not therefore confronted individually with the inevitable necessity of death—but this necessity certainly existed with regard to the mustering up of one or several victims jointly. If no volunteers could be found, the pressure shifted to

[48] Helms 59; Friederich, *Bali* (1850) 11. According to *Dagh-Register* 180, the victims were more or less anaesthetized with drinks on the night before the ceremony. No proofs have been produced so far with regard to the use of drugs.

[49] Friederich, *Gianjar* 425; Friederich, *Bali* (1850) 11; *Encyclopaedie van Nederlandsch-Indië* 1, 118; *Dagh-Register* 181. Moor 92 and Covarrubias 382 deny the possibility of a last-minute revocation. Both these authors probably refer to practice rather than to theory.

[50] For example Friederich, *Gianjar* 425; Friederich, *Bali* (1850) 11; *Dagh-Register* 181; Dubois 21; Helms 59.

[51] Friederich, *Gianjar* 424–5; Zollinger 345.

the widows as a group who had to decide amongst themselves on whom the responsibility should fall.

Interests and Motives of this World and the Other World

What forces worked on the widow and led to her decision either to go happily to her death, or to commit suicide out of desperation and a feeling of hopelessness?

According to the testimony of most of the authors, elements connected to the other world were very important.[52] The widow hoped to be reunited with her husband in the other world[53] in order to maintain her status, even if her personal relationship with the deceased in this world was not characterized by love. Often there was additionally the hope of an improvement in status. It was assumed that concubines would become regular wives, or even the chief or favourite wife (which presupposed that the present favourite did not opt to die), and that women of lower castes would join the upper castes.[54] On the whole, the victim could expect more in the other world than if she had died a natural death later on. Helms wrote about a burning in 1847:

> The courage which sustained them in a position so awful was indeed extraordinary, but it was born of the hope of happiness in a future world. From being bondswomen here, they believed they were to become the favourite wives and queens of their late master in another world. They were assured that readiness to follow him to a future world, with cheerfulness and amid pomp and splendour, would please the unseen powers, and induce the great god Siva to admit them without delay to Swerga Surya, the heaven of Indra.[55]

In 1726 Valentyn linked the belief in the hereafter with the inequality of the sexes:

> One finds more than adequate proof of the affection and submissiveness of these women when their husbands die. When the bodies of

[52] Crawfurd, *Religion* 135–6; Dubois 23; Friederich, *Gianjar* 423, 425; Friederich, *Bali* (1850) 11, 13; van Geuns 66–7. Cf. van der Kraan 120.

[53] For example Zollinger 346.

[54] For example Friederich, *Gianjar* 425; Friederich, *Bali* (1850) 11; van Geuns 66–7; Zollinger 346; cf. Covarrubias 382.

[55] Helms 63.

their husbands are burnt, as is the custom here, the women, adorned in jewellery, jump dancing into the fire to the accompaniment of musical instruments and are burned very cheerfully with their husbands. They firmly believe in the other world and that if they die elsewhere, in their fatherland, the island of Bali, they shall soon be born again, being reunited with their husbands and occupying a far grander position than before. This is why they are willing to follow them into death.[56]

We shall never be able to establish to what extent the participants, both victims and perpetrators, actually believed in such promises. In 1847, Friederich was of the opinion that in recent times mainly concubines, and hardly of the principal wives, had gone to their death. The former came from the lower castes, were hardly educated and therefore superstitious, while the latter came from the upper castes and no longer believed such promises. According to Friederich, the priests believed them even less.[57] However, it is doubtful whether such a rationalistic explanation, which derives from the figure of priestly deceit, is tenable and whether it does not, in fact, read too enlightened a strain into Balinese caste-based society. At any rate, there is hardly any doubt that even in Bali belief in the hereafter constituted the main backdrop for a following of the dead. In addition, there was the guarantee of fame, the guarantee that a widow who had killed herself would be accorded almost divine veneration[58]—an honour that was partially anticipated in this world. As soon as a widow had announced her intention to accompany her husband, she was venerated almost as a goddess. All her desires were fulfilled; her feet were not allowed to touch the ground.[59] While this was definitely a form of control, the veneration, however, appears to have been quite genuine.

The prospect of fame, honour and rewards was undoubtedly of even greater importance for those left behind, especially for the nearest relatives. A family which could claim a heroic widow was held in high

[56] Valentyn 3, 2, 256.

[57] Friederich, *Gianjar* 423–5; Friederich, *Bali* (1850) 10–11; cf. also Helms 63.

[58] Cf. for example *Encyclopaedie van Nederlandsch-Indië* 1, 118; Covarrubias 382; van der Kraan 120.

[59] *Dagh-Register* 180; Helms 59; van Geuns 66; *Encyclopaedie van Nederlandsch-Indië* 1, 118; van der Kraan 120; Covarrubias 382; Friederich, *Bali* (1850) 11.

esteem. Apart from honour, male relatives could also count on significant material rewards in the form of offices, land and other property.[60] As a result, they had a direct interest in the death of their mother, daughter, sister or other relatives. This also lends credibility to the accounts which repeatedly emphasize the importance of the family members, both in the approach to, as well as during the ceremony: they strengthened the widow's resolve, they stabbed her to death if she had chosen this manner of death, and it was generally they who lent a hand and used force if the victim lost her courage at the last minute.[61]

In this process, however, inner conflicts could arise in which other emotions held sway; yet they did not change the victim's fate. In 1846, Zollinger saw how the brother of a young, beautiful, childless widow

> stood before her and asked her in a gentle voice, whether she was determined to die. After she had nodded in agreement, he asked her forgiveness, since he was obliged to kill her. He at once picked up his dagger and pressed it into the left side of her breast, but not very deeply, so that she remained standing. He then threw his dagger away and fled. A man of high esteem stepped up and pushed his dagger all the way into the breast of the hapless woman who collapsed without a sound. The women laid her on a mat, and by dint of rolling and pressing, they tried to let the blood flow out as quickly as possible. Since the victim was not yet dead, another dagger was thrust into her.[62]

Although it is primarily the family members who more or less drive the widow to her death, the role and complicity of the ruler should not be forgotten. The question of incentives for family members only arose because rewards were actually given.

It is not mentioned anywhere whether, and to what extent, the husband's family could appropriate the widow's wealth after her death. At any rate, this possibility has to be taken into account. In practice, however, this aspect would not have been very important, at least in the case of concubines. These came from the lower castes and generally had little which their husband's family did not already have under their control.

[60] Friederich, *Gianjar* 425; Friederich, *Bali* (1850) 11; Dubois 23; van Geuns 66; van der Kraan 120–1.

[61] Friederich, *Gianjar* 425; Friederich, *Bali* (1850) 11; Zollinger 348; *Dagh-Register* 181; Dubois 21; van Geuns 67; van der Kraan 120–1.

[62] Zollinger 347–8.

The statements about the general situation of the widow are partly vague and partly contradictory. Dubois, for example, states that if a woman was menstruating at the time of the ceremony she was not allowed to go to her death and could live peacefully afterwards with no harm done to her reputation.[63] Other authors say that the overall situation for widows was bad,[64] and we can assume that in a society that tied at least some widows closely to their husbands there was little scope for one of them to have an independent position.

Finally, aspects of this and the other world were often firmly linked in the minds of the family members, and according to Dubois they believed that a widow who sacrificed herself was able to effectively protect her family against all dangers.[65]

Frequency

Balinese following into death was an upper-class phenomenon. Its demographic consequences were therefore not very serious. It is not possible to give exact statistical figures, although a certain amount of information was collected by some early authors. Between July 1846 and August 1848 Friederich, for example, learnt of five or six cases each involving four to seven victims. These occurred in Lombok, where only the Balinese, who numbered about 9000, practised the custom.[66] These figures are almost certainly too high, unless, of course, we are looking at extreme exceptions.[67] For the period between 1820 and

[63] Dubois 19–20.

[64] *Encyclopaedie van Nederlandsch-Indië* 1, 118; *Dagh-Register* 181. However, the details given by Oosterwijck on which the statements in the *Dagh-Register* are based are not very reliable since he states that the women concerned went into convents, which never existed in Bali.

[65] Dubois 23.

[66] Friederich, *Bali* (1850) 13; van der Kraan 119.

[67] If one bases oneself on the same assumptions as have been used for India below (see pp. 236–7), then in the course of two years about 90 women would have become widows in Lombok, while the number of widows burned to death would have been between 20 (5x4) and 42 (6x7). The latter number means that almost every second widow would have burnt herself to death. In the districts of India with the highest frequency the number was never more than 1 out of 36. The demographic consequences of such a situation would have been considerable, yet they are not even alluded to in the sources.

1850 Friederich heard of eight cases in the Balinese kingdom of Badung, in each of which between one and nine victims figured.[68]

Even in Bali and Lombok burning alive was not the normal fate of widows. Yet the ceremonies were so frequent that they were present in the general consciousness, especially if one takes into account the high number of onlookers. Dubois' statement that 100,000 people were present[69] is certainly exaggerated, given that in all of Bali, at that time, the population could not have exceeded 500,000. But other authors too speak of tens of thousands of onlookers.[70] A large section of the Balinese people would thus have witnessed at least one burning in the course of their life.

According to eyewitness accounts, the number of victims per case was between one and seven.[71] Authors who were not eyewitnesses give considerably higher figures. If one disregards Valentyn's 270 dead

---

Friederich must have therefore based his figures on rumours, which crossed the boundaries of reality.

[68] Friederich, *Bali* (1850) 13–14; van der Kraan 119. The statement made by Moor 92, that such cases occurred almost every year in Bali, will have to be regarded as less reliable. Crawfurd, *History* 2, 241 states that the custom was more widespread in Bali than in India, but does not substantiate this claim. Similarly Helms 57–8.

[69] Dubois 19; 23.

[70] Friederich, *Gianjar* 429: at least 40,000. Helms 61: 40–50,000. Both authors refer to the same event in 1847, whereby we can assume that they would have spoken to each other about it. Three years later, Friederich, *Bali* (1850) 13 also mentions 50,000 people.

[71] Dubois (1829): 7 (see van der Kraan 96, footnote 17); Zollinger (1846): 1; Friederich and Helms (1847): 3; Schuurman (1840): 1 (cited in van der Kraan 91). According to Prévost (vol. 17, p. 55), in the earliest ceremony witnessed by Europeans in 1633, 22 female slaves were stabbed to death at the funeral of the king's mother. This source, however, has undergone changes. The account in the *Dagh-Register* 179–81, which reproduces the statements of Dutch eyewitnesses, does not mention the number of victims. Van der Kraan 92 (he uses Crawfurd, *History* 2, 244, who for his part translates from Prévost) has simply inserted the number into the translation of the text from the *Dagh-Register*. Prévost's text, which refers to a Dutch manuscript that he translated into French, contains—in contrast to the *Dagh-Register*—several moralizing insets, not found in the original Dutch manuscript and not iden- tified as additions.

widows in Blambangan in 1691,[72] then the highest figure mentioned is 150.[73] More precise accounts record up to 42 victims.[74] From this we can conclude that in the process of repetition the figures became larger. Yet it seems possible that at times a dozen or more women went to their death in the course of a single ceremony.

We cannot draw any definite conclusions about the increase or decrease in frequency over a period of time, although the authors of the sources attempt to do so occasionally. It has been stated that the frequency of the custom decreased during the nineteenth century, but no figures are given.[75] In 1859, van Bloemen Waanders prognosticated that widow burning would die out on its own before the end of the century.[76] In other works it is said that in the nineteenth century the custom was increasingly practised only in the ruling houses, which would indicate an overall decrease.[77] An entirely different theory can also be advanced: that the institutional character of the custom would become less important in the course of time, given that in the nineteenth century slaves and servants were no longer killed, and women were probably not accompanied any more.[78] This meant that the custom could potentially be extended to other social classes.

[72] Valentyn 4, 1, 207.

[73] Junghuhn 2, 342: taken over by Crawfurd, *History* 2, 252. This is a poorer version of the text of 1633 (in which even cases not witnessed by the Dutch are mentioned). The better version, *Dagh-Register* 181 speaks of 120–40 victims. Other cases: Crawfurd, *History* 2, 241 and Crawfurd, *Religion* 135: 74. The same number is mentioned in Raffles 2: ccxxxviii and in the *Asiatic Journal* NS 3/1 (1830), 242, as well as in Helms 58. Humboldt 92: more than 70. Lodewycksz, in Rouffaer/ Ijzerman 202: over 50.

[74] *Dagh-Register* 181: at the funeral of two sons of the King of Bali, 42 women for one and 34 for the other; Crawfurd, *History* II: 241 and Crawfurd, *Religion* 135: twenty in 1813 in Lombok; Raffles, cited in Boon, *Affinities* 38–9: 19; *Asiatic Journal* NS 3/1 (1830) 242: thirteen in 1829; Moor 92: seven in 1825, and in general for rulers ten to twelve; Friederich, *Bali* (1850) 13–14: up to nine.

[75] Zollinger 345; Covarrubias 383.

[76] Van Bloemen Waanders 146.

[77] *Encyclopaedie van Nederlandsch-Indië* 1, 118; Friederich, *Gianjar* 424–5; Moor 92.

[78] Only Moor (1837) 92 makes a vague reference to a following of the dead for queens.

Origins: Bali, India and Hinduism

Quite naturally, we can only speculate about the origins, the causes and the spread of following into death. The question of the relationship between Indian and Balinese widow burning is particularly relevant. Was the development in Bali an independent one, or was the custom taken over from India?

Within the broader framework of following into death there are undoubtedly considerable similarities between India and Bali.[79] The focus is clearly on widow *burning*, which did not occur anywhere else in the same way. While comparing the two more closely, however, the differences surface. In India, generally only one wife burned herself with her husband's body in the same fire, and, at the most, twenty-four hours after her husband's death. Other methods of killing are practically unknown. In Bali, the burning occurs, at the earliest, one week after the husband's death; the number of victims was generally larger; these often consisted more of concubines than wives, and the widow jumped into a separate fire. In addition to burning there was a second method of killing—death by stabbing—which, according to some authors, was used more frequently. Finally, when compared to India, the custom in Bali was an upper-class phenomenon.

Yet there are various aspects that support the assumption that widow burning in Bali was originally taken over from India, or—to put it more precisely—was attendant on Hinduism. In Java, widow burning disappeared along with Hinduism. Similar phenomena cannot be found anywhere else in South East Asia—and Hinduism too cannot be found anywhere else in recent times. The custom as practised in Bali differed to a greater extent from the forms prevalent in South-East Asia than from those that were practised in India. We would have to assume, however, that after the custom was taken over in Bali it followed its own independent course.[80]

[79] Comparative reflections also in Friederich, *Bali* (1850) 9–10 and Helms 57–8.

[80] Humboldt 92–3 assumes that the custom originated in pre-Hindu times in Bali. He cites the fact that the killing of widows was also prevalent in other regions, but does not take the special conditions in Southeast Asia into account. Crawfurd, *History* 2, 242 assumes an independent Balinese origin, but does not give any reasons. Van der Kraan 89 does not attempt to resolve the question.

The End

In Java following into death was evidently suppressed by Islam. In Bali, where Hinduism remains the dominant religion even today, the suppression of widow burning had to wait on the initiative of the colonial power. From the beginning, European observers were shocked and indignant. This was clearly expressed by the prosaic Swiss Zollinger: 'The local onlookers, who stood around me, saw nothing terrible in this slaughter, which took place before our eyes. They laughed and chatted, as if nothing had happened. The man who had carried out the last three thrusts, washed his dagger and sheathed it in the cold-blooded manner of a butcher who had slaughtered an animal.'[81] The Dane, Helms, justified European rule on the basis of such customs:

> This terrible spectacle did not appear to produce any emotion upon the vast crowd, and the scene closed with barbaric music and firing of guns. It was a sight never to be forgotten by those who witnessed it, and brought to one's heart a strange feeling of thankfulness that one belonged to a civilisation which, with all its faults, is merciful, and tends more and more to emancipate women from despotism and cruelty. To the British rule it is due that this foul plague of suttee is extirpated in India, and doubtless the Dutch have, ere now, done as much for Bali. Works like these are the credentials by which the Western civilisation makes good its right to conquer and humanize barbarous races and to replace ancient civilisations.[82]

Despite these outcries, the early observers at first had no means of intervention. Only when the Dutch gradually began to extend their control over the island from the nineteenth century onwards, did they demand that the rulers sign treaties in which the custom was expressly prohibited. Since some princes resisted giving up all claims to the custom for a long time, this policy was completed only at the end of 1904.[83]

With abolition there was at least an end to the big spectacular burnings. The last case of this kind was registered in 1903, when two

[81] Zollinger 349. Cf. also Dubois, in van der Kraan 3; 9; 21–4; Friederich, *Bali* (1850) 13, and footnotes 39–42 above.

[82] Helms 65–6.

[83] Van Geuns 64–5; van der Kraan 89–90; *Encyclopaedie van Nederlandsch-Indië* 1, 118; van Kol 323–4; 359–60.

women were burned at the death of the ruler of Tabanan. The Dutch protested, but they did not prevent the act since they did not have a treaty banning the custom with the princely state.[84] Smaller ceremonies are said to have taken place till the 1920s.[85] Since the underlying views and, especially, the belief in the hereafter had not changed to any great extent, people turned to substitutions. 'Large straw dolls, dressed in expensive robes, symbolise the young women who are cruelly prevented by the new rulers of the country, the Dutch, from following their master in death into the bliss of Indra's heaven.'[86]

Despite the continued traditional belief in life after death, the suppression of the custom seems to have finally been successful. We do not know of any serious attempts to revive it after the colonial power withdrew, and we also must take into account the fact that Indonesia is a state dominated by Islam and has therefore little sympathy for the custom.

[84] Van Kol 323–4; van der Kraan 89; *Encyclopaedie van Nederlandsch-Indië* 1, 118.
[85] Geertz 214, without giving any proof.
[86] Juynboll 232.

PART II

Widow Burning in India

Preliminary Remarks: Sources, Presentation and Terminology

Of all the forms of following the dead that have ever been practiced, widow burning in India is undoubtedly the most famous. It was known even in Ancient Greece and Rome. Later, the Islamic world heard about it, and in modern times awareness of it increasingly became part of the general store of knowledge in Europe and, ultimately, in the whole world. It made its way into poems, novels and stories, into newspapers and schoolbooks and, finally, into film and television.[1]

Such renown presupposes particularly good sources. The situation is in fact unique. For a start there is a substantial body of indigenous written testimony. However, it neither goes so far back in time as in China, nor does historiography play the role it does there. This merely reflects the more modest role of historiography in India as compared to China.[2] Precise descriptions of widow burnings that actually

---

[1] To name only two popular novels: Jules Verne: *Around the World in Eighty Days* (1873) and M.M. Kaye: *The Far Pavilions* (1978), both also filmed. Famous treatments in verse include among others Goethe's ballad *Der Gott und die Bajadere* (1797) and Southey's *Curse of Kehama* (1810). On the literary treatment of the custom see Rajan, *Women*, chap. 2 and Figueira, in Hawley (ed.) 55–72.

[2] See Winternitz, *Geschichte* 3, 80–95.

occurred are as good as non-existent in Indian sources.[3] However, they are often mentioned and described in fiction.[4] Even more important is the treatment of the question in law manuals and commentaries.[5] There is another type of source, which is otherwise found only in China, but which is not as important there: scattered throughout India there are many inscriptions, memorial stones, monuments and temples erected in honour of widows who burnt themselves to death.[6]

Till the nineteenth century local sources are scantier than in China. However, two types of sources stemming from foreigners are far more substantial—accounts written by travellers and by those foreign agencies that wielded power.

The first accounts of Western witnesses were written in antiquity. In medieval times Islamic and even a few European travellers appeared on the scene. After the sea route around the Cape of Good Hope was established, the number and quality of European descriptions registered a big increase. From the first Islamic kingdom in the late twelfth century till 1947, larger or smaller parts of India were ruled by foreigners who did not practise following into death, and who in fact more or less categorically rejected the custom. But not until the end of the eighteenth century do we find any traces of the custom in the official documents of even the Islamic kingdoms or the European holdings. In the beginning of the nineteenth century the British began to regulate widow burning bureaucratically and therefore produced a large body of documents. The regulation led to unusually passionate public debates. After the policy failed, the custom was abolished in 1829. Since individual cases continued to occur, the police and the courts still had to deal with the issue. In connection with a widow burning in 1987 a fierce discussion broke out in India, the likes of which had not been witnessed since 1829.

The nature of the sources determines the structure of this part of the book. Widow burning in India has been attested since 316 BC. This

---

[3] An account written in 1741 by an Indian named Durlabhram and published in 1931 by Dixit is an exception. However it is significant that the author writes in verse and incorporates miraculous stories uncritically.

[4] See for example Arunachalam; Jolly 67ff.; Sprockhoff, *Indien* 421; Winternitz, *Frau* 62.

[5] Fundamental: Kane 2, 1, 625ff. With regard to this Altekar 120ff.; Jolly 67ff.; Winternitz, *Frau* 58ff.; Shastri 118 ff.

[6] See for example Thakur, *History* 148–59 and especially Settar/Sontheimer.

would suggest a chronological presentation. However, for the period till about 1000 AD there are very few sources. They remain scarce till roughly 1500, then become more substantial, and finally take on monumental dimensions in the first decades of the nineteenth century. For the early period it is often only possible to make conjectures on the basis of later sources. This renders a uniform chronological presentation difficult. Instead, chapter 11 gives a brief overview of the spread of the custom. The central chapter 12, on the other hand, is systematically structured. Chapter 13 deals more closely with the background and the determining factors.

More than the extent and spread of widow burning it is perhaps the extent and the fierceness of the debates about its suppression, which give India its special place in the history of following in death. These debates constitute the subject matter of chapter 14. The debates on the abolition of the custom are an instructive example of the relationship between cultural relativism and universal moral claims in political practice. Can religion and tradition sanctify an act that is regarded as a crime in the framework of morals that today base their claim to universality on human rights? And are they able to do so only in theory or in administrative practice as well?[7]

When passionate debates have been conducted on a topic for centuries, indeed for millennia, it inevitably has an effect on the *terminology*. It is therefore surprising that there was never a heated controversy about the concepts, and that the differences in the use of terms generally remain within narrow bounds. Exceptions are most likely to be found in the discussions that led to the abolition of 1829, as well as in the current debates since 1987, where widow burning is characterized by some authors in principle as murder or killing of widows, or as *widow immolation*.[8] However, such linguistic regulations, which

[7] A further imbalance in the presentation arises from the author's limitations. In dealing with sources in Indian languages, someone who is not an Indologist has to rely on translations, which are available only for relatively few texts, and are sometimes controversial with regard to decisive aspects of this study. The author can at best present the controversies, not resolve them. The presentation is therefore based mainly on sources in Western languages.

[8] For example Vaid/Sangari: Institutions, beliefs, ideologies. Widow immolation in contemporary Rajasthan (1991), and the title of the special issue of *Seminar* No. 342 (February 1988): *Sati: A Symposon on Widow Immolation and Its Social Context*. Even in the nineteenth century different authors

tend to eliminate the ambiguous character of the custom, have never gained general acceptance.

The widow who burns herself, or is burnt (such formulations show the problems of terminology, since language is unable to capture not only the openness, but also the contradictory nature of the situation through a single expression), is generally called *sati* (a Sanskrit word) in India both in specialized literature and in popular English accounts. The history of the word is informative.[9] It goes back to the root *as*, 'to be'. From this the present participle *sat* (feminine *sati*), or 'being' is derived, which can be used as an adjective or a noun and means 'that which is', 'that which exists', or 'that which is true'. From this we get the more specific meanings like 'good', 'faithful', 'virtuous', 'honest'. *Sat* refers to virtues that are partly ascribed to both sexes, but chiefly to women. *Sati* therefore embodied the ideal wife (specifically from a male perspective, but also internalized by the women), who is linked with her husband in a relationship of unshakeable devotion and subordination. Expressions of this are found in mythology. The goddess Sati was the wife of Shiva. When Sati's father Daksha gave a large feast he did not invite Shiva. Sati went to her father and demanded an explanation from him, but he refused to change his mind. Sati then produced a fire from within herself, which consumed her. According to other sources she threw herself into a fire.[10]

In this story Sati is portrayed in complete accordance with the ideal of *sati*, but not as a widow. She burns herself to death because her husband has been insulted, not because he has died. The transference to the widow, who dies by burning, possibly occurred relatively late,

---

speak consistently of 'murder', for example Townley and Ward, *Account* and *View*.

[9] For this see especially Weinberger-Thomas (1989) 18 and Weinberger-Thomas (1996) 31–5; Hawley, in Hawley (ed.) 11–15. See also for example Leslie, *Choice* 46, Sutherland 1595 and Thompson, *Suttee* 15–19. For the meaning of *sat* in the broadest sense see Harlan 112ff.

[10] Pathak gives the different versions of the story, as it is found in the Puranas. The different versions however agree on the central points. According to Oldenburg, in Hawley (ed.) 163, in another version Shiva saves Sati. The story is also reproduced in J.D. Anderson 280–2; R.B. Joshi 557–63; Moor 107; Weinberger-Thomas (1989) 33–5; Weinberger-Thomas (1996) 159–61; D.C. Sen; Sutherland 1601.

and, finally, the meaning of the word referred mainly (although never exclusively) to this element.[11]

There are different expressions for the act of (self)-burning in Sanskrit. It distinguishes between the widow burning herself along with her husband's body, which is termed *sahagamana* (to go with), or *sahamaraṇa* (to die with) and the widow burning herself after her husband has been cremated, for which the terms *anugamana* (to go after, to follow), or *anumaraṇa* (to die after) are used.[12]

The Europeans found such expressions difficult to use. This led, probably in the late eighteenth or the early nineteenth century, to an expansion of the meaning of the word *sati*. The term for the person involved was transferred to the act: widow burning was then also called *sati*, or in an Anglicised style, *suttee*.[13] This could lead to confusion, although generally it was clear from the context, whether the widow herself or the burning was being referred to. Some authors in the twentieth century distinguish between *suttee* for the act and *sati* for the widow.[14]

This study chooses to take a slightly different approach. It retains the term 'widow burning', even though it is more unwieldy than *sati* or *suttee*. On the other hand it is self-explanatory, more vivid and less euphemistic. However, if one were to take it literally, it indicates an opinion, since it says that the widow is burnt, and not that she burns herself. The intention behind the choice of the expression is not to resolve the matter, since the question of voluntary death is discussed only in chapter 12.

The woman who burns herself to death, or is burnt to death, is here generally referred to as the *widow,* sometimes also as *sati*. The use of the word 'widow' also implies an opinion (which is intended). According to those Hindu scriptures that propagate widow burning, a *sati* does not become a widow. Through her decision—and the act—she remains continuously linked with her husband as his wife. This view is also expressed in symbolic acts. While, for example, the bangles worn

[11] On the contemporary situation see mainly Harlan 112 ff. and Vaid/Sangari 4–6; 10.

[12] See for example Leslie, *Choice* 46; Thompson, *Suttee* 15; Michaels, *Recht* 102; Weinberger-Thomas (1996) 33.

[13] See Yule/Burnell 878–9; 882–3.

[14] Thompson, *Suttee* 15–16.

by the woman as a mark of her conjugal status are broken when she becomes a widow, the *sati* goes to her death still wearing them. She retains the high prestige of the married woman. According to this view one would then have to logically speak of the burning of wives, or, more correctly, of the self-burning of wives.[15]

Such a definition of a widow is extremely ideological and operates as a justification for the burning. It aims to increase the reputation of the *sati*. This study consciously does not appropriate this viewpoint, and, instead, uses the normal definition: a wife becomes a widow at the death of her husband, regardless of what she does after that. From 1829 to the most recent ban of 1987 the law too has always spoken of widows.[16]

The religio-legal texts in whose ambit widow burning has been primarily mentioned in India, will be referred to as *Dharma texts*.

In the framework of Indian society the concept of caste presents problems that cannot be solved.[17] The concept usually includes two classifications, which are more or less independent of each other. Traditionally, Indian society is divided into four ideal groups, referred to as *varna*, which, however, only have a limited meaning in practice: Brahmins (priests), Kshatriyas (warriors and kings), Vaishyas (traders) and Shudras. In addition there are those without a caste. A person's life is, however, determined to a greater extent by a more varied division into numerous smaller groups known as *jati*. There is no satisfactory terminological differentiation in English. Therefore the terms *varna* and *jati* will be used here.

Transcribing names of places in India into the Latin script is a matter of luck, since a uniform transcription has never been established. As a rule, I have retained the names as given in the sources, and for the better-known names I have used the newer and more common style. Every attempt at establishing uniformity only leads to new inconsistencies.

[15] Weinberger-Thomas (1989) 23–4. Ibid. 24: 'La satî meurt en épouse. [. . .] C'est de crémation des épouses qu'il conviendrait de parler.' See also Leslie, *Choice* 47; Leslie, *Victim* 189.

[16] The subtitle of a collection of essays edited by Hawley (*The Burning of Wives in India*) therefore implies a clear opinion in favour of the orthodox Hindu viewpoint: the customary English formulation (*widow burning*) has been consciously given up.

[17] See especially Dumont, as well as Hutton and Quigley.

CHAPTER 11

The History of Widow Burning

The Early Period: Diodorus, the Mahābhārata and the Rigveda

The oldest account of a widow burning, which is not part of mythology or fiction, comes from the first century BC. It is written by Diodorus of Sicily, a historian who wrote in Greek, and who would have found such an account in earlier Greek sources. Research in classical philology assumes that his source was a text by Hieronymus of Cardia, who was probably an eyewitness to the event.[1]

After the death of Alexander the Great (323 BC) quarrels broke out among his generals. In the battle at Gabiene in Asia Minor in 316 BC, Antigonus won a victory over Eumenes, who had an Indian contingent among his troops. The commander of this contingent, Ceteus, fell in the battle. 'Then an event took place that was amazing and very different from Greek custom. Ceteus, the general of the soldiers who had come from India, was killed in the battle after fighting brilliantly, but he left two wives who had accompanied him in the army, one of them a bride, the other married to him some years before, but both of them loving him deeply.' According to Diodorus, in earlier times women in India often poisoned their husbands in favour of their lovers. This led to a law,

> that wives, except such as were pregnant or had children, should be cremated along with their deceased husbands. [. . .] When these laws had been established, the lawlessness of the women changed into the opposite, for as each one because of the great loss of caste willingly met death, they not only cared for the safety of their husbands as if it were their own, but they even vied with each other as for a very great honour. Such rivalry appeared on this occasion. Although the law ordered only

---

[1] Heckel/Yardley 308. Cf. now also the comprehensive essay by Garzilli, which could not be included in this study.

one of Ceteus' wives to be cremated with him, both of them appeared at his funeral, contending for the right of dying with him as for a prize of valour. When the generals undertook to decide the matter, the younger wife claimed that the other was pregnant and for that reason could not take advantage of the law; and the elder asserted that more justly should the one who had the precedence in years have precedence also in honour, for in all other matters those who are older are regarded as having great precedence over the younger in respect and in honour. The generals, ascertaining from those skilled in midwifery that the elder was pregnant, decided for the younger. When this happened, the one who had lost the decision departed weeping, rending the wreath that was about her head and tearing her hair, just as if some great disaster had been announced to her; but the other, rejoicing in her victory, went off to the pyre crowned with fillets that her maidservants bound upon her head, and magnificently dressed as if for a wedding. She was escorted by her kinsfolk, who sang a hymn in honour of her virtue. As she drew near the pyre, she stripped off her ornaments and gave them to her servants and friends, leaving keepsakes, as one might say, to those who loved her.[. . .] Finally, after taking leave of the household, she was assisted to mount the pyre by her brother, and while the multitude that had gathered for the spectacle watched with amazement, she ended her life in heroic fashion. For the entire army under arms marched three times about the pyre before it was lighted, and she herself, reclining beside her husband and letting no ignoble cry escape her during the onset of the fire, stirred some of those who beheld her to pity, others to extravagant praise. Nevertheless some of the Greeks denounced the custom as barbarous and cruel.[2]

The truth of this passage has never been doubted. Its credibility is underscored by the fact that many of its details match those given in later eyewitness accounts that have been directly transmitted. This is especially true with regard to the course of the ceremony. Occasionally a parallel to the perhaps most spectacular part of the story—the competition between the two widows—has been pointed out.[3] The *Mahā-bhārata*, one of the great popular Indian epics, has a scene that is similar in some respects. King Pandu is burdened by the curse of a Brahmin that he will die in the act of love. Unable to control himself after a long

[2] Diodorus 19, 32, 3–19, 34, 6. Cf. also 17, 91, 3.
[3] Especially by Heckel/Yardley 307–11. See also Garbe 156–8; Winternitz, *Frau* 71; Zachariae, *Witwenverbrennung* 551–2; Dubois, *Moeurs* 2, 24.

time, he dies in the arms of his younger wife Madri who had tried to
stop him from carrying out the act. Madri and Kunti, Pandu's first and
older wife, then argue about who should accompany him in death.
Here too the younger widow wins, arguing that the king died because
of his desire for her, and that this desire should be satisfied in the other
world.[4]

It is not possible to date this passage precisely, and therefore we
cannot determine whether Diodorus or even Hieronymus of Cardia
were influenced by an Indian literary source. What is certain on the
other hand is that both Greek authors had read Herodotus, who describes the quarrel between two Thracian widows for the right to follow
their husband in death.[5] It has been established that this story is probably not based on a verifiable experience. All indications suggest that
Diodorus' account is not a description of a fact, but that he took over
Herodotus' topos. In the numerous eyewitness accounts from later
times such a dispute is never mentioned.[6] Only a few authors speak in
vague terms of a corresponding rule in their times. According to Holwell (1767), only the first wife has the right to burn herself to death;
if she relinquishes her claim, it goes to the second wife. Sometimes
there is a quarrel between them. Although the author did witness many
widow burnings, he does not refer to any concrete experience to substantiate his statement.[7] According to Orlich (1861), it is only the first
wife who has the right to burn herself to death. He cites the Vedas as
the source of his authority without giving any further details.[8]

Nor was there a reason for a contest. None of the many rules and

[4] *Mahābhārata* 1, 116.
[5] Herodotus 5,5. Cf. also above pp. 41–2.
[6] Heckel/Yardley 308 on the other hand doubt that the eyewitness account written by Hieronymus could have been influenced by Herodotus.
However we do not know whether this element was also present in Hieronymus' account, and Heckel/Yardley do not know later accounts of widow
burning in India. They are therefore not aware of the fact that such a dispute
is not a reflection of Indian reality.
[7] Holwell 88–90.
[8] Orlich, *Indien* 2,2,234. Similarly in 1777 Kindersley 127. In 1705
Langhanss 537 speaks only vaguely of the favourite wife. Dubois, *Moeurs* 2,
24 takes the *Mahābhārata* as proof for present times! Herodotus' theme had
lived on in medieval times, especially among authors who did not have close
links with India, as for example in Eyb, *Ehebüchlein* of 1472, p.8, where the
dispute is resolved by a judge.

recommendations found with regard to widow burning in later Indian texts mentioned an upper limit for the number of victims. Widows had to decide, individually, and the decision by one of them to accompany her husband in death did not impinge on a similar decision by the other widows of the same man. It is true that at times some widows were strongly dissuaded from carrying out the act, and family members, priests or bystanders tried to stop them. The intention however was not to pave the way for a competitor. A tendency to restrict numbers never becomes tangible. Such a regulation would also have been incomprehensible from a theological point of view, since it would have amounted to an enforcement of monogamy in the other world, while polygamy was accepted in this world. Some European authors on the contrary even stated that *all* the wives were obliged to kill themselves when their husband died.[9]

The fact that a dispute between the wives is found in the *Mahābhārata*, does not make it more credible. One can easily imagine how such a legend arises. It is a typical product of the wishful thinking and the vanity of men: a quarrel of this kind is the strongest proof of the love and devotion for the deceased. In this way, even those who did not die could be included in the custom: they had wanted to, but were not allowed to.

Even Diodorus' statement that there is a law prescribing widow burning is false. At no point of time was there such a law in India. This does not however mean that the entire account is fictitious. Rather, it proves the spread of the custom in India, and also that it was taken as a matter of course. Had it been rare and controversial in India, it would hardly have been practised by Indians far away from their country, in a place that did not know about the custom, and therefore neither expected nor appreciated it.

Compared to this clear historical description, the Indian sources present far greater problems of interpretation, which begin with the dating of texts, possible only in the rarest of cases. At any rate, it is indisputable that the Rigveda, which encompasses the oldest Indian texts, dates back far beyond the time of Alexander the Great to the second

---

[9] For example Conti 127–8; Fenicio 179; Nuniz 76. What is mentioned more often is that widow burning was obligatory only for certain groups: for example Carré 2, 593; Guichard 382; 387; Manucci 3, 65; Vincenzo 344; Mandelslo, *Reyse-Beschreibung* 117; Dapper 54.

millennium BC and possibly even further back.[10] Till about the middle of the nineteenth century it was unanimously agreed that it contained a passage in which widow burning is at least mentioned, if not recommended, or even prescribed. With regard to the precise ritual guidelines for cremations, widows were mentioned in the following manner according to Colebrooke, who was the first to publish this text in 1795: 'Let these women, not to be widowed, good wives, adorned with collyrium, holding clarified butter, consign themselves to the fire. Immortal, not childless, nor husbandless, well adorned with gems, let them pass into fire.'[11] This translation may be obscure in many details, but women who go into the fire are definitely mentioned. Later research questioned not only the translation, but also the text. It was proved that in the original version a decisive word was different: instead of *agneh* ('fire') *agre* ('earlier', 'first') was written. This did not make the translation easier. However, it became clear that it was not possible to establish a connection with widow burning.[12] The text was probably changed relatively late, possibly only in the fifteenth century AD, at a point of time, when the custom was already widely prevalent and was described and even recommended in many texts.[13] The oft-quoted sentence of Max Müller's, probably the most famous Indologist of the nineteenth century: 'Now this is perhaps the most flagrant instance of what can be done by an unscrupulous priesthood', is thus exaggerated.[14] The change is to be understood more in the sense of an adjustment to reality, or as a correction through a reconstruction of what was considered to be the original text, rather than in the sense of

[10] Cf. the overview of different attempts at dating the texts in Mylius 16–19; Kapadia XXI; Kane 5,2, XI–XVII, as well as Winternitz, *Geschichte* 1, 23–8. Altekar 336 places the Rigveda in the period between 2500 and 1500 BC.

[11] Colebrooke, *Duties* 116 = *Rig-Veda* 10, 18, 7.

[12] This passage has been discussed and interpreted many times over. See mainly Hall; P.N. Bose 2, 65; Jolly 71; Kane 2, 1, 619; 634; M. Müller 2, 29–32; Roth; Sprockhoff, *Indien* 422; Sternbach 17; Winternitz, *Witwe*; Wilson, 271–5; R. Mitra, *Ceremonies* 248–64; Zimmer 328–9. Also see the more recent translation by Geldner, *Rig-Veda* 10,18: 'These women, wives with good husbands, should lie down with their eyes smeared with butter. Without tears, free from disease and decked out in beautiful ornaments, they should climb on to the pyre (again) first.'

[13] Stated by Lanman 2, 383. Weinberger-Thomas (1989) 11 places the change in the text in the tenth century AD.

[14] M. Müller 2, 33. See footnote 16.

a conscious deception, or indeed as the deceit of priests aimed at widows. The distortion did not take place in order to burn widows. Rather the text was adapted after the practice had been prevalent for a long time.[15]

While the problems connected with this verse in the context of widow burning could be solved with the help of philological methods, far more substantial problems of interpretation arose with the verse that directly follows it. Although the translations vary greatly in their details, the core of the subject is not questioned. The widow is told to stand up again after she has lain down near her husband's body. She is supposed to grasp the proffered hand of a man and thus return among the living; she is probably even expected to marry this man.[16]

In the context of debates about the sanctioning of widow burning in Indian texts, this passage is sometimes seen as an indication of a more symbolic form of the custom. The widow is now no longer actually burnt to death; rather she is expressly called upon to continue her life after she has symbolically expressed her devotion to her husband.[17]

This interpretation is possible, but not conclusive. Those who accept it would have to assume that the history of widow burning proceeded in waves. In an indeterminable past it would have been widely prevalent. After that it would have been gradually suppressed, probably under the influence of the Brahminic religion, and replaced by the ritual described above. Later, however, it would have again become prevalent, whereby—and this can be proved—it was increasingly sanctioned and even recommended by the Dharma texts.

The problem with this viewpoint lies mainly in the role assigned to religion, viz. the religious texts, which are first supposed to have helped in restraining the custom, only to favour and promote it later, as has been shown.

From the point of view of the entire history of the custom, an interpretation of the controversial passage as an early form is therefore more plausible (although it cannot be proved). In a symbolic act the widow has to confirm her attachment to her husband. Compared to her re-entry into the world of the living this aspect of the ceremony becomes increasingly more important, till finally the symbol turns

[15] Cf. Winternitz, *Witwe* 178–80.

[16] *Rig-Veda* 10,18,8. For this passage cf. the literature mentioned in footnote 12.

[17] Argued in this manner for example by Kane 2, 1, 619; Oldenberg 586; Thakur, *History* 133; Basham 187.

into reality and the widow is burnt. The dead are victorious over the living.

In the case of India the question of the origin of the custom is linked to the question of the peoples who spread this custom. Is widow burning an indigenous Indian custom, or did migrant peoples bring it in? Some proceed on the assumption that widow burning was also found among the pre-Aryan peoples (whoever they were). The Aryan conquerors and immigrants are supposed to have taken it over from them.[18] Others state, that on the contrary, it was the Aryans who brought the custom with them. In this context they refer to the apparent prevalence of such customs among Indo-Europeans.[19] Some authors merely emphasize that the custom is of foreign and not of Indian origin.[20] In order to explain why it is not mentioned in the earliest texts, the hypothesis is developed further: widow burning is supposed to have gradually gone out of use and to have been reactivated later.[21] How this happened, and under what circumstances, remains unclear. Another theory ascribes the origin to later, Scythian, migrants, on the basis of Herodotus, who describes corresponding customs among the Scythians.[22]

Such debates belong to the realm of speculation.[23] They merely introduce additional unknown quantities in an equation that cannot be solved. One would have to ascertain who constituted the original inhabitants of India and who the migrants were, whether Aryan, Scythian or others. This approach becomes especially problematic when questions of merits and demerits are linked to it. The idea behind such a search for origins is that following into death is a sign of a primitive and barbaric stage of cultural development.[24]

[18] Stated by Kohler 381–2; Zimmer 329–31; Thompson, *Suttee* 23–6; M. Gaur 45; Lommel 384; Mukhopadhyay, *Institution* 99; A.K. Ray 2.

[19] Winternitz, *Frau* 84; V.N. Datta 3–4; Sousa 231; Basham 188; Tawney/Penzer 255–7.

[20] Rahman 111; Shastri 134.

[21] Altekar 116–17; Garbe 149–50; Leslie, *Victim* 175; Thakur, *History* 133; 149; cf. Thompson, *Suttee* 23–6; Zimmer 329–31.

[22] Herodotus 4, 71–2; V. Smith 62; 665; Etter 28; cf. V.N. Datta 4; Narasimhan 123; Chattopadhyay 394; 397.

[23] A critique in Weinberger-Thomas (1989) 11; Kane 2, 1, 625.

[24] Altekar 116; V.N. Datta xvi; 4; Thakur, *History* 133; Thompson, *Suttee* 26; 42; 47; 138.

The Spread of a Custom, 300 BC to 1500 AD

The importance of Diodorus' statements cannot be overestimated. The event that he describes takes place 826 years before the next attested case of widow burning. However, the sources do contain various references to similar events in the intervening period. After an initial slow phase, the custom later appears to have spread more quickly.

In Greek and Roman antiquity knowledge of widow burning in India can be proven since Alexander's campaign in India (327–325 BC). This knowledge seems to have been fairly widespread since the first century BC, in which the earliest sources by Diodorus and Strabo originate.[25] Many authors deal with the custom or at least mention it briefly. One gets the impression that it is more a question of reminding readers of something they already know than of actually informing them about it.

Accounts by foreigners began to appear only in the middle of the ninth century AD. They were written by travellers who had first-hand experience of India and had sometimes also been eyewitnesses to a burning.[26] For the period until about 1500 the Islamic sources are more precise and more reliable than the European ones.

The earliest known account by an Islamic author was written in 851. He refers to Ceylon, where the wives of a ruler are said to burn themselves sometimes with their husband's body. It is emphasized that this happens voluntarily.[27] In the case of India a text from the year 916 mentions another custom: a ruler has a retinue of 300–400 people who during his lifetime have pledged to burn themselves to death when he

[25] Heckel/Yardley give an overview of the history of the text and references to older research. See also Winternitz, *Frau* 69–71; A. Jackson 72–8; *Asiatic Journal* 23 (1827), 621–4. For the Latin texts see André/ Filliozat. The most important passages, which derive from the same sources, but which are much shorter than in Diodorus, are: Propertius 3, 13, 15–22; Cicero, *Tusculanae Disputationes* 5,78; Valerius Maximus 2, 6, 14; Hieronymus, *Adversus Jovinianum* 1, 311; Aelianus, *Variae Historiae* 7, 18; Plutarch, *Moralia* 499c. General mention mainly in Strabo 15, 1, 30 and 15, 1, 62.

[26] Mediaeval travel accounts about widow burning in India are mentioned and cited time and again, but they have never been compiled systematically and therefore could not be evaluated here in their entirety.

[27] Sauvaget 22; Ferrand 66.

dies.[28] The details given in both sources are not necessarily reliable. But they do show that rumours about following into death were in circulation. The customs mentioned do not seem to have been limited to widow burning.

A more reliable and influential account was written around 1030 by Alberuni. A widow in India, he states, may not remarry:

> She has only to choose between two things—either to remain a widow as long as she lives or to burn herself, and the latter eventuality is considered the preferable, because as a widow she is ill-treated as long as she lives. As regards the wives of the kings, they are in the habit of burning them, whether they wish it or not, by which they desire to prevent any of them by chance committing something unworthy of the illustrious husband. They make an exception only for women of advanced years and for those who have children; for the son is the responsible protector of his mother.[29]

Alberuni thus encountered widow burning as a firmly established custom.

Possibly the most detailed and the most precise medieval description is found in the work of the Moroccan traveller Ibn Baṭṭūṭa, who travelled in the region from 1333 to 1347. During this period he witnessed several widow burnings. He emphasizes that the act is recommended, but not prescribed, and describes an incident in the town of Amjhera, in what is today Madhya Pradesh. Three wives of men who had fallen in a battle wanted to burn themselves to death. After preparations lasting three days, a funeral pyre was lit in a pit. Sesame oil had been poured all over the wood. A rug was held high like a curtain between the widow and the fire.

> I saw one of them, on coming to the blanket, pull it violently out of the men's hands, saying to them with a laugh, *mārā mītarsānī az aṭash man mīdānam ū aṭash ast rahā kunī mārā*; these words mean 'Is it with the fire that you frighten me? I know that it is a blazing fire.' Thereupon she joined her hands above her head in salutation to the fire and cast herself into it. At the same moment the drums, trumpets and bugles were sounded, and men threw on her the firewood they were

[28] Ferrand 114 (Abu Zayd).
[29] Alberuni 2, 155 (chap. 69).

carrying and the others put those heavy balks on top of her to prevent her moving, cries were raised and there was a loud clamour. When I saw this I had all but fallen off my horse, if my companions had not quickly brought water to me and laved my face, after which I withdrew.[30]

From the second half of the thirteenth century onward there are also European accounts. They are more general and less precise, but on the whole they confirm the statements made by Islamic authors. The earliest reference to the custom is with regard to Malabar and is written by Marco Polo: 'When a man is dead and his body is being cremated, his wife flings herself into the same fire and lets herself be burnt with her husband. The ladies who do this are highly praised by all. And I assure you that there are many who do as I have told you.'[31] The impression that is first created that all women burnt themselves to death, is thus taken back. Marco Polo also talks of a large number of loyal followers who burnt themselves to death on the funeral pyre of the King of Malabar.[32] A little later Odoricus of Pordenone (1286–1330) described widow burning as voluntary for women with sons and obligatory for all others.[33]

There are no exact descriptions or even eyewitness accounts in the Indian sources, but in other respects they contain more and more precise information than the Western ones. The first established historical evidence of a widow burning after Diodorus is found in an inscription from the year 510 AD. It was found in Eran in the Sagar district of what is today Madhya Pradesh. A ruler had it inscribed that one of his army commanders died at this place in battle and that his widow had followed him into death on his funeral pyre.[34]

Another inscription, also found in Madhya Pradesh, does not have a date, but on the basis of the written characters it can be ascribed to

[30] Ibn Baṭṭūṭa 3, 614–16. Quote: 616.
[31] Marco Polo (ed. Benedetto) 181, chap. 175 (trans. Latham p. 238).
[32] Marco Polo (ed. Benedetto) 180, chap. 175.
[33] Odoricus of Pordenone 139. Further passages in Jordanus 20–1; Conti 126–8; 164–6. Conti's account with important additions also in Tafur (1435–39), 90–1.
[34] Description, text and translation in Fleet 91–3. Another translation in Basham 188. Cf. Rao 233; Thakur, *History* 148. This inscription is mentioned very often in the relevant literature.

the second century AD.[35] In Nepal widow burning is mentioned in inscriptions since 464 AD.[36]

Inscriptions from the following centuries appear time and again in different regions of India.[37]

In addition there was a further form of remembrance which soon became much more frequent. Memorial stones were erected for the widows. For Hinduism, which otherwise rarely erects monuments to the dead, this was conspicuous.[38] These so-called Sati stones display special visual elements. The most common is the raised right arm with a lemon held in the hand; the bangles, symbolising the married woman, are also shown on the arm. Sometimes the stones show the figure of a woman, often accompanied by that of a man. Such portrayals are occasionally accompanied by inscriptions.[39]

A large number of Sati stones are found all over India. However, they are not evenly distributed; in certain regions and in individual places they are present in far greater numbers. Unfortunately, like the inscriptions, they have not been studied systematically as yet. Therefore it is not possible to make any precise statements about the frequency and the regional distribution of the custom. We cannot say

[35] *Archaeological Survey of India* 7 (1878), 136–7. See Walsh 435. Research does not take this finding into account. The interpretation of a finding from the third century AD in Sircar 210–15 is untenable. From the mere mention of two unknown names the author assumes a case of widow burning. Taken over by Saxena, *Reforms* 60–1.

[36] Michaels, *Nepal* 22. Here only a burning that was prevented is mentioned, but the context suggests that burnings actually took place.

[37] Further details in: Altekar 129–31; Arunachalam 92–6 (for Tamil Nadu); Rao 232–7; Settar/Sontheimer; Thakur, *History* 148–59; Thompson, *Suttee* 28–38; Walsh; Winternitz, *Frau* 68–9; Devi 263; Mahalingam 258–60; Shastri 118–35; B.N. Sharma 65–6; Swaminathan 11–13; *Archaeological Survey of India* 9 (1879) 4; 33–4; 39.

[38] Cf. Zachariae 595; Dubois, *Moeurs* 2, 22; Bunsen, *Witwenverbrennung* 459.

[39] Settar/Sontheimer's work on the Sati stones is fundamental. See also Noble/Sankhyan; Sontheimer, *Monuments*; Crooke 1, 186ff.; Hall 191; Longhurst; Malcolm 2, 206–7; Mall; Moor 433; Tawney/Penzer 260–1; Thakur, *History*; Thompson, *Suttee* 28–38; Walsh; Harlan 112–13; Hervey 1, 210–11; 215–16; Mahalingam 258; Parks 1, 95–6; 2, 66; 420; Rao 233; Tod 1, 74–5; Upreti/Upreti 11; Weinberger-Thomas (1989) 24; Weinberger-Thomas (1996) 62–4; Thapar, *Death*; Courtright, in Hawley (ed.) 35–7.

whether it spread all over India simultaneously, or whether it spread in successive stages.[40]

On the other hand, the Sati stones establish beyond doubt that at the very latest since the end of the first millennium AD, and at least in some regions, widow burning was no longer an isolated upper-caste phenomenon. In various places real clusters of memorial stones have been found. In the middle of the eighteenth century, Hall counted several hundred such stones in the radius of one mile near the Narmada River in Central India;[41] some places, especially those near rivers, were regarded as particularly favourable for carrying out the ceremony. In addition, the cases occurred over a period of many years. Yet, at least in such regions, it must have been a relatively widespread phenomenon. At the funeral of rulers attendants seem to have been killed—or to have killed themselves—in large numbers. These were mainly women, but also men, and this is borne out by inscriptional evidence.[42]

After the turn of the millennium, widow burning also figures in historiography. In one of the most famous works, the Rājataraṅgiṇī by Kalhaṇa, a history of Kashmir written in 1148/49, a whole series of cases is mentioned for the tenth to the twelfth centuries.[43] They are not described in detail; rather it is assumed that the readers know what it is all about.

Even in fiction the number of widow burnings mentioned increases slowly, but continuously.[44] It is of course difficult to judge real events on the basis of fiction. If, however, other more reliable sources show

---

[40] Many authors believe that it spread from the north to the south, for example Altekar 126 ff; Gulati 121; Thompson, *Suttee* chap. 3; Winternitz, *Frau* 73–4. However there are early sources even for the south. References for example in Arunachalam. Cf. Bayly 174–5.

[41] Hall 191.

[42] Shastri 132–3 (upto 33 persons mentioned); Rao 236–7; Settar/Sontheimer 177 (upto 77); Weinberger-Thomas (1996) 26.

[43] Kalhaṇa 2, 56; 5, 226; 6, 107; 194–6; 7, 103; 447–81; 724–8; 852–62; 1380; 1484–94; 8, 365–9; 1440–4. Chattopadhyay analyses other authors of this period.

[44] References and overviews among others in Z. Ahmad 149; Altekar 121; Arunachalam (Tamil literature); Coomaraswamy, *Sati*; Coomaraswamy, *Siva* 82ff.; Jolly 67ff.; Kane 2, 1, 626; Schroeder 40–1; 431–4; Sprockhoff, *Indien* 421; Winternitz, *Frau* 62ff.; Sutherland.

the same trend, then fiction can at least be taken as a reinforcing circumstance.

On the other hand the religio-legal texts[45] ignored widow burning even long after the Rigveda had been written. At best there are vague and doubtful references.[46] This is all the more striking since the funeral rites, as well as the position of women and widows, are dealt with extensively.[47] In the most famous and most important book of law, the Manusmṛti, which was probably written between 200 BC and 100 AD, there are detailed passages about the widow who is advised to lead a completely ascetic life.[48]

The absence of widow burning in these texts therefore cannot be attributed to a lack of interest in the general problem. Rather, it is to be understood in the framework of social differentiation. The texts mainly contain instructions for priests, and, in a broader sense, for Brahmins. Accordingly, following into death was not meant for them and it was certainly not prescribed. In fact, as can be deduced from later evidence, it was possibly even forbidden.

[45] Fundamental for these are Kane, Derrett, *Dharmaśāstra* and Lingat. These texts are frequently dealt with extensively. But there has never been a systematic evaluation of the questions that are of interest here. Important overviews in Kane 2, 1, 625ff. and Altekar 117ff. Cf. also Bohlen 1, 293–6; P.N. Bose 2, 65ff.; Colebrooke, *Duties*; Colebrooke, *Digest* 567–80; V.N. Datta 3ff.; Gulati 107ff.; Hall; Jolly 67ff.; Kapadia 171ff.; Krishnamurthy; Lommel 382–8; Michaels, *Recht* 103ff.; Rao 220–32; Schroeder; A. Sharma *et al. Sati*; Shastri 118–35; Sprockhoff, *Indien* 421ff.; Sternbach; Thakur, *History* 128ff.; Ward, *View* 3, 308ff.; Winternitz, *Witwe*; Winternitz, *Frau* 57ff.; Zachariae 549–51; Weinberger-Thomas (1989) 11ff. Relevant editions: Derrett, *Anantarāma*; Leslie, *Wife*.

[46] The Atharvaveda 12, 3, 2 is mentioned most often in this context. For this see Winternitz, *Witwe* 195. Cf. Altekar 117–20; Thakur, *History* 133; Macdonnel/Keith 1, 488; Sarma 2; Upadhyaya 105; Weinberger-Thomas (1989) 11; Deshpande 25–7. Sutherland 1596–1601 deals with a much larger framework. In her work, however, widow burning is placed in the vicinity of (mostly non-ritualised) self-killing for various reasons, whereby the focus is on the preservation or the restoration of the sexual purity of the woman. Only in exceptional cases can one speak of following into death here.

[47] Cf. Altekar 116–17; Winternitz, *Frau* 57ff.; Sprockhoff, *Indien* 421–2; Weinberger-Thomas (1989) 11; Jolly 67.

[48] Manu 5, 156–62; 165–6.

This seems to have changed not long after the beginning of the Christian era. From then on even the Dharma texts talk occasionally of burning as a possibility open to widows. By and by such passages become more frequent and, simultaneously, burning is increasingly portrayed as a worthy, sometimes the sole true path for the really faithful and virtuous wife. The authors mention the rewards that the widow thus obtains in the hereafter for herself and her family. In the end, the custom is portrayed in glowing terms and strongly recommended. But it is never prescribed.[49]

The texts cease to evolve sometime in the first half of the second millennium seeming to settle upon a conclusion of sorts. Widow burning now occupied an important place, although sceptical and even negative opinions were never completely absent.

The course of these events indicates that the authors of the Dharma texts were following developments rather than paving the way for them. The custom had in fact existed long before it was even mentioned in the texts.

Europeans as Observers, 1500–1800

Between about 1500 and about 1800 no decisive changes seem to have occurred. In many regions of India, or, as the case may be, in some branches of Hinduism, the custom had become an established institution. The numerous and often very detailed and precise European accounts[50] of this period enable us to reconstruct the typical course of widow burning in all its details.[51] On the other hand they do not allow us to draw any quantitative conclusions.[52] The travellers were not in a position to make any reliable statements about the frequency of the

[49] Winternitz, *Frau* 61 says that 'in some of the more recent texts accompanying the husband in death' is portrayed 'almost as a duty'. However there is no clear proof of this.

[50] A complete bibliography of European sources has never been undertaken, and even less were they systematically compiled. A useful (although very select) bibliography in Weinberger-Thomas (1989) 44–6. The largest number of older travel accounts has been analysed by Zachariae, who however has often used only contemporary German translations. For European writings on Asia in this period cf. especially Lach.

[51] In exemplary fashion in Weinberger-Thomas (1989) 17–33.

[52] Altekar 133; P.N. Bose 2, 69–70; Weinberger-Thomas (1989) 17; Chidanandamurti, in Settar/Sontheimer 125–6.

burnings. Their remarks in this regard are often overinterpreted. If someone heard that a large number of burnings had occurred in a certain place, it does not necessarily mean that this was a permanent phenomenon, much less that the custom was not prevalent elsewhere. Statements about regions, which were supposedly strongholds of the custom, are often exaggerated. This is especially true of reports from the fifteenth to the seventeenth centuries about Central and South India, according to which hundreds, or even thousands, of women are supposed to have jumped into the fire on the death of a ruler.[53]

Western sources at least allow us to make one fairly definite quantitative statement. During the course of their stay in India an astonishingly large number of Europeans saw one or even several widow burnings. Since these are carried out within twenty-four hours of the husband's death the Europeans could hardly have undertaken any great journeys to witness such an event, which means that the ones they describe must have taken place in their immediate surroundings. Those who lived for a few months or even a year in a large city therefore stood a good chance of witnessing a widow burning. Along with the large number of memorial stones, inscriptions, and monuments this shows us that the custom, although it was not part of the daily experience of the people, was indeed firmly anchored in the collective experience. In many regions, most people witnessed such a ceremony in the course of their lives, or at least heard one eyewitness account of it.

The importance and the spread of widow burning in this period can also be seen from the fact that Indian traders abroad succeeded in carrying out the custom with the help of bribes or threats, in the face of opposition from local rulers. On 15 January 1671, a very rich Indian merchant died in Transcaucasia. By paying a large sum of money his brother received permission to cremate the body. He bought an old Christian female slave, who was tied down on the funeral pyre and burnt to death with the dead man.[54] This was not widow burning, but

[53] For example Conti 127 (2,000–3,000 on the death of the ruler of Vijayanagar); Dellon 111–12 (300–400 in Madurai); Nuniz 61 (500 in Vijayanagar); Vincenzo 344 (11, 000 in Madurai); Barbosa 109 (400–500 in Vijayanagar); Alvares, in Ramusio 1, 645–6 (200–300 in Vijayanagar); Baldaeus 188 (300 in Madurai). An Islamic author too speaks in 1628 of 700 victims in Madurai: Elliot/Dowson 7, 139. Cf. Altekar 131–2.

[54] Struys 265–6. The author claims to have been an eyewitness. Cf. Zachariae 552.

institutional following into death, which by no means corresponded to the Dharma texts.

A different kind of incident occurred in 1722, in Astrakhan, in Russia, where many rich Indian merchants lived in those days. When one of them died, his widow requested the Tsar (probably the local commander) for permission to burn herself with the body of her husband. Permission was denied on account of the 'barbarous' nature of the custom. On hearing this, the Indian merchants threatened to leave the city, and the Russian officials relented.[55]

Europeans as Participants, 1800–1829

As rulers over large parts of India (since 1757), the British at first tried to ignore widow burning. Then, from 1813 to 1829, they regulated it by making a distinction between legal and illegal cases. This required a survey of all planned burnings as early and as fully as possible, so that all illegal cases could be prevented. For a short period, this led to a unique situation in the history of the custom, which also produced a favourable situation with regard to sources: without being banned, the custom was observed and surveyed with the help of modern bureaucratic methods, which resulted in numerous compilations and statistics. For once, qualified statements about frequency, regional distribution, etc. became possible.

The first step towards a systematic registration of, as far as possible, all widow burnings within a certain region was taken by British Baptist missionaries, completely independent of the state and in some regards even secretly, because, till 1813, the East India Company did not tolerate any missionaries in areas under its control. These missionaries had therefore established themselves in Serampore near Calcutta, which was under Danish control.[56] In 1803 they entrusted ten Hindu informants with the task of registering all widow burnings that occurred within a radius of almost 50 kilometres (30 miles) around Calcutta over a period of six months. This was, of course, a fairly rudimentary method of compilation. Despite this, the results could not have been completely inaccurate. Each informant had to cover an area of almost 800 square kilometres. If he knew his way about, it is highly probable that he would have heard about each burning, even if it were only after it had occurred. The ceremonies did, after all, take place publicly, and

---

[55] Bruce 252–3.
[56] For the background cf. Fisch, *Pamphlet war* 24–5.

at this point the British administration was not trying to place any obstacles in their way. The missionaries and their informants were in no position to take any action against those participating in widow burning—rather the former ran the risk of being expelled. Therefore, there was no reason for secrecy, specially since the informants were not acting in any official capacity. Furthermore, as Hindus they could hardly be suspected of Christian propaganda.

Unfortunately, the results of this registration vary greatly in the sources. The lowest numbers are given by Claudius Buchanan. According to him, 275 cases were registered in 1803; between 15 April and 15 October 1804, there were 116 cases in a slightly larger area.[57] William Ward, one of the missionaries, speaks of 438 cases, in 1803, and of 200–300, in 1804.[58] The original material has not been produced till now. From this enumeration one only learns that the number of cases was high, and that in a small area there were at least 200 cases per year. This conclusion is confirmed by later statistics.

If one were to assume a similar frequency in the entire subcontinent, the numbers would be enormous. A maximum estimate on the basis of one area would have meant 100,000 cases per year. In the *Friend of India*, a missionary organ, this number was in fact mentioned in 1819.[59] However, this remained an exception. It was well known that the custom was particularly prevalent in Bengal, which was moreover very densely populated. Nevertheless it was occasionally said that there were many thousands of victims annually. William Wilberforce, for example, stated in 1813 in the House of Commons that in Bengal alone about 10,000 widows were burnt to death every year.[60] The highest estimate for all of India was 33,000 cases annually, of which 15,000 would have been in Bengal.[61] The mission press did not shy away from

[57] Buchanan, *Memoirs* (1812) 125–8.

[58] Ward, *View* 3, 329–30. Cf. Johns 26; Marshman 221–3; Mukhopadhyay, *Institution* 105; Natarajan 30; Potts 146; Robinson 113; Thompson, *Suttee* 60; V.N. Datta 74–5; 187–8; Wilberforce on 22 June 1813 in the House of Commons: *Parliamentary Debates* 26 (1813), 859. For the early period cf. also Yang 84.

[59] Cited from V.N. Datta 185. It could also be a mistake in copying out the figure (instead of 10,000). I did not have access to the original.

[60] Wilberforce 73.

[61] Grant 57. Grant assumed that all widows of Brahmins burnt themselves to death. Further details in: J.W. Cunningham 91 and Maistre 2, 358 (30,000 annually); J. Forbes 1, 284 (several thousand annually); V.N. Datta

tendentially demagogic statements, as, for example, in 1829, when it said that the custom had claimed over a million lives in Bengal alone.[62] Otherwise the missionaries were more cautious. In a work, which first appeared in 1811, Ward mentions at least 3,000 cases every year in all of India,[63] and 2,000 cases in 1821.[64]

However, as we can see from other regions, the calculation of such maximum estimates was inadmissible. The frequency varied enormously from region to region. Because of its limited radius the registration carried out by the missionaries could not take such differences into account. It was only a coincidence (because the missionaries were active in this region) that it was carried out in the area with the highest frequency in all of India.

Registration by the state began in 1815. It took in a much larger area, namely the entire Bengal Presidency. This included not only Bengal (now Bangladesh and the Indian state of West Bengal), but also most of what are today the states of Bihar, Orissa and parts of Uttar Pradesh. It contained 44 per cent of the total population of India (see Table 1).

The registration was organized centrally. Its efficiency has always been a matter of dispute. Some authors assume that the number of unreported cases was considerable, and that it was possibly higher than the number of registered cases.[65] Others presume that most of the cases

---

74; 78; 186–8; Buxton on 6 June 1825, in *Parliamentary Debates* 90 (1825), 1074: in five years 10,000; Johns 84: 5,000 per year; *Appeal* (1831): over 70,000 since 1756; G. Smith 285 (1885): at least 70,000 between 1757 and 1829. A. Mukherjee 283: According to Buchanan (1813) 19,000 every year in India.

[62] [*Friend of India*] NS 1, 366.

[63] Ward, *View* 3, 343. Cf. ibid. 1, CXX: several thousand every year.

[64] Ward, *Letters* 96. The Jesuit Dubois, an enemy of the Baptist missionaries, stated on the contrary in 1821 that south of the Krishna River in Central India with a population of 30 million, less than 30 widows burnt themselves to death every year. Dubois, *Letters* 106.

[65] Cf. V.N. Datta 35–6; 188–9; Weinberger-Thomas (1989) 14; Narasimhan 63. Many contemporaries were even more decidedly of this view, for example: *On the burning of Hindoo widows* 7; *Remarks on the immolations in India* (1821) 14. Ward was of the opinion that the actual figure was several times higher than the number registered: Ward, *View* 1, XXV; cf. ibid., 3, 29–30. Even Governor General Lord Hastings is said to have had

were actually registered.[66] In order to comment on this, we need to look more carefully at the method used.[67]

The unit for registration was the district, the lowest regional unit with a European official at the top. In Bengal, the so-called Lower Provinces, a district spanned, on an average, about 12,000 square kilometres and had a population of about 1.3 million.[68]

The entire police force (which was not very large, and which, except in the upper ranks, consisted entirely of Indians) and its auxiliary organs down to the last village watchman were obliged to report all relevant cases immediately. This could not be achieved overnight, and the figures indeed show an initial phase before the orders were enforced and all concerned had understood their task. Once this had been accomplished, it was difficult to imagine that such spectacular events would not be noticed by at least one of the persons obliged to report them. Did this person report everything that he saw or heard? The incentives, and the pressure to do so, were considerable. Those who did not carry out the orders were liable to be punished, and could even lose their job. Since the burnings were carried out publicly, one could count on the fact that another informant, whether belonging to the police or not, would report the case, thus discrediting the person who was actually obliged to do so. On the other hand, there was no similarly strong pressure not to report the case. This was especially true for the legal cases which constituted the greater part of the cases thanks to a generous official interpretation. The participants often reported the cases themselves although they were not obliged to do so. The advantage of this was that they received official permission, i.e. the guarantee that they could carry out the burning undisturbed. Concealment could, on the contrary, lead to subsequent investigations and punishments. The participants were, therefore, generally not interested in keeping the event secret. It was definitely different in cases involving force, which were illegal. To judge by the sources such cases were very

---

doubts about the figure: Bentinck's minute of 8 November 1829, in: Bentinck 1, 341.

[66] For example Peggs, *Suttee's Cry* (1828) 12.

[67] The most important sources for this are the *Parliamentary Papers,* which, along with the statistical details, also contain an abundant correspondence about the problems of implementation.

[68] Calculated on the basis of two estimates from 1822. D. Bhattacharya (1820–30), 71–2.

rare. However, this impression could well be a result of the secrecy surrounding them. On the other hand, these extreme cases were particularly spectacular, and it would have been difficult to ensure that no reports, or even rumours reached the authorities. Therefore it must be assumed that—either through bribes or pressure on the police and those helping them—the participants ensured that illegal cases were reported as legal ones.

These considerations suggest that after an initial phase the number of unreported cases was relatively low; at any rate, so low that it did not affect the validity of the statistics to any great extent, except possibly that the share of particularly violent and cruel cases was too low. An estimated unknown figure of 10–20 per cent would be rather high.

The results of the registration carried out between 1815 and 1828 are given in Table 2. On an average there were 581 cases every year.

Censuses were carried out for the whole of India only from 1872. For the Bengal Presidency, however, and especially for the Lower Provinces, there are relatively accurate population estimates for the second and third decades of the nineteenth century, which were partly based on house counts.[69] A problem arises regarding the group one would have to base oneself on when working out the frequency of the custom: only the Hindus or the total population? Here a calculation is first presented which refers only to the Hindu population. It is not only adopted by research, but was also often accepted by contemporaries. Since there are no reliable estimates for the ratio of the different religious communities to the total population, further calculations proceed on the basis of the population as a whole.

John Herbert Harington, a judge and a civil servant with long years of experience in different positions, in 1823 estimated the Hindu population in the Bengal Presidency to be about 50 million.[70] He assumed a death rate of 1:33, i.e. 30 per thousand of population, annually.[71] This meant that 1.5 million people would have died every year. Harington assumed that with every sixth death a wife became a widow.[72] Of the roughly 250,000 widows, therefore, one in 430 would

[69] Compiled in D. Bhattacharya. Cf. Tables 1 and 4.

[70] J.H. Harington, Memorandum of 28 June 1823, in PP 1825/24,11, §14.

[71] Such a rate roughly corresponds to pre-modern conditions as recorded for many other regions.

[72] Harington does not say how he arrives at this assumption. The available statistics do not enable us to calculate the ratio of cases, in which wives

have burned herself on an average for the years 1815–28. In 1818, the year with the highest frequency, it would have been one in 298.

Given the figures of about 2.3 (3.4) per thousand of all cases in which wives became widows, and of about 0.4 (0.6) per thousand of all cases of death, widow burning was statistically almost insignificant. Even in extreme cases it retained a marked exceptional character.[73] In the district with the highest number of immolations, Hooghly (see Table 3), with a population of 1, 239,150,[74] one in 43 widows killed herself, in 1818, the year in which the highest number of cases— 141—was registered. From 1815 to 1828, it was one in 66, on an average. Here, therefore, 23.3 (15.1) per thousand widows would have immolated themselves.[75] With respect to all cases of death it would have been 3.8 (2.5) per thousand deaths.

The frequency was even greater in the suburbs of Calcutta, although the absolute figures were lower here. With a population of 360,360 there were on an average 39 widow burnings per year; in 1819 there were 51. This meant that, between 1815 and 1828, one in 47, and, in 1819, one in 36 widows burnt to death (21.3 or 27.8 per thousand respectively). With respect to the total number of deaths, it was 3.6 (4.7) per thousand deaths.

These were extreme figures, even for Bengal, as Table 4 shows. In other parts of India such cases certainly did not occur. In addition, the figures for the districts with the highest frequency contain a significant

---

became widows, with respect to the total number of deaths, especially since this ratio can vary greatly according to the age structure and the marriage customs of the population. Presumably Harington based himself on his long experience of work in the districts.

[73] In the following figures for individual districts the population figures are based on an estimate of 1822 in D. Bhattacharya (1820–30), 71, which however deals only with the Lower Provinces and arrives at a figure of 37.2 million people. Ibid., 72 a further estimate from the same year, this time naming a figure of 39.7 million. The figures take the total population as the point of reference, not just the Hindu population.

[74] Estimate for 1822. D. Bhattacharya (1820–30), 71. Ibid., 72 another estimate for the same year: 1,540,250, which would mean that one of 55 widows immolated herself.

[75] Yang, in *Manushi* 27, arrives at a considerably lower rate for Hooghly, since he assumes a greater proportion of cases, in which wives became widows, within the total mortality figures. He presumes, however, that every adult man left a widow behind, which is not true even for India.

proportion of widows from other districts. The districts with the highest number of burnings all lay in the region of the lower Ganges. It was considered particularly meritorious and auspicious if the ceremony could be carried out on the banks of this river, so that many widows or entire families travelled long distances to gain these advantages.[76] As far as the suburbs of Calcutta are concerned, since widow burning was prohibited within the city, many people went to the surrounding areas.[77]

However, such an approach obviously does not do justice to the matter in hand. On the basis of the statistical insignificance of a phenomenon one cannot assume its social, political, cultural and religious insignificance. If today there are so few victims of terrorism that they do not appear in the death statistics, this does not mean that terrorism is insignificant for the collective consciousness and the collective experience. Widow burning was indeed significant for the collective experience. If one proceeds on the basis of the assumptions given above, in a city of about 100,000 inhabitants one widow burning took place every year. Even in a village with less than 5000 inhabitants one would have occurred every 20 years.[78] Obviously the people of a village also heard of similar events in neighbouring villages. In the course of their lives, therefore, they heard of several widow burnings that had taken place. A considerable number of people had been eyewitnesses, and everyone knew at least one eyewitness whose report he had heard. In the districts with a particularly high frequency the immolations practically constituted an omnipresent phenomenon that hardly anyone could avoid perceiving. In 1818 in the Hooghly district there was one widow burning to every 8,800 persons, and one widow burning to every 13,100 persons, on an average, for the years 1815–28; in the suburbs of Calcutta the corresponding figures were 7,100 (1819) and 9,200 (1815–28).

This statistical analysis corresponds with individual statements in

---

[76] Cf. different reports and comments by magistrates in IOR P/139/34, 482–8; 525–32; 537–54; V.N. Datta 198.

[77] The population of Calcutta was estimated in 1822 at 265,000–300,000. D. Bhattacharya (1820–30), 71–2.

[78] This calculation is not based on the 50 million Hindus assumed by Harington, but on the total estimated population of 57.5 million for the Presidency, since we are concerned with the relative importance of the custom in relation to all inhabitants.

the sources. Europeans who lived for some years in a medium-sized or large city sometimes witnessed several widow burnings.[79]

The regional differences were considerable. This can already be seen at the first administrative level below the Presidency, in the divisions (see Tables 2 and 4). The region around Calcutta, with 62.9 per cent of the cases, constituted the real focus. It was followed by the region of Benares, known as the centre of Hinduism and situated on the Ganges. Although Dacca and Murshidabad belonged to Bengal proper, the number of Muslims was larger here. The Bareilly division included the north-western regions. The differences are even more pronounced at the district level, as can be seen from Table 3 and Map 1.

The statistics show clear variations in frequency over a period of time. In recent times, they have been taken as a point of departure for far-reaching statements about long-term changes. The shocking figures led to the conclusion that around this time Bengal would have reached the highest score in widow burning in Indian history. Some authors speak, in fact, of an 'orgy',[80] a 'pathology'[81] or an 'epidemic'.[82] Various theories have been presented to explain this phenomenon. The content of their statements will be discussed later (see pp. 288–9). However, it must be recorded here that the phenomenon sought to be explained cannot be verified empirically.[83] One cannot derive a long-term trend from figures for 14 years, which moreover were recorded under special conditions. In view of the lack of comparable statistics for the period before 1815 and after 1828, it is absolutely impossible to determine whether at any earlier point of time widow burnings in the Bengal Presidency were more frequent or less frequent.

The Bombay and Madras governments never adopted the Bengal

---

[79] Moor 354–5; Ravesteyn 75; Parks 1, 93; Anon., review Heber 127.

[80] Nandy, *Tale* 170.

[81] Nandy, *Cultures* 264.

[82] Weinberger-Thomas (1989) 13; Weinberger-Thomas (1996) 260, footnote 1; Nandy, in Hawley (ed.) 139–41. Convinced of the increase are also Z. Ahmad 152; Dalmia-Lüderitz 49; Leslie, *Victim* 176; A. Mukherjee 241; R.K. Ray 3; Thakur, *History* 170; Thompson, *Suttee* 36; Das, *Gender* 66–9; Courtright, *Sati* 185 and, earlier, Wilberforce 73.

[83] Doubts about the validity of an assumption that there was a rise are expressed among others by Gupta/Gombrich 254; Altekar 138; S. Singh 21; Stutchbury 28; Yang 85. In 1984 Nandy, *Cultures* 264–5 blithely ignores the empirical problems and persists in his opinion, as also in 1987, in Anand 158, and in 1994, in Hawley (ed.) 139–41.

policy of official regulation.[84] As a result they also never created a comparable system for a survey of widow burnings. The personnel were not instructed in similar terms and were not required to be constantly watchful and to subsequently report cases. If, despite this, figures are available, we would have to take into account the fact that the number of unreported cases would have been significantly higher. In Madras, for example, all districts were required to supply figures for the years 1814–19. The answers show that these were often based on vague conjectures alone.[85] Other figures too were provided by district officials, who were generally unprepared when asked to send reports. Some had carefully observed such cases in the preceding years, others had not bothered to do so. Some wanted abolition as quickly as possible and therefore tended to dramatize and exaggerate, while others wanted to disavow the custom as far as possible and therefore understated the figures.

Despite these reservations the available information conveys the impression that the average frequency was significantly lower than in Bengal. Within each Presidency there were again enormous differences.

The results of the enquiry mentioned for the years 1814–19, which was carried out in 1819–20 in the *Madras* Presidency, are recorded in Table 5 and Map 2. Masulipatam and Chitoor are glaring examples of the fact that the information given is, in parts, grossly inaccurate (which the officials admitted). In Tanjore 17 cases were reported in 1820,[86] although nothing had been heard about widow burnings till then. The absolute figures are therefore definitely too low. At any rate there is a significant North–South divide with regard to frequency.

The data for *Bombay* is even more incomplete, since the government wanted to avoid any discussion of the problem as far as possible.[87] The custom was prevalent at least in the South Konkan district:

[84] For Bombay cf. Ballhatchet 275–305. For Madras a comprehensive account is not available.

[85] PP 1823/17, 69–132 (Compilation: 70–6). In PP 1825/24, 5–6 there are tables for Madras 1814–1821 and Bombay 1815–1823. It is the tabular arrangement with its numerous gaps, which shows us how unsatisfactory the methods were. Many district officials apparently did not send any reports.

[86] PP 1825/24, 5.

[87] In September 1819 however the officials were asked about the significance of widow burning in their districts. But no statistical enquiries were undertaken. PP 1821/18, 253–260.

with a population estimated at 640,875 in 1820/21,[88] 40 cases of widow burning were registered in 1819. In 1820, there were 66 cases. In the meantime, the methods of survey had, admittedly, been improved, which meant that the figure in 1819 would have been higher. For 1821 the information is missing; for the following years the figures reported are:[89]

1822: 47	1825: 32
1823: 38	1826: 28
1824: 27	1827: 27

Apart from this there are only some random references for the Bombay Presidency.[90]

For the *princely states*—under British supervision, but autonomous in internal affairs—even such rudimentary figures are lacking. The British did not want to interfere here, especially so long as their own policy with regard to abolition or a (limited) toleration was not clear. However there are sufficient indications to show that the custom was known in most of these states and was widespread in many of them. The credibility of the figures mentioned in the works of the nineteenth and twentieth centuries is greater, since they are no longer so high and so sweeping as earlier. Indeed, it is also possible that the figures actually fell: the local rulers lost a lot of their power in British times, and it was well known that the British despised widow burning. It was therefore considered advisable to place certain limits on the practice of the custom.

Between 1562 and 1843, a total of 227 persons are said to have been burnt to death at the funerals of 11 rulers in Marwar (Rajasthan). The number of victims in each case is given as being between 2 and 66.[91]

---

[88] Of these 5,97,150 were Hindus. D. Bhattacharya (1820–30) 130; 161.

[89] PP 1825/24, 155; 160; 205–8; PP 1826–27/20, 141; 158–9; PP 1830/28,269.

[90] Correspondence from the Bombay Presidency is to be found in PP 1821/18, 65–6; 245–68; PP 1823/17, 135–9; PP 1824/23, 46–9; PP 1825/24, 155–214; PP 1826–1827/20, 135–59; PP 1828/23, 24–8; PP 1830/28, 253–71. V.N. Datta 189–90 gives other figures for Madras and Bombay. However on the basis of the sources it is not possible to reconstruct how he arrives at these figures. Thompson (*Suttee* 68–9) clearly understates the case, when he says that between 1815 and 1820 there were less than 50 widow burnings every year in Madras and Bombay (it is also unclear whether both presidencies have been counted together or separately).

[91] V.N. Datta 256; Saxena, *Reforms*, Appendix.

In Bundi (Rajasthan) there were 237 satis in nine cases, with up to 75 immolations on the death of a ruler.[92] Large numbers of victims were also common among the Sikhs; once it is said—most probably exaggerated—that 310 women died.[93] When the Raja of Tanjore died in 1802, two women burnt themselves to death on his funeral pyre;[94] in 1808, in Kutch, 15 women;[95] in 1827, in Jaipur, apparently 18 women and 18 men;[96] in 1833, in Idar, 13 women and one man;[97] and, in 1838, in Udaipur, eight women,[98] to just quote a few figures.[99]

Despite all the uncertainties which have been shown, the average frequency of widow burnings in all of India was far lower than in the Lower Provinces of the Bengal Presidency, or even in the Calcutta Division. If one in 150 widows immolated herself in this division, the ratio for the entire Bengal Presidency was roughly 1:400, and, for India as a whole, perhaps between 1:800 and 1:1000.[100]

[92] V.N. Datta 164. For Bikaner cf. also Hervey 1, 216; 238–41.

[93] Griffin 64–7. Cf. Thompson, *Suttee* 96; Chopra.

[94] Mökern 329–31; Dubois, *Moeurs* 2, 29.

[95] Pakrasi 36; Peggs, *Suttee's Cry* (1828) 92.

[96] Thackeray/Richardson 197.

[97] *Asiatic Journal* NS 13/2 (1834), 258–9; A.K. Forbes 2, 201.

[98] Bushby 257.

[99] The funerals of rulers are mentioned very often in the sources and in the relevant literature. In greater detail: V.N. Datta, chap.6; Saxena, *Reforms* 62ff. (upto 68 victims); Mitter; Tod; Narasimhan 119–20.

[100] Most of the estimates, even the contemporary ones, more or less adhere to the given order of magnitude. This is also true for Rammohan Roy, the most active Indian opponent of the custom. In 1831 he believed that 'only one widow out of perhaps 30' immolated herself, while in the Upper Provinces it was one out of 999. Text in J.K. Majumdar 187. Taken over also by Dasgupta 4 and A.Mukherjee 246. In its justification of the abolition of 1829 to the Privy Council in 1831/32, the Court of Directors expressed the opinion that in Bengal itself at the most one of a hundred widows immolated herself, and that for the entire Presidency the ratio was 1:310. IOR L/L/ 13 (1030), vol. 3, 216v. Coomaraswamy, *Sati* 125 assumes a ratio for India as a whole of 1:1000. In the [*Friend of India*] N.S.1, 339 this frequency was considered already in 1829 as the highest. The *Asiatic Journal* 13 (1822), 455 gives estimates of 1:500 and 1:1000. Haafner's (a Dutch author's) assumption in 1808 of a ratio of 1:5000 is definitely too low. Altekar's estimates are very speculative and contradict each other. He first assumes that in the fifteenth to the nineteenth centuries one of every 50 widows became a Sati

Although widow burning was indeed mentioned or recommended in widely accepted texts, the marked regional or even local differences suggest that it was not so much the texts as local and regional customs, practices, and traditions, including particular family traditions, which were decisive when it came to actually carrying out the custom.[101] Yet we would have to talk of an Indian custom and not of a regionally limited custom. At this time, widow burning was not completely unknown in any of the large regions of India. It had a dual character: on the one hand through Hinduism it was situated in an all-India framework, and, on the other hand, its concrete shape was determined by special traditions and customs.

Widow Burning after Its Abolition in 1829

The aim of the policy of regulation and supervision was to effect an immediate reduction in the number of widow burnings and to bring a quick end to the custom. The failure of this policy led to the abolition of 1829/30 in British India. Widow burnings stopped almost overnight. However, now, instead of a frequent occurrence it became a rare one, but not a thing of the past,[102] not even after Indian independence in 1947. Newspapers still reported individual cases on a fairly regular basis.[103] The last known case occurred on 4 September 1987. In the early hours of this day 23-year old Maal Singh died in a hospital in Sikar, a district headquarters in Rajasthan. His body was immediately brought to Deorala, his native village. Barely six months earlier he had

---

(132). In warrior families in Rajasthan he estimates a ratio of 1:10, then among the general population of 1:1000 (no longer 1:50) (138). For Bombay and Madras his estimates are also 1:1000, for Bengal 1:500 (140). Cf. also Anon, review Heber 136; Bayly 174.

[101] Also emphasised by Mani, *Production* 36.

[102] For the early period there are numerous accounts in the *Asiatic Journal*, New Series (NS). See also Bentinck 2, 869–70; 915–16; IOR L/L/13 (1030), vol. 2, 192–211; J.K. Majumdar 169–70; 179–82; P.N. Bose 2, 82–3; K. Datta 122–6; A. Jackson 119–20; Newnham 122–8; Pearce; Robinson 131–2; Thompson, *Suttee* 117–26. For a more detailed description see below pp. 432–6 and 446–50.

[103] For the period after 1947 cf. for example Anand 164–70; V.N. Datta 203; 229–31; Jacobson 133; Narasimhan 6–7; Sangari/Vaid; Vaid/Sangari; S. Singh 81ff.; Thakur, *History* 178–80; Weinberger-Thomas (1996).

married 18-year old Roop Kanwar from Jaipur, the capital of Rajasthan. The couple had lived together for less than a month, since Maal Singh used to work in Jaipur, 60 kilometres away. As soon as news of his death reached Deorala, Roop Kanwar, a girl with 10 years of schooling behind her, announced her intention to accompany her husband in death. The body was cremated in the early afternoon of the same day, and Roop Kanwar burnt to death with it, according to some with a divine smile on a radiant countenance, according to others after she had been thrown into the fire by force. The pyre was set alight by her youngest brother-in-law, 15 years old. Thousands of onlookers followed the proceedings. The police arrived only after the ceremony was over.[104]

This event led to a heated public debate between opponents and supporters of widow burning, and the law banning the custom was tightened.[105] It remains to be seen whether this will actually make the custom disappear. At any rate, confident statements like the one made by Thakur in 1963, that the custom 'is as good as dead',[106] are not heard any more.

It is not possible to give any reliable information about the frequency of the custom for the period after 1829. One would merely have to assume that the number of cases decreased to a fraction of the numbers during 1815–28. Even if all the relevant sources, especially police, court, and administration files, as well as press reports were available, a direct comparison with the statistics for 1815–28 would still not be possible. The framework for a statistical survey had changed. Every immolation was now illegal, and by participating in it one risked punishment. All those who thought of conducting such a ceremony had to try and hide it from official eyes. On the other hand, widow burning without public participation was even less an option

---

[104] The event has been described very often. Cf. for example the survey in *Trial by Fire*; in addition Tully, chap. 7; Anand; Jain *et al.*; Kishwar/Vanita; Kumar 172–81; Leslie, *Victim* 180–3; Mani, *Mediations* 33–5; *Manushi*; Narasimhan, chap.1; Patel/Kumar; Qadeer/Hasan; *Sati and the State*; Upreti 46–63; *Seminar*; Vaid/Sangari; van den Bosch 174ff. A bibliography of the first reactions in *Seminar* 49–52. Numerous press accounts in Anand 81–188.
[105] *The Commission of Sati (Prevention) Act,* 1987. See below pp. 453–7.
[106] Thakur, *History* 180.

than before. Since these events now occurred very seldom, they also had the function of propagating the underlying concept—keeping the tradition alive amongst as many people as possible. As a result, the pressure (to suppress information) on those obliged to report these cases increased. Among the lower levels of the police force, the fear of sanctions on the part of the people, together with material factors in the form of bribes was probably much stronger than the fear of the actions of the employers. In addition, since a large majority of the Indian police force, including high-ranking officers, did not regard widow burning as a crime, but as a meritorious act, their conscience ordered them to remain silent and not to act against the custom. This is valid even today.[107]

One would therefore have to reckon with a high number of un-reported cases. Yet it could hardly be many times higher than the known figure, because at least the spread of rumours could very seldom be prevented. Especially since 1947 such rumours were quickly taken up by a watchful press. Although the police could be prevailed upon to appear late on the scene, and possible witnesses could be pressurized not to say anything that would incriminate the guilty—the fact that an immolation had taken place could not be erased, especially if a temple was erected later.

The figures that are sometimes mentioned (only for the period since 1947) are merely assumptions. According to Vaid and Sangari there were altogether 40 cases since 1947 in Uttar Pradesh, Madhya Pradesh, Maharashtra and Rajasthan, of which 28 were in Rajasthan alone.[108] Such figures and similar ones[109] would be too low. In 1987, an organization that rejected the prohibition and was therefore interested in

---

[107] I am basing myself on observations and discussions in the districts of Sikar and Jhunjhunu (Rajasthan) as well as in Banda (Uttar Pradesh) in autumn 1992 and spring 1995. This fact is also repeatedly mentioned in the relevant literature. Cf. for example Subramaniam, in Anand 164–70; S. Singh 81–7.

[108] Vaid/Sangari 16, footnote 1.

[109] Cf. for example Narasimhan 73: around 30 cases in Rajasthan; Weinberger-Thomas (1989) 14: at least 40 cases since 1979 in Uttar Pradesh, Madhya Pradesh, Bihar and Rajasthan; Weinberger-Thomas (1996) 180: 1943–1987 according to official statements (without naming the source) 28 cases in Rajasthan; ibid., 101: at least 40 cases in India since 1947. *Trial by*

making the matter appear as harmless as possible spoke of 28 cases since 1947.[110] An inspection on the spot in autumn 1992 in a part of the Shekhawati region in Rajasthan showed that at least eight burnings had been carried out between 1954 and 1980 in a range of about 40 kilometres,[111] after which temples had been built in honour of the victims. The police prevented at least one immolation.[112] Naturally it is just as difficult to make an estimate for the entire country on the basis of these figures, as was the case with the figures supplied by the missionaries in 1803/04. Yet one can assume that after abolition several widow burnings took place annually in the whole country.

On the other hand, every statement about an increase or a decrease over a period of time remains speculative. Sometimes it is maintained that the last 10–20 years have seen an increase of the custom in India.[113] It is possible that it is the attention attracted by the custom that has increased, and that the practice, itself, has maintained a constant level.

In statistical terms this means that the custom has become completely insignificant. Now it is no longer one widow in several hundred who burns herself to death, but one in ten thousand, hundred thousand, or, even, a million widows. Since 1829, widow burning has

---

fire: since 1947 38 cases in Rajasthan; elsewhere in this unpaginated text: 22 cases; Tully 224: 28 immolations in Sikar and two other districts since 1947; Upreti 38: 41 cases in Rajasthan since 1947. Sources for these figures are not mentioned anywhere.

[110] Cited by Sangari, in *Seminar* 26. Sangari does not say which region this figure refers to. It is probably related to Rajasthan.

[111] Madho ka Bas (1954); Narsingpuri (1967); Govindpura (1972); Golana (1973); Kotadi (1973); Maonda Kalan (1974/75); Hathideh (1978); Jharli (1980). In addition there is Deorala (1987), where the building of a temple was banned. It cannot be established with any certainty whether the increase in the 1970s can be traced back to a higher frequency, or to the building of more temples, while the frequency remained the same. The effort required to collect reliable information about earlier widow burnings in places without temples or other monuments is not justified by the possible results. Van den Bosch 188, footnote 10, quotes an anti-Sati organization, according to which 40 cases are said to have occurred since 1947 in the Shekhawati region. For general aspects also Weinberger-Thomas (1996).

[112] Devipura (1985).

[113] For example Rajan, *Women* 17.

ceased to be a part of the general experience. However, it is still part of the public consciousness. The frequency is hardly important, so long as the custom does not disappear completely. An isolated immolation simply assumes a greater importance.

CHAPTER 12

Anatomy of a Custom

The Accompanied and the Attendants: Between Institutional and Individual Following into Death

In the form in which it has generally become known, widow burning in India embodies the classical form of individual following into death: in all social strata only husbands are accompanied, while the circle of attendants is limited to widows. The deceased is not accompanied on account of his social position, but on account of his gender.

What is not generally known is the fact that in many regions of India till well beyond the middle of the nineteenth century special forms of following into death were practiced when rulers died. Wives and concubines of the dead ruler, and in isolated cases even members of the princely household immolated themselves, sometimes in large numbers.[1] This was a ruler's privilege and a demonstration of his power—and it was therefore a case of institutional following into death.

As far as can be seen, from an early period onwards the custom in India moves between these two poles. What is important here is, that in all its manifestations it is—to a far greater extent than anywhere else—the killing or self-killing of widows.

Diodorus and the Rigveda

Diodorus' description shows a typical form of institutional following into death in which the circle of the privileged is limited to the ruling class. Ceteus was definitely not the only Indian who died in the Battle

[1] Perhaps the most well-known, and at any rate the best-documented case is the cremation of Ranjit Singh, ruler of the Sikhs, in 1839. Four wives and seven concubines burnt themselves to death on this occasion. The accounts of at least two European eyewitnesses are available: Honigberger 110–13 and Steinbach 17–19. For Indian sources see V.N. Datta 157–8; 179–80. Further contemporary sources are *Asiatic Journal* NS 30/2 (1839), 91–4;

of Gabiene. If other burnings—of the widows of his subordinates—had taken place, or if the Indian soldiers had asked Eumenes for permission to carry them out, and had received a negative response, then Didodorus' informant would have most probably mentioned this as a spectacular element. Despite this institutional character no further categories of attendants were apparently used. Even concubines are not mentioned, let alone a retinue. In India itself there were probably similar conditions around this time. We can hardly assume that the retinue of an army commander, far away from home, therefore not under strong pressure from outside, would allow their leader a privilege which was not his by right.

In the passage from the Rigveda (10, 18, 8), in which the widow lies down next to the corpse on the funeral pyre and then gets up again, the decisive classificatory criterion is gender, not one's position in the social hierarchy. Of course, the elaborate ceremonies described in the Veda could only be carried out by a small section of the wealthy and privileged. The other groups, however, were not expressly excluded from it. Rules were not laid down for the conduct of a spouse from the ruling class on the death of the partner. Rather it is the duty of the widow on the death of her husband that is regulated, and social position is not a consideration. Also, it is the duty of the widow and not of the widower. The deciding factor is gender.

The Development of the Custom, 300 BC to AD 1500

The case described by Diodorus would have us believe that widow burning in Alexander's time was an upper-class phenomenon. However, Diodorus himself maintains that there is a general law in India according to which widows—thus not only those from the upper class—had to burn themselves to death.[2]

The history of the influence of this passage in Western sources is particularly important. Classical Greek and Roman authors speak generally of Indian widows who burn themselves. This tradition continues in the Middle Ages and well into modern times. Although we cannot draw any definite conclusions from such vague formulations,

---

Griffin 64-67; Thorburn 20–1; Eden 309–10; Hügel 4, 809–11; Orlich, *Reise* 103; Osborne 224–5; Prinsep/Thornton 2, 166–7.

[2] Diodorus 19, 33.

we can assume that gradually the very small circle of those entitled to being followed into death was expanded. This is indicated, at any rate, by the earliest eyewitness account that has been directly handed down. Ibn Baṭṭūṭa does not give any details about the social position of the husbands of the three widows whose immolation he witnessed around 1340. From the context it emerges that they were warriors. If they had been of high rank, the author would probably have mentioned it. One can infer from this that the custom had become prevalent among warriors and occurred even among the middle ranks of the military. With reference to the other burnings he witnessed, Ibn Baṭṭūṭa emphasizes that each of the ceremonies was very elaborate. This leads us to assume that they occurred mainly among the wealthy.[3]

Other Western sources that mention only burnings on the death of rulers, sometimes with a large number of victims, give the impression that it was a distinct custom of rulers. Conti recounts that in the fifteenth century, in Vijayanagar, in southern India, 2000–3000 widows would jump into the fire on such occasions.[4] It is striking that even at such mass burnings—whose figures are certainly exaggerated—categories of victims other than women and concubines are hardly ever mentioned. But other authors, and sometimes also the same authors in other contexts, mention a custom in the Middle Ages that has a stronger institutional character: on the death of the ruler, members of the retinue who had long before committed themselves to this step, jump into the fire.[5]

Indian sources stress slightly different aspects, but they do not contradict the foreign accounts.

The early inscriptions would have to be read as evidence of widow burning as an upper-class phenomenon. To favour individuals with such a memorial was rare and, therefore, a privilege, whereas the spread and frequency of sati-stones later could be taken as evidence for the gradual expansion of the custom into other strata of society.

In fiction and historiography, on the other hand, widow burnings appear only among gods and the upper class, mainly in princely families. We cannot conclude from this that they did not occur in other

---

[3] Ibn Baṭṭūṭa 3, 614–16.

[4] Conti 127. Further details in chap. 11, footnote 53.

[5] For example Marco Polo (ed. Benedetto) 180, chap. 175 (for Malabar). For further instances see above, pp. 224–5.

circles, too, as sources deal almost exclusively with leading political, religious and cultural groups. When a ruler died, frequently several
of his wives and concubines killed themselves. In addition, female
and male servants, as well as more important members of the princely
household sometimes jumped into the fire.[6] However, there is neither
an inordinate increase in the number of victims nor an expansion of
the circle from which the victims are taken.

Central to an understanding of the specificity of following into
death in India are the religio-legal texts which mention widow burning
from the first half of the first millennium AD. The most important
distinguishing criterion for all recommendations and rules pertaining
to the custom in these texts is gender and not social standing. Social
distinctions, mainly with regard to caste, are certainly made. But they
are clearly subordinate to the gender-specific stipulations of rights and
duties. In this way following into death acquires—of course only in the
normative sphere—a completely individual character. With the exception of the Brahmins, it is recommended to all widows independent
of their social, and especially their caste position; the accompanied can
only be husbands, and the attendants only wives.

Why did following into death become an object of religious pres-
criptions? And why did these emphasize the individual component so
strongly?

Widow burning in its beginning was not an invention of priests and
scholars. Rather these had to deal with an established custom, and, as
far as can be gathered from the texts, the reaction of the priests and
scholars was late and hesitant.[7] Once begun, they intervened actively
in the events by not just approving the existing practice, but by laying
down recommendations and rules. This was in accordance with the
unusually high religious, ritual and social status of the priestly caste
which stood above the warrior and ruling caste in these matters, even
if it was dependent on the latter with regard to the external means of
power.[8] This led to a rivalry.[9] If priests and warriors had constituted

---

[6] Cf. for example the descriptions in Kalhaṇa 5, 226; 7, 481; 724; 1486;
8, 365–9. References to inscriptions among others in Rao 232ff.; Shastri
131ff.; Weinberger-Thomas (1996) 26.

[7] Cf. for example Jolly 69; Kane 2, 1, 627; Winternitz, *Frau* 55.

[8] Cf. Dumont 96–109.

[9] Cf. Gonda 1, 299; Oldenburg, in Hawley (ed.) 165.

a homogeneous upper class, or if the priests had been clearly subordinate to the warriors, then religious learning would probably not have pervaded the idea and custom of widow burning, and the custom would simply have continued as an upper class practice. Here, however, it became the object of a power struggle. The Brahmins, the caste that provided the priests, and to which the authors of the relevant texts belonged, originally not only left off practising the custom, but also rejected it. At any rate, we know from later times that Brahmin women were forbidden from immolating themselves. The Brahmins would have been too weak to achieve a complete ban in all castes. They would have had to ban a custom, which, although it did not bestow much religious prestige, did go very far in bestowing other types of prestige on their rivals. Instead of prohibiting following of the dead they gave it a stronger religious foundation in the texts, and they permitted, indeed recommended it, in the form of widow burning, to all castes, and even to those without caste, the untouchables.[10] The more the religious character of the custom came to be emphasized, the less the warrior caste could claim it as their own and maintain their monopoly over it. The only way out for them, if they wanted to avoid a direct conflict with the priestly caste, was to carry out the rituals in a particularly conspicuous and elaborate manner with many victims, in order to distinguish themselves from the other castes at least in this regard. A further hindrance was presented by the texts which restricted following into death to only the burning of widows. This could only be ignored in places where the warrior caste was in a position of strength.

Although permission for widow burning was extended to all castes, the ban for the Brahmins themselves was not lifted.[11] In good enlightened tradition some authors have inferred that the selfish Brahmins spared themselves the terrible fate they imposed on others.[12] But this interpretation does not hold. The Brahmins did not spare themselves, but their wives. In the bargain, they deprived themselves of a possible privilege, of an opportunity to win social prestige and demonstrate their power. One would therefore have to ascribe altruism,

[10] PP 1821/18, 123: legal opinion of Mritunjay Vidyalankar, pandit at the High Court in Calcutta (1817); Sontheimer, in Settar/Sontheimer 97; Kane 2, 1, 631; Weinberger-Thomas (1996) 257, footnote 6; Yang 89.

[11] The relevant literature frequently refers to this, for example Kane 2, 1, 627; Leslie, *Victim* 188; Rao 230; Altekar 129; Lommel 383–4; Gulati 126ff.; B.N. Sharma 67.

[12] For example by Narasimhan 20; S. Singh 46.

not egoism to them. Another assumption appears to be more plausible. The Brahmins hadn't invented widow burning; they had only reacted to it. They had not tried to spread it, but to take the monopoly over it away from their rivals. In the process, however, they had provided it with increasing religious prestige, along with its existing worldly prestige. They now became victims of their own actions. Brahmins increasingly started ignoring the ban and practising the custom in order to gain from its religious prestige. Reality overtook the norm again. The ban was never lifted formally, but merely restricted. It was interpreted to mean that only *anumaraṇa*, i.e. burning after the husband had been cremated, remained forbidden to Brahmin women.[13] Even this restriction was not always followed, as later British surveys showed.[14] In many regions, widow burning finally became a distinctly Brahmin custom (see pp. 258–9). Some European authors in fact stated that it was obligatory for Brahmin widows, and them alone.[15]

A further piece of evidence suggests that widow burning was not an invention of the priestly class. The authors of the Dharma texts not only laid down rules for carrying out the custom, they also ensured minimal protection for potential victims. They tried to prevent cases that were sure not to be voluntary from the outset, as well as those that had serious consequences for others. Immolation was not permitted if the widow was too young, if she was pregnant, and if she had small children, the last, however, only in so far as there was no one else to take the responsibility for their care. In passing it must also be mentioned that women were forbidden from immolating themselves if they were menstruating. But this stricture was only valid till three days after the end of menstruation, and sprang undoubtedly less from concern for the possible victims than from reasons of ritual purity.[16]

---

[13] For the gradual acceptance of the custom by the Brahmins see Altekar 129; Gulati 126ff.; Kane 2,1, 630; Leslie, *Victim* 188; Rao 230; A.Sharma *et al.*, *Sati* 25–8; B.N. Sharma 67; Stein, *Women* 253; Thakur, *History* 141. Texts in Colebrooke, *Digest* 2, 574.

[14] The detailed annual compilations for 1815–1828 in the *Parliamentary Papers* contain many cases, in which Brahmin women committed *anumaraṇa*. See also Heber 1, 267. In his well-known legal opinion of c. 1817 Mrityunjay Vidyalankar says that in exceptional cases even *anumaraṇa* is allowed. PP 1821/18, 120. For the early period Chattopadhyay 397.

[15] Mandelslo, *Reyse-Beschreibung* 117; Challe 294; Degrandpré 68.

[16] The British heard of these restrictions in consequence of various questions put to Hindu pandits between 1805 and 1817. PP 1821/18, 26–43;

There is a further reason for the growing importance of the individual component of following into death as compared to the institutional component. Since the late twelfth century large parts of India had been ruled at least at times by foreign conquerors—first Islamic and later European—who not only did not practise following into death, but also abhorred the practice. Therefore its monopolization through the new ruling class was excluded from the beginning. This would have helped the spread of the custom among the middle and even lower classes. Once this had happened, even if a Hindu ruler won the region back, the development could hardly be retracted since it meant that a widely prevalent custom would be forbidden to the people, while it would be practised by the ruling class (now again Hindus). In this respect, therefore, foreign rule helped to spread the custom, inasmuch as it did not take any measures against it.

The Phase of European Observation, 1500–1800

In European eyewitness accounts written between 1500 and 1800 there are hardly any descriptions of funerals of rulers,[17] whereas accounts based on hearsay abound[18] and show a marked tendency to exaggerate the number of victims.[19] Europeans probably stayed more often in regions under Islamic rulers than in those under Hindu rulers. Yet on the basis of these findings one can conclude that elaborate funerals with large numbers of victims were extremely rare. In the other cases witnessed by Europeans, the dead persons came from different social strata. Often, they were merchants, a class that the Europeans dealt with mainly. Brahmins were at least as numerous. The

---

112–44. In Nepal a law of 1854 laid down far more detailed rules. Michaels, *Legislation* 1226–35. See also chap. 14, pp. 371–4.

[17] Only Tavernier can be said—with some degree of certainty—to have been an eyewitness. Around the middle of the seventeenth century he describes the funeral of a Rajah of Velou with 11 women accompanying him in death, as well as that of two Rajahs in Agra, with 13 women all together. On at least one occasion he claims to have been an eyewitness. Both descriptions contain few details. Tavernier 2, 389–91.

[18] For example Rogerius 74: 60 victims on the death of a warrior; Bowrey 39: 27 women and concubines in Mylapore (Madras); Valle 4, 76; Burnell 108.

[19] For instances see chap.11, footnote 53.

majority of the dead had been well-to-do or rich. However, widows of the poor and lower castes also burned themselves.[20]

When not recording their own observations, but making general statements, the European regularly emphasized that the custom was essentially or even exclusively an upper-class or an upper-caste phenomenon.[21] Sometimes they thought that the lower castes had only recently started to practise it.[22] Such statements could not have been based only on the personal experiences of authors. Rather, they would have reflected views that were widely prevalent in India and that were also partly normative. When taken together with the simultaneous eyewitness accounts they strengthen the assumption of a gradual expansion of the custom to all sections of the population. Reality had already overtaken the norm.

The Bureaucratic Registration, 1800–1829

While inferences and assumptions for the early period are only possible on the basis of scattered and more or less random statements, the years 1815–28, at least for the Bengal Presidency, can be statistically assessed and substantiated fairly precisely on the basis of British surveys. The results of this period then also allow us—with due caution—to arrive at conclusions for earlier periods.

From the beginning, the magistrates had to report the wife's age, and the names and the caste of the couple. From 1822 onwards the husband's profession, as well as his income and wealth, also formed part of the survey.[23] Many officials also recorded the number of children, although they were not required to do this. The details are, however, not always complete and possibly not always correct. The data, as a rule, was not gathered by British magistrates, but by subordinate Indian police officers in the field, and the people questioned would often have given information that they thought was expected from them. In addition, there were mistakes of transmission. A case came to

[20] For example Modave 172; Withington 219; Methwold 28–9.
[21] For example Linschoten 18–19; Monserrate 61; Pyrard de Laval 1, 419; Saar 124; Wurffbain 2, 17–18; Varthema 195; Santos 2, 312; Manucci 3, 65; Nunes 47; Dapper 54.
[22] For example Paolino 63 (1, 1, 5)
[23] 15 August 1822 resolution of the Governor General in Council. PP 1824/23, 43.

light of a widow who was registered in the published *Parliamentary Papers* as four years old, which the supporters of abolition used as proof for the cruelty of the system. It was probably just an error in copying.[24] Although these weaknesses are clearly apparent they are not so serious as to call into question the statistical findings of the surveys. From their results it is evident that the division of roles between the sexes is absolute. A woman is never accompanied in death, and a man is never among the attendants.

The survey gives us fairly reliable statistical information on at least five points.[25]

1. In almost all the cases *age* is recorded.[26] The results are listed in Table 6. Admittedly, we are dealing with approximate data which is apparent in the fact that round figures clearly dominate in the age statistics. The officials who gathered the information were therefore aware of the problem. But the mistakes and errors would have balanced each other out since there was no reason for either the family members or the police to make the widow appear any older or younger than she really was. There was one exception. Burning was forbidden to widows under sixteen. This led to the wish to make younger victims appear older. From time to time this was definitely done. But the method naturally had its limits. An eight-year old girl could hardly be made into a sixteen-year old. In view of the relatively small number of satis under twenty the statistical importance of such cases is almost negligible.

A comprehensive evaluation of the results is not possible due to the lack of comparative figures, mainly those concerning the average age

[24] PP 1823/17,45. In 1821 even a two-year old sati was mentioned (13 August 1821 Gazipur district; PP 1823/17,29), and according to PP 1830/28,152 on 13 October 1826 a five-year old widow immolated herself in the Hooghly district.

[25] Unless otherwise mentioned the following information has been obtained from the detailed annual statements in the *Parliamentary Papers* (for 1827 and 1828), or in IOR P/139/34 (see Table 4). The only accurate evaluation of the files undertaken till now is in B.B. Roy 37–80 and 145–208. But Roy limits himself to Bengal 1815-1827 and deals with 5,388 cases. Within this framework, however, the analysis is more detailed than here, but only with regard to regional distribution, caste, age and economic position. The evaluation in Yang 84–91 is far more cursory.

[26] See B.B. Roy 48–9; 167–9.

of widowhood for women. The question therefore, whether younger or older widows immolated themselves more frequently, cannot be answered. Yet it is clear that there were no large deviations from the average. Widow burning was not a phenomenon that was predominantly or even exclusively restricted to a particular age group. Life expectancy was low. The considerable age difference between husband and wife lowered the age of widowhood for women even further. It is therefore not remarkable that a highpoint was reached among the 20–60 year olds, with a peak between 40 and 50. At the most one could assume that the 20–30 year olds were overrepresented, possibly also the 17 or 18 to the 20-year olds.

2. Information about the *number of children* was never a requirement. Despite this, various magistrates supplied the information. Table 7 includes most of the reports.

Here, too, comparative figures are missing for a more precise evaluation of the data, especially those with regard to the average number of children per woman or per widow. Yet a few important results can be noted. The average number of children per sati was 2.28.[27] This was much lower than the average number of children that a woman gave birth to if one takes the high infant and child mortality into consideration. On the other hand the population growth during this period was negligible, which meant that per woman only a little more than two children reached adulthood. The age of the children of satis is seldom mentioned. Yet, from the age of the mothers it follows that all age groups were represented, from infants to older persons. If one took the average of all Indian women, then the number of surviving children per woman at a particular point of time would definitely have been a little more than 2.28. But the difference would not have been very great. That would mean that childless widows burned themselves or were burned more frequently than widows with children. This phenomenon is entirely plausible. The social and economic position of childless widows was particularly bad, their dependence on their husband's family particularly great (see chap. 13). However, one should

[27] K. Datta 79–82 gives the number of children (without mentioning their sex) of 67 satis in Bengal in 1812. On an average it came to 2.66 children for every woman. Johns 37–41 gives statistics of burnings in the vicinity of Serampore in the first half of 1812. There were 185 children of 70 satis, therefore 2.64 per widow.

not attach too much importance to such factors. Table 7 clearly shows that it was not predominantly or even exclusively childless widows who immolated themselves. In particular, the importance of protection by the children should not be overestimated. This becomes apparent when we look at the average number of daughters and sons. A sati had 1.22 sons for every daughter. In Indian society a son offered more protection than a daughter. Therefore widows with sons would have burned themselves less frequently than those without sons, though in reality it was just the opposite. From this one cannot draw the opposite conclusion that sons drove their mothers into death. These factors probably did not play a very important role on the whole.

3. *Caste* was always mentioned (the main caste, as well as the sub-caste). Here the evaluation presents some difficulties. The division into sub-castes varies greatly from region to region. This makes a comparison difficult, and categorization according to main caste groups is also a problem. Taking the entire Bengal Presidency into consideration would require an immense effort. B.B. Roy, however, has carried out this work for Bengal proper for the period 1815–27.[28] Using his findings, only the percentage of Brahmins, which is easier to determine, has been calculated for the entire Presidency and for the whole period (1815–28). They constitute 37.8 per cent of 8,132 cases. For Bengal proper, for the period between 1815 and 1827 (5,388 cases), the figure is 38.4 per cent.[29] The difference between the Upper and the Lower Provinces in this regard was therefore very small, i.e. the percentage of Brahmins was fairly constant. This can also be seen in an official statement which for once calculated the caste-wise distribution for 1823. In this year the percentage of Brahmins in the entire Presidency was 40.7 per cent (of 575 cases).[30] This clearly indicated an over-representation of Brahmins who constituted about 5–10 per cent of the entire population.[31] They had therefore not only taken over a custom that they had originally rejected, but had made it into their own favoured

[28] B.B. Roy 36–48; 148–66.
[29] B.B. Roy 148.
[30] PP 1825/24, 153.
[31] Cf. J.M. Datta 439–40. According to the census of 1931 6.4 per cent of Hindus in all of India were Brahmins: Killingley 10. In 1881 the corresponding figures were 6.1 per cent in Bengal and 7.3 per cent in all of India. *Census of India* 1881, 240–1.

domain, although the prohibition of *anumaraṇa*, which did not apply to the other castes, still existed for Brahmins.

The second main caste, the Kshatriyas, were responsible for 14.8 per cent of widow burnings in Bengal; in 1823, the corresponding figure was only 6.1 per cent in the entire Presidency. However, the first figure, which is based on a larger selection, would be more representative. The third main caste, the Vaishyas, accounted for 3.9 per cent of satis in Bengal; in 1823, the corresponding figure for the Presidency was 2.4 per cent.[32] The Kshatriyas were therefore also over-represented, the Vaisyas on the other hand under-represented.[33]

The percentage that fell to the fourth main caste, the Shudras, as well as to those without caste, was therefore 42.9 per cent, in Bengal proper, and 50.8 per cent, in 1823, in the entire Presidency. This clearly meant that they were under-represented. But it indicated that the custom did not occur only among the three main upper castes. It also strengthens the assumption that the custom gradually extended from the upper to the lower castes.

4. Similarly, widow burning was not limited to the rich. This can be seen from the information given on the *status of income and wealth*, although these figures have a limited interpretative value. They vary from district to district and are often compiled rather carelessly. Any attempt at formulating more precise statistics would be inappropriate. The general impression, on the other hand, is clear. One finds the entire spectrum from immense wealth to utter poverty. All professions are represented.[34] But the wealthy are clearly over-represented.

5. Finally, the survey also gives us information on the *number of victims per death*. The findings here are clear. Of 8132 widows whose immolation was registered between 1815 and 1828, 8004, i.e. 98.4 per cent mounted the funeral pyre alone. Only 128, i.e. 1.6 per cent, burnt to death along with one or several other widows of the same husband. In 52 cases there were two women, in four cases three, and finally on three occasions there were four widows all of the same husband.

[32] B.B. Roy 148; PP 1825/24,153.

[33] According to the *Census of India* 1881, 240–1, the Kshatriyas constituted 3.1 per cent of the Hindu population in 1881. In all of India the figure was 3.8 per cent.

[34] A detailed classification of 2, 124 cases in B.B. Roy 61–80; 170–209.

However, we must remember that these findings are not valid for all of India, since in areas under British control there were no cremations of rulers, which in other places still demanded large numbers of victims.[35] But even in the princely states their statistical significance would have been negligible. The measure of attention that these extreme cases attracted far outweighed their quantitative importance. This can be seen in the case of Bengal in another context. The so-called Kulin Brahmins often had many wives. Isolated cases have been handed down in which women burned themselves in large numbers when such a man died. The accounts are quite plausible. On the other hand, the survey for the period 1815–28 does not register a single case with more than four victims. One can hardly suppose that a spectacular event like a mass immolation escaped the notice of British officials. Therefore we can only conclude that such events occurred very rarely, far more infrequently in fact than the numerous references and descriptions would have us believe.

Widow Burning since 1829

The abolition of 1829/30 in the areas directly administered by the British had a strange result. With respect to India as a whole, the number of widow burnings outside the ruling class was drastically reduced. In the princely states, on the other hand, nothing really changed at first. Most of the rulers were Hindus, and in many Hindu states following into death was customary when rulers died. The percentage of such cases therefore, again taking India as a whole, sharply increased, while the percentage of burnings in the middle and lower classes decreased. Thus for the first time the abolition led in a decisive way to the relative strengthening of institutional following into death as opposed to individual following into death.[36]

At the funerals of rulers both wives and concubines were burnt to death. Other categories of victims are not mentioned. In 1839, however, at the funeral of the Sikh ruler, Ranjit Singh, his Prime Minister Dhyan Singh wanted to jump into the fire, 'but the welfare of the

[35] One of the three registered cases with four victims actually occurred in connection with the funeral of the semi-autonomous Rajah of Cuttack on 28 September 1827.

[36] An overview of funerals of rulers between 1829 and 1862 in V.N. Datta, chap. 6; Saxena, *Reforms* 86–143; Thompson, *Suttee*, chap. 8. See also pp. 242 above and 439–44 below.

country depending at that time solely on him, he was prevented from undergoing this terrific ceremony,' as Ranjit Singh's personal physician, a German, reports.[37] Thompson is convinced that Dhyan Singh feigned the entire scene, that he had in fact never intended to kill himself.[38] This sounds plausible because a male attendant would have, at the time, gone completely against tradition.

After the ban was extended to the princely states, the conditions changed again. In view of the British abhorrence of the custom it would have been politically unwise and also very risky to carry out widow burnings at funerals of rulers. Consequently, this did not occur any more. Yet the custom did not disappear completely. Burnings were most likely to occur in rural areas, which were difficult to control, and principally among members of the middle and the lower classes. This was true even after Independence.[39]

This marks the end of a tendency in India, apparent from the beginning, to move away from institutional following into death to its individual form. Since the end of the campaign for its abolition around 1862, and very likely much before that, widow burning has become virtually the only form of individual following into death in India. However, it still remains to be shown that on another level it has, in equal measures, maintained and partly gained a marked political character.

Summary

In conclusion, the different categories of people involved must be looked at systematically.

1. Among the *attendants*, widows clearly dominate. Following into death in India is first and foremost the killing or the self-killing of widows. Normally one can assume a close personal relationship between the attendant and the person being accompanied. However this was not a necessary pre-condition. Rather, the roles of the persons involved were decisive. This can be seen from the fact that sometimes wives who had scarcely known their husbands went to their death,[40] but even more from the fact that time and again women burned

---

[37] Honigberger 1, 97. Cf. Steinbach 19.

[38] Thompson, *Suttee* 94–5.

[39] Cf. for example Vaid/Sangari; Anand 164–70; V.N. Datta 203; 229–31; S. Singh 81ff.

[40] Especially wives of Kulin Brahmins: see below, p. 266.

themselves on the death of a fiancé, although they had either never seen him, or at best only briefly.[41] The objective criterion of an (intended) marital bond, not the subjective individual attitude, was the decisive factor.

Occasionally, the sources also name other attendants who had a particularly close connection to the dead person, generally in the framework of a family relationship. Mostly it is the case of mothers killing themselves with the body of their sons. Some authors are of the view that this, in a way, is the prototype and the highest form of sati.[42] Although this is often mentioned in general terms,[43] precise descriptions of concrete cases are very rare;[44] in eyewitness accounts they are never mentioned. From 1815 to 1828 the British registered merely two such cases.[45] As only self-immolation of widows was legal,[46] it must have made family members talk of widows, even when the victim had a different relationship to the dead person. Had such cases been widespread, they would not have remained completely secret. It is possible that they occurred more frequently in earlier times, before the custom acquired its final form as widow burning. Such cases are testified to both in monuments[47] and in early Indian historiography.[48]

[41] PP 1830/28; 190; J.K. Majumdar 112; *Burning of a . . . Bride* 119; *Asiatic Journal* 9 (1820), 71; Chidanandamurti, in Settar/Sontheimer 121–2; 129; Altekar 136; Harlan 141; S. Singh 21; Mukhopadhyay, *Institution* 103.

[42] Weinberger-Thomas (1989) 28; Weinberger-Thomas (1996) 132–3; Saxena, *Reforms* 57.

[43] References in: Crooke 1, 188; D'Gruyther; Malcolm 206; Modi 423; I. Mukherjee 132; Mukhopadhyay, *Institution* 103; Narasimhan 112; S. Singh 29; Saxena, *Reforms*, Appendix; B.N. Sharma 66; Stein, *Women* 254; Thompson, *Suttee* 37; Winternitz, *Frau* 68; PP 1826–1827/20; 41.

[44] A case registered by the police in 1843 is described in *Measures* 128–9. Bishnoi 83 identified four cases in Rajasthan between 1842 and 1845, in which Brahmin women burned themselves with their son's body. See also Postans 75.

[45] PP 1825/24,70 (Ghazipur no. 42); PP 1830/28,203 (28 September1826 Ghazipur; probably not a ritualized case).

[46] The case of 28 September 1826 (see previous footnote) came before a court.

[47] References in D'Gruyther and in Arunachalam 70.

[48] For example Kalhaṇa 7, 1380.

In addition, the self-killing of sisters on the death of a brother, of grandmothers on the death of a grandson, and of daughters-in-law on the death of the father-in-law are mentioned.[49]

In some cases, along with the widow additional attendants were killed who did not have a particularly close relationship with the dead person. Here mainly female and male servants and slaves are mentioned, but also high officials and ministers, most of whom were members of the princely household.[50] As far as these categories are concerned, it is even clearer that their importance diminishes in the course of time. They are mentioned occasionally in inscriptions and monuments and in early Indian historiography.[51] Under non-Hindu rulers, on the other hand, such practices would scarcely have been prevalent, and there are only a few vague accounts of it, even for Hindu states in the eighteenth and nineteenth centuries.[52] In the cases handed down there are always one or several wives and concubines burnt to death along with the other victims.

As far as the relationship between the sexes is concerned, only widows and concubines accompanied their husbands; never widowers their wives or concubines. Even in cases of close, personal family relationships, the attendants were apparently always women. Although in 1843 the British registered a case in which a grandfather accompanied his grandson in death,[53] there does not seem to have been any elaborate

[49] Sister with brother: PP 1825/24,80 (1822 in Saran district). Regarding the same case: *On the burning of Hindoo widows* 7; *Papers* (1868) 256–7. Cf. also Mukhopadhyay, *Institution* 103; S. Singh 29; B.N. Sharma 66; Stein, *Women* 254; Arunachalam 70.

Other relatives: for example Kalhaṇa 7, 103; 1486 (daughters-in-law); Altekar 127; Gulati 114; Rao 232ff.; S. Singh 29–30; Sontheimer, in Settar/ Sontheimer 84.

[50] V.N. Datta 9; Altekar 127; Jolly 68; Kane 2, 1, 630; Krishnasvami 129–30; Mukhopadhyay, *Institution* 103; 111; Rao 232ff.; Swaminathan 11; Settar/Sontheimer 126; 196–7; Sontheimer 274; Thakur, *Self-immolation* 118–23; Thakur, *History* 46; Winternitz, *Frau* 83–4; Balbi 83; Burnell 108; Dellon 1, 112; Wurffbain 18.

[51] Historiography: Kalhaṇa 5, 226; 7, 481; 724; 1486. Inscriptions and monuments: Rao 235; Shastri 131ff.; Hervey 1, 216.

[52] Postans 72–4; Orlich, *Indien* 2, 2, 235; Saxena, *Reforms*, Appendix; Thackeray/Richardson 197.

[53] *Measures* 129.

ritual associated with this case. One would therefore have to speak of a transition to common suicide.

In the context of institutional following into death, on the other hand, men are often mentioned: servants, slaves, ministers, members of the retinue in general, but also friends.[54] Probably the proportion of their percentage in the total figure went down to the extent to which the individual form established itself. In later times, at any rate, such cases were extremely rare. An enumeration of following into death at eleven funerals of rulers in the Kingdom of Marwar in Rajasthan in the years 1562–1847 arrives at 222 females and five males.[55]

2. The conditions among the *accompanied persons* are clearer and more uniform. From the point of view of the social position it was originally probably exclusively, or at least predominantly, a case of members of the ruling group.[56] Their monopoly was increasingly breached, not least as a result of rivalries between the priestly and the warrior caste, till the custom finally established itself at all levels of society.

In this process the deciding criterion too changed from social position to gender. There is no reliable proof that any woman in her role as a wife was accompanied by her husband.[57] This completely one-sided relationship between the sexes is generally true for the custom in its individual form. Even when other persons close to the dead, mostly relatives, function as attendants, the person accompanied is never a woman: the mother never accompanies her daughter instead of her son, for example, nor does the sister ever accompany her sister, instead of her brother.

The stronger the institutional character of the custom, the greater the probability that at one time even women were accompanied. Early

[54] See footnote 50.

[55] Saxena, *Reforms*, Appendix; V.N. Datta 256.

[56] Cf. Sontheimer in Settar/Sontheimer 279; Thakur, *History* 137ff.

[57] Arunachalam 100 speaks of such a case in 1964 in Bilaspur. However this generally uncritical article does not mention any further details. The reference cannot function as a counter-evidence. The basis for the author's statement was probably a non-ritualized suicide. It is also typical that Mandeville (2, 327), notorious for his lack of credibility, states that some-times widowers immolated themselves with their wife's body. Similarly vague: Ovington 201; Orlich, *Indien* 2, 2, 235; Narasimhan 112; Weinberger-Thomas (1996) 242, footnote 84.

sources sometimes mention a queen or a highly-placed woman being accompanied in death by a retinue comprising both sexes.[58] However, there is not a single concrete description, and such accounts are completely missing from the sixteenth to the nineteenth centuries.[59] Already in the first half of the fifteenth century Pero Tafur expressed the 'logic' of the system in unambiguous terms: 'If the man dies first the woman has to burn herself, in the same way as the heathen burn bodies. But if the woman dies first the man does not have to burn himself, for they say that woman was made for the service of man, but not man for the woman; and if the principal should perish, the accessory is not worthy even of mention.'[60]

The Time of Killing

The relevant texts recommended or laid down that the widow burn herself along with her husband's body on the same funeral pyre.[61] In India cremation traditionally takes place within twenty-four hours of death.

In this respect, reality coincided with the norm. In most cases widow burning occurred at the latest on the day after the husband's death, generally on the same day.[62] In no other region of the world was following into death carried out so quickly. The ceremony was meant

[58] D'Gruyther 45; Rao 237–9; Saxena, *Reforms* 57; Krishnasvami 129; Swaminathan 11.

[59] The only exception is Postans 72–4, who, in 1839, tells us how long before, on the death of the mother of the Rao of Kutch, an old female servant had herself buried alive.

[60] Tafur 90. The author says that he has taken this passage from Conti, in whose book, however, this statement is not to be found.

[61] Compiled among others in: Colebrooke, *Digest* 2, 567–74 and Colebrooke, *Duties.*

[62] In earlier times a postponement was probably granted more easily. Various sources indicate this; however the statements they make are vague and partly also contradictory. According to Fedrici 36 the immolation is often delayed by 1–3 months on the widow's request. Guichard 388; 391 and Franck ccix talk of a delay of upto 15 days, without giving any further proof. Holwell, who was an eyewitness several times, first states (2, 88) that the widow could not take a decision till 24 hours after her husband's death. A few pages later (2, 93) on the other hand he says that the wife must make up her mind immediately. Manucci 3, 65 also gets entangled in contradictions when he explains that the widow has three days to decide; in case of a refusal however

to bind the wife as closely as possible to her husband and to ensure that the separation caused by death was overcome as soon as possible. This intention is expressed particularly well in the fact that the sati is not considered or treated as a widow, but as a wife.

All other aspects were subordinated to overcoming the separation of the couple as soon as possible. A tendency to extend following into death into a long drawn-out process is not evident anywhere. The idea of an enduring connection between this world and the other does not play an obvious role. After a proper cremation, the dead have no influence on the events of this world. They do not have to be propitiated through continuous efforts; they cease posing any danger.[63] Messengers do not need to be sent after them to keep them abreast of events in this world, although this element is sometimes found as occasionally family members or even bystanders are said to have given the widow messages for the dead.[64] The widow could, for example, promise her son to tell his father that he had been brave.[65] Sometimes she was given letters and gifts.[66]

Even where following into death had a stronger institutional character there were no basic deviations from this pattern. The funerals of rulers with a larger number of victims were also carried out within 24 hours. In Bengal the Kulin Brahmins, as mentioned earlier, had several wives. The wives lived with their families scattered throughout the country. When such a Brahmin died, sometimes a number of his wives killed themselves. Ward tells of a case, in 1799, in which a Brahmin who had more than a hundred wives died near Nadia. His funeral pyre burnt for three days. During this time, 37 of his widows jumped into the fire.[67] It did not occur to anyone to conduct a large elaborate ceremony for such immolations as in Bali, for example.

---

she is coerced, in which case one cannot speak of a decision any more. Castanheda 1, 243 and Fenicio 179 write that only poor widows were burnt with their husband's body, rich ones were immolated a few days later.

[63] The blessing and the curse of the sati are indeed said to be very powerful. However, the widow utters both before her death. After that she can be called on for help from this world, but she does not act on her own. A detailed discussion in Harlan 112–81. For sources see below p. 277, footnotes 106–9.

[64] Ibn Baṭṭūṭa 3, 615; Stavorinus 2, 48; Tafur 91.

[65] Latif 518 (1843 in Punjab).

[66] Careri 3, 139; Tavernier 2, 387.

[67] Ward, *View* 3, 317. Further cases: ibid., 314–18; Robinson 113; 123;

Yet, all widow burnings did not occur immediately after the husband's death. The texts also provided for a second form, *anumarana*, the death of a widow by burning after her husband's cremation with an article that had belonged to him. These cases were clearly a minority, but they happened from time to time.[68] Sometimes many years had passed since the husband's death. In 1827 a widow in the district of Shahabad went to her death forty-eight years after her husband had died.[69] On 11 August 1820 a 45-year old woman, whose husband had died thirty-five years ago, burnt herself to death.[70] An 80-year old woman who wanted to immolate herself twenty-five years after her husband's death was prevented from doing so in 1822 in Ghazipur district.[71] In 1819 a 72-year old widow decided to become a sati seventeen years after her husband's death.[72] Repeatedly, cases were reported in which the burning occurred ten to sixteen years later.[73] Here the reference to the dead husband could often just be the means to endow a suicide, which was committed for other reasons, with greater sanctity. At any rate, the reasons given were apparently accepted by society.

Normally, the time frame even with *anumarana* was much shorter. The reasons for choosing this form were mostly of a practical nature. If the husband died in a place far away from his wife it was generally not possible to bring his body home. He was cremated at the place of death, often even before his wife received news of his death. And once this was received then widow burning normally occurred within 24 hours. This custom sometimes had tragic consequences, when, for example, the news of death subsequently proved to be false.[74] In addition the custom could be misused by hostile relatives or neighbours

---

Johns 37; 41; 59; *Appeal* 35–6; K. Datta 78; cf. V.N. Datta 197. Ward's reports have been frequently quoted.

[68] The *Parliamentary Papers* frequently note whether it is a case of *sahamarana* or *anumarana*. From this one gets the impression that in perhaps between one fourth and one third of the cases the burning of the widow was carried out only subsequently, with large regional differences in frequency.

[69] 8 August 1829, comments of the Nizamat Adalat. IOR P/139/34, 197.

[70] PP 1823/17,47.

[71] 11 April 1822. PP 1823/17,70.

[72] 28 February 1819. PP 1823/17, 21. Cf. PP 1821/18,95 for an immolation which is said to have happened 32 years later.

[73] Cf. Yang, in *Manushi* 28–9.

[74] A case of 1788 is described in *Papers* (1868) 223, another in Sleeman 27–8.

spreading rumours about the husband's death, who then returned after his wife had burnt to death, but such a case has not been attested to with any degree of certainty. In yet another case a woman declared that she had seen the spirit of her absent husband and burnt herself to death.[75]

The second combination of factors that led to *anumaraṇa* arose when the widow did not fulfil the conditions for an immolation at the point of time when her husband died, i.e. if she had her monthly period, if she was pregnant, or if she had small children. Although these restrictions were not always strictly observed and women with infants[76] or even pregnant women burnt themselves or were burnt to death,[77] they often led to a postponement—up to the third day after menstruation, till the birth of the child, till the infant had been weaned, or till the child grew up. It is not possible to determine how often the decision taken at the time of the husband's death was subsequently abandoned. It is most likely to have happened when the initial sorrow had passed. Isolated cases have been handed down.[78] *Anumaraṇa* did not constitute an extension, a more elaborate form of widow burning, but merely a poor substitute for the same. This lower status expressed itself most clearly in the fact that it remained forbidden to Brahmin women, members of the highest caste.

As will be shown in the next section, in individual cases widows were buried alive. Here, too, the ceremony occurred just as soon after the husband's death as the burning.

The Manner of Killing

Nowhere else does a single manner of killing dominate in the way widow burning does in India. Norm and reality coincide completely with one another in this case. The Dharma texts speak only of burning. There was one specific and rare exception—burial alive—(yet to be

[75] Around 1823. PP 1830/28, 12–14.

[76] For example Ravesteyn 73: 3 months; Twist 33: 4 months; Pelsaert 330: 1 year; PP 1825/24, 15: 6 days; IOR L/L/13 (1030), vol. 2, 209: 6 weeks.

[77] A.K. Forbes 2, 206; Weinberger-Thomas (1989) 27. Accounts about attempted self-immolations by pregnant women that were prevented are far more frequent, which shows that this was not really accepted by society. See for example *Asiatic Journal* 16 (1823), 345; Tod 2,58; Ray 129.

[78] For example *Essays* 23–4.

discussed) which is mentioned at least by the descriptive texts. In special situations, however, when the burning could not be carried out 'properly', especially when the victim resisted, other means were used. Cases have been recorded in which the victim was killed with a sword or another weapon after she had jumped off the pyre several times.[79] In some cases, a woman who had escaped to a nearby river was drowned in it.[80] As a rule, widows who were caught after an attempted escape were thrown back into the fire.

It was mainly regional differences that manifested themselves in the execution of the burning. Social, religious, caste and material differences, were apparent mainly in the expenditure: in the quality of material used for the funeral pyre, in the number and the importance of the participating priests, in the number of musicians, in the splendour of the clothes, in the value of the gifts distributed to the people present, etc. Regionally at least three forms can be distinguished, with manifold variations and combinations in practice.[81]

1. The best-known and the most prevalent form was found in large parts of northern India. A funeral pyre was set up as in a normal cremation, consisting of wood, to which were added flammable materials like brushwood, resin and oil, and precious essences. The use of clarified butter was customary. The widow sat down on the funeral pyre and laid her husband's body on her lap. According to the rules of the ritual it was the task of the eldest son to light the pyre. This was generally followed. If the widow did not have any sons, this task was usually carried out by another family member; sometimes it could also be an outsider or a priest. In this form it is rarely mentioned that the widow

---

[79] The most famous case took place on 20 November 1820; PP 1821/ 18,54. Description in PP 1823/17, 67–8 (see below, pp. 306–7). Cf. also Johns 43 (1813); PP 1828/23, 3–17 (1823). The records frequently mention similar cases.

[80] For example Thackeray/Richardson 63–4 (1825); *Emperor vs. Vidyasagar Pande* 500 (1927; prevented by the police).

[81] Similar classifications were also undertaken by early European observers, most clearly by Tavernier 2, 385–8, and also by Dapper 56–7; Careri 3, 231–2; Geleynssen de Jong 86; Thevenot 5, 255–6; Schouten 2, 99–100; *Breve relação* 20 (chap. 19). Cf. also Ahuja 81; S. Chaudhury, *Society* 42ff.; Saxena, *Reforms* 64–5; Winternitz, *Frau* 73–4; Thompson, *Suttee* 39–43; PP 1823/17,93. The most accurate description is in Weinberger-Thomas (1989) 29–30.

lit the fire herself.[82] In order to prevent her from escaping, she was often tied to the corpse, or big pieces of wood were placed on top of her, or else she was held down with long bamboo rods.

2. A variation and further development of this form was used mainly in Central India. Here, too, a normal funeral pyre was set up. On this a kind of small hut or sometimes a canopy of wood, straw and other flammable material was built. The widow sat down inside the hut and laid the corpse on her lap. The entrance to the hut was then closed and generally barricaded with large logs of wood, making escape impossible. A substantial amount of wood was placed on the roof of the hut, while the pillars that supported this roof were very weak. They tended to collapse immediately after the fire was lit and the victim was thus buried under the wood that had been placed on the roof. Often the roof would be brought down with the help of ropes tied to the pillars. However, things didn't always work out as planned. The construction sometimes held out longer, or only one side collapsed next to the widow, so that she could escape.[83]

In this form it was not unusual for the widow to light the fire herself. It was easier in this case, since there was flammable material above her. She held a lighted brand in her hand and set the roof on fire. On the whole, such cases seem to have been exceptions. They were particularly appreciated and admired by the onlookers. The event came very close to the ideal, in which the enormous virtue and strength of the widow made it possible to produce fire from within herself without any external help. Through this her *sat* became evident. After all, the Sati of the legend had produced the fire, in which she burnt, out of herself. That this was the ideal to aspire to could also be seen from the fact that with the passing of time the statements made by the participants increasingly tended to replace natural sources of fire with supernatural ones. This is valid even today. In autumn 1992 and in spring 1995 I visited the districts of Sikar and Jhunjhunu in Rajasthan, where a number of widow burnings had taken place since 1954. The further back in time the events lay, the more the witnesses—whether actual or alleged—emphasized that the fire broke out 'automatically', although

---

[82] For example in PP 1830/28, 189; *Asiatic Journal* 22 (1826), 441; Drummond 38; Postans 68; Parks 1, 91; Bunsen, *Briefe* 673.

[83] A case of 1804: *Interesting facts* 115; *Remarks* 20–1; Poynder 180–2.

in most cases it was known that a clearly identifiable person had carried out the task.

The enormous prestige associated with this kind of ignition could lead to attempts to help the matter along. At least one case gained legal notoriety. On 22 November 1927, a widow in the village of Barh in Bihar sat down on the funeral pyre with her husband's body on her lap. Her left hand was hidden in her clothes. A moment later flames broke out from her clothes. The judges were convinced that a mechanism to light the fire was hidden in the folds of her clothes, but it is not clear whether the widow knew about it or not. At any rate, she did not behave as expected, but jumped down, badly injured, before the pyre caught fire and tried to save herself. The organizers were caught in a dilemma. The mechanism did not allow for a repetition of the trick. If the woman had been thrown back onto the pyre, and the fire had been ignited externally, the deception would have been all-too evident. The persons responsible for this therefore tried to throw her to the crocodiles, and, when this was not successful, they tried to drown her, when the police appeared on the scene at the last minute. The victim succumbed to her injuries three days later.[84]

3. In the third form, chiefly used in South India, but sometimes also in the North, a pit was dug. It was then filled with materials used for a normal funeral pyre. The corpse was placed on it, and the fire was lit. The widow was separated from the pit by a curtain or a kind of folding screen. When the fire was blazing, and when the husband's corpse had already burnt, the curtain was drawn aside and the widow jumped into the fire, or was thrown into it. The bystanders immediately tossed wood and other flammable materials onto the victim. Often large blocks of wood were also thrown over her.[85]

For most people death by fire, with its associated images, is undoubtedly the most horrible manner of death. This is characteristic for notions of the hereafter in religions which envision a place of punishment and damnation in which fire plays a prominent role. The tortures of hell are almost always the tortures of fire.

---

[84] *Emperor vs. Vidyasagar Pande* 497–500; Hirst 2–12; Lovett 314. On self-ignition in general Weinberger-Thomas (1996) 135–7.

[85] For this form of immolation see for example Ibn Baṭṭūta 3, 615–16; Fedrici 38–9; Haafner 89–92; Rogerius 77; *Chronica* 76–7.

This assessment does have a basis in reality. During the course of one's life everyone burns themselves lightly. This is very painful. The thought of experiencing such pain in an intensified form all over, when it already seems unbearable on a small part of the body, is what gives death by burning its special character.

It appears that in the case of Indian widow burning there was a discrepancy between the notions of the uninvolved persons and the actual course of the burning. If one goes by the most reliable and most detailed accounts, especially those written by eyewitnesses with medical knowledge, then one gets the impression that the death throes usually did not last very long. The time between the first flaring up of the fire and the death of the victim is only a few minutes.[86] Qualified observers agree that death almost always occurred due to suffocation and not due to burning.[87] Mandelslo described it in less scientific terms in the seventeenth century. He saw how the widow sat down on the funeral pyre and how the fire was lit, 'and how without a cry or a sign of suffering she was killed in a split second as if struck by lightning.'[88]

These details are by no means an attempt to trivialize the process. But it is important to see that the moral condemnation of the custom in Europe was based primarily on general ideas about death by fire, and less on knowledge of the actual process. An anonymous author stated in 1827: 'Much of the horror of the sacrifice itself is the effect of the imagination of the spectators, which has no foundation in reality.'[89] The difference in comparison to other forms of death or killing was smaller than popular imagination believed it to be. One would even have to proceed from the fact that many of these forms involved a

---

[86] Almost immediately: PP 1826–1827/20, 147 (1825 in Poona). Less than a minute: *Asiatic Journal* 17 (1824), 665; PP 1826–1827/20, 145–6; Lawrence, in Edwardes/Merivale 37 (1845 in Nepal). About 1 1/2 minutes: PP 1826–1827/20,152. The person reporting, Robertson, wanted to make the suffering last as long as possible, as a deterrent, (see below, p. 274) and therefore would definitely not have mentioned a very short time. Less than 3 minutes: IOR L/L/13 (1030), vol. 3, 159; Bunsen, *Witwenverbrennung* 460. A few minutes: *Asiatic Journal* 18 (1824), 316; Honigberger 113; Kennedy 50. The two last named authors were doctors.

[87] For example *Asiatic Journal* 17 (1824), 665; Kennedy 50; PP 1826–1827/20, 145–6.

[88] Mandelslo, *Reyse-Beschreibung* 81 (book 1, chap. 23).

[89] *Asiatic Journal* 24 (1827), 406.

longer period of suffering. These few minutes, however, would have been horrible for the victim. Many women, who till the moment the fire was lit, had displayed the most amazing steadfastness, determination and composure, and had insisted on dying, were suddenly seized by the desire to live and tried, often already half-burnt, to save themselves. On the other hand, many widows remained unflinching and firm in the flames.

Even when the voluntary nature of the act is doubtful, it does not automatically follow that sadism was the motivating factor. The manner of killing was prescribed. But within this framework there was an attempt to reduce the victim's suffering. It is never reported, for example, that a woman was consciously roasted on a small fire, as did happen in Europe when heretics and witches were burnt alive, or also in the torture of prisoners in America. Rather, one tried to rake the fire as much as possible. As soon as the person designated had ritually lighted it, people came from all sides to light a large number of small fires, so that the funeral pyre burst into flames at once. Yet there were shocking and agonizing scenes. These were not intended, but a result of poverty or unfavourable circumstances. Bad weather could make it difficult to carry out the burning—generally one did not dare to postpone it. Some families also did not have the means to erect a sufficiently large pyre or to buy an adequate quantity of flammable material. It could then happen that the widow was singed all over, and succumbed to her burns only hours or even days later.[90]

Yet the problem of inflicted pain remained virulent in Indian society and could be seen in the efforts to suppress it. The *sat*, the special power that enables the widow to become a sati, has the effect, according to popular view, of making her immune to pain and not letting her feel the flames at all.[91] This could, of course, be based on the experience that with the help of Yoga or autosuggestion it is possible to achieve a relative immunity to pain.[92] But it was undeniable to any, that extreme pain was being inflicted on someone.

Making the victim suffer, on the other hand, even if it was but a consequence of good intentions, only occurred under British rule. All

[90] Cf. for example the accounts in Johns 28; 36 and *An old inhabitant* 487. Bowrey 40 is not clear.

[91] Rajan, *Women* 20; Vaid/Sangari 6; Weinberger-Thomas (1989) 28; Haafner 83; Postans 69.

[92] Emphasized by Bunsen, *Witwenverbrennung* 460.

officials found the custom horrible, and they were united in their desire to abolish it. But many of them were afraid that abolition could lead to disturbances and opposition and thus to an end of British power in India. Therefore, they initially looked for less radical possibilities of intervention.

In 1823 a particularly brutal widow burning took place in Poona, in the Bombay Presidency. The district officer, Robertson, called some pandits for a discussion on the question of the use of violence. The debate ended inconclusively. Robertson had the Hindu-texts enquired into and came to the conclusion that the burning was only allowed on a pyre which burnt slowly to make escape possible. By prolonging the suffering he hoped to achieve a stronger deterring effect, and also counted on the widow's fear of the shame of bringing the ceremony to a premature end. The pandits accepted the suggestion to allow only such funeral pyres, as did Robertson's superiors, although with some reservations, in Poona, Bombay and London. In individual districts the British now began to experiment with the new policy. After some initial success the results were disappointing. One or two widows actually abandoned their resolve after they had seen the new pyre. The majority, however, did not allow it to affect themselves, whether out of a sense of heroism or because they felt that they could not resist the pressure of family members. On 6 June 1825 Robertson first witnessed a burning which was carried out according to his regulations: 'The conduct of this extraordinary old woman when preparing for death was characterized by the most determined bravery and coolness.' She refused to be deterred. To Robertson's horror the funeral pyre burst into flames at once, and the woman was dead in less than one and a half minutes—his calculations proved to be completely wrong. He decided to construct a pyre the next time which would burn much more slowly, in order to frighten and turn away prospective victims.[93]

[93] 7 October 1825 Robertson to Chaplin. PP 1826–1827/20, 152–3. The sources for the entire proceedings: PP 1825/24, 163–9; 184; 190–214; PP 1826–1827/20, 135–53; PP 1828/23, 27–8; PP 1830/28, 253–8; 263; IOR F/4/920, no. 25884, 154–9. Summary in Ballhatchet 284–90. Cf. V.N. Datta 56–7 and Weinberger-Thomas (1996) 200–5. An anonymous author made a similar demand in Bengal in 1826: *An old inhabitant* 482–7; *Asiatic Journal* 28 (1829), 149. In this Presidency J.J. Harvey, the magistrate of the district Nugwan, arbitrarily (and illegally) laid down rules in 1828 similar to those propagated by Robertson. According to his own statements he had

Why was this manner of dying or killing chosen in India? The idea was to bind the wife as closely as possible to the husband. Given that burning of the dead was almost certainly an older custom than widow burning, this binding together of man and wife was sought through a joint funeral, an act soon formalized. Therefore, as long as burning of the dead continued, widow burning was the logical outcome of following into death.

The only notable exception to the rule of burning serves to confirm that the chief concern was binding the wives to the husbands, and not the manner of killing in itself. In different regions of India widows were sometimes buried alive.[94] This custom was limited to those castes that practised burial of the dead. This shows that the manner of killing was a function of the funeral rites.

In early times, burying widows alive seems to have been fairly widespread. Inscriptions also provide proof of this.[95] In modern European sources, on the other hand, it has only been confirmed for the Jogis, a weaver caste.[96] The close link between burial practices and burial alive is also indicated by the fact that, at times, Muslims were said to have practised this custom.[97]

In burial alive the widow sat in the pit that had been dug and laid her husband's body on her lap. Earth was then thrown in till only the woman's head was free. The statements about what came next vary. Sometimes more earth would simply be heaped upon the woman till even her head was covered. Then the bystanders trampled the earth down firmly over her head.[98] In other cases the widow was strangled

---

some success. However, the time till 1829, when the custom was completely abolished, was not enough to judge the long-term effect. IOR P/139/34, 526–34.

[94] Cf. Garbe 174; Thompson, *Suttee* 39; Weinberger-Thomas (1989) 32; Zachariae 554.

[95] Devi 265; Mahalingam 260; Settar, in Settar/Sontheimer 197.

[96] In the statistics for the years 1815–1828 burial alive is only mentioned for the district of Tipperah, with about 10 cases per year. Contemporary accounts (and more so older ones) give the impression that this form was occasionally also found in other places.

[97] Johns 65–70; Modi 423; I. Mukherjee 132; Thakur, *History* 169.

[98] *Remarks* 8; Robinson 128–9; Ward, *View* 1, XLVII; 2, 110; 3, 323; *Chronica* 77; Stavorinus 2, 53–4; Tavernier 2, 388; Gonçalves 67; Nuniz 77; Methwold 28–9; Johns 67.

to death;[99] some authors say that her neck was broken,[100] and others maintain that she had been given poison earlier.[101] It was always a brutal ceremony. But one can hardly speak of a conscious act of cruelty that went beyond the requirements of a common funeral for the spouses. It is never said that the burial took place in tombs, which would have caused the victim to struggle with death for a long time.[102] In the seventeenth century Rogerius was convinced that the widow was given poison 'to shorten her suffering and pain'.[103] Other forms of killing or self-killing cannot be established.[104]

Aspects of This World

The Widow

After announcing her decision to burn herself the widow generally had only a few hours to live. Therefore we would have to assume that motives and interests which came into play after her death were more important than those which were valid only for the short time remaining to her in this life.

The idea of posthumous fame could indeed have played a role, although there is no direct proof of this. Outwardly other motives had to be emphasized, particularly loyalty to the husband and the desire to be reunited with him. In this case, fame and honour were not merely a hope but a certainty. Every sati was revered in some form or the other. Yet there were considerable differences in the extent of fame after death. A widow from a poor family, and of a low caste, generally did

[99] Careri 3, 232; Dellon 1, 111; Thevenot 5, 257.

[100] Bernier 120; Fryer 153; Fedrici 40. According to Valentyn 5, 1, 52 (who was not an eyewitness) first a cloth was thrown over the widow's head, and sometimes she also received a blow on the head.

[101] Dapper 58; Sonnerat 1, 95; Rogerius 81–2.

[102] Guichard 390 states however that the widow's head remained outside the pit and that she was left to die a slow death. But Guichard was never in India, so one can only assume that he had not read the sources carefully. Barbosa 111 is also alone in stating that the widow was killed by placing a big stone on her head.

[103] Rogerius 82.

[104] R.S. Gandhi 152 mentions a special custom, which is said to have been practised in eighteenth century Gujarat: very young widows, even small girls, would be poisoned at a meal out of a sense of pity. Then their bodies were burnt along with those of their husbands. This was not a public ritualised killing and therefore not really following into death.

not receive the same posthumous honours as did a widow of a rich, respectable, religiously highly-placed family, or indeed the wife of a ruler. Along with the social position of the widow her individual conduct also played a role. The more heroic her act, the greater her steadfastness and ability to bear pain, the more people would remember her.

In addition, the extent of fame after death was also influenced by the frequency of immolations. Where they were widely prevalent, the individual case did not get much attention, and the number of people who honoured the widow after her death, prayed to her and set up memorial stones or monuments to her, was smaller.[105] It is significant that hardly any sati temples were built in Bengal. The landscape would otherwise have been dotted with tens of thousands of temples, for which not enough pilgrims and donors would have been found. It would appear that not even a memorial stone was erected for every sati.

Yet even in the few hours left to the widow, the incentives of this world were not missing. The sati received a measure of veneration, even power, that a woman could otherwise only get if she was a ruler. She became the focal point of a large, elaborate ceremony. People crowded around to get her blessings.[106] Her prophecies were highly valued[107], and her curse was feared.[108] Because of this fear no one dared to interfere and prevent the widow from carrying out her intentions, but, on the other hand, it could also serve as a useful excuse to justify inaction or even passive encouragement.[109]

Along with such positive factors, which made death appear more attractive to the widow, there were also negative factors which made her life miserable. The most obvious of these, the effect of the husband's death, cannot be generalized. Here one would have to expect all the different stages from sorrow and despair to a sense of liberation and

[105] Harlan 171 points out that there is no competition between the satis to be honoured, and that each additional sati is a gain for a family. This does not change the fact that the relative importance of the individual sati diminishes with increasing numbers.

[106] Cf. Thakur, *History* 159; Garbe 166; Harlan 134–8.

[107] Cf. Sangari/Vaid 1286; Garbe 166; Zachariae 595; Hügel 2,402; Lutfullah 175; Sleeman 23; Dubois, *Moeurs* 2,27; Valentyn 5, 3, 300.

[108] Crooke 1,188; Harlan 139–46; Narasimhan 90–1; Prinsep/Thornton 2, 168–9; Chidanandamurti, in Settar/Sontheimer 130; Weinberger-Thomas (1989) 26; Tod 2, 497; 499; 623; Bushby 261.

[109] For example *Measures* 133–4; Thompson, *Suttee* 123–5; PP 1830/28; 189; *Emperor vs. Ram Dayal.*

release. With regard to such feelings the differences when compared to other regions of the world, where following into death was not practised, would not have been too large. However, practically nowhere else was the wife so dependent on her husband as in India. Even if his wife had hated him, the death of the husband was—objectively seen—a big loss for her, because many possibilities were now barred to her, and her social status worsened considerably. The fact of her husband's death did not necessarily drive the wife to despair, but what did was the fact that she had become a widow. This leads to the general question regarding the status of the wife and the widow which is discussed in the next chapter.

The Relatives

From a material point of view widow burning was ambivalent for the relatives. On the one hand they lost a potential worker, on the other hand they had one less mouth to feed. If one wanted to go strictly according to economic criteria, we would have to clarify whether the value of the work done by the widow was higher than the cost of her upkeep. If one takes such considerations seriously, then we would have to assume that widows who were old, weak and in bad health were encouraged to burn themselves, whereas the relatives would be interested in keeping young and strong widows alive. But the statistics do not show a predominance of old satis. The individual accounts seldom mention particularly infirm widows.[110] The authors, on the other hand, frequently stress the youth and beauty of the victim.

Another material factor was probably more important: not the widow's capacity to work, but her wealth. It scarcely needs to be emphasized that the husband's relatives were interested in getting the widow's possessions. Here everything depended on the legal framework. There were two different legal systems in modern India.[111] In both the widow could only inherit if she did not have any sons.

1. The *Mitākṣarā* law of inheritance was valid in most parts of the country. According to it a widow would only inherit her husband's property if he had taken his share during his lifetime from the common property of the extended family, which very seldom happened. Normally

[110] For example Vigne 1, 82.

[111] Of central importance for the following is Sontheimer, *Joint Hindu Family*. Cf. also Vishnoi 164–7; Altekar, chaps 8–9; Narang 1–15; Manjushree 180 and below, p. 335.

the husband's family, i.e. his father or brothers, therefore retained control over the property, and the widow merely had the right to maintenance. She did not impede a shift in the ownership of the property. The question for the relatives from a material point of view came down to weighing the value of her work against the cost of her upkeep.

2. In Bengal and a few other regions of India the *Dāyabhāga* law of inheritance was valid. According to this, even in the case of undivided family property the widow was entitled to her husband's share. If she died, her share went back to his family. These relatives would therefore have a definite stake in her death.

In fact, as we have seen, widow burnings took place in far greater numbers in Bengal than in most other regions of India. This suggests a connection with the greed of the relatives. Such an explanation has in fact been put forward frequently, perhaps most notably by the first important modern Indian opponent of widow burning, Rammohan Roy, who in 1831 accused Bengali families of killing their widows out of greed.[112]

It is necessary to exercise caution with respect to such an interpretation. A considerable number of widows came from poor families with hardly any, or without significant wealth. In addition, widow burning did not occur with greater frequency in districts in which the *Dāyabhāga* law of inheritance was valid, just as, conversely, there were large numbers of immolations in some areas governed by the *Mitākṣarā* law of inheritance. Since the husband's family could only get the power of attorney over the widow's property if she did not have any sons, it would have to be established whether in areas under the *Dāyabhāga* law of inheritance large numbers of widows without sons were burnt to death. In this regard the statistics for the whole Bengal Presidency do not show any major differences, although the *Mitākṣarā* law of inheritance was valid in some regions. Satis, in fact, had, on an average, 20 per cent more sons than daughters (see Table 7).

All this does not eliminate the possibility that the relatives, tempted

---

[112] R. Roy, *Some remarks* 273 (also in Anand 75–6). A similar argumentation in: Kane 2,1, 635–6; Altekar 139; 261; R.S. Gandhi 153; Spivak 300; R.Thapar, in *Manushi* 8; Nandy, *Tale* 172; Gulati 123; 139; Woodruff 253; Rogerius 80; Haafner 83. More cautious: B.B. Roy 40; 72ff. Even the Court of Directors emphasized the connection in their representation to the Privy Council: IOR L/L/13 (1030) vol. 3, 215v (around 1831/32).

by the prospect of getting the widow's wealth, were less persuasive in their attempts to stop her, or that they even encouraged her. They might have behaved differently without the material incentive. In 1828, in Jaunpur, the burning of a widow who had been instigated by her brothers to take this step, was prevented. She stood to inherit the large sum of about Rs 3,500.[113] In 1824, an Indian non-commissioned officer died in the Madras Presidency. His widow wanted to burn herself. She was prohibited from doing so inside the garrison, and abandoned her intention of doing so. Her son-in-law, also a military person, came, and tried to make her burn herself by threatening her. He would have then inherited about Rs 4,000. He was subsequently dismissed from service.[114] Even at the immolation of Roop Kanwar in 1987 reference was made to the large dowry which the husband's family would have lost if the widow had stayed alive.[115]

Yet it would be problematic to make such indisputable phenomena into general explanatory factors.[116] If the widow's inheritance had really been the central issue, why was it that in other parts of the world, where a widow's inheritance rights were just as good or even better, widow burning did not occur? It seems fair to assume that in Bengal widows were no more frequently driven into death than widows of families in other parts of the world were killed out of greed and avarice.

The position of a widow within the family depended only indirectly on material factors. The most important factor was undoubtedly children, and, in particular, sons. A widow with sons had a better position in the family than one who had only daughters, or indeed one without children. Sons represented protection. Although this matter is undisputed, it appears to have had hardly any effect on widow burning. Occasionally it is claimed that it was predominantly childless widows who immolated themselves.[117] But this assumption has been proved incorrect (see pp. 257–8).

[113] *Asiatic Journal* 28 (1829), 478.
[114] PP 1830/28, 242–4. Other comparable cases: PP 1825/24, 102: Rangpur, 3,000–4,000 Rupees; *Asiatic Journal* 11 (1821), 508; 21 (1826), 83; 22 (1826), 441–2; *Friend of India* 3 (1820) , 131–2; Parks 1, 93. Cf. also Vaid, in *Seminar* 23, about a case of 1954.
[115] *Trial by fire.*
[116] Scepticism also in Narasimhan 116; M. Bhattacharya 670, and specially in Thakur, *History* 182–3. Earlier also in Elphinstone 359.
[117] For example Orlich, *Indien* 2,2, 260; Tavernier 2, 384; Valentyn 5,1,52; Rogerius 71; Honigberger 110; Patnaik 97.

An obvious motive for the relatives was to control the widow's sexuality and especially her reproductive abilities. For this burning constituted the most radical 'solution'. In practice, the role of this factor would have been negligible because there does not seem to have been an unusually large percentage of young satis (see pp. 256–7).

The motive of honour and fame existed not only for the widow, but also for the relatives. They were merely participants in this, but in contrast to the widow they could enjoy fame during their lifetime. Each widow burning lent considerable prestige to the family concerned.[118] In principle this possibility was open to every family, but the effects differed according to social status. As we have seen, the relative frequency of the custom increased with the importance of the social class. The higher the status of a family, the less an immolation contributed to a gain in status, serving merely to maintain it. And the more this was the case, the greater was the pressure to actually carry out the immolation. In this the families of rulers constituted an extreme example. Their status could not be raised any more through widow burning; rather the latter formed an integral part of this status. This is also why widow burning had to be carried out. Below the level of the ruler, a custom had been established in some upper-class families to provide at least one sati in every generation.[119] The pressure on widows here was therefore not quite so great as in families of rulers. But it became stronger, the further back the last immolation in the family lay in time. Less highly placed families, and more so those from the middle and lower classes, in which the custom was rare, could on the other hand gain in status with the help of a sati.

However, this had its limitations. The really important status differences, especially those of caste, could not be negotiated through this.[120] The fame and honour that belonged to a family remained linked to its status.

Finally it is also important to note that the state, even the Hindu state, did not provide any incentives for following into death. In this respect it was a 'liberal' state. It neither awarded honours like the Chinese honorary gates, temple inscriptions and annual sacrifices, nor did

[118] This has always been emphasized in the relevant literature. Cf., for example, Sangari/Vaid 1287 and B.B. Roy, chaps 2–3.

[119] See for example Griffiths 218; Parks 1,93; *Remarks* 7; Saxena, *Reforms* 76; Ward, *View* 3,310; Winternitz, *Frau* 72.

[120] Something like this is at any rate never mentioned. It would also have completely contradicted the caste system.

it grant the relatives rewards in the form of official positions, promotions, landownership or other assets like in Bali. This is true at least for later times and for following into death in its individual form. With the institutional form, on the other hand, the state would not always have been neutral. According to an inscription of *c.*1130 in Karnataka, the secretary followed a ruler into death in accordance with an oath given earlier. The new ruler rewarded his family.[121]

The Wider Circle of Participants

Widow burning in India was a public ceremony. Unfortunately, the sources seldom give precise details about the number of spectators. Really large events, in the manner of Balinese immolations, with tens of thousands of onlookers seem to have occurred only very rarely. Most likely such large numbers were found at the funerals of rulers. If one disregards an obviously exaggerated newspaper report of 1985, which speaks of 50,000 onlookers,[122] then the highest figure mentioned is 15,000.[123] As a rule, only a few thousand and sometimes just a few hundred spectators are mentioned.[124] From time to time there were

---

[121] Shastri 131.

[122] *Guardian* (London) of 15 March 1985 with reference to an immolation that was prevented in Devipura, Rajasthan. Devipura, where the widow still lives in a small temple, is a tiny village without any larger towns or villages in the immediate vicinity.

[123] Given by Fedden 19–20 according to a report in the *Daily Telegraph* (London) of 31 August 1937. For the nineteenth century the highest (and best-testified) number of onlookers is 10,000–12,000: 6 October 1828 in Jellalabad, in Shahjehanpur district. The widow was 15 years old. According to British regulations therefore the immolation was illegal. IOR P/139/34, 408.

[124] Parks 1, 95; 8,000 (at a case that was a 'false alarm'); Peggs, *Suttee's cry* (1828) 11–12: 6,000–8,000 (also in Thompson, *Suttee* 148–52); PP 1828/23, 24–5: 5,000–7,000 (police report); Wilkens 387: 5,000; Parks 1, 92: about 5,000; *Asiatic Journal* NS 36/2 (1841), 344–5: about 3,000; Johns 50–2: 1,000–4,000; *Tejsingh vs. The State* (1958) 171: 3, 000–4,000. *Emperor vs. Ram Dayal* (1913) 28: 1,500–2,000; Kennedy 51: about 500; Ray 124: several hundred; *Asiatic Journal* 17 (1824), 665: only a few hundred; PP 1823/17, 68: about 200. For the latest widow burning of 1987 V.N. Datta XI speaks of about 3,000 onlookers and *Trial by fire* of 4,000–5,000; otherwise generally several thousand are mentioned.

even fewer onlookers. On 5 November 1845, Henry Lawrence observed in Nepal that 'about a hundred spectators, chiefly beggars and old women, were collected to view the spectacle.'[125]

The number of onlookers would have depended on the frequency of such immolations, and on the status of the dead person which determined how elaborate the ceremony would be. European observers sometimes describe how at first they tried everything to be able to witness a burning, whereas later they restricted themselves to observing from a distance, for example from the other side of a river. Sometimes they even turned their faces away from the spectacle.[126]

Only some Europeans have written about their motives for wanting to take part in such a ceremony. It was mainly curiosity which drove them to do this, the attraction of the unknown, the horror of the situation, but sometimes also the intention to intervene, or at least the vague hope of being able to achieve something.

For the masses of indigenous onlookers the motive was probably first and foremost sensationalism, but for many there was also the hope of being blessed by the widow. European authors often hold forth about the spectators at such events, who are said to have been apathetic or even sadistic, who looked on, at best indifferently, even during the most horrible scenes,[127] and often even showed signs of pleasure.[128] A British officer compared the event to a bullfight.[129] In a trial dealing with the violence against a widow who had jumped down from the funeral pyre, Indian witnesses testified that the spectators had asked the participants to kill the victim.[130]

In view of the different cultural backgrounds it is difficult to make a direct comparison of European and Indian reactions, and to morally

[125] Edwardes/Merivale 2, 36. See Anon., review Heber 127: about 100 people in Poona; Hodges 82.

[126] Moor 354–5; Parks 1,93; Anon., review Heber 127; Ravesteyn 75.

[127] For example *Essays* 15; *Quarterly Review* 37 (1828), 130; Kennedy 16; 34; 39; 52; Thompson, *Suttee* 51; 157–8; Hodges 82; Stavorinus 1,447; Twining 467.

[128] Thompson, *Suttee* 123; Lawrence, in Edwardes/Merivale 2, 37; Parks 1, 93.

[129] 20 December 1828, Major W.S. Beatson. IOR L/L/13 (1030), vol. 3, App. 46. Z. Ahmad 162 speaks in 1968 of bullfights as well as gladiator fights.

[130] Case of 7 September 1823; Trial of 27 June 1826. PP 1828/23, 14–17.

qualify certain emotional reactions. It is true that an element of sadism cannot be ruled out among the Indian spectators. However, it would be more appropriate to make comparisons, not with the reactions of the few Europeans in India, but with the attitude of spectators at public executions and at the burning of witches and heretics at the stake in Europe. In the Indian case in which the onlookers cried for the death of the victim, the perpetrators later testified that they feared the consequences of not carrying the immolation to its end.[131]

It is better to keep to the unquestionable facts. The crowd, at any rate, never tried to prevent a widow burning. The spectators almost always helped to stoke the fire, and sometimes they actively helped when a widow was thrown back on the funeral pyre. Objectively seen, the crowd clearly had an intensifying effect, even when it behaved apathetically. In front of the public it would have been more difficult for a widow to explain that she had changed her mind at the last minute, or even to jump down from the pyre, than if she had been in front of a small private circle. For the relatives, too, it would have been a far greater disgrace to accept this in front of a crowd. In a manner of speaking therefore the onlookers constituted an iron framework which indirectly enforced the immolation once it had been decided upon.

On the other hand, one normally cannot speak of an aggressive, bloodthirsty, fanatical crowd, which stifled all resistance, and, if necessary, enforced immolation. Before the abolition of 1829 spirited Europeans often intervened and prevented a burning, even when it was legal. The mere appearance in 1804 of two British women at the site of a widow burning in Bihar caused the organizers to run away. The widow was able to save herself from the burning pyre, and the two ladies took her under their protection.[132] European men sometimes rushed into the crowd with their weapons drawn, and nothing happened to them either.[133] The romanticism associated with such actions is not an invention of later fiction writers. In 1801 Degrandpré describes in detail how he organized an expedition to save or abduct a widow, almost in military fashion, with two Indians, two European officers, twenty European sailors, twelve rifles, eight pistols and twenty sabres. The landing (from the river) at the site of the immolation went

[131] PP 1828/23, 15.
[132] *Interesting Facts* 115–16; *Remarks* 20–1; Poynder 180–2.
[133] For example Bowrey 40; Manucci 2, 97; Crawfurd 273; Johns 56.

according to plan, but the widow had already been burnt on the previous evening. 'I felt sorry for the woman, especially in view of the pleasure that I would have got from rescuing her, and in view of the mental images that I had of her youth and beauty.'[134] Others succeeded with threats and persuasion.[135] From time to time Indians helped,[136] sometimes even taking the initiative themselves.[137] Frequently the widow refused to be dissuaded from carrying out her decision,[138] but some did refuse to die at the last minute. They jumped down from the pyre, which was possibly already in flames, and requested strangers present (if they had not already acted on their own) for protection and help.[139] Such a rescue could even lead to the rescuer marrying the widow, although such accounts could indeed frequently be just legends.[140] The most famous case (though not completely substantiated) is that of Job Charnock, the founder of Calcutta. In 1694, he saved a widow from the pyre, and he is said to have lived with her till she died.[141]

The intervention of Europeans is never said to have led to violent exchanges. The onlookers would certainly have been most displeased at such an ending, but they appear to have accepted it even at a time when the Europeans did not have the power of the state behind them.[142]

[134] Degrandpré 71–5. Quote: 75.

[135] For example Bernier 107–10.

[136] A. Sharma *et al.*, *Sati* 54; Ray 123–9; PP 1821/18, 258.

[137] Ray 129.

[138] Relevant accounts are available in large numbers, for example van den Broecke 167; Ravesteyn 74; Johns 23–4; 51; 67; Ward, *View* 3, 325; Buckland 1, 160–2; Hervey 1, 218–21; *Asiatic Journal* 20 (1825), 145–8; Elliot 3; Lutfullah 175–6; Mökern 1, 329–32; Townley 139–41; Vigne 1, 83–4; Nunes 48.

[139] Absolutely reliable accounts are available only for the period after 1757: Elphinstone 190; *Interesting facts* 115–16; *Remarks* 20–1; IOR P/139/34, 244–52 (1828); PP 1823/17, 26; Massie 2, 175–6.

[140] Manucci 2, 97; Navarrete 2, 335.

[141] Holwell 2,100; Hamilton 2, 5; Orlich, *Indien* 2, 2, 239; Peggs, *Suttee's cry* 92; A. Sharma, *Thresholds* 86; V.N. Datta 23.

[142] *On the burning of widows* 472; Holwell 2, 99–100; Wintergerst 118;
Further accounts about successful interventions by Europeans: *Asiatic Journal* 16 (1823), 343–5; Peggs, *Suttee's cry* (1828) 71–2; Prinsep/Thornton 1, 171; PP 1823/17, 76ff.; IOR L/L/13 (1030), vol. 3, App. 37; 61; 65; 69;

Before 1829 the police often intervened in illegal cases,[143] and after the abolition they were expected to stop all planned immolations that came to their notice on time (although the policemen were not always enthusiastic, since not many of them were convinced that this was a crime, and because they also feared the sati's curse). Before 1829 disputes occasionally began when the crowd hindered the police from interfering.[144] More serious clashes took place only in a few cases immediately after 1829. They had a clear political character and will be described later (see pp. 433–5). Subsequently, in only one case of 1927 is the crowd reported to have pushed the police away from the immolation site, not, however, harming them in any way.[145]

The inhabitants of the village, the city or the region, or the members of the same caste not only basked in the glory of the widow's fame, but often also benefitted from the substantial material interests involved. This, however, was essentially a phenomenon of the post-1947 period. Whereas earlier only modest memorial stones or monuments had been erected for the sati and she had been worshipped in a local cult, now an increasing number of proper temples were constructed, sometimes on a significant scale.[146] An attempt was made to turn them into places

---

90; 95; 98–9; 107; J. Forbes 2, 394–6; Manucci 3,157; Navarrete 335; J.K. Majumdar 130.

It is difficult to fit in a statement which is made by only one author, into this context. Bernier 117–18 insists having observed several times how young, beautiful widows managed to save themselves. They rushed into the arms of untouchables, who, knowing about the attractive widow, had positioned themselves near her. The widows were then saved from further persecution. Although Bernier is generally considered to be reliable, one can scarcely assume that a widow was often in a position to break out of a crowd consisting of several hundred people, or that this crowd allowed untouchables to come that close.

[143] Numerous cases are recorded in the annual compilations in the *Parliamentary Papers*. Cf. also Poynder 138ff.; PP 1821/18, 36–7; 95; 228. On 1 December 1829 the government informed the Nizamat Adalat that in 1827 and 1828 the police had prevented 34 cases each without any problems. IOR L/L/ 13 (1030), vol. 3, App. 129.

[144] See PP 1821/18, 35–6 (case of 1813); *Asiatic Journal* 23 (1827), 671; IOR P/139/34, 416 (1827/28).

[145] *Emperor vs. Vidyasagar Pande* 498–500; Hirst 2–6; cf. *Tejsingh vs. The State* 169 (1958).

[146] Cf. van den Bosch 180ff.; Vaid/Sangari; Sangari/Vaid; S. Singh 89–96;

of pilgrimage. This could mean considerable advantages and profits, both for the inhabitants of the place as well as for possible investors from other places.

But this material motive should not be projected back onto burnings in the past, and even in the present the possibilities linked with it are limited. Large successful ventures of this kind remained rare. Some temples were never completed, either for lack of money or for lack of initiative.[147] It is also remarkable that by far the most successful place of pilgrimage associated with sati-worship, the Rani Sati temple in Jhunjhunu, Rajasthan, is not linked to a recent occurrence, but to a mythical event, apparently from the thirteenth or fourteenth century.[148] One would therefore hardly be able to see such material interests as the driving force behind the staging of widow burnings.

Research in the last two decades seeks occasionally to emphasize a more political motivation, both on the part of the relatives, and on the part of society in general. The point of departure for this is a thesis put forward by Ashis Nandy in 1975. Nandy proceeds from a significant increase in the number of widow burnings in Bengal in the late eighteenth and the early nineteenth centuries. He interprets it as a means of population control in view of famines. This thesis is, on account of the statistical evidence, definitely not tenable. For Nandy, however, the increase is primarily to be seen as a reaction to colonial rule. For the old elite British rule meant the loss of their traditional power bases. Those

---

Upreti 108ff.; *Seminar* 20–30; Weinberger-Thomas (1996) 116ff.; 176ff.; 188ff.

[147] Of the eight places with new temples which I could find in 1992 in a circle of about 40 km in the districts of Sikar and Jhunjhunu, at the most five can be termed reasonably successful. What is particularly striking is the contrast between Hathideh, where a widow burnt to death in 1978 and where a temple in her honour remains incomplete, and Jharli, only a few kilometres away, where after an immolation in 1980 a successful temple operation was begun. For Jharli see Vaid/Sangari 3–6. Other entrepreneurial failures in the region are Govindpura and Maonda Kalan. Kumar's statement (175) 'Sati is big business' is an exaggeration, at least in this context.

[148] Van den Bosch 180-185; Vaid/Sangari 9–12; Vaid, in *Seminar* 20–3; *Trial by fire*; Upreti 108ff.; Sangari, in *Seminar* 24–30. 'Branches' of this temple were established in large numbers all over India. According to Vaid/Sangari 10 there were 105 such 'branches' in 1991; Weinberger-Thomas (1996) 177 speaks of 111.

who wanted to stay at the top had to adapt themselves. This meant, even for the new, upwardly mobile groups, working together with the new rulers. These shifts led to a widespread feeling of instability. It was the groups that had successfully adapted that now tried to prove their link with tradition by practising a custom that was considered the quintessence of orthodox Hinduism. Widow burning became an act of self-confirmation and self-affirmation,[149] in some respects almost a form of anti-colonial resistance (since it was known that the new rulers despised the custom).[150] According to Nandy widow burning was 'a pathology primarily produced by colonialism but perceived as a pure product of traditions.'[151]

The presupposition for this thesis, the increase in the number of cases in the first decades of British rule, cannot be substantiated empirically, as has already been shown (see p. 239). It is true that the opposite cannot be proved either. Yet in such a case the burden of proof must lie on those who state that there was a change. The thesis therefore can only be considered hypothetically. At least a few more reasons can be stated as to why it should not be given too much importance so long as its premises are not substantiated empirically.

The basic structure of this argument has often appeared in the history of following into death. The custom is, from this point of view, principally a reaction to invasions from outside, or it is even considered a foreign import. The assertion of the non-Chinese or non-Indian origins of early following into death in China and India (see pp. 146 and 223) argues along similar lines. Even closer to the Nandy thesis is the statement that in Africa the custom was practised on a greater scale only as a reaction to European incursions, first of the slave traders and then of the colonial conquerors (see pp. 78–9). One could argue similarly for Oceania (although this has not yet been done) and declare following into death to be essentially a reaction to missionary activities.

[149] Nandy, *Tale* 168–80; Nandy, in Anand 158–9; Nandy, in Hawley (ed.) 137–42. Cf. Michaels, *Recht* 108; Michaels, *Nepal* 29–30; R.K. Ray, in V.C. Joshi (ed.) 103–5; Bayly 174; Crawford 74; Narasimhan 117; Weinberger-Thomas (1989) 13–14; Spivak 298–300; Das, *Gender* 69. Somewhat more restrained: Kopf 270. Clearly rejected by: V.N. Datta 200; Gupta/Gombrich; Embree, in Hawley (ed.) 149–59. More cautiously: Thapar, in *Seminar* 17.

[150] V.N. Datta 37; Chowdhury-Sengupta 41.

[151] Nandy, *Cultures* 264; Nandy, in Anand 158: 'A pathology of colonialism not of Hinduism'.

With a little bit of imagination even the Southeast Asian forms could be interpreted in the same way.

So far no proof has been offered anywhere. Everywhere we can assume that the supposed increase in the number of cases was merely a result of increased reporting by Europeans. In general it seems problematic to explain a custom that is found in so many parts of the world, in the most varying contexts and forms, predominantly as a reaction to relatively weak external influences as compared to the importance of the indigenous culture. The tendency to view following into death as a pathological phenomenon and not as a normal part of a culture is, for its part, a consequence of European influence in the form of particular notions of morality. European norms are used to assess non-European traditions. So long as it is only a case of assessment this is legitimate, but it is misleading in the case of historical explanations.

Aspects of the Other World

For the survivors, the interests and motives of this world were more numerous and played a more important role than for the widow, for whom the aspects of the other world held greater significance. However, a simple contrasting model, which sets the deceitful perpetrators against the deceived victims, is inappropriate here. In this model the perpetrators invent a glowing after-life and indoctrinate the victim who allows herself to be driven to death in this manner. It is the classic model of priestly deceit.[152] The Dutchman Adolph Bassing expressed it particularly radically in 1677: 'With such sweet temptations these women are seduced by the men, and especially by the cunning Brahmins, to carry out such a horrible deed, whereas the men are so cowardly and scared that they almost die when they just see another person's blood.'[153] The model presupposes that the perpetrators know more than the victim because otherwise it would be difficult to understand why they do not believe their own promises like the victims do. The perpetrators in the case of widow burning were not only educated people or priests, but came from all classes. In addition, this juxtaposition

[152] This statement is found very often among European observers and commentators. Some examples: Vigne 1,88; Challe 294; Dubois, *Moeurs* 2, 34; Dapper 55; *Breve relação* 20 (chap.19). Cf. V.N. Datta, chap. 8.

[153] Valentyn 5, 3, 300, who prints an account by Bassing. The style indicates that Valentyn edited the text.

of the educated and the uneducated reduces belief to superstition, and, from the point of view of the educated, it is declared as simply a means to an end, which was certainly never true of India in general. Concepts of the hereafter can never be perceived in the context of specific groups that have been defined in an ad-hoc manner. They are shared by a people as a whole, or by those belonging to the same religion or the same culture. If the widows, who burnt themselves to death, believed in a particular concept of the hereafter, then this was merely a reflex of corresponding notions within their society. Such notions do not appear overnight, nor can they be manipulated at will. The widow's belief, when faced with a funeral pyre, that she will be reunited with her husband in the other world, is not a result of last minute indoctrination, but of a process that has continued for years and decades; it is an influence of her surroundings. A society that produces such a belief will, for its part, be affected by it.

In the early period, the notion of the hereafter as a continuation of this world seems to have been widely prevalent in India too. Ceteus' widow apparently assumed that after immolating herself she would continue to live with her husband as before. This is expressed more vividly in the *Mahābhārata* when Madri takes it for granted that after her death she can resume the act of love with Pandu.

In the course of time, however, more differentiated notions of the hereafter were formed, and they gained moral overtones. The good were rewarded, the evil punished. Such views most likely existed, parallel to the earlier ones, long before Ceteus and the *Mahābhārata*, but gained more importance gradually. Following into death was not compatible with such views. Wherever they established themselves the custom disappeared, or it did not come into existence in the first place. Christianity and Islam are only the most prominent examples of this.

It is here that the separate development in India began, and widow burning acquired a character that clearly distinguished it from all other forms of following into death. The belief in the hereafter did not lead to the suppression of widow burning, but the view that it was based upon was adjusted to fit the new belief in the hereafter. This was the work of the authors of the Dharma texts, and it took place very slowly over the course of many centuries.[154]

The authors made the new belief in the hereafter the basis of the custom, by giving it moral underpinning. Till then the act merely

[154] Cf. I. Singh 192.

entailed following someone into death. Now it became a morally deserving act.[155] Through this act the woman gained eternal bliss, not only for herself, but also for her husband, even had he deserved the worst of all possible fates on account of his deeds. Through her act the widow was indeed in a position to cleanse other relatives of their sins.

The reunion of the couple that was endangered by the morally-based belief in the hereafter was ensured again through the morally deserving act of the woman. Nowhere else was there such a thorough and systematic adaptation of following into death tied to more elaborate notions of the hereafter. This resulted in a particularly strong, primarily religious anchoring of the custom, which partly explains the tenacity with which it has held.

Along with religious feelings more human emotions were sometimes brought into play, for example, when the view was expressed in Kannaḍa literature that, left alone, a man would enjoy himself in the other world with heavenly maidens. The wife on earth could only prevent this by following him immediately into death.[156]

As a result of this process, the attempt to morally disqualify the institution of widow burning as a criminal act was always met with the counter-argument that, seen from the point of view of the individual, it was a morally deserving act.

This opposition exists even today. In 1987, after the immolation of Roop Kanwar, a private investigation report categorically stated: 'No practice that is so cruel and inhuman can be defended on the ground that it has religious sanction.'[157] In 1982, on the other hand, Stutchbury stated that 'Sati was not murder, but sacrifice.'[158] Both texts, therefore, pretended that the question which can only be answered on the basis of the intellectual background of the observer was capable of being answered objectively.

The new point of view was sometimes expressed in a drastic fashion in the Dharma texts:

> She who follows her husband in death dwells in heaven for as many years as there are hair on the human body, viz. 3 1/2 crores of years. Just as a snake-catcher draws out a snake from a hole by force, so such a

[155] Cf. Lommel 386.

[156] Settar/Sontheimer 22–3; 125.

[157] *Trial by fire.* For the elimination of the religious background among the opponents of the custom see also below, pp. 450–3.

[158] Stutchbury 43.

woman draws her husband from (wherever he may be) and enjoys bliss together with him. In heaven she being solely devoted to her husband and praised by bevies of heavenly damsels sports with her husband for as long as fourteen Indras rule.[159] Even if the husband be guilty of the murder of a brāhmana or of a friend or be guilty of ingratitude, the wife who dies (in fire) clasping his body, purifies him (of the sin). That woman, who ascends (the funeral pyre) when the husband dies, is equal to Arundhatī [exemplary mythological figure of a woman] in her character and is praised in heaven. As long as a woman does not burn herself in fire on the death of her husband she is never free from being born as a woman (in successive births).[160]

Another author was of the view that 'that woman who follows her husband in death purifies three families, viz. of her mother, of her father and of her husband.'[161]

In a later text this ability to rescue the husband from the fires of hell is more clearly emphasized: 'Even in the case of a husband who has entered into hell itself and who, seized by the servants of Death and bound with terrible bonds, has arrived at the very place of torment; even if he is already standing there, helpless and wretched, quivering with fear because of his evil deeds [. . .]—even then a women who refuses to become a widow can purify him: in dying, she takes him with her.'[162]

This new view led to a peculiar, dialectical relationship between the sexes. The wife, as it turned out, was far superior to the husband from the point of view of the possibility of meritorious action. Through her deed she was in a position to save both of them, while the husband was often not even able to take care of himself. The price for the morally superior position of the wife in the other world was however her life in this world. The wife had to die in order to realize her superiority, whereas the husband's life on earth was secure because of his inferiority.

The effects of this division of functions not only became apparent

[159] According to *Remarks* 5 this corresponds to 30 million years.

[160] Śaṅkha and Aṅgiras, quoted in Kane 2, 1, 631.

[161] Hārīta, quoted in Kane 2, 1, 631.

[162] Tryambakayajvan (eighteenth century), quoted in Leslie, *Victim* 185. Cf. also Colebrooke, *Digest* 2, 567–74; Leslie, *Wife* 293–5; Lommel 385–6; Thakur, *History* 144–7; Ward, *View* 3, 308–10; Wilkins 379; IOR L/L/13 (1030), vol. 2, 135–9; Böhtlingk, no. 2568; 2882; 4803; 4947–8; 5477; 6466.

in the views about the position in the other world, but also in the consequences of widow burning in this world. They enabled the woman to achieve a kind of honour in her last hours on earth and to enjoy a form of cult-worship after her death, for which there were no equivalents for a man. Equivalents of this also do not exist in the history of following into death in other parts of the world. Nowhere else do the attendants become objects of such a cult. Even the honours bestowed on widows in China did not approach this deification.

Politically speaking: the position of men in this world was ensured with the help of considerable concessions to women with regard to the other world. But it was only possible to redeem these concessions at the cost of life which confirmed the subjugation of women in this world. However, we do not need to impute that the authors consciously intended this. The changes occurred very slowly, and the actual consequences were probably never conceived of by anyone.

Notions of the hereafter underwent further shifts in Hinduism. The Karma theory in particular became more important.[163] According to this theory every soul had to go through countless rebirths till it could finally be released. The form of each rebirth was determined by actions in the previous life. The view that widow burning could influence the husband's fate contradicted the strict apportioning of rebirth according to sins and merit, which in turn led to the assumption that married couples generally went different ways after death. There was never any systematic clarity on this point.[164] Yet one can understand that beliefs which showed a way out of the rigid determinism of the Karma doctrine were not unwelcome. Thus, it was, on the other hand, the Indian opponents of widow burning who denied that it was possibile to catch up with the dead in the other world.[165] In addition, the views wavered between the belief that the widow would enter an unlimited period of bliss and the assumption that the couple would be reborn together in improved circumstances.[166] A combination of both views then led to

[163] On the Karma doctrine and its consequences for notions of the hereafter in general see for example Michaels, *Reinkarnation*; Horsch; Neufeldt; O'Flaherty; Gonda 1, 204ff.; 279ff.

[164] Altekar 125; Leslie, *Victim* 186; S. Singh 11; Thapar, in *Seminar* 16–17; Thakur, *History* 140; Narasimhan 121.

[165] Mainly Bāṇa (seventh century), quoted in Winternitz, *Frau* 64. For the actual text of the quote see below p. 346. Cf. also Arunachalam 67–8.

[166] Cf. Derrett, *Religion* 69.

the opinion that salvation occurs only after a widow has burned herself five or seven times. Some widows declared that they had already burned themselves several times with the same husband, and that they would have to repeat the act till the figure of five or seven had been reached, after which their final salvation would be possible.[167] However, a widow is never reported as having said that the present immolation was her last one.

The aspect of the reunion with the husband was also emphasized in the burning ceremony which was staged as a symbolic affirmation or even as a repetition of the marriage ceremony. The sati often wore her wedding clothes.[168]

There is no doubt that for the victims the belief in or the hope of a reunion with the husband played an important role. Many European authors depict how they tried to dissuade the widow from carrying out her intentions and how she told them that her only aim was to be reunited with her husband.[169] At least as far as the widows—who paid for their beliefs with their lives—were concerned, it is difficult to believe that they were merely following a mindlessly repeated formula. Some even rebuked the British officials for the delay which prevented them from attaining salvation with their husbands.[170]

It is more difficult to determine the importance of factors of the other world for the survivors because they were not required to affirm their beliefs in the same way through their actions. However, there are indications for the views of the public at large. What is particularly symptomatic is the fact that the spectators sometimes gave the widow messages for the dead (see p. 266). The Sati-cult is also a part of this,

---

[167] Kennedy 40 (five times); Parks 1, 93 (six times); Sleeman 21 (three times); ibid. 27–31: the author describes how a married woman burns herself with the corpse of a man who was not her husband, but to whom she maintains she was married in a previous life; Marshman 2, 357–8 (six times); Bernier 112 (five times); Statham 135 (several times). Occasionally such cases are mentioned in the *Asiatic Journal*, for example 25 (1828), 264–5 (five times). See Weinberger-Thomas (1989) 31.

[168] This is emphasized in older texts as well as in modern research, for example Manrique 78; Tavernier 2, 385; Vincenzo 344; Fedrici 36–7; Challe 293; Zachariae 557; Sontheimer, in Settar/Sontheimer 97–8; Weinberger-Thomas (1989) 24.

[169] For example in van den Broecke 168; Nunes 48.

[170] For example in Sleeman 18–24.

as well as the belief in the effectiveness of the widow's blessings and chiefly her curse, although here older notions of the dangers emanating from the spirits of the dead could also have played a role.

Free Choice and Coercion

The Absence of Resistance

If the concept of resistance is understood politically to mean organized and collective action, then we cannot speak of this in the context of widow burning. It is never reported that women organized themselves in any form to escape immolation, or that they set up far-reaching demands for the restriction or the abolition of the custom. It is true that widow burning in India sometimes sparked controversy, but it was never so in the political sense between the widows and the organizers. This is true even today. The women's movement in India is carrying out a determined struggle against the revival of the custom.[171] But the potential victims, who generally belong to the poorer, less-educated rural sections, hardly ever constitute a part of this movement.

The main cause for the lack of resistance would have to lie in the pronounced individual character of this kind of following into death. If institutional following into death has the tendency to lead to class struggle, then the individual form of the custom is gender struggle. The satis came from all social classes. What they had in common was only their gender. Generally social or class struggle is more frequent in history and more intensive than gender struggle. For the discriminated sex to rise in open resistance there have to be very unusual conditions, not because women lack the power of resistance, but because of the objectively difficult conditions arising chiefly from their extreme isolation. In the present case this was intensified by various circumstances.

Women, who clearly knew what they wanted and who were determined to act accordingly, could almost always escape immolation. Seen from an individual perspective, therefore, a form of action which did not lead to (collective) resistance, was more attractive for them, because they could thereby ensure their own survival more easily. Thus a possible resistance lacked the most determined elements from the very beginning.

[171] Cf. for example the special issues of *Manushi* and *Seminar* after the death of Roop Kanwar (1987), as well as *Trial by Fire*, Sangari/Vaid and Kumar.

The individual character of following into death also resulted in the fact that there was no tendency to increase the number of victims and that in most cases only a single widow burnt to death. This would have made the rise of solidarity difficult. Each time it was only one woman who was directly concerned; the fate of all others was completely open. If they died before their husbands, the matter was settled. If they became widows, there was after all—with reference to the entire country— a 99.9 per cent probability of not becoming a sati; and even in areas with the highest frequency this probability lay around 97–98 per cent.

But widow burning in India also had partly institutional features, particularly at the funerals of rulers. Generally, however, not all wives of the dead ruler were required to kill themselves. If there weren't enough volunteers, the issue was shifted to the wives, among whom a quarrel about who should become the victims could ensue. This would have hindered the rise of solidarity among the wives. Solidarity was sometimes also discouraged because the element of compulsion was not strong enough to drive women into death if they were determined to survive. When the Maharajah of Udaipur died in 1861, all his wives refused to accompany him in death, and finally it was only possible, by exerting considerable pressure, to send a concubine to her death.[172] So, in the end, it was the weakest who were the victims.

The rise of solidarity was even more difficult on the death of a Kulin brahmin, although sometimes widows killed themselves in large numbers on such occasions. However, they lived in different places, sometimes at great distances from one another, and did not even know each other.

Finally, the possibility of resistance was also reduced on account of the brief span of time between the death of the husband and the burning.

In recent years a far more politically oriented form of resistance has been discussed according to which widow burning had an anti-colonial thrust. That this argument does not have an empirical basis, and is inherently questionable, has already been shown (see pp. 239–40 and pp. 288–9). In the context being dealt with here, the crucial point is that such resistance would be due more to the organizers of the immolations than to the widows. At any rate it would not lead to a restriction of the custom.

[172] M.Gaur 64; Thompson, *Suttee* 106; 112–13; Altekar 141–2; V.N. Datta 165. Cf. also Saxena, *Reforms* 66; Dubois, *Moeurs* 2, 21.

Was Free Choice Possible?

No other question regarding widow burning in India has been discussed as often, as intensively and as controversially as the one about free choice, coercion and violence. This is true even today, and is completely understandable, because the opinion about the actions of the participants and about the custom as a whole depends on the answer to this question.

On the one hand the basically voluntary nature of widow burning is emphasized time and again. Naturally exceptions are not denied. But they do not, the argument states, dispute the rule.[173]

It is true that this view can base itself only on some of the eyewitness accounts, but it also appears to be confirmed by the surveys undertaken by the British in Bengal. The overwhelming majority of the over 8,000 registered cases were legal ones. At any rate, this is what the district officers reported. In order to be legal in the eyes of the British they had to be voluntary acts. One can assume that the unknown figure for illegal cases was higher. However from the point of view of the statistics this would not have been very important (see pp. 235–6).

Whereas in earlier times in India it was generally assumed that sati was predominantly a voluntary act, the opposite view was more frequent among foreign observers who felt that coercion and violence were used in most of the cases. Sometimes, particularly in recent times, this argument was intensified. It was basically denied that there could be something like a voluntary widow burning.[174] In 1987 an author stated: 'There is no such thing as a voluntary sati.'[175]

Paradoxically even the view expressed in 1987 can at least indirectly refer to the colonial power. When the British abolished widow burning in 1829, suicide was a criminal offence according to English law. The

[173] This view—frequently with more or less far-reaching modifications—can be found for example in: Bunsen, *Witwenverbrennung* 458–61; Harlan, chaps 4–5; Leslie, *Victim* 179ff.; Mukhopadhyay, *Institution* 114; Nandy, *Tale* 170; Newnham 122–8; A.Sharma, *Thresholds* 87; A. Sharma, *Sati* 74; 108; Sousa 2; Thakur, *History* 144; 180–3; Thomas 92; Winternitz, *Frau* 72.

[174] For example Kishwar/Vanita 21; Ray 14; *Trial by Fire*; Walker 462–5; Daly 115–19; Woodruff 255. For older authors see chap.14.

[175] Title of an article by Kumkum Sangari in the *Times of India* of 25 October 1987. Same phrase in Narasimhan 101. Similarly: Dhagamwar, *Saint* 37; I.P. Singh 365; *Sati and the State*; Upreti 15; *Anti Sati Bill* 19.

abolition was valid for every form of widow burning, however (in contrast to the law of 1987/88), it did not provide for any punishment for the widow, but only for the other participants. In the course of enforcing the ban no widows were penalized. We cannot assume that in the eyes of the British suicide suddenly became a legitimate act. Rather we would have to conclude that they placed the responsibility for widow burning on the spectators. This ruled out the possibility of free choice.

Through their survey the British therefore shored up the argument regarding the voluntary nature of the act, but with abolition they placed themselves on the side of those who assumed coercion. This shows the complicated nature of the problem which was expressed in an unsurpassable, though unintended, paradox as early as the sixteenth century. According to Brás de Albuquerque 'the woman had to burn herself willingly.'[176]

We must first clarify what is meant by free choice and by coercion. Here we will have to refer to the statements made in the Introduction. There the terms were considered to be a contradictory opposition. They are mutually exclusive, and a third possibility is ruled out. An action is either voluntary or forced; it cannot be both or something completely different. The criterion for making the distinction in the present case is whether the subject (or the victim) could have stayed alive if she had acted differently. What kind of life this would have been is not the focus of interest. The criterion corresponds to the central content of following into death, which of necessity implies the death of the attendant.

Free choice is therefore not just a formal characteristic, but one concerning the content, defined by its consequences. Every person can act somewhat differently in every situation, even if only with regard to insignificant details. However, this does not necessarily mean that there will be any fundamental changes in his/her fate. It would be inappropriate to speak of a voluntary act in this context. This can even refer to the killing itself. If a woman kills herself because she knows that otherwise others would kill her in a far more agonizing manner, then it would be inappropriate to describe her action as a voluntary one.

[176] Albuquerque 1, 116 (part 2, chap. 20): '*A mulher se avia de queimar por sua vontade.*'

From this point of view one can only say that an action was either voluntary or coerced. We do not need to make any further distinctions regarding coercion since, in any case, it leads to the death of the victim. Regarding a voluntary act, however, one can and must search for the factors that influenced this decision or led to it. In circumstances where the widow was pressurized by all those around her and where she was faced with the certainty of a miserable life, we cannot speak of free choice in the same way as we would in circumstances where the widow had prospects of a life in honour and comfort, and where her relatives and others tried to dissuade her from carrying out her intentions.

The search for the reasons for the widow's decision to burn herself, or to allow herself to be burnt to death, leads to the antinomy of causality and freedom which is valid for every historical explanation. It is particularly apparent in a controversial question like the voluntary nature of following into death. When we talk of a voluntary act, we presuppose freedom and therefore free will. The search for causes, on the other hand, is complete when we have fully explained what motivated the person to his/her action, and thus determined the action. The determining factors are fully established. Neither view is compatible with the other. Whether free will can be attributed to human beings is not an empirical question. The answer depends rather on a decision that precedes all experience. If one assumes freedom, as is the case here, then an action can never completely be explained on the basis of causes—the person could in fact have acted differently.

The question of free choice and coercion should only refer to the immediate conditions of the action being examined, and should be linked neither with its moral character nor with its purpose. There are many good reasons for the complete rejection of widow burning and of following into death as a whole. These reasons, however, are not an argument against the possibility of dying of one's own free will. Anyone can voluntarily die for a bad cause, or can be forced into death for a good cause.

An essential precondition for widow burning is its public nature. This automatically gives the participants, from the relatives and the priests to the mere onlookers, a kind of collective veto.[177] They can refuse to set up the funeral pyre or to light the fire, or they can simply stay away. From this we cannot conclude that the widow, therefore,

---

[177] Emphasized in *Essays* 23.

cannot act freely. One can accuse the onlookers of making the immolation possible in the first place, and also of lending a hand, for example, by stoking the fire. The attitude of aiding and abetting however cannot be equated with coercion, but at best with complicity. As long as the onlookers act in accordance with the widow's demands and do not dictate her actions, the conditions for the possibility of free choice continue to exist.

Observers and the Observational Situation

Preconceived notions influenced even the most reliable and incorruptible observers. Those who rejected widow burning as a barbaric and cruel act were generally also convinced that coercion and violence played a role in it. They therefore tended to see and note those aspects which suggested the use of force and not the exercise of free choice. On the other hand, those who admired widow burning as a heroic and morally deserving act assumed that it was voluntary and therefore saw those aspects that confirmed this view. Neither side needed to tell lies or conceal anything. Since even the most careful and the most detailed description of an event can never be complete, a selection of the elements to be described is required, and this occurs mainly subconsciously.

A large majority of Indian, particularly Hindu, authors till the nineteenth century belong to the second group, whereas Europeans and Muslims are to be included, almost exclusively, in the first group. This has to be taken into consideration in the interpretation.

For the period until about AD 1500 we have only one eyewitness account that has been directly handed down, i.e. that of Ibn Baṭṭūṭa. His testimony indicates that coercion and violence were not ubiquitous phenomena. Till they jump into the fire, the three widows act voluntarily. Only subsequent attempts to escape (which anyway are hardly possible on account of the blazing fire) are prevented by throwing big blocks of wood.[178]

The other relevant information from the period before 1500 is probably based on details given by interested parties. This information clearly shows the manipulation in favour of free choice based on wishful thinking, especially in the fictitious account of the competition among the widows. Inscriptions do not narrate the course of the incident, but they glorify the widows, who *must* have therefore carried out

[178] Ibn Baṭṭūṭa 3, 615–16.

a heroic act. Finally, the Dharma texts detail what should happen and not what happened.

For the period from the sixteenth to the early nineteenth centuries, on the other hand, there are a large number of detailed accounts by Europeans who could observe the ceremony unhindered and who probably did not emphasize too much the element of free choice.

With regard to the conditions of observation, and, therefore, also with regard to present conditions of knowledge, the abolition of 1829 led to a radical change. Everyone who now participated in widow burning was culpable. The reaction to this was one of self-protection, which resulted from the solidarity of complicity. Immediately after the event a kind of 'official' version was developed by the participants, in which the aspect of free choice was emphasized as much as possible and coercion and violence were not spoken of at all. All participants adopted this version, both because they were afraid of reprisals from their accomplices, and also out of fear of being prosecuted by the officials.[179] The fact of having been an eyewitness was no longer significant; each one reported what had (tacitly) been agreed upon, and not what he had seen. This can be easily verified even today by questioning people who have participated in widow burnings of the last decades. Subsequent attempts at establishing the true nature of events regularly proved and still prove to be impossible.

The 'official' version given by the participants can only be countered by conjectures and assertions of those who rightly suspect an attempt to hush up the matter. This impossibility of arriving at the truth is the price of abolition, as long as it is not completely effective.

Every form of widow burning was prohibited. The question of the willingness to die was not important. Otherwise one would have had to distinguish again between legal and illegal cases, which would have meant that the custom was allowed in principle. The role of an independent observer was therefore ruled out. Apart from the fact that the organizers tried as far as possible to keep reporters and journalists away, these observers for their part would have made themselves culpable through their participation and would therefore have had a vested interest in confirming the 'official' version of the participants. The law required them to prevent the immolation, not describe it. The effects on the investigation of the events can best be seen among the

---

[179] Cf. Vaid/Sangari 6; 15.

police. If they arrived on the scene too late, they could only rely on the partisan statements of those involved. If they arrived on time they had to prevent the immolation. On the rare occasions on which they were unable to prevent the ceremony despite their presence, there was a particularly thorough investigation, in the course of which the suspicion that they had allowed themselves to be bribed by the organizers could never be ruled out.[180]

Since 1829 therefore it would be difficult to say with any certainty how a concrete case takes its course. This became particularly apparent in the last, and also the most famous case—in the immolation of Roop Kanwar on 4 September 1987.[181] Completely varying accounts of the event are in circulation, ranging from a heroic willingness to die, to open murder. None of these versions have been proved beyond doubt. It is significant that there are no photographs, although many pictures were put together after the event and other pictures were distributed which show the victim in the classic cheerful and calm pose. The event immediately takes on an ideal form which gives us no clues about its real nature.[182]

Because of these consequences of abolition the following analysis concentrates on the sources of the sixteenth to nineteenth centuries. Finally, we have to ask whether abolition and modern influences have fundamentally changed the framework for free choice and coercion.

The Theory

In the Dharma texts, widow burning is only recommended, never prescribed. From this it follows that the authors took free choice for granted. No one can be forced to do something which he/she is not obliged to do. The widow therefore can only be burnt to death if she agrees to it.

[180] Cf. for example the case *Emperor vs. Vidyasagar Pande* of 1928. Also: Anand 164–70; S. Singh 87.

[181] For more details see above, pp. 243–4.

[182] Similar hypothesis in Rajan, *Women* 25, who on p.18 emphasizes that today all immolations are voluntary acts for the believers and acts of violence for the opponents. The fundamental impossibility of arriving at the truth emerges indirectly (and probably unintentionally) from the portrayal in *Trial by fire*, and also from a newspaper article by Modhumita Majumdar in *Mainstream* of 26 December 1987, reproduced in Anand 145–50. It can also be found in Tully 220, and in Vaid/Sangari 4–5.

One can also introduce a content-oriented, though not completely compelling, argument. The texts declared widow burning to be a singularly deserving act in moral terms. Generally an action is considered morally deserving only when it is voluntary. Of course it cannot be ruled out that the results of the act, i.e. the reunion with the husband in a better life or in everlasting bliss, are ascribed to the act as such, independent of the accompanying circumstances. Yet such a view, that a forced immolation is considered to have the same effect as a voluntary one, seems to have been advocated only rarely, and only tentatively.[183]

The aspect of free choice can be related to different decisions or actions over a period of time: to the announcement of the decision after the husband's death (or after receiving news of his death), to taking part in the procession to the cremation site and in the preparatory ceremonies at the funeral pyre, to the mounting of the pyre or the leap into the fire, and finally to holding out in the flames. Is a new, voluntary decision required for each of these acts, or does a single decision at the beginning suffice?

The announcement of the decision to burn oneself is the most important. One can regard it as the self-commitment of the widow before the family or the community, but also as an agreement with them. The community pledges to take all the measures necessary for carrying out the ceremony while the widow expresses her willingness to take on the main role, which means at the same time that she claims this role for herself. The question now is whether such a contractual agreement is terminable, and if so, under what conditions? According to a view prevalent chiefly, but not only, in modern Europe, an agreement in which a contracting party disposes of his/her own life is invalid from the outset because it is not compatible with the fundamental, inalienable freedom of the individual. Under no circumstances can adherence to such a contract be demanded. This point of view is based on preconditions which did not obtain everywhere and at all times. A voluntary commitment to die can also be regarded as irreversible. The other party then has the right to claim fulfilment of the conditions of the contract, if necessary by force. This force is then only a consequence of the initial, free decision. It does not violate this decision, much less dissolve it. Rather it is inherently necessary for the system, just as the repayment of a loan by a debtor has to be enforced if necessary, in order

---

[183] Leslie, *Wife* 293–6; Leslie, *Victim* 186; Altekar 126.

that the institution of credit is not destroyed. In such a case, refusal is not actually a free decision, but only the non-fulfilment of an obligation.

The fact that the authors of the Dharma texts did not apply this strict point of view speaks for their relative 'liberal-mindedness'. Moreover, most of them granted the widow the right to revoke her decision even at the last minute.[184] At any rate, the claims of the other party were also considered to some extent. A widow who subsequently withdrew from the burning had to do penance and go through an elaborate ritual cleansing. The later the withdrawal occurred, the larger the extent of these obligations. However, the widow could not be expelled from the community forever.[185]

There was no similarly clear opinion expressed regarding the question which became decisive for the actual extent of the use of force. The last, irrevocable decision about life and death had to be taken by the widow when the flames seized her. Was one allowed to prevent her from escaping with the help of force? Such measures undoubtedly contradicted the principle of free choice till the last moment. They could, however, also be declared as normal aspects of the ceremony. It seems that the texts did not really deal with these questions; but they did not reject preventive force unequivocally.[186] If one had repeatedly

[184] Garbe 163; Kane 2,1,633; Ward, *View* 3, 327; Weinberger-Thomas (1989) 18; Weinberger-Thomas (1996) 46; PP 1821/18,29; 105; 118 (legal opinion of pandits). The same holds true for the Nepalese law of 1854. Michaels, *Legislation* 1229–34. According to Jolly 68 some authors did not permit this.

[185] In the Bombay Presidency the British, in order to increase the deterring effect, laid down that widows who subsequently changed their minds would lose their caste. This did not conform to the rules of Hinduism and was not approved by the Court of Directors in London. PP 1825/24, 192; 195–6; PP 1828/23, 28. What normally happened was that the British forced the caste members to take the widow in again after due penance had been done, because in practice expulsions do in fact appear to have taken place. Cf. PP 1821/18, 164; PP 1825/24: 109; 115; PP 1830/28, 169. Mitter 128 reports of a widow being taken back into the family after she had saved herself. In a case of 1817 this happened only reluctantly after the court had ordered it. PP 1821/18, 164. Parks 1, 93: widow not taken in again.

[186] In the literature at any rate no relevant statements are mentioned. Even in the detailed Nepalese law of 1854 the question is not dealt with. Michaels, *Legislation* 1226–35.

allowed the ceremony to be broken off in this way, the prestige of the custom would have suffered badly. On the other hand, there is no doubt about the fact that till the widow mounted the pyre theory demanded free choice.

As opposed to this, many contemporary authors write that it was not possible to revoke the decision, either at the beginning, or once the ceremony had begun.[187] This statement is generally made by eye-witnesses. Obviously the latitude available to the widow in practice was far less than in theory,[188] as will be shown now.

The Practice

Witnesses who can be trusted repeatedly talk about cases in which a woman exercised her free choice in the face of all opposition. In November 1829, the British official John Henry Sleeman prohibited a 65-year old widow from burning herself. He had the body of her husband cremated at a far away place. The woman sat down on a hunger strike. Sleeman promised her all kinds of support for the rest of her life and at the same time threatened to confiscate the family property if she killed herself. She remained unmoved and declared that, as far as this world was concerned, she was already dead. Her relatives also tried, unsuccessfully, to dissuade her from the act. After five days Sleeman yielded to her wishes. The widow, 'casting her eyes upward, said, "Why have they kept me five days from thee, my husband?" She ordered the pyre to be lit. "She then walked up deliberately and steadily to the brink, stepped into the centre of the flame, sat down, and leaning back in the midst as if reposing upon a couch, was consumed without uttering a shriek or betraying one sign of agony." '[189]

The event occurred a few weeks before the ban in Bengal was announced. Sleeman could not have had an interest in exaggerating the aspect of free choice and suppressing the elements of coercion. He despised the custom himself and was aware of the government's efforts to put an end to it.

The event was not an exception. Time and again, widows of all ages mounted the pyre astonishingly calm and composed, after many

[187] Some examples: Vigne 1, 84; Bowrey 40; Holwell 2,88; Dubois, *Moeurs* 2, 23; Rogerius 77.

[188] Emphasized by Weinberger-Thomas (1989) 18; Weinberger-Thomas (1996) 46, and also earlier by Ward, *View* 3,327.

[189] Sleeman 18–23. Quote: 22–3.

people had tried to make them give up their plan. Around 1810 a British eyewitness writes about a 17- or 18-year old widow in Poona who burnt herself to death with her husband's shoes, after her husband, a soldier, had died in a far away place. She seemed serious and composed and showed not 'the slightest degree of agitation or disturbance.' Even when she mounted the pyre and sat down in the small hut, she appeared to be

> entirely unmoved. Not the slightest emotion of any kind was perceptible. There was no effort, no impatience, no shrinking. To look at her, one would have supposed that she was engaged in some indifferent occupation; and although I was within a few yards of her, I could not, at any moment, detect, either in her voice, or manner, or in the expression of her countenance, the smallest appearance of constraint, or the least departure from the most entire self-possession.

She was not under the influence of drugs, and no one tried to persuade her, to incite her, or to encourage her. 'She herself took the lead throughout, and did all that was to be done, of her own accord.' She lit the fire with her own hands and lay down. The roof of the hut collapsed, 'the weight of which was insufficient either to injure or to confine the victim.' The woman was by no means prevented from escaping. Her death showed 'no outward appearances to excite horror; no struggle, no violence, none of the contortions, or agonies of death.'[190]

In contrast to this there were cases involving the most brutal use of force, as, for example, on 20 November 1820, in Gorakhpur district:

> One Seetloo, a brahmin, died when absent from his family. A fortnight afterwards, his widow, Hoomuleea, a girl of about fourteen years of age, proceeded to burn herself, the pile being prepared by her nearest relations then at the village she resided in. Her father, Puttun Tewarrey, was in another part of the country, and does not appear to have been made acquainted with what was passing. Whether the sacrifice was originally a voluntary one, has not been ascertained; it must be presumed it was so.
>
> The preparatory rites completed, Hoomuleea ascended the pile, which was fired by her uncle, the prisoner Sheolol. The agony was soon

[190] Anon.: Review Heber 127–9.

beyond endurance, and she leaped from the flame, but seized by Sheolol Bhichhook, and others, she was taken up by the hands and feet, and again thrown upon it; much burnt, and her clothes quite consumed, she again sprang from the pile, and running to a well hard by, laid herself down in the watercourse, weeping bitterly. Sheolol now took a sheet, offered for the occasion by Roosa, and spreading it on the ground, desired her to seat herself upon it: 'No!' she said, 'she would not do this, he would again carry her to the fire, and she could not submit to this; she would quit the family, and live by beggary; any thing, if they would have mercy upon her!' Sheolol upon this, swore by Ganges, that if she would seat herself on the cloth, he would carry her to her home. She did so; they bound her up in it, sent for a bamboo, which was passed through the loops formed by tying it together, and carrying it thus to the pile, now fiercely burning, threw it bodily into the flames. The cloth was immediately consumed, and the wretched victim once more made an effort to save herself, when, at the instigation of the rest, the Moosulman Buraichee, approached near enough to reach her with his sword, and cutting her through the head, she fell back, and was released from further trial by death.[191]

The large majority of cases lie between these two extremes. Their analysis has to proceed from the chronological course of events. For this widow burning is looked at as a process which begins with the husband's death and reaches its conclusion with the death of the widow. Theoretically, the question of free choice and coercion has to be considered separately for every point of time in this process.

The sources provide numerous and detailed statements about the final phase, but say hardly anything about the initial phase. Generally Europeans could participate in the public part of the ceremony unhindered. But they were never present during the earlier phases—the death of the husband, the announcement of the widow's decision, and the first preparations for the ceremony. Here, only local people

---

[191] 25 May 1821, letter from the judge R.M. Rattray to the Nizamat Adalat, in PP1823/17, 67–8, as well as in PP 1830/28, 7–9. Case first reported: PP 1823/17, 54. Some further extreme examples: *Asiatic Journal* NS 19 (1836), 263; PP 1823/17, 26; PP 1825/24, 4–6; 162–90; PP 1828/23, 10–12; PP 1830/28, 7–21; 197; Bowrey 40; 303; Johns 25; 31; Peggs, *Suttee's cry* (1828) 18–19; Thackeray/Richardson 63–4; Thompson, *Suttee* 118; Massie 2, 175–6.

were witnesses, and they have not left behind any accounts. Yet it is possible to make some general statements. In doing this a clear asymmetry between the cases described becomes evident.

One can assume with a degree of certainty that both the widow Sleeman talks about and the one in Poona acted of their own free will in the early phase. When free choice is undisputed in the face of death, then it follows without additional proof that it was also given in the early phase, when the direct confrontation with the agonies of death was not yet present.

On the other hand, the fact that Hoomulea was murdered in a brutal manner, as the judge himself emphasized, should not lead to the assumption that the case involved violence and coercion from the beginning. Sometimes European eyewitnesses write that the widow at first displayed an extraordinary steadfastness and immense courage, and that she upheld her decision in the face of all objections. But when she was supposed to mount the pyre, she would suddenly break down,[192] or she simply refused to do what was expected of her.[193] Sometimes her instinct for survival proved to be stronger than her will power when the flames shot up.[194] At this point violence began; the widow was prevented from leaving the pyre, or she was thrown back onto it again. Till then, however, violence had not been necessary at all.

In the early phase violence would certainly have been rare, especially because it did not serve any purpose. After the husband's death the question at first was whether the widow would decide to accompany him. This decision could not be obtained through coercion. The widow could be pressurized and threatened, but her consent could not be wrested from her by force. If she refused, there was no alternative but to drag her to the cremation site and tie her onto the pyre, or throw her into the fire. This appears never to have happened, or only in exceptional cases. At any rate, the sources—even the court records—never mention it. Opponents of the custom would not have missed the opportunity of pointing out such cruelty. Such a procedure would also have gone completely against the substance of the ritual in which the widow played such an important role. At least upto the mounting of

[192] For example Dubois, *Moeurs* 2, 28–31. Cf. Garbe 165.

[193] Caunter 94–8.

[194] For example *Emperor vs. Vidyasagar Pande* 501; Peggs, *Suttee's cry* (1828) 18–19; PP 1821/18, 164; PP 1823/17,26; J.K. Majumdar 131; IOR P/139/34, 244–52.

the pyre it would have been absolutely impossible to conduct the ceremony with a widow who put up a fierce resistance. The ritual rules and practices therefore ensured that the widow had to co-operate at least to some extent. It is true that it is occasionally mentioned that the widow was not completely conscious, or that she suffered an attack of weakness and had to be supported.[195] But that did not indicate a use of force.

From this we can conclude what is also emphasized in the sources: the necessity of obtaining the widow's consent after her husband's death. If the widow refused firmly enough, nothing further happened. As a rule, if the widow refused to honour her commitment after the announcement of the decision, but before the start of the actual ceremony, her refusal also appears to have been accepted.[196]

The sources contain very few precise details about a factor that further complicates the question of willingness and coercion. It appears that some widows pledged themselves, while their husbands were still alive, to burn themselves with his body after his death. Different forms of this commitment are mentioned.

Naturally we can know very little about cases in which the wife gave her husband the promise privately and without witnesses.[197] None would know about this obligation so long as her husband did not tell anyone about her promise. This only became known if the widows themselves referred to such promises at the moment of cremation, in order to silence the voices trying to dissuade them from the act.[198]

What is mentioned more often is the more or less public announcement of the decision while the husband is still alive.[199] This promise could have been given to the family.[200] Occasionally it is also said that during a widow burning other women declared that they would do the

---

[195] Thus Dubois, *Moeurs* 2, 28–9; S.C. Bose 276; Vigne 1, 82; Moor 355.

[196] Such a case is described already in Kalhaṇa 6, 194–6.

[197] Ward, *View* 3, 310; Valentyn 5, 1, 84–5.

[198] Mökern 1, 331; IOR P/206/82, no. 9.

[199] Without mentioning the exact circumstances: Dapper 54; Mukhopadhyay, *Institution* 104; Ward, *View* 3, 314–15; Haafner 81–2; 87; Wurffbain 2, 17. There is no proof given for the statement by Weinberger-Thomas (1989) 19, that the promise was frequently given while the husband lay on his deathbed.

[200] For example Hügel 2, 401.

same if their husbands died.[201] Older authors even say that such promises were often already given at the time of marriage.[202] The possibility of expressly stating that a widow burning was out of the question is also said to have existed.[203]

Relevant accounts are never very precise, nor do they enable us to estimate the frequency of such occurrences. But there are some indications that they became rarer in the course of time. The practice can possibly be traced back to that form of institutional following into death in which vassals, on entering service, pledged themselves to accompany their master into death. Such a context is sometimes mentioned.[204] This was a clear contractual relationship which was not suited to a marital relationship, and therefore with time it probably lost its importance in individual following into death. In the older sources the relevant references are at any rate more frequent than in the later ones. An obligation that was linked with a particular position in the court became a personal obligation with regard to the husband, one which was apparently formally complied with less and less in the course of time.

To what extent can such promises and obligations be looked upon as circumstantial evidence for free choice or coercion? To a certain extent, at least it means a shift in the announcement of the decision from the moment of the husband's death to an earlier point of time. In this situation it is easier to speak of a free and considered decision than in the moment of deepest sorrow and greatest numbness. On the other hand, there was the danger of taking a rash decision, since the time to carry out the promise seemed far away (if the wife died first, the necessity to carry it out would not arise at all). We also cannot say how seriously one took the nature of obligation of such promises. There was a strong moral pressure to keep a promise given earlier, one moreover that could have the religious character of a vow. But generally it would not have been forced on the widow against her declared will. Some authors are of the opinion that such a promise was not binding.[205] Ward, on the other hand, relates how in 1802 a woman near Calcutta

[201] For example Kennedy 19–20; Sleeman 24 (promise given 13 years ago).
[202] Conti 127–8; 166; Guichard 382; Tafur 91; Rogerius 71.
[203] Schouten 2, 100.
[204] Rao 238; Shastri 133.
[205] Haafner 87; Dapper 54.

who did not want to fulfil her promise was tied to her husband's body and burnt to death.[206]

The nature of the ceremony and the role that the widow had to play in it therefore ruled out the use of physical force to a large extent until the widow had to mount the pyre or leap into the flames. Alongside this there is another possible form of violence, which is far more effective in some respects, and which is frequently mentioned both in the sources and in modern research. In a country in which the use of opium and other drugs was widely prevalent, the use of such means would seem likely. If the widow was given an intoxicant, it was generally easier to obtain her consent. The effect of the drug also made the widow more pliant later.

Although such considerations sound plausible, the use of drugs cannot be proved.[207] We do not possess a single account in which an eyewitness notes having seen intoxicants being administered. Many contemporary and also modern authors are convinced that drugs were used,[208] others deny this.[209] With reference to the most recent case of 1987, most accounts assume that drugs were used.[210] Medically educated eyewitnesses frequently tried to identify the symptoms through accurate observation: however they could never offer definite proof. In the 1820s or 1830s Marianne Postans, who observed the extreme apathy of a widow during the entire ceremony, presumed that she was under the influence of drugs. She had the approximately 30-year old woman examined by two doctors who could not find anything.[211] In 1824, when a British observer asked a magistrate to stop a burning

---

[206] Ward, *View* 3, 314–15. Hügel 2, 401 states with reference to Kashmir that some wives and concubines of a ruler would promise him during his lifetime to accompany him in death, in order to win his favour. In return the other wives would then insist on the promise being fulfilled.

[207] This is also emphasized by Garbe 165.

[208] For example Elphinstone 360 (in Gujarat); Hervey 1, 212; Macdonald 221; Statham 133; Lutfullah 176; Patnaik 99–101; Saxena, *Reforms* 74; A. Sharma *et al.*, *Sati* 27; Sousa 2; Bishnoi 80; Vigne 1, 82; 93; Weinberger-Thomas (1989) 25; Winternitz, *Frau* 72–4; IOR L/L 13, 1030, vol. 3, 215v: c. 1831/32 Court of Directors to the Privy Council; Manrique 78; Manucci 3, 156; Monserrate 62; Sonnerat 1, 94; Bowrey 37; Caunter 94–6.

[209] For example Hügel 2, 402–3; IOR P/139/34,251; Campbell 245.

[210] For example Modhumita Mojumdar, in *Mainstream* 26 December 1987, reproduced in Anand 150; Upreti 70; 88.

[211] Postans 65.

because he believed to have established beyond doubt the effect of drugs, the official refused to do anything for lack of proof.[212]

It is indeed probable that drugs were used from time to time. Their use presented itself so obviously that we can hardly assume that there was a conscious effort to avoid them. That the problem was known can also be seen from the fact that in some Dharma texts the use of drugs was prohibited.[213] On the other hand, it is improbable that intoxicants were used regularly, or even in a majority of the cases. This would have become known with time and would have been recorded by Europeans.

Even if the use of drugs could be proved beyond doubt, one would not be justified in automatically assuming the use of force. The advantages described could also make the widow reach for the intoxicants herself. She was determined to die, but knew how painful and torturous it was. It would therefore have been quite natural to reduce the suffering with the help of drugs.

Zachariae believes that drugs were not administered to break the widow's resistance or to minimise suffering, but to induce an ecstatic condition in which the widow would be in a position to utter prophecies.[214]

Several circumstances that led the observers to infer that drugs were used can also be explained differently in view of a situation which was fit to make the widow numb. Thompson says that 'the intoxication was of the spirit, not the body,' and he speaks of 'a psychological intoxication.'[215] In 1840 Hügel had already given detailed reasons for his view that opium was not being used:

> The sudden transition from a condition of anxiety and hope at her husband's deathbed to the certainty of her husband's death as well as her own, the pain of being parted from her husband, the horror of the approaching terrible moment brought about by a moral necessity, the noisy ceremonies and the high honours bestowed on the unlucky woman by holy men, who earlier would have recoiled at her touch: all this affects the uneducated mind of Hindu women in a way, which

[212] Patnaik 100–1; cf. also *Asiatic Journal* 17 (1824), 570.

[213] Cf. the legal opinion of pandits for the Nizamat Adalat, *c.* 1803–5. PP 1821/18,28. There was a very strict ban in the Nepalese law of 1854 to regulate widow burning. Michaels, *Legislation* 1230–1.

[214] Zachariae 597.

[215] Thompson, *Suttee* 50–1.

makes them believe that they already belong to another world. These events, which happen in quick succession, would be calculated to confuse and deaden a stronger mind than that of an Indian woman. Fear of death is moreover unknown to most Hindus, and the conviction of a higher joy which, according to their belief, awaits the person sacrificing herself, makes her, if she really begins to think, disregard the painful moment that is so close. There is no time for reflection.[216]

Coercion, and especially violence, were mainly used in the final phase, in the actual burning. Brutal scenes like the murder of Hoomuleea were extremely rare. They might be dismissed as criminal exceptions. Another form of less spectacular, yet more effective, force, which was far more prevalent, has repeatedly been mentioned: preventive force in the form of devices that were meant to prevent the widow from escaping. To name only some of these methods that have often been attested: the widow was tied to her husband's body[217] or to a stake;[218] heavy blocks of wood were laid over her and the corpse;[219] she was held down with long bamboo sticks;[220] the entrance to the hut was locked;[221] heavy pieces of wood were piled up on the roof of the hut and the pillars constructed in such a way that they either soon collapsed in consequence of the fire,[222] or could be made to come down while the

[216] Hügel 2, 403.

[217] For example Challe 293; Johns 48; Burnell 108; Campbell 245; Stavorinus 2, 50; Twining 466; *An Old Inhabitant* 487; *Sketch* 46; *Asiatic Journal* 9 (1820), 387–8; 17 (1824), 192; 26 (1828), 215; Ward, *View* 3, 311ff.; Careri 3, 231; J.K. Majumdar 203; Ray 83–5.

[218] For example Careri 3, 138–9; Manucci 3, 60; Tavernier 2, 385; Coverte 57.

[219] For example Bogaert 376–7; Ravesteyn 74; Rogerius 79; Edwardes/Merivale 2, 36–7; Campbell 245; Manucci 3, 60; Twining 466; Wurffbain 2, 17–18; Andersen/Iversen 209; Elliot 5; *Friend of India* 3 (1820), 207; Ward, *View* 3, 311ff; Fryer 33.

[220] For example Edwardes/Merivale 2, 36–7; Johns 23–4; 48; Mundy 2, 34; Twining 466; *An Old Inhabitant* 487; *Sketch* 46; *Asiatic Journal* 9 (1820), 387–8; Johns 23–6; Ward, *View* 3, 311ff.; Bowrey 40; Manucci 3, 65–6; 165; Monserrate 62; J.K. Majumdar 203; G. Smith 108–9.

[221] For example Mökern 326–8; Modave 172–4; Mundy 2, 34; Rennefort 316; PP 1825/24, 213.

[222] Holwell 2, 97; *Asiatic Journal* 20 (1825), 147; NS 2/1 (1830), 206; PP 1825/24, 213; Lutfullah 176.

fire was lit by pulling away the supports.[223] If the burning took place in a pit, the spectators threw heavy blocks of wood on the widow after she had jumped in.[224] The European eyewitness accounts and even the Indian sources leave us in no doubt about the fact that such things happened frequently in a more or less routine fashion. This is even valid for the case described by Kennedy.[225]

Some remarks give the impression that preventive force was the rule.[226] Yet sometimes they are not written by disinterested witnesses. Rammohan Roy particularly emphasized this aspect of violence.[227] In the British surveys of the years 1815–28, it is not mentioned very often, yet the most reliable eyewitness accounts speak astonishingly frequently about arrangements to prevent the victim from escaping. One would rather have to assume that the use of such means was taken so much for granted in many places that it ceased to be mentioned. According to the British understanding the use of any kind of coercion was illegal. If necessary these means could be declared as part of the normal procedure, especially since their use was not clearly regulated in the normative texts. Moreover, it would have to be assumed that they were sometimes used with the widow's consent, as in the case observed by Kennedy.[228]

Apparently most of the participants assumed that it was legitimate to use such force. The basis for this seems to have been the belief that the widow did not have the right to revoke her decision at the last moment. This could be seen in a case of 1841 (thus after abolition). Although the widow was not tied down, she was expressly warned that if she tried to escape she would be thrown back onto the pyre.[229] The

[223] For example Mökern 326–8; J. Forbes 1, 282–3; Peggs, *Suttee's cry* (1828) 12; *Interesting facts* 115; Dubois, *Moeurs* 2, 31.

[224] For example Rogerius 79; Schorer 58; Schouten 2, 100; Twist 32; Hamilton 1, 157–8; Methwold 29; Haafner 91–2; Nuniz 76–7.

[225] Kennedy 46. Cf. above, p. 3.

[226] *Essays* 9–10; *Remarks* 8; *Friend of India* 2 (1819), 308–9; 3 (1820), 208; PP 1821/18, 227–9 (W. Ewer).

[227] R. Roy, *English Works* 3, 95–6. William Wilberforce maintained in the House of Commons that preventive force was always used. *Parliamentary Debates* 26, 859 (22 June 1813).

[228] Kennedy 46. Cf. also S.C. Bose 276; Campbell 241–6; Careri 3, 231; Challe 292–4; Johns 23–4; Lutfullah 175–7; Ray 83–5; Thompson, *Suttee* 157.

[229] *Asiatic Journal* NS 36/2 (1841), 344–5.

event was seen as a ritual, complete in itself, that could not be arbitrarily discontinued. Once begun, all participants had to adhere to their roles, not least because they had obligations to the powers of the other world. If they did not fulfil these obligations, it could have negative consequences for all. In the general interest, therefore, this meant the right to force recalcitrant widows to fulfil their role.

The widespread use of preventive force allows for a further inference. Apparently the number of cases, in which the widow tried to save herself at the last moment, was not small. Obviously the arrangements to prevent her escape were only used where it seemed necessary. They harmed the prestige of the institution, which was essentially based on the stated voluntary nature of the act and the presumed heroism of the widow. In popular imagination the ceremony certainly did not have the reputation of a murder or a ceremonial slaughter. Rather it was associated with the belief that the true sati did not feel any pain. If the ceremony was stopped too often at the last moment, the determination of the widow proved to be an illusion and the prestige of the custom suffered greater harm than with the use of preventive force. One therefore merely chose the lesser of two evils.

However, even this conclusion is not always true. The cases in which the widow was able to escape show that preventive force was not always used, or at least not to a sufficient degree.

The dilemma led to a further attempt to find a solution. Before the widow was allowed to mount the pyre, her capability to bear suffering was tested. For this she had to put a finger, a hand, or an arm into a flame without showing the slightest sign of pain. Many European observers, who were otherwise by no means well-disposed towards the custom, report this with unconcealed admiration.[230] Sometimes the widow herself asked for the test, in order to be able to prove her determination and to silence those who wanted to dissuade her from carrying out her intention.[231] But even this method does not always

[230] Ganguly 57; Patnaik 100–1; Ward, *View* 1, xlv; Tavernier 2, 392. Cf. Lutfullah 176. Weinberger-Thomas (1989) 26; Weinberger-Thomas (1996) 45–54 presumes that this test was introduced by the Moghuls in order to frighten the widow, or at least to probe the seriousness of her intentions. However no supporting evidence is given, and it is possible that this method is much older.

[231] S.C. Bose 274 (the author's aunt); Halliday, in Buckland 1, 160–1. Tully 217 speaks of a case that is supposed to have happened in Jodhpur in 1954. However he does not provide any supporting evidence.

seem to have been successful. Otherwise it would probably have been used everywhere as an alternative to preventive force. The sources do not say whether this lack of success resulted from the widows' refusal to undergo the test of fire, or whether some of them, despite having passed the test, subsequently lost courage in the blazing flames of the pyre. Some women lost their courage even before the test of fire and gave up, which, as a rule, was accepted.[232] Others displayed a marked inconsistency in their last moments. Different kinds of forces, impressions and emotions affected them, so that sometimes, immediately after being saved, they wanted to jump into the flames again. In 1822, a sati jumped down from the pyre at the magistrate's feet. Although she would have been saved, she wanted to go back into the fire, which the magistrate finally allowed her to do.[233] In 1817, a widow screamed for help. The police officer brought her down from the pyre. She later accused him 'with having forced her from the pile against her will.'[234]

Finally, the frequent use of preventive force leads to the assumption that opium could not solve all problems. Otherwise it would definitely have been used in preference to more violent methods.

In order to determine the role of free choice and coercion more precisely, widow burning must be looked at as a process which over a period of time—even if this is mostly limited to a few hours—undergoes a fundamental change of character.

The first phase culminates in the announcement of the widow's decision to die with her husband. In most of the cases one would have to speak of a voluntary decision here (the reasons for it will be explored later). The decision itself could not be forced, and generally it was respected.

Once the widow had taken the decision to die, the conditions changed. This became evident in two opposite trends. If she adhered to her decision, the widow found that increasingly the demands on her became greater. The closer death advanced, the more horrible it appeared, and the more the desire to live prevailed. The climax came just before the end, when the woman was seized by the flames. The longer the ceremony (and the agony) lasted, the more she tended to

---

[232] *Papers* (1868), 256; PP 1823/17,19; Elliott 4. In the case last mentioned the widow was burnt to death despite this.

[233] PP 1823/17, 50–1 (quote: see below, p. 390).

[234] PP 1821/18, 164.

relinquish the idea of burning. Indeed, the widows mostly shrank back at the last minute—sometimes waiting until it was too late, so that they died days later of their burns.[235]

Society viewed the matter in exactly the opposite way. As long as the widow had not announced her intention to immolate herself, one hoped perhaps that this would happen. But it was not always expected from her. With the announcement of the decision the expectation was awakened, and it grew stronger by the hour. The further the preparations had advanced, the greater the effort that had gone into these, the more people assembled, the more obvious it seemed to all that a burning would now actually take place. What was simply the result of the passage of time was intensified by the fear of the adverse consequences, if the ceremony was brought to a premature end. The closer the time for lighting the pyre approached, the more it was to be expected that, if necessary, the widow would be forced to die. However, the preparatory ceremonies were usually conducted with a widow who was willing to die.

The point of sudden change, when both these lines crossed each other, came only with the mounting of the pyre, at the latest, when the fire was lit. At this point force came to the surface and the widow was no longer allowed to escape. In some cases, however, one had to talk of free choice till the end, since the widow held out in the flames without the use of force. One could argue that it is no longer justified to speak of free choice, especially in the way it is used here, since the widow would have been killed either way. But even at the moment of immolation force was not always used in case of a refusal, and some widows were able to save themselves against all odds.

Therefore it is not correct to talk in an undifferentiated manner of widow burning as an institution based purely on force. On the other hand, the fact has been established that even in India the custom was linked to a considerable extent with force and violence. Without the elements of violence it would hardly have endured in the form as we know it. Perhaps it would not have died out completely, but it would certainly have become rarer if its prestige had suffered due to frequent, tumultuous discontinuance at the last moment.

A view rejected by theory was thus to a large extent established by

[235] This could however also have been because the widow had to free herself with a tremendous effort, for example by pushing aside the wood piled upon her.

practice. The widow's decision to burn herself with her husband's body in a public ceremony was treated as an irrevocable obligation which in case of a subsequent refusal would be carried out with force if necessary, and the later the point of time at which consent was withdrawn, the more likely that force would be used. From a permanently valid right, consent became a one-time decision.

In popular imagination, and even in research, the prevalent view is that widow burning in Rajasthan was predominantly voluntary, while in Bengal it was mostly associated with force. Even Thompson asserts: 'Suttee reached its most magnificent and least squalid form among the Rajputs.'[236] The image of martial, heroic Rajputs and frail, cowardly Bengalis belongs to the standard myths of the British in India, which was frequently taken over by Indians. At least with regard to widow burning it is empirically not tenable; the sources do not suggest a regional distinction in the concentration of magnificence or squalidness (however they may be defined).

In very rare cases the widow got involved in the violence used against her. In the 1670s Thomas Bowrey observed the following near Hooghly:

> The Woman wold not at all deny to burne, knowinge any deniall to be of noe Effect, and although She was unwillinge thereto, yet She knew it now fell to her lot, therefore bore it patiently, and Stood very couragiously neare the place of torment (the fiery flames); whereupon the Brachmans gave Order for the fire to burne very furiously that the Sooner she might be dispatched, and they were very Joyfull to See the woman Undaunted; but when she was, according to theire Expection, to have leaped into the fire, she refused it. Whereupon the Brachmans were very yeare [desirous] to take hold of her; but the first that laid hands on her, She laid as Sure hands upon him, and threw herselfe headlonge into the fire and the Brachman with her, where they both perished in a moment. Thus one of those Diabolicall Priests perished in the Pitt he had digged for another.[237]

Violence on the part of the widow could also be directed against her enemies. A case in the second half of the seventeenth century became

[236] Thompson, *Suttee* 42. Cf. ib., 52–3; Bayly 174; Upreti 30; Sangari, in *Seminar* 26; Vaid/Sangari 13; Weinberger-Thomas (1996) 242, footnote 85.
[237] Bowrey 204.

famous. A woman had a lover, for whose sake she poisoned her husband. The lover refused to marry her, whereupon the woman made preparations to burn herself with her husband's body. In front of the pit filled with combustibles she took leave of her friends and relatives. Her lover was among them. She threw a golden chain around his neck and dragged him into the blazing fire.[238]

What Led the Widow to Choose Death?[239]

The widow's decision to burn herself, or to allow herself to be burnt to death, was influenced by a range of forces and factors, most of which have already been dealt with, especially with regard to aspects of this and the other world. Others are discussed in the next chapter. The focus here is on whether, and to what extent, they are capable of explaining the actions and behaviour of the widow. In this a distinction will be made between positive and negative factors. The former make death appear attractive to the widow, the latter drive her into death.

The most important positive factor was undoubtedly the belief in the hereafter in all its facets, and with all the hopes associated with it. Along with this was the desire for fame and honour, for oneself, for one's relatives, and for the larger community, as well as the will to prove one's virtue and strength. Even the prospect of being in the centre of public attention for once, if only for a short time, and of being able to exert power and influence over the participants, would have sometimes played a role.

The negative factors were more numerous and varied, although it is not clear whether their effect was stronger than that of the positive factors. First the sorrow and despair at the husband's death must be

[238] Manucci 2, 96 (eyewitness); Bernier 114–16; a slightly different version in Hamilton 1, 157–8.

[239] The question of motives is understandably repeatedly asked by earlier authors as well as in modern research, and attempts at more or less comprehensive explanations are made. Some differentiated reflections by earlier authors: *Essays* 17ff.; A Bengal civilian 60; Johns 85–6; Jordanus 20; Dubois, *Moeurs* 2, 21; Challe 294; Rogerius 80; Bernier 114; *Friend of India* 2 (1819), 319ff.; Ward, *View* 3, 328. Modern authors: Chaudhury, *Society* 51ff.; Gulati; Mukhopadhyay, *Institution* 11–12; Nandy, *Tale* 171ff.; Narasimhan 80ff.; Saxena, *Reforms* 69ff.; Michaels, *Recht*; Sternbach; Thompson, *Suttee* 44–51; V.N.Datta, chaps 7–8.

mentioned. Independent of this, however, his death brought on a considerable loss of status for the widow and worsened the conditions of her life. This will be dealt with in the next chapter. In addition, there was the influence of society. The relatives applied pressure; the widow knew that they had an eye on her property, and that they possibly even wanted to be rid of her. Priests extolled the exemplary nature of a sati. She felt as if she had been abandoned by all the forces that had protected her. All through her life she had been taught that the highest ideal of a woman was to become a sati. Once she had taken her decision to die, she was confronted with the expectations of society, and to revoke the decision would have brought on scorn, disgrace and poverty, in fact a loss of honour. In short: a life dragged out endlessly in misery and contempt was contrasted to a glorious death. The list could be extended. However it gives sufficient indication of the various powers and influences that affected the widow's decision.

Now we face a paradox. If these factors are taken seriously and understood as the actual causes, then it follows that widow burning would have been a widespread phenomenon at all times in most parts of the world. It was not only Indian widows who mourned their husbands, and belief in a better life after death was not only prevalent in India, just as the position of the widow in matters of inheritance, where the relatives stood to gain from her death, was not peculiar to India. Even the desire for fame and honour is not limited to India.

By regarding these factors as causes, we arrive at a marked overdetermination of the phenomenon to be explained. In giving too many explanations, little or nothing is actually explained. Causes, which have the effects ascribed to them only in the rarest of cases, are not really causes. Both in popular as well as in academic treatments of the theme the following argument is often found: in view of the miserable fate that awaited her, the widow had no choice but to kill herself,[240] or, in a milder version: was it surprising that widows killed themselves in view of such conditions?[241] Such explanations must be prepared for the counter question: If the situation of widows was really so unbearable, why is it that for every widow, who burned herself, 999 others stayed alive? The 999 also did not subsequently regret the decision to stay

[240] For example in Tavernier 2, 383.

[241] For example Terry 322–3; Bogaert 376; Pasquier 319–20; *On the burning of Hindoo widows* 18–19; Le Bon 652; Winternitz, *Witwe* 85; S. Chaudhury, *Society* 51; Stein, *Women* 255; Basham 186–7. Critique: Elphinstone 358; Sprockhoff, *Indien* 427.

alive to such an extent that large numbers burned themselves after they had experienced the reality of a widow's existence. The possibility was open to them. Non-Brahmin women at least could immolate themselves at a later point of time.

The conclusion is obvious. One cannot explain an exceptional case with phenomena representing the rule. The explanation would have to have recourse to special and unusual circumstances, to exceptional factors. It is relatively easy to explain the special position of India in the matter of following into death. The subordination of the wife to the husband, her dependence on him, was more pronounced than in most other parts of the world. Marital bonds were supposed to exist even beyond death. In addition, following into death had been adapted to an elaborate belief in the hereafter which took the merits and demerits of this world into consideration. Foreign rulers showed no interest in institutional following into death. This meant that the individual form could be realized more easily. The competition between the priestly caste and the warrior caste also favoured the spread of the custom.

It is more difficult to explain the exceptional position of widow burning within India. It was principally an upper-class or upper-caste phenomenon. In these circles the widow's labour power was not a consideration, while notions of honour, focused around the preservation of an all-encompassing chastity, played an important role. The desire to appropriate the widow's wealth, as well as hopes for a gain in status and prestige for the family, also had an effect.

Here, the method reaches its limits. It is true that widow burning occurred particularly frequently in the upper classes. Yet even among these it represented a rare exception; besides it was also found among the lower classes. Whichever way one looks at it—in India, even with reference to caste and social classes, it is not a regular phenomenon, but an exception that has to be explained. Therefore, these factors do not have the status of causes, but merely of basic conditions. Taken together, they can at least be regarded as conditions that make widow burning possible. Even when all of them materialize together, it does not follow in the least that immolation will occur. In other words: these factors cannot really explain the individual case. For that the specific situation at hand will have to be considered. The sources do not contain sufficient information to undertake this. The question therefore will have to remain unanswered as to what led one widow to her decision in contrast to 999 others. This does not mean that the decision was taken without external influences. But the external factors did not affect every widow in the same way. Women who could count on a prosperous and respectable life surrounded by their children killed themselves, while others, who had nothing but misery and scorn to look forward to, remained alive.

These difficulties and methodological limitations are true not only for the analysis of following into death, but also for every comparable, exceptional phenomenon, as also for suicide and for varied forms of deviant behaviour including crimes. A statistical explanation based on probability cannot explain the individual case, but can only make it plausible. It explains why it could happen, and not why it actually happened.

The Period After Abolition

With abolition the course of events leading up to burnings, which still took place, could no longer be reconstructed with any degree of certainty (see pp. 301–2). The impossibility of objective knowledge primarily concerns the question of free choice and coercion which was particularly controversial because the extent of culpability of the participants depended on the answer. Here one can only weigh arguments of plausibility against one another. We must also ask whether the changes that occurred in the position of women and widows since 1829 favoured free choice or coercion.

1. The prohibition increased the risk of punishment for those who took part in widow burnings. This led to a decrease in the violence used. Moreover, burnings now became much rarer. Therefore, the probability was greater that a widow went to her death with steadfast determination upto the last minute. But this argument is not conclusive. On account of this increased rarity the exemplary nature of such events was also lost to a great extent. They became isolated cases which referred less and less to living traditions.

Abolition had a two-edged effect also on the actual ceremony. The people associated with a burning constantly stood under the threat of an interference by organs of the state and had to run through the event as quickly as possible, which could lead to the use of force.

2. The position of women, and especially of widows, clearly changed on paper from 1829. The extent of legal subordination to the husband particularly became less. In practice however this was only valid for a small group of women of the upper and middle classes.

Other determining factors have changed even less, from the widow's sorrow to the relatives' desire to inherit her property. Only the belief in the hereafter would have lost its persuasive power—and that too only in a relatively small group.

For the overwhelming majority of widows the original conditions for free choice and coercion remain more or less unchanged. Widow burning still takes place in its traditional framework. This can also be seen in the fact that since 1829, and especially in the recent decades, it has generally taken place in remote rural regions.

Yet even the assumption that the views would have changed fundamentally at least in the 'new' classes has proved to be problematic. This is one of the reasons why the last well-known case of widow burning of 4 September 1987 had much stronger after-effects than earlier cases. 18-year old Roop Kanwar came from a well-to-do middle-class family in the large city of Jaipur. She had gone to school for ten years, which represents an above-average level of education in Rajasthan, where the literacy rate among women is extremely low.[242] She married into a family in a village, but it was a teacher's family, and her husband worked in Jaipur.[243] This background makes one understand why in this case the—insoluble—dispute about free choice and coercion was particularly fierce. If Roop Kanwar had gone voluntarily to her death, it proved that the old views were deeply embedded even in the 'new' classes. If, on the other hand, force was used, the responsibility could be shifted to reactionary forces.

Problems of a Special Form: *Jauhar*

In 1295, the Hindu defenders of the city of Jaisalmer found themselves in an inextricable situation after a long siege by a Muslim army. They could only choose between surrender and a fight to death. Honour demanded of them that they die. The leaders agreed that first the honour of the women should be protected, and then that of the men

---

[242] Literacy rates 1991, in percent

	female	male
Rajasthan	20.84	55.07
All India	39.42	63.86

The female literacy rate in Rajasthan was the lowest in all of India. Source: Aggarwal/Chowdhury 1–2.

[243] For details about relevant literature see chap. 11, footnote 104.

upheld. They called all the women of the city together and killed them without exception. 'Twenty-four thousand females, from infancy to old age, surrendered their lives, some by the sword, others in the volcano of fire. Blood flowed in torrents, while the smoke of the pyre ascended to the heavens: not one feared to die.' When the job had been completed, 'three thousand eight hundred warriors, with faces red with wrath, prepared to die with their chiefs', by plunging into the last battle against the besiegers.[244]

Many accounts about such events and similar ones can be found, mainly from Rajasthan, in the context of battles between the Hindu princely states and their Muslim enemies, but partly also between Hindus. An army, which is also supposed to protect women—this is most likely the case in besieged forts or cities—finds itself in a situation which according to the concept of honour of the military aristocracy only allows for death as a way out, even for the women. They are on no account to fall into the hands of the enemy. Therefore, they are all killed, preferably on a large pyre or in a big building filled with combustible material, or also individually with the weapons of war. After this the men go to their death in battle. If they are not killed, or if they are in danger of being taken prisoner, they either kill each other or kill themselves. In an 'ideal' case not one of the besieged remains alive.[245]

In research this occurrence called *jauhar*[246] is generally studied in connection with widow burning, as a kind of intensification of the same.[247] According to the criteria used here, one cannot speak of following into death. The most important difference lies in the fact that those who follow the dead (here, the women) first kill them with their own hands, whereas otherwise those who are to be accompanied are never killed by the attendants. In addition there are no ceremonies conducted when the men die.

[244] Tod 2, 251–2.

[245] Further descriptions for example in Tod 1, 266; 311–12; 327; 639–41; 2, 60; Elliot/Dowson 3, 546; Nand 176–8; Ashraf 161–3; Srivastava 202–3; Pelsaert 79; Thakur, *History* 161–9. Thakur has taken his examples, as have most other authors, from Tod.

[246] For the term cf. Ashraf 161; Leslie, *Victim* 176; Oldenburg, in Hawley (ed.) 164.

[247] For example Leslie, *Victim* 176; Thakur, *History* 161–8; Thompson, *Suttee* 37; Tod 1,639; A. Sharma, *Thresholds* 98; Deshpande 28; Narasimhan 118–19; Manjushree 184; Nand 176–8; Saxena, *Reforms* 68; B.N. Sharma 68; Srivastava 202–3.

Judging from the outward events men therefore follow women into death—the idea, however, is exactly the opposite. The analogy to following the dead, and especially to widow burning, lies in this idea. But here the men enforce the following into death of women in advance. This indeed shows a clear intensification of the custom in comparison with widow burning. While in the latter the husband can only hope that his wife accompanies him in death, or that others urge her to it, with *jauhar* he takes care of it himself.

Of all the traditional forms of following into death *jauhar* is the most violent, cruel and bloody. The number of victims mentioned surpasses all known figures from normal ceremonies of the custom.[248] It is impossible to talk of free choice as a general rule, even if the sources like to state it. At best it is mass hysteria. The assurance itself that all victims, without any exception, went to their death voluntarily, that not even one of them refused, shows it to be a stylized version, especially when we take into consideration that not only the wives of the soldiers, but apparently all women, married and unmarried, young and old, were killed. The stated motive was to protect the honour of the women, but actually it was a matter of preserving the honour of the men, an honour that was essentially defined by the undisputed possession of women. The manner of killing was particularly brutal. Even though the sources try to give the impression that all the victims died on the spot, we can be sure that in such mass slaughters in many cases death occurred only after a long time, since some women, for example, were only just touched by the flames of the large pyre. During the siege of Chitor in 1534 13,000 women were sent into caverns filled with explosives and then blown up.[249] We can assume that the conquerors found many women still in the throes of death.

It is astonishing that this obvious violence in connection with *jauhar* has hardly been mentioned.[250] The events are often stated without any comment.[251] Time and again, and till today *jauhar* is highly praised as the most wonderful, most noble, most honourable and most selfless form of widow burning, as an expression of unparalleled heroism and selfless obedience to a sublime notion of honour, especially on

[248] Cf. for example Tod 1, 311–12: 13,000 victims; 1,266: thousands.

[249] Tod 1, 311–12. Similarly ib. 2,60 (1680 in Delhi).

[250] Attempts at an explicit critique now in Oldenburg, in Hawley (ed.) 163–6.

[251] For example A. Sharma, *Thresholds* 96; Nand 176–8; Srivastava 202–3; Narasimhan 118–19.

the part of the women, to whom free choice is attributed uncritically. For V.V. Deshpande *jauhar* offered in 1977 'the most glorious episodes of purest chastity and exemplary loyalty of Hindu wifehood,'[252] and even for Thompson in 1928 it was a case of 'suttee in its noblest form.'[253] Khushwant Singh, one of the most respected contemporary Indian authors, stated on 11 October 1987 that he felt 'a glow of pride' with regard to *jauhar*, whereas he condemned widow burning as 'a remnant of medieval barbarity.'[254] In 1990 Manjushree stated: 'We in our heart of hearts feel deep reverence, admiration and pride for those Rajput ladies who performed "Jauhar".'[255]

One of the consequences of this attitude has been that *jauhar* has not even been analysed with the most elementary methods of historical criticism. The case described in the beginning definitely did not take place in the manner specified. The number of victims would have been grossly exaggerated. This is suggested by the fact that there are supposed to have been 24,000 women to 3,800 men fit for active service (of whom only 700 fell in the final battle). Even the most incapable commander would hardly have allowed himself to be manoeuvred into such a situation. It is also difficult to imagine how women in such great numbers are supposed to have been killed in such a short time. In a dry region like Jaisalmer, with hardly any wood, the fuel alone would not have been available—especially after a long siege—to burn thousands of women.

The accounts quoted most often have been handed down by James Tod in his *Annals of Rajasthan* which appeared in 1829. In this work Tod proves himself to be a glowing admirer of the Rajput warrior culture with its strict notions of honour and heroism.[256] In Rajasthan his work almost has the function of a national epic. In the case of *jauhar* this admiration has led to the absence of a critical attitude with regard to the sources. We do not have a single eyewitness account about a jauhar nor a halfway realistic description, but only idealized stories

[252] Deshpande 28.

[253] Thompson, *Suttee* 37. Cf. also Thakur, *History* 162; 167–8. Ashraf 161–3 is somewhat more reserved.

[254] Quoted in *Trial by Fire*.

[255] Manjushree 184. Cf. also B.N. Sharma 68.

[256] Tod also narrates stories uncritically about how a curse uttered by a sati came true. Tod 2, 497; 499; 623.

characterized by wishful thinking. Apart from Tod's stories there are generally only brief mentions in contemporary historical works.[257]

Yet there is probably a factual core. In the undoubtedly often merciless warfare in North India there must have been hopeless situations from time to time. It is not implausible that women were killed by their husbands or by other men so that they would not fall into the hands of the enemy, or that some women allowed themselves to be killed or killed themselves. The estimated numbers would have to be much lower and the heroic aspect would have to be toned down.

---

[257] Cf. the compilation in Ashraf 161–3 as well as footnote 247 above.

CHAPTER 13

Background and Origins

Many of the factors that are normally regarded as explanations of widow burning in India, are also found in places outside India, where however they would not lead to widow burning. Therefore we must now ask, what conditions of a general nature have to be fulfilled to make widow burning conceivable at all. What was the background of the custom? In what soil could it first grow?

The question is so vast and therefore so undefined, that it is impossible to deal with it in a thorough and systematic manner, and it is possible to give only a few indications. Four aspects are highlighted.

1. One of the most conspicuous characteristics of widow burning in India in comparison with other forms of following into death, is the almost complete polarization between the sexes. Widower burning is absolutely inconceivable. This extreme asymmetry and inequality would be a result of the prevailing relationship between the sexes, and of the position of women and the widow.

2. Controversy reigns over the extent to which widow burning can be considered a religious ceremony.[1] Undeniably, the custom has a much stronger religious background than any other form of following into death. This is most evident in its adjustment to more complex forms of belief in the hereafter. The origins of the custom did not lie in Hinduism, but particular streams of Hinduism adopted the custom and gave it a religious framework. It therefore seems to be justified to ask about the influence of religious concepts, which originally stood in a different context.

3. All indications suggest that widow burning in India first spread among the warrior caste. Did therefore views associated with personal courage and individual heroism have a special influence on it?

[1] Along with literature on the Vedic and the Dharma texts mentioned in chap. 12, footnotes 12 and 45, see also Bhasin/Menon, in *Seminar* 12–13; *Trial by fire* for present-day debates, as well as Deshpande for a counterposition. For general aspects see Mani, *Production* 35; 39.

4. It is true that the three questions mentioned above have been formulated systematically. But they are directed at matters that were subjected to many historical changes. A historical study of the background leads to the question of its origins, which can no longer be grasped historically, and, thus, to the origins of widow burning itself.

The Position of Women and Widows[2]

Both the normative as well as the descriptive sources on the position of women in India well into modernity, refer, de facto, largely to the upper classes, even when they talk of women in general. In pre-modern times school education for example was relevant only for a very small minority. Elaborate funeral rites could not be carried out by the masses, and the poor could not afford to lock their women up at home.

When, despite this, in the interests of brevity, we still simply speak of women and widows, these qualifications have to be kept in mind. In any case, the rules given in the texts and the practices among the upper classes or castes were decisive. Those who wanted to rise in society, whether as individuals or as a caste, had to strive to emulate this model. There was therefore a tendency among a steadily increasing part of the population to observe these rules. This is valid even today.[3]

In research there is agreement about the fact that the position of women has changed considerably since Vedic times. Generally these changes are perceived as a more or less continuous loss of independence.[4] The Vedic times have probably been portrayed in too idyllic a fashion, especially since the reality of those times is only tangible through the glorified veil of normative texts. This kind of treatment of early periods generally has a political and ideological background. It is meant to

---

[2] The best overall representation of the history of the position of women in India with regard to the aspects that are of interest here, is still Altekar. In addition there is Winternitz, *Frau*. Other general literature: Baig; P.N. Bose, vol. 1; A.R. Gupta; Kane 2, 1, 550–623; Kapadia; Kohler; Manjushree; Narang; Shastri; Upadhyay; Vishnoi.

[3] This process, which has come to be defined as *Sanskritisation*, was first described by Srinivas.

[4] The best summary is to be found in Altekar. Similar hypothesis: Winternitz, *Frau*; Mookerji and Panikkar in Baig 1–13; A.R. Gupta 6; Kane 2, 1, 550–623; Manjushree; Narang 1–15; Shastri; Upadhyay; Vishnoi; Chattopadhyay.

show that the modern conditions, which the authors reject, cannot be based upon the ancient tradition, which is also considered the most holy in India. It is also meant to prove in a nationalist sense that an improvement in the position of women would not—or at least not exclusively—mean having to take recourse to foreign ideas. Despite these reservations a good part of the positive view of the early period has been taken over here. It dominates in the relevant literature and can only be questioned on the basis of a through study of the sources.

In early times[5] the highly placed woman seems to have had a significant measure of religious independence. She could carry out the ceremonies and rituals she required, either alone or together with her husband. Along with this went the fact that formal education at all levels was open to her. There are isolated cases of women even among the most famous authors. This indicates that women participated in public life and took on important public functions. The age of marriage was between 16 and 17 years, which is low, according to today's standards, but relatively high compared to later times in India, and at any rate high enough, that the woman's wishes could not be completely ignored at the outset. The dissolution of marriage was possible, and the woman could also take the initiative in this. A widow was allowed to remarry. In addition there was the institution of *niyoga*.[6] If a man died without leaving behind any sons, his brother could have children with the wife/widow for him and in his name. In comparison to a normal re-marriage this left the widow in a position of subordination, but it at least ensured that she continued to be part of the family.

Although these conditions changed very slowly over many centuries, the final result was radical.[7] In matters of religion the woman was increasingly dependent on the services of her husband or of priests, possibly also on her sons or male relatives, to carry out the rituals she required. Simultaneously she was largely excluded from all types of formalized education. This lasting effect can be seen even today in the

[5] The following remarks are based mainly on Altekar, chaps 1–7; and on Winternitz, *Frau*. See apart from this: Narang, Upadhyay and Vishnoi.

[6] For *niyoga* see: Altekar 143ff.; Kane 2, 1, 599–607; Gulati 102–3; 130; Kapadia 171; Rao 220ff.; Sprockhoff, *Indien* 425; Winternitz, *Frau* 57; Upadhyay 100; 108–9; 216.

[7] For the following see, apart from the literature mentioned in footnote 5, also: Baig; A.R. Gupta; Kane 2, 1, 550–623; Kapadia; Manjushree; Shastri; Thomas; Nadarajah; Saraswati 69–93.

difference in the rate of female and male literacy. In 1991 63.86 per cent of the male population was literate as opposed to 39.42 per cent of the female population.[8] The same picture emerges, when one considers the enrolment figures.[9]

Enrolment figures in India 1981, in percentages

Age	6–11	11–14	14–17
Male	95.8	54.3	24.8
Female	64.1	28.6	11.5

This was accompanied by the displacement of women from all spheres of public life. But this was only possible to a limited extent in the lower classes, where women had to look for jobs outside the house. The change in the upper classes went much further with the introduction of *purdah*, with the complete segregation of women, not only from everything that happened outside the house, but also within the house, where they had to remain in the part of the house meant for them.

The marriageable age of women was gradually lowered. It became an established rule to marry off a girl at the latest with the onset of puberty. In this way the husband had complete control over his wife's reproductive capacity. This practice too received religious sanction. Control over the reproductive capacity also meant control of sexuality and this again led to a further lowering of the marriageable age, before the onset of puberty; to child marriage, not exclusively, but predominantly for girls. With this the age difference between the couple increased. Dissolution of marriage was still possible, but now almost only on the man's initiative.

The trend in all these changes was clear: the wife, indeed every woman, was supposed to be completely and irrevocably subordinated to a man. Until marriage or, in the case of child marriage, till the marriage was consummated, it was the father, after that the husband.

These rules got an ideological and religious underpinning, not only in the Dharma texts, but also in creative literature. The wife had to honour and care for her husband, regardless of whether he was a pious man or a criminal. The Manusmṛti says:

[8] Aggarwal/Chowdhry 1.
[9] P.P. Singh 170.

A girl, a young woman, or even an old woman should not do anything independently, even in (her own) house. In childhood a woman should be under her father's control, in youth under her husband's, and when her husband is dead, under her sons'. She should not have independence. A woman should not try to separate herself from her father, her husband or her sons, for her separation from them would make both (her own and her husband's) families contemptible. [. . .] A virtuous wife should constantly serve her husband like a god, even if he behaves badly, freely indulges his lust, and is devoid of any good qualities. Apart (from their husbands), women cannot sacrifice or undertake a vow or fast; it is because a wife obeys her husband that she is exalted in heaven.[10]

If the husband died before the wife—in view of the large age difference that often existed between the couple, this happened far more frequently than the early death of the wife—a dilemma arose. If the aim were to subjugate every woman to the complete control of a man, then re-marriage would have been the best option. Since polygamy was allowed, this indeed could have been the answer. Here however the concerns of this world collided with those of the next. In a society with a marked belief in the hereafter, the possibility of breaking off marriage after death would have been unjust, since in this way those men who died early would have lost their wives to other men. It was therefore important to maintain the husband's control over his wife beyond death. But even independent of the belief in the hereafter, the need could have existed to maintain power beyond the grave and to put one's wife out of the reach of another man. In this context we would have to look at the position of the widow.[11]

A compelling conclusion at first was to stop re-marriage and *niyoga*. Both were increasingly considered to be in bad taste and were finally practically prohibited. The ban however was limited to the upper classes and the higher castes. The poor could hardly afford such a custom, because it meant added expenditure on the control of the widow.

In order to understand the problems that arose from the ban on re-marriage, we would have to point out to the very low average age of

[10] Manu 5, 147–9; 154–5.

[11] On the position of the widow see Altekar, chaps 4–5; U. Chakravarti; Winternitz, *Frau* 55–105; Kane 2, 1, 583–636; Sprockhoff, *Indien* 425–6; Stein, *Women*; Wilkins 364–76, and the literature mentioned in footnotes 5 and 7. For the present-day situation see for example Chen/Dreze (1995).

widowhood as compared to present-day industrialized countries. Widowhood was not limited to old-age. In view of the low life expectancy in pre-modern Europe too, widowhood generally occurred earlier than today. In India the large age difference between the couple and the custom of child marriage were additional factors. If a ten-year-old girl was married, and if the husband died on the same day, then the girl was considered to be a widow in the same way as an eighty-year-old woman after seventy years of marriage. This resulted in an imbalance in the relationship between the sexes as far as widowhood and marriage were concerned, as is evident from the following data for 1881:[12]

Marriage and Widowhood in the Indian Population 1881

	Single	%	Married	%	Widowed	%	Total
Women	36,254,160	32.3	54,878,999	49.0	20,938,626	18.7	1,12,071,782
Men	56,521,018	48.4	54,518,665	46.7	56,791,937	4.9	1,16,731,620

The percentage of boys among married people in the age group 0–14 in 1881 was 6.3 per cent, and of girls in the same age group it was 18.7 per cent.[13] In 1901 there were 19,487 widows under the age of five in India, 1,15,285 widows under the age of 10, and 3,91,147 widows under 15.[14] The upper castes were clearly more strongly affected than the lower castes. In 1931, in Bengal, 23 per cent of the 15–40-year old women of the upper castes were widows, whereas in the lower castes the corresponding figure was 15 per cent.[15]

The problem therefore was that the widow in a way had to be kept under the control of her dead husband. Therefore she had to be kept out of the reach of other men and had to become unattractive to them. In addition, her own needs and desires, which could undermine her faithfulness to her dead husband, had to be suppressed and deadened. To this end, extremely strict rules of conduct were set up. In general the widow had to lead a life of asceticism.[16] Total sexual abstinence, 'sexual death'[17] was taken for granted. The widow was not allowed more than

[12] *Census of India* (1881) 34–5. The first census was conducted in 1872.
[13] P.P. Singh 84.
[14] Winternitz, *Frau* 87.
[15] Stein, *Women* 263.
[16] Source texts: *Digest* 2, 575–80.
[17] U. Chakravarti 2249.

one proper meal a day, and many kinds of food were completely prohibited. She had to sleep on the ground, undergo many religious rituals and had to fast often; she was not allowed to wear any jewellery and could only wear the simplest of clothes of the roughest material. In many places her hair was regularly shorn.[18]

Naturally such rules (which have by no means been listed here completely) were not observed everywhere in the same way. But they represented the norm, which could be used to remind the widow of her duties. These rules, as against those concerning widow burning, occupied a central place in all the texts, even the most authoritative ones, especially the Manusmṛti.[19] This treatment of the widow was completely uncontroversial in Indian society (at least to the extent that views of this society are tangible in texts, which means that women do not have a direct voice in it). Even in the nineteenth century the most determined Indian opponents of widow burning never questioned the demand that the widow should lead an ascetic life.[20] The whole thing was then given a religious and moral underpinning. The focus of this was the blame attached to the widow for her husband's death, because she had allegedly neglected her duties.[21] Although in most cases these accusations were absurd—the contrary could hardly ever be formally proved, leaving the blame to have its effect. Probably older magical views, which explained a person's death as a consequence of other peoples' influences, also played a role here. This view was extended into the perspective that the widow generally brought bad luck. Encounters with her were to be avoided as far as possible. She was not allowed to participate in happy events and in festivals, especially not in marriages. Socially she was already dead.[22]

[18] Many early travellers frequently noticed this custom, for example: Burnell 108; Fryer 33; Herport 123; Withington 220; Andersen/Iversen 208; Tavernier 2, 383; Ravesteyn 72; Twist 32; Haafner 83; Herbert 310; Rogerius 80; Hügel 2, 400. On the prevalence of the custom see for example B.N. Sharma 69 and Kane 2,1, 587; 592. Dealt with extensively in U. Chakravarti 2248–52.

[19] Manu 5, 156–65. The conditions here however remain fairly general.

[20] Rammohan Roy, the most important among them, always emphasized the importance of the rules regarding asceticism for widows. See for example R. Roy, *English Works* 3, 91–2; 108ff.; 131–6.

[21] See for example A. Sharma *et al., Sati* 77; Stein, *Women* 255.

[22] Sprockhoff, *Indien* 425; Stutchbury 36; U. Chakravarti 2248ff.

This far-reaching expulsion of the widow from society, which was supposed to guarantee posthumous control by the husband, developed a peculiar dialectic. The isolation deprived the widow of protection and made her particularly vulnerable and dependent. If she was living in a large household, she was often exposed to the unwelcome advances of her male relatives.[23] If she did not have any relatives, or if she was living alone, or, if in addition she also had children to take care of, this ostracism made it difficult for her to earn a living. Widows therefore frequently found themselves being forced to do the lowest jobs, including prostitution,[24] which made a complete mockery of the claim made by the rules, that they kept the widow completely under her husband's control.

At least in one sphere there was an improvement, in the sense of a more pronounced independence.[25] From the beginning Hindu law incorporated women's property (*strīdhanam*). On the other hand women originally did not have any share in the common family property and therefore could not inherit any part of it. Later they were allowed a share in it. A satisfactory explanation for this development, which ran counter to the increasing subjugation of women under men, has not yet been offered. One could possibly speak of a measure meant to absorb the shock of the progressive isolation and separation of the widow from society.[26] Yet, within a system of control, it would have been more plausible if the relatives had been made responsible for the widow's upkeep. It therefore seems likely that this had to do with the relations between the husband's family and the wife's family. If the property remained with the widow it would be easier for her family to have access to it, than if the husband's family got complete control over it.

[23] See for example Mazumdar *Comment* 273; Winternitz, *Frau* 87.

[24] This is often emphasized by older authors, for example: Fryer 33; Mandelslo, *Journal* 30; Manucci 3, 60; Paolino 63; Pires 377; Santos 313; Schouten 1, 293; Dapper 55. See Altekar 156; Sousa 2; Winternitz, *Frau* 88; Wilkins 365.

[25] On property and inheritance rights see Altekar, chaps 8–9; Kane 2, 1, 573ff.; Vishnoi 157ff. and specially Narang as well as Sontheimer, *Family*. See above pp. 278–81.

[26] Altekar 252 presumes that the right to inheritance was introduced as a kind of compensation for the ban on re-marriage and *niyoga*. Similary Narang 12–14.

In the matter of individual fates widowhood represented a greater break for women of the upper classes than it did for those of the lower classes. The former were cast out of all their social points of reference and were isolated—they could have just as easily been made redundant—while the latter for the most part retained their economic functions, which is why they could not be completely excluded from society. This would also partly explain the much higher frequency of widow burning among the upper classes.

The rules about the life and the treatment of the widow were an attempt to square the circle. According to the Hindu scriptural view of marriage, the wife had to remain under her husband's control, his private property, even after his death. In order to establish this claim however, the dead man had to depend on the help of other persons, not least other men, who were at the same time potential competitors for the same woman. The only real 'solution' of the problem, which cut the knot with one blow, was following into death.[27]

What were the causes for the deterioration in the position of women? Literature offers only a few hypothetical considerations.[28] The situation at the beginning can be considered typical for a society of conquerors in its early phase. All efforts have to be concentrated on maintaining power. Differences among the conquerors, even between the sexes, would endanger their survival. Society is dependent on women and therefore grants them an independent status. All this however is only valid for the small class of conquerors.

The gradual deterioration could therefore be explained with the consolidation of power and the melting away of differences between the conquerors and the conquered. The conquerors also increasingly married women from among the conquered. These women could not claim a position of equality with their husbands. The effective subjugation of the conquered also ensured a sufficient labour force for the conquerors. Therefore the economic importance of women diminished, and they could be taken out of the production process and removed from the public sphere. The conquerors felt less threatened after they had consolidated their power and therefore did not have to rely on the co-operation of their women in public matters.

So long as the conquerors constituted a small and a more or less

[27] This aspect of the subjugation of women is also reiterated for example by Thapar, in *Seminar* 16.
[28] Summarized in Altekar 342–5.

isolated group, safeguarding their reproduction as a group, and, there-fore, their women, was of utmost importance. Widows therefore had to be re-married as soon as possible or brought into a *niyoga* relationship. After the opposition between the conquerors and the conquered dimi-nished, the concept of the woman as the husband's personal property, even after his death, prevailed. The idea of the life-long faithfulness and chastity of the widow corresponded to this.

Asceticism and Religious Suicide

Suicide was originally strictly rejected in Indian religions.[29] This view was later modified on account of the growing importance of asceticism in religious practice.[30] With the help of asceticism it was possible to earn, indeed even extort gains as well as advantages and rewards for the hereafter, or for the next life. In this the concept of a special, final phase of life meant for asceticism, played an important role. Such an exist-ence as a *saṃnyāsin* should, according to the Dharma texts, be em-barked upon after a person had fulfilled his duties towards society in the family and public sphere.

In this context the function and estimation of suicide changed. As long as it was carried out in the right spirit and with the proper goal in mind, it no longer represented a despicable act, but the ultimate and most worthy act of asceticism. An interpretation of the act as a renun-ciation of life would not be wrong. With the help of strict requirements with regard to its cast of mind, place, time and method, attempts were made to distinguish it from normal suicide. The most prevalent method was to drown oneself in a holy river at a particular spot. How-ever, other methods of suicide were also allowed, and self-immolation was among them.[31] It appears that the new views were first established

---

[29] On suicide in India see especially Thakur, *History*; Thakur, *Self-immolation*; Stietencron; Sternbach 16–19. R. Roy, *English Works* 3, 89 reite-rated that the ban was also valid for widow burning. See also *Cremation* 17; S. Singh 36.

[30] Along with the literature mentioned in the above footnote, see especially Sprockhoff, *Askese*; Rüping; Shee; Gonda 1, 283–8; Michaels, *Recht* 122–3; Olivelle; A. Sharma *et al.*, *Sati* 78ff.; Weinberger-Thomas (1989) 12; Winternitz, *Frau* 82; Devi 260–3; Sutherland 1597–1601. For Jainism see Settar.

[31] Detailed information in Thakur, *History* 77–105 and Stietencron 14–20. Accounts also in Johns 69–77 and in Krishnasvami.

in practice and the sanctioning of the practice in the texts followed only slowly—as in the case of widow burning too.

Such forms of asceticism, particularly the life of a *saṃnyāsin*, which in principle was limited to Brahmins, were not, at least in theory, open to women.[32] Otherwise a wife would have had the right to leave her husband. Widows, of course, were even further removed from such independence. On the other hand, the particular form of asceticism, which was thrust upon the widow, could be more easily justified by comparing it with the asceticism of the *saṃnyāsin*.[33] Chiefly, however, widow burning could now be placed in a religious context. It appeared as a religiously sanctioned, indeed as a religious suicide. It could be integrated into a general feature of Hinduism—the importance of asceticism—and in time gained prestige and popularity. Many authors did not consider it to be suicide, but a legitimate, indeed a meritorious act, and on the whole this view established itself among the masses.[34] In this process it did not remain at the level of a mere parallel to the religious suicide of men, but was clearly intensified. The religious merit that a widow earned through self-immolation was much greater than that which a man was capable of achieving through suicide. He could merely influence his own future fate. The widow on the other hand ensured immeasurable happiness in the other world, not only for herself, but also for her husband, and in addition she improved the fate of her relatives. Her deed was also honoured in this world. Widows received memorial stones, monuments and temples; long after their death they were revered as goddesses; large numbers of admiring onlookers were present at the immolation. Their superiority can also be seen in the sati stones. On these the figure of the woman is generally larger than that of the man, whereas the proportions in Indian art are otherwise the opposite.[35] All these honours were not accorded to

[32] Altekar 210; Hawley, in Hawley (ed.) 181. In practice however there were also isolated cases, in which women lived as ascetics. See Gonda, 1, 285; Shee 397; Sutherland 1598. In Jainism especially, religious suicide by women occurred frequently: Settar 65–6.

[33] For this see especially Leslie, *Choice* 49–59 and Leslie, *Wife* 298–304. See also Gulati 121; Michaels, *Recht* 122; A. Sharma *et al.*, 78ff; Hawley, in Hawley (ed.) 181–5; Weinberger-Thomas (1996) 26–7; 62–4.

[34] See Colebrooke, *Duties* 118–19; Leslie, *Wife* 293; Mukhopadhyay, *Institution* 115; Olivelle; Sternbach 16–19; Winternitz, *Frau* 82–3; Stietencron 18–23; Michaels, *Nepal* 30–1.

[35] In Jainism on the other hand monuments for those who had committed

people, who had committed religious suicide, and generally their post-humous fame hardly ever equalled that of a sati.[36]

The price for this privileged position of the sati was an increased subordination of the woman to the man. The woman could only become a sati, if her husband died—therefore in this respect too she was dependent on him.[37] The husband's death was also the cause for the ascetic life of the widow, who did not become a sati. Through the act of self-immolation the wife brought about the reunification with the husband, as a result of which her subordination again became complete and direct. The extra merits that she earned for herself in comparison with the ascetic man served to bind her in the other world (or in the next life in this world) to her traditional role.

Gender-specific Heroism

There are many indications that widow burning was initially limited to a large extent to the caste of warriors and rulers. In this group the men often died in war. Thus Ceteus lost his life in a battle.[38] The oldest verified inscription also narrates how the husband of the sati died in a battle.[39] The husbands of the three widows, whose immolation Ibn Baṭṭūṭa described, had also died while fighting a war.[40]

Death in battle is traditionally portrayed as a heroic death. In this case it was even less possible to treat a woman as an equal than it was in the case of asceticism and religious suicide. However a parallel could indeed be drawn, and this allowed a call to imitate the original. Even widow burning could be made into a heroic act. In reality, voluntary death in the flames of the pyre generally requires far greater heroism than the so-called heroic death in battle. Much greater reserves of strength are demanded from the widow than from the warrior. The latter is active. He does not concentrate on his own death, but on battle and on the death that he will mete out to others, and not on the dangers threatening him. His own death is at best a result of this effort, and normally the chances of his survival are good. Death for him is only

---

religious suicide (including many women) were common. Settar 65–6; 187–237.

[36] Chidanandamurti, in Settar/Sontheimer 129.

[37] Also reiterated by Leslie, *Choice* 57.

[38] Diodorus 19, 33, 1.

[39] Fleet 93 (AD 510/11).

[40] Ibn Baṭṭūṭa 3, 615.

a possible, perhaps a probable result of his heroism, not its actual object.

In the case of a widow it is quite different. Once she takes the decision to die, the goal and purpose of all her actions is her own death, which she has to confront. There is nothing, which distracts her attention from it. She cannot fight, and she cannot defend herself. If she does, then her actions can perhaps also be heroic, but they are not in accordance with widow burning. She has no other possibility but to concentrate on her fear, her suffering and her death, and this requires far greater steadfastness and resolve than the actions of a warrior.

Wars are certainly older and more prevalent than widow burning. Therefore we can assume that the heroism of the widow was seen in analogy to that of the warrior and not vice versa. An incentive and simultaneously a justification for widow burning arose from this. The women strove to emulate the men and to prove their own heroism.[41] This was reflected in sayings like the following: 'Brahmins, who are afraid of the cold, warriors, who are afraid of battle, and a woman, who is afraid of the fire (i.e. of the pyre): all three do not attain heaven.'[42] With the figure of the Brahmin the parallel to asceticism is also drawn.

The incentive to imitate male heroism probably played an important role in early times. The sources do portray this. The imagined competition among the widows for the honour of accompanying their husband in death thus serves as proof of their courage in analogy to the martial retinue. On sati-stones the sati is often portrayed together with her husband, who is in full battle dress.[43] In some regions the parallel was emphasized even in later periods, especially where martial traditions were kept up, for example in Rajasthan.[44] In other regions widow burning became independent of this analogy, without however losing the heroism immanent in it, or, in other words, female heroism was

[41] The connection between heroism and widow burning is pointed out by: Leslie, *Choice* 49–51; Thakur, *History* 138–9; Harlan 123; Stein, *Women* 253; Weinberger-Thomas (1989) 12; Weinberger-Thomas (1996) 78; Michaels, *Recht* 116. The relationship between memorial tablets for heroes and satis is documented in the book by Settar/Sontheimer.

[42] Böhtlingk 3, 378 (No. 6466).

[43] Longhurst 35; Chidanandamurti, in Settar/Sontheimer 130; Walsh 431–4; Thapar, in *Seminar* 16; Thapar, *Death*; Upreti 11.

[44] Tod 1, 503; Upreti 30; Woodruff 254; Sangari/Vaid 1287; Sangari, in *Seminar* 28; *Trial by fire*.

still a requirement, when the male version had long since become a myth. The more the custom was extended to other castes and classes, the less likely it was that the men being accompanied had died in battle. Among the more than 8,000 cases of widow burning registered by the British between 1815 and 1828 in the Bengal Presidency, there is not a single case in which it can be proved that the man had died in a military operation; on the whole the number of soldiers among the accompanied is very small.

Over time therefore the sati no longer imitated her husband's heroism, but only what was generally regarded as male heroism, without ever having seen it practised in her immediate environment.

Here too the differences between the sexes are decisive for the character of widow burning. To a great extent they are the same as those mentioned in the context of religious suicide. Parallels are drawn on the basis of the difference between the sexes, which is not bridged by the parallels, but on the contrary, strengthened. The condition for the possibility of the woman's heroism was the death of her husband, and with this her complete subordination to her husband was re-established.

The relationship between the sexes is therefore identical in asceticism, religious suicide and heroism. This points to the underlying mechanism. Since widow burning is based upon the strict division of gender roles, the woman does not become equal to the man when she imitates him, but submits to him.

The Origins

Speculations about the origin of widow burning in India are as old as accounts of it. Didodorus already considered it necessary to enlighten his readers about the deeper causes of the custom before describing the immolation of Ceteus' widow:

> It is an ancient custom among the Indians that the men who marry and maidens who are married do not do so as a result of the decision of their parents but by mutual persuasion. Formerly, since the wooing was done by persons who were too young, it often happened that, the choice turning out badly, both would quickly regret their act, and that many wives were first seduced, then through wantonness gave their love to other men, and finally, not being able without disgrace to leave the mates whom they had first selected, would kill their husbands by poison. [. . .] But when this evil became fashionable and many were

murdered in this way, the Indians, although they punished those guilty of crime, since they were not able to deter the others from wrongdoing, established a law that wives, except such as were pregnant or had children, should be cremated along with their deceased husbands, and that one who was not willing to obey this law should not only be a widow for life but also be entirely debarred from sacrifices and other religious observances as unclean.[45]

This explanation must have already been prevalent in antiquity. It is given at roughly the same time by Diodorus as well as by Strabo.[46] Both authors probably took it over from an earlier source. Later in antiquity too it is mentioned from time to time.[47] In modern times as well, many authors, among them a large number of eyewitnesses, oblige us with the same story.[48] A crass version can be found in 1638 in Mandelslo's account: 'This custom has come about, because earlier the wives, out of lust, killed their husbands with poison or other secret means, in order to get other husbands, who could tend better to their lust. Therefore an Indian king issued these orders, so that the wives may fear the death of their husbands. If the wife however does not wish to burn herself to death, she has to become a prostitute and is no longer welcome in honest society.'[49]

Obviously one European simply told the story to the next one. Yet it is difficult to imagine that some Europeans had not occasionally also heard it from Indians; in individual cases this has even been testified.[50] We can assume that this explanation was not invented by foreigners, but was offered by the creators of the custom or by their descendants, and was then accepted everywhere.

Many European authors found the explanation convincing. Others refrained from commenting on it, which can at least be interpreted as a discreet agreement. From time to time doubts were also expressed,

[45] Diodorus 19, 33, 2–3.

[46] Strabo 15,1,30.

[47] Heckel/Yardley 309.

[48] A selection: Dow 1, xxxv; Linschoten 19; Paolino 63; Balbi 83; Carletti 255; Wintergerst 119; Withington 221; Langhanss 538; Coverte 56; Dellon 1,102–3; Fedrici 41; Herport 124; Methwold 28; Schouten 2, 99; Herbert 310; Lord 68–9; Ovington 201.

[49] Mandelslo, *Journal* 30. Cf. Mandelslo, *Reyse-Bescheibung* 81–2.

[50] Fedrici 41; Methwold 28.

as early as by Strabo: 'However the law is not stated in a plausible manner, nor the cause of it either.'[51] It was only in the nineteenth and twentieth centuries that the story lost its status of a standard explanation, although even then it never went out of use completely.[52]

This is not a case of historical fact, but only of a myth, which is meant to explain why something, which one knows but doesn't understand, arose in a time, of which one knows nothing anymore. Even in the early period the origins were historically no longer accessible.

From its inner contradictions and lack of logical consistency we can deduce that even as a myth this narrative does not possess a true core. If these measures were to fulfil their purpose, then widow burning would have to be obligatory, if not for all widows, then at least, if the dead man or his relatives had demanded it. At any rate the decision would not lie with the widow. Otherwise the guiltiest widows would escape punishment, and the measures would not have their intended effect of deterring others from similar actions. Yet even Diodorus emphasizes the voluntary nature of the act with his story of the competition among the widows. Indeed through this he even suggests that not everyone who wanted to, was allowed to immolate herself. He also has an explanation for the apparent contradiction. Since the supposed law prohibited re-marriage and imposed an ascetic life on the widow, 'the lawlessness of the woman changed into the opposite, for as each one because of the great loss of caste willingly met death.'[53]

In the seventeenth century Nicholas Withington portrayed the change in even more naïve terms: 'But then they were forced unto yt; but nowe they have gotte such a custome of yt that they doe yt moste willinglye.'[54]

What appears here as an explanation is nothing more than a pious wish that criminally-minded women would undergo such a change of heart. The entire myth should not therefore be read as an account of factual events, but as an indication of the mind-set that obtained at the

[51] Strabo 15, 1, 30. Doubts expressed before the nineteenth century for example by Holwell 2, 88; Le Couteur 323–4; Grose 1, 92.

[52] Still found in Hervey 1, 213–14; 217 (1892); Thomas 89–90 (1939) and Walker 2, 465 (1968). Rejected by Deshpande 18–24, who insists it was voluntary.

[53] Diodorus 19, 33, 4.

[54] Withington 121 (1612-1616). Similarly Linschoten 19; Coverte 56; Methwold 28; Lord 68–9.

origin of the custom. It does not reflect the behaviour of women, but the fears and desires of men, and can thus give us an indication of the origins of the custom. The focus is on the obsession that men have about controlling their wives, especially their sexuality. The myth was supposed to provide the justification for the measures taken. It shifts the responsibility onto the woman and portrays the actions of men in a rather maudlin fashion as self-defence. It would be just as problematical to try and construct an alternative story of the origin of the custom by imputing that men had invented and introduced it with such a clear purpose. The beginning was not an invention, but a gradual, fumbling development.

CHAPTER 14

The Struggle Against
Widow Burning: End Without
an End

India is the only region in the world in which following into death can be proved to exist even today. In many parts of Asia, and in most of the regions of Africa and Oceania, the colonial powers (among them also Great Britain) began to suppress following into death much later than in India, but with quicker and more convincing results. What caused this particular resistance in India?

An important reason is the marked individual character of widow burning in India. While suppressing the institutional form of the custom, the practices of only a small group have to change. The individual form on the other hand permeates the entire society. The rulers, whether indigenous or foreign, find it less easy to influence the views of the broad masses than those of the upper class. Rational arguments do not carry much weight; deeply embedded religious convictions have to be changed, and, in addition, state control is greatly reduced in far-flung regions and among the lower classes.

During the last 800 years, India has been ruled longer and more intensively than other similarly large regions by foreigners who practised other religions. Both foreign religions, Islam and Christianity, rejected following of the dead. However, the conquerors always constituted a small group which could remain in power only with the cooperation of important sections of the indigenous upper classes. Therefore they were afraid of taking measures that could antagonize their allies and provoke unrest or even resistance among the people over whom they ruled. This situation made matters more difficult for Indians. Those who spoke out against widow burning were suspected of denying their own religion. Maintaining the custom could therefore acquire the character of resistance, indeed even of an anti-colonial struggle which, however, should not be over-estimated. It cannot be assumed that such a custom was practised for centuries only to defy the conquerors.

Early Indian Opponents

Following into death was never undisputed in India. At first, the priestly caste had problems accepting it. Long before Islamic and European rule, this caste displayed a strangely indecisive attitude by ignoring such customs and thereby excluding them from the funeral rites that they sanctioned, while never condemning them directly. Subsequently, a polarization took place. Some approved of widow burning, indeed even glorified it, while others now clearly spoke out against it. The poet Bāṇa articulated this rejection very clearly in the early seventh century AD:

> This following another to death is most vain! It is a path followed by the ignorant. It is a mere freak of madness, a path of ignorance, an enterprise of recklessness, and a blunder of folly, that one should resign life on the death of father, brother, friend or husband. If life leaves us not of itself, we must not resign it. For this leaving of life, if we examine it, is merely for our own interest, because we cannot bear our cureless pain. To the dead man it brings no good whatever. For it is no means of bringing him back to life, or heaping up merit, or gaining heaven for him, or saving him from hell, or seeing him again, or being reunited with him. For he is led helplessly, irresistibly to another state meet (sic) for the fruits of his own deeds. And yet he shares in the guilt of the friend who has killed himself. But a man who lives on can help greatly, by offerings of water and the like, both the dead man and himself; but by dying he helps neither.[1]

Bāṇa thus anticipated many of the arguments of later Indian and foreign, Hindu and non-Hindu opponents of widow burning, specifically the denial of the component of the other world, and in general the religious component. He was by no means the only opponent.[2] Opposition to the custom was not limited to isolated thinkers. Different currents of Hinduism with large numbers of followers rejected widow burning, or at least did not practise it. These included the

---

[1] Bāṇa 136–7; (338–9).
[2] Cf. Winternitz, *Frau* 61–5; Rao 230–2; B.B. Roy 82ff.; A. Sharma *et al.*, *Sati* 15ff.; Upreti 16–17.

Tantric sects,[3] the Shakti cult[4] and the followers of Vishnu.[5] One cannot say that the opposition was ineffective. Yet if one refers strictly to the suppression of the custom, one would have to talk of a failure. The opponents were not only not in a position to implement a ban, they were also unable to prevent the increasing spread of the custom well into modernity, along with its underlying ideologies, religious beliefs and social conditions. The single exception is only apparently an exception. It seems that on the Malabar Coast, in what is today Kerala, burnings did not take place.[6] However, this was not a result of modern opposition, but of the continuing existence of old customs. As matrilineal law prevailed, the women here were in a stronger position than their sisters in other parts of the country.

In China and in Japan indigenous opposition groups were more successful. But the differences with India are smaller than they seem at first glance. In China only institutional following into death could be suppressed, not the individual form of the custom which, on the contrary, often received official sanction. Funerals of rulers and the self-killing of widows were seen as two clearly separate matters. This was not the case in India. Here, even at the funerals of rulers, following into death mainly took the form of widow burning, making it difficult to do away with one while retaining the other. In Japan, on the other hand, along with the institutional form of the custom, the special form, in which a military retinue accompanied the dead, was also suppressed. Given the clear hierarchies of power and the fact that the custom here was less bound up with religion, this was relatively easy.

The Islamic Conquerors

From the thirteenth century large parts of India were under Islamic rule for varying periods of time. From the sixteenth to the eighteenth centuries a Muslim dynasty, the Mughals, ruled over almost the entire

---

[3] Mukhopadhyay, *Institution* 108; Thapar, in *Seminar* 18; A. Sharma *et al.*, *Sati* 16–17; Weinberger-Thomas (1989) 12; Gupta/Gombrich 254; Vaid/Sangari 4; Oldenburg, in Hawley (ed.) 171.

[4] Thapar, in *Seminar* 17; A. Sharma *et al.*, *Sati* 16–17; Gupta/Gombrich 254. Negated by Nandy, *Cultures* 266–7.

[5] Gupta/Gombrich 254.

[6] Narasimhan 54; Thakur, *History* 171; Thompson, *Suttee* 29; Gonçalves 66. A survey conducted in 1819/20 in the Madras Presidency among the district officers came to the same conclusion. PP 1823/17, 123; 128–9.

sub-continent. In most of the areas, however, Islam as a religion was always limited to a minority of the population.

Following into death does not exist in Islam.[7] The sources leave us in no doubt that the Muslims despised the custom of widow burning. When Akbar (1556–1605), the greatest of the Mughal rulers, heard of plans to burn a widow in Bengal against her will, he is said to have galloped there at full speed in order to prevent the immolation, and was even successful.[8] This was apparently not the only such incident in his life.[9] Such stories are probably not authentic. But as legends they clearly indicate the widely prevalent attitude of the Muslims.

This private attitude did not correspond at all to the official political stance. There is no credible proof that widow burning was banned in even one of the many Islamic kingdoms in India, let alone a ban that was subsequently enforced.

Details of the policies of the early Islamic kingdoms are not known. It is sometimes mentioned that the Sultans of Delhi (thirteenth to sixteenth centuries) banned widow burning.[10] What is more frequently stated is that permission had to be sought to carry out the custom, and that this was only granted if the act was going to be voluntary.[11] But there is no conclusive evidence. Possibly it is a case of backward projection from Mughal times.[12] A formal and uniform regulation is not likely to have existed. Rather, we can expect that the rulers—as Akbar later—expressed their displeasure with the custom spontaneously, and prevented burnings in their immediate environment. The efficacy of such measures would have been negligible outside the royal court and the large cities, and outside the circles dependent on the ruler.[13]

[7] Cf. Chittick, *Muslim Understanding*; Chittick, *Eschatology*; Smith/ Haddad.

[8] Abu-l-Fazl 595–6; also in Elliot/Dowson 6, 68–9. The event is not dated.

[9] Ashraf 160. Monserrate 61 on the other hand maintains that Akbar asked the Jesuit missionaries to witness a burning. This is probably an invention.

[10] Ahuja 81–2; Crawfurd 259; Dubois, *Moeurs* 2, 18.

[11] Arunachalam 72; Ashraf 160; S. Chaudhury, *Society* 55ff.; S. Chaudhury, *Institution* 220; Dapper 57; Nand 173; Saxena, *Reforms* 27; Srivastava 232.

[12] This surmise is not valid for Ibn Baṭṭūṭa who in 3, 614 mentions the obligation to seek permission, but at the same time states that permission is always granted.

[13] Cf. Hügel 2, 401.

More is known about the Mughal Empire (sixteenth to eighteenth centuries). Both contemporary authors, especially Europeans, and modern scholars frequently state that widow burning was permanently or at least temporarily banned under the Mughals.[14] However, the information proves to be either mere conjecture or simply groundless assertions. No relevant document has been presented thus far. The most precise information mentions a ban under Humayun (1530–56) which is said to have been revoked even before it came into force. It would have been limited to women who were past the age of conceiving.[15] It is also often said that Aurangzeb abolished the custom in 1663, but only for women with children.[16] Other authors state that Jahangir had already issued a prohibition in 1620.[17] In both cases conclusive evidence is lacking. This is even truer for bans supposedly issued under Akbar.[18] At any rate the burnings did not stop. The Mughals were apparently satisfied with introducing the requirement of official sanction.[19] Permission for a burning had to be obtained from the Governor of the province.[20] Particular significance was attached to the voluntary nature of the act.[21]

It has always been assumed that Islamic rulers laid down this requirement out of the desire to curb the custom as far as possible. While

[14] Burnell 108; Manucci 2, 97; *An account* 12; Johns 1; Leslie, *Victim* 176.

[15] Ashraf 160; Cf. Leslie, *Victim* 176; S. Chaudhury, *Society* 56; S. Chaudhury, *Institution* 220; Saxena, *Reforms* 27.

[16] Z. Ahmad 150; Arunachalam 72; M. Gaur 50; S. Chaudhury, *Society* 58; S. Chaudhury, *Institution* 221; R. Misra 134; Saxena, *Reforms* 79.

[17] Arunachalam 72; Garbe 177; S.Chaudhury, *Institution* 220; Mukhopadhyay, *Institution* 101; O'Malley 340 (on capital punishment); Thakur, *History* 158; Thompson, *Suttee* 57; Mundy 2, 179 (on capital punishment).

[18] Thakur, *History* 158.

[19] Such a rule is mentioned very often, both by contemporary authors and in modern research. The following is only a small selection: V.N. Datta 11–14; Modi 413; Saxena, *Reforms* 78–9; Biervillas 78ff.; Pelsaert 329; Reis 60; Tavernier 2, 384; Careri 3, 138. Relevant legal documents are, however, not available.

[20] Wherever a competent authority is mentioned, it is always the ruler or the governor of the province. We can assume that in remote places even less highly placed functionaries had a similar competence—provided they were asked.

[21] Emphasized for example by Abu-l-Fazl 595 and Buchanan, *Establishment* 137.

such a motive was certainly important, the political aspect should not be overlooked. Even in some Hindu kingdoms widow burning was subject to an official sanction.[22] This regulation can probably be traced back to a time in which only highly placed families were allowed to practice widow burning. The restriction was no longer valid, and the regulation could hardly have been aimed at keeping the number of victims as small as possible. Rather it allowed the ruler to exercise his sovereignty. If he relinquished this right, it could be interpreted as weakness. With their regulations both the Mughals and the British continued an indigenous tradition, although their aims were different.

This measure placed the Mughals in a dilemma. The obligation to seek permission led to the distinction between permissible and forbidden, between legal and illegal widow burnings. From the perspective of the rulers and their high Islamic officials, however, all burnings were despicable. If necessary, the policy could be justified by saying that it helped in making the custom gradually disappear. If this did not happen, the distinction between legal and illegal cases would become untenable. One could not expect Islamic officials to constantly act against their beliefs. In course of time aversion and even resistance would have appeared in their ranks.

The Mughals were saved from such dangerous consequences of their actions by the corruption immanent in the system. Contemporary European authors agree that it was not legal or moral considerations that determined whether permission was granted for a burning or not, but the amount of money paid as a bribe.[23]

The British often prided themselves on having done away with the corruption that had been rampant under their predecessors.[24] At the level of the highly paid European civil servants this would have to a great extent been true. In the case of widow burning, however, it proved to be a stumbling block for them. Here corruption was a practical necessity for the system, for the moral exoneration of the foreign rulers. By turning the permission for widow burning into a question of money, the distinction between legal and illegal cases could be

[22] PP 1821/18, 253; 258; IOR F/4/665, § 185 (Marathas); Settar/Sontheimer 126 (Karnataka).

[23] See for example Crawfurd 259; Dapper 57; PP 1823/17, 104; Careri 3, 138; 232; Fraser 60; Biervillas 48ff.; Burnell 108; Tavernier 2, 384; Johns 1-2; Saxena, *Reforms* 78; Ahuja 81–2; Vincenzo 344; Valentyn 5,1, 52; Ovington 201.

[24] For example PP 1823/17,104.

undermined—a distinction which in any case was senseless and indeed immoral in the eyes of the Muslims. Such exoneration was not available to the British because of their lack of corruption.

Many contemporary European authors emphasize that the number of burnings decreased in the Mughal Empire, and that on the whole it became very small.[25] However, there is no proof of this. The authors do not even try to make extrapolations on the basis of random samples. Generally they were only familiar with a few cities. In these, and especially in the vicinity of the imperial court, the effects of the measures would have been strongest. The presence of many highly-placed Islamic dignitaries had a deterring effect. The lack of reliability of the statements made can also be seen in the fact that some authors maintain that the custom went out of use entirely in the Mughal Empire.[26] This is definitely not true. Other authors maintain—again without proof—that widow burnings did not become rarer under the Mughals,[27] and that many cases occurred even in the central areas of the Empire.[28] According to Pelsaert (1627) two or three burnings took place every week in the capital, Agra.[29]

It is possible that the number of cases decreased because of the need to obtain permission and to pay bribes. However, the effects should not be overestimated. Bribery apart, the British had very little success with similar, or even more restrained measures. Some modern authors, who maintain that immolations were rare in the Mughal Empire mainly because of the zeal of the rulers, assume that the number of cases increased under the British.[30] This increase is often traced back to the consequences of the regulations: the people took official permission to be encouragement of the custom.[31] The argument, which is not supported by any statistics, would also be valid for the Mughal Empire.

---

[25] For example Careri 3, 232; Mundy 2, 35; Thevenot 5, 257–8; Tavernier 2, 384; Bowrey 39; Burnell 108; Mandelslo, *Reyse-Beschreibung* 60; Ovington 201; Vincenzo 344; Herbert 309; Andersen/Iversen 208; Dubois, *Moeurs* 2, 18; Twist 32; Bernier 106–7.

[26] Sonnerat 1, 93; Mundy 2, 179–80 (contradicts ibid. 2, 35).

[27] For example Hawkins 119; Holwell 2, 94; Modave 172.

[28] Burnell 108.

[29] Pelsaert 328–9.

[30] Weinberger-Thomas (1989) 13–14 (with reservations); Leslie, *Victim* 176.

[31] V.N. Datta 36; Dalmia-Lüderitz 49; I. Singh 197; Kaye 530–2. See below pp. 382–3.

In reality, its measures would in any case hardly have been effective in remote areas. The administration was not efficient enough for this. Practice in British times leads us to assume that in the countryside burnings were carried out without official permission. The cases in which European authors mention permission given by high officials in the Mughal Empire, were, significantly, always in cities.[32] The fact that a ban was never issued leads us to assume that the implementation of the measures and the observation of the obligation to register immolations were not taken very seriously. If the Mughals had been willing to make the effort and accept the risks connected with it, then they could well have implemented a total ban.

How can one explain this largely tolerant attitude toward a custom despised by Islamic rulers? It was most probably the fear—of a relatively small group of conquerors—of angering large sections of the conquered with measures, which, when considered in political terms, were unimportant. The continued existence of widow burning might have preyed on the conscience of some rulers, but the custom did not pose any danger to their rule. A determined attempt to suppress it, on the other hand, might have led to dissatisfaction and unrest, maybe even to revolts.

At any rate, widow burning did not lose its importance even under Islamic rule; indeed, its importance probably grew. It even penetrated Islam.[33] It is not clear whether immigrant Muslims practised it. But some Indians who had converted to Islam definitely practised it, and apparently not only those of the first generation.

The Individual Attitude of Europeans[34]

Till the middle of the eighteenth century only a few Europeans ruled over small regions in India. The bulk of them were in India as private individuals. Their perception of widow burning and their views

[32] For example Twist 32; Pelsaert 329; Withington 219; Rennefort 315; Careri 3, 138.

[33] Ahuja 82; Ashraf 160–1; S.Chaudhury, *Society* 59; Fraser 45; 59–60; Modi 423; I. Mukherjee 132; Mukhopadhyay, *Institution* 110; Nand 176; Pakrasi 136; Thakur, *History* 141; 169; Weinberger-Thomas (1996) 226, footnote 94. In accordance with the manner of disposing of the dead, burial alive was prevalent.

[34] Cf. A. Sharma, *Thresholds* 83–111; Figueira, in Hawley (ed.) 55–72; Weinberger-Thomas (1996) 95–102.

about it were therefore not influenced or even determined by political motives and responsibilities.

In the beginning Christian positions dominated. From the eighteenth century secular views that ignored or rejected Christianity were expressed more frequently. Both positions agreed in their opinion of widow burning: it could not be reconciled with European legal, moral and religious views.

For Christianity following into death was an object of horror. It contradicted Christian notions of the hereafter and seemed to threaten the idea of a Last Judgement carried out according to moral criteria. The custom was considered to be murder or suicide, and the latter was almost as sharply condemned as the former.[35] It went against important divine commandments and contradicted all true religion.

In views with a more secular orientation the rejection was just as pointed. From a Christian perspective there was at least the possibility of speaking of a misplaced religious zeal and a false notion of the hereafter. For those who ignored the hereafter there was no possibility of justification.

The incompatibility of widow burning with their own intellectual and cultural background was never a matter of doubt for the Europeans. The question of their accepting, or even propagating and glorifying the custom in their own society never arose. This did not necessarily mean a clear public rejection and condemnation of the conditions in India. Following into death could also be understood as the outcome of a different intellectual and cultural background which had to be accepted at least as long as one's own Christian–European background had not been established. This was, as has been shown, a widely prevalent view in the European Middle Ages. At first the existence of the custom among non-Christians, especially in Eastern Europe, had been more or less accepted. Boniface had even held it up as a mirror for the Christians.[36] The accounts about India at first also described widow burning as a curiosity, not as a matter of disgrace. Marco Polo, for example, makes no value judgements. He merely remarks that the people praise the satis a lot.[37] A determined rejection of following into death arose only very slowly, and at first only with reference to Europe.

---

[35] For the rise of a firm rejection of suicide (not derived from the Bible) in Christianity see Droge/Tabor.

[36] Boniface 220/221 (Letter 73). See above, p. 46.

[37] Marco Polo (Ed. Benedetto). 181 (chap. 175).

India still seemed to be very far away and too different to be measured with a European yardstick.

Both these strands are tangible in European accounts about India in the sixteenth century. The authors regularly mention widow burning, often without commenting on it.[38] Along with the view that one was reporting on something exotic—and therefore something that could not be judged with one's own yardstick—there were two other reasons for this. The authors concerned were not eyewitnesses, and they or their European sources had generally got their information from Indians who, for their part, approved of the custom and idealized it. In such a situation it would have been difficult to formulate an opinion. Despite this we also find the custom being condemned in the sixteenth century, among others by eyewitnesses and by ecclesiastical authors.[39]

In the seventeenth and eighteenth centuries only a few authors refrain from expressing an opinion.[40] A clear rejection of the custom is now normal, and often it is condemned outright. Terry for example spoke in the early seventeenth century of a 'hellish sacrifice'[41] and Careri at the end of the century of a 'barbaric inhumanity'.[42] Ecclesiastic authors were convinced that the widow would land in hell.[43] India lost its exotic status and was subjected to the European yardstick.

Such opinions were based, at least in the case of eyewitnesses, primarily on their own experiences, as could clearly be seen in occasional physical reactions. Ibn Baṭṭūṭa, who in this respect can be compared

[38] For example *Chronica* 76; Varthema 155; Castanheda 1, 243; Nuniz 61; 76–7; 350; 365; 372; 377; Albuquerque 1, 116 (part 2, chap. 20); Alvares 645–6; Sassetti 386–7; Resende 31–2 (verses 82–5).

[39] For example Balbi 82–3 (eyewitness, very restrained in his condemnation); Fedrici 36 ('I saw strange and bestial things'); Nunes 47 (priest, not an eyewitness); Franck CCIX verso; Barbosa 107–9 (109: 'abominable custom').

[40] Mundy 2, 34–6; 5, 62–3; Pyrard de Laval 1, 419–20; Saar 124–5; Rennefort 315–16; Hamilton 1, 157–8; Bogaert 376–7; Schorer 58.

[41] Terry 323.

[42] Careri 3, 232. Further voices of rejection are for example: Baldaeus 188; Biervillas 55; Bowrey 35; *Breve Relação* 20 (chap. 19); van den Broecke 167–8; Carletti 257; Valle 4, 197; Dellon 1, 108; Haafner 1, 93; Manrique 1, 78–9; Monserrate 61; Thevenot 5, 255; Bernier 106–19; Tavernier 2, 383–92; Fenicio 1, 179; Gonçalves 66–8; Coverte 56–7; Methwold 30; Ovington 201; Ravesteyn 74; Rogerius 71–81; Schouten 2, 99; Herbert 310.

[43] Carré 2, 507; Kircher 150–1.

to the Europeans, fell unconscious.[44] However, it was rare for someone to even lose his mind over it. Johann Sigmund Wurffbain wrote after an experience of 1638: 'Such an act is indeed very cruel and horrible to see. An English merchant living in Agra, having been present at such an imprudent act, was so distressed that his mind became affected and he was unable to overcome this for the rest of his life.'[45] Some were so shocked that they refused to ever witness such a scene again.[46] More robust natures, who frequently witnessed widow burnings, tended, on the other hand, to react indignantly, like the French doctor François Bernier in 1667: 'Sometimes I was so filled with rage against these accursed Brahmins, that I would have strangled them had I only dared.'[47] Pelsaert is an exception with his mix of cynicism and irony: 'It is not a very pleasant spectacle.'[48]

After 1757, there was a general condemnation of widow burning as an institution. Standard phrases came into existence like *horrid rite, horrible custom, abominable practice, horrible practice, inhuman and dreadful custom, horrid custom.* The indignation reached a climax with William Ward, a Baptist missionary, who published an important work on Hinduism in 1811:

But what shall we say of the murder of widows on the funeral pile?—this too is an act of great piety. The priest assists the poor wretch, in her last moments, before she falls on the pile, with the formulas given by the Hindoo legislators; and, to complete this most horrible of all religious customs, the son of this wretched victim kindles the fire in the very face of the mother who gave him birth. Can there possibly be a greater outrage on human nature? Is there any thing like it in all the records of the most wild and savage nations? The North American Indian proceeds with the utmost coolness, it is true, in the work of scalping and murder, but the victim is his enemy, taken in battle; here the victim is an innocent woman—a mother—a widow, her heart fresh bleeding under the loss of the companion of her youth—the murderer, her own child—dragged to the work by the *mild* bramhun, who dances, and shouts, and drowns the cries of the family and the victim in the horrid sounds of the drum. Such is the balm which is here poured into the

---

[44] Ibn Baṭṭūṭa 3, 616.

[45] Wurffbain 2, 18.

[46] Withington 220; Ravesteyn 75; Henry Lawrence, in Edwardes/Merivale 2, 37.

[47] Bernier 118.

[48] Pelsaert, *India* 78.

broken heart of the widow. Nor are these unheard of, unparalleled murders, perpetrated in the night, in some impenetrable forest, but in the presence of the whole population of India, in open day.[49]

This unanimously negative attitude constituted the framework within which the struggle for the abolition of widow burning was fought out, and which no one could avoid. The opponents of abolition had to prove that they found the custom just as horrible as those who were in favour of it and that their misgivings did not arise from a misconceived tolerance of the intolerable, but merely out of consideration of the higher goals that could be attained by British rule, which in their view would be endangered by abolition.

With this, a kind of social compulsion to condemn the custom arose, a pressure to conform, which exists till today. Those who did not conform risked being excluded from the discourse, as today if someone were to propagate the use of torture he would be hushed up, treated as if he were not of sound mind or prosecuted. Yet the evidence suggests that the rejection almost always sprang from a deep conviction.

Deviations from this conformity stand out very clearly. Paolino da San Bartolemeo wrote in 1796: 'If this law [which earlier supposedly required widows to burn themselves with their husband's body] were to be introduced in Europe, then so many good husbands would not wander around restlessly, and the rule of women in northern countries would come to an end, a rule, which is so despised in Oriental countries, where the women either remain behind closed doors or burn themselves to death with their husband.'[50] Paolino addressed his report to Pope Pius VI. It is unlikely that he wanted to introduce widow burning in Christianity by means of a law. Rather, his comments are indicative of considerations that were quite common and found in numerous anecdotes, but seldom expressed so clearly in accounts about India: European men dream of having the position of power that their Indian counterparts supposedly or actually have thanks to widow burning. It is significant that Paolino never witnessed an immolation.

In 1690, Robert Challe wrote: 'If the women in Europe were obliged to burn themselves after their husbands' death, then sudden cases of death would not be so frequent, and our France in my time would

---

[49] Ward, *View* 1, CXIX–CXX. In a similar vein on 9 January 1807 Ward's colleague John Marshman. Johns 28–9.

[50] Paolino 63 (1, 1, 5).

not have brought forth any monsters like a Constantin [. . .] and many others.'[51] Just before expressing this opinion, the author gives an eyewitness account in which he condemns the custom in no uncertain terms.[52]

In general reflections on widow burning some authors drew parallels with the burning of witches and heretics, and even with the custom of fighting duels, especially when they wanted to exonerate the Indians to some extent by proving that not so long ago people in Europe too had been no less cruel, indeed even more cruel.[53] Jacob Grimm was particularly vehement in 1849: 'It is therefore not the heathens, whose wives were allowed to be burnt with their husbands, who should be called barbaric and cruel, but the Christians, among whom large numbers of heretics and witches are cruelly consigned to the flames. The former is based on the holy bond of nature, the latter on the deluded fervour of priests.'[54] Yet these comparisons were in no way a justification of widow burning. In addition it is striking that eyewitnesses do not use them. For them the shock was evidently too great to allow the issue to be toned down indirectly in this manner.

In 1821, the French Jesuit Dubois, who worked in South India and was a sworn enemy of the Baptist missionaries, went especially far in his attempts to qualify the matter. He accused the Baptists of having driven the Hindus to resistance with their unbridled zeal, this causing an increase in the number of immolations. According to him more people died in France and England every month through suicide and duelling than widows burnt to death in a year in India. 'Are suicides and duelling in Europe less nefarious than suttees in India?' Dubois had witnessed immolations. But his dubious comparison stood apart from the concrete descriptions, and even he hastened to add that the burnings were 'execrable sacrifices' and 'horrid excesses of superstition and fanaticism'.[55]

[51] Challe 294.

[52] Challe 292–4. Cf. Herbert 310 and Mandelslo, *Reyse-Beschreibung* 82, who quotes Englishmen as saying that 'there are enough women and others of the species [whores and dancing girls] in India, and there would be no harm if some of the parasites were burnt.'

[53] Witches: Bohlen 1, 301; *Friend of India* 2 (1819), 454; Thompson, *Suttee* 131; Thomas 89. Heretics: *Friend of India* 2 (1819), 454. Duels: *Calcutta Journal* 1822, quoted in Ray 91–4.

[54] Grimm 308.

[55] Dubois, *Letters* 105–6. Cf. Dubois, *Moeurs* 18–34.

Yet at no point in time was this determined rejection the only reaction of Europeans. Along with it there was often a strong fascination. The two attitudes were not mutually exclusive. It was mainly this fascination that made Europeans take part in burnings.

Witnessing an immolation led not only to anger, grief and disgust, but in many cases to admiration for the heroism of the widow, not only among romantics. Holwell wrote in 1767:

> When people have lived together to an advanced age, in mutual acts of confidence, friendship and affection, the sacrifice a Gentoo widow makes of her person (under such affecting circumstances as the loss of friend and husband) seems less an object of wonder;—but when we see women in the bloom of youth, and beauty, in the calm possession of their reason and understanding, with astonishing fortitude, set at nought, the tender considerations of parents, children, friends, and the horror and torments of the death they court, we cannot resist viewing such an act, and such a victim, with tears of commiseration, awe and reverence.[56]

This mix of disgust and admiration is not a contradiction. The admiration was for the widow. Disgust was, on the one hand, often directed at the behaviour of the participants, and, on the other hand, it was always directed at the institution. In not one of the European accounts does the widow's heroism lead the author to wonder whether there was something good about the custom after all. On the other hand there is often an unwilling admission that despite the horrible nature of the institution the widow's behaviour would sometimes have to be considered admirable. Ward, one of the fiercest critics of widow burning, wrote: 'The desire of Hindoo women to die with their husbands, and the calmness of many going through the ceremonies which precede this horrible death, are circumstances almost, if not altogether unparalleled.'[57] The historian Kaye, who was strongly influenced by Evangelicalism, wrote in 1853: 'Even a Christian writer may say, that there was often an unearthly grandeur in the bearing of the deluded woman, which filled the spectator with scarcely less of admiration than of pity.'[58] Authors often exclaim that some widows behaved like martyrs. Admiration for a resoluteness, which was in every way equal to the greatest Christian examples, was mingled with regret that this

---

[56] Holwell 2, 91–2. Cf. also Della Valle 4, 232–3; Stavorinus 47–51.
[57] Ward, *View* 3, 327.
[58] Kaye 524.

strength of will was in the service of a bad cause and a false belief. The Jesuit missionary Roberto Nobili wrote, in 1606, that the widows would have made excellent Christian martyrs.[59] Mountstuart Elphinstone, the Governor of Bombay from 1819 to 1827, wrote: 'One is humiliated to think that so feeble a being can be elevated by superstition to a self-devotion not surpassed by the noblest examples of patriots or martyrs.'[60]

What is distinctive in 1903 in Marie von Bunsen's account is the combination of understanding and admiration for the widow, and the sharp critique of the underlying conditions:

> The death of the widow in India corresponded so well to religious views and beliefs, to the joy of self-sacrifice inherent in every woman, to the widely prevalent respect for her valiant courage, to caste pride, to the instinct for dramatic effect, that—assuming the belief—it seems to be almost ideally beautiful despite the possibly extremely painful minutes. Only the end of the most favoured Christian martyrs can compare with its moral-aesthetic effect. Therefore it seems to me not to be psychological to always make the infinitely smaller evil into the main thing because of its sensational effect, which arouses the imagination. The unspeakable, unimaginable cruelty lay in the general male-egotistic failure to respect women. If the woman was no longer required on earth but wanted in the other world, her violent death appeared to be indicated beyond doubt. If she did not grasp this opportunity, she was subjected to the most miserable contempt, 'to an unimaginable sorrow lasting unto death'. Under these conditions the poetic-symbolic apotheosis did not represent cruelty, but rather joy.[61]

The classical formulation had been found almost a century earlier by one of the first British admirers not only of past, but also contemporary Indian culture, by the later general, Charles Stuart. Widow burning, he said, was 'an instance of deluded heroism, that we cannot but admire, while we condemn.'[62]

---

[59] Cronin 53–5.

[60] Elphinstone 1, 360. In a similar vein, partly by eyewitnesses: *Asiatic Journal* 26 (1828), 730–1; Coomaraswamy, *Sati* 123–4; Grose 1, 195; Kaye 524; Postans 67; Le Bon 652; Rajan, *Women* 46; Stein, *Women* 268; IOR P/139/34, 251; Holwell 2, 99; Vincenzo 345; Lord 68. The comparison is emphatically rejected in *Friend of India* 2 (1819) 301–2.

[61] Bunsen, *Witwenverbrennung* 461.

[62] Stuart 72. For this see Fisch, *Vindicator*.

In many cases, in which force was obviously used, pity for the victim took the place of admiration. The reaction could even be sentimental, as for example when Schroeder in 1887 spoke of 'the terrible, but yet so moving and pathetic custom of widow burning.'[63]

A problem arises with regard to the assessment of the widow. In recent times it has sometimes been critically mentioned in research that the European observers, and especially the British officials, had always viewed the widow as a poor, helpless victim without a will of her own who required the assistance of strong men. In doing so they had merely projected their own European image of the dependent woman, who was entirely under her husband's protection, onto the Indian widow, and had in a way deprived her of her agency.[64] This may indeed have often been the case. An extreme form of this attitude was evident in a letter to the editor of the *Oriental Herald* in 1826, in which 'an old inhabitant of Bengal' stated 'that a woman in India, ninety-nine times out of a hundred, is, without exaggeration, little better than a child, and that, in this particular act of burning themselves with their husbands' bodies, they can scarcely be said to have any will of their own.'[65] At any rate, we see that along with this, admiration for the widow's heroism is seldom missing in European opinion, even if it is evident only in the emphasis placed on the voluntary nature of the act.[66] The real reason for portraying the widow as weak and helpless does not lie in the image of women that the authors have, but in the structure of European opinion about widow burning and about following into death in general. Those who reject such customs, or even demand that they be abolished, have to declare the widow to be either a victim or a criminal. If the widow is acclaimed as an independent, active agent of legitimate deeds, then the custom has also to be acclaimed, which presupposes a distinction between praiseworthy and blameworthy—between legal and illegal cases. The demand for a comprehensive ban cannot be reconciled with this, because it presupposes that all cases are to be rejected without any distinction. If the widow

---

[63] Schroeder 432.

[64] Especially Mani, *Production* 35–6 and Mani, *Traditions* 136; 152. Similarly Dalmia-Lüderitz 52–4; Rajan, *Women* 18ff.; 40–63; Stein, *Women* 259–61; Courtright, 185; Metcalf 96–8; Das, *Gender* 64–9.

[65] *An old inhabitant* 479.

[66] This is also seen by Mani, *Traditions* 152 and Stein, *Women* 261.

is perceived as an independent, active agent, the responsibility for the despised custom falls on her. This is an unavoidable consequence and is not linked with the image of women that one may have. It can be seen very clearly today. The most committed Indian opponents of widow burning, who certainly cannot be suspected of wanting to render a dependent status to Indian women, portray the sati to a much greater extent as a helpless victim than did the British officials in the nineteenth century, since they also dispute any kind of heroism. They deny the possibility of a voluntary widow burning from the outset.[67] The opinion about the sati does not depend on the opinion about the widow, but on the opinion about widow burning.

The Europeans did not confine themselves to opinions. Sometimes they also tried to confirm their opinions through deeds. They sought contact with the widow in order to convince her of the sinfulness of her actions and to try and stop her from carrying out her plans.[68] Sometimes they promised to support her in case she decided to live.[69] They often required the services of an interpreter for such a conversation.[70] Even if they spoke the language, they were sometimes prevented by relatives or priests from having direct contact with the widow, making them dependent on mediators.[71] Their message therefore often reached the widow only in a garbled and distorted form. Yet, even if a direct and unhindered conversation was possible, both sides probably often did not understand what the other was saying, since the

[67] For example Sangari, *Myth*. The radical feminist Mary Daly consistently insists in a most determined manner on the role of victim for the sati. Daly 115–33. Gandhi too wanted to hear nothing about the 'courage' of the sati in the face of this 'barbarous [. . .] practice'. M.K. Gandhi 122.

[68] For example *Asiatic Journal* 28 (1829), 217–18; [*Friend of India*] NS 1, 271; van den Broecke 1, 167; Ravesteyn 74; Ray 83–5; 123–9; Elliot 3; Statham 128–36.

[69] For example Challe 293; Twining 465–6; Lutfullah 175; Bernier 108–10; *Asiatic Journal* 20 (1825), 145–8; Statham 130.

[70] For example *Asiatic Journal* 16 (1823), 343–5.

[71] For example Thompson, *Suttee* 150; Townley 139–41; Bowrey 37; Twining 465–6; Statham 130–5. According to some authors, if a European happened to touch the widow, she was not allowed to burn herself. Stavorinus 2, 51–2; cf. Weinberger-Thomas (1989) 29. This would not have been a general rule. In many cases Europeans were not prevented from approaching the widow. Wilkins 386 mentions other restrictions.

arguments of a well-meaning European would hardly have made sense to the widow. At any rate, Europeans were seldom successful in making the woman stop the ceremony unless they used force or the authority of the state.[72] The strong counter pressure on the widow from her relatives has also to be taken into consideration.

Later, the combination of the condemnation of the institution and the admiration for the individuals also became common in India, although with an apologetic slant. P.V. Kane, the most important scholar of the Dharma texts in the twentieth century, wrote in 1941:

> Modern India does not justify the practice of sati, but it is a warped mentality that rebukes modern Indians for expressing admiration and reverence for the cool and unfaltering courage of Indian women in becoming satis or performing the 'jauhar' for cherishing their ideals of womanly conduct. If Englishmen can feel pride in their ancestors who grabbed one fourth of the world's surface or if Frenchmen can feel pride in the deeds of their Emperor Napoleon who tried to enslave the whole of Europe and yet are not held up to ridicule or rebuke, there is no reason why poor Indians cannot express admiration for the sacrifices which their women made in the past, though they may condemn the institution itself which demanded such terrible sacrifice and suffering.[73]

The Political Attitude of Europeans till the Middle of the Eighteenth Century

In the few regions ruled by them before the middle of the eighteenth century, the Europeans could, and indeed had to deal with widow burning as a political issue, since they were after all responsible for such matters. The Portuguese made a beginning. They acted with a consistency hitherto unknown in India.[74] Shortly after conquering Goa in 1510 they prohibited widow burning there. In 1560 the Viceroy issued a formal ban in all Portuguese territories. It appears that the measures were successful from the start. Several factors contributed to this.

---

[72] Exceptions: J. Forbes 2, 394–6; Bernier 108–10; *Asiatic Journal* 16 (1823), 343–5. For the active intervention of Europeans see above, pp. 284–6.

[73] Kane 2, 1, 636. Similarly, but more concisely: Chidanandamurti, in Settar/Sontheimer 125; Chandra 114 (1988).

[74] Albuquerque 1, 116–17 (part 2, chap. 20); Saldhana 371; Sousa 233; Thompson, *Suttee* 57; Della Valle 4, 77–8; Zachariae 566.

1. Widow burnings had been rare in the Goa region even earlier.[75]

2. In the sixteenth century the Portuguese conducted intensive missionary campaigns linked with different kinds of pressure, leading to the emigration of a part of the Hindu population.[76] Among them were certainly many of the orthodox people, who practised customs like widow burning.

3. An external factor was probably the most important. The Portuguese territories were so small that it was easy to shift the immolations to neighbouring regions. A modus vivendi appears to have been found here: the Portuguese did not prevent this evasion, and the Hindus refrained from provoking the Portuguese by carrying out burnings in the regions under their control.

The first two factors did not apply to the other European holdings. In some of the European held areas immolations were particularly frequent, as, for example, in Bengal. In addition the other European powers were extremely cautious where missionary activity was concerned. The third factor was therefore all the more important. The territories were even smaller than Goa. It appears that although no formal ban was issued, the custom was generally not permitted.[77] At any rate, immolations have been recorded directly or indirectly for Danish Serampore and for French Karikal.[78]

---

[75] Saldanha 371. This was portrayed differently in the early sixteenth century by Pires 377, who states that in Goa almost all widows burned themselves (which is also definitely not true).

[76] Cf. D'Costa.

[77] The information in the sources and in the relevant literature is not very precise. The most reliable information seems to be that provided by the missionary William Carey to Governor General Bentinck on 31 October 1829, after consulting with the governor of the Danish territory of Serampore. According to this information widow burning was banned (although nothing is known of a formal ban) in the French and the Dutch territories, whereas in the Danish territory only individual cases were prevented. *Bentinck Papers,* PwJf 2620/I. Included by Bentinck into his minute of 8 November 1829. Bentinck 1, 105. Cf. Salahuddin Ahmed 163: banned in the territories of all three European powers; Thompson, *Suttee* 59: banned only by the Dutch, whereas the French and the Danes suppressed the custom de facto to a large extent; Olafsson 136: prevention by the Danes; Wintergerst 118: Dutch ban; Modave 171–2: opposition by Europeans everywhere, least among the British.

[78] *Sketch of popular ideas* (1825) 44–7: burning in Serampore, at which

The Contestations of a Colonial Power:
Regulation to Abolition, 1757–1829

The British abolition of widow burning has always been celebrated as a great humanitarian achievement, as one of the few acts of a colonial power that was motivated by noble intentions and was without doubt a blessing for the subjects.[79] At least outside, but partly also within India, Charles Metcalfe, a member of the government in Calcutta, proved to be right with the prophecy he made three weeks before abolition: 'I expect that the time will come, when it will be universally acknowledged by the people of India as the best act performed by the British government.'[80]

Since the estimation of the act was hardly ever disputed, the discussion from the beginning, which continues till today, was centred on the question of who should be given the main credit for it: Governor General Bentinck, British public opinion in general or the Protestant missionaries in particular, or the opposition within India around Rammohan Roy?

The special feature of the abolition of 1829 is not that it was enacted, but that it was enacted so late. By concentrating on the search for persons to whom credit is due, one does not see that the abolition represented the inevitable consequence of a policy which had been doomed from the outset, because it ignored the specific situation of the colonial power. Tolerating any form of following into death under European rule was bound to lead to a moral conflict, since Europeans, as rulers, had to sanction acts that were crimes according to their own concepts of morality. Such conflicts could only be avoided through a complete prohibition. In all other regions of the world the colonial powers—among them also the British—therefore actually implemented a ban (or a de facto suppression) immediately after they had established their rule. In India, however, the British tried to avoid this right up to the end, and in the process only got themselves more deeply entangled in conflicts and contradictions till abolition became the only way out.

---

even force is used. Pasquier 322: In 1829 a French official suceeds in persuading a woman not to burn herself. A ban therefore apparently did not exist and prevention was not always attempted.

[79] Cf. A. Sharma, *Thresholds* 91ff.

[80] Minute of 14 November 1829. IOR L/L/13 (1030), vol. 3, App. 128.

It was not so much a great humanitarian achievement as a late acknowledgement of a failed policy. It resulted from the very measures that were taken to avoid abolition, thus demonstrating that under a modern bureaucratic administration, a custom that cannot be reconciled with the moral code of the administrators, cannot in the long run either be ignored or regulated.

Such a perspective does not change the nature of the abolition, nor its salutary effect, but its estimation in the historical context.

In what follows, the question is not who gets the credit for the abolition. Rather it is a question of describing a process that began with the timidity of a colonial power that was unwilling to understand the character of its own rule, and that finally caught up with its authors.

This revision of the existing view is also a dictate of historical justice. The European suppression of following into death in all other parts of the world is disregarded and taken for granted, whereas the abolition of 1829, which only became necessary in this form because the colonial rulers had shied away from it for decades, is portrayed as an act of great merit.

The argument being presented here runs counter to the accepted view both in academic research as well as in public opinion in India and Great Britain. This necessitates a somewhat more extensive presentation and substantiation.

The Policy of Disregard, 1757–1789

By gaining control over Bengal, Bihar and Orissa in 1757 the British had brought an important and prosperous part of India under their rule. They contented themselves with a lax supervision of affairs and concentrated their energies on the economic exploitation of the country. But the attempt to enjoy the fruits of power without taking on political responsibility ended in chaos and famine. From 1772 onwards the British took the administration into their own hands and changed it fundamentally—a process that was more or less completed by the beginning of the 1790s. In view of the extremely small number of European officials, direct control was wide-meshed. Yet the British were quite efficient when it came to carrying out measures that were in their own interests, particularly tax collection and the enforcement of law and order.[81]

---

[81] For the early phase of British rule in India and for the organization of

This means that it would have been easily possible to take measures against widow burning. Yet nothing happened. Almost all important British civil servants were of the view that the country had to be ruled as far as possible according to its own laws. In this context religion, and especially customs and traditions based on religion were considered to be all-important. It was assumed that the Indians, or the Hindus, would fervently cling to them. Changes in this area were therefore regarded as extremely risky.[82]

This was in contrast to the fundamental and uncompromising condemnation of all forms of following the dead by the Europeans. They thus had to overlook something which in their eyes was immoral, cruel and criminal. Their opinion could not change overnight, indeed not even over a medium space of time, since it sprang from a mental background that had grown over centuries.

Since the assessment of the custom could not be changed, the only thing to do was to pretend it did not exist. Such an attitude was relatively easy for someone who lived in London. Even the senior officials in Calcutta could easily maintain the illusion that there was no real problem, especially since widow burning was not allowed in the city of Calcutta (as also in Bombay). Both cities had come under British control before 1757, and here the British had acted like the other Europeans in their territories.[83] Matters would have been more difficult for the junior officials in the districts. Sooner or later they would have come into contact with the custom. They too could naturally close their eyes and their ears. But it is doubtful whether they could have managed to continue in this fashion permanently, since such an attitude contradicted all traditional European concepts of good governance. The state was responsible for the welfare of its subjects. If it tolerated practices that it considered to be cruel and criminal, it was not fulfilling its self-appointed duties, or, as W.H. Macnaghten stated

---

the administration cf. D.N. Banerjee; Aspinall; B.B. Misra; Marshall. A brief useful overview in Bearce 239–40.

[82] Cf. Stokes; Cassels, *Religion*; Fisch, *Pamphlet war*.

[83] Calcutta: Ingham 45; Bentinck 1, 340; V.N. Datta 28. Bombay: Johns VII; 88; Buchanan, *Establishment* 132. For Madras a ban is not mentioned before 1830, nor are widow burnings in the city mentioned. In Calcutta a formal ban was in force only since 1798. But apparently it was enforced to a large extent even earlier.

clearly in 1828: 'Considered as an abstract question of morality, the ruling authority is criminal, where it neglects to exercise that power for the suppression of practices which are inimical to the welfare of the people committed to its protection.'[84]

The Court of Directors in London, the executive body of the East India Company, had sensed the danger at the very latest by 1818. When the Bengal regulation of widow burning was sought to be imposed on the Madras Presidency, it was first intended that the magistrate be present at the burnings. Someone noted in the margins of the draft that he considered this to be an 'unwise stipulation', since it would give official blessing to the ceremony. Chiefly one should reconsider 'the hardship of subjecting an European to the necessity of witnessing so cruel an exhibition.' The clause was cancelled.[85]

Already in 1813 William Wilberforce had emphasized in the House of Commons how important spatial distance was for the opinion of the public, even if he had a different aim in mind. People in Great Britain had not yet undertaken anything against widow burning because they still did not regard India as part of the British Empire, and Indians as fellow citizens:

> The vast distance also of the scene of these barbarities tends considerably to deaden the impression which they would otherwise produce. If these transactions took place in any part of England, instead of the indifference with which they have been too long regarded by men, I am sensible, not inferior in humanity to ourselves, the public zeal would be called forth, and every possible endeavour would be used to put an end to them. But here again, Sir, we see the effects of that strange delusion by which our countrymen are led into adapting one set of morals, and principles, and even feelings, for this country, and another for India.[86]

As will be shown, the reproach concerning inactivity was not valid against the district officers.

With its policy of disregarding the custom, the government was engaged in a dangerous game in which it would have to expect increasing

---

[84] 14.12.1828. IOR L/L/13 (1030), vol. 3, App. 53.

[85] 4.3.1818. IOR E/4/920, 749.

[86] 22.6.1813 Wilberforce, in *Parliamentary Debates* 26 (1813), 861–2. Similarly:[Peggs], *Meeting* 539 (1826).

resistance—not from the Indians, but from its own civil servants, not to mention public opinion in Great Britain.

At first everything went well. In the early phase the district officers had numerous other problems to contend with, so that they actually did not bother very much about widow burning, although it occurred frequently enough. At least they did not report it to the higher authorities. This changed even before the administrative reforms had been completed.

The Path to Regulation, 1789–1815

In 1789 a widow in the district of Shahabad turned to the local British official, M.H. Brooke, with the request for permission to burn herself to death. According to existing laws, permission was not required. Yet, even in other parts of British India, permission was later frequently sought from the administrators. It is possible that the obligation to seek official permission, which had existed in the Mughal Empire and in other Islamic and also in some Hindu states, had remained in peoples' minds.

According to official policy, Brooke should have declined to take on the responsibility. Instead, he prohibited the burning. He reported this to the government in Calcutta and justified his action on 'being impressed with a belief that this savage custom has been prohibited in and around Calcutta. [. . .] The rites and superstitions of the Hindu religion should be allowed with the most unqualified tolerance, but a practice at which human nature shudders I cannot permit within the limits of my jurisdiction, without particular instructions.'[87]

With this Brooke transferred the responsibility onto the government: if it wanted its officials to suppress natural feelings of humanity, it would have to expressly order them to do so.

The government accepted the implicit reproach. It approved of Brooke's action, but also made it clear that it was pursuing another policy:

> Though they [the government] are desirous he [Brooke] should exert all his private influence to dissuade the natives from a practice so repugnant to humanity and the first principles of religion, they do not deem it advisable to authorize him to prevent the observance of it by coercive measures, or by any exertion of his official powers; as the

[87] 28.1.1789 Brooke to the government. PP 1821/18,22.

public prohibition of a ceremony, authorized by the tenets of the religion of the Hindoos, and from the observance of which they have never yet been restricted by the ruling power, would in all probability tend rather to increase than diminish their veneration for it; and, consequently, prove the means of rendering it more prevalent than it is at present. That it is hoped the natives themselves will, in the course of time, discern the fallacy of the principles which have given rise to this practice, and that it will of itself gradually fall into disuse.[88]

These statements contain the nucleus of the debates that were conducted during the following decades with increasing intensity and severity. The focus of controversy was whether the assessment and the political handling of widow burning should be in accordance with British or Indian standards.[89]

At first two similarities become evident. Both, the government as well as Brooke, call for an all-encompassing tolerance, and they agree in their spontaneous opinion of widow burning. This is regarded as a barbaric custom that flies in the face of the principles of true religion and humanity. On this point there was always unity. No Briton seriously tried to justify the custom with European standards.

These two positions could not be maintained to their full extent at the same time. If one wanted to establish European standards in areas where they came into conflict with Indian ones, then tolerance would have to be sacrificed. If one wanted unconditional tolerance, then Indian standards would have to be accepted in practice. Brooke wanted tolerance to end where actual practices which went against humanity and against norms that were postulated as universally valid were concerned. What constituted humanity or human nature was determined according to his own, European standards. The government, on the other hand, restricted the validity of European standards. In political practice there was an effort to maintain Indian standards.

Universalists and relativists thus stood on opposite sides. The universalists demanded that their standards be established without any restrictions. The relativists, on the other hand, were relativists only in action, not in opinion. They were willing to deal with widow burning according to Indian standards, but they were not willing to accept Indian standards as their own, and with it Indian opinion about widow

---

[88] 4.2. 1789. PP 1821/18,22.
[89] Cf. Griffiths 217 on the question of standards.

burning. They were no less convinced than the universalists that their standards were correct.

The conflict between the two groups was therefore not concerned with finding, but merely with pushing through the truth. If necessary, the universalists were willing to use compulsion in the form of a ban, whereas the relativists insisted on free choice. They placed great hopes on the influence of European education. In 1823, for example, the government in Bombay wrote with considerable enthusiasm: 'The prejudices of the natives are rapidly giving way to the effect of our example; at no very distant period the worst of their delusions will we trust vanish of themselves before the general diffusion of knowledge.'[90]

The relativists too were therefore concerned with the relationship between a true and a false standard, and not with the conflict between two equal standards. In a sense they had to use different yardsticks in order to keep their personal convictions and the standards for their political actions apart. The less such situations arose, the easier it was to maintain a relativist policy.

In the following years the government maintained silence on the question of widow burning. However, in the course of time, the moral conflicts with which the district officers were involved found their bureaucratic path to the top.

In 1797, a magistrate tried—as it seems unsuccessfully—to stop a nine-year-old widow from burning herself to death.[91] His action contradicted the sacred principle of non-interference in religious matters. Despite this, the government approved of his act. This can only have been the outcome of moral shock. In European eyes, the burning to death of a child was such a monstrous act that if the official had been rebuked, it would have morally disqualified the government in the eyes of its European subjects. On the other hand, none of the perpetrators appear to have been arrested or indeed punished.

In 1805, a twelve-year-old widow was supposed to be burnt to death in Gaya district (Bihar). Some relatives secretly informed the police officer that they were against this plan. The officer reported this to the magistrate who paid the widow a visit, and was able to persuade her to give up her plan.[92]

[90] 25.6.1823 Government of Bombay to the Court of Directors PP 1824/23, 47. The hopes linked with the effect of the 'diffusion of knowledge' were part of the standard argument of the opponents of the ban till the end.

[91] 17.5.1797 James Battray, magistrate of Midnapur. PP 1821/18,23.

[92] 4.1.1805 J.R.Elphinstone, magistrate Gaya. PP 1821/18,23.

This episode seems to have awakened doubts and misgivings in Calcutta. Shortly thereafter the government turned to the highest criminal court, the *Nizamat Adalat* (which, despite its Persian name, consisted entirely of British judges). It asked the court, whether widow burning could be prohibited, or, if this did not appear practicable, whether measures could be taken to ensure that it was voluntary.[93] To aid its decision, the court was asked to get a legal opinion from Hindu pandits, in order to determine 'how far the practice above noticed is founded in the religious opinions of the Hindoos.'[94]

There was a tradition of asking the pandits for their legal opinion.[95] But the decision to rule the Indians according to their own laws led to enormous practical problems. One could not simply fall back on a codified legal system. It was difficult to say what Hindu law was. The point of departure was a large number of older texts, in which the rules, or even merely recommendations, often either contradicted one another or were vague. Moreover these texts included only the smaller part of legal reality. Important aspects of the administration of justice, especially among the lower castes, were regulated according to unwritten laws which varied greatly from region to region. This task was beyond the capabilities of a colonial power whose officials generally did not even know the regional languages. Therefore they concentrated on the written laws which were easier to ascertain. For this they took help from the pandits who were asked to give the prevailing view on certain points. This gave the pandits considerable power.[96] The British were able to free themselves from this dependence only in the course of the nineteenth century, when sufficient European experts had been trained.

There were advantages as well in consulting the pandits. The colonial power could rid itself of part of the responsibility by pointing out that the laws it had introduced and applied were based on the views of traditional authorities on the subject. Especially in cases where it feared that the changes could lead to unrest, it was natural to safeguard its position in this manner.

Actually, by referring the matter to the pandits, a decision had

[93] 5.2.1805. PP 1821/18, 24.

[94] PP 1821/18, 24.

[95] Cf. Derrett, The British as patrons of the Śāstra, in: Derrett, *Religion* 225–73; Derrett, The administration of Hindu law by the British, ibid., 274–320; Mani, *Production* 36–8; Mani, *Traditions* 130–4; 140–50.

[96] Emphasized for example by Poynder 28. Cf. PP 1825/24, 104–6; for conflicts cf. PP 1821/18, 39–40.

already been taken. No one could seriously expect the experts to say that widow burning had no basis in Hinduism and that it was just an ordinary crime. This means that the decision to ask for a legal opinion was simultaneously a decision against the prohibition of widow burning and in favour of regulation.

The pandits came to the conclusion that under certain circumstances widows of all four main castes were allowed to burn themselves to death. It was not permitted if her children were still small, unless someone took on the responsibility for their care. The widow should not be pregnant; she should not be of a pre-pubescent age, and she should not be menstruating. The act had to be voluntary. Therefore the use of drugs was prohibited and the decision to die could be revoked up to the last minute. If this happened after the end of the preparatory ceremonies, an extensive penance would have to be undergone.[97]

With these legal opinions the hands of the Nizamat Adalat were tied, as it declared rhetorically: 'The practice, horrid and revolting even as a voluntary one, should be prohibited and entirely abolished.' But 'the prejudices in favour of the custom, are at present so strongly impressed on the minds of the inhabitants [. . .], that all casts of Hindoos would be extremely tenacious of its continuance.' At the present juncture a ban would 'in all probability excite a considerable degree of alarm and dissatisfaction' among the Hindus; therefore it would be 'highly inexpedient.'[98] What formally appeared to be conditions laid down by the pandits, was in reality their blessing to what the court had wanted. It could now shelter itself behind their authority.

By linking permission for widow burning to certain conditions, the legal opinion nevertheless brought home the necessity of taking action if the administration was to take its task seriously. The Nizamat Adalat suggested police surveillance.[99] By ensuring that the conditions were observed, at least the worst cases could be prevented, and, perhaps, in time, the custom could be completely abolished.

Regulating the custom also had problematic consequences. It led to a distinction between legal and illegal cases. British magistrates and judges required a great deal of acumen to decide whether a burning could be permitted or not. In concrete terms this could mean, for

[97] Answers of the pandits, undated [1805]. PP 1821/18, 28-29. For detailed rules that partly deviate from this, cf. the law passed in Nepal in 1854. Michaels, *Legislation* 1226–35.
[98] 5.6.1805 Nizamat Adalat to the government. PP 1821/18, 27.
[99] PP 1821/18, 28.

example, that burning to death without the husband's body was legal in the case of a non-Brahmin, but illegal for a Brahmin widow. It could not be assumed that an European official would find the burning more acceptable in one case than in the other. An anonymous author wrote in 1868 of 'getting into a dilemma by attempting to introduce justice and law into what was, in itself, the highest kind of illegality, the most palpable injustice, and the most revolting cruelty.'[100] A modern author stated: 'The whole notion of drawing a fine line of distinction between voluntary and involuntary Suttees was an essay in hypocritical pedantry intended to cover up a cowardly evasion of the real issue.'[101]

The distinction between legal and illegal cases was bound to increase the number of moral conflicts in the administration of justice. It was likely that the responsible officials would increasingly experience feelings of revulsion and would demand a general prohibition because the path back was blocked. Restrictions, once decreed, could only be revoked with a considerable loss of prestige.

The government possibly recognized these dangers. At any rate, it did not take any action. The Nizamat Adalat does not appear to have been unhappy about this. More than seven years later only, on 3 September 1812, it ventured to ask the government about the fate of its proposals.[102] A district officer had once again requested guidelines for action in such cases.

The government informed the court on 5 December 1812 that in view of the legal opinion presented by the pandits, it would appear that the only correct policy—in accordance with the principles of tolerance—would be to permit the custom in cases where it was approved by Hinduism, and to prohibit it in all other cases.[103]

Accordingly, guidelines were issued on 29 April 1813 to all police officers.[104] It was stated that certain cases were 'contrary to the Shaster [Hindu law], and perfectly inconsistent with every principle of humanity.' Once again the dilemma of the British is evident. It is not enough that such cases contradict Hindu law—they also clash with the principles of humanity. If the members of the government and the court had been asked whether legal burnings did not clash with these

---

[100] *Papers* (1868) 235.
[101] I. Singh 197.
[102] 3.9.1812 Nizamat Adalat to the government. PP 1821/18, 29–30.
[103] 5.12.1812 Government to the Nizamat Adalat. PP 1821/18, 31–2.
[104] 11.3.1813 Draft of the Nizamat Adalat, sent out on 29.4.1813. PP 1821/18, 32–4. Quote: 32.

principles, they certainly would have protested against such insinuations.

In the future, the police were supposed to attempt their best to find out as early as possible about intended widow burnings and reach the place immediately in order to find out whether the conditions of legality had been fulfilled. Except for one point, these conditions were set out less restrictively than in the legal opinion of the pandits of 1805. A burning was to be considered illegal only if the widow was pregnant, if she was not yet 16 years old, if she was under the influence of drugs, or if the act was not voluntary. The question of menstruation appeared to be too delicate to be handled administratively. The same could not be said of the requirement that the widow was without small children, a point that was nonetheless dropped. The minimum age of the widow was, however, higher than that mentioned by the pandits.

If the conditions were not fulfilled, the police were supposed to try to prevent the burning from being carried out and the British authorities were supposed to take penal action. If, on the other hand, all conditions were fulfilled, then the police officer was to let the organizers 'know that it is not the intention of the government to check or forbid any act authorized by the tenets of the religion of the inhabitants of their dominions, or even to require that any express leave or permission be required.'[105] The absence of an obligation to report planned burnings must have made the job of the police exceedingly difficult.

The extreme caution exercised by the government and the Nizamat Adalat could be seen in yet another point. The guidelines did not constitute a law, but merely orders given by the magistrate to the police which were not even published. Legally, the prohibited acts were therefore not crimes, so that, strictly speaking, no one could be punished. The legal character of the new rules was, to put it cautiously, questionable. This is all the more striking, since British administration of justice in India was otherwise meticulously concerned with maintaining legality.[106]

From the beginning the rules led to moral conflicts, and they also proved in need of greater precision and more details. In October 1813, a widow in the district of Burdwan, who had a two-and-a-half-year-old child, wanted to burn herself on her husband's pyre. The police

[105] PP 1821/18, 33.
[106] Cf. Fisch, *Cheap Lives.*

officer present was of the opinion that this was illegal and tried to prevent the act. However, the crowd stopped him from doing so.[107]

The Nizamat Adalat's reply to the report concerning the incident showed where the official distinction between legal and illegal cases could lead. Bayley, the magistrate, whose Indian police officer had obviously taken pity on the widow, was told—quite correctly—that according to the rules this was not an illegal case. He should therefore 'issue the strictest injunctions' to the police 'prohibiting their interference on such occasions.'[108] This was undoubtedly the correct position, but it hardly presented suitable guidance for resolving moral conflicts. The case showed that even Hindus (the police officers and their subordinates) were not spared such conflicts. Bayley protested in vain that in four similar cases he had successfully prevented the burnings.[109] Seen from the perspective of good administration, it was not a question of simply preventing cases of widow burning, but of preventing illegal cases only.

In the same year two further problems arose. In Purnea district in Bihar a widow allowed herself to be buried alive. The magistrate did not take any steps to prevent this, but requested instructions for the future.[110] In Bundelkhand (Madhya Pradesh) a woman wanted to burn herself to death 17 years after her husband's death. The police prevented her from carrying out the act, and the magistrate also asked for instructions.[111]

The Nizamat Adalat took recourse to the tested method of asking for legal opinions. The pandits stated that a widow with children under three years of age was not allowed to follow her husband in death unless someone was prepared to take care of the orphans. Burial alive was allowed among certain castes. *Anumaraṇa* was prohibited to Brahmin widows, but allowed among other castes.[112]

On the basis of this information, additional instructions were sent

---

[107] 28.10.1813 W.B. Bayley, magistrate of Burdwan, to the Nizamat Adalat. PP 1821/18, 35–6.

[108] 9.12.1813 Nizamat Adalat to Bayley. PP 1821/18, 36.

[109] 18.12.1813 Bayley to the Nizamat Adalat. PP 1821/18, 36–7.

[110] PP 1821/18, 38–9.

[111] PP 1821/18, 39–40.

[112] 14.9.1814 Nizamat Adalat to the government. PP 1821/18, 33–5. 4.10.1814 Government to the Nizamat Adalat. Ibid., 40–1. Cf. also ibid., 37–40.

out on 21 March 1815.[113] In one point the consequences of the timidity of the Nizamat Adalat had already caught up with it. In their first legal opinion the pandits had stated that mothers of small children were not allowed to follow their husbands into death. This statement had been ignored in the first set of instructions—now it was to be included. The act was also prohibited if the widow was menstruating. The question of burial alive, however, remained unresolved.[114]

These events clearly show the immanent tendencies of the new policy. Once the distinction between legal and illegal immolations had been drawn, it was seized by the bureaucratic machinery and constantly perfected. It was not important, whether the additional distinctions made sense or not. It was only important that the rules did not contradict each other and were able to cover all the cases that occurred.

The Politics of Regulation, 1815–1829

In the meantime the first results of the survey to determine the frequency of the custom were available. They have already been discussed, and it has been explained why the figures are more or less reliable. The information about questions of legality is less reliable. If the police decided that a case was legal, there was nothing more to be done. In illegal cases, however, there was the duty to prevent, or, if that was not possible, then the case had to be subsequently investigated. Interrogations had to be conducted, and, under certain circumstances, arrests had to be made, which could arouse the ire of the local population. Since the government wanted to avoid such situations, there was no cause for exaggerated zeal on the part of the police. If the police arrived on the scene too late, it was even more difficult to determine whether the case had fulfilled all the conditions of legality. Many authors and even British administrators suspected that the police were often bribed to report that the conditions of legality had been fulfilled.[115] Even though there is no evidence, it is at least probable that the zeal of the police was further reduced by this factor.

On the other hand, corruption would not have played a significant

[113] 21.3.1815. PP 1821/18, 41–3 (along with the expert opinion of the pandits, which were also regarded as rules).

[114] As late as on 8.8.1829 the Nizamat Adalat explained that burial alive had never been expressly declared as illegal. IOR P/139/34, 197.

[115] For example 18.11.1818 W. Ewer, Superintendent of Police of the Lower Provinces, to the government in Calcutta. PP 1821/18,229, § 13;

role in this context at the level of the British officials. However, one case (obviously an exception) has been handed down. In 1818, a magistrate by the name of Sage is said to have taken a bribe of 800–900 rupees for granting permission to a young widow to follow her husband into death. He is said to have been dismissed.[116]

Yet some illegal cases were reported in 1815 and 1816. The Nizamat Adalat registered the violations and demanded that they be prevented in future. Criminal proceedings were not initiated, however, and nor were the magistrates or police reprimanded.[117]

On the other hand, the court did not say anything about illegal actions of the state. Magistrates occasionally imposed fines and prison sentences of up to one and a half months on people who had not reported a planned widow burning to the police. Since an obligation to report did not exist, such actions were clearly illegal. In 1815, a widow was not allowed to burn herself to death because she belonged to a caste that allegedly did not have a right to widow burning.[118] The existing rules did not offer a basis for such measures.

The question as to whether burial alive was permitted according to Hindu law was still a matter of controversy. The Nizamat Adalat asked for further legal opinions, which arrived at different conclusions. This custom was not mentioned anywhere in the Dharma texts, but it had a basis in customary law. The Nizamat Adalat proposed a ban (which never came into effect).[119] This demonstrated its heightened sense of power, because here it decided against a practice that was firmly established among the people. But the risk was small since the custom was not widely prevalent. Every year only five to ten cases were registered.

In 1816, the magistrate of Benares prohibited two burnings, since the women had not been the wives of the deceased.[120] The Nizamat

---

236. Cf. also PP 1821/18, 255–6; IOR L/L/13 (1030), vol. 3, App. 57; 86; Poynder 19.

[116] January 1830 Calder to Benson. Bentinck 1, 377–8. Cf. V.N. Datta 137. Given the high salaries of British civil servants, the bribe mentioned seems very low. The case is not mentioned in the official files.

[117] 25.6.1817 Nizamat Adalat Proceedings. PP 1821/18, 101–2.

[118] Detailed statements 1815. PP 1821/18, 80.

[119] 25.6.1817 Nizamat Adalat Proceedings. PP 1821/18, 105. Different expert opinions: ibid., 112–14 (1815–17). Demand for a ban: ibid., 131 (25.6.1817) and 141 (9.9.1817).

[120] 23.7.1816 W.W. Bird, magistrate of Benares to the Court of Circuit Benares. PP 1821/18, 133–4.

Adalat resolved to include this point in the new rules, without first seeking the legal opinion of the pandits.[121] The extent of politically motivated consideration for the ruled was being reduced.

From now, this attitude was consistently maintained. On 25 June 1817, the court presented a draft of the new rules.[122] They were no longer going to be issued as internal orders, but as a formal law. However, the relativist position was still maintained, and was emphasized in the preamble of the draft in such a way as to make the moral conflict of the British authorities very clear:

> The government, actuated by its general principle of toleration, however anxious for the voluntary discontinuance of a custom so repugnant to the feelings of humanity, deemed it proper, [. . .] to authorise the interference of public officers, so far only as appeared absolutely necessary, under experience of gross abuses and irregularities, for maintaining a more strict observance of the ordinances of the Hindoo law.[123]

Whereas the guidelines of 1813 had placed humanity and the Hindu law on the same level, now humanity was subordinated to the Hindu law. As far as details are concerned, the rules of 1813 and 1815 were partly maintained and stated more precisely, partly they were extended and made more stringent. The most important change was the obligation to report planned burnings.

If this bill had been passed, it would have probably reduced the number of widow burnings considerably. But it would not have been able to stop them completely and would have implicated the British administration even more deeply in the matter. The government was obviously afraid of this. It therefore approved of most of the suggestions made by the court, but felt that the rules should be issued again as guidelines for the police, not as a law.[124] Two months later the government again retracted its position, which amounted to an about-turn. It felt that the international situation made it appear desirable to delay the law 'until a period of greater tranquillity.'[125] In reality, the government had in the meantime had serious misgivings about the direction it had taken. It had 'considerable doubts with regard to the actual

[121] PP 1821/18, 139.
[122] PP 1821/18, 126–31. Final version of 9.9.1817, ibid., 137–42.
[123] PP 1821/18, 126.
[124] 9.9.1817 Government to the Nizamat Adalat. PP 1821/18, 142–4.
[125] 5.11.1817 Government Resolution. PP 1821/18, 241–2. Quote: 241.

effects which have been produced by the circular orders [. . .] with a view to diminish the prevalence of the practice of suttee.' It was 'reluctantly led to express the apprehension that the greater confidence with which the people perform this rite under the sanction of government [. . .] combined with the excitement of religious bigotry by the continual agitation of the question, may have tended to augment, rather than diminish, the frequency of these sacrifices.' If the number of cases did not decrease, the government even considered giving up official interference altogether.[126]

The government was successful in so far as the new guidelines never came into effect. On the other hand an about-turn also did not take place. As long as widow burning was legal, the orders of 1813 and 1815 remained valid.

The Nizamat Adalat also continued its arbitrary manner of dealing with legality and the principles of the rule of law, by acting as if some of its proposed regulations of 1817 had in fact come into effect. In May 1819, it summarized the supposedly valid rules for the use of the police. According to these rules *anumaraṇa* was not allowed, unless the widow carried out the act immediately after receiving the news of her husband's death.[127] The rule had never been laid down in this manner. Nor did the court maintain such a position consistently. When it mentioned an *anumaraṇa* that had taken place 48 years after the husband's death in its annual report of 1829, there was no mention of illegality.[128] As a rule, however, magistrates who went against the law by not granting permission for such ceremonies were not reprimanded.[129] Some of them also applied the proposed ban of 1817 on the burning of women who were not wives of the deceased. They too were not censured.[130]

Meanwhile, a first voice in the administration demanded an absolute prohibition. In April 1816, E. Watson, judge in Alipur, a suburb of Calcutta, submitted a proposal in this matter to the Nizamat

[126] PP 1821/18, 241–2.

[127] 21.5.1819 Nizamat Adalat Proceedings. PP 1821/18, 222. Cf. PP 1830/28, 239 and PP 1821/18, 42–3.

[128] 8.8.1829. IOR P/139/34, 197.

[129] Cf. for example PP 1825/24, 70; 121; PP 1830/28, 94; 204.

[130] After a concubine had burnt herself to death on 18.12.1818 in Bundelkhand, the Court of Circuit even punished the police officer because he— and correctly so—had not prevented the ceremony. PP 1821/18, 205. Cf. IOR P/139/34, 70–1 (28.9.1827 Cuttack).

Adalat.[131] Burnings occurred very frequently in his district. The arguments presented by him were also used later, both by members of the administration and by critical voices from outside. The framework of demands for a prohibition always consisted of humanitarian, universalistic views. For the actual debate, however, the more specific arguments were of greater importance. The focus was on the attempt to convince the government by pointing out precedents in its own policy. Watson reminded the court that ever since the British administration had taken criminal legislation into its hands in 1790, it had, successfully and without resistance, abolished practices that it regarded as inhuman or unjust. Among these was infanticide (mainly of girls), and child sacrifice at holy rivers ensuing from religious oaths. In a somewhat different context (not mentioned by Watson, but otherwise often used) stood the abolition of the privilege of the Brahmins not to be subjected to the death penalty under any circumstances. The court argued that these examples, in contrast to widow burning, were not religiously sanctioned practices.[132] This was only partly correct. The privilege of Brahmins occupied a central place in the Dharma texts. It is true that the other practices were not mentioned in the texts. But they were firmly established customs and, apart from infanticide, also had a fairly distinct religious character in the consciousness of those involved. If the British were really concerned with sparing the religious feelings, and not only the religious laws of the Hindus, they would have to tolerate such practices also. The court, on the other hand, pointed at a more important difference. In all these examples it was a question of murder, whereas widow burning, at least in theory, was suicide. The less this premise was accepted, the more difficult it must have been to oppose abolition.

The results of the surveys for 1817 and 1818 were bound to be sobering and indeed disappointing or even shocking for all those who had expected that the policy of regulation would be a quick success. The number of registered widow burnings increased from 442 in 1816 to 707 in 1817 and 839 in 1818 (see Table 2). This was more than double the number of cases in 1815 (378). In 1818, the Nizamat Adalat still stood firm in its opinion: it attributed the increase to the better

---

[131] 16.4.1816. PP 1821/18, 99–100.

[132] The counter-arguments of the Nizamat Adalat in its Proceedings of 25.6.1817. PP 1821/18, 107–9.

methods of bureaucratic registration.[133] In 1819, it named the cholera epidemic that had raged in Bengal in 1817/18 as a further reason. In addition, the rapid increase did 'unavoidably excite a doubt whether the methods publicly adopted, with the humane view of diminishing the number of these sacrifices, [. . .] have not rather been attended with a contrary effect than the one contemplated.' There was a fear of 'a spirit of fanaticism, rather inflamed than repressed by the interference of the public authorities.'[134]

Thus the Nizamat Adalat was subjected to the same doubts as the government. This predetermined its attitude during the following years. On the one hand, there was no desire to introduce new regulations, and the court rejected all relevant suggestions from the administration. On the other hand one did not dare to revoke the rules that had already been introduced. The government, as well as the Nizamat Adalat, persevered in their inaction. At the same time the existing rules had their effect and progressively implicated the administration in the matter of widow burning.

The explanation for the rapid increase in the number of cases in 1817 and 1818 is still controversial.[135] The improved methods of bureaucratic registration would definitely have played an important role. Yet we cannot assume that the jump from 1816 to 1817 can be wholly attributed to this. The cholera epidemic could have been another reason. This assumption, however, cannot be proved due to a lack of sources. Within the administration too there was no unity on this point. The district officers would have known best about it. In an enquiry conducted at the end of 1818 among eleven magistrates in Bengal and Bihar,[136] three magistrates were of the view that cholera was responsible for the increase,[137] while one of them denied this.[138] His

[133] 4.6.1818 Nizamat Adalat Proceedings. PP 1821/18, 177.

[134] 21.5.1819 Nizamat Adalat Proceedings. PP 1821/18, 222.

[135] The question is often dealt with in the relevant literature. Yet there are no arguments that go beyond the contemporary debate carried out within the administration, and generally even this debate is not taken up in all its aspects.

[136] PP 1821/18, 232–41.

[137] The magistrates of Patna, Burdwan and 24 Parganas. PP 1821/18, 233; 234; 238.

[138] The magistrate of Hugli. PP 1821/18, 236. The other seven magistrates did not reply to this question. On 4.4.1818 a judge in the Circuit Court of Calcutta had even told the Nizamat Adalat that in 1817 the number of widow

statement was especially important, because his district, Hooghly, had the largest number of registered widow burnings. But he did not give any sound justifications for his view, and the magistrate of Burdwan district, in which widow burnings were almost as frequent, took the opposite view. It is also not possible to distinguish between them on the basis of ideology. Among those who saw a connection between the epidemic and the frequency of widow burnings, there were two opponents and one supporter of abolition.[139] As long as no better reasons are presented, it seems at least plausible to assume that the epidemic had a certain influence on the figures.[140] This is also supported by the fact that later figures were never so high as those of 1817/18.

What has always been mentioned most frequently, as a third possible cause for the increase in the number of widow burnings, is British interference itself. The argument runs as follows: the debates about the question of legality and police control gave widow burning far more publicity than before. At the same time they awarded greater prestige to it. Therefore more widows decided to carry out the act, or the relatives urged them to it more often and with greater force. The distinction between legal and illegal cases also meant that legal cases were expressly sanctioned by the government, if not in theory then in practice. The word is thus said to have circulated that 'they were burning the widow according to the Regulations.'[141] The argument could be intensified: the sanctioning of widow burning could easily be misunderstood or interpreted as an invitation to the act.

This view plays an important role even today. At the time it was yet more dominant. Even the highest bodies adopted it, at least for a while. As has been shown, the government in Calcutta was the first to do so in 1817,[142] followed in 1819 by the Nizamat Adalat.[143] The governments in Madras and Bombay also supported this view.[144] In 1823 even the

---

burnings in the districts not affected by cholera had increased even more. PP 1821/18, 176.

[139] Opponent of abolition: Patna. Supporters of abolition: Burdwan and 24 Parganas. No clear position: Hooghly.

[140] In modern research B.B. Roy 38 and Yang 88 also take this view.

[141] 21.3.1829 W. Ewer. IOR L/L/13 (1030), vol. 3, App. 102.

[142] 5.11.1817 Government Resolution. PP 1821/18, 241–2. Repeated 1.2.1820 Government to the Court of Directors. J.K. Majumdar 119–20.

[143] 21.5.1819 Nizamat Adalat Proceedings. PP 1821/18, 222.

[144] Madras: PP 1823/17, 130 (6.4.1821); 69 (4.1.1822). Bombay: cf. PP 1821/18, 254ff. (since 1819); PP 1824/23, 49.

Court of Directors joined them: 'To us, however, it appears very doubtful, (and we are confirmed in this doubt by respectable authority) whether the measures which have already been taken, have not tended rather to increase than to diminish the frequency of the practice.'[145] Even after the ban, the directors maintained this view and further emphasised it:

> Prior to the year 1828, it had become matter of common experience, that the circular orders not only had not been productive of the benefits which were expected to be derived from them but had given birth to most serious and unforeseen evils. [. . .] The impression actually produced upon the natives was, that, to a certain extent at least, the practice of Suttee was sanctioned and approved of by the Government: an impression that was strongly displayed, by the light in which the mere permission of the magistrate for the performance of the ceremony appears to have been regarded; in so much that what, in fact, amounted to a simple acknowledgement by the Magistrate that there were no circumstances in the case which, under the circular orders, could give him a right to interfere, was considered by the people as equivalent to a command that the Suttee should be consummated.[146]

Such statements by the highest authorities merely reflect the opinion that was being advocated at all levels of the administration, and by an increasing number of people. Their standpoint became more determined the longer they advocated this view.[147] The arguments also increasingly spread to public discussions of the matter,[148] and they dominate modern research as well.[149]

Some isolated voices—till 1819 even the missionaries—took the

---

[145] 17.6.1823 Court of Directors to the government in Calcutta. PP 1824/ 23, 45. More emphatically: draft of 18.3.1824. PP 1826–27/20, 2.

[146] Undated (*c.* 1831/32) Court of Directors to the Privy Council. IOR L/L/13 (1030), vol. 3, 214r/v. Similarly 8.11.1829 Governor General Bentinck. Bentinck 1, 337. Cf. ibid. 92.

[147] A selection of relevant passages: Poynder 44–57; PP 1821/18, 212; 254ff.; PP 1823/17, 67; PP 1825/24, 148–9; PP 1826–27/20, 148–9; PP 1830/28, 19; 126–7; 233; IOR L/L/13 (1030), vol. 3, App. 101–2.

[148] For example *Burning* (1824) 557; *On the Burning of Hindoo Widows* 6; *Papers* (1868) 259; Grimshawe 6; Kaye 530–2; Poynder 22; 30; J.K. Majumdar 158.

[149] For example Dalmia-Lüderitz 49; V.N. Datta 36; I. Singh 197; Stutchbury 42.

opposite view, that the administrative measures had reduced the number of cases.[150]

Neither side could present convincing evidence. The opinion was generated not so much by information as by a sense of dismay. The more frequently someone witnessed widow burnings the more convincing seemed to him the hypothesis that the increase in frequency was the result of British regulation. This could also be seen in the above-mentioned enquiry conducted among magistrates at the end of 1818. Four magistrates were of the opinion that the custom had become more frequent because of police interference.[151] Three expressed the opposite view,[152] and four others believed that neither was the case.[153] No one had really convincing reasons for his hypothesis. Three of the four magistrates who believed in the negative influence of the interference, worked in districts, in which the number of widow burnings in the preceding two years had greatly increased, while in the fourth district (Sylhet) not even one case had occurred (see Table 8). In two of the three districts, whose magistrates expressed the opposite view, the number of cases in 1818 was far less than in 1817. The belief that police interference made the custom either less or more frequent therefore appears not so much to spring from rational arguments as from frustration at the failure, or euphoria about the success of measures taken. The opinion could also be determined by aspects of political expediency, as was shown after abolition. The orthodox Hindus, who rejected any kind of interference by the state, used the same hypothesis in their petition against the abolition as was being advocated by the supporters, namely that state interference had led to an increase in the number of widow burnings.[154]

There are important reasons for not assuming that British interference made the custom more popular, because, whatever the early difficulties, the pattern from 1819 shows a slow, but almost continuous decrease (see Table 2). After an initial phase the method seems to have had a certain restrictive or deterring effect.

[150] In the administration: PP 1825/24, 16; IOR L/L/13 (1030), vol. 3, App. 20; 31–2; 114; Mitter 128. Missionaries: *Essays* 11–12; *Friend of India* 2 (1819), 311. In modern research: Mukhopadhyay, *Movement* 26.

[151] Hooghly and Jessore categorically, Sylhet and 24 Parganas as an assumption. PP 1821/18, 232–41.

[152] Bakarganj, Birbhum and Dacca.

[153] Bihar, Burdwan, Chittagong and Patna.

[154] 19.12.1829. Bentinck 1, 369.

On the other hand, widow burning was a tradition that had been firmly entrenched for centuries. Behaviour determined by tradition cannot be influenced so easily, which in the present case means that without evidence we cannot assume a rapid increase or decrease in the number of cases. For the rest, the effects of British interference that were visible and tangible to the people were probably not very strong. No law had been framed, in order not to have to publicize the guidelines. There is nothing to suggest that the people were aware of the distinction between legal and illegal cases. As late as in 1821, a magistrate maintained that he was unaware of the fact that the burning of a fourteen-year-old widow was illegal.[155] In 1822, a British salt agent witnessed a widow burning, at which the widow was prevented by force from jumping down from the pyre. He did not interfere, because he claimed he did not know that the use of force was prohibited.[156] In 1825, an Indian police officer in the Hooghly district, where widow burnings were almost a daily phenomenon, was suspended because he had allowed the burning of a fifteen-year-old widow. He claimed not to have known about the age limit.[157]

This general ignorance was expressed particularly dramatically in a case witnessed by the missionary John Statham. The police officer allowed a ceremony to take place only after permission had been granted by a judge, which caused a delay of three days. Since the judge actually granted permission, he too did not seem to know that permission was not required. When the ceremony finally took place, the widow was tied down to the pyre while the police looked on, although this was in fact illegal. The actions of the police officer were neither dictated by the desire to save the widow, nor by the intention of letting her die, but merely by his conscientious ignorance, which was shared by the judge as well as by the reporting missionary.[158]

There is no evidence to show that the measures were discussed outside the administration and outside of a small circle of the educated elite in Calcutta. The fear that a debate on widow burning could

[155] PP 1824/23, 16.
[156] 1.6.1822 R.C. Plowden to the Magistrate of 24 Parganas. PP 1824/23, 4–5.
[157] PP 1830/28,41.
[158] Statham 128–36. The author neither mentions the place nor the date. He was in India from 1818 to 1827. Till the abolition of 1829 there are many cases which show that a large part of both the Indian and the British officials did not know the guidelines.

increase the frequency of the custom was just as unjustified as the hope that it could be made to disappear through 'the dissemination of knowledge' once Indians understood the 'right' morals and ethics.

With time, the number of voices in the administration asking for abolition increased.[159] In 1817, R.M. Bird, the Magistrate of Ghazipur, expressed the attitude behind this demand with all the pathos that official language was capable of:

> If it were desired to portray a scene which should thrill with horror every heart, not entirely dead to the touch of human sympathy, it would suffice to describe a father, regardless of the affection of his tender child, in having already suffered one of the severest of the miseries which flesh is heir to, with tearless eye leading her forth a spectacle to the assembled multitude, who with barbarous cries demand the sacrifice, and unrelentingly delivering up the unconscious and unresisting victim to an untimely death, accompanied by the most cruel tortures.[160]

In 1818, a memorandum of the Superintendent of Police for the Lower Provinces, Walter Ewer, had greater influence.[161] His main contention was that at most one percent of widow burnings were really voluntary, while in all others direct or indirect force was used. Therefore 99 per cent of the cases went against Hindu law, which required free choice. Ewer felt that abolition was not only necessary, but also possible, as it would not lead to any serious unrest among the Indian population. He pointed out the number of times ceremonies had been stopped without any resistance.

The results of a survey conducted by Ewer at the end of 1818 among 11 magistrates were revealing (see Table 8).[162] Five of them supported abolition,[163] while six rejected the idea.[164] Four of the supporters represented the districts with the highest number of cases; only the fifth came from a district with relatively few cases (Chittagong), and he spoke in favour of abolition with far less determination than his

[159] For example PP 1821/18, 176; 212; 218–19; 243; PP 1825/24, 122. Cf. *Papers* (1868) 243ff. and V.N. Datta, chap. 1.

[160] 31.7.1817 R.M. Bird to the Nizamat Adalat. PP 1821/18, 136, § 8.

[161] 18.11.1818 Ewer to the government. PP 1821/18, 227–9.

[162] PP 1821/18, 232–41.

[163] Burdwan, Hooghly, 24 Parganas, Jessore and, to a limited extent, Chittagong.

[164] Bakarganj, Bihar, Birbhum, Dacca, Patna, Sylhet.

counterparts in the other districts. Among the opponents, matters were just the opposite. Widow burnings were relatively frequent only in Dacca, with a clear tendency towards an increase; in the districts of the other magistrates opposing abolition they were rare. Taken together, the six who were against abolition represented districts in which, according to the official survey of 1815 to 1818, 102 widow burnings had taken place, whereas in the five districts of the supporters of abolition 861 widows had burnt to death.[165]

The rejection of abolition resulted from the entire tradition of British policy in India, from the principle of tolerance and non-interference in everything that was connected with religion, or might be connected with it. This attitude was only questioned under the effect of great shocks. Apparently the frequent debates about widow burning and, even more, the witnessing of the ceremony was a shock for many officials. The government in Calcutta saw the connection in 1828. Officials, in whose districts widow burnings were frequent, considered 'the evil to be of so crying a nature that it ought to be put down at all risks, while others in a different quarter, where the rite is rarely observed, think it scarcely deserving the hazard of interference.'[166]

The results of the surveys for 1819 and 1820 actually allowed for a cautious optimism. For the first time since the introduction of regulation the number of cases had gone down; from 839 in 1818 to 650 in 1819 and 597 in 1820 (see Table 2).

The spirit of opposition now also seized the Nizamat Adalat. Its second judge, Courtney Smith, stated laconically on 25 May 1821: 'My opinion is, that the toleration of the practice of suttee is a reproach to our government, and that the entire and immediate abolition of it would be attended with no sort of danger.'[167] He did not consider it necessary to give reasons for his view. The other judges found it too radical. Yet doubts arose among them too. Only the third judge, S.T. Goad, held on to the existing view.[168] The first judge, W. Leycester, advocated a ban in those regions in which the custom seldom or

---

[165] At the time of the survey (December 1818) the magistrates naturally did not know all the figures for 1818. But they would have known the trends. For Table 8 I have taken the later official figures instead of the figures given by the magistrates in the survey. The differences, however, are very small.

[166] 10.4.1828. Bentinck 1, 23–4.

[167] PP 1823/17, 63.

[168] 25.5.1821 S.T. Goad. PP 1823/17, 63.

never occurred. However, violations would not be punished.[169] Judge W. Dorin also spoke in favour of a kind of trial prohibition, but of a completely different kind. He wanted to begin with the Hooghly district, in which the largest number of cases occurred. A formal ban was not to be announced, but the magistrates would simply receive instructions to prevent every ceremony.[170] In view of the alleged problems and risks, even the highest judges were not prepared to take the question of legality seriously.

Now only a single body was still completely in favour of the existing policy of non-intervention: the government in Calcutta. It was not impressed with the Nizamat Adalat's change of heart, and declared itself to be both against total and partial prohibition; both 'would tend to excite a spirit of fanaticism, and eventually to produce very injurious consequences.'[171]

The results for 1821 again cast the shadow of doubt on even cautious optimism. The number of cases had increased, from 597 to 654. At the same time, a change in the attitude of the authorities became evident. The number of illegal cases was significantly higher than in previous years. All indications suggest that this was not so much an actual increase, as it was the result of better methods of registration. The police and the British officials apparently no longer allowed themselves to be convinced so easily that everything was in order, or had been in order. The caution exercised till then made way for a stronger feeling of self-confidence. Various illegal cases were handed over to the courts. In a counter-move the Nizamat Adalat also began to control British actions more strictly. If the authorities meted out punishments for not reporting a ceremony to the police, they received a sharp reprimand. In several cases, the court even ordered fines to be refunded.[172] But lashes and prison sentences already served could not be taken back, and the court did not go so far as to award compensation.[173]

In 1823, the highest body of the East India Company, the Court of Directors, looked into the question of widow burning for the first

[169] 25.5.1821. PP 1823/17, 63–4.

[170] 25.5.1821. PP 1823/17, 63–4.

[171] 17.7.1821 Government Resolution. PP 1823/17, 64–5.

[172] For example PP 1824/23, 39 (Banda district). Cf. also ibid. 37 and V.N. Datta 50.

[173] For example PP 1830/28,30; IOR P/139/34, 321ff.; 491ff. Cf. Singha 208.

time. The results showed that doubts and distaste had also made their appearance in London: 'It is, moreover, with much reluctance that we can consent to make the British government, by a specific permission of the suttee, an ostensible party to the sacrifice; we are averse also to the practice of making British courts expounders and vindicators of the Hindoo religion, when it leads to acts which, not less as legislators than as Christians, we abominate.' A radical group had managed to make its voice heard. But only rhetorically, because in the subsequent instructions a more cautious tone was used. A general prohibition was only envisaged as a perspective for a distant future. At the end the letter even arrived more or less at the government's position: 'The most acceptable form of success would be, that which would be brought about by such an increase of intelligence among the people as should show them the wickedness and absurdity of the practice; next to this, we should rejoice to see the abolition effected by influence, and the co-operation of the higher order of natives.'[174]

The government thus still had a free hand. Yet, a careful reading of the letter showed the writing on the wall. There were many indications that the period of grace was limited.

The opposition against the policy, which had existed since 1813, had now clearly spread from the lower to the upper rungs of the hierarchy. The further a body was from the scene of action, the longer it defended a policy of non-intervention. In this regard, the Court of Directors in London had now overtaken the government in Calcutta. The agitation for a stricter procedure had already attained considerable proportions in Britain. In London, unlike in Calcutta, this had to be taken into consideration, if problems in Parliament were to be avoided.

After 654 cases in 1821 there were 583 cases in 1822 and 575 in 1823 (see Table 2). The proportion of illegal cases, which continued to increase, indicated a greater alertness on the part of the police. Yet, their attitude still left a lot to be desired. In Ghazipur district, for example, they often reported that the widow's clothes, and with it the pyre, had self-ignited.[175]

As the statistical surveys continued to record the fact that matters had hardly changed, the uncertainty and nervousness, often even the

[174] 17.6.1823. PP 1824/23, 44–5.
[175] PP 1825/24, 115–20; 128–34.

aversion in the administration, grew stronger. The actual phenomenon could not be portrayed with the help of statistics, as one case on 1 December 1822 shows. In Bhagalpur (Bihar), a wealthy twenty-six-year-old widow, whose husband had died in a place far away, decided to burn herself to death.

> The magistrate [. . .] immediately repaired to the scene of action, and, after having spent some hours in ineffectual endeavours to dissuade the widow from her purpose, at length permitted her nearest of kin to light the pile. The widow behaved with the utmost calmness and composure as long as the attacks of the flames were confined to her lower extremities, but when they reached her breast and face the torture seemingly became intolerable, and her fortitude gave way; by a violent exertion she disengaged herself from the faggots with which she was encumbered, and springing from the pile fell down nearly insensible at the feet of the magistrate, who had remained standing close beside it. In a few moments, however, she revived, when the magistrate seized the opportunity of again urging her to abandon her design, and renewed his promises of maintaining and protecting her in future if she would consent to quit the spot. This attempt was as unsuccessful as the former had been; so far from yielding to the magistrate's entreaties, the widow exclaimed vehemently against his interference, insisted on being allowed to go back into the fire, and breaking from his hold attempted to regain her position on the pile, by climbing up the logs of which it was composed, and which were by that time burning with the greatest fury. The magistrate finding that her resolution to complete the ceremony was unconquerable, and being of the opinion that any further opposition to her will might, under the existing regulations, be considered as illegal and improper, permitted some of her relations, whose assistance she invocated with loud cries, to lift her again into the flames, which speedily consumed her to ashes.[176]

In the face of such events discussions about the relationship between interference and non-interference would have appeared academic. Despite its immense pathos, the statement of the Nizamat Adalat was not able to hide the prevailing sense of helplessness: 'The sacrifice in question affords, perhaps, the most striking instance on record of this species of infatuation, and sufficiently exhibits the force of the

[176] PP 1825/24, 50–1.

superstitious motives which actuate the devoted females on these occasions.'[177]

Such experiences led not only to an increase in demands for abolition among the magistrates, but also changed the mood of the Nizamat Adalat. In December 1824, the judges again stated their views. As before, Smith demanded an immediate and unrestricted ban.[178] This time two other judges supported him.[179] What was more indicative of the general attitude was the position taken by J.H. Harington, who acted for the first judge. His position is also particularly important because he was by far the most learned among the judges, the best authority on Anglo-Indian law at that time. In a minute of 1823 he had optimistically stated that 'the entire and immediate abolition [. . .] would be attended with no sort of danger.' But with regard to the actual measures to be taken, he had only proposed that the stricter rules of 1817 should at last be put into force.[180] Now, in 1824, when he was speaking as the highest judge, he retreated even further. He expressly stated that abolition should be postponed, and dropped the demand to enforce the rules of 1817. Instead he merely proposed the obligation to report cases.[181]

This timid vacillation definitely betrayed his sense of opportunism, but also his uncertainty. On the one hand there is a clear personal opinion, on the other the sense of responsibility of the judge and the scholar who believes he has the duty to respect indigenous customs. Between both there is the administrator who is concerned with safeguarding British rule in India.

Harington's attitude is characteristic of the uncertainty of these years. Yet neither doubts nor resistance were able to influence the government, which again refused to take any measures.[182] It defended its position against the Court of Directors: 'We entirely participate with your honourable court in the feelings of detestation with which you view the rite, and in your earnest desire to have it suppressed; and

[177] PP 1825/24, 78.
[178] 3.12.1824. PP 1825/24, 148.
[179] 3.12.1824 J.T. Shakespear and J. Ahmuty. PP 1825/24, 149.
[180] 28.6.1823. PP 1825/24, 8–18. Quote: 18. Cf. also Harington's 'Remarks' of 30.5.1822, in which he still did not risk expressing a definite opinion. Ibid., 18–20.
[181] Undated (c. 23.7.1824). PP 1825/24, 147–8.
[182] 3.12.1824 Government Resolution. PP 1825/24, 150–4.

we beg to assure you, that nothing but the apprehension of evils infinitely greater than those arising from the existence of the practice, could induce us to tolerate it for a single day.' This was an opportunity to stress the principles of a politically motivated relativism: 'In the eyes of the natives the great redeeming point in our government, the circumstance which reconciles them above all others to the manifold inconvenience of foreign rule, is the scrupulous regard we have paid to their customs and prejudices.' The government claimed decision-making powers for itself by indirectly hinting that the Court of Directors lacked the authority to do so. 'The safety and the expediency of suppressing the practice must be judged by reference chiefly to native, and not to European habits of thinking.' Although 'even the best informed classes of the Hindoo population are not yet sufficiently enlightened to recognize the propriety of abolishing the rite', yet hopes continued to be placed in the spread of education.

The position taken by the government showed that it now felt that it was being pushed into the defensive. Despite this, displaying an almost stubborn attitude, it did not make any concessions. 'We do not wish to pledge ourselves for the future, even by sketching any specific plan for the approbation of your honourable court.'[183]

An event that had occurred several months previously showed that the days of such a high-handed position were numbered. On 19 March 1824, a party placed a draft in the Court of Directors for new orders to be issued to the government. This draft did not actually order abolition. But the latitude given to the government would have been very small, since 'nothing short of an absolute overruling necessity can justify the toleration of the practice by the British, or by any Christian government.'[184]

This proposal prompted the opponents of abolition to come forward with a counter proposal. Neither of the proposals could get a majority.[185] But it had become clear that the attitude of the Court of Directors might soon change.

Radical views were now being represented even by some of the directors. In a dissenting vote against the decision to leave matters alone, J.Hudleston and W.T. Money broke with a taboo. Till then it had been taken for granted in the Company that there was no question

[183] 3.12.1824 Government to the Court of Directors. PP 1825/24, 6–8.
[184] PP 1826–27/20, 1–31, esp. 29–31. Quote: 31.
[185] 19.3.1824. PP 1826–27/20, 32.

of abolition if it were to seriously endanger British rule in India. The dissenting opinion denied this danger. But 'even admitting that there would be danger in prohibiting the practice, we should doubt our having a moral right to permit any natives, become British subjects, male or female, to burn themselves, or to be burnt alive in British India, from fear of the consequence of preventing it.'[186] Universalism would no longer accept any limits.

The statistical surveys for 1824–28 were more precise, more comprehensive and more reliable than in the previous years. Despite this, they only played a minor role in the discussions. This was chiefly because of the numbers (see Table 2). In 1824, 572 widows burnt themselves to death as against 575 in the previous year. In 1825, the corresponding figure was 639, in 1826 it was 518. In 1827 the figure remained constant at 517, while in 1828 it again went down to 463. This constituted a decrease of almost 45 per cent as compared to the 'record year' 1818. If the more 'normal' year 1819 was taken as the point of comparison, however, then the decrease constituted only 29 per cent. Even in the most favourable circumstances an end could not be foreseen for many years. The debates in the meantime had attained a level of bitterness and urgency which excluded such far-reaching perspectives. Everyone knew that this situation could not continue much longer. The pent-up anger and antipathy inside and outside the administration was too large to be contained.

This led to many new proposals which its authors hoped would lead to the disappearance of the custom, or at least to a considerable decline in cases, without having to take recourse to the dreaded abolition. R.N.C. Hamilton for example, the Magistrate of Benares, demanded that first the rules of 1817 should be enforced and also made more stringent. For this he wanted to introduce a package of far-reaching measures. A person, for example, who came from a family in which a widow had burnt herself to death, would not be eligible for a government job; no official would be allowed to associate with such families. The property of the widow, or of her husband, would fall to the state, whereby the informant would receive half of it.[187]

Both the Nizamat Adalat and the government, rejected this and all

---

[186] 31.3.1824. PP 1826–27/20, 32–4. Quote: 32.
[187] 12.8.1826. PP 1830/28, 119–21. Although Hamilton stated, ibid. 119, that he was in favour of a total ban, this could only have been meant rhetorically, given his proposal.

similar proposals.[188] In the meantime it had become clear that abolition was the only viable alternative to the existing rules. The basic problems of regulation could not be eliminated with new restrictions.

From the beginning of 1827 there was also opposition within the government. In 1813 W.B. Bayley, magistrate of Burdwan, had been reprimanded by the Nizamat Adalat for excessive interference in cases of widow burning.[189] Subsequently he had been Secretary to the government for many years. As a result, he knew all the reports on widow burnings. This makes it easy to understand his position, and at the same time confirms the hypothesis that the rejection of widow burning came from the lower rungs of the administration and gradually penetrated the upper rungs. With a single remark he demonstrated the absurdity of the argument that the spread of European education would gradually make the custom disappear: nowhere in India, he stated, were widow burnings as frequent as in the region around Calcutta. The aim of the policy would therefore have to be a blanket prohibition. However, Bayley still considered it to be too risky at present. He recommended a kind of trial prohibition in those regions in which the rules of 1813 were not valid, in which therefore a distinction between legal and illegal cases could not be made.[190]

In the government, consisting at that time of four members, Bayley was not only supported by Harington, a judge in the Nizamat Adalat,[191] but also by Combermere, the Commander-in-Chief of the army.[192]

With this, the circle of uncompromising supporters of the existing policy had become even smaller, and was essentially limited to Governor General Amherst.[193] Soon even he lost the support, or at least the

[188] PP 1830/28, 119. A few other plans: PP 1826–27/20, 149 (1825 Bombay: tax on the construction of a pyre to finance pensions for surviving widows); IOR P/139/34, 228-244; IOR L/L/13 (1030), vol. 3, App. 55–7; *A Bengal Civilian* 61–2; Macdonald; *An Old Inhabitant*; Shepherd 67.

[189] PP 1821/18, 35–9. See above, pp. 374–5

[190] 13.1.1827. PP 1830/28, 123–7.

[191] 18.2.1827. PP 1830/28, 127–32.

[192] 1.3.1827. PP 1830/28, 132.

[193] 18.3.1827. PP 1830/28, 133. Amherst's motivation would have been primarily determined by concern about the protection of British power and less by indifference to the victims. At any rate his wife grappled with the problem of widow burning, and she probably witnessed one in 1825. Cf. references to her diary in Thackeray/Richardson 63–4 and 197.

tacit connivance of the Court of Directors, which clearly gave to understand that it wanted abolition quickly, even though it left the decision to the government.[194]

In November 1827, Bayley repeated his demands.[195] This time he was supported by another, recently appointed and highly respected, member of the government, Charles Metcalfe, who felt: 'If the first act of our administration, on any new conquest, had been to abolish the practice of burning widows, the abolition would have been effected every where with ease.' This opportunity, he felt, had been lost by choosing instead to distinguish between legal and illegal cases; therefore one would now have to proceed more cautiously and in stages.[196]

Despite all opposition, Amherst maintained his position that the disappearance of the custom could and would be brought about only by the good judgement of the Indians. But he now also placed his hopes on the 'unostentatious exertions of our local officers.'[197] With this, the most determined supporter of the existing policy had also paid his first tribute to abolition.

The demand for prohibition not only spread quickly, it was also put forward more aggressively. The Nizamat Adalat was symptomatic of this. In November 1826 Courtney Smith mounted a sharp attack which demonstrated the growing self-confidence of large circles within the administration. He cited as his authority

> the experience which every successive year has afforded of our power to do exactly what we please in India, without any likelihood of resistance. [. . .] The most decidedly and atrociously cruel rite that anywhere exists at this moment upon the face of the globe is carried on by the express sanction of the ruling power, whose officers are liable to censure and other consequences if they interfere to prevent its performance. The plea, and the only plea, for this is, that prohibition might cause discontent and create disturbance among the natives. Discontent at hundreds of human beings, and those of their own tribe

[194] 25.7.1827. PP 1828/23, 21. The meeting of the Court of Proprietors in March had passed a much stricter resolution (see below pp. 405–6). A motion to have this included in the Court of Directors' letter was blocked by the Board of Control, the highest body responsible for Indian affairs. IOR E/4/719, 1252–1254.

[195] 28.11.1827. PP 1830/28, 214.

[196] 29.12.1827. PP 1830/28, 214–15.

[197] 4.1.1828. PP 1830/28, 216.

and persuasion, being rescued yearly from the most excruciating and lingering torment, terminating in death! Disturbance, because we showed a disinterested sympathy with human suffering; because we had enacted a law in strict accordance with two of the strongest feelings that sway the heart of man, the dread of pain and the fear of death, a law forbidding the infliction of pain and prolonging the duration of life!

Universalism celebrated its triumph here, ending on a challenging note: 'So long as, having the power, we want the will, or having the power and the will, we want the energy to abolish it, it may fairly be doubted whether we are de jure rulers of the country.'[198] Yet, even in 1827, the opinions of the judges were still divided.[199] Although in 1828 the voices in favour of abolition were more pronounced, there was still no unanimity. Only in August 1829 did the court support a prohibition in one voice and without any reservations, writing 'that the practice of suttee may be prohibited without danger, and that it should therefore be prohibited.'[200]

No Governor General could postpone abolition indefinitely against the will of the overwhelming majority of the civil servants. This was demonstrated by some cases of insubordination during this time.[201]

In April 1828, the authorities in Dacca prohibited a widow burning.[202] They quoted the legal opinion that the Nizamat Adalat had been given by the pandits in 1805. In this, they said, widow burning was only permitted to members of the four main castes. The widow mentioned did not belong to any of these castes. In addition, they stated that neither the death of the husband, nor the voluntary decision of the widow could be established with any certainty.[203] This was only an excuse. Both aspects could have been easily clarified. The restriction to the four main castes did not correspond to the regulations that were in force. Magistrates and judges were not supposed to follow the opinion of the pandits, but the orders of the government. In Dacca too

[198] 1.11.1826. PP 1830/28, 32.
[199] 19.10.1827. PP 1830/28, 142.
[200] 9.8.1829. IOR L/L/13 (1030), vol. 3, App. 142.
[201] References also in Marshman 2, 400; Thompson, *Suttee* 66.
[202] The documentation of this case is in PP 1830/28, 223–40, as well as in IOR L/L/13 (1030), vol. 3, App. 143ff.
[203] 15.4.1828 Proceedings Foujdary Court Dacca. PP 1830/28, 225.

they would have been aware of this. All indications suggest that the authorities in Dacca were only looking for excuses to prevent the case. The humanitarian motive and not legal protocol was what decided the matter.

This attitude led to conflict. Two Indians complained to the Nizamat Adalat and requested permission for the planned burning.[204] The court asked the authorities in Dacca to explain the reasons for the prohibition, and came to the—undoubtedly correct—conclusion that these reasons were not valid. Permission would have to be granted. In the meantime however, the widow had given up her intention to die. The authorities in Dacca had achieved their goal.[205]

Two months later, Cracroft, a judge in the Dacca Court of Circuit, deigned to inform the Nizamat Adalat that the prohibition of widow burning for the lower castes, which was in force in his region, had not been lifted despite orders from Calcutta. There was, he said, no doubt about the validity of the legal opinion of 1805. The existing prohibition, he further stated, did not have any negative consequences, whereas, if it were lifted, it would cause tremendous evils. The court would then be guilty of abetting suicide. Beside, since the orders of the Nizamat Adalat had been signed only by two, instead of five judges, it had never had the weight of the law.[206]

This was an open, indeed defiant insubordination. That it was at all possible in the strict bureaucratic hierarchy of the East India Company shows how important the question of widow burning had become, and the aversion to the policy among the civil service.

The Nizamat Adalat could not let this defiance go unnoticed. The statements of the individual judges in this regard were very severe.[207] Yet they also betrayed a certain sense of helplessness. They showed that the court had been manoeuvred into a defensive position. No one denied the humanitarian motives of the officials in Dacca. Therefore one could only cite the principle of legality and the dangers associated with prohibition. The second argument was weak and could only refer to total abolition, since a partial one had already been successfully enforced in Dacca. Leycester, the First Judge, commented on Cracroft's

---

[204] Undated. PP 1830/28, 223.

[205] The correspondence is in PP 1830/28, 224–8.

[206] 14.7.1828 W. Cracroft, Second judge at the Court of Circuit Dacca, to the Nizamat Adalat. PP 1830/28, 226–8.

[207] August/September 1828. PP 1830/28, 228–9; 231–8.

reference to the fact that a life had been saved: 'As a man I rejoice, but as a judge of this court I cannot rejoice in any result obtained by a contempt of the rules and orders established by government; the due execution of which, and their enforcement, are entrusted to us in our oaths.'[208]

The government, which had passed on the decision to the Nizamat Adalat, wholly supported it, and Dacca had to revoke the ban.[209]

This was the most blatant, but by no means the only case of high-handedness in the last years before abolition. In 1824 already, the Magistrate of Chota Nagpur had not only prohibited a widow burning which was legal according to the rules, but had even recommended that the police use force if necessary. He was well aware of the fact that his action went against the rules. 'Be it so, the consolation is mine that lives apparently have been saved by such interference.' His motives were respected, but he was urged to adhere to the rules.[210]

H.M. Pigou, Magistrate in Cuttack (Orissa), implemented a de facto prohibition in his area in 1828. He used all possible chicanery against participants in widow burnings, even when the conditions of legality were fulfilled, and his punishments were fairly indiscriminate. He was reprimanded by his superior, who clearly stated: 'The humanity of your motives I do not mean to question, but the feelings of public officers must be controlled by their duty.' Pigou was not as rebellious as Cracroft. He confessed his mistakes, the cause of which, he stated, had been 'over anxiety to discourage the practice.'[211]

Pigou's example was effective. In July 1829, his successor, H. Brownlow, was so shocked by a widow burning he had witnessed, and which he had not been able to prevent because it was legal, that he decided not to allow any such ceremonies, well aware of the fact that he was acting against the law. A few days later he actually intervened in another case, had the husband's body cremated and handed over the widow to her father's care. His superiors did not agree with his actions, but till abolition in December no decisive steps were taken.[212]

[208] Undated (*c.* August/September 1828). PP 1830/28, 229.

[209] 10.10.1828 Government to the Nizamat Adalat. PP 1830/28, 240.

[210] 21.4.1827 Report of S.T. Cuthbart, Magistrate Ramghar. PP 1830/28, 240–1.

[211] The correspondence is in IOR P/139/34, 491–513. Quotes: 507; 512.

[212] IOR L/L/ 13 (1030), vol. 3, App.158–60; Mitter 130–1; K. Datta 95–7.

The hierarchy thus still functioned to some extent: in other similar cases the higher authorities were also able to establish their authority against insubordinate civil servants.[213] Nevertheless, in the long run such a situation was bound to become intolerable, especially since the longer it lasted, the more one could only fall back on purely formal arguments of hierarchy and legality, as the good intentions and the humanitarian motives of the insubordinate civil servants were never questioned. The government machinery stood in danger of suffering a loss of authority.

Judicial Practice

Once orders for the restriction of widow burning had been issued, the success of British measures depended not least on judicial practice. However, the legal situation was very ambiguous, since the orders merely represented guidelines for the administration.

At first the courts decided as much as possible in favour of the perpetrators. Till 1820 formal legal proceedings were never initiated for taking part in a widow burning. It was only at the lowest level that the magistrates sometimes imposed penalties for not reporting planned ceremonies to the police. This contradicted the orders, and later the higher authorities generally took exception to it.[214] From 1821 onwards the courts sometimes dealt with cases of widow burning which would not have been permitted according to the regulations of 1813 and 1815. Therefore these were now considered, in a rather doubtful interpretation, to be valid laws. The courts remained cautious. Proceedings were initiated only in a minority of the illegal cases, and after 1825 most of them were not pursued. This attitude was the result of a debate within the Nizamat Adalat: should these trials be used as deterrents with drastic penalties, or should one, in traditional fashion, make special allowances in matters of religion?

The ground was already laid in the first case in August 1821. A fourteen-year-old Brahmin widow had climbed the pyre without her husband's body. She was under the legally permissible age and also violating the prohibition of *anumaraṇa* for Brahmins. The widow

[213] Further cases of insubordination in the files:
IOR L/L/13 (1030), vol. 3, App. 97–100: 1828 Allahabad.
IOR P/139/34, 478: 1828 Azamgarh.
IOR P/139/34, 526–34: 1829 Nugwan.
[214] For example PP 1823/17, 28. Cf. also footnotes 172 and 173.

jumped down from the burning pyre thrice. Twice she was thrown back onto the pyre, and after her third attempt to escape a Muslim killed her with a sword.[215]

Even in the Hindu view this was a case of murder. The judge in the Court of Circuit, who could not conceal his revulsion, felt that all the six accused deserved to die, but then demanded the death penalty for only three of them and life-imprisonment for the others.[216] In the appeal, Leycester, the First Judge in the Nizamat Adalat recommended two death sentences and life-imprisonment for four.[217] Courtney Smith, the Second Judge, contradicted both of them emphatically.[218] The widow's decision, he felt, had been a voluntary one. At least some of the defendants had by no means been ill-disposed towards the victim. Since the discontinuance of a ceremony, once begun, not only brought dishonour to the family, but was also regarded as a bad omen for all participants and onlookers, it almost became an obligation to ensure that the custom was carried out 'properly'. Without saying it directly, Smith was arguing here in favour of extending the notion of tolerance from written Hindu law to local traditions and customs which in this case would have justified the use of force. It was difficult to determine whether this was actually a tradition or simply a unique case of brutality.

Smith's arguments concerning the British were more important. He stated that although the rules were violated time and again, no one had been punished till now. The proposed penalties were therefore too severe. The existing attitude of the British administration had given the Indians the impression that widow burning was regarded with indifference, if not in fact with benevolence. Smith demanded only five years imprisonment for the main perpetrator and three years for the main accomplice; he asked that the other four be acquitted. The final verdict incorporated the first two suggestions made by Smith, while the other four accomplices got a prison sentence of two years each: 'Making allowance, however, for the superstitious prejudices of

[215] The sources in PP 1823/17, 66–8 and in PP 1830/28, 7–9. These official records do not mention either the place or the time of the event. The burning took place on 20.11.1820 in Gorakhpur district: PP 1823/17, 54. For the details see above, pp. 306–7.

[216] 25.5.1821 R.M. Rattray to the Nizamat Adalat. PP 1823/17, 67–8.

[217] Undated (August 1821). PP 1823/17, 66.

[218] 2.8.1821. PP 1823/17, 66–7.

the Hindoos concerned, and for the ignorance of the Mahomedans, the court do not discern, in any of them, the guilt of murder.'[219]

With this the fronts had been peculiarly reversed. Smith was one of the most uncompromising opponents of the custom, and was already demanding an unrestricted prohibition.[220] Here an occasion presented itself to achieve a deterring effect through a harsh verdict. Leycester on the other hand categorically rejected a ban at this time.[221] From his point of view a lenient verdict would have been more justified, since his main argument against prohibition was the fear of unrest among the people. Even a harsh verdict could lead to unrest.

Smith obviously did not want to jeopardise the quick implementation of abolition. The elimination of the custom was, in his view, the task of the legislature and not of the courts. A partial success with the help of a harsh judicial practice would only have stolen momentum from the demand for total prohibition. For Leycester the same was true in the reverse. A partial success would have strengthened his position as an opponent of the ban, and would have proved that widow burning could also be fought through other means.

With the verdict, however, Smith had been successful. The Nizamat Adalat had made it clear that it was not willing to take on a task that the government, which was also the legislative body, was afraid of carrying out.[222]

After a lenient verdict had been passed in a case of unmatched brutality, a precedent had been established which narrowed down the scope for later decisions. During the following years cases of a less serious nature were dealt with.[223] The constellation of 1821 repeated itself.

[219] 7.8.1821. PP 1823/17, 66.

[220] 25.5.1821. PP 1823/17, 63.

[221] 25.5.1821. PP 1823/17, 63.

[222] Dhagamwar, *Law* 131–3 sharply criticizes the verdict. Her criticism misses the target however, because it does not take into account the dialectical correlation of the differing positions with the demands for a ban. For Smith, leniency was a means to achieve a quicker implementation of the ban and anything but an expression of complicity with the murderers.

[223] A compilation of the cases dealt with by the Nizamat Adalat between 1821 and 1825 can be found in PP 1830/28, 7–21. In the *Parliamentary Papers* numerous cases at the level of the district and circuit courts are mentioned, especially with regard to *anumaraṇa* of Brahmin widows. Singha's hypothesis (p. 209) that the British took legal action against the perpetrators only when they used force is not correct.

The judges of the Courts of Circuit demanded comparatively harsh punishments, with up to 14 years imprisonment.[224] Smith mostly pleaded for acquittal. Although he did not define the rules of 1813 and 1815 as illegal, he did not consider them to be binding, since they did not have legal force.[225] If, however, a pandit from the region, in which the burning had occurred, declared it to be legal, he adhered to this legal opinion. The final verdicts of the Nizamat Adalat were between one year and three years' imprisonment.[226] In a brutal case of 1821, in which the widow was thrown back into the fire twice, the court in 1824 acquitted all the accused for lack of evidence—some witnesses stated that the accused had merely thrown the widow's corpse into the fire again. As improbable as this was, the strict rules of evidence were adhered to.[227]

In 1826 a special court dealt with a case of 1823, in which a widow who had jumped down from the pyre, was first thrown back and finally stabbed to death by two of her relatives. The spectators were afraid of negative consequences for the village in case the ceremony was broken off. The court wanted to sentence two accused to deportation for life. However, the government pardoned them, probably on the basis of the previous verdicts of the Nizamat Adalat.[228]

Such extreme leniency could not even cite Hindu law as its authority. This became evident a few decades later, when a comprehensive law was enacted in Nepal to regulate widow burning. It contained, especially in cases when force was used, very harsh penalties, including capital punishment.[229] British caution was a consequence not of legalistic considerations but of the fear of hurting the religious sentiments of the Indians and thus provoking unrest. This became negatively evident in a case in 1822. A woman burnt herself to death, not on the death of her husband, but of her brother. Her father lit the pyre. There

---

[224] 11.8.1823 Government vs. Sheo Suhai. PP 1830/28, 15.

[225] 16.7.1823 Government vs. Surnam Tewary. PP 1830/28, 15.

[226] In 1824/25 Smith passed three judgements on his own with imprisonment ranging from one month to a year. PP 1830/28, 19–21.

[227] PP 1828/23, 10–12. A similar case of 1823 in Gorakhpur district. 10.10.1823 R.W. Bird, Magistrate of Gorakhpur, to the Nizamat Adalat. PP 1825/24, 5–6.

[228] PP 1828/23, 3; 14–17. Cf. ibid. 3 the reasons given in justification by the government to the Court of Directors on 12.7.1827.

[229] Michaels, *Legislation* 1226–35.

are many indications that force was not used. The woman was not following any religiously motivated custom. Her father was merely acting on her request. However, the absence of a generally accepted religious legitimization sealed his fate. The Nizamat Adalat sentenced him to seven years imprisonment, more than even the most brutal murderers of widows had ever received.[230]

British Public Opposition to the Custom

Europe had known about widow burning for a long time from numerous accounts. But as yet it had not been a topic of discussion, much less an object of political debate. In this regard public discussion lagged remarkably behind the debates in the administration. This is due to the fact that the public at large was not affected by the custom. The subordinate officials came into contact with widow burning more often and more directly than other British in India or authors in Great Britain.

Within the general public the first to speak out were those who had dealt intensively with Hinduism and its customs: the Baptist missionaries working in Bengal. But they did not appear before the public with the results of the statistical surveys they had conducted in 1803/04 with regard to the frequency of burnings. They presented their findings to the government, but did not demand a ban.[231] As far as we know, the government did not reply. Occasional sharp words in distant places had no effect, as when Mitchell demanded an 'immediate and unrestricted prohibition ' in a prize essay of 1805.[232] Authors who knew the conditions in India were more cautious.

Even in the years that followed, the general public did not enter the picture. The situation changed in 1811, when the missionary William Ward published a comprehensive work on Hinduism. In this he sharply rejected widow burning, without however demanding that the

---

[230] 14.5.1822 Saran district. PP 1825/24, 80. Trial: 31.3.1823 Government vs. Degumber Pande. PP 1830/28, 10–11.

[231] Marshman 1, 221–3; 2, 399; Potts 146ff. G. Smith 279–85 speaks of a demand for prohibition in 1808 by the missionary Carey, but does not provide evidence for this statement. The results were published only in 1805 by Buchanan—not on their own, but as a part of his book on Christian missions in India. He was not in favour of abolition either, but suggested a regulation of the custom. Buchanan, *Memoirs* (1805), 99–100.

[232] Mitchell 113.

government declare a prohibition.[233] The same is true for William Johns, a doctor, who in 1816 published the first book devoted almost entirely to widow burning. He quoted many voices which expressed the hope that the government would intervene to put a quick end to widow burning.[234] Yet there was no clear demand for abolition. The clearest remarks in this context had been made in 1813 by the *Christian Observer*. A custom such as this, it stated, 'ought not to exist under a British Government, and which it might be proved that Government have it in their power easily and safely to suppress.'[235] Proof of this was not given. John's own views displayed a similar tendency. He merely declared that he was 'convinced that, when these opinions shall have obtained their just influence, the horrid practices of homicide, infanticide and matricide will be for ever abolished.'[236]

From about 1818 public discussions about widow burning increased in extent and intensity, and they reached their peak between 1827 and 1829. Pamphlets and articles in journals and newspapers appeared in large numbers, both in Great Britain and in India.[237]

Between 1818 and 1822 several articles in *The Friend of India*, a journal published by the Baptist missionaries, functioned as outriders.[238] The authors were decidedly against the custom, and it was clear that they were aiming for total prohibition. However, they did not demand it directly, but simply presented it as something that was possible without any risks—and this only in 1822,[239] whereas concrete demands for abolition had been made within the administration since 1816. Even Ward had not joined in the demand for abolition in 1821.[240] The same is true for an anonymous pamphlet published in the same year which sharply condemned widow burning. The author even referred to demands for abolition made by the civil service which had come to the

---

[233] Ward, *View*, 1, CXIX–CXX; 3, 308–30. Cf. above, pp. 355–6.

[234] Johns 45; 88–92.

[235] *Christian Observer* March 1813, quoted in Johns 92.

[236] Johns 104. Cf. ibid. VII.

[237] The relevant volumes of the *Asiatic Journal* provide a good overview. For the many articles and pamphlets cf. the bibliography.

[238] Compiled in 1823 in: *Essays Relative to the Habits, Character, and Moral Improvement of the Hindoos* 1-86.

[239] Similarly, but in more decisive terms, also in 1822 in *The Friend of India*, the essay *On the Criminality of Burning Widows Alive*.

[240] Ward, *Letters* 98.

notice of the public through the Parliamentary Papers.[241] This showed how public discussions lagged behind those within the administration and were at the same time influenced by these. The lag was made up only in 1823, when T.S. Grimshawe demanded a general and statutory prohibition.[242]

The new, determined attitude of a part of the public affected a meeting of the Court of Proprietors of the East India Company in March 1827. Two shareholders went into action. After a speech lasting several hours, John Poynder succeeded, despite resistance from the Court of Directors, in having a resolution passed, in which the demand for abolition was made.[243] Such resolutions were not binding. The Court of Proprietors did not have the power to issue orders to the Court of Directors, which received its orders from a state body, the Board of Control. The shareholders, on the other hand, elected the Court of Directors, which meant that their opinion could not be disregarded entirely. At any rate the Court of Directors quoted this resolution in July in its draft orders for the government in Calcutta, but the Board of Control struck out the passage.[244]

Randle Jackson was able to add more political weight to the matter in hand. The basis for this was the experience that one could now draw the attention of wide circles to the question. In some places meetings were held which formulated petitions to Parliament demanding a quick end to widow burning. Bedford began with this in 1823 and managed to collect about 2400 signatures.[245] Crail, near Edinburgh, followed in 1825. After these precursors a regular movement arose in 1827. Many similar petitions came in from numerous other cities.[246]

Based on these events, Jackson threatened the Directors with the people's anger in case effective measures were not adopted quickly.

---

[241] *Remarks* 17–25.

[242] Grimshawe 35–9. Cf. from the following years: R.H.; *On the Burning of Widows;* Elliott 9–13. On the other hand voices of warning persisted till the end. As late as in 1828 John Briggs decidedly rejected any interference. Briggs 136–42.

[243] 28.3.1827. Poynder III–IV. For the date: IOR E/4/719, 1252–4.

[244] IOR E/4/719, 1252–4.

[245] *Parliamentary Debates* NS 9 (1823), 1017 (18.6.1823 Buxton).

[246] For the list see Peggs, *Suttee's Cry* (1828) 93–4. For a detailed description of the proceedings of such a meeting see *An Account . . . York.* In York the mayor called the meeting; only supporters of abolition were allowed to speak.

They should, he stated, do 'that spontaneously, which outraged humanity would otherwise soon force upon their adoption.'[247] Everyone knew what he had in mind, since there was a precedent for this. The Charter of the Company had to be renewed by Parliament every 20 years, and on these occasions conditions could be attached to the renewal. In 1813, the economic opponents of the Company, who wanted to end its trade monopoly, joined forces with the philanthropic-missionary opponents, who wanted the freedom to carry out missionary activities. By flooding it with petitions from all corners of the country, they had wrested from Parliament permission for missionaries to work in India.[248] The next renewal of the Charter was to take place in 1833. Jackson took up the argument brought forward by those defending dissenting opinions in 1824 in the Court of Directors. There was no risk involved in abolition and it would not lead to any unrest. Yet, even if this were not the case, Britain was nevertheless morally obliged to abolish the custom in order not to forfeit its (moral) mandate over India by immoral actions.[249]

This assessment of public debates is confirmed by the role of Parliament. When the renewal of the Charter of the East India Company was debated in the House of Commons in June/July 1813, widow burning did not constitute a separate theme of discussion. Despite this, several speakers touched upon the matter, among them William Wilberforce, the protagonist of the abolition of slavery. He merely hinted at the possibility of a future abolition of widow burning.[250] Other members of Parliament went much further. They put forward the view that the custom could be abolished—but they did not demand it.[251]

It was only in June 1821 that widow burning was placed on the agenda in the House of Commons.[252] Thomas Fowell Buxton, the initiator of the debate, merely demanded that Hindu law be strictly

[247] R. Jackson 26.

[248] Cf. Fisch, *Pamphlet War* 25. Contemporary opinions: [Peggs], *Meeting*. This pamphlet narrates how in a meeting in Coventry in 1829 there was an open threat by the opponents of widow burning to join forces with the textile industry (p. 540).

[249] R. Jackson 7; 26.

[250] Wilberforce 46–113; especially 73–6.

[251] *Parliamentary Debates* 26 (1813), 828–9; Johns 93–104.

[252] 20.6.1821. The entire debate in *Parliamentary Debates* NS 5 (1821), 1217–22.

adhered to, which in fact meant that the rules of 1813 and 1815 were to be followed. He placed his hopes, as did the government in Calcutta, on European education. Wilberforce expressly stated that he was against any kind of compulsion. Therefore, the Foreign Secretary, Canning, had no difficulty in closing the debate on a reconciliatory note: everyone was against the custom and hoped that it would soon be eliminated. But everyone was also against the use of force, which meant that it was advisable to proceed carefully in stages while relying on the 'diffusion of knowledge'.

Compared to those of 1813, the statements of 1821 appear to be distinctly cautious. From this we cannot assume that the extent of opposition to the custom had decreased in the intervening period. In 1813 widow burning had not really been a political issue. The indication of a demand for abolition was not linked with the idea that the government should take immediate action. Rather it had merely been an expression of an explicit condemnation of the custom. This had changed in 1821. Now widow burning had in fact become a political matter—therefore the members of Parliament were more cautious.

Two years later, in June 1823, the mood had changed completely.[253] Buxton, seconded by Wilberforce, now clearly articulated the demand for abolition. He based himself on the petition from Bedford mentioned earlier. But this was still an isolated phenomenon, and the majority of speakers was against abolition.

This too changed in the course of the next two years. When the question was debated for a third time in June 1825, a majority of the debaters now spoke in favour of abolition.[254] The matter was not put to vote, but the change of mood was still obvious.

However, the debates were not repeated during the following years. It was only in March 1830 that Buxton placed widow burning on the agenda again—just to find out that the custom had already been abolished in December 1829.[255] In the following months it became apparent that a new campaign had begun. Between March and July several petitions for a ban were submitted to the House of Lords.[256]

---

[253] 18.6.1823. The entire debate in *Parliamentary Debates* NS 9 (1823), 1017–21.

[254] 6.6.1825. The entire debate in *Parliamentary Debates* NS 13 (1825), 1043–7.

[255] 16.3.1830. *Parliamentary Debates* NS 23 (1830), 390.

[256] *Parliamentary Debates* NS 23 (1830), 157 (11.3.1830); 1118 (1.4.1830); 1189 (2.4.1830); 1265 (5.4.1830); *Parliamentary Debates* NS

They all ran aground—public debates within and outside Parliament almost always lagged behind the debates in the administration.

Indian Opposition to the Custom

Many groups and movements within Hinduism did not practise widow burning and even rejected it. However, at the beginning of the nineteenth century there was no question of a real opposition which condemned the custom in its entirety and sought to eliminate it.

British rule placed potential Indian opponents in a dilemma. On the one hand their position was strengthened by the uncompromising rejection of widow burning by the Europeans. On the other hand this very aspect made them appear as betrayers of their own cause. Such a situation demanded restraint.

In 1817 it became apparent that the custom did not always arouse enthusiasm among the Indians. Mrityunjay Vidyalankar, the pandit of the Nizamat Adalat in Calcutta, made it clear in his legal opinion that he did not consider widow burning as a central element of Hinduism. He was of the view that an ascetic life was a greater act of merit on the part of the widow than burning to death.[257]

The Indian supporters of widow burning opposed the planned tightening of the restrictions in 1817 (see pp. 378–9). Orthodox Hindus in Calcutta submitted a petition in 1818 in which they not only protested against the new restrictions that were being planned, but also against the regulation of the custom as a whole, and demanded that these measures be revoked.[258] The Indians could hardly maintain

---

24 (1830), 1 (8.4.1830); *Parliamentary Debates* NS 25 (1830), 947 (5.7.1830).

[257] Undated (1817). PP 1821/18, 119–25. Excerpts in A.K. Ray 86–90. In the relevant literature it is often stated that Vidyalankar justified abolition, or indeed, demanded it; for example: Mani, *Production* 38; Mukhopadhyay, *Movement* 24; R.C. Majumdar, *Rammohun Roy* 219; Kopf 205–6. This view is not supported by Vidyalankar's report. More cautious assessments in: V.N. Datta 125–6; B.B. Roy 83; Salahuddin Ahmed 112; A. Sharma *et al.*, *Sati* 49–56. V.N. Datta 125 writes of a separate tract by Vidyalankar, in Sanskrit, in which the custom is possibly condemned more sharply. However, he only refers to excerpts from the legal opinion of 1817. Till now the existence of another work has not been proved. Rammohan Roy later cited Vidyalankar as an authority: R. Roy, *Some remarks* 274.

[258] The petition is mentioned in the petition quoted in the following

that Hindu law was being disregarded, since the restrictions were based on the legal opinion of pandits. But they could portray the regulations as being inconsistent with the policy of non-interference in religious matters. Paradoxically, it was their protests that launched an indigenous anti-sati movement.

After this petition a counter-petition was submitted in which the government was asked not only to retain the existing rules and to introduce the planned ones, but also to implement further restrictions in the future. The signatories argued on an exegetic and on a universal level, in order to be able to speak to the Hindus as well as to the British. Widow burning, they stated, was never prescribed in the Dharma texts, but only permitted, though in some places it was recommended as being a greater act of merit than an existence as a widow. In the oldest and most authoritative texts the custom was never mentioned. The most important text, the Manusmṛti, did not tell the widow to commit suicide, but to lead an ascetic life. All these texts rejected the use of compulsion and violence, which was why the restrictions imposed by the British were completely justified. From this, the petition stated, it followed that those 'who signed it [the first petition] must be either ignorant of their own law, or amongst the most inhumane of any class of the community.' This provided the transition to the universalist argument. Widow burnings carried out by force, the petition stated, were murder 'according to every shastur, as well as to the common sense of all nations.' The burning of mothers of small children was 'contrary to the dictates of nature and morality.' The demands of their opponents were 'an insult to the known humanity of the British nation.'[259]

Both the petitioning parties were talking at cross-purposes. The opponents of the British restrictions were not defending the legality of illegal burnings, but were principally opposed to British interference. They were by no means generally conservative. Among them were many supporters of reforms in other spheres.[260] In contrast to this, the

---

footnote, according to which it had appeared in newspapers. *Asiatic Journal* 8 (1819), 15. I could not find the text anywhere. Similarly Collet 87.

[259] *Asiatic Journal* 8 (1819), 15–17. Quotes: 16. Also in J.K. Majumdar 115–17. The petition is not dated; the editors date it around the beginning of August 1818.

[260] Kopf 193; 206; Mukhopadhyay, *Movement* 32–3. Mani, *Production* 32; 35 argues rightly against aligning them in the debate on modernization.

supporters of abolition did not address the general question as to whether the British had a right to interfere. From a political perspective one could speak of a confrontation between collaboration and resistance. But this shift to the political sphere, whether one should principally be against the British, or whether one should support them in this point, did not occur. Although the aspect of collaboration was sometimes mentioned on the margins of the debate,[261] it was not extended to other spheres. The nationalistic potential of the issue was not exhausted. That was due less to a fear of British sanctions than to the fact that a comprehensive resistance could still scarcely be imagined.

Rammohan Roy, the most important Bengal reformer in the early nineteenth century, evidently authored the counter-petition.[262] Around 1811 his sister-in-law is said to have burnt herself to death—force was probably used.[263] It is possible that he was present at the burning.[264] At any rate he became a determined opponent of the custom. It seems that he also fought against it in practice and was not always successful. In March 1818 missionaries reported that an Indian, 'we believe, Ram Mohun Roy' had tried to prevent the burning of two widows of a doctor. The 23 year-old elder widow went into the fire unmoved, while the 17 year-old younger widow addressed him with the following words: 'You have just seen my husband's first wife perform the duty incumbent on her, and you will now see me follow her example. Henceforward, I pray, do not attempt to prevent Hindoo women from burning, otherwise our curse will be upon you.'[265]

[261] J.K. Majumdar 124–5 (Letters to the editor of 1822); 180–1 (1830). Compare this to the sharp attacks mounted on the opponents of sati as collaborators by Kulkarni 1987.

[262] There is an extensive literature on Rammohan Roy. For the aspects that are of interest here cf. for example Collet; J.K. Majumdar; V.C. Joshi.

[263] The event is dated differently: Collet 33–4; 58: 1812; K. Datta 99: 8.4.1810; Kotnala 26: 1811; A. Sharma, *Thresholds* 107: 1811. Other authors doubt that it took place at all: R.C. Majumdar, *R. Roy* 218; V.N. Datta 120; Nag 44.

[264] Mukhopadhyay, *Movement* 30; Natarajan 31 as well as the passages mentioned in the previous footnote.

[265] *Missionary Intelligence* March 1818, quoted in *Asiatic Journal* 5 (1818), 291. The missionaries would hardly have been interested in maligning Rammohan Roy, who was well disposed towards them, and who shared their rejection of widow burning. The story therefore could not be a complete invention.

What was more important was Rammohan Roy's media campaign against widow burning. In 1818 he published a pamphlet in the form of a dialogue between a supporter and an opponent of widow burning.[266] In this he argued as he had done in the petition. At the same time the pamphlet demonstrated the limits of his reform movement. The long-term goal was evidently the abolition of widow burning. But this would not necessarily change the fate of the widow; indeed this fate was actually sealed by the demand that the widow lead a life of renunciation. The aims of Indian reformers were just as selective as those of the British.

In 1820 Rammohan Roy published a second pamphlet.[267] In this he again argued exegetically. Along with this, he took up another point which had not been dealt with in this manner by the Europeans. He insinuated that his opponents considered a woman to be of inferior intellect and character. Since she was neither capable of real loyalty, nor of real education or of real asceticism, only the shortcut of burning remained open to her if she wished to gain the same merits as her husband. Rammohan Roy instead attributed the same abilities to women as to men. He was not preaching emancipation but rejecting widow burning—but a path had been indicated which could lead to an improvement in the position of women even in other spheres.

The potential of these views for the future should not blind one to the actual weakness of Rammohan Roy's campaign. It did not extend beyond Calcutta and its immediate surroundings, and even here the conservatives remained in the stronger position.

Abolition in the Bengal Presidency (1829)

When Lord William Bentinck took up office as governor general in July 1828, widow burning had finally become a political issue that was hotly debated in public both in India and in Britain. Bentinck had not received any orders which obliged him to abolish the custom. But the

[266] *Conference between an Advocate for, and an Opponent of, the Practice of Burning Widows Alive*, Calcutta 1818. Reproduced often, among others by Anand 20–30; quoted here from the edition in R. Roy, *English Works* 3, 88–97. Anantarāma wrote a counter-tract (ed. Derrett).

[267] *A Second Conference between an Advocate for and an Opponent of the Practice of Burning Widows Alive*, Calcutta 1820. Reproduced often, among others by Anand 31–57; quoted here from the edition in R. Roy, *English Works* 3, 101–27.

Court of Directors, in a letter of 1827 to the then government in Calcutta, had hinted that it expected quick and effective measures,[268] and this position had been confirmed with Bentinck before his departure.[269] He himself wrote later that even before arriving in India he had decided to take up the matter immediately.[270]

In Calcutta all members of the government that Bentinck was going to head supported abolition in one form or the other, as did the judges of the supreme criminal court. The overwhelming majority of the civil service was in favour of total abolition. Bentinck himself spoke in 1829 of 90 percent, which was probably an exaggeration.[271] This increasingly led to high-handedness of the subordinate bodies, to illegal interventions and prohibitions, and even to open insubordination. It is true that the country was not yet threatened by ungovernability. But administration would suffer in the long run, if the lower bodies of state had to be more or less forced to carry out orders, and that too by senior officials who found the attitude they were meant to suppress morally superior.

These dangers were indeed acknowledged and taken seriously. W. Bird, a judge in Gorakhpur, urgently warned against the highhandedness of the local authorities: 'It is not to be wondered at that their feelings as men should get the better of their duty as public officers, and that they should be unable to resist the natural impulse to exert themselves, beyond what may be strictly authorized, in order to save sometimes the young, and always the deluded, victim from being sacrificed, in the most cruel of all modes, on the altar of prejudice and superstition.' Finally, he stated further, they would disregard all consequences and all political considerations if they could only save this one victim. 'I speak from experience. The painful emotions excited by being officially a party to the performance of the rite in question, can never be got rid of.'[272] Bentinck knew of the different high-handed actions,[273] and in 1831/32 the Court of Directors in its communication to the Privy Council referred explicitly to the risks associated with

[268] 25.7.1827. PP 1828/23, 21–2.

[269] Cf. Ingham 49; V.N. Datta 90-91, but especially 12.11.1828 Bentinck to Combermere. Bentinck 1, 94.

[270] 12.1.1829 to William Astell. Bentinck 1, 140.

[271] Minute of 8.11.1829. Bentinck 1, 340.

[272] 4.4.1829 Bird to Benson. Bentinck 1, 181–2. Cf. also 25.11.1828 Porderi to Benson. Ibid., 1, 162.

[273] 8.11.1829. Bentinck 1, 340.

these actions. The experiences of the magistrates were, it said, 'calculated to produce a collision of opinions between them and the supreme Authorities, and a deviation from strict subordination, which might prove injurious to the reputation and dangerous to the stability of the Government.'[274]

No one in India could force the Governor General to declare abolition. But it was difficult to imagine that in the long run he would be willing, or in a position, to work against his entire administration. The statement that is sometimes made, that without Bentinck the issue of abolition would have been postponed for some more decades, overlooks these aspects.[275] Only someone with an extremely strong and independent will could have continued to ignore the demands for abolition, someone who at the same time took a completely relativist position, and who therefore considered unjust and wrong interference in customs and traditions which were not compatible with his own values. In practice this meant that he was indifferent to moral questions. This did not apply to Bentinck at all. He definitely wanted to do away with widow burning which he despised. But these intentions were in marked contrast to deep-seated fears that can be partly explained with Bentinck's biography.[276] From 1803 to 1807 he had been Governor of the Madras Presidency. In July 1806 an Indian garrison in Vellore, in his jurisdiction, had revolted, allegedly because the soldiers had been prohibited from wearing certain caste marks. Bentinck had approved of the relevant orders and had been dismissed on those grounds.[277] It certainly was this experience in the first place which led him to adopt an extremely cautious procedure.

The supreme criterion for assessing all government measures in India was always securing British rule, even if this was embellished with humanitarian motives. Bentinck himself stated this very clearly in 1828: 'The whole and sole justification [for the delay of abolition] is state necessity—that is, the security of the British empire, and even that justification, would be, if at all, still very incomplete, if upon the continuance of the British rule did not entirely depend the future

---

[274] Undated (c. 1831/32). IOR L/L/13 (1030), vol. 3, 214v.

[275] Thus V.N. Datta 111and Cassells, review of Datta 78.

[276] Cf. Boulger; Rosselli; J.C. Joshi and Philips' introduction to Bentinck.

[277] Bentinck stresses the connection with Vellore in his well-known minute of 8.11.1829. Bentinck 1, 336. For the Vellore Mutiny cf. Boulger 29-35; M. Ahmad; Chinnian; M. Gupta; J.C. Joshi 22–35; Fisch, *Pamphlet War* 28.

happiness and improvement of the numerous population of this eastern world.'[278]

The most important instrument of power was the army, the lower ranks of which consisted mostly of Indians. Therefore it was advisable to ensure their loyalty. On 10 November 1828, Bentinck asked fifty senior officers and three civilians whether they were for or against abolition, and whether they were afraid of the negative consequences on the army.[279] Although such measures were understandable from the perspective of power, they were unnecessary in the context of the matter at hand. It was well known that the army had nothing to do with widow burning. The people questioned were therefore not experts at all in this matter.[280] Bentinck was not looking for their knowledge, but for their support. The survey was merely a means of opinion polling. Bentinck's cautiousness could also be seen in the fact that he forbade the addressees to discuss the questions with Indians.[281]

The results were clear. Only four people were against abolition.[282] Ten were against direct abolition, but supported forms of careful interference.[283] Eleven wanted to eliminate the custom without legal abolition, but with the interference of the magistrates.[284] The remaining 28 were for a more or less unrestricted abolition.[285] Only two officers feared serious repercussions on the army, not in the form of a rebellion, but in the sense of a reduced reliability.[286] Another warned of unforeseen consequences in an indefinite future.[287] The only reply, in which

---

[278] 10.11.1828 government circular to Army officers. Bentinck 1, 91. Similarly Bentinck in his minute of 8.11.1829. Ibid., 1, 355. Also, without humanitarian frills, *c.* 1831/32 Court of Directors to Privy Council. IOR L/L/13 (1030), vol. 3, 217r.

[279] Bentinck 1, 90–2. The circular with all the replies is in IOR L/L/13 (1030), vol. 3, 231r–264r (=Appendix 16-81).

[280] This could be seen in the many factually incorrect or distorted statements in the replies to the questions.

[281] Bentinck 1, 92.

[282] IOR L/L/13 (1030), vol. 3, App. 18–24.

[283] Ibid. 25–8; 29–36.

[284] Ibid. 28–9; 36–44.

[285] Ibid. 45–81. Various statements were not as clear and far more cautious than the official division in five categories would have us believe.

[286] Brigadier General A. Knox and Brigadier General J.R. Lumley. Ibid. 23–4.

[287] Captain J. Cowslade. Ibid. 21–3.

abolition was unequivocally rejected, came from a civilian, the great Sanskrit scholar H.H. Wilson, who firmly advocated the traditional relativist position of non-intervention.[288] This was certainly not a coincidence. As a scholar, Wilson could concentrate on the theoretical aspects of relativism while ignoring the conflicts that arose in practice.

Despite this unambiguous result Bentinck once again hit upon a means of postponement by asking thirteen civil servants in February 1829 what they thought of the idea of combining the abolition of widow burning with a simultaneous abolition of the pilgrim tax in order to diminish the effect of the former.[289] The British had taken over the practice of levying such taxes at some places of pilgrimage from their predecessors.[290] The reaction was clear. Only a single official found something positive in the proposal, although he too was by no means enthusiastic.[291] All the other respondents recognized it for what it was, a crude attempt at bribery. They made their views fairly clear,[292] and stated at the same time that not only would the Indians not be taken in by such a measure, but that it would also harm British prestige.[293] Bentinck had explained in the circular that he himself did not think much of the proposal.[294] If, despite this, he still carried out the survey, risking disgrace in the eyes of his own administration, which in fact promptly set in, then this can only be seen as a desperate attempt to postpone the decision at any cost.

As far as the central point was concerned, eight respondents were in favour of complete abolition.[295] Two wanted measures to be initially

[288] Ibid. 18–21.

[289] 16.2.1829 circular on *sati* and the pilgrim tax. Bentinck 1, 153–4. The circular along with all replies is in IOR L/L/13 (1030), vol. 3, 264r–282v (=App. 81–118). One of the officers included in the previous survey had suggested the abolition of the pilgrim tax. 2.12.1828 Lieutenant Colonel L.H. Todd. Ibid. 73.

[290] On general aspects of the pilgrim tax Cassels, *Religion*.

[291] 30.3.1829 A. Stirling, Secretary in the Persian department. IOR L/L/13 (1030), vol. 3, App. 107–9.

[292] Ewer even spoke of an 'intention to bribe'. Ibid. 102.

[293] Ibid. 82–106; 109–18.

[294] Ibid. 81–2, also in Bentinck 1, 153–4; repeated in the minute of 8.11.1829. Ibid. 343.

[295] W.W. Bird; R.M. Bird; G.F. Brown; J. Calder; W. Ewer; R.N.C. Hamilton; A. Stirling; A. Trotter. IOR L/L/13 (1030), vol. 3, App. 91–118. Hamilton had been afraid of abolition in 1826. (See above, p. 393.)

introduced at the district level and abolition implemented only later.[296] Two were against abolition, although they considered it to be free of risk,[297] and only one was against any kind of measures.[298]

No further consultations or clarifications were now possible on the British side. However, Bentinck met with Rammohan Roy in July 1829, who spoke against abolition.[299]

Bentinck set this opinion aside and followed the recommendations of his officers and civil servants. Caution remained the guiding principle. In a draft law presented by the government, widow burning was prohibited. Yet a distinction was made between two kinds of cases: those permitted according to Hindu law, and those prohibited even according to Hindu law. The first were to be treated as misdemeanours and let off with mild punishments. Only cases belonging to the second category were regarded as actual crimes of culpable homicide.[300] With this the government, as also Bentinck, showed that they had not learnt even the simplest lesson from the experiences to date. The distinction between legal and illegal cases, which had got the British so hopelessly entangled in the matter, would have continued to exist, even though in a milder form; along with abolition there would still have to be strict regulation. British assessment of the custom would have been only partially established, and the British would have continued to depend on the pandits.

The Nizamat Adalat saved the government from the consequences of its own blindness and insisted on total abolition.[301] This was issued in the form of a law on 4 December 1829.[302] The preamble was distinctly defensive and self-justifying, and once again it demonstrated

[296] H. Douglas and J. Dunsmure. Ibid. 89–91.

[297] Th. Pakenham and W. Wilkinson. Ibid. 82–4.

[298] W. Blunt. Ibid. 85–9.

[299] *Calcutta Monthly Journal* of 27.7.1829, reprinted in J.K.Majumdar 138. No precise records of this often mentioned meeting between Rammohan Roy and Bentinck exist. Not even the date is known. Rammohan Roy does not speak of it anywhere, while Bentinck only mentions the conversation briefly in his minute of 8.11.1829. Bentinck 1, 338.

[300] Undated (probably November 1829). IOR L/L/13 (1030), vol. 3, App. 119.

[301] Observations of the Nizamat Adalat, undated. Ibid. 120. Accepted by the government in its letter of 1.12.1829 to the Nizamat Adalat. Ibid. 129.

[302] Bengal Regulation 17, 1829. The law has been printed often, for example in Bentinck 1, 360–2.

the dilemma between relativism and universalism into which the British had manoeuvered themselves. The preamble first emphasized that the custom was 'revolting to the feelings of human nature'. Then it brought in a supporting argument: widow burning, it stated, is 'nowhere enjoined by the religion of the Hindoos as an imperative duty'; in fact a life of asceticism was considered to be a greater act of merit, and in any case a large majority of the population did not follow the custom. The preamble therefore admitted that political aspects were the most important ones. The British wanted to prove that only few people would be affected by the abolition. The preamble went on to state that the ban did not intend to 'depart from one of the first and most important principles of British government in India, that all classes of the people be secure in the observance of their religious usages, so long as that system can be adhered to'—and here came the decisive universalist restriction—'without violation of the paramount dictates of justice and humanity.'

After this preamble widow burning was unconditionally abolished, independent of the question of willingness, and abetment, indeed even participation was made punishable by law. Not even capital punishment was excluded. Yet here too, caution was exercised. Internally it was decided to proceed very carefully during the initial phase, and to restrict oneself to very mild punishments.[303] Orders to this effect were therefore sent along with a copy of the abolition to the officials at all levels of the administration and to the police.[304]

If one follows this depiction of events, then the traditional image of Bentinck as the determined reformer, who decreed the abolition of widow burning with tremendous dedication and courage against many odds and risking great dangers out of a genuine humanitarian concern,[305] appears to be an idealization. Later, this reputation was further cultivated by Bentinck's famous minute.[306] In reality abolition had become inevitable in 1829, and Bentinck only led the somewhat

[303] Thus for example 1.12.1829 Government to the Nizamat Adalat. IOR L/L/13 (1030), vol. 3, App. 129–30. Similarly Bentinck in his minute of 8.11.1829. Bentinck 1, 343.

[304] IOR L/L/13 (1030), vol. 3, App. 132–4.

[305] This view has become a recurring theme in the relevant literature. Cf. for example V.N. Datta 99; Altekar 141.

[306] 8.11.1829, but first published only in 1892 in Boulger 96–111; quoted here from Bentinck 1, 335–45.

ordered retreat, hesitantly and timidly. Even within this movement he was driven rather than being the driving force. At the most, one can give him credit for insisting on legal abolition and rejecting informal—and therefore illegal—interference.[307] It was alarming, however, that he was not able to understand important aspects of the matter, as demonstrated by the disgrace he suffered on account of the proposal to do away with the pilgrim tax as also the proposal to continue with the distinction between legal and illegal cases (according to Hindu law).

It is even more difficult, however, to regard the establishing of the law as a consequence of a public campaign in Great Britain and in India. This has to be stressed even against Bentinck, who stated that the abolition of the custom did not mean that the government was over-taking public opinion, but was merely following it slowly.[308] Although this was true, public opinion for its part lagged behind the administration.

The third candidate, the opposition movement in India under Rammohan Roy, cannot claim credit for the abolition either. The manner in which Bentinck proceeded puts the perspective in order. Rammohan Roy was the last to be approached, and his advice was not heeded. This does not mean that there was no concern for Indian opinion. The question of possible unrest as a result of abolition was the decisive factor in all deliberations. It means, however, that not much importance was attached to the Indian opposition. The view frequently expressed that Rammohan Roy first paved the way for abolition by weakening Indian resistance to it, indeed that Bentinck would not have dared to implement the abolition without the preliminary work done by Rammohan Roy[309] does not stand up to scrutiny, as will be shown when discussing the consequences of abolition. He did indeed fight with great determination against the custom, but his movement hardly reached beyond a small section of the Indian elite in Calcutta. On the other hand, large sections of the Indian people, and important currents of Hinduism had never practised widow burning.

The fact that abolition is considered to be such a deserving act is the result of a legend constructed by the participants: the legend of the

[307] Bentinck 337.
[308] Bentinck 344.
[309] This hypothesis is naturally mainly prevalent in the Indian literature on the subject (although it is by no means generally accepted), for example Basu 39–40; Kotnala 48; Dasgupta 14–21; Pant, in Barua 119; Nag 44; 52.

dangers of abolition, with which government inactivity was meant to be justified. Subsequent generations believed this alibi and therefore forgot to examine the actions and views of the participants. The idea that abolition became possible because of a change in public opinion in India, is also part of this legend. There had hardly been any changes in this sphere till 1829, and the custom could just as easily have been abolished in 1770, perhaps even more easily, since the matter had not been so controversial then. Walter Ewer, Superintendent of Police of the Lower Provinces, stated in August 1828: 'If it [sati] be considered a question of importance by any small portion of our subjects it is ourselves who have made it so by our strong expressions of abhorrence of the custom, the extreme length and serious character of our discussions and the total absence of decisions and efficient measures to abolish it.' Twenty years ago there would have been no opposition to the abolition of the custom.[310] In the letter, which the government sent along with the text of the abolition to London, it declared that there was 'no reason whatever' to assume that there had been 'any change of opinion amongst the people at large.'[311]

The facts told a story that was completely different from the legend of the dangers of abolition, and it speaks in Bentinck's favour that he did not conceal these facts. It is just that no one took notice of them later. Since the beginning of British rule in India no serious incidents had ever occurred in the context of widow burning, despite repeated— sometimes even forceful—interferences on all levels.[312]

The official British attitude has always been criticized, sometimes very sharply.[313] Bentinck himself used the prevalent image of 'an act, which is to wash out a foul stain upon British rule.'[314] The criticism, however,

---

[310] 15.8.1828 Ewer to the government. *Bentinck Papers* PwJf 2599 III § 4. Similar hypothesis in Lovett 317.

[311] 4.12.1829 Government to the Court of Directors, § 5. J.K. Majumdar 154.

[312] 8.11.1829. Bentinck's minute. Bentinck 1, 339–41. The varied eyewitness accounts confirm this statement, as do the yearly surveys and the official correspondence in the *Parliamentary Papers*. Cf. above pp. 284–7.

[313] Examples are: Thompson, *Suttee* 66; 77; Marshman 2, 359.

[314] 8.11.1829. Bentinck 1, 344. For this formulation, see for example *Bentinck Papers* PwJf 2623/I (May 1829 missionaries: 'the foulest stain in the history of man'); *On the Burning of Hindoo Widows* 1; PP 1830/28,32; J.K. Majumdar 114; 138.

generally proceeded from a different point. Missionaries, civil servants, and later authors usually focused on humanitarian considerations. Here moral questions are not open to debate. The argument is not that the British were morally obliged to suppress widow burning. Rather it is, that in the long run they could not rule India without abolishing the custom, so long as they were not willing to give up their entire intellectual and cultural background and their concepts of morality, as well as their notions of a good and just administration and good government. If they did not want to do this, and if, despite this, they still wanted to have nothing to do with such customs, then logically they also should not interfere in the governance of the country. Bentinck decided, understandably so, to abolish the custom and not to retreat from India.

That the abolition was primarily a result of the contact of civil servants with widow burning, and that therefore the main credit for it goes neither to Bentinck, nor to Rammohan Roy, nor to the missionaries or some pamphleteers, was once seen by contemporaries, but later forgotten. The annual report of the Missionary schools for Indian girls in Serampore stated at the end of 1829:

> It will long be matter of wonder how the British government could endure for so many years to make legal provision for the perpetration of these horrors, and to bring down even their European servants to the shame and the distress of giving them their sanction. [. . .] Our gratitude, as far as men are concerned, is naturally directed first to the illustrious nobleman at the head of the present government [Bentinck]. [. . .] But were we required to specify the class of men to whom we are most indebted for this triumph, we should not hesitate to say that they were the gentlemen of the Honourable East India Company's Civil Service. They were made to sign the death-warrants of the thousands of widows who have been murdered on the pile for these many years past; and they keenly felt the disgrace that was thus put upon them, whilst all their feelings of humanity and religion were constantly galled beyond endurance. Hence the almost unanimous, and frequently indignant, character of the Reports which they have of late years presented to their superiors on the subject of Suttees. By these they took away every pretence from the government at home for perpetuating the late system. And hence, too, numbers of these gentlemen have for years, at their own personal risk and responsibility, been anticipating the recent act of government [i.e. the abolition], some by preventing

Suttees occasionally, and others by entirely abolishing them in the districts under their charge. We speak of facts brought to our knowledge by the gentlemen themselves to whom we refer, and not upon hear-say. We say, therefore, that these gentlemen dared the most, and effected the most, in this glorious enterprise.[315]

Madras

In the Madras Presidency, too, the government tried to keep out of the matter. Since widow burning was rarer than in Bengal, this was not difficult at first. It was only in August 1813 that a magistrate asked for guidelines. The government rejected the informal local prohibition of the custom suggested by him and encouraged him to try persuasion, although this had always been unsuccessful in his district.[316] While replying to a question from Bombay in 1818, the government spoke against any kind of interference.[317] A few weeks later, however, the Court of Directors asked it to adopt the regulations valid in Bengal.[318] The government in Madras reacted with careful deliberation. More than a year later it first conducted a survey among the magistrates in which it enquired about the frequency of the custom and the existing views of the administration.[319] The replies showed the situation that obtained prior to interference from higher authorities, and which till 1813 had certainly also obtained in Bengal. They clearly demonstrated that long before any kind of regulation, British involvement in the matter was much greater than what was apparent from the few cases that were reported to superiors. On no account can one talk of a policy

---

[315] 31.12.1829 *Fourth Report of the Serampore Native Female Schools.* [*Friend of India*] NS 1, 338–9. Less unambiguously: Shore 2, 217–18. In his detailed description of the history preceding the abolition V.N. Datta praises the role of the civil service. In his overall assessment however he focuses on the question of credit for the abolition, and leaves the civil service, as actors, out of the picture. V.N. Datta, chaps 1–5. Cf. also Natarajan 33 and Marshman 2, 400.

[316] 14.8.1813 C.M. Lushington, Magistrate of Combaconum, to the Government; 31.8.1813 Government to Lushington; 1.3.1815 Government to the Court of Directors. IOR F/4/522, No. 12457; PP 1821/18, 248.

[317] 28.1.1818. PP 1821/18, 248.

[318] 4.3.1818. PP 1823/17, 69.

[319] 23.6.1819 Questionnaire. PP 1823/17, 76. The replies, some of which were sent only by April 1820, ibid. 78-124.

of non-interference, or indeed, avoidance. Much depended on local conditions and on the person and temperament of the magistrate. In order to prevent individual cases, some of them adopted measures that would have been considered illegal according to the Bengal guidelines and according to Hindu law. One magistrate had detained the widow while her husband's body was being cremated, and he had occasionally also prevented onlookers from being present.[320] Others were more cautious, but they tried to dissuade the widow from carrying out her plans by talking to her or deputing Indians to do the same, or by stationing police for surveillance.[321] Even those, who did not undertake anything themselves, were dragged into the matter: time and again the organisers of widow burnings asked for permission. If the magistrate refused to give permission, he was overstepping the limits of his authority. If he gave it, he was supporting the custom. If he refused to give an answer, he was lowering the reputation of the colonial power, and his attitude could still be interpreted as tacit agreement and support. Some magistrates tried to evade responsibility by stating that in their districts widow burnings were 'perfectly voluntary.'[322]

The Foujdary Adalat, the highest criminal court in Madras, drafted some guidelines at the end of 1820 on the basis of the results of the survey, and after getting a legal opinion from pandits. To a great extent these guidelines adhered to the rules implemented in Bengal in 1813 and 1815, which were made more precise, and partly also tightened.[323] However, the government in Madras refused to give its consent,[324] not least because of the negative experiences with regulation in Bengal.[325] Since the Court of Directors also increasingly doubted the benefits of official intervention, it did not insist on its demands. Thus the legal situation in Madras remained open. The magistrates were more or less

[320] 16.8.1819 P.R. Cazalet, Magistrate of Berhampore. PP 1823/17, 79. Cf. also 19.7.1819 W. Thackeray, Collector Bellary, ibid. 89 and 3.9.1819 J. Hanbury, Magistrate Cuddapa, ibid. 90.

[321] For example 13.4.1820 J. Dacre, judge in Chitoor. PP 1823/17, 100.

[322] Thus on 4.12.1819 J. Smith, Magistrate of Vizagapatam. PP 1823/17, 81. Similarly on 30.10.1819 F.W. Robertson, Magistrate of Rajahmundry. Ibid. 83. Robertson had once permitted the burning of an eleven year-old girl. Ibid. Cf. also ibid. 86 (Russell, Masulipatam); 88 (Fraser, Nellore); 106–7 (Ogilvie, Tanjore).

[323] 18.12.1820 Minutes of the Foujdary Adalat. PP 1823/17, 73–4.

[324] 6.4.1821 Government to the Foujdary Adalat. PP 1823/17, 130.

[325] 4.1.1822. PP 1823/17, 69.

given a free hand. Those who did not undertake anything, even in problematic cases, could be certain that their conduct would be approved. Over-enthusiastic officials, on the other hand, who went beyond the limits set by the Bengal regulations, even if they tried to be extremely cautious, were admonished from time to time. The sub-magistrate of Combaconum, for example, delayed the burning of a widow in 1825 on the pretext of awaiting orders from above. He had the husband's body cremated, upon which the widow (a Brahmin who was not allowed *anumaraṇa*), gave up her intentions.[326]

The situation remained like this till 1829. The abolition in Bengal created a new situation in Madras too. If the British tolerated a custom in some regions, which they had abolished by law in others, saying it conflicted with all principles of humanity, their credibility would be lost. Since the government in Madras had until now mostly kept out of the debates, it could take over the law without any loss of prestige. On 2 February 1830 it enacted a law which was identical with the Bengal Regulation of 4 December 1829.[327]

Bombay[328]

In the Bombay Presidency too the principle of non-interference was practised, and widow burning was much rarer than in Bengal. If, despite this, in some ways the conditions developed differently to those in Madras, then this was chiefly due to the personalities of the main actors. The governors, Mountstuart Elphinstone (1819–27) and especially John Malcolm (1827–31), were among the most uncompromising supporters of the policy of non-interference. But the government also included supporters of abolition, and some magistrates showed an inclination to resolute interference. This led to many fierce debates.

In 1817 a magistrate in Bassein prevented a widow burning. The government could not make up its mind whether the official should be praised or reprimanded for his action. It enquired in Calcutta and in Madras how such questions were dealt with there.[329] In the following year an Indian police officer, who had prevented a widow burning, was reprimanded.[330]

[326] PP 1826–27/20, 130–1.
[327] Madras Regulation 1 (1830). IOR V/8/28.
[328] An overview in Ballhatchet 275–305.
[329] Bombay Judicial Consultations 5.11.1817, PP 1821/18, 245–7.
[330] PP 1821/18, 249.

Apparently the Court of Directors had also asked the government in Bombay in 1818 to adopt the Bengal guidelines.[331] In contrast to Madras, the government sent the orders to the magistrates,[332] some of whom did not forward these to the police.[333] Some feared that the custom, which till then had been almost or completely unknown in their district, would become popular and would be practised because of the regulations.[334] Others were of the view that the additional power given to (Indian) police officers would only lead to increased corruption, in that they would more or less sell permissions and would be interested in an increase in the number of cases.[335]

The government neither insisted on an official announcement of these guidelines, nor on the implementation of the rules. These were in fact formally revoked in 1823.[336] The principle of non-interference came into force again. The government continued to receive requests for guidelines as well as reports about particularly brutal cases. On 29 September 1823 a widow in Poona jumped down from a burning pyre. According to some accounts she climbed back voluntarily; according to others she was thrown on to the pyre again. She jumped down again, and now there was no doubt that she was forced back. On her third attempt to escape, she succeeded in jumping into the river nearby. Her relatives wanted to drown her. Although a European saved her, she died of her burns on the following day. An indignant magistrate and an outraged press demanded that the guilty be punished.[337]

[331] A corresponding document is not published anywhere, and even Ballhatchet does not mention anything. The actions of the government in Bombay however do not allow us to draw any other conclusion.

[332] 1.10.1818. PP 1821/18, 252.

[333] See the results of a survey of 4.9.1819 in which the government enquired about the effects of the implementation of the new rules. PP 1821/18, 253–60.

[334] In this vein 4.10.1819 V.Hale, judge in Southern Konkan, to the government. PP 1821/18, 258–9. Cf. also 25.9.1819 C. Shubrick, Magistrate of Broach (ibid. 255), and 25.9.1819 C. Norris, judge in Ahmedabad (ibid. 256–7).

[335] In this vein 25.9.1819 S. Marriott, Magistrate of Northern Konkan to the government. PP 1821/18, 256.

[336] 25.6.1823 Government of Bombay to the Court of Directors. PP 1824/23, 46–7. Reservations and objections were already given in the letter sent by the government to the Court of Directors on 16.5.1821. IOR F/4/665, §§ 186–91.

[337] PP 1825/24, 162–74. Cf. Ballhatchet 283–4.

This was one of the cases, in which the principle of non-interference, as convincing as it might have been in theory, could not be maintained in practice among Europeans. A trial took place, in which the court found two of the three defendants guilty.[338] Before deciding its sentence the court asked the pandits whether the deeds which the defendants were accused of were punishable according to Hindu law. The answer was: 'The throwing into the fire, and the other acts [. . .] do not constitute a crime; because, although such acts are not explicitly sanctioned by the Shaster, yet there have been instances of their enactment on similar occasions, while the practice of suttee itself has been continued from the most remote antiquity.' The incriminating deeds 'are not mentioned in the Shaster as crimes, so that there can be no punishment.' Asked whether there was any other legal foundation for the actions of the defendants, the pandit of the court answered: 'I have only learnt from common report that it is usual to throw suttees into the fire [. . .] but there is no clear authority in the Shaster on the subject.'[339]

These statements almost made a mockery of the court. The legal opinions given in Bengal had always stressed that force was not allowed.[340] It was easy to 'prove' that the incriminating acts were not crimes, if the event was not described simply as throwing a person into the fire against her will. Even the practice of citing tradition and local customs, which the British often used to justify their own inactivity,[341] did not help here, especially since the pandits did not really say that acts like the one in Poona had ever been approved of by the Hindu community.

The court accepted the frivolous arguments, although it recognized them as such, and allowed the two defendants, who had initially been found guilty, to go free. The reasons it gave were hardly suited to strengthen the authority of the new rulers:

> You [. . .] stand convicted of having attempted the murder of your relation, [. . .] in a way which is not declared to be consonant with the principles of your religion, or with your laws; for the pandits of the city have exposed their inability to quote any passage from your Shasters, wherein the acts you have perpetrated are recommended, or declared

[338] The documents in PP 1825/24, 186–90.

[339] Undated (before November 1823). PP 1825/24, 188–9.

[340] Even the Nepalese law of 1854 prohibited all use of force, explicitly the throwing back into the fire. Michaels, *Legislation* 1229–30.

[341] Particularly pronounced in an undated comment made by Elphinstone on this case. PP 1825/24, 183–4.

to be excusable. The impossibility of a legal sanction being adduced in support of what you have done, would warrant this court in sentencing you to the punishment due to those who commit murder, while the well-known fact that you are nearly related to the deceased heightens the feeling of your cold-blooded cruelty, and would prevent the extension of mercy towards you. Fortunately for you, however, the pundits and shastrees consulted by this court have declared, that there prevails a notion or belief among your caste, that after the enactment by the victim of a certain ceremonial before the pile is in flames, it is incumbent on those who officiate to put her to death, should she retract from the full performance of suttee; [They had not said it in this way, and had certainly not talked of a duty.] and although their exposition that this illegal practice has been heretofore customary is both vague and uncircumstantial, and, therefore, in a corresponding degree unsatisfactory, yet this court is pleased to allow the exposition great weight on this occasion, choosing rather to lean to the side of mercy in a case wherein it cannot precisely balance between the degree of guilt attachable to you for an intent to kill, and that of merely a desire to finish a sacrifice which you may have deemed it to be incumbent on you, and justifiable from the general belief among your people to bring to a conclusion by putting the victim to death. You are, therefore, indebted to the lenity of the court rather than to the merits of your case in being sentenced to no punishment.[342]

The government approved of these proceedings with a comment that carried caution to extremes: 'It is of more importance in a case like the present to attend more to the feelings of the people, than to the degree of solidity belonging to the arguments by which their erroneous notions may be supported.'[343]

On a superficial level the case showed how the British had manoeuvred themselves into a position of dependency on the pandits. In reality these legal opinions only served as an alibi for their own inactivity. The court could easily have formulated the questions put to the pandits in a way that would have made such a shoddy evasion impossible. It should also be recorded that a few months later other pandits stated in their report that the use of force in widow burning should receive half the punishment meted out for murder.[344]

[342] Sentence of 5.11.1823. PP 1825/24, 189.
[343] 11.12.1823. PP 1825/24, 189.
[344] Undated [1824], contained in a letter of 1.3.1824 written by Robertson to Chaplin. PP 1825/24, 201–2.

To soothe British conscience, the official in charge announced, with the approval of the government, that in future the use of force in widow burning would be punished as murder.[345] Here the views of the pandits were no longer of interest. Despite this, a brutal case in 1824 in South Konkan was again dealt with leniently, accompanied once more by the stated intention of strict measures in the future.[346]

The timidity in the manner of dealing with the terrible case in Poona did not however meet with the approval of the Court of Directors: 'It is deeply to be regretted, that under a British government, deeds of such atrocity have been perpetrated with such impunity.'[347] A sharper condemnation could hardly be imagined in an official framework.

The leniency of the court was a direct outcome of the fear of unrest. It thus had a function that was completely different from the one in the case of 1821 in the Nizamat Adalat in Calcutta, in which Courtney Smith wanted to force the government to abolish the custom by refusing to pronounce harsh judgements (see pp. 400–1).

In the following years the government of Bombay firmly adhered to its policy, even in the face of opposition from its own ranks.[348] In order to defend itself against criticism, it undertook or supported initiatives that required minimal interference or that, for other reasons, appeared to offer the best guarantee against unrest.

One of the possibilities was to appeal to the widow's material interests by promising her a pension. However, since it was not rare for widows, who could have survived comfortably without financial cares, to burn themselves to death, it was to be expected that such promises would not always have the desired effect. The risk of misuse was more serious. Widows could have announced their intention to follow their husband in death, in order to be bought off later with a pension.

Nevertheless, this method seems to have been used occasionally from early times. A German author reports at the beginning of the eighteenth century that the Dutch instituted a monthly pension for all

---

[345] 15.12.1823 Chaplin to the government. PP 1825/24, 190. The proclamation is also mentioned in the sentence. Ibid.189.

[346] PP 1825/24, 211–14.

[347] 13.10.1827 Court of Directors to the government in Bombay. PP 1828/23, 28.

[348] Cf. the documents PP 1825/24, 191–214; PP 1826–27/20, 135–59; PP 1828/23, 24–8; PP 1830/28, 253–71; *Bentinck Papers* PwJf 2617 and also Ballhatchet 283ff.

widows in their territories, independent of their expressed intention to burn themselves to death.[349] This is probably exaggerated, but it can at least be seen as an attempt to improve the fate of widows. Pelsaert mentions the unsuccessful offer of a pension on the part of a Mughal official in 1627 in Agra.[350] At the turn of the nineteenth century a British traveller also failed with a similar offer.[351] A few years later a widow rejected such an offer from two European ladies 'with indignant looks and words'.[352] For obvious reasons the method at first does not appear to have been used officially in the British territories. This changed in 1818 in the Bombay Presidency. Here the method had repeated success in getting widows to give up their intentions with the promise of a pension. The government approved of this method.[353] The hope of achieving something without risking the people's anger made the government blind to the most obvious consequences. These appeared very quickly,[354] and the government stopped the practice in 1819.[355] Despite this, Governor Elphinstone suggested in 1825 that the method be tried again, especially since pensions had sometimes been promised even in the intervening years, although this was prohibited. His suggestion was not accepted.[356]

This method was never used in Madras or in Bengal.[357] Only once, a widow, who had been rescued by the police from a burning pyre, received a pension—the risk of imitation was not very great here.[358]

A second method was to gain Indian support. The attempt was to get Indians to portray the custom as being prohibited in some, or even

---

[349] Wintergerst 2, 119.

[350] Pelsaert 329.

[351] Twining 466 (between 1798 and 1805).

[352] Statham 130 (between 1818 and 1827).

[353] Ballhatchet 281.

[354] A case of 1819/20 in Baroda, in which a widow threatened to burn herself to death, although she did not mean to do so, is described in PP 1823/17, 135–9.

[355] PP 1821/18, 264–8; Ballhatchet 287; cf. ibid. 290.

[356] PP 1826–27/20, 153.

[357] For Madras at least there is no such information. Replying to an enquiry, the government in Calcutta informed the government in Bombay on 1 September 1825 that it had never used these means for fear of 'abuse and frauds'. PP 1826–27/20, 154.

[358] 28.5.1821 Muradabad. PP 1823/17, 26. Cf. also Pasquier 322 (French in Karikal, 1829) and Murray, in Prinsep/Thornton 1, 171 (Sikhs, 1826).

in all cases. The responsibility for failures or for unrest could then be shifted onto them. The episode already described concerning the 'correct' form of the pyre, which not only guaranteed escape at all times, but also prolonged suffering, was part of this attempt (see pp. 273–5). In this case, the fear of abolition led to a virtually perverse attitude at the cost of the victims.

Despite the highly questionable 'success' of this policy, Governor Malcolm tried as late as in 1828/29 to shift the responsibility onto the Indians. He asked the pandits associated with the government to do what he himself was afraid of, supporting a restriction of the custom by interpreting Hindu law in as narrow a manner as possible. If, he told them, widow burning could not be abolished, then India's reputation in Britain would increasingly become worse. 'The continuance of this custom weakens the power of persons like me, who are their [the Hindus'] friend and advocate, to be useful to them in England, when the practice of Suttee is held in such abhorrence, that all our praises of Brahmins and men of wisdom and piety in India are slighted, because you do not exert yourselves to abolish this usage.'[359] This was a mix of flattery, blackmail and intimidation, together with the willingness to subject oneself to some extent to the standards of the other side. The success of this measure cannot be gauged, because widow burning was prohibited shortly thereafter. Yet even with willing pandits, the custom would certainly not have been completely eliminated in this manner.

In its need to dispel all fears that it imagined Indians had, the government in 1827 went a step further than Madras or Calcutta had ever been willing to go. A law stated that neither the suspicion of sorcery nor the desire of the victim to be killed excused murder, 'but assisting at any rites of self-immolation, as directed by the religious law of the person performing such immolation, shall not subject any one to the penalty of murder.'[360] Although widow burning was not mentioned

[359] 26.11.1829 Malcolm to the pandits. *Bentinck Papers* PwJf 2617/II. Cf. 20.9.1828 Malcolm's minute. PP 1830/28, 269–70. On this also see Ballhatchet 301–4. Even Robertson, the author of the policy of the 'correct' pyre, wanted, according to his own statement, to shift the responsibility onto Indians: 9.10.1823 Robertson to Chaplin. PP 1825/24, 168.

[360] 1.1.1827 Bombay Regulation 14 (1827), Section 26, Clause 2. IOR V/8/24. Cf. Ballhatchet 290–1. A parallel to the first part of the paragraph existed in Bengal since 1799. Regulation 8 (1799), Section 3 laid down that the desire of the victim to be killed was irrelevant for legal purposes. This clause was simply not used in cases of widow burning; it was not, like in

expressly, it was clear what was meant. With this the government had officially given its blessing to the custom.

The abolition in Bengal put the government in Bombay in an uncomfortable position. In the long run it would not be possible to avoid a similar measure. A straightforward adoption of the Bengal abolition would however have meant a serious loss of face. At first the government firmly refused to change its existing policies. Instead, in February 1830, it adopted the suggestions made by the pandits in answer to Malcolm's appeal.[361]

These were, however, rearguard actions. The success of the abolition in Bengal made references to risks obsolete. Nevertheless Malcolm tried till the end to wash his hands of the matter. On 18 April 1830 he stated that in India abolition would have to be portrayed as having been forced on the British government in India against its will by the British people.[362]

In the meantime a method had been found which allowed the government to save face to some extent. Instead of adopting the Bengal abolition, as the government in Madras had done, the above-quoted clause of 1827 was simply abolished. In addition, assistance at a religiously motivated self-immolation was to be regarded as manslaughter, and, in the case of the use of force, as murder.[363] With this the legal situation was the same as in Madras and Bengal. The manner of its introduction however was extremely unjust *vis-à-vis* the people. Widow burning was again not mentioned, and the whole procedure was so technical that one cannot assume that its contents were known to all. Because of its timidity, and its desperate attempt to save face, the government failed to stand openly and honestly by the abolition.

The fact that the British themselves in the end failed to understand the legal situation, becoming victims of their own tactics of erecting a smoke-screen, shows that the accusations are not unfounded.

In 1835/36 several widow burnings in neighbouring princely states demonstrated the powerlessness of the authorities of the Bombay

Bombay, formally abolished. Cf. Fisch, *Cheap Lives* 54 and Singha 184–5; 204.

[361] *Bentinck Papers* PwJf 2617/III–IV; 2617/IV–V. Ballhatchet 302–4.

[362] 18.4.1830 Malcolm's minute. *Bentinck Papers* PwJf 2621; also in IOR L/L/13 (1030), vol. 2, 196–9.

[363] 29.5.1830 Bombay Regulation 16 (1830). IOR V/8/25. Cf. Ballhatchet 304–5.

Presidency.[364] Legally they could neither prevent the widows from escaping to a princely state, nor could they stop them from burning in British territory, as long as they did it alone. What no one had thought of in 1830, now suddenly became clear: only the abetting of widow burning had been declared a crime, not the act of the widow itself. This was now seen as a shortcoming, and many senior civil servants demanded an outright ban, including the escape to a princely state. It would otherwise have been difficult to ask these states to abolish the custom.

The government in Bombay then had a relevant law drafted. It was rejected in Calcutta on the grounds that soon a new penal code for the whole of India with relevant clauses would be promulgated (which, however, only happened in 1862). Cases like the one described were said to be so rare that it was not worth taking any action on such a basis, especially since every public discussion carried with it the risk of a renewed increase of widow burnings.[365]

These were weighty and plausible arguments that everyone understood. By treating Bombay as a special case, however, Calcutta showed that it understood the legal situation as little as Bombay did. The government in Bombay assumed that in Bengal and Madras an effective prohibition had been in force since 1829 and 1830 respectively. Bombay should simply follow suit. Otherwise, a widow from the two other Presidencies could come to Bombay, in order to burn herself to death without fear of punishment. This was true—but it was equally true for the other side. In contrast to Bombay where the law did not even mention the custom by name, the laws in Madras and Bengal expressly declared widow burning to be illegal. But they only made abetting punishable, i.e. they included only burning, not self-burning. The difference between Bombay and the two other Presidencies was therefore not of a material–substantial, but merely of a linguistic-rhetorical nature. No one in the entire administration of British India appears to have noticed this.

In the case of Bengal and Madras, the lack of prohibition of the widow's act itself was not an omission, but the consequence of the public nature of widow burning (see above, pp. 299–300). In Bombay

---

[364] The sources: IOR P/206/81, nos 1–3; P/206/82, nos 5–10 (India Legislative Consultations 18.1 and 23.5.1836).

[365] 18.1.1836. IOR P/206/81, No. 3; P/206/82, No. 10. The draft law itself is missing in the files.

this had not been noticed because of the fear of any kind of prohibition, and this led in turn to confusion in Bengal and Madras too. If the widow killed herself alone, then one could not talk of widow burning in the usual sense, but only of suicide or of widow *self*-burning. The widow burning that was encompassed by the law was, without it being expressly stated, a public act. Therefore, by definition, other persons were involved. Since any kind of abetment was prohibited, someone always became punishable when a widow burning was carried out, and hence the act itself had to be considered as prohibited. Without noticing it, the Bombay government, in 1835/36, wanted to abolish not widow burning, but normal suicide.

Effects of Abolition in British India

Success showed that it was correct to term the measures of 1829/30 as abolition. It surpassed the wildest expectations. It had been assumed that implementation would take some time. Instead widow burnings stopped practically overnight.[366] Attempts to violate the ban were rare.[367] In such cases the police often appeared in time and were able to prevent the burning.[368] Sometimes even other people interfered successfully.[369]

In other cases the police arrived on the scene too late, or they heard of the incident only after it had happened.[370] They could then only try

[366] See for example the letter of 20.12.1830 from the Government to the Court of Directors, IOR L/L/13 (1030), vol. 2, 195, and the undated letter (*c.* 1831/32) from the Court of Directors to the Privy Council, ibid. vol. 3, 215r.

[367] For cases in the first years after abolition see especially *Asiatic Journal,* New Series (NS); in addition Thompson, *Suttee* 117–26 and IOR L/L/13 (1030), vol. 2, 192–211. See also footnote 375.

[368] For example *Asiatic Journal* NS 3/2 (1830), 10; NS 4/2 (1831), 182; NS 11/2 (1833), 10–12; NS 21/2 (1836), 226; *Bentinck Papers* PwJf 2614; 2616/ix; IOR L/L/13 (1030), vol. 2, 193–4.

[369] For example *Asiatic Journal* NS 4/1 (1831), 119; NS 13/2 (1834), 151; *Calcutta Monthly Journal* March 1930, 12–13; J.K. Majumdar 179; 181.

[370] Some cases: *Asiatic Journal* NS 4/2 (1831), 188; NS 13/2 (1834), 100; NS 32/2 (1840), 109; NS 36/2 (1841), 344–5; *Calcutta Monthly Journal* June 1830, 9–10. V. Mazumdar 269 writes in 1978 that her great-great grandmother burnt herself to death shortly after 1829 against the will of her relatives who were afraid of official reprisals.

to investigate the case and to arrest the main perpetrators, who were tried, but dealt with leniently.[371]

There were a few untoward incidents. Sometimes the crowd held back the police who had arrived only at the last minute, or it even turned violent, and the burning took place despite the presence of the police.[372] On 14 August 1830 a policeman was fatally wounded in Muradabad district, and two more were injured.[373] On no account could such scenes be equated with the reactions that the British had always feared in case of interference with the religious customs of the Hindus. They did not crystallize into general dissatisfaction. The violence was not to be understood as protest against the abolition in general, but as a sign of annoyance due to the fact that a ceremony that had already begun was to be interrupted at the last minute. In the worst incident on record the police had behaved particularly incompetently. Instead of Hindu policemen, as prescribed, Muslim policemen appeared on the scene.[374]

Success, however, also had its limits. Widow burning did not disappear completely. This is true even of present times.[375]

What were the reasons for the success of abolition and for the limits of this success?

The success was only astonishing if one accepted the fear that had been stoked for decades by the opponents of abolition, in order to justify their own inaction: the fear of the reactions of a mass of people,

[371] Cf. for example *Asiatic Journal* NS 25/2 (1838), 208–9: three accused receive three years imprisonment each; IOR L/L/13 (1030), vol. 2, 200–2: the main defendant receives two years, three others one year each. Bentinck supported leniency after the abolition and recommended pardon: Bentinck 2, 915. Cf. also Thompson, *Suttee* 218–26.

[372] *Calcutta Monthly Journal* February 1830, 139–40: case of January 1830 in Tirhut district (also in *Asiatic Journal* NS 2/2 [1830], 197); *Asiatic Journal* NS 10/2 (1833), 9–10 (Gaya); NS 23/2 (1837), 109–10 (Bihar district).

[373] The documents are in IOR L/L/13 (1030), vol. 2, 202–9.

[374] The officer in charge of the police station was dismissed. According to some accounts the police in fact appeared on the scene only after the widow had died. Ibid.

[375] In the sources and in the relevant literature there is scattered information on burnings that took place after the 1830s. This information has never been compiled. Some references: P.N. Bose 2, 82–3; K. Datta 122–6; A.V.W. Jackson 119–20; Narasimhan 71ff.; Pearce; Robinson 131–2; Thakur, *History* 155; 177; Thompson, *Suttee* 118–26. Cf. also below, pp. 446–9 for the court cases.

who easily became fanatical when it came to questions of religion. If, on the other hand, one went by the fact that European interference had never led to serious untoward incidents or to widespread dissatisfaction, then the results of abolition were less remarkable.

More than any scientific study and any legal opinion, the success of abolition demonstrated that widow burning was not a central and necessary component of Hinduism, and that its suppression would not lead people to despair because they feared for their salvation. It also showed that too much importance should not be attached to material factors. If the attempt to gain control over the widow's property had been the driving force behind widow burnings, then such hopes would not have been relinquished so quickly and so completely. In addition, it was important to remember that the overwhelming majority of widows had always remained alive. Precise religious rules and firmly established social conventions existed which governed the manner of treatment of widows and the organization of their lives. In this regard abolition of the custom did not create a vacuum. One still knew how to deal with widows.

Finally, the success of abolition was also linked to the manner in which widow burning was carried out. Even when it was a voluntary act, it was not a simple suicide, but required the help of the community. If they wanted to, the onlookers could have prevented each and every act of widow burning. Since the law threatened all participants with punishment, they were now far more interested in preventing the act. On the other hand, it was seen that preventing the public from attending generally meant preventing the ceremony itself. This had been observed occasionally even before abolition. Around 1829 a British official heard of a burning planned in the vicinity of Bassein (near Bombay). The widow did not respond to attempts to dissuade her from the act. The official thereupon got the crowd to disperse, with the exception of two Brahmins and an old woman. The widow then refused to mount the pyre.[376] The effect would be greater if from the beginning there was no chance for a public ceremony. In 1828 W.H. Macnaghten stated: 'The people would not care for the performance of the rite if they were compelled to stealth and secrecy. [. . .] The very essence of it [widow burning] consists in publicity; take away the

---

[376] *Asiatic Journal*, NS 1/1 (1830) 259–61. Similarly: PP 1823/17,79 (1819 Ganjam district).

pomp and circumstance, the ostentation and display, and it would soon cease to be the imposing and alluring ceremony which now dazzles and destroys the infatuated victims who fall within the sphere of its influence.'[377]

The comparatively loose religious anchoring of the custom partly explains the quick success of abolition. On the other hand, the limits of success can be explained by the fact that a connection with religion actually existed. While contemplating the limits of success, the first factor to be considered is British policy. If the British had banned or simply suppressed the custom everywhere at the beginning of their rule, then it would not have gained such a prominent place in India. Instead, endless debates were carried on; pandits had to keep supplying legal opinions; all the relevant texts were unearthed, and the religious foundation and background of the custom were of particular interest. Far more was now known about these aspects than at any previous point of time. Since the British were so afraid of interfering in religious customs, they explored the religious character of widow burning, thereby partly creating this character in practice.

Yet the original anchoring in religion, which goes back much further, would have definitely been of greater importance. It went so deep, that abolition was not able to eliminate it. In many streams of Hinduism widow burning retained its character as a meritorious act. A court verdict laconically stated in 1918 that 'the feelings and beliefs which prompt a sati still exist.'[378] One could always be a Hindu and not practice the custom. But it was difficult to maintain that it was completely irreconcilable with Hinduism. It could always be recalled.

Along with the religious there were the social factors. The custom reflected a certain relationship between the sexes. So long as the extreme subordination of women was not reduced, it was highly improbable that it would cease to find support and sympathy.

The fact that the custom remained socially acceptable was demonstrated in scholarship. A.S. Altekar, who wrote a fundamental work on women in Hinduism in 1938, reported in the second edition of 1959 (which is reprinted till today) that his sister became a sati on 17 January

---

[377] 14.12.1828, reply to Bentinck's enquiry of 10.11.1828. IOR L/L/13 (1030), vol. 3, App. 53.

[378] *Emperor vs. Ram Dayal* 31. Similar formulation ibid. 32. Nandy, *Kaliyuga*, mentions, but without naming a source, a survey of 1987, according to which the majority of Indian Hindus and Muslims supported the custom.

1946. Apparently the author considered it more useful than harmful for his reputation to mention the event.[379]

The abolition had a political sequel.[380] The orthodox Hindus among the Indian elite in Calcutta, who had occasionally protested against British measures even before 1829, convened meetings, and on 19 December 1829 they addressed a petition to Bentinck with 652 signatures in which they demanded that abolition be revoked. They did not defend widow burning as much as they reminded the British of their promise of tolerance and non-interference in religious matters. They maintained that old rights and customs were being violated and that they regarded this only as the first step in the process of a general attack on Hinduism. It would be received everywhere 'with horror and dismay'. An underlying threat also became audible: the Hindus should not be pushed into a situation in which they would have to choose between loyalty to the government and loyalty to their religion.[381]

Bentinck firmly rejected the demands.[382] His position was made easier by the fact that Indian opponents of the custom also became active under the leadership of Rammohan Roy, who loyally supported abolition once it had been decreed. He wrote an address of thanks to Bentinck, which was signed by about 300 Indians, asking him to hold on to abolition.[383] The Europeans in Calcutta also added their weight to this with a letter of thanks that had about 800 signatures.[384]

[379] Altekar 137.

[380] Most of the documents mentioned and quoted here in the context of protests against abolition and its rejection are reproduced in Bentinck 1, 367ff, in J.K. Majumdar 156–219 as well as in the *Asiatic Journal*. For a depiction of the events: V.N. Datta, chap. 5.

[381] Published many times and often incorrectly dated 14.1.1830 (Bentinck's reply). Quoted here from Bentinck 1, 367–70, quote: 368. The original in *Bentinck Papers* PwJf 2950, with 652 signatures. In the relevant literature 800 signatures are generally mentioned, as for example in *Asiatic Journal* NS 2/2 (1830),136 and in J.K. Majumdar 159. A statement from 120 pandits was attached to the petition. In addition a further petition from the province with 346 signatures and a statement from 28 pandits was presented. J.K. Majumdar 159–62.

[382] 14.1.1830. Also often published. Quoted here from Bentinck 1, 470 (incorrectly dated 14.7.1830).

[383] 16.1.1830. *Asiatic Journal* NS 2/2 (1830), 138–9.

[384] 16.1.1830. Ibid. 76; 138; 140; J.K. Majumdar 172–3.

The opponents of abolition were thus able to mobilize a much larger following among Indians than the supporters. It is true that they were sometimes accused of using compulsion.[385] This cannot be ruled out, but it is difficult to imagine that all or even a large part of the signatures came about in this manner.

Bentinck had pointed out to the opponents of abolition that they could appeal to the highest authority in Great Britain, to the Privy Council. They resolved to do this in a meeting on 17 June 1830, collecting the considerable sum of Rs 11,260, and asked the British lawyer Francis Bathie to represent their case, since their religion did not permit them to cross the sea.[386] In a petition addressed to the King, they launched a frontal attack on universalist arguments. Bentinck, the petition said, cited the

> common voice of mankind. [. . .] But by what right are the holy dictates of our religion brought down to be measured by so low and vague a standard? We appeal from the common voice (if voice it be) of all mankind to the voice of the creator of man, to the words of the Almighty Ruler of the universe, delivered by him to our holy sages, and by them to us in our sacred books; we deny the right of our rulers to judge, to reason, or to feel for us on such points.[387]

The petitioners never received a reply. It was not possible to put forward any arguments here, one could only decide between two opposing and incompatible approaches.

Rammohan Roy took the matter so seriously that he travelled to Britain (where he died in 1833), in order to support the case of abolition. He wrote a counter petition to the House of Commons, without mincing his words either, and tried to appeal to the honour of the British. 'Your petitioners cannot permit themselves to suppose that such a practice, abhorrent to all the feelings of nature, the obligations of society, and the principles of good government, will receive the sanction of your Honourable House, much less that, having been abolished, the British name and character will be dishonoured by its re-establishment.'[388]

[385] *Bentinck Papers* PwJf 2616; J.K. Majumdar 172; Salahuddin Ahmed 123.
[386] J.K. Majumdar 173–4.
[387] 17.6.1830. IOR L/L/13 (1030), vol. 2, 151–9. Quote:159.
[388] Undated petition to the House of Commons. Rammohun Roy, *English*

On 11 July 1832, the matter was taken up in the Privy Council, of which Amherst was a member.[389] The appeal was rejected by 6:4 votes.[390] Any other outcome was simply unimaginable. The highest judicial body in Great Britain would otherwise have openly disowned the government in India. British authority would have been wantonly endangered, and British prestige would certainly have suffered. The conservative Hindus would have received a kind of veto in the interpretation of the promise of non-interference. In addition, one knew that abolition had not led to unrest.

In the meantime a fierce conflict of opinion broke out in Calcutta, mainly in the press,[391] which subsided after the Privy Council had announced its decision. The conservative Hindus did not try to create a kind of mass movement. They could never have imagined working together with sections of the population from whom they were worlds apart. This was also true for the supporters of abolition. The debates within India remained restricted to a small group in Calcutta; even in Madras and in Bombay comparable debates did not take place.

After 1832 widow burning was no longer a political topic in British India. The situation, however, was different in the princely states.

Works 3, 137–8. For the position of the supporters of abolition cf. also *Appeal* 355–8.

[389] There are few sources. The official documents in the Public Record Office PC/2/213, 404–19; 432 and PC/7/2, 417; 423; 441–2; 506 are very brief. They merely note the rejection, first by the Commission and then by the Council, without giving the reasons, without naming those present and without any details of the proportion of votes. The details that follow would have become known through informal channels, and the information could be wrong.

[390] The information about the procedure of the Privy Council is not very precise and partly contradictory. The most detailed accounts, from an Indian newspaper and from the *Asiatic Journal*, with information about the composition of the Council, but not about the proportion of votes, are in J.K. Majumdar 194–9. Ray 50; Mukhopadhyay, *Movement* 40; J.K. Majumdar 209 speak of a rejection by 6:4 votes. According to a letter to the editor in the *Times* of 26.8.1936 from Philip Morell, the proportion was 5:4 (IOL Ms. Eur.165, No. 171, 3). According to J.K. Majumdar 212 and Greville 2, 314–15 Amherst was against abolition—he had thus remained true to himself. In general V.N. Datta 142–4.

[391] A cross-section in J.K. Majumdar 165–220, as well as in the relevant issues of the *Asiatic Journal*.

Abolition in the Princely States, 1829–1862[392]

With 83 million out of a total of 131 million, British India contained a good 63 per cent of the total population of India in 1820, as well as 45 per cent of the total area—1,432,000 of 3,151,000 square kilometres (see Table 1).[393] The rest of the area was taken up by a few independent and by several hundred princely states. These were formally independent, but they were more or less under British control, generally on the basis of a feudal relationship, or of an unequal alliance. The British controlled mainly external affairs and the military. In internal matters, however, the princely states were autonomous. Widow burning was an internal matter par excellence, so that legally the British had no means of extending the abolition of 1829/30 to the princely states. The Indian rulers, especially the Hindus, could not be expected to abolish the custom on their own in the foreseeable future. On the other hand the British, by virtue of their superior power, could achieve almost anything they wanted in these states with the help of pressure tactics. Such interventions, however, put a strain on the alliance with the rulers, and were therefore used only in matters of great importance. Widow burning was definitely not included in this. The possibility of unrest or even resistance, in case abolition was established more or less by force, was significantly higher in the princely states than in British India, not so much on account of widow burning itself, but to defend the autonomy of the rulers. In addition, there was also the institutional character of the custom to contend with in many of these states: widow burning occurred here mainly at the funerals of rulers, where the number of victims was also the largest. Abolition would have required the ruler or the dynasty to renounce a privilege, which functioned as a means of demonstrating and consolidating power.

Yet it was clear that such a situation could not carry on forever. If the British treated a custom that they obviously despised as a crime in their territory, but allowed it to be practised freely in neighbouring territories that were under their suzerainty, then in the course of time

---

[392] The implementation of the prohibition in the princely states is discussed in: Bushby; V.N. Datta 151–84; Saxena, *Reforms* 77–143; Thompson, *Suttee* 82–116; Thompson, *Suppression*; M. Gaur 51–65; Bishnoi 86–8. In particular for Orissa: K. Mitra; Mitter; Patnaik, chap. 2.

[393] On the princely states in general Fisher and the older works of Tupper, Lee-Warner and Malleson.

their credibility would have suffered, and they would have found it difficult to maintain abolition in their own territories. The burning of widows who went from British territories to the princely states constituted a special provocation.[394] In addition, pressure from British civil servants could develop, as had been the case before 1829 in the directly administered territories. The colonial power had residents (or agents) in the princely courts who looked after British interests and at the same time functioned as a supervisory body. If they came into contact with widow burning frequently, or even had to be present, aversion to the custom could gradually arise, and with it demands for counter-measures. If no steps were undertaken officially, there could be arbitrary actions on the part of the British residents. The British therefore again found themselves in the dilemma they had been in before 1829. For reasons of the stability of their rule they would have preferred not to do anything, but with time they found that they were compelled to take action. In view of the legal situation they could not declare abolition unilaterally, but only make their influence felt. A staggered action that would prevent solidarity among the rulers was required. Islamic rulers could be won over more easily to abolish a custom that they too despised. Hindu ruling houses that did not practice widow burning were also more willing to suppress it than those in which the custom had a long tradition. One could begin with the weakest states and thus gradually isolate the larger ones.

The first major successes occurred in 1833, when bans were issued in the important kingdom of Oudh, which had an Islamic ruler and in which the custom was rare, and in Assam.[395]

In other places the British proceeded less reluctantly, as for example in 1832 or 1833 in Patiala in Punjab, where several people were punished for taking part in a widow burning, although there had been no ban till then.[396]

Shortly thereafter, this energetic method was less successful. On the death of the Rajah of Idar (near the Bombay Presidency), on 5 September 1833, seven wives, two concubines, four female slaves and a male servant of the ruler were burnt to death. In February 1835, the Rajah of the neighbouring Ahmadnagar state died, a state which for some

---

[394] For example IOR P/206/81, no. 2; P/206/82, nos 5–6; Klemm 7, 147; Thompson, *Suttee* 87.

[395] V.N. Datta 153; Thompson, *Suttee* 83; Orlich, *Indien* 2, 2, 235.

[396] *Asiatic Journal* NS 11/2 (1833), 66. Patiala had approximately 1–1.5 million inhabitants.

time had been a part of Idar and had the same traditions. By chance, 300 British troops were stationed just outside Ahmadnagar in order to fight local rebels. Their commander, Erskine, asked the persons in charge to forego widow burnings. He only received an assurance that force would not be used. In the meantime armed men were brought into the city and the British troops were driven out of its immediate surroundings. On the night of 8 February, five of the seven wives of the dead ruler were burnt to death. In the days that followed the fighting between British troops and the troops of Idar continued and claimed a considerable number of lives. It was only in 1836 that the new ruler pledged to renounce widow burning in future.[397]

Had the opponents of abolition been correct in their warnings? Was there the danger of a serious rebellion if vigorous action against the custom continued? The case could hardly be generalized. The British had been very inept in their handling of the issue. No ban had been in existence at the time of the ruler's death. If the successor was forced to give up a custom just when it was to be carried out, it meant humiliation and a loss of prestige for him. Erskine had clearly overstepped the limits of his authority. His offensive behaviour had made the issue into a question of power, a question of the autonomy of the state. In addition, there were the rivalries between different indigenous groups which were also fought out on this occasion. A repetition of such events could be avoided with a somewhat skilfully conceived policy. In fact, serious clashes occurred again only in 1850, when an over-enthusiastic British official deployed troops to prevent a widow burning in Gwalior. He was reprimanded by his superiors.[398]

Understandably enough the British proceeded very cautiously after 1835.[399] Sometimes official protests were lodged and disapproval was expressed when burnings took place at the funerals of rulers or other important men.[400] At other times the British residents had to maintain

[397] The sources: A.K. Forbes 2, 206–7; 211–25; *Asiatic Journal* NS 13/2 (1834) 258–9; 17/2 (1835), 236–7; 18/2 (1835), 16. Cf. the accounts in Thompson, *Suttee* 84–6; Thompson, *Suppression* 274–6; V.N. Datta 154.

[398] V.N. Datta 170–1.

[399] For the following see: Bushby; V.N. Datta 151–84; Saxena, *Reforms* 77–143; Thompson, *Suttee* 81–116; M. Gaur 51–65; *Measures*. Several cases of 1835/36 in the Bombay Presidency in IOR P/206/81, nos 1–2 and P/206/82, No. 5–6; 8–9. For a case of 1852 in Kutch Jacob 139–51.

[400] For example IOR P/206/82, no. 9 (1836 Bhooj); M. Gaur 53 (1838 Mewar).

silence; in their official capacity at least they could not demand abolition.[401] But they tried to use favourable opportunities. This included in particular the British right to confirm new rulers. On such occasions at least the smaller ones among them had to pledge to abolish the custom.[402]

Despite the stringent restrictions that the British residents were subject to, it was still important whether they were indifferent to the custom or whether they secretly tried to agitate against it. A particularly well-known attempt was the one by Major Ludlow, resident at the court of the Maharajah of Jaipur, to convince the pandits and the important men of the state that the custom had no basis in Hinduism. After a few years he was successful, even if it remains uncertain whether the change of heart sprang from genuine conviction or rather from the desire to win the favour of the colonial power. At any rate the custom was banned in Jaipur in 1846.[403]

With this the British had gained ground in the remaining core area of widow burning, in the princely states of Rajasthan. In the next two years a whole series of Rajput states joined in abolition. Others stubbornly refused to do so. The British made it clear that they would not tolerate the custom for long. In 1847 Governor General Hardinge issued a proclamation that stated in unambiguous terms what the British wanted.[404] Governor General Dalhousie (1848–56) further increased the pressure. Mewar (Udaipur) was the last to issue a ban in 1860 which, however, only provided for fines and was rarely adhered to. This provoked renewed British pressure, which led to a stricter law in 1862. Again there was only limited adherence to it, so that the British intervened directly a few times, although they were not entitled to do so. From about 1868 widow burnings seem to have occurred only rarely.[405]

---

[401] In 1842, for example, Governor General Ellenborough rejected the offer made by the British resident at the court of the Nizam of Hyderabad to use his influence to have the custom legally abolished. Bushby 263; V.N. Datta 170. The Islamic Nizam was one of the most powerful Indian rulers.

[402] Bishnoi 88, footnote 35 describes a case of 1849 in Panna.

[403] Bushby 267–9; Saxena, *Reforms* 102–3; V.N. Datta 169; Thompson, *Suttee* 108.

[404] V.N. Datta 163; 174.

[405] Saxena, *Reforms* 121–35.

When the British had conquered and annexed a princely state, they sometimes acted much more firmly. In 1843, the year in which Sind was annexed, its conqueror, General Charles Napier, the veteran of many campaigns,

> hearing of an intended burning, he made it known that he would stop the sacrifice. The priests said it was a religious rite which must not be meddled with—that all nations had customs which should be respected and this was a very sacred one. The general affecting to be struck with the argument replied: 'Be it so. This burning of widows is your custom; prepare the funeral pile. But my nation has also a custom. When men burn women alive we hang them, and confiscate all their property. My carpenters shall therefore erect gibbets on which to hang all concerned when the widow is consumed. Let us all act according to national customs!' No suttee took place then or afterwards.[406]

Even if this episode is fictitious, it shows the clash of irreconcilable views.

By about 1862 abolition had been established everywhere.[407] This time the success was due to an even larger extent to the efforts of the administration than in 1829. Public opinion had lost interest in the matter after Bentinck's abolition.

Although there are no figures available, one can assume that the burnings in the princely states did not stop immediately after abolition as they did in the British territories. The administrative apparatuses were less efficient and consisted to a large extent of people, who, even if they did not exactly admire the custom, regarded it as an element of Hinduism, and, at any rate, not as a crime. They would therefore have frequently tried to prevent interference. Yet here too the public nature of the ceremony would have had an effect. The British would have definitely heard of widow burnings on the occasion of a royal funeral. Such a ceremony would have been a breach of promise and an open provocation after the ruler had entered into an agreement for legal

---

[406] Napier 35.

[407] One can argue whether the year 1862 should be considered as the terminal point of legal widow burning. The details about this in the relevant literature are fairly unspecific. Yet the order of magnitude would at least be correct. Thompson, *Suttee* 115 also places the end in 1862, while V.N. Datta and Saxena do not make any definite statements.

abolition. In order to retain power, dynasties were therefore forced to give up the custom and to renounce their privilege after a prohibition. With this the rulers were also no longer interested in helping their subjects to (secretly) retain the same privilege. We can thus assume that widow burning in the princely states lasted longer than in the British territories,[408] but that subsequently the adherence to abolition was hardly less.

The abolition of 1829/30 has occasionally been regarded as one of the long-term causes of the great rebellion of 1857/58. It is argued that the British demonstrated here that they were willing to take action against customs sanctioned by religion. Further steps followed in the next decades. Taken together they created the impression that the British wanted to Europeanize society. The fears arising from this finally led to the rebellion.[409]

The entire hypothesis cannot be examined here. As far as the effects of the abolition of widow burning are concerned, the British officials who were responsible for pushing this through in the last of the princely states between 1858 and 1862 obviously did not share this view—otherwise they would have certainly waited for a few years. On 23 December 1859, Viceroy Canning expressly stated that Queen Victoria's proclamation of 1 November 1858, in which all Indians were assured of the free exercise of their religion, did not include widow burning.[410] There are further considerations which speak against the custom being given such an eminently political significance. The abolition of 1829/30 had essentially led to protest only in Calcutta and here only among the middle and upper classes. The burnings had been most frequent in Bengal, especially in and around Calcutta. These regions did not take part in the rebellion. In the core areas of the rebellion, the Upper Provinces, widow burning had been of little importance before 1829.

There are many indications that the hypothesis about the connection between abolition and the rebellion is only the renewal or the after-effect of the statement used by the British to justify their own inaction:

[408] Violations of the bans are mentioned mainly by V.N. Datta 153–78 and by Saxena, *Reforms* 103–43.

[409] V.N. Datta 105; 147; Rahman 141; A. Sharma *et al.*, *Sati* 9; 91; Biswas/Ganguli, in Collet 258; S.N. Sen 5.

[410] V.N. Datta 172.

that the Hindus would consider abolition as interference with their religion and would resist it.

Widow burning as a legal institution in Hindu regions now existed only outside the British sphere of influence. The special case of Bali has already been discussed.

The only exception in South Asia after 1862 was the kingdom of Nepal, in which the custom in 1854 had not been banned, but regulated. A law laid down meticulously under what conditions a widow was allowed to burn herself to death.[411] The rules were stricter than those framed by the British in 1813 and 1815. Thus the widow was not allowed to burn herself if she had sons under 16 and daughters under five years. The possibility of backing down was guaranteed until the last moment. The law contained comprehensive and strict penalties. There have been no studies till now as to whether the law merely codified the legal situation which had been in force for a long time, or whether the restrictions were made more stringent as a result of the British campaign for abolition in India. However, we can assume that the rules did not deviate too much from the existing customary law, since otherwise it would have been difficult to establish them. Here, this task fell not to a foreign power, but to a Hindu state, so that there were no moral conflicts within the administration.[412]

Time and again reports on widow burning in Nepal had reached India.[413] Following upon the abolition of 1829 and especially after 1862 the British tried to exert pressure. When the Prime Minister Jung Bahadur died on 25 February 1877, three of his widows killed themselves three days later. Viceroy Lytton protested. When a general died in 1884, the Prime Minister prevented a burning. He received a letter of thanks from the Viceroy.[414] Yet such expressions of praise and censure could not effect abolition—in resisting this, Nepal demonstrated its independence in contrast to the princely states, as a result of which it became a model for orthodox Hindus. In the end, however, local

[411] Text and translation in Michaels, *Legislation*; cf. Michaels, *Recht* 111–15 and Michaels, *Nepal* 25–9.

[412] However, the application of the law has not been studied till now.

[413] Cf. for example *Asiatic Journal* 2 (1816), 599 (case of 1813); 5 (1818), 221–2 (royal funeral with many victims); 20 (1825), 88 (diverse cases); Peggs, *India's cries* 267. A report of 1845 is mentioned in Edwardes/Merivale 2, 36–7.

[414] V.N. Datta 171; Thakur, *History* 177; Jolly 69.

political considerations were overtaken by moral ones that were being established world-wide: in 1920 Nepal too declared abolition, using a similar justification as the British in 1829.[415]

Widow Burning under the Indian Penal Code, 1862–1987

In the same year in which widow burning was abolished in the last of the princely states, a uniform penal code came into effect in the territories directly administered by the British. After Indian independence in 1947 it was extended to the former princely states, and it remains valid till today. Henceforth all criminal offences had to be tried in accordance with this code. It did not mention widow burning.[416] On the other hand, the abolition of 1829/30 was never revoked. Indirectly it also formed the basis for abolition in the princely states. Since the British attitude to the custom had not changed, we can assume that the intention of the old decree of abolition remained in force, while the sentences had to be determined on the basis of the new code. Widow burning had to be subsumed under other offences: murder and homicide (Sec. 299–300; 302; 304), abetment of suicide (Secs 305–6), and attempted suicide (Sec. 309).[417]

With regard to the worst offences, murder and homicide, there was a change compared with 1829. At that time it had been stressed that the question, whether the act had been voluntary or not on the part of the victim, was immaterial for judging the deeds of other persons involved.[418] Now it had been laid down that the killing of a person would not be regarded as murder, but only as homicide, if the victim was at least 18 years old and had given his or her consent. The maximum punishment for this was deportation for life instead of the death penalty (Sec. 304). In contrast to 1829 this made the question of willingness

[415] For this and about Nepal in general Michaels, *Recht* 111–15 and Michaels, *Nepal*, especially 27–9.

[416] These questions are touched upon, but not answered by Dhagamwar, *Law* 124–6; 295–6 and Dhagamwar, *Saint* 34–7. Cf. also Anand 171–2 and Agnes 30–1.

[417] These and the following references in brackets refer to the Indian Penal Code. Cf. also Hirst 1; S. Singh 75.

[418] Bengal Regulation 17 (1829), Section 4.2. Printed for example in Bentinck 1, 361.

legally material to the case. It was a problematic decision, since the question of free will could hardly be established with any degree of certainty. Making the victim accountable meant a potential exoneration of the perpetrators.

In practice these rules were irrelevant. Convictions for participating in widow burnings were never for murder or homicide, but always for abetment of suicide.[419] The maximum penalty for this was 10 years imprisonment (Sec. 305); for abetment of suicide of minors and the insane even the death penalty was possible (Sec. 306), whereby the consent of the victim was immaterial. For attempted suicide the maximum penalty was one year's imprisonment (Sec. 309). In 1829 punishment of the widow had not been mentioned. Yet even this change was irrelevant in practice, since, as far as can be seen, a widow, who had survived an attempt at burning, was never put on trial.

There were no fundamental changes in the way the administration of justice dealt with widow burning after 1862. On the whole, one finds rather an increase in stringency over the course of time, with the court of appeal either confirming or increasing the measure of punishment given by the lower court. This was in contrast to the years before 1829, when the Nizamat Adalat had regularly reduced the sentences of the courts of circuit. The principal accused normally received 4–5 years imprisonment. In a particularly sensational case of 1928, five of the accused were each sentenced to 10 years imprisonment, the maximum penalty for abetment of suicide.[420]

The tendency to greater stringency was probably connected with the political background. Widow burning had become so rare that the state did not need to be afraid of creating unrest by interfering. Yet there were no really fundamental changes in the caution employed by the British. It was still difficult to imagine that the main actors involved in a widow burning could be sentenced to death and executed as murderers, or at least be deported for life.

After Independence the Indian State not only took over the penal code from the British, but also the firm, official condemnation of

[419] Dhagamwar, *Law* 124–6 and Dhagamwar, *Saint* 36–7, who was the first to point out the difference, overlooks this. Similarly Singha 213–14.

[420] Five other accused received between one and seven years. 13.6.1928. *Emperor vs. Vidyasagar Pande*. The Privy Council rejected an appeal on 5.2.1929. Hirst 9. Cf. also 9.9.1871 *Queen vs. Mohit Pandey* and 1.11.1913 *Emperor vs. Ram Dayal*.

widow burning. A verdict of 1958 shows that despite this the framework had changed. In 1955 the police were prevented from intervening in a widow burning in Rajasthan. Twelve people were arrested. The judge in the court of original jurisdiction acquitted five of them, while the other seven were each sentenced to six months imprisonment. The appellate court took him to task:

> The reasons he has given for this ridiculously lenient sentence are rather strange in the middle of the 20th century. He is still not sure whether the people are wrong or right in their adoration of Sati, though the law in this country has declared abetment of suicide to be a crime for over a hundred years. He seems to sympathise with the view of the people that it is their religious duty to help a woman who wants to become a Sati. He has also made the observation that the custom of Sati is a well known custom and judicial notice can be taken of it. We are surprised at this. This custom which was prevalent upto 1833 [he means 1829] was forbidden more than 100 years ago by law. We are, therefore of opinion that a sentence of six months' rigorous imprisonment for such a barbarous act of abetment of Sati is ludicrous. It is essential that people should respect the law which has been in force for over a hundred years. In such cases of Sati therefore, which off and on take place, we are of opinion that a deterrent sentence is called for.

All twelve accused were sentenced to five years' imprisonment.[421]

Such a discrepancy between verdicts given in the first and those given in the second instance would hardly have been possible under the British. It showed the fundamental problem of the independent Indian State. The overwhelming majority of the civil service right to the top ranks—not to speak of the broad masses—showed understanding and frequently also admiration for widow burning as a meritorious act. Under colonial rule it would not have been worthwhile if Indian judges had passed lenient sentences in the first instance, since these would have definitely been set aside by the higher courts. After all, it was the British who set the tone in this matter, and it was well known that they completely rejected the custom. From 1947 onwards the conditions were less clear, since, even at the higher level, not all officials despised the custom. One could therefore attempt to pass a lenient sentence. Those who defended the official attitude of the State had to react all the more firmly. Once the colonial power had left, the

[421] 1958 *Tejsingh vs. the State*. Quote: 172, § 11.

debates between Indian opponents and supporters of the custom intensified.

Very little is known about conditions in the princely states between abolition and 1947.[422] Occasionally there were trials, in which the sentence was sometimes considerably harsher than in the British territories. In 1852 the chief perpetrator in a widow burning was sentenced to 12 years of imprisonment in Gwalior; in addition, all his property was confiscated.[423] In 1859 several people who had taken part in a widow burning in Alwar were sentenced to 11 years of imprisonment and a large fine of Rupees 13, 200.[424] In 1880 the chief perpetrator in a widow burning in Mewar (Udaipur) received a prison sentence of 14 years.[425]

Such verdicts were not the direct outcome of British interference, but they resulted from the fear of arousing the displeasure of the colonial power. Conversely this made it possible for the colonial power to recommend greater leniency in individual cases in order to divert the possible anger of the people away from itself.[426]

Widow Burning as an Object of Populist Politics and the Renewed Abolition of 1987[427]

The official policy of independent India adopted the British position on widow burning. It did not need to be as apprehensive as the colonial power that its policy could be interpreted as an attack on religion, or as an attempt at Europeanization. As has already been shown, this advantage, on the other hand, made it difficult to implement abolition, since most of the officials were not convinced that it was necessary.

---

[422] Cf. particularly V.N. Datta 151–84; Saxena, *Reforms* 77–143; Thompson, *Suttee* 82–116.

[423] V.N. Datta 171.

[424] V.N. Datta 176.

[425] Saxena, *Reforms* 135; cf. ibid. 135–40.

[426] Cf. Saxena, *Reforms* 134 (case of 1868 in Mewar).

[427] For the following: A.M.; Anand 81–188; van den Bosch; Jain *et al.*; Kumar 172–81; *Manushi*; *Seminar*; Patel/Kumar; Narasimhan; Qadeer/Hasan; Ram; *Sati and the State; Trial by fire*; Tully 210–36; Upreti/Upreti; Vaid/Sangari; Weinberger-Thomas (1996) 175 ff.; Nandy, *Kaliyuga*; Nandy, in Hawley (ed.) 131–49; Oldenburg, in Hawley (ed.) 101–30; Mani, *Mediations*. Cf. also the bibliography in *Seminar* 49–52.

Time and again there was the suspicion that the police had done too little or nothing at all.[428]

There were some attempts at further changes in the 1960s which were intensified in the seventies and mainly in the eighties. The Sati-cult, hitherto found mostly on a local level, increasingly mobilized people in larger areas and longer periods of time.[429] Simultaneously the political conditions also changed. With independence, the masses gained a new political significance in the framework of democracy. They had to be addressed as voters. While at first most of the politicians had stressed the secular character of the new State, in the seventies and eighties more and more of them increasingly tried to win supporters with religious slogans.

The Sati-cult, and through it finally also widow burning, gained a new political potential under the conditions of Indian democracy. Since at first the potential was hardly transformed into actuality, the underlying changes were not really perceived. This situation suddenly changed as a result of Roop Kanwar's burning on 4 September 1987.[430] The event received nation-wide, indeed world-wide publicity. Within a few days hundreds of thousands streamed to the place where the immolation had taken place, and large sums of money were donated for the construction of a temple. This reaction was partly spontaneous, and politicians who hoped to gain supporters by defending the custom, then intensified it. They portrayed widow burning as a unique embodiment of the traditional values of Hinduism which had to be maintained and nurtured. They stated that devotion, faithfulness, heroic courage and willingness to make sacrifices manifested themselves in the custom (whereby it was taken for granted that the act was completely voluntary). Those who were against it, destroyed the foundations of Hinduism and therefore also of India. In this way widow burning became the banner under which conservative Hindu politicians gathered their supporters—among them many women. They condemned the prohibition of the custom as a violation of religious freedom and simultaneously attacked the secular foundations of the Indian State.[431]

Till now the political function of the custom of following the dead in all parts of the world had consisted in demonstrating the power of

[428] Cf. S. Singh 81–7; Subramaniam, in Anand 164–70.

[429] Cf. Noble/Sankhyan.

[430] For a more detailed description with references see above, pp. 243–4.

[431] An example for a particularly committed defence of the custom is Kulkarni.

the ruler, or the ruling group, by actually carrying out the relevant ceremonies. Here, on the other hand, interest groups tried to gain power and influence with the help of the mental attitude associated with widow burning. It was primarily the symbolic character which was important. A large number of actual burnings would have been a hindrance for the intentions of such politicians. Their supporters would have probably dwindled as a result. For them an isolated event like the burning of Roop Kanwar was much more useful. In this way they could focus public attention more easily on one point. In order to strengthen their political position, they accepted the fact that widow burnings occurred. They must have been aware of the fact that the revocation, or at least the non-implementation of the prohibition that they were demanding, could lead to an unforeseeable increase in the number of cases, not least because they propagated such convictions.

There were striking parallels and important differences to the actions of the opponents of the abolition in 1829/30. As had happened then, arguments were not presented in support of widow burning, but in rejection of state interference in religious customs. In contrast to 1829, however, the opponents of the ban were now able to lend considerable political weight to their opposition by successfully taking their movement to the people.

As had happened in 1829, the activities of the opponents brought the supporters of abolition onto the scene, led this time by women's organizations and a section of the intellectuals. In 1987, the opponents of the custom could hardly be accused of collaborating with foreign rulers, nor could they be characterised as a kind of Fifth Column of Christian missionary activity. Yet structurally similar arguments were used to discredit them. They were now regarded as intellectuals corrupted by decadent Western ideas, and alienated from the Indian tradition, who had no support among the people and did not understand their feelings and concerns.[432] The arguments against the custom had not changed very much in relation to 1829,[433] since the issue had not changed either. Mostly it was universalist views that were put forward. Only, religion was now replaced by natural law and human rights: 'The issue is not whether any religion sanctions Sati or not, but whether society will tolerate the murder, torture and degradation of widows in

---

[432] Even Nandy, *Kaliyuga* argues in this manner, although he certainly cannot be termed an orthodox opponent of abolition, or indeed a supporter of widow burning. Tully 235–6 mainly criticizes the women's movement.

[433] Also stated by Upreti VI; 112.

the name of religion. [. . .] The issue of women's rights is one which overrides any religious customs, rite or practice.'[434] One women's organisation stated: 'The rights of women are inalienable and derived not from religious sanction but from the Constitution of India.'[435] However, these forces were not in a position to carry the same political weight as their opponents. There was no question of a mass movement. When women's organizations led a silent march in Jaipur on 6 October 1987 to protest against the burning of Roop Kanwar, they were able to mobilize only about 3, 000 people. Two days later their opponents marched with about 70,000 people.[436]

In view of such debates the government was faced with an unpleasant situation. If it condemned the opponents of the ban, or even took action against them, it would have created powerful internal enemies for itself and risked alienating large sections of the people. If they allowed the conservative Hindus to carry on, or indeed if they support-ed them, they would of course lose the sympathy of a much smaller number of voters. But they would also have harmed India's reputation abroad. In 1829, Bentinck had already emphasised this aspect: 'When they [the Hindus] shall have been convinced of the error of this first and most criminal of their customs, may it not be hoped, that others which stand in the way of their improvement may likewise pass away, and that with this emancipation from those chains and shackles upon their minds and actions, they may no longer continue as they have done, the slaves of every foreign conqueror, but that they may assume their just place among the great families of mankind.'[437]

In 1868 an anonymous author stated in more concrete, naïve and self-assured terms: 'Advancement of natives to high posts of emolument or responsibility, was simply impossible, while such relics of dark ages and dark superstitions were fostered or endured. [. . .] Imagine a native gentleman dying, who was a member of the Governor-General's Council for making Laws, and the Viceroy, on sending a message of condolence to his family, being quietly told that his wives had all burnt themselves the day before.'[438]

While such formulations cannot be used today, the attitude under-lying them has completely established itself only now: in the universal

[434] *Anti Sati Bill* 18–19.
[435] Ibid. 21.
[436] Hawley, in Hawley (ed.) 9.
[437] Minute of 8.11.1829. Bentinck 1, 344.
[438] *Papers relating to East India Affairs* (1868), 260.

discourse on human rights. India has consistently supported this policy since 1947. The legalization of widow burning would ruin its international reputation, or, expressed in terms of the nineteenth century, which are no longer politically correct, but which actually play a far greater role today than at that time, India would leave the community of civilised states. Rammohan Roy had stated this very clearly in 1830: 'We should not omit the present opportunity of offering up thanks to Heaven, whose protecting arm has rescued our weaker sex from cruel murder, under the cloak of religion, and our character, as a people, from the contempt and pity with which it has been regarded, on account of this custom, by all civilized nations on the surface of the globe.'[439] In 1987, after Deorala, two commentators were of the view that 'this particular incident has happened, [. . .] because the government is not willing to enforce the norms and laws of a modern and civilised state,'[440] and in 1988 V.N. Datta, author of one of the most important works on the topic, wanted to regard the custom 'as a sort of barometer of the society's position in the scale of human civilization.'[441]

Faced with this dilemma the state government of Rajasthan and the central government in Delhi were at first silent. However, like the British earlier, they were not able to keep out of the matter completely. On 15 September the Chief Minister of Rajasthan condemned the event, and on 27 September the Indian Prime Minister, Rajiv Gandhi, followed suit. Both expressed themselves in a relatively mild manner.[442] Gandhi at least spoke of a 'national shame'.[443] Both governments continued to avoid taking direct action against the opponents of abolition. In order to prove their good intentions, they took the path of legislation, which was less risky, at least for the moment. In October 1987, a law was passed in Rajasthan which was extended to the entire country at the end of the year. The only object of this law was the prevention

[439] R. Roy, *English Works* 3, 136 (Abstract of the arguments regarding the burning of widows, 1830, final paragraph). Similarly in the address of thanks to Bentinck of 16.1.1830. *Asiatic Journal* NS 2/2 (1830), 138–9.

[440] Qadeer/Hasan 1947.

[441] V.N. Datta XVI. Cf. also Griffiths 225; Mukhopadhyay, *Institution* 99; Thompson, *Suttee* 129–34; K.D. Gaur 205 (1993): 'A cruel society [. . .] that claims to be civilized.'

[442] Jain *et al.* 1893; Upreti 53; 86. For later debates about the role of politicians who approved of the custom see Joseph.

[443] Upreti 53.

of widow burning.[444] Opponents of the custom were not completely unjustified in accusing the governments of trying to cover up their inaction.[445] Yet, laws can develop their inherent dynamics and lead to effects not foreseen by their authors who are then forced into action. Therefore, it becomes necessary to take a look at the law all the same.[446]

That the basic problem had not changed since 1829 can be seen from the preamble which, although much shorter, was taken over almost verbatim from the old law.[447] The same holds true for the essence of the prohibition, which makes participation in such ceremonies a criminal offence, but considerably increases the punishment. If the burning actually takes place, the penalty laid down is death or life imprisonment (Section 4.1). If the attempt at burning is prevented, the penalty is life imprisonment (Section 4.2). In both cases there is no provision for a milder sentence. The legislative organ was not afraid of direct interference in matters of religion—something the British would never have risked: abetment to widow burning also includes 'making a widow or woman believe that the commission of sati would result in some spiritual benefit to her or her deceased husband or relative or the general well being of the family.' (Section 4.2.b) The law also ensures that no one involved in a widow burning can inherit the victim's property (Section 18).

Taking the changed framework into account, the law also prohibits the glorification of widow burning. This refers to those aspects which constitute the political importance of widow burning: acts which help in making the custom the point of departure and the crystallizing point for the mobilization of the masses. This includes ceremonies and

---

[444] *The Rajasthan Sati (Prevention) Act,* 1987 (Act no. 40 of 1987), passed as a decree on 1.10.1987, as a law on 10.11.1987. For India: *The Commission of Sati (Prevention) Act,* 1987 (Act No. 3 of 1988), passed on 16.12.1987, published on 6.1.1988. Both laws, which differ only slightly, are printed, for example, in Narasimhan 168–83. The law for Rajasthan is quoted here from Narasimhan, the Indian law from the edition of Delhi Law House 1990. For the enactment of both laws and their coming into force different dates are mentioned.

[445] For example Agnes 30–1; van den Bosch 179; Kishwar/Vanita; *Anti Sati Bill* 18–21; cf. Tully 232.

[446] The following analysis and the references to sections refer, unless mentioned otherwise, to the federal law. Cf. the treatment of the subject in Dhagamwar, *Saint* 34–9 and Dhagamwar, *Law* 296–302.

[447] The Rajasthan law does not contain this preamble.

processions in the framework of widow burning, as well as their support, justification and propagation. Also included are events to glorify a sati, the establishing of trusts, collecting money and the building of temples or other places of worship, as well as all forms of a Sati-cult (Section 2.1). The penalty for this is between one and seven years along with a heavy fine (Section 5).

The new law also contains two further sections that are not so easy to classify.

1. In case of a charge of abetment, the burden of proof falls on the accused (Section 16). It is doubtful whether this provision, which is highly questionable from the point of view of the rule of law, will contribute to the suppression of the custom.

2. Whereas the threat of punishment in 1829 extended only to the organizers, it now also includes the widow who is sentenced to one year's imprisonment and a fine (Section 3). In this case the provision in the Penal Code for attempted suicide was simply taken over. But in contrast to the Penal Code it referred here expressly to widow burning. The actions of the widow, which had not been taken into consideration in 1829 and had to be indirectly inferred in the Penal Code of 1862, now gained a much greater importance. The clause only makes sense if one assumes that at least in some cases the widow is not the victim, but that she actively seeks her death and is therefore also the perpetrator. If she were always a victim, then it would make no sense to punish her after she has been able to save herself, or has been saved by the police.

Staunch opponents of the custom, who reject the possibility of the voluntary nature of the act, protested against this view. They were only able to have the provision mitigated, but could not establish their principled stand. The law for Rajasthan provided for 1–5 years' imprisonment and heavy fines. Apart from this it placed the burden of proof—a truly perverse provision—on the widow (Rajasthan, Sections 3; 16). The Indian law did away with this. In addition, punishment was no longer obligatory, and it was considerably more lenient (Sections 3; 16).

Even if one does not share the view that there can never be a voluntary widow burning, the modified provision still remained problematic. Its deterring effect would be minimal, and it can, on the other hand, be used by the opponents of abolition who maintain that the burnings are always voluntary.

Both these problematic clauses clearly reveal what is true of the entire law. It is a display piece, meant to prove the good intentions of the state, rather than an instrument for practical use.[448] One can hardly imagine that the legislative was not aware of this. In view of the sympathy that widow burning still enjoys, and in view of the tradition of extremely lenient sentences going back to the period before 1829, life-imprisonment as minimum punishment for all forms of abetment appears to be grossly exaggerated. The idea that such a sentence, or indeed the death-sentence, could actually be implemented, is somewhat preposterous.

This assumption is strengthened by what has happened since then. The main organizers of the burning of Roop Kanwar were arrested a few days later, but were subsequently released.[449] On 13 October 1996 they were acquitted for lack of evidence.[450]

The debates regarding the question of glorification are more diverse and more political. Here the law itself became an object of politics. Some of its clauses favoured this process, and possibly such a function was intended from the beginning. The law contains a number of far-reaching discretionary provisions. The district magistrate *may* have temples and other sati-monuments pulled down, and confiscate all the property of the concerned trusts (Sections 6–8). The law for Rajasthan had excluded existing institutions from this provision (Sections 6–8; 19) and women's organizations had protested against this.[451]

The threat of the law was therefore present. However, it did not need to be realized. Indeed there was a kind of tacit agreement about what the authorities would allow, although they could prohibit it.[452] Compared to pre-1987, considerable restrictions were imposed. At present the construction of temples and the organization of pilgrim festivals, i.e. the organizing of mass events is banned. Holding public events, in which the custom is propagated in any form, is also banned, as is the dissemination of propaganda through words and pictures. Finally, the collection of funds is also prohibited. Existing funds were

[448] Nandy, in Hawley (ed.) 133 speaks of a 'public gesture'.

[449] Cf. Narasimhan 4.

[450] BBC World Service. According to *Newsweek* 2.12.1996, p. 31, the case will be carried on.

[451] Narasimhan 74.

[452] The following statements are based mainly on conversations and observations in the districts of Sikar and Jhunjhunu (Rajasthan) in autumn 1992 and in spring 1995. Cf. also Weinberger-Thomas (1996) 175ff.

placed under government administration and frozen. The continued running of existing temples and pilgrimages outside of large festivals are not considered to be banned. Various controversial points are being dealt with at present by the courts.

But the success or failure of the new ban will finally depend on the general framework and not on these details. Scepticism is in order, although officially there have been no new cases since Deorala. The ban appears to have had an effect despite all its shortcomings, although scepticism is still justified. In March 1995 I heard of two failed attempts at widow burning a short while before in Banda district (Uttar Pradesh). On 26 September 1994 the police prevented an intended burning in Pailani. The widow, who was about twenty years old, was apparently pressurized by her relatives and welcomed the interference of the police. On 21 December 1994 a widow in Kalyanpur, who was twenty years old according to the police, but only sixteen years old according to the villagers, allowed herself to be dissuaded from burning with her husband's body. She died at home, either on the same or on the following day, according to the police of shock or sorrow, and according to the villagers of love. No medical reasons were given for her death. According to the police her body was cremated one day after that of her husband, but at the same spot; according to the villagers both bodies were cremated at the same time. The cremation ground immediately became a place of pilgrimage.

The second case in particular shows the precarious nature of the adherence to the ban, if one wants to speak of adherence at all. The ban continues to be a necessity, since the mental background of the custom still exists. To what extent the potential for burnings is realised would depend chiefly on political factors. If politics, as has happened in the last years, continues to use religion for purposes of mobilisation, then we can be sure that despite the new ban the political potential of the custom will continue to be exploited in the future. It would create an atmosphere favourable to burnings. If, on the other hand, religion and politics are successfully separated again, the prospects for the ban are better. Without such changes the ban alone will never be able to make the custom disappear completely. Widow burning is a subject that India has not yet put behind it forever.

Summary and Conclusion

In *Ancient Egypt* and in the *Ancient Near East* following into death probably did not play a major role, since it is not mentioned in written records. Excavations, on the other hand, indicate that it was not completely unknown. The most significant finds are from Ur in Sumer in southern Mesopotamia, from the period between *c.* 2600 and 2450 BC. In the larger graves, rulers or important persons were found with an entire retinue consisting of dozens of people.

The finds in Egypt are far more numerous but less obvious, and rather unevenly distributed in time and in space between *c.* 2900 BC and the sixth century AD. The tombs, which contain the bodies of up to 500 people, clearly show the hierarchy of the court of a king or some other high dignitary. However, it is not certain if all the dead were buried at the same time, or whether the complex of tombs arose over a long period of time.

In *Europe*, following into death plays a minor role. It cannot be established for Western and Central Europe, including Ancient Greece and Rome. The situation is different for Eastern Europe. It seems that among the Scythians some rulers were followed into the grave by a retinue consisting of several people. Later accounts mention the killing of a concubine among the Rus on the Lower Volga after the death of her lover in the tenth century, and also the killing of servants in the thirteenth century among the Prussians and the Cumans (on the Black Sea). This increases the credibility of more general statements in the sources about the occurrence of the custom among the Slavs and the Lithuanians till the fifteenth century.

In Europe the role of Christianity in the suppression of the custom was modest. Following into death did not exist in the Roman Empire even in the pre-Christian era. It is true that there was never any doubt about the fact that Christian teachings, and especially Christian ideas of the hereafter, could not be reconciled with following into death. But in the Middle Ages this did not immediately lead to a struggle against the custom among non-Christians. Rather, the attitude early on was relatively benevolent. Later, such customs were at least tolerated, and an increasingly determined rejection becomes noticeable only with the Late Middle Ages.

There are relatively few accounts of following into death in *America*. The Natchez of the Lower Mississippi constitute a special case. Among them this custom represented an important element of the social order, in the sense that it not only emphasized and cemented existing boundaries between the social classes, but to some extent even regulated social advancement. Its almost exclusively institutional character was also demonstrated by the fact that the difference between the sexes did not play any role in the custom. Nowhere else has it been established that men had to accompany women into death in the same way that women had to accompany men.

Elsewhere in North America highly placed persons, mostly men, are reported to have been frequently accompanied by one or several of their wives and/or by male and female slaves.

In the larger kingdoms and empires of Central and South America members of the royal household as well as victims provided by subordinate chiefs and vassals are said to have been killed, sometimes in large numbers, on the death of a ruler, and occasionally on the death of another important person.

In *sub-Saharan Africa* following into death seems to have been widely prevalent. Primarily, rulers were followed into death, and in most states, besides them, also other highly placed persons. Thus the custom gained an eminently political character. Its chief function was to demonstrate and strengthen power structures, partly in relation to other states, but mainly within the state. It drastically symbolized the subordination of the subjects under the ruler.

This institutional-political character caused a tendency to expansion by increasing the number of victims. While those who had a more personal relationship with the deceased constituted the core of his retinue in death, anonymous persons were used when a larger number of victims were required: prisoners of war, criminals, slaves bought for this purpose and persons taken seemingly indiscriminately from the crowd.

Following into death was meant to establish as lasting a link as possible between this world and the other. Therefore it was often extended into a lengthy process with repeated killings, chiefly on anniversaries, but also by sending messengers at other points of time. The underlying belief in the hereafter was closely linked with ancestor worship. The custom was used to propitiate the dead, who were believed to have substantial influence over events in this world. Following into death thus had a clear sacrificial character without becoming a mere sacrifice. If the custom was not carried out, the dead could withdraw their support, and this affected the entire community. The subjects therefore also considered the custom to be indispensable, in fact they sometimes insisted more firmly than the rulers that it was carried out, although they had to provide the victims. However, those who were directly affected sometimes resisted when the demand for victims was too high.

The institutional character of the custom also meant that it was not used to differentiate between the sexes, i.e. to subordinate women to men.

In pre-colonial times European attempts to suppress following into death failed on account of its political character. Those who questioned the custom also threatened the community in question. This political character became indirectly evident when the ceremonies disappeared quickly and almost completely after colonial rule had been established. The religious background continued to exist at first, but the public-political framework was no longer available. This was sufficient to eliminate the custom. The result was confirmed by the spread of Islam and Christianity.

Following into death was practised on most groups of islands in *Oceania* before European rule was established. It focussed on the killing of wives and concubines on the death of their husband and also of relatives on the death of a family member. Only women accompanied the dead, and only men were accompanied. No social class seems to have been completely excluded from the custom. In addition to women, sometimes slaves, servants and members of the retinue of both sexes were killed on the death of an important person.

Although self-killing is frequently reported only for New Zealand, free will would have definitely played a role in Oceania, at least in the case of personal attendants. Those who refused were generally allowed to live. There is no evidence of organized resistance.

In *China* two different forms of following into death are found in temporal succession, although they partly overlap.

On the death of rulers, members of the ruling house and high officials, wives, concubines, slaves, servants, members of the court and occasionally also other people, more or less indiscriminately chosen, were killed as a retinue for the other world. This probably happened since the fourth, and to a greater extent since the second millennium BC. The number of victims sometimes ran into hundreds.

Intellectual opposition to following into death becomes tangible earlier than in any other part of the world, since the second millennium BC. From the second century BC onwards it led to the suppression of the custom by the state. Human beings as burial objects were replaced by figures. The fact that this was regarded as necessary shows that the underlying belief in the hereafter still existed, and that the custom could therefore be easily reactivated. The reactivation took the form of individual following into death, especially the self-killing of widows. It was available in principle to all social classes and was fairly widely prevalent in modern times, well into the twentieth century. It required the voluntary decision of the widow, at least formally. In principle the state maintained its rejectionist stance, which was not very popular with its functionaries. In practice it frequently encouraged the custom by bestowing honours and creating an official cult for women who had followed the dead.

The history of the custom in *Japan* at first runs more or less parallel to that in China, with however a certain delay in individual phases. Since the third century AD at the latest the institutional form of following into death for rulers and their families has been recorded. Opposition, which began around the seventh century, led to effective suppression by the state with the help of substitution. As in China the custom was revived later, and simultaneously a change occurred. It was now practised in favour of the high military nobility. On the death of one of its members, part of the military retinue sometimes killed themselves. This custom was successfully suppressed in the seventeenth and eighteenth centuries—although at least the underlying concepts of honour and loyalty, but probably also corresponding forms of a belief in the hereafter, survived well into the twentieth century.

Very little is known about following the dead in *Central Asia*. We can assume that sometimes rulers and important men were given a mainly male retinue in death. The prevalence of such customs is also indicated by the fact that Chinese dynasties that originally came from Central Asia continued to practise them to some extent between the tenth and seventeenth centuries, although they had been suppressed in China long before.

For the larger states on the mainland of *Southeast Asia*, with the exception of Assam, there are no verified proofs of following into death. However, particularly on the islands, two special forms were widely prevalent. Although head-hunting is not a following into death in the strict sense of the term, for the people involved it gained this function in many places in the course of time. The people killed were regarded as servants or slaves in the hereafter. This function becomes indisputable when, on the death of an important person, a head-hunt is carried out in order to procure heads for the deceased and not for the hunter.

In addition, there was a second, also predominantly institutional, form of following the dead, which was sometimes practised along with head-hunting and sometimes instead of it—the killing of slaves on a person's death. It was often extended into a lengthy process with different people being killed at different points of time to follow the same person. The attitude of the victim was irrelevant.

Java and *Bali* mark a sharp contrast to the rest of South East Asia. For both, the killing or self-killing of widows has been recorded. In Bali the custom was only suppressed at the beginning of the twentieth century by the Dutch, while in Java it disappeared probably between the fifteenth and seventeenth centuries under the influence of Islam.

Although it was not forbidden to any caste, both in Java and in Bali following into death is mentioned only in the context of the death of highly placed persons, especially rulers. The circle of attendants was increasingly narrowed in the course of time to wives and concubines. The victim's consent was required. The closer the moment of burning approached, the more difficult it was to revoke the given agreement.

The fact that the custom disappeared in Java at the same time as Hinduism did, and that it survived in Bali together with Hinduism, allows us to suppose that its origins were Indian. This is also supported by the fact that it assumed completely different forms in the surrounding non-Hindu regions.

There is evidence for following into death in *India* since the fourth century BC. Rulers and members of the upper classes, especially warriors, were accompanied in death by their wives, and also by members of the court and of their retinue, the latter sometimes having to commit themselves at the time of entering service.

The transformation of this custom into widow burning occurred very slowly and came to a certain conclusion around AD 1500. Two factors have to be emphasized here.

1. The rivalry between the caste of warriors and rulers on the one hand and the priestly caste on the other. The priestly scholars rejected the custom at first, especially for their own caste, but they did not openly combat it, or at least were unable to eliminate it. In the course of time they accepted widow burning in the legal-religious texts they wrote, and in the end they often recommended or even propagated it, without ever making it obligatory. They gave widow burning a religious substance and opened it to all castes except the Brahmins, thus depriving the warrior caste of their monopoly. The prestige linked with the custom was so great that even the Brahmins slowly took it over, and finally they practised it more than all other castes.

2. When notions emerged that made the position in the hereafter dependent on one's actions in this world, following into death did not disappear as it happened everywhere else. Instead it was adapted to the new conditions by being moralized itself. Burning was now regarded as a meritorious act by the widow, which ensured the reunion of the couple. The widow thus gained a much more prominent position than the husband, both during the ceremony of burning and in the later cult.

The increasing occurrence of widow burning was based on the inequality of the sexes, which entailed the complete subordination of women to men lasting beyond death.

More or less reliable statements about the frequency of the custom are only possible for the years 1815–28. With reference to India as a whole, perhaps one of every thousand widows burnt herself to death. In the regions where widow burning was most prevalent, the ratio in some districts could vary between 1:100 and 1:50.

The widow's decision to burn to death, which as a rule she announced immediately after her husband's death, was generally voluntary, in the sense that, if she refused to die, she could continue to live, even if it was under wretched conditions. On the other hand there was a tendency among the participants to consider the decision, once taken, as irrevocable, and to demand that it be carried out even against the widow's will. The closer the time of burning approached, the more frequently one saw coercion and violence being used.

Widow burning, and following the dead in general, often met with rejection and resistance in India and within Hinduism. There was however never any really successful opposition, which would have led to a remarkable reduction, or even to the disappearance of the custom in a larger region.

It is true that Muslim and European-Christian conquerors abhorred widow burning. Yet they hardly undertook any measures against it till the nineteenth century. On the one hand this was because of their fear of creating unrest, on the other hand it was a result of the fact that the administrative apparatus was too wide-meshed and lacked efficiency. This made control difficult. Islamic rulers at least suppressed the custom in the immediate surroundings of their court. Everywhere else their attempts generally failed.

The British at first tried to ignore the custom. This proved impossible in the long run, given the fact that such a public ceremony shocked Europeans severely. They then tried to regulate the custom by making a distinction—according to Hindu law—between legal and illegal cases. With this the British perspective separated legality and morality, since even the legal cases were immoral and criminal in the eyes of British officials. Particularly among the lower rungs of the civil service, which frequently witnessed widow burnings, this led to moral conflicts and soon also to protest and open insubordination. In addition, a public protest movement arose in Great Britain and in India, and even Indians began to agitate against the custom. In 1829/30 the government was left with no option but unrestricted prohibition, and this was extended to all of India by 1862.

The abolition worked quickly and thoroughly, but not completely. Isolated cases still occurred and continue up to the present. The law had not been able to eliminate either the mental-religious roots of the custom or its social preconditions in the form of the strict subordination of women to men. Widow burning remained a custom that could easily be reactivated. In the last few decades this fact has gained greater significance. Groups that base their politics on religion have discovered the potential of political mobilization in claiming widow burning as a valuable Indian tradition.

Following into death thus occurred in many regions of the world. Only in the case of Central and Western Europe can one say with a sufficient degree of certainty that the custom did not occur in historic times.

At the same time, this widely prevalent phenomenon was a distinctly rare exception wherever it occurred. Very few of the dead were actually followed in death. Serious demographic consequences of the custom are mentioned only in the nineteenth century in Oceania, and even here it was more in the form of apprehension than actual proof. The custom never had the function and much less the purpose of population control.

In the search for causes two *necessary conditions* (not in the logical but in the empirical sense) can be mentioned.

1. Following into death presupposes a relationship lasting beyond death between the persons being accompanied and the persons accompanying them. This indicates a specific *belief in the hereafter* or a *belief in reincarnation,* which proceeds on the assumption that a person's position in this world is carried over into the other world or into the next life. Otherwise the custom cannot be justified and becomes a crime. Since it is carried out as a public ritual, it has to be legitimized by the society concerned. This does not mean that all those who participate in the ceremony, and much less that all members of that society, have to share these views. What is necessary however is that they play an important role in that society. Time and again the sources record statements of those going to their death, who were convinced that they would be reunited with the deceased after their own death.

This condition presupposes a religious element. The custom cannot be reduced to religious and otherworldly aspects, but without these even the most determined interests and motives of this world could not have given rise to it.

There is only one case in which following the dead did not end along with the belief that the other world was merely a reproduction of this world. This was in India, where the custom was adapted to the idea that one's position in the other world was determined by actions in this world. Following into death was declared a meritorious act, which ensured that those separated by death were reunited. With this the basic pattern of the continuation of this life in the other world (or in a new life in this world) was maintained.

2. A general application of the custom leads to a quick extinction of the society practising it. Restrictions are unavoidable. Given its existential significance, it is not surprising that the selection of those

entitled to being followed, as well as of those obliged to follow others into death, is never a matter of pure chance. Someone must have the power or the influence to force others to accompany a dead person. Following into death therefore presupposes a minimum level of *social inequality*. According to the kind of inequality present, two types of following the dead were distinguished. If the circle of those entitled to be accompanied is determined by the class based position in the social hierarchy, in the sense that only highly placed persons are accompanied, then we speak of *institutional following into death*. If the entitlement is a result of status based differentiation, normally on the basis of gender, in the sense that men are followed into death by their wives (the inverse case that men follow women into death is not found anywhere), we speak of *individual following into death*.

Since the number of those entitled to be followed is higher in places where the individual form is practised, the number of cases is normally also higher than in those regions where the institutional form predominates. But the number of attendants per case is generally higher in the latter form, and it has a tendency to expand to new categories of victims.

The second condition thus presupposes inequality. Here the institutional form of the custom is to be seen in connection with the struggles between groups, classes, estates, etc. Therefore it is, if one understands the term broadly enough, an element of class struggle, while individual following into death constitutes an element of gender struggle.

The *interests* and *motives* of those accompanying the dead are only important if free will can be presupposed. Otherwise they are merely objects. The voluntary nature of the act means that the victim would have had a real chance of survival had she decided otherwise. If one accepts this criterion, free will played a considerable role in following into death, although this will was frequently subjected to external pressure. Where a relatively close personal relationship existed between the person being followed and the person following him into death, one would normally have to proceed on the basis of free will. Once the decision to follow the dead was taken, however, it was usually regarded by society as a more or less irrevocable obligation. Its fulfilment was therefore often enforced.

For the people accompanying the dead the motive of a reunion with the dead person was linked with the hope of the maintenance or even an improvement of status in the other world. In addition, the loss of the previous protector led to the fear that one's status in this life would become worse. There was also the expectation of fame and honour before and after death, often linked with notions of honour and their corresponding obligations, and the effects of pressure from relatives and society. Finally, sorrow, grief and despair at the loss of a loved person should not be underestimated.

For the organizers in the broadest sense there was first the belief that the deceased had to be satisfied, so as to prevent his harassment of the living. Along with this, piety for the dead person could play a role, supplemented possibly by the hope of likewise being followed into death later. The relatives of the victim could also gain fame and honour, and sometimes even received material rewards from the ruler. If, in addition, they could gain control over the victim's property while being rid of the responsibility for her upkeep, the material incentives even became stronger. In other cases political rivals could be disposed of in this manner.

The above enumeration of motives is by no means complete. What is common to all is that they cannot be taken as the actual causes of the custom, because they overdetermine a phenomenon they claim to explain. They are present in many cases when someone dies, and despite this following into death is carried out only in a very small number of cases. As an exceptional phenomenon the custom cannot actually be explained on the basis of normal phenomena; it can only be made statistically plausible.

The *functions* of the custom can essentially be traced back to aspects concerning the safeguarding of power. The custom is a product, but at the same time also a factor of certain structures of inequality. It emphasizes, as the case may be, the leading position of a dynasty, a ruling class or of men in general in a symbolic and at the same time very real act. Symbolic insofar as it is not the lower classes as such, or all the women who have to die with the rulers or with men, real insofar as the subordination is again and again sealed with blood in individual cases. To achieve this, mechanisms are important, which partly integrate excluded and subjected persons, without mitigating the basic inequality. This happens in different ways in institutional and individual following into death.

When a dead person, especially a ruler, is believed to have the ability and the will to continue to exercise power and influence over matters of this world, then one of the functions of following into death is to appease him or to try and gain his support. The custom therefore also gains the character of a sacrifice. Since the anger or the displeasure of the deceased affects the entire community everyone has an interest in maintaining the custom, even those who have to provide the victims.

In the institutional form of the custom the focus is generally on the person being followed. In his lifetime he was already a leading figure who is remembered and venerated after his death. The contrast to anonymous, interchangeable victims, whose will and actions are of no importance, is extreme. In the perspective of those who remain behind, even the personal attendants who go to their death voluntarily, are normally clearly subordinated to the person being followed. This is different in individual following into death. The dead man here is frequently an insignificant person, since the ritual is available to members of all classes. Generally this is also true of the persons following the dead, who are normally women. But they can overcome this insignificance through the very act of following into death, and in fact more so, when the voluntary nature of their act is more pronounced. The dead man is at best a prop during the ceremony; sometimes he is even completely absent, especially in China. He is scarcely mentioned and subsequently remembered even less, while the woman who has followed him into death increasingly becomes the object of a cult. No one remembers the people who had to follow a king of Dahomey into the grave. Roop Kanwar, on the other hand, became known around the world overnight in 1987, whereas no one was interested in her husband Maal Singh. But a woman can achieve this importance only if she dies, or kills herself, which in turn again confirms her subordination to men. The concessions concern the dead, not the living; the system is not endangered, but stabilised.

A function that is not linked with the safeguarding of power is only found in places where following into death constitutes an aspect of the relations between different societies, where, in a way, it has an international character. This applies to head-hunting and to wars conducted for the procurement of victims.

The *origins* of following the dead cannot be historically determined anywhere. Where it appears in written sources, it is always found in a fully developed form. The archaeological finds lead us into a more distant past, but they do not provide any answers to questions regarding the genesis of the custom.

This fact seems to suggest that the custom was always present and is therefore a kind of structural characteristic of many human societies, which has to be explained anthropologically rather than historically.

This is a mistaken assumption as is demonstrated by the necessary conditions. Neither the specific belief in the hereafter nor the inequality based on a certain social differentiation can be presupposed for all societies at all times. Nor is the custom a given stage of development that all societies have to go through. Rather it arises out of very specific situations.

1. Most frequently, the beginnings appear to be characterized by efforts to concentrate political power in the hands of an individual, a dynasty or a group. Assuming the corresponding belief in the hereafter as given, institutional following into death offers itself as a means to enforce and demonstrate the subjugation of the ruled by the rulers. This process can be presumed for India, China and Japan and probably also in many regions of Africa and perhaps of South and Central America.

2. It appears justified to assume that in all societies persons of both sexes killed themselves out of sorrow, grief or despair on the death of a relative, a spouse or another intimate person. In the course of an increasing differentiation between the sexes, especially in the process of the subordination of women to men, this more or less private event can be taken over by society and sanctioned with the help of rituals and by making it a public event—but only on the death of men, and with women as victims. With this individual following into death is constituted. In Oceania and in some regions of North America this was presumably the situation at the beginning.

3. Head-hunting is an exception. The outer event probably arose before the idea of following the dead became associated with it. One would therefore have to speak of a subsequent reinterpretation, which probably also served as a justification.

The fact that following into death is not a fixed phase or a stage in the general pattern of development of human societies can be seen more clearly in the transformation of one type into another. In the final analysis the custom is always also the result of power struggles, which on the surface are concerned with the right to be followed in death and with the obligation to follow the dead, while in a broader sense they have to do with the social and political distribution of power. If this changes, it is also reflected in the custom.

Viewed from the outside the custom is murderous or at least suicidal. It is therefore not surprising that in the course of history it repeatedly encountered *criticism, rejection and resistance.* Here we have to distinguish between opposition immanent to the system and opposition that breaks open the system, depending on how it is related to the two necessary conditions of the custom.

1. Following into death is based on structures of inequality, which for their part are consequences of power struggles. The weaker sections of the population, i.e. those obliged to follow the dead, always try—individually or collectively—to improve their position. The most common form is escape. Organized resistance on the other hand is rare, and it is even more rare for it to be successful. It is found in the context of institutional rather than of individual following into death. In the former the number of victims per case, as well as the extent of coercion and violence, is generally greater. This encourages solidarity among the victims. In individual following into death, on the other hand, a certain freedom of choice is guaranteed, so that the most determined among the possible victims can escape their fate by refusing to die. Solidarity among the victims is difficult because of their extreme isolation and the social differences between them. There is little common ground between a casteless widow and the widow of a rich Brahmin.

2. Opposition against the custom as such begins with its most important precondition, the belief in the hereafter. One can distinguish between a religious and a rational critique, depending on whether the specific belief in the hereafter, which makes the custom possible, is to be replaced by another kind of belief that excludes the custom, or whether any kind of belief in the hereafter is disputed. A further distinction also has to be made between opposition from within the concerned society and that from outside.

Internal criticism, and one that is successful, can be established only relatively seldom. At the same time it has always proved more difficult to suppress the individual form of following into death, which penetrates down to the lower classes, than the institutional form, which is limited to a small upper class, concentrated on a few spectacular cases and based much more on force.

An effective suppression of all forms of following the dead generally occurred only when a new religion, coming from outside, which excluded such customs on the basis of its own notions of the hereafter, established itself in the concerned society. To what extent this happened with the spread of certain Asian religions, especially Buddhism, remains unanswered. Islam and Christianity became decisive in this process. Both advocated beliefs in the hereafter that could not be reconciled with following into death, and they also rejected the custom with increasing determination. Wherever they prevailed, it disappeared. But this was not always a gradual suppression in the process of the conversion of the indigenous population. Often prohibitions were more or less established long before conversion, after an Islamic or a Christian power had conquered a region. This was especially true for the European expansion overseas since the sixteenth century. From the late eighteenth century onwards a shift became evident. Measures against the custom were intensified without the colonial power having simultaneously increased missionary activities. By the twentieth century this had led to the worldwide disappearance of the custom, even in regions that had only partly or not at all become Christian. This was linked to the spread of rationalism since the Enlightenment. Here the focus was not so much negatively on the denial of a belief in the hereafter, as positively on the argument of equality derived from natural law and human rights. If an unrestricted exercise of free choice is not possible, then following into death contradicts an assumed right to life. In addition, individual human life had an extremely unequal value in the framework of the custom. This contradicted the increasing demands for equality. Moreover, in the European view participation in a ritual killing was always a crime, independent of the victim's will.

There was another reason for the fact that in the nineteenth and twentieth centuries Europeans tried to eliminate following into death without first spreading their religion. By now their rule had been established and strengthened. In the long run one could not expect a modern bureaucratic administration run by Europeans to administratively control a custom that flew in the face of their own moral views without provoking insubordination and resistance on the part of the civil service. European rule and following the dead increasingly became mutually exclusive.

It is true that success in suppressing the custom presupposed European rule, especially in regions where the custom played an important political role, as for example in West Africa. In the long run however it was not based simply on force, but also on changes in the views of people. This became evident after the end of colonial rule, when there were no serious attempts at restoration. European views were by no means the only determining factor, but they had gained a dominant position. Especially in international discourse, they had established themselves totally. This placed ruling groups in the individual countries under growing pressure to abide by them. Despite all multicultural declarations there is no doubt about the fact that if today a country would regularly tolerate, allow or even favour following into death, it would lose its standing as a respected member of the international community. The suppression of such customs has become an unspoken, but nevertheless compelling 'standard of civilization'.

The worldwide suppression of following into death by Europeans was thus no longer based on the spread of a religion with a universal claim, but on their success in establishing a universal claim based on human rights, which placed itself above all religions and became a standard for measuring them.

The fact that movements which favour following into death have not completely disappeared can be seen in India, where numerous bans have not been able to abolish widow burning even now. The adaptation of the custom to more elaborate beliefs in the hereafter anchored it deeply in the religious views of large sections of the population. This enables a reactivation, especially when there is an attempt to exploit religious feelings for political gains. Elsewhere, however, there seem to be practically no attempts at present to reactivate following into death, even though it cannot be ruled out completely in view of the fact that new religious movements and sects are emerging in quick succession.

Appendix
Tables, Maps and Illustrations

Table 1: India: Area and Population in 1820

	Area sq.km.	%	Population	%
I. British India				
1. Bengal Presidency	849,000	26.9	57,500.000	43.9
2. Madras Presidency	399,000	12.7	15,000,000	11.5
3. Bombay Presidency	184,000	5.8	10,500,000	8.0
British India (total)	1,432,000	45.4	83,000,000	63.4
II. Princely States	1,424,000	45.2	40,000,000	30.5
III. Independent States	295,000	9.4	8,000,000	6.1
All India	3,151,000	100.0	131,000,000	100.0

Calculated on the basis of D. Bhattacharya (1820–1830) 4–5. Unlike in Bhattacharya, Nepal and Kabul have not been counted among the independent states, because, in contrast to the other independent states existing in 1820, they did not come either directly or indirectly under British rule later.

Table 2: Widow burnings registered by the British administration in the Bengal Presidency, 1815–1828

Division	1815	1816	1817	1818	1819	1820	1821	1822	1823	1824	1825	1826	1827	1828	Total	%
Calcutta	253	289	442	544	421	370	392	328	340	373	398	324	337	308	5119	62.9
Dacca	31	24	52	58	55	51	52	45	40	40	101	65	49	47	710	8.7
Murshidabad	11	22	42	30	25	21	12	22	13	14	21	8	9	10	260	3.2
Patna	20	29	49	57	40	42	69	70	49	42	47	65	55	55	689	8.5
Benares	48	65	103	137	92	103	114	102	121	93	55	48	49	33	1153	14.2
Bareilly	15	13	19	13	17	20	15	16	12	10	17	8	18	10	203	2.5
Bengal Presidency	378	442	707	839	650	597	654	583	575	572	639	518	517	463	8134	100.0

Source: IOR L/L/13, vol. 3, folio 309r (App. p. 171).

Table 3: Widow burnings registered by the British administration in the districts of the Bengal Presidency, 1815–1828

District	1815	1816	1817	1818	1819	1820	1821	1822	1823	1824	1825	1826	1827	1828	Total	Average per year	Population (estimated: 1822)	Ratio persons to one burning per year
Agra		1	2	1	1	1	1				1	1	1	1	11	0.8		
Aligarh		1	2	2					1	1	2	1	2		12	0.9		
Allahabad	3	2	5	3	4	4	4			5	2	3	1	2	38	2.7		
Azamgarh			9	2	5				1	8	3	5	2	3	38	2.7		
Bakarganj	1	5	9	1	6	3	3	18	11	23	63	45	29	32	249	17.8	686,640	38,575
Balasore						2	1	1	1				1	2	8	0.6		
Balundashahur						1			1						2	0.1		
Banda							5								5	0.4		
Barasut									1	4	20	8	13	11	57	4.1		
Bareilly	2	1						2	1	1					7	0.5		
Baugundi								2							2	0.1		
Benares	13	12	16	15	18	11	12	11	18	16	17	15	15	11	200	14.3		
Bhagalpur	3		2					1	1				1		8	0.6	797,790	1,329,650
Bhetora										1		1			2	0.1		
Bhitowra									4		2				6	0.4		
Bihar				2	4	1	2	4	4	1	1	3	3	2	27	1.9		
Bilah														1	1	0.1		
Birbhum	1	3	5	4	5	5	3	3	6	3	9	4	6	6	67	4.8	1,267,065	263,972
Bundelkhand	7	4	5	11	5	4	3	3	4	7	1	2	5	2	63	4.5		
Burdwan	50	67	97	132	75	57	62	40	45	56	63	45	60	68	917	65.5	1,187,580	18,131

Contd.

Tables

District	1815	1816	1817	1818	1819	1820	1821	1822	1823	1824	1825	1826	1827	1828	Total	Average per year	Population (estimated: 1822)	Ratio persons to one burning per year
Chitagong	5	5	6	3	7	3	4	1		2	9	1		3	49	3.5	700,800	200,229
Chota Nagpur							1	2							3	0.2		
Cuttack	8	9	14	11	13	17	18	14	19	11	14	10	12	16	186	13.3	1,984,620	149,220
Dacca City	4	6	18	25	16	18	26	9	14	7	18	12	7	5	185	13.2	512,385	38,817
Dacca Jalalpur	1	1	5	5	6	8	7	7	2	2	2	3	1	1	51	3.6	588,375	163,438
Dinajpur	1	4	6					1							12	0.9	2,341,420	2,601,578
Etawah	3		3	3	2	3	4	2	1		5	1	7	2	36	2.6		
Farukhabad	1		1				1	2				1	1	1	8	0.6		
Fatehpur			1	1		1						1			4	0.3		
Ghazipur	8	15	27	43	26	34	35	47	55	33	21	19	14	7	384	27.4		
Gorakhpur	14	23	24	50	23	32	44	28	32	17	9	22	14	16	348	24.9		
Hooghly	72	51	112	141	115	93	95	79	81	91	104	98	111	81	1324	94.6	1,239,150	13,099
Jaunpur	1	3	2	3	1	4	2	4	4	1			2	3	30	2.1		
Jessore	7	13	21	23	16	25	31	21	14	30	16	3			220	15.7	1,183,950	75,411
Jungle Mehals	34	39	43	62	31	18	39	24	27	16	9	11	7	10	370	26.4	1,304,740	49,422
Kalpi		2	9	4											15	1.1		
Kanpur	5	4	3	5	3	6	5	4	4	5	6	2	6	4	62	4.4		
Khurdah/Puri					20	14	9	13	11	14	16	35	20	3	155	11.1		
Maldah			1	1	1	2		2	1	1	1	1			11	0.8		
Mangalour									1						1	0.1		
Meerut									1						1	0.1		
Midnapur	4	11	7	22	13	12	6	16	15	22	22	14	15	15	194	13.9	1,914,060	137,702

Contd.

District	1815	1816	1817	1818	1819	1820	1821	1822	1823	1824	1825	1826	1827	1828	Total	Average per year	Population (estimated: 1822)	Ratio persons to one burning per year
Mirzapur	2	4	5	5	8	3	9	8	3	6	9	3	10	6	81	5.8		
Monghyr			1						1						2	0.1		
Moradabad	3			1	3	1	1								9	0.6		
Murshidabad	3	7	7	6	6	3		5	2	8	6	4	1	2	60	4.3	762,690	177,370
Mymensingh															3	0.2	1,454,670	7,273,350
Nadia	50	56	85	80	47	59	59	50	59	73	60	44	44	60	826	59.0	1,187,160	20,121
Noakhali								3	3			1	2		9	0.6		
Nugwan															4	0.3		
Patna	2	3	5	3	2	5	5	1	1		2	4	1		34	2.4	255,705	106,544
Purnea	2	2	4	1	2	2				1					14	1.0	1,362,165	1,362,165
Puttegurh (Tullohpur)					2										2	0.1		
Rajshahi			1	2	1						2				6	0.4		
Ramgarh	2		2	4	5	4	6	14	5	10		3	10	3	68	4.9	2,252,985	459,793
Rangpur	1	5	11	16	13	8	9	10	2	1	1		1	2	80	5.7	1,340,350	235,149
Saharanpur		7	7	1	6	6	2	2	2	1	1	3	1		39	2.8		
Saran	12	16	25	23	10	11	15	12	7	12	15	10	11	11	190	13.6	1,464,075	107,653
Shahabad	4	9	14	25	18	19	39	36	30	18	20	22	15	22	291	20.8	908,850	43,695
Shahjahanpur						2		3	1	1	1	1	1	1	11	0.8		
Suburbs	25	40	39	43	51	47	39	43	46	34	48	35	35	24	549	39.2	360,360	9,193
Calcutta																		
Sylhet				1		1	1	1	1						5	0.4	1,083,720	2,709,300

Contd.

District	1815	1816	1817	1818	1819	1820	1821	1822	1823	1824	1825	1826	1827	1828	Total	Average per year	Population (estimated: 1822)	Ratio persons to one burning per year
Tipperah (Tripura)	20	7	13	22	21	17	11	6	9	6	8	4	7	9	160	11.4	1,372,260	120,374
Tirhut		3		1	1	2	1	1	3	1		1	1		15	1.1		
24 Parganas	2	3	20	31	39	26	33	25	21	22	26	20	21	16	305	21.8	599,595	27,504
Total	376	442	703	840	650	597	654	582	575	572	639	518	520	464	8132			

Sources: 1815 PP1821/18, 67–81; 1816 ibid., 82–98; 1817 ibid., 148–75; 1818 ibid., 184–211; 1819 PP 1823/17, 7–26; 1820 ibid., 32–54; 1821 PP 1824/23, 6–32; 1822 PP 1825/24, 28–74; 1823 ibid., 86–138; 1824 PP 1826–1827/20, 61–123; 1825 PP 1830/28, 34–111; 1826 ibid., 143–206; 1827 IOR P/139/34, 3–170; 1828 ibid., 260–442.

Population figures: D. Bhattacharya (1820–1830) 16

The total figure in this table and in Table 6 is 8132, whereas the better known Table 2 proceeds from 8134 cases. In addition there are small differences in the total yearly figures. This is because the figures in the detailed accounts in the above-named sources were sometimes silently corrected in the annual compilations on the basis of new information. An exact localization of differences is therefore not possible. In any case, they are statistically irrelevant.

During the period of survey the division of districts sometimes changed. All districts mentioned in the sources have been included.

Table 4: Population of the divisions of the Bengal Presidency, 1822

Division	Population
Calcutta	10,960,855
Dacca	6,398,850
Murshidabad	11,958,635
Patna	7,919,925

Source: D. Bhattacharya (1820–1830) 71. For the divisions of Bareilly and Benares comparable estimates are not available.

Table 5: Widow burnings in the Madras Presidency, 1814–1819

District	1814–1816	1817–1819	1814–1819
Ganjam	45	37	82
Vizagapatam	6	17	23
Rajahmundry	3 (?)	9	12
Masulipatam	1 (?)	43	44
Guntoor	No information	14	14
Nellore	1 (?)	12	13
Bellary	–	–	-
Cuddapah	1	6 (4 prevented)	7
Chingleput	–	4	4
Chittoor	3	13	16
Trichnipoly	–	2	2
Combaconum	20	22	42
Verdachellum	–	–	–
Salem	–	–	–
Coimbatore	–	–	–
Madura	–	–	–
Tinnevelly	–	–	–
North & South Malabar	–	–	–
Canara	–	4	4
Seringapatam	–	–	–
Tanjore	No information	No information	No information
Total	80	183	243

(?) In these cases the district officials considered the information to be incomplete.
Sources: PP 1823/17, 70–132; PP 1825/24,5.

Table 6: Age of the satis in the Bengal Presidency, 1815–1828

Age / Year	<10		11-15		16-20		21-30		31-40		41-50		51-60	
	Number	%	Number	%	Number	%	Number	%	Number	%	Number	%	Number	%
1815	0	0.0	1	0.3	21	5.6	66	17.6	64	17.0	67	17.8	75	19.9
1816	1	0.2	5	1.1	26	5.9	52	11.8	70	15.8	92	20.8	90	20.4
1817	2	0.3	2	0.3	53	7.5	121	17.2	113	16.1	142	20.2	117	16.6
1818	0	0.0	10	1.2	58	6.9	144	17.1	166	19.8	167	19.9	137	16.3
1819	2	0.3	3	0.5	51	7.8	96	14.8	111	17.1	138	21.2	115	17.7
1820	1	0.2	4	0.7	43	7.2	111	18.6	108	18.1	124	20.8	94	15.7
1821	2	0.3	11	1.7	43	6.6	112	17.1	116	17.7	119	18.8	107	16.4
1822	1	0.2	10	1.7	42	7.2	113	19.4	104	17.9	111	19.1	90	15.5
1823	1	0.2	8	1.4	48	8.3	107	18.6	84	14.6	111	19.3	109	19.0
1824	2	0.3	6	1.0	33	5.8	95	16.6	106	18.5	122	21.3	111	19.4
1825	0	0.0	6	0.9	29	4.5	116	18.2	140	21.9	125	19.6	125	19.6
1826	3	0.6	5	1.0	34	6.6	115	22.2	82	15.8	99	19.1	80	15.4
1827	0	0.0	3	0.6	25	4.8	78	15.0	109	21.0	108	20.8	92	17.7
1828	0	0.0	2	0.4	31	6.7	80	17.2	95	20.5	88	19.0	80	17.2
Total	15	0.2	76	0.9	537	6.6	1406	17.3	1468	18.1	1613	19.8	1422	17.5

Contd.

Age Year	61–70		71–80		81–90		91–100		>100		Age not mentioned		Total
	Number	%	Number	%	Number	%	Number	%	Number	%	Number	%	Number
1815	35	9.3	24	6.4	6	1.6	1	0.3	0	0.0	16	4.3	376
1816	51	11.5	34	7.7	8	1.8	1	0.2	0	0.0	12	2.7	442
1817	87	12.4	42	6.0	12	1.7	4	0.6	1	0.1	7	1.0	703
1818	79	9.4	59	7.0	11	1.3	3	0.4	0	0.0	6	0.7	840
1819	81	12.5	40	6.2	8	1.2	0	0.0	0	0.0	5	0.8	650
1820	63	10.6	41	6.9	2	0.3	3	0.5	0	0.0	3	0.5	597
1821	74	11.3	48	7.3	14	2.1	1	0.2	0	0.0	7	1.1	654
1822	59	10.1	41	7.0	8	1.4	2	0.3	0	0.0	1	0.2	582
1823	61	10.6	39	6.8	5	0.9	1	0.2	0	0.0	1	0.2	575
1824	48	8.4	39	6.8	8	1.4	1	0.2	0	0.0	1	0.2	572
1825	52	8.1	38	5.9	6	0.9	1	0.2	1	0.2	0	0.0	639
1826	46	8.9	47	9.1	4	0.8	3	0.6	0	0.0	0	0.0	518
1827	63	12.1	34	6.5	7	1.3	1	0.2	0	0.0	0	0.0	520
1828	51	11.0	27	5.8	6	1.3	4	0.9	0	0.0	0	0.0	464
Total	850	10.5	533	6.8	105	1.3	26	0.3	2	0.0	59	0.7	8132

Sources: See Table 3.

Table 7: Number of children of satis in selected districts and years

District	Year	Sons	Daughters	Children Sex not known	Number of cases
Barasut	1825	27	21		20
Barasut	1826	8	12		8
Barasut	1827	10	11		13
Barasut	1828	14	10		11
Burdwan	1815	57	47	2	50
Burdwan	1816	58	30	7	67
Burdwan	1826	47	54	5	45
Burdwan	1827	74	63	9	60
Burdwan	1828	76	85		68
Hugli	1822	106	41	9	79
Hooghly	1823	125	85		81
Hooghly	1824	123	112	9	91
Hooghly	1825	136	114	6	104
Hooghly	1826	124	126		98
Hooghly	1827	144	121		111
Hooghly	1828	102	97		81
Jessore	1823	16	12		14
Jessore	1824	42	33		30
Jessore	1825	16	15		16
Midnapur	1822	9	5		16
Midnapur	1823	14	3		15
Midnapur	1824	18	12	12	22
Midnapur	1826	24	8		14
Midnapur	1827	18	8		15
Midnapur	1828	16	6		15
24 Parganas	1819	53	55		39
24 Parganas	1820	22	14		26
24 Parganas	1821	46	44		33
24 Parganas	1822	37	24		25
24 Parganas	1823	32	29		21
24 Parganas	1824	17	21		22
24 Parganas	1825	25	22	2	26
24 Parganas	1826	24	9	2	20
24 Parganas	1827	22	15		21
24 Parganas	1828	24	16		16
Suburbs Calcutta	1815	28	21		25
Suburbs Calcutta	1816	60	51		40

Contd.

Table 7 (*contd.*)

District	Year	Sons	Daughters	Children Sex not known	Number of cases
Suburbs Calcutta	1817	42	46		39
Suburbs Calcutta	1818	56	45		43
Suburbs Calcutta	1819	60	50		51
Suburbs Calcutta	1820	76	53		47
Suburbs Calcutta	1821	41	56		39
Suburbs Calcutta	1822	53	54		43
Suburbs Calcutta	1823	71	44		46
Suburbs Calcutta	1824	31	35		34
Suburbs Calcutta	1825	45	42		48
Suburbs Calcutta	1826	40	32		35
Suburbs Calcutta	1827	60	29		35
Suburbs Calcutta	1828	22	26		24
Total		2391	1964	63	1942

Total number of children: 4418
Number of children per sati: 2.27
Number of sons per sati: 1.23
Number of daughters per sati: 1.01
Number of daughters to one son: 0.82
Number of sons to one daughter: 1.22

Sources: see Table 3.

Table 8: Widow burnings in the districts of Bengal included
in the survey conducted at the end of 1818

District	1815	1816	1817	1818	1815–1818
Bakarganj	1	5	9	1	16
Bihar	–	–	–	2	2
Birbhum	1	3	9	4	17
Burdwan	50	67	97	132	346
Chittagong	5	5	6	3	10
Dacca City	4	6	18	25	53
Hooghly	72	51	112	141	376
Jessore	7	13	21	23	64
24 Parganas	2	3	20	31	56
Patna	2	3	5	3	13
Sylhet	–	–	–	1	1

Sources: see Table 3.

Map 1 Frequency of widow burning in Bengal Presidency, 1815 - 28

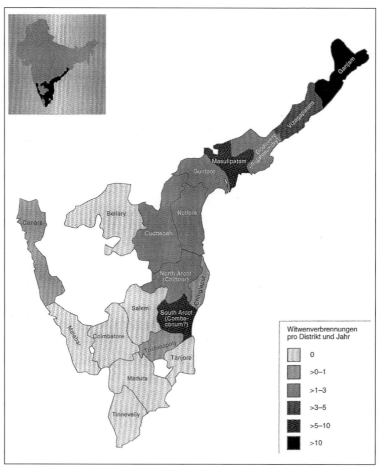

Map 2 Frequency of widow burning in Madras Presidency, 1814 - 19

1. A widow being almost burned to death among the Talkotin Indians in North America. *Source*: Yarrow 145.

2. Funeral of Chief Serpent Piqué and strangling of eight attendants in death among the Natchez Indians in North America. Detail. *Source*: Le Page du Pratz 3, 55.

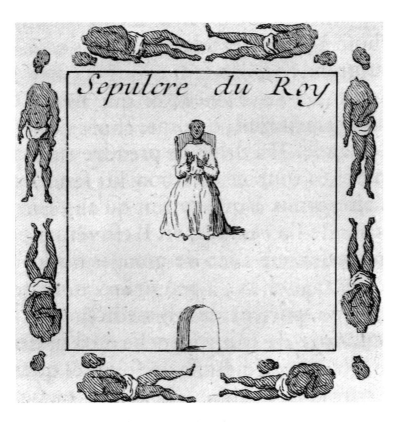

3. Grave of the King of Juda (Whydah, Dahomey).
Source: Des Marchais 2, 94.

4. Human sacrifice in Dahomey. *Source:* F. E. Forbes 2, 44 and 2, 52.

5. Human sacrifice in Dahomey. *Source*: F. E. Forbes 2, 44 and 2, 52.

6. Honorary gate for a chaste widow in China. *Source*: De Groot 2, 746.

7. Widow burning in Bali. *Source*: Helms 61.

8. Memorial stone for a man with two satis in Capka, Gujarat, India.
Source: Settar/Sontheimer.

9. Sati memorial stones in Saurashtra, India. *Source*: Settar/Sontheimer.

10. Memorial stone for three satis in Kandar, Maharashtra, India.
Source: Settar/Sontheimer.

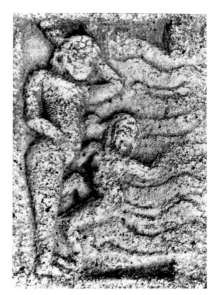

11. Detail of a sati memorial stone in Kumbharvalan, Maharashtra, India.
Source: Settar/Sontheimer.

12. Widow burning. Painting by an Indian artist for a British official, Tanjore, around 1800. *Source:* Victoria & Albert Museum, London, AL.8805. Reproduced by kind permission of the museum.

14. Widow burning. Painting by an Indian artist, Tanjore, around 1800.
Source: British Library, Oriental and India Office Collections, Add.Or. 2533.
Reproduced by kind permission of the British Library.

16. Widow burning. Sketch by the British captain Thomas Bowrey, between 1669 and 1679. *Source:* Bowrey 86.

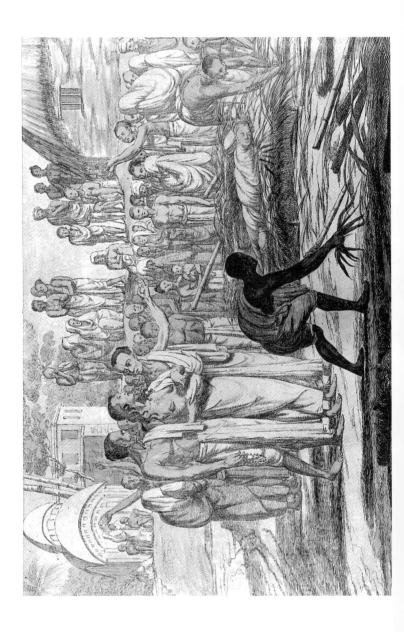

18. Widow burning II (1799). *Source:* Ibid., section 12, no. 14.

20. A widow is buried alive (1799). *Source:* Ibid., section 12, no. 16.

22. A fresco in the sati temple of Maonda Kalan. Photographed by the author.

24. A sculpture in the sati temple in Govindpura. Photographed by the author.

25. Sculptures at a memorial site for a sati in Pangara, Banda district, Uttar Pradesh, India. Photographed by the author.

26. Sculptures at a memorial site for a sati in Pangara. Photographed by the author.

Sources and Literature

Since in older works the information on sources is generally not very precise, and since interpretations in the context of following into death are often uncritical, the present study on principle goes back to the original sources and, as a rule, does not consider passages quoted in the literature unless they could be found in the original source.

1. Following into Death in General

Following into death as a universally prevalent phenomenon has never been an object of serious research. Its universality is usually merely emphasised, and a list of examples is given. The broadest and most useful overview is the article *Human Sacrifice* by A.E. CRAWLEY *et al.* (1913). In WAITZ/GERLAND and in WISSE relevant information is scattered throughout the works. More concise surveys can be found, for example, in SPENCER 1, 186–9, TYLOR 1, 458–67, and DURKHEIM 233ff. In the most recent works on Indian widow burning the universal aspects are almost totally absent.

2. Following into Death Outside India

Older compilations, especially the works of WISSE and WAITZ/GERLAND, are particularly useful for locating the widely scattered source material which could only be studied to a limited extent here.

a) Egypt and the Ancient Near East

GREEN (1975) offers the best modern overview. Important supplementary material can be found in GADD. For Egypt the most detailed accounts are given by REISNER, for Mesopotamia by WOOLLEY.

b) Europe

The older archaeological material has been studied and evaluated most thoroughly by MARINGER. The author has the tendency to infer too quickly on following into death. EBERT presents the results of many excavations in different publications. For Greece there is the thorough work of HUGHES (1991); a corresponding study for Rome is unfortunately lacking—SCHWENN is not really a substitute. The works of ROLLE are useful as an introduction to the Scythians. For the European Middle Ages there is no comprehensive study.

c) America

The sources for following into death in America are located to a large extent in European travel accounts and historical works. They have never been systematically collected. Useful compilations are available mainly in BANCROFT and in the *Handbook of South American Indians.* The custom has never been comprehensively studied. While there is a complete lack of relevant studies for Latin America, for the North the works of MACLEOD as well as the study by YARROW are an important beginning, even though these authors do not focus on the custom.

d) Africa

The wealth of material on following into death in Africa has never been systematically collected. At any rate some useful, although uncritical older compilations exist, as for example in IRSTAM 34–6; 153–5 and in SCHNEIDER, Religion 118–23; 133–5; 143–67. The Islamic sources can be found in LEVTZION/HOPKINS.

Following into death has figured somewhat more prominently in more recent research on African history, and led to controversies. The best overview is in LAW, *Human sacrifice.* The works of COQUERY-VIDROVITCH and CAMPION-VINCENT are relevant in the special context of Dahomey; for Asante cf. along with the studies of RATTRAY (1989) and MCCASKIE (1995) the controversy about the function of following into death between CLIFFORD WILLIAMS (1988) and WILKS (1988 and 1989).

e) Oceania

The material for Oceania has not been collated, and there are no scientific studies. Therefore one has to fall back on the compilations of WISSE and WAITZ/GERLAND as well as on monographs on individual islands and groups of islands. Only SCHOCH mentions a larger body of relevant material. The work by WILLIAMS/CALVERT contains many references to contemporary accounts

f) China

The sources on China have neither been collected nor dealt with comprehensively. It is particularly difficult to record them, since archaeology and the opening up of regional and local sources constantly come up with new material. The most important classification and evaluation of the relevant material to date is found in DE GROOT 2, 721–827. BRINKER/GOEPPER and CHANG provide a good overview of the archaeological evidence. ELVIN has evaluated written sources of the modern period.

g) Japan

At least western academic research appears to have hardly taken note of following into death in Japan. Consequently the sources have not been collected. Brief overviews are available in BITŌ (1983) and in the article *Junshi* of the *Dictionnaire historique du Japon* (1984). PINGUET discusses relevant questions in a broader framework. Contemporary European voices have been recorded by KAPITZA.

h) Central Asia

On following into death in Central Asia there are neither comprehensive collections of source materials nor significant scientific studies.

i) Southeast Asia

Sources on the history of the custom in Southeast Asia are first and foremost old travel accounts and ethnological studies of the nineteenth and twentieth centuries. They have hardly been evaluated with regard to the present theme. On the other hand, head-hunting, which to a large extent overlaps with following into death, has been studied intensively for a long time. However, in more recent times it is rare to find comparative treatments or fundamental theoretical reflections of the theme. Among the older literature HEINE-GELDERN gives the best and the broadest overview. For modern studies cf. for example HÖLL-MANN; BOELAARS; SCHUSTER; ROSALDO; WAGNER, Chap.5; MCKINLEY; JENSEN, Mythos 191–5. There is no work that deals comprehensively with all of Southeast Asia. The unpublished dissertation by SCHUSTER (1956) has the broadest scope, and it deals with a relatively large number of sources, but the critique of sources is mostly lacking. Much relevant material from different regions of Southeast Asia can also be found in WILKEN, Animisme 90–101. The most accurate studies on individual regions have been produced by SCHÄRER.

j) Java and Bali

Like Indian widow burning, Balinese widow burning has also been relatively well researched. VAN DER KRAAN gives a very useful compilation of important sources. His article is also significant for questions of interpretation. In addition, there is now WEINBERGER-THOMAS (1996), 13–25. More general aspects are covered in BOON and GEERTZ.

3. *Widow Burning in India*

There are many more sources available for widow burning in India, and much more has been written about it than about any other form of following into death. However, only a part of the sources has been compiled in an easily accessible form. There is no collection of inscriptions and memorial stones related to the custom. The book by SETTAR/SONTHEIMER contains the largest amount of relevant information. Accounts of burnings, as well as literary and legal sources have to be gleaned from a large, scattered mass of material. Administrative records are more easily accessible, although only for the British period, while hardly anything from earlier periods has been preserved. The most important records are the *Parliamentary Papers* which were published for the British House of Commons between 1821 and 1830. These papers enable researchers to compute statistics, and they also provide an insight into the many forms of the custom as well as into the administrative dealings of the British. With particular reference to questions of their use cf. the article by DALMIA-LÜDERITZ (1990). The Parliamentary Papers are only a small part of a much larger range of material in British and South Asian archives. Of the utmost importance for a study that focuses on the entire country, especially on the events at the top, are the collections of the *India Office Records* (IOR) and the *India Office Library* (IOL), both now under the name *Oriental and India Office Collections* part of the *British Library* in London. The archives in South Asia, which were not used for this study, are, on the other hand, more important for regional and local studies. Particularly for Bengal they have been evaluated by B.B. ROY, while some other authors have used them for studies on the suppression of widow burning in the princely states, for example SAXENA (1975).

On the whole, archives in Europe and Asia still contain a large amount of material which has not been evaluated as yet. The use of these sources is particularly difficult, since the relevant documents have hardly been compiled by the administration.

J.K. MAJUMDAR has produced an important source publication with regard to Rammohan Roy and the abolition of 1829. While this work deals with the Indian side, the published correspondence of Governor General BENTINCK is essential for the British perspective.

A useful reference work is the bibliography by SAKALA (1980).

Research on the topic begins in a certain sense in the early nineteenth century in connection with the struggle for the abolition of widow burning. Even if the material available was limited and most of the publications had a political or an agitational purpose, yet sources were evaluated comprehensively for the first time, not least the *Parliamentary Papers*. There is for example the first work devoted almost exclusively to widow burning, by WILLIAM JOHNS in 1816: *A Collection of facts and opinions relative to the burning of widows*. In the 1820s further important pamphlets based on a large amount of material were published, especially by JAMES PEGGS and JOHN POYNDER. From 1818 till the abolition of the custom, *The Friend of India*, published by the Baptist missionaries, became a platform for publications about widow burning. References to more specific publications of this time are given in chapter 14.

Academic interest in the topic initially faded away after the abolition of 1829. There was only an extensive retrospective in 1868 (*Papers*). This changed gradually in the course of the twentieth century. A provocative essay, published in 1913 by ANANDA K. COOMARASWAMY in a distinguished journal, triggered off the debate. The author defended widow burning as an important element of Indian tradition. In 1928 EDWARD THOMPSON published the first scientific monograph, although on the basis of a rather limited amount of sources. In some respects, V.N. DATTA'S comprehensive book of 1988 is in the tradition of Thompson. Datta's work focuses mainly on the history of the abolition of 1829. B.B.ROY's work of 1987 is narrower in its scope, but more precise; it has a strong tendency to quantification and is restricted to Bengal. After NARASIMHAN's short, popular overview of 1990, there followed the last of the larger monographs in 1996: the book by CATHERINE WEINBERGER-THOMAS (English translation 2000). It is strongly oriented towards the history of mentalities and religion. For general historical aspects the article of 1989 by the same author is more important. So far it offers the best summary of the subject matter. About Classical Antiquity and early Indian texts there is now the detailed article by GARZILLI (1997).

In addition to these comprehensive overviews two strands of more specific publications can be identified in the last decades. The first, more academically oriented, was strongly influenced by the hypotheses put forward by ASHIS NANDY in various essays (contradicted for example in GUPTA/GOMBRICH 1984). His views were later linked with feminist and post-modern approaches. The works of LATA MANI, DOROTHY STEIN and R.S. RAJAN belong to this category. The different trends are included in the two volumes edited by HAWLEY (1994) and HARLAN/COURTRIGHT (1995). Increasingly traditional methods of empathic understanding are becoming important again, as shown particularly by HARLAN's monograph of 1992. The studies by JULIA LESLIE have a more Indological perspective. A.SHARMA illuminates very diverse aspects. For the debate on Durkheim, cf. along with Sharma also R.S. GANDHI.

The second strand of publications is also academically productive, but it is primarily politically motivated. It was triggered off by the burning of Roop Kanwar in 1987. Only a few representative names can be mentioned here (further information is given in chapter 14). The special issues of the journals *Manushi* (1987) and *Seminar* (1988) are seminal. Attention needs to be drawn to the contributions by KUMKUM SANGARI and SUDESH VAID as also, for example, to those by UPRETI/UPRETI and KISHWAR.

Alongside this, there are finally also studies on more specific aspects of the history of widow burning. The abolition in the princely states has been touched upon time and again. An early treatment of the theme is found in 1855 in BUSHBY, while among the newer works SAXENA (1975) has to be mentioned.

As far as more general aspects are concerned, KANE is still central for an understanding of the Dharma-texts, while THAKUR's history of suicide in India opens up an important background, as does ALTEKAR's work on the position of women. Questions of criminal law are dealt with in some detail only by DHAGAMWAR, to be supplemented by SINGHA (1993).

As compared to the nineteenth and twentieth centuries in India, other places and periods have hardly been researched. SUSHIL CHAUDHARY has supplied two small contributions on the Mughal period. For widow burning in Nepal the works of MICHAELS now have to be consulted.

Bibliography

Bibliography for Part I

Acosta, José de, Historia natural y moral de las Indias. 1590. In: Acosta, *Obras*, ed. Francisco Mateos, Madrid 1954, 1–247.

Adams, John, *Remarks on the country extending from Cape Palmas to the River Congo, including observations on the manners and customs of the inhabitants.* London 1823.

Addison, James Thayer, *Life beyond death in the beliefs of mankind.* London 1933.

Adriani, N./Kruijt, Alb. C., *De Bare'e-sprekende Toradja's van Midden-Celebes.* 3 vols, Batavia 1912–1914.

———, *De Bare'e sprekende Torjadas van Midden-Celebes (de Oost-Toradjas).* 3 vols, 2nd ed. Amsterdam 1951.

Allen, William/Thomson, T.R.H., *A narrative of the expedition sent by her Majesty's government to the river Niger, in 1841, under the command of Captain H.D. Trotter.* 2 vols, London 1848.

Allier, Raoul, *Le non-civilisé et nous. Différence irréductible ou identité foncière?* Paris 1927.

Altunian, Georg, *Die Mongolen und ihre Eroberungen in kaukasischen und kleinasiatischen Ländern im xiii. Jahrhundert.* Berlin 1911.

Alvear, Diego de, Relación geografica e historica de la provincia de Misiones. In: Pedro de Angelis (ed.), *Colección de obras y documentos relativos a la historia antigua y moderna de la provincia del Río de la Plata*, vol. 4, Buenos Aires 1836.

Ankermann, Bernhard, *Ostafrika.* Stuttgart 1929.

Apollonius, Levinus, *De Peruviae, Regionis, inter Noui Orbis provincias celeberrimae, Inventione: et rebus in eadem gestis, libri v.* Antwerpen n.d. [1566 or 1567].

Arhin, Kwame, The missionary role on the Gold Coast and in Ashanti: Reverend F.A. Ramseyer and the British take-over of Ashanti 1869–1894. In: *Research Review 4* (1967/68), 1–15.

Arnkiel, M. Trogillo: *Cimbrische Heyden-Religion.* 4 parts, Hamburg 1702.

Ashe, Robert Pickering, *Two kings of Uganda or, life by the shores of Victoria Nyanza, being an account of a residence of six years in eastern equatorial Africa.* 1889. 2nd ed., ed. John A. Rowe, London 1970.

Aston, W.G., *Shinto (The way of the gods).* London 1905.

Ayscough, Florence, *Chinese women yesterday and today.* Boston 1937 (reprinted New York 1975).

Baal, J. van, Offering, sacrifice and gift. In: *Numen* 23 (1976), 161–78.

Bacon, R.H., *Benin. The city of blood.* London 1897.

Baden-Powell, R.S.S., *The downfall of Prempeh. A diary of life with the native levy in Ashanti.* London 1896.

Baikie, William Balfour, *Narrative of an exploring voyage up the rivers Kwo'ra and Bi'nne (commonly known as the Niger and Tsádda) in 1854.* London 1856.

Baker, Samuel W., *Ismailia. A narrative of the epedition to Central Africa for the suppression of the slave trade organized by Ismail, Khedive of Egypt.* 2 vols, London 1874.

Ball, J. Dyer, Art. Human Sacrifice (Chinese), in: *Encyclopaedia of Religion and Ethics*, ed. James Hastings, vol. 6, Edinburgh 1913 (reprinted 1964), 845–7.

———, *Things Chinese, being notes on various subjects connected with China.* 2nd ed., London 1893.

Bancroft, Hubert Howe, *The native races of the Pacific States of North America.* 5 vols, New York 1875–1876.

Barbot, Jean, *Barbot on Guinea. The writings of Jean Barbot on West Africa 1678–1712.* Ed. P.E.H. Hair *et al.*, 2 vols, London 1992.

Barthold, W./Boyle, J.A., Art. Hulagu, in: *Encyclopédie de l'Islam, Nouvelle éd.*, vol. 3, Leiden 1971, 589.

Bastian, Adolf, *Die Culturländer des alten America.* 3 vols, Berlin 1878–89.

———, *Die deutsche Expedition an der Loango-Küste, nebst älteren Nachrichten über die zu erforschenden Länder.* 2 vols, Jena 1874–1875.

Bauer, Wolfgang, *China und die Hoffnung auf Glück. Paradiese—Utopien—Idealvorstellungen.* München 1971.

Baumann, Hermann *et al.*, *Völkerkunde von Afrika. Mit besonderer Berücksichtigung der kolonialen Aufgabe.* Essen 1940.

Bayol, Jean, *Exposition d'éthnographie coloniale. Les Dahoméens au Champs de Mars. Moeurs et coutumes.* Paris n.d. [1893].

Becker, Die Gehülfen der Missionare auf Borneo und die Dajak-Paris. In: *Das Missionsblatt.* Ed. Missions-Gesellschaft zu Barmen 23, No. 6 (20.3.1848; n. pag.).

Beecham, John, *Ashantee and the Gold Coast: being a sketch of the history, social state, and superstitions of the inhabitants of those countries: with a notice on the state and prospects of Christianity among them.* London 1841.

[Begert, Johann Jakob], *Nachrichten von der amerikanischen Halbinsel Californien: mit einem zweyfachen Anhang falscher Nachrichten. Geschrieben von einem Priester der Gesellschaft Jesu, welcher lang darinn diese letztere Jahre gelebt hat.* Mannheim 1772.

Bentinck, William Cavendish, *The Correspondence of Lord William Cavendish Bentinck Governor-General of India 1828–1835.* Ed. C.H. Philips. 2 vols, Oxford 1977.

Bernheim, Pierre-Antoine/Stavrides, Guy, *Welt der Paradiese—Paradiese der Welt.* Trans. Wieland Grommes. Zürich 1992.

Bieber, Friedrich J., *Kaffa. Ein altkuschitisches Volkstum in Inner-Afrika. Vol.2: Das Gemeinleben der Kaffitscho oder Gonga.* Wien 1929.

Bijdragen tot de kennis van het eiland Nias. In: *Tijdschrift voor Nederlandsch Indië 10* (1848), 171–99.

Bitō, Masahide, Art. *Junshi.* In: *Kodanska Encyclopaedia of Japan*, vol. 4, Tokyo 1983, 84–5.

Blair, Emma Helen/Robertson, James Alexander, ed., *The Philippine Islands, 1493–1803.* 55 vols, Cleveland 1903–1909.

Bloemen Waanders, P. L. van, Aanteekeningen omtrent de zeden en gebruiken der Balinezen, inzonderheid die van Boeleleng. In: *Tijdschrift voor Indische Taal-, Land-en Volkenkunde 8* (Batavia 1859), 105–259.

Blumentritt, Ferd., *Versuch einer Ethnographie der Philippinen.* Gotha 1882.

Böhl, Franz M. Th., Das Menschenopfer bei den alten Sumerern. In: *Zeitschrift für Assyriologie 39* (1930), 83–98.

Boelaars, J.H.M.C., *Head-hunters about themselves. An ethnographic report from Irian Jaya, Indonesia.* Den Haag 1991.

Bösch, Fr., *Les Banyamwezi. Peuple de l'Afrique orientale.* Münster 1930.

Boniface, *Briefe des Bonifatius. Willibalds Leben des Bonifatius. Nebst einigen zeitgen. Dokumenten.* Unter Benutzung der Übersetzungen von M. Tangl und Ph. H. Külb neu bearb. v. Reinhold Rau. Darmstadt 1968.

Bonnet, Charles, Excavations of the Nubian royal town of Kerma: 1975–1991. In: *Antiquity* 66 (1992), 611–25.

———, ed., *Kerma, royaume de Nubie. Mission archéologique de Genève à Soudan.* Genéve 1990.

Boon, James A., *Affinities and extremes. Crisscrossing the bittersweet ethnology of East Indies history, Hindu-Balinese culture, and Indo-European allure*. Chicago 1990.

——, *The anthropological romance of Bali 1597–1972. Dynamic perspectives in marriage and caste, politics and religion*. Cambridge 1977.

Borhegyi, Stephan F., Archaeological synthesis of the Guatemalan Highlands. In: Gordon R. Wiley (ed.), *Archaeology of Southern Mesoamerica*, vol. 1, Austin 1965, 3–58.

Bosman, Willem, *Nauwkeurige Beschryving van de Guinese Goud-, Tand- en Slavekust*. 2 vols, 2nd ed., Amsterdam 1709.

Bouche, Pierre, *Sept ans en Afrique occidentale. La Côte des esclaves et le Dahomey*. Paris 1885.

Bowdich, Thomas Edward, *Mission from Cape Coast Castle to Ashantee*. London 1819 (reprinted London 1966).

Bradbury, R.E./Lloyd, P.C., The Benin Kingdom. London 1957.

Brain, Jeffrey P., The Natchez 'Paradox'. In: *Ethnology* 10 (1971), 215–22.

Brandon, S.G.F., *The judgment of the dead. An historical and comparative study of the idea of a* post-mortem *judgment in the major religions*. London 1967.

Brandt, Max von, *Sittenbilder aus China. Mädchen und Frauen. Ein Beitrag zur Kenntnis des chinesischen Volkes*. Stuttgart 1990 (first published 1895).

Braun, Hans-Jürg, *Das Jenseits. Die Vorstellungen der Menschheit über das Leben nach dem Tod*. Zürich 1996.

Brinker, Helmut/Goepper, Roger, *Kunstschätze aus China. 5000 v.Chr. bis 900 n.Chr. Neue archäologische Funde aus der Volksrepublik China*. Zürich 1980.

Brunschwig, Henri, *L'avènement de l'Afrique noire du XIXe siècle à nos jours*. Paris 1963.

Bryant, A.T., *Olden times in Zululand and Natal, containing earlier political history of the eastern-Nguni clans*. Reprint Cape Town 1965. First published London 1929.

Buchholz, R., *Land und Leute in Westafrika*. Berlin 1876.

Burton, Richard F., *A mission to Gelele, King of Dahome*. 2 vols, London 1864.

——, *The Lake Regions of Central Africa. A picture of exploration*. 2 vols, London 1860.

Caesar, Caius Iulius, *De bello Gallico/The Gallic war*. Trans. by H.J. Edwards. Cambridge, Mass. 1969.

Callaway, Henry, *The religious system of the Amazulu.* Cape Town 1970.

Cameron, Verney Lovett, *Across Africa.* 2 vols, London 1877.

Campion-Vincent, Véronique, L'image du Dahomey dans la presse française (1890–1895). Les sacrifices humains. In: *Cahiers d'études africaines* 7 (1967), 27–58.

Caron, François, *François Carons und Jod. Schouten wahrhaftige Beschreibungen zweier mächtiger Königreiche Jappan und Siam.* Nürnberg 1663.

Carver, Jonathan, *Travels through the interior parts of North-America, in the years 1766, 1767 and 1768.* Dublin 1779.

Catlin, George: *Letters and notes on the manners, customs, and condition of the North American Indians, written during eight years' travel amongst the wildest tribes of Indians in North America.* 2 vols, New York 1841.

Cavan, Ruth Shonle, *Suicide.* Chicago 1928.

Cavazzi da Montecuccolo, Giovanni Antonio, *Istorica descrittione de' tre regni Congo, Matamba, et Angola situati nell'Etiopia inferiore occidentale e delle missioni apostoliche esercitatevi da religiosi Capuccini.* Milano 1690.

Černý, Jaroslav, *Ancient Egyptian Religion.* London 1952.

Chamisso, Adelbert von, Tagebuch der Reise um die Welt mit der Romanzowischen Entdeckungs-Expedition in den Jahren 1815–1818 auf der Brigg Rurik, Kapitän Otto v. Kotzebue. In: *Chamissos sämtliche Werke,* ed. Rod Böttcher, Berlin n.d., 113–547.

Chang, Kwang-Chih, *The archaeology of ancient China.* 4th ed., New Haven 1986.

———, *Art, myth and ritual. The path to political authority in ancient China.* Cambridge, Mass. 1983.

Chang, Tsung-Tung, *Der Kult der Shang-Dynastie im Spiegel der Orakelinschriften. Eine paläographische Studie zur Religion im archaischen China.* Wiesbaden 1970.

Charlevoix, Pierre François-Xavier, *Histoire du Paraguay.* 6 vols, Paris 1757.

———, *Histoire et description générale de la nouvelle France.* 3 vols, Paris 1744.

Chinesische Wittwenopfer (All the Year Round). In: *Das Ausland* 33, no. 44 (27.10.1861), 1051–3.

Cieza de León, Pedro, La crónica del Perú. In: *Biblioteca de autores españoles. Historiadores primitivos de Indias.* Ed. Enrique de Vedia, vol. 2, Madrid 1853, 349–458.

Cipolletti, Maria Susana, *Jenseitsvorstellungen bei den Indianern Südamerikas*. Berlin 1983.

Clapperton, Hugh, *Journal of a second expedition into the interior of Africa, from the Bight of Benin to Soccatoo. To which is added the journal of Richard Lander from Kano to the sea-coast, partly by a more eastern route*. London 1829.

Cobo, Bernabé, Historia del nuevo mundo. In: Francisco Mateos, ed., *Obras del Padre Bernabé Cobo*. vol. 2, Madrid 1964.

Codrington, R.H., *The Melanesians. Studies in their anthropology and folk-lore*. Oxford 1891 (reprinted Oxford 1969).

Cole, Fay-Cooper, *The Tinguian. Social, religious, and economic life of a Philippine tribe*. Chicago 1922. (Field Museum of Natural history, Publication 209, Anthropological Series vol. XIV, no. 2, pp. 227–493.)

Colenso, William, *On the Maori races of New Zealand*. N.p. 1865.

Colin, Francisco, *Labor evangélica* (Madrid 1663). Excerpts in Eng. transl. in: Blair/Robertson 40, 37–98.

Collins, Edmund, The panic element in nineteenth-century British relations with Ashanti. In: *Transactions of the Historical Society of Ghana* 5/2 (Legon 1962), 79–144.

Connah, Graham, *The archaeology of Benin. Excavations and other researches in and around Benin City, Nigeria*. Oxford 1975.

Cook, James, *The journals of Captain James Cook on his voyages of discovery*. Ed. J.C. Beaglehole. 4 vols, Cambridge 1955–1974.

Coquery-Vidrovitch, Catherine, La fête des coutumes au Dahomey: historique et essai d'interprétation. In: *Annales* 19 (1964), 696–716.

Coquilhat, Camille, *Sur le Haut-Congo*. Paris 1888.

Corney, Bolton Glanvill, ed., *The quest and occupation of Tahiti by emissaries of Spain during the years 1772–1776 told in dispatches and other contemporary documents*. 3 vols, London 1913–1919.

Covarrubias, Miguel, *Island of Bali*. New York 1950.

Cox, Ross, *Adventures on the Columbia River, including the narrative of a residence of six years on the western side of the Rocky Mountains, among various tribes of Indians hitherto unknown: together with a journey across the American continent*. 2 vols, London 1831.

Crawfurd, John, *History of the Indian Archipelago. Containing an account of the manners, arts, languages, religions, institutions, and commerce of its inhabitants*. 3 vols, reprinted London 1967 (first published London 1820).

————, On the existence of the Hindu religion in the island of Bali. In: *Asiatick Researches* 13 (Calcutta 1820), 128–70.

Crawley, A.E. *et al.*, Art. Human Sacrifice. In: James Hastings, ed., *Encyclopaedia of Religion and Ethics* 6 (Edinburgh 1913), 840–67.

Cruickshank, Brodie, *Ein achtzehnjähriger Aufenthalt auf der Goldküste Afrika's*. Leipzig n.d. [c. 1854/55].

Cruise, Richard A., *Journal of a ten months' residence in New Zealand*. 2nd ed., London 1824 (reprinted Christchurch 1974).

Cunningham, J.F., *Uganda and its peoples*. London 1905 (reprinted New York 1969).

Dagh-Register gehouden int Casteel Batavia vant passerende daer ter plaetse als over geheel Nederlandts-India Anno 1631–1634. Ed. H.T. Colenbrander. Den Haag 1898.

Dalrymple, Alexander, Essay towards an account of Sooloo. In: Alexander Dalrymple, ed., *Oriental Repertory*, vol. 1, London 1808, 499–578. (Also in: *Journal of the Indian Archipelago and Eastern Asia*, ed. J.R. Logan, vol. 3, Singapore 1849, 512–31; 545–67.)

Dalton, Edwart Tuite, *Descriptive ethnology of Bengal*. Calcutta 1872.

Dalzel, Archibald, *The history of Dahomy, an inland kingdom of Africa; compiled from authentic memoirs*. London 1793 (reprinted London 1967, ed. J.D. Fage).

Dapper, Olfert, *Naukeurige beschryvinge der Afrikaensche gewesten*. 2 parts in 1 vol., Amsterdam 1668.

————, *Umbständliche und eigentliche Beschreibung von Africa und denen darzu gehörigen Königreichen und Landschaften*. 2 parts in 1 vol., Amsterdam 1670.

Davidson, Basil, *Black Mother. Africa: the years of trial*. London 1961.

Davies, Nigel, *Human sacrifice in history and today*. London 1981.

De Groot, J. J. M., *The religious system of China, its ancient forms, evolution, history and present aspect. Manners, customs and social institutions connected therewith*. 6 vols, Leiden 1892–1910.

De Guignes, *Voyages a Pékin, Manille et l'île de France faits dans l'intervalle des années 1784–1801*. 3 vols, Paris 1808.

Denis, Jules, Notes sur l'organisation de quelques tribus aux environs du Lac Léopold II. In: *Anthropos* 35/36 (1940/41), 815–29.

Des Marchais, *Voyage du chevalier Des Marchais en Guinée, isles voisines, et à Cayenne, fait en 1725, 1726 et 1727*. Ed. Labat. 4 vols, Amsterdam 1731.

Devereux, George, *Mohave ethnopsychiatry and suicide: the psychiatric knowledge and the psychic disturbances of an Indian tribe.* Washington 1961.

Dieck, Alfred, Selbsttötung bei den Germanen. In: *Archiv für Religionswissenschaft* 36 (Leipzig 1939), 391–7.

Dieffenbach, Ernest, *Travels in New Zealand; with contributions to the geography, geology, botany, and natural history of that country.* 2 vols, London 1843.

D'Ohsson, Constantin, *Histoire des Mongols, depuis Tchinguiz-Khan jusqu'à Timour Bey ou Tamerlan.* Vol. 1, Den Haag 1834.

Doke, Clement M., *The Lambos of Northern Rhodesia. A study of their customs and beliefs.* London 1931.

Doolittle, Justus, *Social life of the Chinese: with some of their religious, governmental, educational, and business customs and opinions.* 2 vols, New York 1865 (reprinted Taipei 1966).

Dorman, Rushton M., *The origin of primitive superstitions and their development into the worship of spirits and the doctrine of spiritual agency among the aborigines of America.* Philadelphia 1881.

Downs, R.E., Head-hunting in Indonesia. In: *Bijdragen tot de Taal-, Land- en Volkenkunde* 111 (1955), 40–70.

Dubois, Pierre, Légère idée de Balie en 1830. Lettre VIII (Ms.). In: *Algemeen Rijksarchief*, Den Haag, MvK 3087.

Dumont de Montigny, *Mémoires historiques sur la Louisiane contenant ce qui est arrivé de plus mémorable depuis l'année 1687 jusqu'à présent.* 2 vols, Paris 1753.

Dumont d'Urville, Jules, *Voyage de la corvette l'Astrolabe, exécuté par ordre du roi, pendant les années 1826–1827–1828–1829.* Vol. 4, Paris 1832.

Duncan, John, *Travels in western Africa, in 1845 & 1846, comprising a journey from Whydah, through the kingdom of Dahomey, to Adoffodia, in the interior.* 2 vols, London 1847.

Dunn, John, *History of the Oregon territory and British North-American fur trade.* London 1844.

Durán, Diego, *Historia de las Indias de Nueva España e isles de la tierra firme.* Ed. Angel Maria Garibay K. 2 vols, 2nd ed., Mexico 1984.

Durand, Jean-Baptiste-Léonard, *Voyage au Sénégal.* 2 vols, Paris 1802.

Durkheim, Emile, *Le suicide. Etude de sociologie.* Paris 1969.

Earl, George Windsor, *The Eastern Seas, or voyages and adventures in the Indian Archipelago, in 1832–33–34.* London 1837.

Ebert, Max, ed., *Reallexikon der Vorgeschichte.* 14 vols, Berlin 1925–1929.

———, *Südrußland im Altertum.* Bonn 1921.

————, Art. Südrußland. In: Max Ebert, ed., *Reallexikon der Vorgeschichte* 13 (1928), 32–114.

Eckardt, M., Die Salomo-Inseln. In: *Globus* 39 (1881), 314–16; 334–6; 349–51; 363–6; 376–9.

Eine portugiesische Expedition nach dem Reich des Cazembe (Südafrika). In: *Das Ausland* 31 (1858), 259–62.

Elbert, Johannes, *Die Sunda-Expedition des Vereins für Geographie und Statistik zu Frankfurt am Main*. 2 vols, Frankfurt am Main 1911–12.

Ellis, A.B., *The Ewe-speaking peoples of the Slave Coast of West Africa. Their religion, manners, customs, laws, languages, etc.* Reprinted Oosterhout N.B. 1966 (first published 1890).

————, *The Tshi-speaking peoples of the Gold Coast of West Africa. Their religion, manners, customs, laws, languages, etc.* Reprinted Oosterhout N.B. 1966 (first published 1887).

————, *The Yoruba-speaking peoples of the Slave Coast of West Africa*. 2nd ed., London 1974 (first published 1894).

Ellis, William, *Narrative of a tour through Hawaii, or Owhyhee: with observations on the natural history of the Sandwich Islands, and remarks on the manners, customs, traditions, history and language of their inhabitants*. 2nd ed., London 1827.

Elshout, J.M., *De Kenja-Dajaks uit het Apo-Kajangebied. Bijdragen tot de kennis von Centraal-Borneo*. Den Haag 1926.

Elvas, Fidalgo de, *Expedición de Hernando de Soto a Florida*. Spanish trans. Miguel Muñoz de San Pedro. 3rd ed., Madrid 1965 (first published in Portuguese 1557).

Elvin, Mark, Female virtue and the state in China. In: *Past and Present* 104 (1984), 111–52.

Emery, Walter B., *Archaic Egypt*. Harmondsworth 1961.

————, *Egypt in Nubia*. London 1965.

Encyclopaedie van Nederlandsch-Indië. Vol. 1, 2nd ed., Den Haag 1917.

Engster, Hermann, *Das Problem des Witwenselbstmordes bei den Germanen*. PhD thesis Göttingen 1970.

Erkes, Eduard, Menschenopfer und Kannibalismus im alten China. In: *Der Erdball* 1, 1 (1926), 1–6.

Erskine, John Elphinstone, *Journal of a cruise among the islands of the Western Pacific, including the Feejees and others inhabited by the Polynesian Negro races*. London 1853.

Euripides, Supplices/Suppliant Women. In: *Euripides*. Vol. 3, trans. by David Kovacs, Cambridge, Mass. 1998, 12–139.

Faber, Karl-Georg *et al.*, Art. Macht, Gewalt. In: Otto Brunner *et al.*, eds, *Geschichtliche Grundbegriffe*, vol. 3, Stuttgart 1982, 817–935.

Falkenhausen, Lothar von, Ahnenkult und Grabkult im Staat Qin. Der religiöse Hintergrund der Terrakotta-Armee. In: Lothar Ledderose/ Adele Schlombs, eds, *Jenseits der Großen Mauer. Der erste Kaiser von China und seine Terrakotta-Armee.* Gütersloh 1990, 35–48.

Farberow, Norman L., ed., *Suicide in different cultures*. Baltimore 1975.

Fedden, Henry Romilly, *Suicide. A social and historical study*. London 1938.

Ferdon, Edwin N., *Early Tahiti as the explorers saw it 1767–1797*. Tucson 1981.

Fernandes, Valentin, *O manuscripto*. Ed. António Baião. Lisboa 1940.

Fernández de Oviedo, Gonzalo, *Historia general y natural de las Indias*. Ed. Juan Pérez de Tudela Bueso. 5 vols, Madrid 1959.

Field, Margaret Joyce, *Religion and medicine of the Gâ people*. London 1937.

Fisch, Jörg, Jenseitsglaube, Ungleichheit und Tod. Zu einigen Aspekten der Totenfolge. In: *Saeculum* 44 (1993), 265–99.

Forbes, Frederick E., *Dahomey and the Dahomans: being the journals of two missions to the King of Dahomey, and residence at his capital, in the years 1849 and 1850*. 2 vols, London 1851.

Forrest, Thomas, *A voyage to New Guinea, and the Moluccas, from Balambangan, including an account of Magindanao, Sooloo, and other islands … during the years 1774, 1775, and 1776*. London 1779.

Frähn, C.M., ed., *Ibn-Foszlan's und anderer Araber Berichte über die Russen älterer Zeit*. St. Petersburg 1823.

Frässle, Joseph, *Meiner Urwaldneger Denken und Handeln*. Freiburg i. B. 1923.

François, Curt von, *Die Erforschung der Tschuapa und Lulongo. Reisen in Centralafrika*. Leipzig 1888.

Franke, Otto, *Geschichte des chinesischen Reiches*. Vol. 1, 2nd ed., Berlin 1965. Vol. 3, Berlin 1937.

Frazer, James George, *The Golden Bough. A study in magic and religion*. 9 vols, 3rd ed., New York 1951.

Freeman, Richard Austin, *Travels and life in Ashanti and Jaman*. New York 1898.

Freeman, Thomas Birch, *Journal of various visits to the kingdoms of Ashanti,*

Aku, and Dahomi in Western Africa. 3rd ed., ed. Harrison M. Wright, London 1968 (first published 1844).

[Friederich R.], Een fest in de hoofdplaats van het rijk Gianjar op het eiland Bali. In: *Tijdschrift voor Nederlandsch Indië 1849,* 421–9.

———, Voorloopig verslag van het eiland Bali. In: *Verhandelingen van het Bataviaasch Genootschap van Kunsten en Wetenschappen* 22 (1849); 23 (1850). Engl. Trans.: An account of the island of Bali, in: *Journal of the Royal Asiatic Society,* NS 8 (1876), 157–218; NS 9 (1877), 59–120; NS 10 (1878), 49–97.

Friederici, Georg: *Skalpieren und ähnliche Kriegsgebräuche in Amerika.* Braunschweig 1906 (reprinted Kassel 1991).

Fries, E., Das, 'Koppensnellen' auf Nias. In: *Allgemeine Missionszeitschrift* 35 (1908), 73–88.

Frobenius, Leo, *Und Afrika sprach . . .* 3 vols, Berlin 1912–1913.

Fülleborn, Friedrich, *Das Deutsche Njassa- und Ruwuma-Gebiet, Land und Leute, nebst Bemerkungen über die Schire-Länder.* Berlin 1906.

Fuller, Francis, *A vanished dynasty. Ashanti.* London 1921.

Furness, William Henry, *The home-life of Borneo head-hunters. Its festivals and folk-lore.* Philadelphia 1902 (reprinted New York n.d.).

Fynn, Henry Francis, *The Diary.* Ed. James Stuart/D. McK. Malcolm. Pietermaritzburg 1950.

Gadd, C.J., The spirit of living sacrifices in tombs. In: *Iraq* 22 (1960), 51–8.

Gaerte, Wilhelm, Witwenverbrennung im vorordenszeitlichen Ostpreußen. In: *Prussia* 29 (1931), 125–34.

Gait, Edward A., *A history of Assam.* 1st ed., Calcutta 1906. 2nd ed. ibid., 1926.

Galtung, Johan, Violence, Peace and Peace Research. In: *Journal of Peace Research* 6 (1969), 167–91.

Garcilaso de La Vega, *Comentarios reales de los Incas.* Ed. Aurelio Miro Quesada. 2 vols, n.p. 1976.

Garnier, Jules, *Océanie. Les Iles des Pins, Loyalty et Tahiti.* Paris 1871.

Geertz, Clifford, *Negara. The Theatre State in nineteenth-century Bali.* Princeton 1980.

Gerhards, Gisela, Das Bild der Witwe in der deutschen Literatur des Mittelalters. PhD thesis Bonn 1962.

Geuns, M. van, Door Badoeng en Tabanan. Een en ander over Bali en zijne bewoners. In: *Soerabajaasch Handelsblad* 24., 27., 29. 11. and 1., 4., 6., 11., 14., 17.12.1906.

Gibbs, George, Tribes of western Washington and northwestern Oregon. In: *Contributions to North American Ethnology* 1 (Washington 1877), 157–241.

Gill, William, *Gems from the Coral Islands; or, incidents of contrast between savage and Christian life in the South Sea islands*. London n.d. [ca.1855].

Göckenjan, Hansgerd, Art. Kumanen. In: *Lexikon des Mittelalters* 5 (München 1991), 1568–1569.

Gohain, Bikash Chandra, *Human sacrifice and head-hunting in northeastern India*. Gauhati 1977.

González Torres, Yólotl, *El sacrificio humano entre los Mexicas*. Mexico 1985.

Graham, James D., The slave trade, depopulation and human sacrifice in Benin history. The general approach. In: *Cahiers d'études africaines* 5 (1965), 317–34.

Grakow, B.N., *Die Skythen*. Berlin 1978.

Grandidier, Alfred/Grandidier, Guillaume, *Histoire physique, naturelle et politique de Madagascar*. Vol. 4: *Ethnographie de Madagascar*. Tome 3: *Les habitants de Madagascar*. Paris 1917.

Granet, Marcel, *Danses et légendes de la Chine ancienne*. 2 vols, Paris 1926.

Gravier, Jacques, Relation ou journal du voyage du Père Gravier, de la Compagnie de Jésus en 1700 depuis le pays des Illinois jusqu'à l'embouchure du fleuve Mississippi. In: *Jesuit Relations* 65, 100–78.

Gray, John Henry, *China*. 2 vols, London 1864.

Green, Alberto Ravinell Whitney, *The role of human sacrifice in the Ancient Near East*. Missoula, Montana 1975.

Grimm, Jacob, *Deutsche Rechtsaltertümer*. Vol. 1, 4th ed., Leipzig 1899 (reprinted Darmstadt 1965).

———, Über das Verbrennen der Leichen. In: Jacob Grimm: *Kleinere Schriften* 2 (Berlin 1865, reprinted Hildesheim 1965), 211–313 (first published 1849).

Groeneveldt, W.P., Notes on the Malay Archipelago and Malacca, compiled from Chinese sources. In: *Verhandelingen van het Bataviaasch Genootschap van Kunsten en Wetenschappen* 39 (1880).

Grosier, Jean Baptiste G.A., ed., *Histoire générale de la Chine ou annales de cet empire; traduites du Tong-kien-kang-mou*. Vol. 1, Paris 1777.

Große Ada (Sitte) in Abomey, Die. In: *Das Ausland* 34 (1861), 407–8.

Grubauer, Albert, *Unter Kopfjägern in Central-Celebes. Ethnologische Streifzüge in Südost- und Central-Celebes*. Leipzig 1923.

Guevara, José, Historia del Paraguay, Río de la Plata y Tucuman. In: Pedro de Angelis, ed., *Colección de obras y documentos relativos á la historia antigua y moderna de las provincias del Río de la Plata*. Vol. 2, Buenos Aires 1836.

Guppy, H.B., *The Solomon Islands and their natives*. London 1887.

Gyamfi, Kwaku Effah, *Traditional history of the Bono State*. Legon 1979.

Haarhoff, Barend Johannes, Die Bantu-Stämme Süd-Afrikas. PhD thesis Leipzig 1890.

Haddon, Alfred C., *Head-hunters. Black, white and brown*. London 1901 (reprinted New York 1978).

Hale, Horatio, *Ethnography and philology*. (United States exploring expedition. During the years 1838, 1829, 1840, 1841, 1842. Under the command of Charles Wilkes, U.S.N., Vol. 6.) Philadelphia 1846.

Handbook of South American Indians. Ed. Julian H. Steward. 7 vols, Washington 1946–1959.

Hardeland, A., Borneo. In: *Das Missions-Blatt*. Ed. Missions-Gesellschaft zu Barmen 17, no. 16 (8.8.1842), n. pag.

Harmon, Daniel Williams, *A journal of voyages and travels in the interior of North America*. Ed. W.L. Grant. Toronto 1911 (first published 1820).

Hart, C.W.M., A reconsideration of the Natchez social structure. In: *American Anthropologist* NS 45 (1943), 374–86.

Hartmann, Robert, *Die Völker Afrikas*. Leipzig 1879.

Harttmann, Hermann, Ethnographische Studie über die Baja. In: *Zeitschrift für Ethnologie* 59 (1927), 1–61.

Hassler, Peter, *Menschenopfer bei den Azteken? Eine quellen- und ideologiekritische Studie*. Bern 1992.

Hecquard, Hyacinth, *Reise an die Küste und in das Innere von West-Afrika*. Leipzig 1854.

Hehn, Victor, *Kulturpflanzen und Hausthiere in ihrem Übergang aus Asien nach Griechenland und Italien sowie das übrige Europa*. 6th ed., ed. O. Schrader, Berlin 1894.

Heine-Geldern, Robert, Kopfjagd und Menschenjagd in Assam und Birma und ihre Ausstrahlungen nach Vorderindien. In: *Mitteilungen der Anthropologischen Gesellschaft in Wien* 37 (1917), 1–65.

Helfrich, Klaus, *Menschenopfer und Tötungsrituale im Kult der Maya*. Berlin 1973.

Helms, Ludvig Verner, *Pioneering in the Far East and journeys to California in 1849 and to the White Sea in 1878*. London 1882.

Henninger, Joseph, Art. Sacrifice, in: *Encyclopedia of Religion*, ed. Mircea Eliade, 12 (New York 1987), 545–57.

Heinrichs, Albert, Human sacrifice in Greek religion: three case studies. In: Jean Rudhardt/Olivier Reverdin, eds, *Le sacrifice dans l'antiquité*, Genève 1981, 195–235.

Henry, Teuira, *Ancient Tahiti*. Honolulu 1928.

Herodotus, *Historiai/The Persian War*. 4 vols, trans. by A.D. Godley, Cambridge, Mass. 1969.

Herrera, Antonio de, *Historia general de los hechos de los castellanos en las islas y tierra firme del mar oceano. Década Quinta*. Madrid 1728.

Herskovits, Melville J., *Dahomey. An ancient West African kingdom.* 2 vols, New York 1938.

Hirt, Herman, *Die Indogermanen. Ihre Verbreitung, ihre Urheimat und ihre Kultur.* 2 vols, Strassburg 1905–1907.

Hirzel, Rudolf, Der Selbstmord. In: *Archiv für Religionswissenschaft* 11 (1908), 75–104; 243–84; 417–76.

Hoang, Pierre, *Le mariage chinois du point de vue légal.* Shanghai 1898.

Hocart, A.M., The cult of the dead in Eddystone of the Solomons. Part I. In: *Journal of the Royal Anthropological Society of Great Britain and Ireland* 52 (1922), 71–112.

Höllmann, Thomas O., Wahrlich 'mannhafte' Taten? Von der Kopfjagd bei den austronesischsprachigen Ethnien Taiwans und den Möglichkeiten historischer Konfliktforschung. In: *Saeculum* 45 (1994), 105–25.

Hofmayr, Wilhelm, *Die Schilluk. Geschichte, Religion und Leben eines Niloten-Stammes.* Mödling bei Wien 1919.

Home, Robert, *City of Blood revisited. A new look at the Benin expedition of 1897.* London 1982.

Homer, *Ilias/The Iliad.* 2 vols, trans. by A.T. Murray, Cambridge, Mass. 1969.

Hose, Charles/McDougall, William, *The pagan tribes of Borneo.* 2 vols, London 1912.

Hrdlčka, Aleš, *Physiological and medical observations among the Indians of south-western United States and northern Mexico.* Washington 1908.

Hsieh, Andrew C.K./Spence, Jonathan D., Suicide and the family in pre-modern Chinese society. In: Arthur Kleinman/Tsung-Yi Lin, eds, *Normal and abnormal behavior in Chinese society.* Dordrecht 1981, 29–47.

Huc, Evariste Regis, *Souvenirs d'un voyage dans la Tartarie, le Thibet et la Chine pendant les années 1844, 1845 et 1846.* 2 vols, Paris 1850.

Hughes, Dennis D., *Human sacrifice in Ancient Greece*. London 1991.

Human Sacrifice, Art. In: *Encyclopaedia of Religion and Ethics*, ed. James Hastings, vol. 6, Edinburgh 1913, 840–67.

Humboldt, Wilhelm von, *Über die Kawi-Sprache auf der Insel Java*. Vol. 1, Berlin 1836

Huntley, Henry, *Seven years' service on the Slave Coast of West Africa*. 2 vols, London 1850.

Hupperts, Letter on Borneo of 26.10.1841. In: *Das Missions-Blatt*. Ed. Missions-Gesellschaft zu Barmen 18, no. 7 (3.4.1843), n. pag.

Hutton, William, *A voyage to Africa: including a narrative of an embassy to one of the interior kingdoms, in the year 1820; with remarks on the course and termination of the Niger, and other principal rivers in that country*. London 1821.

Ibn Baṭṭūṭa, *The travels A.D. 1325–1354*. Ed. and trans. H.A.R. Gibb. 5 vols, London 1958–2000.

Ibn Faḍlān, *Ibn Faḍlān's Reisebericht*. Ed. A. Zeki Validi Togan. Leipzig 1939.

———, La relation du voyage d'Ibn Fadlân chez les Bulgares de la Volga. Ed. M. Canard. In: *Annales de l'Institut d'études orientales* 16 (Algier 1958), 41–146.

Ihle, Alexander, *Das alte Königreich Kongo*. Leipzig 1929.

Irstam, Tor, *The King of Ganda. Studies in the institutions of sacral kingship in Africa*. Stockholm 1944.

Isert, Paul Erdmann, *Neue Reise nach Guinea und den Caribaischen Inseln in Amerika in den Jahren 1783–1787*. Berlin 1790.

Isichei, Elizabeth, *History of West Africa since 1800*. London 1977.

———, *The Ibo people and the Europeans. The genesis of a relationship— to 1906*. London 1973.

———, The quest for social reform in the context of traditional religion: a neglected theme of West African history. In: *African Affairs* 77 (1978), 463–78.

Ivens, W.G., *Melanesians of the South-east Solomon Islands*. London 1927.

Jacquet, Mélanges malays, javanais et polynésiens. In: *Nouveau journal asiatique* 8 (1831), 3–45.

Janssen, Hans-Lüitjen, Mittelalterliche Berichte vom Totenbrauch der Balten. In: *Prussia* 33 (1939), 192–200.

Jean de Joinville, *Histoire de Saint Louis*. Ed. Natalis de Wailly. Paris 1868.

———, *Histoire de Saint Louis. Texte rapproché du français moderne*. Ed. Natalis de Wailly. 2nd ed., Paris 1865.

Jensen Ad. E., *Die drei Ströme. Züge aus dem geistigen und religiösen Leben der Wemale, einem Primitiv-Volk in den Molukken.* Leipzig 1948.

——, *Mythos und Kult bei Naturvölkern. Religionswissenschaftliche Betrachtungen.* 2nd ed., Wiesbaden 1960.

Jesch, Judith, *Women in the Viking Age.* Woodbridge, Suffolk 1991.

Jesuit relations and allied documents. Travels and explorations of the Jesuit missionaries in New France, 1610–1791. Ed. Reuben Gold Thwaites. 73 vols, Cleveland 1896–1901.

Johnson, Samuel, *The history of the Yorubas from the earliest time to the beginning of the British Protectorate.* London 1921.

Johnston, Harry, *The Uganda Protectorate.* 2 vols, London 1902.

Jones, Adam, Four years in Asante: one source or several? In: *History in Africa* 18 (1991), 173–203.

——, *German sources for West African history 1599–1669.* Wiesbaden 1983.

——, *Zur Quellenproblematik der Geschichte West Afrikas 1450–1900.* Stuttgart 1990.

Jonge, J.K.J. de, ed., *De opkomst van het Nederlandsch gezag in Oost-Indië (1595–1610).* Vol. 3, Den Haag 1865.

Jordanes, *Romana et Getica.* Ed. Theodor Mommsen. Berlin 1883.

——, *Gothengeschichte nebst Auszügen aus seiner römischen Geschichte.* Trans. Wilhelm Martens. Leipzig n.d.

Journal des missions évangéliques. Vol. 36, Paris 1861.

Junghuhn, Franz, *Die Battaländer auf Sumatra.* 2 vols, Berlin 1847.

Junker, Wilhelm, *Reisen in Afrika 1875–1886.* 3 vols, Wien 1889–1891.

Junshi, Art. Junshi, in: *Dictionnaire historique du Japon*, Fascicule X: Lettre J, Tokyo 1984, 78–9.

Justinus, Marcus Junianus, *Epitoma historiarum Philippicarum Pompei Trogi*, ed. Otto Seel, Leipzig 1935.

Juynboll, H.H., Een Deensch bericht over eene vorstelijke lijkverbranding op Bali in het midden der 19e eeuw. In: *De Indische Gids 49/1* (1927), 226–32.

Kalous, Milan, Human sacrifices in Benin history. In: *Archiv Orientální* 37 (1969), 365–76.

Kane, Paul, *Wanderings of an artist among the Indians of North America from Canada to Vancouver Island and Oregon through the Hudson's Bay Company's territories and back again.* London 1859.

Kapitza, Peter, *Japan in Europe. Texte und Bilddokumente zur europäischen Japankenntnis von Marco Polo bis Wilhelm von Humboldt.* 3 vols, München 1990.

Karageorghis, Vassos, *Salamis in Cyprus. Homeric, Hellenistic and Roman.* London 1969.

———, *et al.*, *Salamis.* 12 vols, Nicosia 1964–1978.

Katscher, Leopold, *Bilder aus dem chinesischen Leben. Mit besonderer Rücksicht auf Sitten und Gebräuche.* Leipzig 1881.

Kees, Hermann, *Totenglauben und Jenseitsvorstellungen der alten Ägypter. Grundlagen und Entwicklung bis zum Ende des Mittleren Reiches.* 2nd ed., Berlin 1956.

Kennedy, R. Hartley, *The Sutti, as witnessed at Baroda, November 29th, 1825.* London 1855. First published as: The suttee: the narrative of an eye-witness. In: *Bentley's Miscellany* 13 (1843), 241–56.

Kidd, Dudley, *The essential Kaffir.* 2nd ed., London 1925.

Kingsley, Mary H., *West African Studies.* London 1899.

Kleiweg de Zwaan, J.P., *Die Heilkunde der Niasser.* Den Haag 1913.

Klimkeit, Hans-Joachim, ed., *Tod und Jenseits im Glauben der Völker.* Wiesbaden 1978.

Kol, H.H. van, *Driemal dwars door Sumatra en zwerftochten door Bali.* Rotterdam 1914.

Kowalska, Maria, Ibn Faḍlān's account of his journey to the State of the Bulgars. In: *Folia Orientalia* 14 (1972/73), 219–30.

Krafft, Max, Die Rechtsverhältnisse der Ovakuanjama und der Ovandonga. In: *Mitteilungen aus den deutschen Schutzgebieten*, ed. H. Marquardsen 27 (1914), 17–35.

Kramer, Samuel Noah, The death of Gilgamesh. In: *Bulletin of the American School of Oriental Research* 94 (1944), 2–12.

———, *The Sumerians. Their history, culture and character.* Chicago 1963.

Kranz, M., *Natur-und Kulturleben in Süd-Afrika. Zululand–Natal und seine Bewohner.* Wiesbaden 1880.

Krickeberg, Walter *et al.*, *Die Religionen des alten Amerika.* Stuttgart 1961.

Krieger, Maximilian, *Neu-Guinea.* Berlin n.d. [1899].

Krohn, William O., *In Borneo jungles. Among the Dyak headhunters.* Indianapolis 1927.

Kruyt, Alb. C., De Soembaneezen. In: *Bijdragen tot de Taal-, Land- en Volkenkunde van Nederlandsch–Indië* 78 (1922), 466–608.

———, De Timoreezen. In: *Bijdragen tot de Taal-, Land- en Volkenkunde van Nederlandsch–Indië* 79 (1923), 347–490.

———, *De West-Toradjas op Midden-Celebes.* 3 vols, Amsterdam 1938.

———, Het koppensnellen der Toradja's van Midden-Celebes, en zijne beteekenis. In: *Verslagen en Mededeelingen der Koninklijke Akademie der Wetenschappen, Afd. Letterkunde, vierde reeks, derde deel*, Amsterdam 1899, 147–229.

———, De Toradja's van de Sa'dan-, Masopoe- en Mamasa-Rivieren. In: *Tijdschrift vor Indische Taal-, Land- en Volkenkunde 63* (Batavia 1923), 93–175; 259–356.

Kuhn, Dieter, *Status und Ritus. Das China der Aristokraten von den Anfängen bis zum 10. Jahrhundert nach Christus.* Heidelberg 1991.

———, Totenritual und Beerdigungen im chinesischen Altertum. In: *Das alte China*, München 1995, 45–67; 445–8.

Kurtz, Donna C./Boardman, John, *Greek burial customs.* London 1971.

Labarthe, Pierre, *Voyage à la côte de Guinée, ou description des côtes d'Afrique, depuis le cap Tagrin jusqu'au cap de Lopez-Gonzalves.* Paris 1803.

———, *Reise nach der Küste von Guinea.* Trans. Theophil Friedrich Ehrmann. Weimar 1803.

Lahontan, *Mémoires de l'Amérique septentrionale ou la suite des voyages de Mr. Le baron de Lahontan.* Vol. 2, Den Haag 1703.

Lander, Richard, Journal from Kano to the sea-coast, partly by a more eastern route. In: *Clapperton* 255–327.

Lander, Richard/Lander, John, *Journal of an expedition to explore the course and termination of the Niger; with a narrative of a voyage down that river to its termination.* 3 vols, London 1832. German trans.: *Reise in Afrika zur Erforschung des Nigers bis zu seiner Mündung.* 3 vols, Leipzig 1833.

Landolphe, *Mémoires du capitaine Landolphe, contenant l'histoire de ses voyages pendant trente-six ans, aux côtes d'Afrique et aux deux Amériques, rédigés sur son manuscript par J.S. Quesné.* 2 vols, Paris 1823.

Lang, Bernhard/McDannell, Colleen, *Der Himmel. Eine Kulturgeschichte des ewigen Lebens.* Frankfurt a.M. 1990.

Las Casas, Bartolomé de, *Apologética historia.* Ed. Juan Pérez de Tudela Bueso. 2 vols, Madrid 1958.

Lateiner, Donald, *The historical method of Herodotus.* Toronto 1989.

Law, Robin, Human sacrifice in pre-colonial West Africa. In: *African Affairs* 84 (1985), 53–87.

———, 'My head belongs to the king', On the political and ritual significance of decapitation in pre-colonial Dahomey. In: *Journal of African History* 30 (1989), 399–415.

Ledderose, Lothar/Schlombs, Adele, eds, *Jenseits der Großen Mauer. Der erste Kaiser von China und seine Terrakotta-Armee.* Gütersloh 1990.

Legrand, M.-A., *Au pays des Canaques. La Nouvelle-Calédonie et ses habitants en 1890*. Paris 1893.

Le Hérissé, A., *L'ancien royaume du Dahomey. Moeurs, religions, histoire*. Paris 1911.

Leonard, Arthur Glyn, *The lower Niger and its tribes*. London 1906.

Le Page du Pratz, *Histoire de la Louisiane*. 3 vols, Paris 1758.

Le Petit, Mathurin, Lettre du Père le Petit, Missionaire, au Père d'Avangour, Procureur des Missions de l'Amérique Septentrionale. Nouvelle Orléans 12.7.1730. In: *The Jesuit Relations* 68, 120–222.

Levtzion, N./Hopkins, J.F.P., eds and trans, *Corpus of early Arabic sources for West African history*. Cambridge 1981.

Lewin, Thomas J., *Asante before the British. The Prempean years, 1875–1900*. Lawrence, Kansas 1978.

Lifton, Robert Jay *et al.*, *Six lives, six deaths. Portraits from modern Japan*. New Haven 1979.

Lî kî, Trans. James Legge. Vol. 1, Oxford 1885.

Linck, Gudula, Die Phönixe tanzen zu zweit—Weiblichkeits- und Männlichkeitsideale im früh- und spätkaiserzeitlichen China. In: Jochen Martin/Renate Zoepfel, eds, *Aufgaben, Rollen und Räume von Frau und Mann*, Freiburg i. B. 1989, 341–70.

Linck-Kesting, Gudula, China, Geschlechtsreife und Legitimation zur Zeugung. In: Ernst Wilhelm Müller, ed., *Geschlechtsreife und Legitimation zur Zeugung*, Freiburg i.B. 1985, 85–176.

Lincoln, Bruce, On the Scythian royal burials. In: Bruce Lincoln: *Death, war and sacrifice. Studies in ideology and practice*, Chicago 1991, 188–97.

Lloyd, Alan, *The drums of Kumasi*. London 1964.

Loarca, Miguel de, Relacion de las yslas Filipinas [1582]. In: *Blair/Robertson* 5 (1903), 34–186.

Logan, J.R., Memoirs of Malays. In: *Journal of the Indian Archipelago and Eastern Asia*, ed. J.R. Logan, vol. 2, Singapore 1848, 353–61.

López de Gómara, Francisco, *Historia de la conquista de México*. Ed. Jorge Garria Lacroix. Caracas 1979.

———, *Historia general de las Indias*. 2 vols, Madrid 1982.

Lucian, De Luctu/On Sacrifices. In: *Lucian*. Vol. 3, trans. by A.M. Harmon, Cambridge, Mass. 1969, 153–71.

Lumholtz, Carl, *Through Central Borneo. An account of two years' travel in the land of the head-hunters between the years 1913 and 1917*. 2 vols, London 1920.

Macdonald, James, *Religion and myth*. London 1893.

Mackay, A.M., *Pioneer missionary of the Church Missionary Society to Uganda. By his sister.* London 1890 (reprinted with an introduction by D.A. Low, London 1970).

Mackenzie, Alexander, *Voyages from Montreal, on the River St. Laurence, through the continent of North America, to the frozen and pacific Oceans; in the years 1789 and 1793.* London 1801.

Mackenzie, D.R., *The spirit-ridden Konde.* London 1925.

Maclean, John, *Notes of a twenty five years' service in the Hudson's Bay Territory.* Ed. W.S. Wallace. Toronto 1932.

MacLeod, William Christie, Certain mortuary aspects of Northwest Coast culture. In: *American Anthropologist* 27 (1925), 122–48.

——, The distribution and process of suttee in North America. In: *American Anthropologist* NS 33 (1931), 209–15.

——, Natchez political evolution. In: *American Anthropologist* NS 26 (1924), 201–29.

——, On Natchez cultural origins. In: *American Anthropologist* NS 28 (1926), 409–13.

——, The origin of the state reconsidered in the light of the data of aboriginal North America. PhD thesis. Philadelphia 1924.

——, The Suttee in North America: its antecedents and origins. In: *Journal de la societé des américanistes de Paris* NS 20 (1928), 107–20.

Magyar, Ladislaus, *Reisen in Süd-Afrika in den Jahren 1849 bis 1857.* Trans. from the Hungarian Johann Hunfalvy. Vol. 1, Pest 1859.

[Maning, F.E.], *Old New Zealand: being incidents of native customs and character in the old times by a Pakeha Maori.* London 1863.

Marco Polo, *Il Milione. Prima edizione integrale.* Ed. Luigi Foscolo Benedetto. Firenze 1928.

——, *The travels.* Trans. Ronald Latham. Harmondsworth 1958.

——, *The Book of Ser Marco Polo the Venetian.* Ed. and trans. Henry Yule and Henri Cordier. 2 vols, reprinted New Delhi 1993.

Margry, Pierre, ed., Mémoires et documents pour servir à l'histoire des origines françaises des pays d'outre-mer. Découvertes et établissements des Français dans l'ouest et dans le sud de l'Amerique septentrionale (1683–1724). Vol. 5: Première formation d'une chaîne de postes entre le fleuve Saint-Laurent et le Golfe du Méxique (1683–1724). Paris 1887. 377–586: *Les premiers postes de la Louisiane. Relation de Pénicaut (1698–1699).*

Mariner, William, *An account of the natives of the Tonga Islands, in the South Pacific Ocean.* Ed. John Martin. 2 vols, London 1817 (reprinted Westmead 1972).

Maringer, Johannes, Menschenopfer im Bestattungsbrauch Alteuropas. Eine Untersuchung über die Doppel-und Mehrbestattungen im vor- und frühgeschichtlichen Europa, insbesondere Mitteleuropa. In: *Anthropos* 37–38 (1942–43), 1–112.

Marquardsen, Hugo, *Angola*. Berlin 1920.

Mason, Carol, Natchez class structure. In: *Ethnohistory* 11 (1964), 120–33.

Matignon, J.-J., *La Chine hermétique. Superstition, crime et misère*. Paris 1936.

Maurikios, *Das Strategikon des Maurikios*. Ed. George T. Dennis. Trans. Ernst Gamillscheg. Wien 1981.

Mayer, Brantz, *Captain Canot; or, twenty years of an African slaver*. London 1855.

McCaskie, Thomas C., Death and the Asantehene: a historical meditation. In: *Journal of African History* 30 (1989), 417–44.

———, *State and society in pre-colonial Asante*. Cambridge 1995.

McCoy, Isaac, *History of Baptist Indian missions: embracing remarks on the former and present condition of the aboriginal tribes; their settlement within the Indian territory, and their future prospects*. Washington 1840.

McKinley, Robert, Human and proud of it! A structural treatment of headhunting rites and the social definition of enemies. In: G.N. Appell, ed., *Studies in Borneo societies: social process and anthropological explanation*, Detroit 1976, 92–126.

Meek, C.K., *A Sudanese kingdom. An ethnographical study of the Jukun-speaking peoples of Nigeria*. London 1931 (reprinted New York 1969).

———, *Tribal studies in Northern Nigeria*. 2 vols, London 1931.

Mensen, Bernhard, ed., *Jenseitsvorstellungen verschiedener Völker*. St. Augustin 1985.

Merolla, Girolamo, *Breve, e succinta relatione del viaggio nel regno di Congo nell'Africa Meridionale*. Ed. Angelo Piccardo da Napoli. Napoli 1692.

Metcalfe, G.E., ed., *Great Britain and Ghana. Documents of Ghana history 1807–1957*. Legon 1964.

Meyerowitz, Eva L.R., *The sacred state of the Akan*. London 1951.

Michelena y Rojas, Francisco, *Viajes científicos en todo el mundo (en los años 1822–1842)*. Madrid 1843 (reprinted Caracas 1971).

Miquel, André, *La géographie humaine du monde musulman jusqu'au milieu du 11e siècle*. Vol. 2: *Géographie arabe et représentation du monde: la terre et l'étranger*. Paris 1975.

Mjöberg, Eric, *Durch die Insel der Kopfjäger. Abenteuer im Innern von Borneo*. Leipzig 1929.

M'Leod, John, *A voyage to Africa with some account of the manners and customs of the Dahomian people.* London 1820.

Mockler-Ferryman, A.F., *British Nigeria.* London 1902.

Modigliani, Elio, *Un viaggio a Nías.* Milano 1890.

Monrad, H.C., *Gemälde der Küste von Guinea und der Einwanderer derselben, wie auch der Dänischen Colonien auf dieser Küste; entworfen während meines Aufenthaltes in Afrika in den Jahren 1805 bis 1809.* Trans. from Danish H.E. Wolf. Weimar 1824.

Moor, J.H., *Notices of the Indian Archipelago and adjacent countries.* Part 1, Singapore 1837.

Morenz, Siegfried, *Ägyptische Religion.* 2nd ed., Stuttgart 1977.

Morse, Jedidah, *A report to the Secretary of War of the United States on Indian affairs, comprising a narrative of a tour performed in the summer of 1820.* New-Haven 1822 (reprinted New York 1970).

Motolinia, Toribio, *Memoriales e historia de los Indios de la Nueva España.* Ed. Fidel de Lejarzu. Madrid 1970.

Müller, Wilhelm Johann, *Die africanische auf der guinesischen Gold-Cust gelegene Landschafft Fetu.* Graz 1968 (first published Hamburg 1676).

Murray, M.A., Burial customs and beliefs in the hereafter in predynastic Egypt. In: *Journal of Egyptian Archaeology* 42 (1956), 86–96.

Nachtigal, Gustav, *Sahara und Sudan. Ergebnisse sechsjähriger Reisen in Afrika.* Vol. 2, Berlin 1881.

Nadler, Patricia, *Better Life Programme for Rural Women im Rahmen ländlicher Entwicklung und Frauenförderung in Nigeria.* Diploma thesis, Geographical Institute of the University of Zürich, 1994.

Néel, H., Note sur deux peuplades de la frontière libérienne, les Kissi et les Toma. In: *L'Anthropologie* 24 (1933), 445–75.

Neuhauss, R., *Deutsch Neu-Guinea.* 3 vols, Berlin 1911.

Nieuwenhuis, A.W., *Quer durch Borneo. Ergebnisse seiner Reise in den Jahren 1894, 1896–97 und 1898–1900.* 2 vols, Leiden 1904–1907.

Nieuwenhuis, J.T./Rosenberg, H.C.B. von, *Verslag omtrent het eiland Nias en deszelfs bewoners.* Verhandelingen von het Bataviaasch Genootschap van Kunsten und Wetenschappen 30 [1863].

Nihongi. Chronicles of Japan from the earliest times to AD 697. Trans. W.G. Aston. 2 parts in 1 vol. London 1896 (reprinted London, 1956).

Nippel, Wilfried, Ethnographie und Anthropologie bei Herodot. In: Wilfried Nippel: *Griechen, Barbaren und 'Wilde'. Alte Geschichte und Sozialanthropologie,* Frankfurt a.M. 1990, 11–29; 152–6.

Norris, Robert, *Memoirs of the reign of Bossa Ahádee, King of Dahomey, an inland country of Guiney.* London 1789 (reprinted London 1968).

————, Reise nach dem Hoflager des Königs von Dahomey, Bossa Ahadi, im Jahre 1772. In: *Neue Beiträge zur Kenntniß von Afrika, mit Anm. v. Johann Reinhold Forster*, Berlin 1791, 159–224.

Oberländer, Richard, *Ozeanien II. Die Inselwelt des Stillen Ozeans in Melanesien, Polynesien und Mikronesien*. Leipzig 1873.

————, ed., *Westafrika vom Senegal bis Benguela*. 3rd rev. ed., Leipzig 1878.

Obeyesekere, Gananath, *The apotheosis of Captain Cook. European mythmaking in the Pacific*. Princeton 1992.

Oldendorp, C.G.A., *Geschichte der Mission der evangelischen Brüder auf den caraibischen Inseln S. Thomas, S. Croix und S. Jan*. Ed. Johann Jakob Bossart. Barby 1777.

Oliver, Douglas L., *Ancient Tahitian Society*. 3 vols, Honolulu 1974.

Omboni, Tito, *Viaggio nell'Africa occidentale*. Milano 1845.

Parry, N.E., *The Lakhers*. Ed. J.H. Hutton. Calcutta 1976 (first published London 1932).

Partridge, Charles, *Cross River natives, being some notes on the primitive pagans of Obubura Hill District southern Nigeria*. London 1905.

Peiffer, Karlheinz, Menschenopfer in Lateinamerika und der übrigen Welt. In: *Universitätsjahrbuch Düsseldorf 1969/70*, 335–50.

Pénicaut, see Margry.

Perelaer, M.T.H., *Ethnografische beschrijving der Dajaks*. Zalt-Bommel 1870.

Pérez, Domingo, *Relation of the Zambals* (1680). In: Blair/Robertson 47, 287–332.

Peter von Dusburg, *Chronik des Preußenlandes*. Latin and German. Ed. Max Toeppen, trans. Klaus Scholz/ Dieter Wojtecki. Darmstadt 1984.

Petrus Martyr de Angleria, De orbe novo . . . decades. In: Petrus Martyr de Angleria: *Opera*, ed. Erich Woldan, Graz 1966, 35–273.

Pigafetta, Antonio, *Magellan's voyage around the world*. Italian and English. Ed. and trans. James Alexander Robertson. 2 vols, Cleveland 1906.

Pinguet, Maurice, *Der Freitod in Japan. Ein Kulturvergleich*. Berlin 1991.

Pires, Tomé, *The Suma Oriental. An account of the East, from the Red Sea to Japan, written in Malacca and India in 1512–1515*. Ed. and Engl. trans. from the Portugese Armando Cortesão. Reprinted Nendeln 1967.

Playfair, A., *The Garos*. London 1909.

Pleyte, C.M., De geographische Verbreiding van het koppensnellen in den Oost Indischen Archipel. In: *Tijdschrift van het Koninklijk*

Nederlandsch Ardrijkskundig Genootschap, 2nd series, vol.8 (1891), 908–46.

Plutarch, Philopoemen. In: Plutarch, *Vitae Parallelae/Parallel Lives*. Vol. 10, trans. by Bernadotte Perrin, Cambridge, Mass. 1969, 255–319.

Polack, J.S., *Manners and customs of the New Zealanders; with notes corroborative of their habits, usages, etc., and remarks to intending emigrants*. 2 vols, reprinted Christchurch 1976 (first published London 1840).

Pomar, Juan Bautista, Relación de Tezcoco. In: *Nueva colección de documentos para la historia de México*, vol. 3, México 1891, 1–69.

Pommegorge, Pruneau de, *Description de la Nigritie*. Amsterdam 1789.

Pomponius Mela, *De situ orbis A.D. 43/Geography*. Trans. by Paul Berry, Lewiston 1997.

Posern, Thomas, *Strukturelle Gewalt als Paradigma sozialethisch-theologischer Theoriebildung*. Frankfurt a.M. 1992.

Potratz, Johannes A.H., *Die Skythen in Südrussland. Ein untergegangenes Volk in Südosteuropa*. Basel 1963.

Prahl, Über Selbstmorde bei den Chinesen unter beesonderer Berücksichtigung des deutschen Schutzgebiets Kiautschou und der Provinz Schantung. In: *Archiv für Rassen- und Gesellschafts-Biologie* 5 (1908), 669–706.

Preidel, Helmut, Die Witwenverbrennung bei slawischen Völkern. In: *Stifter-Jahrbuch* 7 (1962), 275–92.

Preuss, Konrad Theodor, Menschenopfer und Selbstverstümmelung bei der Todtentrauer in Amerika. Eine Darstellung der Natur des Gewissens vermittelst der vergleichenden Völkerpsychologie. In: *Festschrift Adolf Bastian Zum 70. Gebuststag*, Berlin 1896, 197–230.

Preußisches Urkundenbuch. Vol. 1, 1st half, ed. Philippi. Reprinted Aalen 1961 (first published 1882).

[Prévost, Antoine-François, ed.], *Histoire générale des voyages*. Vol. 17, The Hague 1763.

Pritchard, James B., ed., *Ancient Near Eastern texts relating to the Old Testament*. 2nd ed., Princeton 1955.

Procopius, *History of the Wars*. 7 vols., trans. by H.B. Dewing and Glanville Downey, Cambridge, Mass. 1969.

Pryer, W.B., On the natives of British North Borneo. In: *Journal of the Anthropological Institute of Great Britain and Ireland* 16 (1886), 229–36.

Raffles, Thomas Stamford, *The History of Java*. 2 vols, London 1817 (reprinted Kuala Lumpur 1978, ed. John Bastin).

Ramseyer, Friedrich August/Kühne, Johannes, *Vier Jahre in Asante. Tagebücher aus der Zeit ihrer Gefangenschaft.* Ed. H. Gundert. Basel 1875.

———, *Vier Jahre in Asante. Tagebücher der Missionare Ramseyer und Kühne.* Ed. H. Gundert. 2nd improved and extended ed., Basel 1875.

———, *Four years in Ashantee.* New York 1875.

Ramusio, Giovanni Battista, *Navigazioni e viaggi.* Ed. Marica Milanesi. Vol.1, Torino 1978.

Ranke, Kurt, *Indogermanische Totenverehrung.* Vol. 1, Helsinki 1951.

Rathbone, Richard, *Murder and politics in colonial Ghana.* New Haven 1993.

Rattray, R.S., *Religion and art in Ashanti.* Oxford 1927.

Ray, Benjamin, Death, kingship and royal ancestors in Buganda. In: Frank E. Reynolds/Earle H. Waugh, eds, *Religious encounters with death. Insights from the history and anthropology of religions,* University Park, Pennsylvania 1977, 56–69.

Reade, Winwood W., *Savage Africa, being the narrative of a tour in Equatorial, Southwestern and Northwestern Africa.* New York 1864.

Realencyclopädie der classischen Altertumswissenschaft. Eds August F. Pauly/ Georg Wissowa *et al.* 83 vols, Stuttgart 1894–1997.

Reisner, George Andrew, *The development of the Egyptian tomb down to the accession of Cheops.* Cambridge, Mass. 1936.

———, *Excavations at Kerma.* 3 vols, Cambridge, Mass. 1923 (reprinted Millwood, New York 1975).

Relacion de las ceremonias y ritos, poblacion y gobierno de los indios de la provincia de Mechuacan. In: *Colección de documentos inéditos para la historia de España,* ed. Marques de Miraflores/Miguel Salva, vol. 53 (Madrid 1869, reprinted Nendeln 1966), 5–293.

Remy, Jules, *Voyages au pays des Mormons.* 2 vols, Paris 1860.

Ricketts, H., *Narrative of the Ashantee War; with a view of the present state of the colony of Sierra Leone.* London 1831.

Rolle, Renate, *Totenkult der Skythen.* Part I: *Das Steppengebiet.* 2 vols, Berlin 1979.

———, *Die Welt der Skythen. Stutenmelker und Pferdebogner: Ein antikes Reitervolk in neuer Sicht.* Luzern 1980.

Rosaldo, Renato, *Ilongot headhunting 1883–1974. A study in society and history.* Stanford 1980.

Roscoe, John, *The Baganda. An account of their native customs and beliefs.* London 1911.

———, *The Bakitara or Banyoro.* Cambridge 1923.

————, *The Banyakole*. Cambridge 1923.

————, The Negro-Hamitic people of Uganda. In: *Scottish Geographical Magazine* 39 (1923), 145–59.

————, *The Northern Bantu. An account of some Central African tribes of the Uganda Protectorate*. Cambridge 1915.

Roth, Henry Ling, *Great Benin. Its customs, art and horrors*. Halifax 1903.

————, *The natives of Sarawak and British North Borneo*. 2 vols, London 1896 (reprinted Kuala Lumpur 1968).

Rouffaer, G.P./Ijzerman, J.W., eds, *De eerste schipvaart der Nederlanders naar Oost-Indië onder Cornelis de Houtman 1595–1597*. Vol. 1: *D'eerste boeck van Willem Lodewycksz*. The Hague 1915.

Ruhstrat, Ernst, *Aus dem Lande der Mitte. Schilderungen der Sitten und Gebräuche der Chinesen*. Berlin n.d. [1899].

Rutter, Owen, *The pagans of North Borneo*. Reprinted Singapore 1985 (first published London 1929).

Ryce, Tamara Talbot, *The Scythians*. London 1957.

Ryder, A.F.C., *Benin and the Europeans 1485–1897*. London 1969.

Sahagún, Bernardino de, *Historia general de las cosas de Nueva España*. Ed. Angel María Garibay K. 3rd ed., Mexico 1975.

St. John, Spenser, *Life in the forests of the Far East*. 2 vols, London 1862.

San Nicolas, Andres de, *General history of the discalced Augustinian Fathers* (1664). In: Blair/Robertson 21 (1905), 111ff.

Santa Cruz Pachacuti-Jamqui Salcamayhua, Juan de, An account of the antiquities of Peru. In: Clements R. Markham, ed. and trans., *Narratives of the rights and laws of the Yncas*, London 1873, 65–120.

Sarasin, Fritz, *Ethnologie der Neu-Caledonier und Loyalty-Insulaner*. München 1929.

Sarasin, Paul/Sarasin, Fritz, *Reisen in Celebes ausgeführt in den Jahren 1893–1896 und 1902–1903*. 2 vols, Wiesbaden 1905.

Schärer, Hans, Die Bedeutung des Menschenopfers im Dajakischen Totenkult. In: *Mitteilungsblatt der Gesellschaft für Völkerkunde* 10 (Leipzig 1940), 3–30.

————, Das Menschenopfer bei den Katinganern (Ein Beitrag zum Opferdienst der Katinganer). In: *Tijdschrift voor Indische Taal-, Land- en Volkenkunde* 78 (Batavia 1938), 536–78.

Schebesta, Paul, *Vollblutneger und Halbzwerge. Forschungen unter Waldnegern und Halbpygmäen am Jturi in Belgisch Kongo*. Salzburg 1934.

Schebesta, P.P., Die Zimbabwe-Kultur in Afrika. In: *Anthropos 21* (1926), 484–522.

Schellong, O., Über Familienleben und Gebräuche der Papuas der Umgebung von Finschhafen (Kaiser-Wilhelms-Land). In: *Zeitschrift für Ethnologie* 21 (1889), 10–25.

Schetelig, Haakon, Traces of the custom of 'suttee' in Norway during the Viking age. In: *Viking Society for Northern Research. Saga Book of the Viking Club* 6/2 (London 1910), 180–208.

Schlegel, G., Iets omtrent de betrekkingen der Chinezen met Java, voor de komst der Europeanen aldaar. In: *Tijdschrift voor Indische Taal-, Land- en Volkenkunde* 20 (1873), 9–31.

Schneider, K., Art. Gladiatores, in: *RE, Suppl.* 3 (1918), 760–84.

Schneider, Wilhelm, *Die Religion der afrikanischen Naturvölker.* Münster 1891.

Schoch, Alfred, Rituelle Menschentötungen in Polynesien. PhD thesis. Freiburg i.Üe. 1953, Ulm 1954.

Schoolcraft, Henry R., *Historical and statistical information, respecting the history, condition and prospects of the Indian tribes of the United States.* 6 vols, Philadelphia 1851–1857.

Schreuer, Hans, Das Recht der Toten. Eine germanistische Untersuchung. In: *Zeitschrift für vergleichende Rechtswissenschaft* 33 (1915), 333–432; 34 (1916), 1–208.

Schröder, E.E.W.Gs., *Nias. Ethnographische, geographische en historische aantekeningen en studien.* 2 vols, Leiden 1917.

Schütt, Otto H., *Reisen im südwestlichen Becken des Congo.* Ed. Paul Lindberg. Berlin 1881.

Schuster, Meinhard, Kopfjagd in Indonesien. Ph.D. thesis, Frankfurt am Main, typescript, n.d. [1956].

Schwenn, Friedrich, *Die Menschenopfer bei den Griechen und Römern.* Gießen 1915.

Schynse, August Wilhelm, *Zwei Jahre am Congo. Erlebnisse und Schilderungen.* Ed. Karl Hespers. Köln 1889.

Seligman, C.G./Seligman, Brenda Z., *Pagan tribes of the Nilotic Sudan.* London 1932.

Shooter, Joseph, *The Kafirs of Natal and the Zulu country.* Reprinted New York 1969 (first published 1857).

Sibree, James, *The great African island. Chapters on Madagascar.* London 1880 (reprinted New York 1969).

Skertchly, J.A., *Dahomey as it is; being a narrative of eight months' residence in that country, with a full account of the notorious annual customs, and the social and religious institutions of the Ffons; also an appendix on Ashantee, and a glossary of Dahoman words and titles.* London 1874.

Smet, Pierree Jean de, *Voyages aux montagnes rocheuses et séjour chez les tribus indiennes de l'Orégon (Etats-Units).* 2ⁿᵈ ed., Bruxelles 1873 (first published 1848).

Smith, Jane Idleman/Haddad, Yvonne Yazbeck, *The Islamic understanding of death and resurrection.* Albany 1981.

Smith, Sidney, Assyriological notes. A Bablyonian fertility cult. In: *Journal of the Royal Asiatic Society* 1928, 849–75.

Snelgrave, William, *Nouvelle relation de quelques endroits de Guinée, et du commerce d'esclaves qu'on y fait.* Amsterdam 1735.

Solinus, Gaius Julius, *Collectanea rerum memorabilium.* Berlin 1864.

Sonnerat, *Voyage aux Indes orientales et à la Chine, fait par ordre du Roi, depuis 1774 jusqu'en 1781.* 2 vols. Paris 1782.

Speiser, Felix, *Ethnographische Materialien aus den Neuen Hebriden und den Banks-Inseln.* Berlin 1923.

———, *Südsee/Urwald Kannibalen. Reisen in den Neuen Hebriden und Santa-Cruz-Inseln.* Stuttgart 1924.

Speleers, Louis, *Les figurines funéraires égyptiennes.* Bruxelles 1923.

Spencer, Herbert, *The Works.* Vol. 6: *A system of synthetic philosophy; The principles of sociology*, vol. 1, reprinted Osnabrück 1966 (first published 1904).

Spuler, Bertold, *Die Mongolen in Iran. Politik, Verwaltung und Kultur der Ilchanzeit. 1220–1350.* Leipzig 1939.

Stannard, David E., *Before the horror. The population of Hawai'i on the eve of western contact.* Honolulu 1989.

Steinmetz, S.R., *Ethnologische Studien zur ersten Entwicklung der Strafe, nebst einer psychologischen Abhandlung über Grausamkeit und Rachsucht.* 2 vols, 2nd ed., Groningen 1928 (first published 1894).

———, Der Selbstmord bei den afrikanischen Naturvölkern. In: S.R. Steinmetz: *Gesammelte Schriften zur Ethnologie und Soziologie*, vol. 2, Groningen 1930, 354–81 (first published 1907).

Stöhr, Waldemar, Totenreise und Totendorf in der Kunst der Ngadja-Dajak aus Kalimantan. Ein Beispiel altindonesischer Jenseitsvorstellung. In: Mensen, ed., 41–66.

Streck, Maximilian, *Assurbanipal und die letzten assyrischen Könige bis zum Untergange Ninivehs.* Vol. 2: Texts. Leipzig 1916.

Stresemann, E., Religiöse Gebräuche auf Seran. In: *Tijdschrift voor Indische Taal-, Land- en Volkenkunde* 62 (1923), 305–424.

Suetonius, Augustus. In: *De vita Caesarum/The Lives of the Caesars.* Vol. 1, trans. by J.C. Rolfe, Cambridge, Mass. 1969, 122–287.

Swanton, John R., *Indian tribes of the lower Mississippi Valley and adjacent coast of the Gulf of Mexico.* Washington 1911 (reprinted New York 1970).

Talbot, P. Amaury, *Life in Southern Nigeria. The magic, beliefs and customs of the Ibibo tribe.* London 1923.

Tauern, Odo Deodatus, *Patasiwa und Patalima. Vom Molukkeneiland Seram und seinen Bewohnern.* Leipzig 1918.

Taylor, Richard, *Te ika a maui, or New Zealand and its inhabitants.* London 1855.

Theal, George McCall, *History and ethnography of Africa south of the Zambesi.* Vol.1: *The Portuguese in South Africa from 1505 to 1700.* London 1907.

Thietmar von Merseburg, *Chronik.* Ed. and German trans. Werner Trillmich. 5th ed., Darmstadt 1974.

Thomas, Thomas Morgan, *Eleven years in Central South Africa.* 2nd ed., ed. by Richard Brown, London 1971 (first published London 1872).

Thompson, Edward, *Suttee. A historical and philosophical enquiry into the Hindu rite of widow-burning.* London 1928.

Thomson, Basil, *The Fijians. A study of the decay of custom.* London 1908.

Thomson, Joseph, *To the Central African lakes and back: The narrative of the Royal Geographical Society's East Central African Expedition, 1878–1880.* 2 vols, London 1881.

Tönjes, Hermann, *Ovamboland. Land Leute Mission. Mit besonderer Berücksichtigung seines größten Stammes Oukuanjama.* Berlin 1911.

Tooker, Elizabeth, Natchez social organization: fact or anthropological folklore? In: *Ethnohistory 10* (1963), 358–72.

Torquemada, Juan de, *Monarquía Indiana.* Vol. 2, 5th ed., ed. Miguel León Portilla, Mexico 1975.

Tregear, Edward, *The Maori race.* Wanganz, N.Z. 1904.

Tremearne, A.J.N., *The tailed head-hunters of Nigeria. An account of an official's seven years' experiences in the northern Nigerian pagan belt, and a description of the manners, habits, and customs of the native tribes.* London 1912.

Turner, George, *Nineteen years in Polynesia: missionary life, travels, and researches in the islands of the Pacific.* London 1861.

Tylor, Edward B., *Primitive culture. Researches into the development of mythology, philosophy, religion, language, art and custom.* 2 vols, 4th ed., London 1903.

Valdez, Francisco Travasses, *Six years of a traveller's life in Western Africa.* 2 vols, London 1861.

Valentyn, François, *Oud en Nieuw Oost-Indiën.* 5 vols, Dordrecht 1724–1726.

Valeri, Valerio, *Kingship and sacrifice. Ritual and society in ancient Hawaii.* Chicago 1985.

Van der Kraan, Alfons, Human sacrifice in Bali: sources, notes and commentary. In: *Indonesia* No. 4 (Cornell Southeast Asia Program 1985), 89–122.

Velde, Liévin van de, La région du Bas-Congo et du Kwilou-Niadi. Usages et coutumes des indigènes. In: *Bulletin de la Société Royale Belge de Géographie* 10 (1886), 347–412.

Volhard, Ewald, *Kannibalismus.* Stuttgart 1939.

Volmering, Th, Het koppensnellen bij de volken in den Oost-Indischen Archipel. In: *Koloniaal Tijdschrift* 3 (1914), 1153–84; 1319–37; 1461–91.

Waddell, Hope Masterton, *Twenty-nine years in the West Indies and Central Africa. A Review of missionary work and adventure 1829–1858.* 2nd ed., ed. by G.I. Jones, London 1970 (first published London 1863).

Wagner, Ulla, *Colonialism and Iban warfare.* Stockholm 1972.

Waitz, Theodor/Gerland, Georg, *Anthropologie der Naturvölker.* 6 vols, Leipzig 1859–1872.

Ward, Herbert, *Fünf Jahre unter den Stämmen des Kongo-Staates.* Trans. H.v. Wobeser. Leipzig 1891.

Weeks, John H., *Among the Congo Cannibals.* London 1913.

Weinberger-Thomas, Catherine, *Cendres d'immortalité. La crémation des veuves en Inde.* Paris 1996. Engl. trans. by Jeffrey Mehlman and David G. White, Chicago 2000.

Wells, William V., Wild life in Oregon. In: *Harper's New Monthly Magazine* 13 (1856), 588–608.

West, John, *The substance of a journal during a residence at the Red River Colony, British North America; and frequent excursions among the North-West American Indians, in the years 1820, 1821, 1822, 1823.* London 1824 (reprinted Wakefield 1966).

Westermann, Diedrich, *Die Kpelle. Ein Negerstamm in Liberia.* Göttingen 1921.

———, *The Shilluk people. Their language and folklore.* Philadelphia 1912.

White, Douglas R. *et al.*, Natchez class and rank reconsidered. In: *Ethnology* 10 (1971), 369–88.

Wijngaarden, J.K., Naar Soemba. In: *Mededelingen van wege het Neder-landsche Zendelinggenootschap* 37 (1893), 352–76.

Wilken, G.A., *Het animisme bij de volken van den Indischen Archipel.* Leiden 1885. Also in: G.A. Wilken: *Verspreide Geschriften* 3 (Semarang 1912), 1–287.

————, Über das Haaropfer und einige andere Trauergebräuche bei den Völkern Indonesiens. In: G.A. Wilken: *Verspreide Geschriften* 3 (Semarang 1912), 399–500 (first published 1886–1887).

Wilkerson, S. Jeffrey, In search of the Mountain of foam: human sacrifice in Eastern Mesoamerica. In: Elizabeth Boone (ed.), *Ritual Human Sacrifice in Mesoamerica. A Conference at Dumbarton Oaks, 13th and 14th October 1979.* Washington 1984, 101–32.

Wilkes, Charles, *Narrative of the United States exploring expedition, during the years 1838, 1839, 1840, 1841, 1842.* Vol. 3, New York 1856.

Wilks, Ivor, Asante: human sacrifice or capital punishment? A rejoinder. In: *International Journal of African Historical Studies* 21 (1988), 443–52.

————, *Asante in the nineteenth century. The structure and evolution of a political order.* 2nd ed., Cambridge 1989.

Williams, Clifford, Asante, Human sacrifice or capital punishment? An assessment of the period 1807–1874. In: *International Journal of African Historical Studies* 21 (1988), 433–41.

Williams, F.E., *Orokaiva Society.* London 1969 (first published 1930).

Williams, Mary Wilhelmine, *Social Scandinavia in the Viking age.* New York 1920.

Williams, Thomas/Calvert, James, *Fiji and the Fijians.* Ed. George Stringer Rowe. 2 vols, London 1858.

Wing, van, *Études Bakongo. Histoire et sociologie.* Bruxelles n.d. [1921].

Wisse, Jakob, Selbstmord und Todesfurcht bei den Naturvölkern. PhD thesis Amsterdam 1933, Zutphen 1933.

Wissmann, Hermann von, *Meine zweite Durchquerung Äquatorial-Afrikas vom Congo zum Zambesi während der Jahre 1886 und 1887.* Frankfurt a.O. n.d. [c. 1890].

————, *et al. Im Innern Afrikas. Die Erforschung der Kassai während der Jahre 1883, 1884 und 1885.* 3rd ed. Leipzig 1891.

Witte, J., *Das Jenseits im Glauben der Völker.* Leipzig 1929.

Woolley, C. Leonard, Excavations at Ur, 1927–8. In: *The Antiquaries Journal* 8 (1928), 415–48.

————, *Ur excavations.* Vol. II: *The royal cemetery.* 2 parts, London 1934.

————, *Ur 'of the Chaldees'. The final account, 'Excavations at Ur', revised and updated by P.R.S. Moorey.* London 1982.

Worcester, Dean C., Head-hunters of Northern Luzon. In: *National Geographic Magazine* 23 (1912), 833–930.

Wüst, Ernst, Art. Polyxena. In: *RE* 21, 2 (1952), 1840–1850.

Yang, Hsi-Chang, The Shang dynasty cemetery system. In: K.C. Chang, ed., *Studies of Shang Archaeology,* New Haven 1986, 49-63.

Yang Shushen, *Liao shi jiaubiau* [Introduction to the history of the Liao]. Shenyang 1984.

Yarrow, H.C., A further contribution to the study of the mortuary customs of the North American Indians. In: J.W. Powell, ed., *First annual report of the Bureau of Ethnology to the Secretary of the Smithsonian Institution 1879–80,* Washington 1881, 87–203.

Yule, Henry, *Cathay and the way thither, being a collection of medieval notices of China.* 2nd ed., ed. by Henri Cordier, 4 vols, reprinted Nendeln 1967 (first published 1913–1916).

Zárate, Agustín de, Historia del descubrimiento y conquista de la provincia del Peru [1555]. In: *Biblioteca de autores españoles 26,* Madrid 1886, 459–574.

Zollinger, H., Het eiland Lombok. In: *Tijdschrift voor Nederlandsch Indië* 9 (1847), 301–83.

Bibliography for Part II

1. UNPUBLISHED SOURCES

Only the most important collections consulted are listed here. References to less relevant collections, cited only once, are given in the footnotes.

a) India Office Records (IOR), London (now Oriental and India Office Collections, British Library, London)

L/L/13 (1030) Documents on the appeal against the abolition of 1829.

P/139/34 } Widow burnings in the
P/139/35 } years 1827 and 1828.

P/206/81
P/206/82 } Questions concerning the implementation
F/4/665 } of the abolition in the Bombay Presidency.
F/4/920
P/V/798

E/4/920 ⎱ Questions concerning the implementation
F/4/522 ⎰ of the abolition in the Madras Presidency.

b) India Office Library (IOL), London (now Oriental and India Office Collections, British Library, London).

Various manuscripts, including
Mss. Eur. D 814 Ludlow Papers.
Mss. Eur. F 140 Amherst Papers.

c) Public Record Office (PRO), Kew/London.

PC/2/213 ⎱ Documents on the appeal against the
PC/7/2 ⎰ abolition of 1829.

d) University Library, Nottingham
Bentinck Papers

2. PARLIAMENTARY PAPERS, GREAT BRITAIN AND IRELAND, HOUSE OF COMMONS (CITED AS PP)

The page numbers given here refer to the handwritten pagination in the collections of the British Library. All page numbers in the footnotes, however, refer to the printed, separate pagination of the individual Parliamentary papers, which appear here in brackets.

1821, vol. 18, pp. 295–565: Paper no. 749 (pp. 1–271).
1823, vol. 17, pp. 157–295: Paper no. 466 (pp. 1–139).
1824, vol. 23, pp. 311–71 (pp. 322-332 are missing in the pagination): Paper no. 443 (pp. 1–51).
1825, vol. 24, pp. 225–30: Paper no. 508 (pp. 1–6).
1825, vol. 24, pp. 231–444: Paper no. 518 (pp. 1–214).
1826–1827, vol. 20: Paper no. 354 (pp. 1–161).
1828, vol. 23: Paper no. 547 (pp. 1–28)
1830, vol. 28: Paper no. 178 (pp. 1–275).
1830, vol. 28: Paper no. 550 (pp. 1–10).

All these papers are compiled in the IOL under the catalogue number W 2263.

3. PUBLISHED SOURCES AND LITERATURE

The bibliography for this part contains—in contrast to Bibliography I—not only all the works quoted in the footnotes, but also further relevant titles for the topic.

Aelianus, *Variae Historiae/Historical Miscellany*. Trans. by Niegel G. Wilson, Cambridge, Mass. 1997.

A.M., Calcutta Diary. In: *EPW* 22 (1987), 1729–1731.

Abstract of the arguments regarding the burning of widows considered as a religious rite. Calcutta 1830.

Abu-l-Fazl, *The Akbar Nama (History of the reign of Akbar including an account of his predecessors)*. Trans. H. Beveridge. 3 vols, reprinted New Delhi 1979.

Acworth, H.A., On the Marathi ballad written on the suttee of Ramaba, widow of Madhavrao Peshwa. In: *Journal of the Anthropological Society of Bombay* 2 (1891), 179–92.

Aelianus, *Variae Historiae / Historical Miscellany*. Trans. by Nigel G. Wilson, Cambridge, Mass. 1997.

Aggarwal, J.C./Chowdhry, N.K., *Census of India 1991: Historical and world perspective*. New Delhi 1991.

Agnes, Flavia, Protecting women against violence? Review of a decade of legislation 1980–9. In: *EPW* 27 (1992), 19–33.

Ahmad, Monazir, *Lord William Bentinck*. Allahabad 1978.

Ahmad, Zakiuddin, Sati in eighteenth century Bengal. In: *Journal of the Asiatic Society of Pakistan* 13 (1968), 147–64.

Ahuja, S.K., The legend that was sati. In: *Folklore* 11/3 (Calcutta 1970), 77–85.

Aitken, R.H., *Suttee*. Bombay 1872.

Alberuni, *Alberuni's India. An account of the religion, philosophy, literature, geography, chronology, astronomy, customs, laws and astrology of India about AD 1030*. Ed. and trans. Edward C. Sachau. 2 vols, London 1888.

Albuquerque, Brás de, *Comentarios de Afonso de Albuquerque*. 4 parts in 2 vols, 5th ed., Lisboa 1973.

Altekar, A.S., *The position of women in Hindu civilization from pre-historic times to the present day*. 3rd ed., Delhi 1962.

Alvares, Pedro, Navigazione. In: Ramusio, Giovanni Battista: *Navigazione e viaggi*. Ed. Marica Milanesi, vol. 1 (Torino 1978), 619–53.

An account of the proceedings at a public meeting held at the City of York, on the 19th January 1827, to take into consideration the expediency of petitioning Parliament on the subject of Hindoo widows in British India. York 1827.

Anand, Mulk Raj, *Sati. A writeup of Raja Ram Mohan Roy about burning of widows alive*. Delhi 1989.

Andersen, Jürgen/Iversen, Volquard, *Orientalische Reise-Beschreibungen in der Bearbeitung von Adam Olearius*. Ed. Dieter Lohmeier, Tübingen 1980 (first published Schleswig 1669).

Anderson, J.D., The legend of Sati. In: *Asiatic Quarterly Review* NS 1 (1913), 277–92.

Anderson, Michael Roy, *Sati: The social history of a crime.* Typescript London, School of Oriental and African Studies, LL M Essay 1988.

André, Jacques/Filliozat, Jean, *L'Inde vue de Rome. Textes latins de l'Antiquité relatifs à l'Inde.* Paris 1986.

An old inhabitant of Bengal, Plan for abolishing human sacrifices in India. In: *Oriental Herald* 8 (London 1826), 479–88.

Anon., Review: Reginald Heber, Narrative of a journey through the Upper Provinces of India, from Calcutta to Bombay. In: *Quarterly Review* 37 (1828), 100–47.

Anti Sati Bill and the Women's Movement. In: *Women's Equality* Jan.-March 1988, 18–21.

Appeal to the Privy Council for permission to bury or burn Hindoo widows alive. In: *Alexander's East India Magazine* 2 (1831), 355–8.

Appendix to the statement submitted on the part of the Court of Directors of the East-India Company, in support of the regulation of the Governor General in Council, declaring the practice of Suttee illegal and punishable by the criminal courts. N.p., n.d.

Archaeological Survey of India. Vol. 7, Calcutta 1878; vol. 9, Calcutta 1879.

Arunachalam, M., The sati cult in Tamilnadu. In: *Institute of Traditional Cultures (Madras) Bulletin* July/December 1978, 59–104.

A select bibliography on women in India. Bombay n.d. [ca.1975].

Ashraf, Kunwar Muhammad, *Life and conditions of the people of Hindustan (1200–1550 AD).* Karachi 1978.

Aspinall, A., *Cornwallis in Bengal.* Manchester 1931.

Baig, Tara Ali, ed., *Women of India.* Delhi 1958.

Balbi, Gasparo, *Viaggio dell'Indie orientali.* Venice 1590.

Baldaeus, Philippus, *Nauwkeurige en waarachtige ontedekking en wederlegginge van de afgoderye der oost-indische Heidenen.* Amsterdam 1672.

Ballhatchet, Kenneth, *Social policy and social change in western India, 1817–1830.* London 1957.

Bāṇa, *The Kādambarī.* Trans. C.M. Ridding. London 1896.

Banerjee, D.N., *Early administrative system of the East India Company in Bengal.* Vol. 1, 1765–1774, London 1943.

Banerjee, Sudanshu Mohun, Rammohun Roy and the abolition of the sati rite. In: *Journal of the Asiatic Society* 19 (Calcutta 1977), 59–61.

Barbosa, Duarte, *Livro em que dá relação do que viu e ouviu no Oriente.* Ed. Augusto Reis Machado. Lisboa 1946.

Barua, B.P., ed., *Raja Rammohun Roy and the new learning.* Calcutta 1988.

Basham, A.L., *The wonder that was India. A survey of the culture of the Indian Sub-continent before the coming of the Muslims.* London 1954.

Basu, Krishna, Movement for emancipation of women in the nineteenth century. In: Ray, Renuka *et al.: Role and status of women in Indian Society,* Calcutta 1978, 36–51.

Bayly, C.A., From ritual to ceremony: death ritual and society in Hindu North India since 1600. In: Whaley, Joachim, ed., *Mirrors of mortality. Studies in the social history of death,* London 1981, 154–86.

Bearce, George D., Lord William Bentinck: the application of liberalism to India. In: *Journal of Modern History* 28 (1956), 234–46.

Bengal Civilian, A, On the practice of Suttee. In: *Asiatic Journal* 27 (1829), 57–63.

Bentinck, William Cavendish, *The correspondence of Lord William Cavendish Bentinck Governor-General of India 1828–1835.* Ed. C.H. Philips. 2 vols, Oxford 1977.

Bentinck Papers, see unpublished sources.

Bernier, François, Lettre à Monsieur Chapelain, envoyé de Chiras en Perse, le 4 Octobre 1667. In: *Suite des Mémoires du Sr. Bernier sur l'empire du Grand Mogol.* Paris 1667.

Bhattacharya, Durgaprasad, ed., *Census of India 1961. Report on the population estimates of India (1820–1830)* [1965]. *Vol. II: 1801–1810* [1982], *Vol. III: 1811–1820* [1989]. New Delhi n.d.

Bhattacharya, Malini, Sati in Bengal: the socio-economic background. In: *EPW* 24 (1989), 669–70 (Review of B.B. Roy: Socio-economic impact of Sati in Bengal).

Biervillas, Innigo de, *Voyage d'Innigo de Biervillas, Portugais, à la côte de Malabar, Goa, Batavia, et autres lieux des Indes Orientales.* 2 vols, Paris 1736.

Bishnoi, Brij Lal, Sati and its suppression in the Rajput states (1800–1857). In: Ganshyam Lal Devra, ed., *Socio-economic study of Rajasthan* (Jodhpur 1986), 79-89.

Böhtlingk, Otto, *Indische Sprüche.* 3 vols, 2nd ed., St. Petersburg 1870–1873.

Bogaert, Abraham, *Historische Reizen door d'oostersche deelen van Asia.* Amsterdam 1711.

Bohlen, P. von, *Das alte Indien, mit besonderer Rücksicht auf Aegypten*. 2 vols, Königsberg 1830.

Bose, Pramatha Nath, *A history of Hindu civilization during British rule*. 3 vols, London 1894–1896 (reprinted New Delhi 1975).

Bose, Shib Chunder, *The Hindoos as they are. A description of the manners, customs and inner life of Hindoo society in Bengal*. London 1881.

Boulger, Demetrius C., *Lord William Bentinck*. Oxford 1892.

Bowrey, Thomas, *A geographical account of countries round the Bay of Bengal, 1669 to 1679*. Ed. Richard Carnac Temple. Cambridge 1905.

Breve relação das escrituras dos gentios da India Oriental, e dos seus costumes. In: *Collecção de noticias para a historia e geografia das nações ultramarinas que vivem nos dominios portuguezes, ou lhes são visinhos*. Vol. 1, Lisboa 1812, 1–59.

Briggs, John, *Letters addressed to a young person in India; calculated to afford instruction for his conduct in general, and more especially in his intercourse with the natives*. London 1828.

Bruce, Peter Henry, *Memoirs of Peter Henry Bruce, Esq., a military officer, in the services of Prussia, Russia, and Great Britain. Containing an account of his travels in Germany, Russia, Tartary, Turkey, the West Indies etc*. London 1782.

Buchanan, Claudius, *Colonial ecclesiastical establishment: being a brief view of the state of the colonies of Great Britain and of her Asiatic empire, in respect to religious instruction: prefaced by some considerations on the national duty of affording it*. 2nd ed., London 1813.

———, *Memoir of the expediency of an ecclesiastical establishment for British India*. 2nd ed., London 1812 (1st ed. London 1805).

Buckland, Charles Edward, *Bengal under the Lieutenant-Governors, being a narrative of the principal events and public measures during their periods of office, from 1854 to 1898*. 2 vols, 2nd ed., New Delhi 1976 (first published Calcutta 1901).

Bunsen, Marie von, Briefe aus Indien. In: *Die Frau* 22 (Berlin 1915), 665–78.

———, Zur indischen Witwenverbrennung. In: *Deutsche Rundschau* 105 (1903), 458–61.

Burnell, John, *Bombay in the days of Queen Anne, being an account of the settlement*. Ed. Samuel T. Sheppard. London 1933.

Burning of a young betrothed bride. India—Chandernagore. In: *The Missionary Register*, London 1820, 119–20.

Burning of Hindoo Widows. In: *Oriental Herald* 1 (1824), 551–60.

Bushby, Henry Jeffreys, Widow-burning: a narrative. London 1855. First published in: *Quarterly Review* 89 (1851), 257–76.

Campbell, Donald, *A narrative of the extraordinary adventures, and sufferings by shipwrecks and imprisonment, of Donald Campbell.* 4th ed., London 1801.

Careri, Gio. Francesco Gemelli, *Giro del mondo. Vol. 3 (Indostan)*, Napoli 1700.

Carletti, Francesco, *Ragionamenti di Francesco Carletti Fiorentino sopra le cose da lui vedute ne' suoi viaggi sì dell' Indie Occidentali, e Orientali, come d'altri paesi.* 2 vols, Firenze 1701.

Carré, Abbé, *The travels of the Abbé Carré in the Near East 1672 to 1674.* Ed. Charles Fawcett, trans. Lady Fawcett. 3 vols, London 1947–1948.

Cassels, Nancy Gardner, Bentinck: humanitarian and imperialist – the abolition of Suttee. In: *Journal of British Studies* 5 (1965), 77–87.

———, *Religion and Pilgrim Tax under the Company Raj.* New Delhi 1988.

———, Review: V.N. Datta: Sati. In: *Journal of Asian History* 23 (1989), 85–6.

Castanheda, Fernão Lopes de, *História do descobrimento e conquista da India pelos Portugueses.* Ed. Pedro de Azevedo. 3rd ed., 4 vols, Coimbra 1924–1933.

Caunter, Hobart, *The Oriental Annual, or scenes in India.* [Vol. 1,] London 1834.

Census of India 1881. Statistics of Population. Vol. 2, Calcutta 1883.

Chakravarti, Uma, Gender, caste and labour. Ideological and material structure of widowhood. In: *EPW* 30 (1995), 2248–57.

Challe, Robert, *Journal d'un voyage fait aux Indes orientales (1690–1691).* Ed. Frédéric Deloffre/Melâhat Menemencioglu. Paris 1979 (first published 1721).

Chandra, Sudhir, Sati, the dharmic fallacy. In: *New Quest* No. 6 (March/April 1988), 111–14.

Chattopadhyay, Aparna, Position of widows in early medieval India in the light of the Kathāsaritsāgara. In: *Journal of the Oriental Institute* 24 (Baroda 1975), 393–402.

Chaudhury, Sushil, Medieval Indian society, state and social custom. Sati as a case study. In: *Calcutta Historical Journal* 8 (1983), 38–60.

————, Sati as social institution and the Mughals. In: *Indian History Congress. Proceedings of the 37th session.* Calicut 1976.

Chen, Marty/Dreze, Jean, Recent research on widows in India. Workshop and conference report. In: *EPW* 30 (1995), 2435–50.

Chinnian, P., *The Vellore Mutiny—1806 (The first uprising against the British).* Self-published 1982.

Chittick, William C., Eschatology. In: Seyyed Hosein Nasr, ed., *Islamic spirituality.* London 1987, 378–409.

————, 'Your sight today is piercing': the Muslim understanding of death and afterlife. In: Hiroshi Obayashi, ed., *Death and afterlife. Perspective of world religions* (New York 1992), 125–39.

Chopra, Barkat Rai, *Kingdom of the Punjab 1839–45.* Hoshiarpur 1969.

Chowdhury-Sengupta, Indira, The return of the sati: a note on heroism and domesticity in colonial Bengal. In: *Resources for Feminist Research* 22, Nos. 3/4 (1993), 41–4.

Chronica dos reis de Bisnaga. Manuscripto inedito do seculo XVI. Ed. David Lopes. Lisboa 1897.

Cicero, Marcus Tullius, *Tusculanae disputationes/Tusculan Disputations.* Trans. by J.E. King, Cambridge, Mass. 1969.

Colebrooke, H.T., trans., *A Digest of Hindu law on contracts and successions.* 4 vols, Calcutta 1797–1798.

————, On the duties of a faithful Hindu widow. In: H.T. Colebrooke: *Essays on history, literature and religions of ancient India* 1, New Delhi 1977, 114–22. (First published in: Asiatic Researches 4 [Calcutta 1795], 209–19.)

Collet, Sophia Dobson, *The life and letters of Raja Rammohun Roy.* 3rd ed., ed. by Dilip Kumar Biswas/Prabhat Chandra Ganguli. Calcutta 1962 (1st ed. 1900).

Commission of Sati (Prevention) Act (Act No. 3 of 1988). Delhi 1990.

Conti, Nicolò de', *Viaggi in Persia, India e Giava.* Ed. Mario Longhena. Milano 1929.

Coomaraswamy, Ananda K., *The dance of Siva. Fourteen Indian essays.* New York 1924.

————, Sati: a vindication of the Hindu woman. In: *Sociological Review* 6 (1913), 117–35, with a commentary by H.M. Swanwick, ibid., 136–8.

Courtright, Paul B., Sati, sacrifice, and marriage: the modernity of tradition. In: Harlan/Courtright, eds 184–203.

Coverte, Robert, *The travels.* Ed. Boies Penrose. Philadelphia 1931 (first published 1612).

Crawford, Cromwell, Ram Mohun Roy on sati and sexism. In: *Indian Journal of Social Work* 41 (1980), 73–91.

[Crawfurd, Quintin], *Sketches chiefly relating to the history, religion, learning, and manners, of the Hindoos, with a concise account of the present state of the native powers of Hindostan.* London 1790.

Cremation of widows. Counter petition of the Hindu inhabitants of Calcutta. In: *Asiatic Journal* 8 (1819), 15–17.

Cronin, Vincent, *A pearl to India. The life of Roberto de Nobili.* London 1959.

Crooke, William, *The popular religion and folk-lore of northern India.* 2 vols, Delhi 1968.

Cunningham, John William, *Christianity in India. An essay on the duty, means and consequences, of introducing the Christian religion among the native inhabitants of the British dominions in the East.* London 1808.

Dalmia-Lüderitz, Vasudha, Über die Verwendung der 'Parliamentary Papers on Widow Immolation in India, 1821–1830'. In: Adam Jones, ed., *Außereuropäische Frauengeschichte. Probleme der Forschung.* Pfaffenweiler 1990, 41–65.

Daly, Mary, *Gyn Ecology. The metaethics of feminism.* Boston 1978.

Dapper, Olfert, *Asia, of naukeurige beschryving van ht rijk des Grooten Mogols en een goot gedeelte van Indië.* Amsterdam 1672.

Das, Veena, Gender studies, cross cultural comparison and the colonial organization of knowledge. In: *Berkshire Review 21* (1986), 58–76.

———, Shakti versus Sati. A reading of the Santoshi Ma cult. In: *Manushi 49* (1988), 26–30.

Dasgupta, B.N., *Raja Rammohun Roy. The last phase.* New Delhi n.d. [ca.1980].

Datta, Jatindra Mohan, Some sociological facts about 'suttees'. In: *Modern Review 71* (Calcutta 1942), 439–41.

Datta, Kalikinkar, *Education and social amelioration of women in pre-mutiny India.* Patna n.d. [ca. 1936].

Datta, V.N., *Sati. A historical, social and philosophical enquiry into the Hindu rite of widow burning.* New Delhi 1988.

Davidson, C.J.C., *Tara, the Suttee: an Indian drama, in five acts: with copious notes, explanatory, original, and selected.* London 1851.

D'Costa, Anthony, *The Christianisation of the Goa Islands 1510–1567.* Bombay 1965.

Degrandpré, L., *Voyage dans l'Inde et au Bengale, fait dans les années 1789 et 1790.* 2 vols, Paris 1801.

Dellon, *Relation d'un voyage des Indes orientales*. 2 vols, Paris 1685.

Derrett, J. Duncan M., Anantārama's defence of suttee (*c.* 1818–1820). In: *Calcutta Sanskrit College Research Series No. 119: Our Heritage. Special number, 150th Anniversary Volume (1824–1974)*, Calcutta n.d. [1980], 47–76.

———, *Dharmaśāstra and juridicial literature*. Wiesbaden 1973.

———, *Religion, Law and the State in India*. London 1968.

Deshpande, V.V., Comments on 'a note on origin of sati' by Shri Bani Prasanna Misra. In: *Hindutva 7/11* (February 1977), 18–28.

Devi, Konduri Sarojini, *Religion in Vijayanagara Empire*. New Delhi 1990.

D'Gruyther, W.J., Panjab—Rajputana—Pataudi—Jesalmer—Burning with dead by men and women—Sati—Satu. In: *Indian Notes and Queries 8, 39* (London, Dec. 1886), 44–5.

Dhagamwar, Vasudha, *Law, power and justice. The protection of personal rights in the Indian Penal Code*. 2nd ed., New Delhi 1992.

———, Saint, victim or criminal. In: *Seminar 342* (Feb. 1988), 34–9.

Diodorus Siculus, *Bibliotheca historical / Library of Histories*. Vol. 9, trans. by Russel M. Geer, Cambridge, Mass. 1969.

Dixit, S.C., An account of widow immolation in Gujarat in 1741 AD. In: *Journal of the Anthropological Society of Bombay 14* (1931), 830–3.

Dow, Alexander, *The history of Hindustan, translated from the Persian*. 2nd ed., 2 vols, London 1970.

Droge, Arthur J./Tabor, James D., *A noble death. Suicide and martyrdom among Christians and Jews in Antiquity*. San Francisco 1992.

Drummond, Robert, *Illustrations of the grammatical parts of the Guzerattee, Mahratta and English languages*. Bombay 1808.

Dubois, J.A., *Letters on the state of Christianity in India, in which the conversion of the Hindoos is considered as impracticable*. Ed. Sharda Paul. New Delhi 1977 (first published 1821).

———, *Moeurs, institutions et cérémonies des peuples de l'Inde*. 2 vols, Paris 1825.

Dumont, Louis, *Homo hierarchicus. Le système des castes et ses implications*. Paris 1966. Engl. trans. by Mark Sainsbury, *Homo hierarchicus. The caste system and its implications*. London 1970.

Eden, Emily, *Up the country. Letters written to her sister from the upper provinces of India*. London 1983.

Edwardes, Herbert Benjamin/ Merivale, Herman, *Life of Sir Henry Lawrence*. Vol. 2, London 1872.

Elliott, Charles Boileau, *Two letters addressed to the supreme government of British India, regarding the abolition of suttees; and the best means of ameliorating the moral and intellectual conditions of the natives of India.* Salisbury n.d. [1827].

Elliot, Henry M./Dowson, John, *The history of India told by its own historians. The Muhammadan period.* Vol. 6, London 1875.

Elphinstone, Mountstuart, *The history of India.* 2 vols, London 1841.

Emperor v. Ram Dayal. In: *Indian Law Reports, Allahabad* 36 (1914), 26–33.

Emperor v. Vidyasagar Pande. In: *All India Reporter 1928 Patna*, 497–502.

English version of a song or hymn sung by a Hindoo woman, on the point of being burned on the pile with her husband's body. In: *Oriental Herald* 28 (1828), 286.

Essays relative to the habits, character, and moral improvement of the Hindoos. London 1823.

Etter, Annemarie, Wie kam es zur Sati in Indien? In: *Unipress 78* (Bern, Oct. 1993), 26–30.

Eyb, Albrecht von, *Ehebüchlein* (1472). Ed. Max Hermann. Berlin 1890.

Fedden, Henry Romilly, *Suicide. A social and historical study.* London 1938.

Fedrici, Cesare, *Viaggio di M. Cesare de i Fedrici nell'India Orientale, et oltra l'India.* Venezia 1587.

Fenicio, Jacobo, *Livro da seita dos Indios orientales.* Ed. Jarl Charpentier. Uppsala 1933.

Ferrand, Gabriel, ed. and trans., *Voyage du marchand arabe Sulaymân en Inde et en Chine rédigé en 851 suivi de remarques par Abû Zayd Hasan (vers 916).* Paris 1922.

Fisch, Jörg, A pamphlet war on Christian missions in India 1807–1809. In: *Journal of Asian History* 19 (1985), 22–70

————, A solitary vindicator of the Hindus: the life and writings of General Charles Stuart (1757/58–1828). In: *Journal of the Royal Asiatic Society* (1985), 35–57.

————, *Cheap lives and dear limbs. The British transformation of the Bengal criminal law 1769–1817.* Wiesbaden 1983.

————, Jenseitsglaube, Ungleichheit und Tod. Zu einigen Aspekten der Totenfolge. In: *Saeculum* 44 (1993), 265–99.

Fisher, Michael, *Indirect rule in India. Residents and the residency system 1764–1858.* Delhi 1991.

Fleet, John Fithfull, *Corpus Inscriptonum Indicarum. Vol. III. Inscriptions of the early Gupta kings and their successors.* Varanasi 1970.

Forbes, Alexander Kinloch, *Râs Mâlâ. Hindu annals of the Provinces of Goozerat in Western India.* Ed. H.G. Rawlinson. 2 vols, London 1924 (first published London 1856).

Forbes, James, *Oriental memoirs.* 4 vols, London 1813.

Foster, William, ed., *Early travels in India 1583–1619.* London 1921.

Franck, Sebastian, *Wahrhafftige Beschreibunge aller theil der Welt.* N.p. 1567.

Fraser, James, *The history of Nadir Shah, formerly called Thamas Kuli Khan, the present Emperor of Persia. To which is prefixed a short history of the Moghol Emperors.* 2nd ed., London 1742.

Friend of India, The, containing information relative to the state of religion and literature in India, with occasional intelligence from Europe and America. 3 vols, Serampore 1818–1820 (see also *Essays*).

[Friend of India] = *Periodical accounts of the Serampore Mission.* New Series. Vol. 1, London 1834.

Fryer, John, *A new account of East India and Persia, in eight letters. Being nine years travels, begun 1672. And finished 1681.* London 1698.

Gandhi M.K., *Women and social injustice.* Ahmedabad 1958.

Gandhi, Raj S., Sati as altruistic suicide. Beyond Durkheim's interpretation. In: *Contributions to Asian Studies 10* (Leiden 1977), 141–57.

Ganguly, Narendranath, A note on Sati. In: *Bengal, Past and Present 70* (1951), 55–7.

Garbe, Richard, *Beiträge zur indischen Kulturgeschichte.* Berlin 1903.

Garzilli, Enrica, First Greek and Latin documents on *sahagamana* and some connected problems. In: *Indo-Iranian Journal 40* (1997), 205–43; 339–65.

Gaur, K.D., Poor victim of uses and abuses of criminal law and process in India. In: *Journal of the Indian Law Institute 35/2* (1993), 183–232.

Gaur, Meena, *Sati and social reforms in India.* Jaipur 1989.

Geleynssen de Jongh, W., *Remonstrantie.* Ed. W. Caland. Den Haag 1929.

Gonçalves, Diogo, Historia do Malavar. Ed. Josef Wicki. Münster 1955.

Gonda, Jan, *Die Religionen Indiens.* 2 vols, Stuttgart 1960–1963.

Grant, Charles, Observations on the state of society among the Asiatic subjects of Great Britain, particularly with respect to morals; and on the means of improving it. Written chiefly in the year 1792. In: *PP* 1812–1813/10, 31–146, Paper No. 282.

Greville, Charles C.F., *The Greville Memoirs. A journal of the reigns of King George IV, King William IV and Queen Victoria.* Ed. Henry Reeve. A new edition, 8 vols, London 1888.

Griffin, Lepel, *Ranjit Singh.* Delhi 1967 (first published London 1892).

Griffiths, Percival, *The British impact on India.* N.p. 1965 (first published 1953).

Grimm, Jacob, Über das Verbrennen der Leichen. In: Jacob Grimm: *Kleinere Schriften 2* (Berlin 1865, reprinted Hildesheim 1965), 211–313 (first published 1849).

Grimshawe, T.S., *An earnest appeal to British humanity in behalf of Hindoo widows; in which the abolition of the barbarous rite of burning alive, is proved to be both safe and practicable.* London 1825.

Grose, John Henry, *A voyage to the East Indies.* 2 vols, London 1772.

Guichard, Claude, *Funérailles, et diverses manieres d'ensevelir des Rommains, Grecs, et autres nations, tant anciennes que modernes.* Lyon 1581.

Gulati, Saraj, *Women and society. Northern India in 11th and 12th centuries.* Delhi 1985.

Gupta, A.R., *Women in Hindu Society (a study of tradition and transition).* New Delhi 1976.

Gupta, Maya, *Lord William Bentinck in Madras and the Vellore Mutiny, 1803–1807.* New Delhi 1986.

Gupta, Sanjukta/Gombrich, Richard, Another view of widow-burning and womanliness in Indian public culture. In: *Journal of Commonwealth and Comparative Politics 22* (1984), 252–8.

Haafner, J., *Reize in eenen Palanquin; of lotgevallen en merkwaardige aantekeningen op eene reize langs de Kusten Orixa en Chormandel.* 2 vols, Amsterdam 1808.

Hall, Fitzedward, The source of Colebrooke's essay 'On the duties of a faithful Hindu widow'. In: *Journal of the Royal Asiatic Society of Great Britain and Ireland, NS 3* (1867), 183–98.

Hamilton, Alexander, *A new account of the East Indies.* Ed. William Forster. 2 vols, reprinted Amsterdam 1970 (first published 1727).

Harlan, Lindsey, *Religion and Rajput women. The ethic of protection in contemporary narratives.* Berkeley 1992.

Harlan, Lindsey/Courtright, Paul B., eds, *From the margins of Hindu marriage. Essays on gender, religion and culture.* New York 1995.

Hawkins, William, in: Foster 70–121.

Hawley, John Stratton, ed., *Sati, the blessing and the curse. The burning of wives in India.* New York 1994.

Heber, Reginald, *Narrative of a journey through the upper provinces of India, from Calcutta to Bombay, 1824–1825*. 2 vols, London 1828.

Heckel, Waldemar/ Yardley, John C., Roman writers and the practice of suttee. In: *Philologus 125* (1981), 305–11.

Herbert, Thomas, *Some yeares travels into Africa and Asia the Great*. London 1638.

Herodotus, *Historiai/The Persian War*. 4 vols., trans. by A.D. Godley, Cambridge, Mass. 1969.

Herport, Albrecht, *Reise nach Java, Formosa, Vorder-Indien und Ceylon 1659–1668*. Ed. S.P. L'Honoré Naber. Den Haag 1930 (first published 1669).

Hervey, Charles, *Some records of crime (being the diary of a year, official and particular, of an officer of the Thaggee and Dacoitie Police)*. 2 vols, London 1892.

Hieronymus, Eusebius Sophronius, Adversus Jovinianum. In: *Opera Omnia. Magna Patrologia Latina*, ed. Jean-Paul Migne, vol. 23, Paris 1883, 221–352.

Hillebrandt, Alfred, Der freiwillige Feuertod in Indien und die Somaweihe. *Sitzungsberichte der kgl. Bayer. Akad. d. Wiss., Philos.-philol. u. histor. Klasse 1917, 8. Abh.*, München 1917.

Hirst, R.J., *Suttee: a modern instance. Extracted from The Police Journal vol. II*, 1929, pp. 297/309. In: IOL, Ms. Eur. F. 161/171.

Hodges, William, *Travels in India during the years 1780, 1781, 1782, and 1783*. London 1793.

Holwell, John Zephaniah, *Interesting historical events, relative to the provinces of Bengal, and the Empire of Hindostan*. 3 vols, London 1766–1771.

Honigberger, Johann Martin, *Früchte aus dem Morgenlande*. Wien 1851. Eng. trans.: *Thirty-five years in the East. Adventures, discoveries, experiments, and historical sketches, relating to the Punjab and Cashmere*. 2 vols, London 1851.

Horsch, Paul, Vorstufen der indischen Seelenwanderungslehre. In: *Asiatische Studien 25* (1971), 99–157.

Hough, James, Immolation of Hindoo widows. In: William Ellis, ed., *The Missionary; or Christian's New Year's gift*. London n.d. [1833], 13–21.

Hügel, Carl Freiherr von, *Kaschmir und das Reich der Siek*. 4 vols, Stuttgart 1840–1848.

Hutton, J.H., *Caste in India. Its nature, functions and origins*. Cambridge 1946.

Ibn Baṭṭūṭa, *The travels AD 1325–1354*. Ed. and trans. H.A.R. Gibb. 5 vols, London 1958–2000.

Indian Penal Code (Act XLV of 1860), ed. R. Ranchhoddas and D.K. Thakore. 27th ed., Nagpur 1994.

Ingham, Kenneth, *Reformers in India 1793–1833*. Cambridge 1956.

Interesting facts respecting the self-immolation of females. In: *The Missionary Register*, London 1821, 115–17.

Jackson, A.V. Williams, ed., *History of India. Vol. 9: Historic accounts of India by foreign travelers classic, oriental, and occidental*. London 1907 (reprinted New York 1975).

Jackson, Randle, *Substance of the speech at a general court of the proprietors of East-India stock, on Wednesday, March 28th, 1827*. London 1827.

Jacob, George Le Grand, *Western India before and during the mutinies*. 3rd ed., London 1872 (reprinted Delhi 1985).

Jacobson, Doranne, The chaste wife: cultural norm and individual experience. In: Sylvia Vatuk, ed., *American studies in the anthropology of India*, New Delhi 1978, 97–138.

Jain, Sharada *et al.*, Deorala Episode. Women's protest in Rajasthan. In: *EPW 22* (1987), 1891–1894.

Johns, William, *A collection of facts and opinions relative to the burning of widows with the dead bodies of their husbands, and to other destructive customs prevalent in British India: respectfully submitted to the consideration of Government, as soliciting a further extension of their humane interference*. Birmingham 1816.

Jolly, Julius, *Recht und Sitte (einschließlich der einheimischen Literatur)*. Straßburg 1896. (= Grundriss der indo-arischen Philologie und Altertumskunde, ed. Georg Bühler, vol. II, part 8.)

Jordanus, Friar, *Mirabilia descripta. The wonders of the east (ca. 1330)*. Ed. and trans. Henry Yule. London 1863.

Joseph, Ammu, Political parties and 'sati'. In: *EPW 26* (1991), 1025–6.

Joshi, J.C., *Lord William Bentinck. His economic, administrative, social and educational reforms*. New Delhi 1988.

Joshi, Rao Bahadur P.B., The festival of the cuckoos and the origin of the name and practice of sati. In: *Journal of the Anthropological Society of Bombay 9/8* (1912), 554–67.

Joshi, V.C., ed., *Rammohun Roy and the process of modernization in India*. Delhi 1975.

Kalhaṇa, *Rājataraṅgiṇī. A chronicle of the kings of Kashmir*. Ed. and trans. M.A. Stein. 2 vols, Westminster 1900.

Kane, Pandurang Vaman, *History of Dharmaśāstra (ancient and mediaeval civil and religious law of India)*. 2nd ed., 5 vols, Poona 1968–1975.

Kapadia, K.M., *Marriage and family in India*. 2nd ed., Bombay 1958.

Kaye, John William, *The administration of the East India Company. A history of Indian progress*. London 1853.

Kennedy, R. Hartley, *The Sutti, as witnessed at Baroda, November 29th, 1825*. London 1855. First published as: The suttee: the narrative of an eye-witness. In: *Bentley's Miscellany* 13 (1843), 241–56.

Killingley, Dermot, Varna and caste in Hindu apologetic. In: Dermot Killingley *et al.*, eds, *Hindu ritual and society*. Newcastle upon Tyne 1991, 7–31.

Kindersley, Jemima: *Letters from the island of Teneriffe, Brazil, the Cape of Good Hope, and the East Indies*. London 1777.

Kircher, Athanasius, *China monumentis . . . illustrata*. Amsterdam 1667.

Kishwar, Madhu/Vanita, Ruth, The burning of Roop Kanwar. In: *Manushi* 42/43, September–December 1987, 15–25.

Klemm, Gustav, *Allgemeine Cultur-Geschichte der Menschheit. Vol. 7: Das Morgenland*. Leipzig 1849.

Kohler, Josef, Indisches Ehe- und Familienrecht. In: *Zeitschrift für vergleichende Rechtswissenschaft 3* (1882), 342–442.

Kopf, David, *British Orientalism and the Bengal Renaissance. The dynamics of Indian modernization 1773–1835*. Berkeley 1969.

Kotnala, Mohan Chandra, *Raja Ram Mohun Roy and Indian awakening*. New Delhi 1975.

Krishna Murthy, K., The sati sacrifice and its lithographic vestige at Nagarjunakonda, Andhra Pradesh. In: *Orissa Historical Research Journal 11* (1963), 201–5.

Krishnasvami Aiyangar, S., Self-immolation which is not sati. In: *Indian Antiquary 35* (Bombay 1906), 129–31.

Kulkarni, Jeevan, Sati—shame or pride? In: *Organiser*. New Delhi 22.11.1987, 10–11.

Kumar, Radha, *The history of doing. An illustrated account of movements for women's rights and feminism in India 1800–1990*. London 1993.

Lach, Donald F., *Asia in the making of Europe*. 3 vols in 10 ports, Chicago 1965–93.

Langhanss, Christoph, *Neue Ost-Indische Reise / worinnen umständlich beschrieben werden unterschiedene Küsten und Inseln in Ost-Indien*. Leipzig 1705.

Lanman, Charles Rockwell, *A Sanskrit reader*. 2 vols, Boston 1884–1889.

Latif, Syad Muhammad, *History of the Punjáb from the remotest antiquity to the present time*. Calcutta 1891.

Le Bon, Gustave, *Les civilisations de l'Inde*. Paris 1887.

Le Couteur, John, *Letters chiefly from India, translated from the French*. London 1790.

Lee-Warner, William, *The native states of India*. 2nd ed., London 1910.

Leslie, Julia, *The perfect wife. The orthodox Hindu woman according to the* Strīdharmapaddhati *of Tryambakayajvan*. Delhi 1989.

————, A problem of choice: the Heroic Sati or the Widow–Ascetic. In: Julia Leslie, ed., *Rules and remedies in classical Indian law*, Leiden 1991, 46–61.

————, Suttee or Sati: victim or victor? In: Julia Leslie, ed., *Roles and rituals for Hindu women*, London 1991, 175–81.

Lingat, Robert, *Les sources du droit dans le système traditionnel de l'Inde*. Paris 1967.

Linschoten, Jan Huygen van, *Itinerario. Voyage ofte schipvaert van Jan Huygen van Linschoten naer Oost ofte Portugaels Indien 1579–1592*. Ed. H. Kern. Vol. 2, 2nd ed., Den Haag 1956.

Lommel, Herman, Die aufopferungsvolle Gattin im alten Indien. In: Herman Lommel: *Kleine Schriften*, ed. Klaus L. Janert, Wiesbaden 1978, 374–88. First published in: Paideuma 6 (1955), 95–109.

Longhurst, A.H., *Hampi ruins*. 3rd ed., Delhi 1993.

Loomba, Ania, Dead women tell no tales: issues of female subjectivity, subaltern agency and tradition in colonial and post-colonial writings on widow immolation in India. In: *History Workshop* (1993), 209–27.

[Lord, Henry,] *A discoverie of the sect of the Banians. Containing their history, law, liturgie, casts, customes, and ceremonies*. London 1630.

Lovett, H. Verney, Suttee. In: *Asiatic Review NS 24* (London 1928), 314–20.

Lutfullah, *Autobiography of Lutfullah, a Mohamedan gentleman; and his transactions with his fellow-creatures; interspersed with remarks on the habits, customs, and character of the people with whom he had to deal*. Ed. Edward B. Eastwick. Leipzig 1857.

Macdonald, John, On the Hindoo laws respecting the burning of widows. In: *Asiatic Journal 13* (1822), 220–6.

Macdonnell, Arthur Anthony/Keith, Arthur Berriedale, *Vedic index of names and subjects*. 2 vols, London 1912.

Mahābhārata. Vol. 1, The book of the beginning. Ed. and trans. J.A.B. von Buitenen. Chicago 1973.

Mahalingam, T.V., *Administration and social life under Vijayanagar*. Madras 1940.

Maistre, Joseph de, *Le soirées de Saint-Pétersbourg ou entretiens sur le gouvernement temporel de la providence suivies d'un traité sur les sacrifices.* 2 vols, 8th ed. Lyon 1862 (first published 1821).

Majumdar, Jatindra Kumar, ed., *Raja Rammohun Roy and progressive movements in India. A selection from records* (1775–1845). Calcutta 1941 (reprinted Delhi 1988).

Majumdar, R.C., Raja Rammohun Roy—a historical review. In: *Calcutta Review 3* (1972), 209–26.

———, Tenth annual conference. Presidential address. In: *The Quarterly Review of Historical Studies 11, 2* (1972/73), 79–83.

Malcolm, John, *A memoir of Central India, including Malwa, and adjoining provinces, with the history, and copious illustrations, of the past and present condition of that country.* 2 vols, London 1823.

Mall, Chaina, Tombs of Satis. In: *Punjab Notes and Queries 30/3* (Allahabad, March 1986), 92.

Malleson, George Bruce, *A historical sketch of the native states of India in subsidiary alliance with the British government. With a notice of the mediated and minor states.* London 1875.

Mandelslo, Johann Albrecht von, *Morgenländische Reyse-Beschreibung.* Ed. Adam Olearius. Schleswig 1658.

———, Journal und Observation (1637–1640). Ed. Margarete Refslund-Klemann. Copenhagen 1942.

Mandeville, John, *Mandeville's travels. Texts and translations.* Ed. Malcolm Letts. 2 vols, London 1953.

Mani, Lata, Contentious traditions: The debate on Sati in colonial India. In: Kumkum Sangari/Sudesh Vaid, eds, *Recasting women. Essays in colonial history.* New Delhi 1989, 88–126. Slightly modified version in: *Cultural Critique 7* (1987), 119–56.

———, Multiple mediations: feminist scholarship in the age of multi-national reception. In: *Feminist Review 35* (Summer 1990), 24–41.

———, The production of an official discourse on Sati in early nineteenth-century Bengal. In: Francis Barker *et al.*, eds, *Europe and its others, Vol. 1*, Colchester 1985, 107–27. Also in *EPW* 21 (1986), WS 32–WS 40.

Manjushree, *The position of women in the Yājñavalkyasmṛti.* New Delhi 1990.

Manrique, Sebastian, *Travels of Fray Sebastian Manrique, 1629–1643.* Ed. and trans. C. Eckford Luard/H.Hosten. 2 vols, Oxford 1927.

Manu, *The Laws of Manu*: Ed. and trans. Wendy Doniger/Brian K. Smith. London 1991.

Manucci, Niccolao, *Storia do Mogor or Mogul India 1653–1708*. Ed. and trans. William Irvine. 4 vols, London 1906–1907.

Manushi, No. 42–43 (1987): Special issue on Sati.

Marco Polo, *Il Milione. Prima edizione integrale*. Ed. Luigi Foscolo Benedetto. Firenze 1928.

———, *The travels*. Trans. Ronald Latham. Harmondsworth 1958.

Marshall, Peter J., *Bengal: the British bridgehead. Eastern India 1740–1828*. Cambridge 1987.

Marshman, John Clark, *The life and times of Carey, Marshman, and Ward, embracing the history of the Serampore Mission*. 2 vols, London 1859.

Massie, J.W., *Continental India. Travelling sketches and historical recollections, illustrating the antiquity, religion, and manners of the Hindoos, the extent of British conquests, and the progress of military operations*. 2 vols, London 1840.

Mazumdar, Vina, Comment on Suttee. In: *Signs. Journal of Women in Culture and Society 4* (1978), 269–73.

Measures for the prevention of Suttee in the Pahlumpoor districts. In: R. Hughes Thomas, ed., *Selections from the records of the Bombay Government, NS, No. 25*, Bombay 1856, 128–36 (IOR P/V/798).

Metcalf, Thomas R., *Ideologies of the Raj*. Cambridge 1994.

Methwold, William, Relations of the Kingdome of Golchonda, and other neighbouring nations (1625). In: W.H. Moreland, ed., *Relations of Golconda in the early seventeenth century* (London 1931), 1–49.

Michaels, Axel, The legislation of widow burning in 19th century Nepal. Edition and translation of the chapter *Satijānyako* of the Muluki Ain. In: *Asiatische Studien 48* (1995), 1213–40.

———, Recht auf Leben und Selbsttötung in Indien. In: Bernhard Mensen, ed., *Jenseitsvorstellungen verschiedener Völker*, St. Augustin 1985, 95–124.

———, Reinkarnation—ein morgenländisches 'Dogma'? In: *Der Evangelische Erzieher 47* (1995), 159–70.

———, Widow burning in Nepal. In: Toffin, Gérard, ed., *Nepal, past and present*, Paris 1993, 21–34.

Misra, B.B., *The central administration of the East India Company 1773–1834*. 2nd ed., Manchester 1959.

Misra, Rekha, *Women in Mughal India, 1526–1748 AD*. Delhi 1967.

Mitchell, John, *An essay on the best means of civilizing the subjects of the British Empire in India, and of diffusing the light of the Christian religion throughout the eastern world*. Edinburgh 1805.

Mitra, Kalipada, Suppression of Suttee in the Garhjat States of Orissa. In: *Bengal, Past and Present 48* (1932), 133–6.

Mitra, Rájendrála, On human sacrifices in ancient India. In: *Proceedings of the Asiatic Society of Bengal 45* (1876), 76–118.

———, On the funeral *ceremonies* of the ancient Hindus. In: *Journal of the Asiatic Society of Bengal 39/1* (1870), 241–64.

Mitter, Kalipada, Suppression of Suttee in 'the Province of Cuttack'. In: *Bengal, Past and Present 46* (1933), 125–31.

Modave, Louis Laurent de Féderbe, Comte de, *Voyage en Inde 1773–1776 (Nouveaux mémoires sur l'état actuel du Bengale et de l'Indoustan).* Ed. Jean Deloche. Paris 1971.

Modi, Jivanshi Jamshedji, The antiquity of the custom of sati. In: *Journal of the Anthropological Society of Bombay 13/5,* 412–24.

Mökern, Philipp van, *Ostindien, seine Geschichte, Cultur und seine Bewohner.* 2 vols, Leipzig 1857.

Monserrate, *The commentary of Father Monserrate,* S.J. Ed. S.N. Banerjee, trans. J.S. Hayland. London 1922.

Moor, Edward, *The Hindu Pantheon.* London 1810.

Müller, Max, *Chips from a German workshop.* 2 vols, London 1867.

Mukherjee, Amitabha, *Reform and regeneration in Bengal 1774–1823.* Calcutta 1968.

Mukherjee, Ila, *Social status of North Indian women (1526–1707 AD).* Agra 1972.

Mukhopadhyay, Amitabha, Movement for the abolition of Sati in Bengal in the 19th century. In: *Bengal, Past and Present 77* (1958), 20–41.

———, Sati as a social institution in Bengal. In: *Bengal, Past and Present 76* (1957), 99–115.

Mundy, Peter, *The travels of Peter Mundy, in Europe and Asia, 1608–1667.* Ed. Richard Carnac Temple. 5 vols, Cambridge/London 1907–1936.

Mylius, Klaus, *Geschichte der altindischen Literatur.* Leipzig 1988.

Nadarajah, Devapoopathy, *Women in Tamil society. The classical period.* Kuala Lumpur 1966.

Nag, Jamuna, *India's great social reformer. Raja Rammohun Roy.* New Delhi 1972.

Nagesh, H.V., ed., *Widowhood in India.* Ujire 1988.

Nand, Lakesh Chandra, *Women in Delhi Sultanate.* Allahabad 1989.

Nandy, Ashis, *At the edge of psychology. Essays in politics and culture.* Delhi 1980.

———, Cultures of politics and politics of cultures. In: *Journal of Commonwealth and Comparative Politics 22* (1984), 262–74.

———, Sati: a nineteenth century tale of women, violence and protest. In: V.C. Joshi, ed., 168–94 and in Nandy, ed., *Edge* 1–31.

————, Sati in Kaliyuga. In: *EPW 23* (1988), 1976.

Napier, William, *History of General Sir Charles Napier's administration of Scinde, and campaign in the Cutchee Hills.* London 1851.

Narang, Bhim Sain, *Concept of Strīdhana in ancient India.* Delhi 1991.

Narasimhan, Sakuntala, *Sati. A study of widow burning in India.* New Delhi 1990.

Natarajan, S., *A century of social reform in India.* 2nd ed., London 1962.

Navarrete, Domingo, *The travels and controversies of Friar Domingo Navarrete 1618–1686.* Ed. and trans. J.S. Cummins. 2 vols, Cambridge 1962.

Neufeldt, Ronald W., ed., *Karma and rebirth: post classical developments.* Albany 1986.

Newnham, H., *East India question. Facts and observations intended to convey the opinions of the native population of the territory of Bengal respecting the past and the future.* 2nd ed., London 1833.

Noble, William/Sankhyan, Ad Ram, Signs of the divine: satī memorials and satī worship in Rajasthan. In: Karine Schomer *et al.*, eds, *The idea of Rajasthan. Explorations in regional identity. Vol. 1: Constructions,* New Delhi 1994, 343–89.

Nunes, Baltasar, Letter of 1551 from Goa to Portugal. In: António da Silva Rego, ed., *Documentação para a historia das missões do Padroado português do Oriente,* vol. 5, Lisbona 1951, 45–59.

[Nuniz, Fernão], *Chronica dos reis de Bisnaga. Manuscripto inedito do seculo XVI.* Ed. David Lopes. Lisboa 1897. (Eng. trans. in: Robert Sewell: *A forgotten empire. Vijayanagar.* Reprinted Delhi 1962, 279–380).

Odoricus of Pordenone, in: Henry Yule, ed. and trans.: *Cathay and the way thither, being a collection of medieval notes on China.* Vol. 2, 2nd ed., London 1913 (reprinted Nendeln 1967).

O'Flaherty, Wendy Doniger, ed., *Karma and rebirth in classical Indian traditions.* Berkeley 1980.

Olafsson, Jón, *The life of the Icelander Jón Olafsson, traveller to India, written by himself and completed about 1661 AD, with a continuation, by another hand, up to his death in 1679.* Ed. and trans. Bertha S. Phillpotts and Richard Temple. 2 vols, London 1923–1932.

Oldenberg, Hermann, *Die Religion des Veda.* 2nd ed., Stuttgart 1917 (reprinted Darmstadt 1977).

Olivelle, Patrick, Ritual suicide and the rite of renunciation. In: *Wiener Zeitschrift für die Kunde Südasiens und Archiv für indische Philosophie 22* (1978), 19–44.

O'Malley, L.S.S., *History of Bengal, Bihar and Orissa under British rule.* Calcutta 1925.

On the burning of Hindoo widows. In: *Oriental Herald 8* (1826), 1–20.

On the burning of widows. In: *Friend of India 4* (Serampore 1826), 449–77.

On the criminality of burning widows alive, with a brief view of what has been already published on this subject. In: *Friend of India (Quarterly series)* 2 (Serampore 1822), 254–84.

Orlich, Leopold von, *Indien und seine Regierung.* 2 vols, Leipzig 1859–1861.

———, *Reise in Ostindien in Briefen an Alexander von Humboldt und Carl Ritter.* Leipzig 1845.

Osborne, W.G., *The court and camp of Runjeet Singh, with an introductory sketch of the origin and rise of the Shik State.* London 1840.

Ovington, John, *A voyage to Suratt, in the year 1689.* Ed. H.G. Rawlinson. London 1929 (first published London 1699).

Pakrasi, Kanti B., *Female infanticide in India.* Calcutta 1970.

Paolino da San Bartolomeo, *Viaggio alle Indie orientali umilita alla Santità di N.S. Papa Pio Sesto, Pontefício Massimo.* Roma 1796.

Papers relating to East India affairs, viz., Hindoo widows and voluntary immolation. Ordered by the House of Commons to be printed. 1821–1825. In: *Calcutta Review 46* (1868), 221–61.

Parks, Fanny, *Wanderings of a pilgrim in search of the picturesque, during four-and-twenty years in the East; with revelations of life in the Zenana.* 2 vols, London 1850.

Parliamentary Debates, vol. 26, London 1813. New Series, vol. 5–25, London 1822–1830.

Pasquier, L.M.C., *Précis de l'histoire de l'Hindoustan.* Paris 1843.

Patel, Sujata/Kumar, Krishna, Defenders of Sati. In: *EPW 23* (1988), 129–30.

Pathak, Madhusudan M., Dakṣayajñavidhvaṁsa-episode in Purāṇas. A comparative study. In: *Purana 20* (Benares 1978), 204–23.

Patnaik, Nihar Ranjan, *Social history of 19th century Orissa.* Allahabad 1989.

Pearce, George, *Suttee or Sati.* Talk given to the 'Friends in Council', a Cheltenham group of intelligencia. N.d. IOL Ms. Eur. F 161/170.

Peggs, James, *India's cries to British humanity, relative to infanticide, British connection with idolatry, Ghaut murders, suttee, slavery, and colonization in India; to which are added hints for the melioration of the state of society in British India.* 3rd ed., London 1832.

———, *The Suttee's cry to Britain; containing extracts from essays published in India and Parliamentary Papers on the burning of Hindoo widows: shewing that the rite is not an integral part of the religion of the Hindoos, but a horrid custom, opposed to the Institutes of Menu, and a violation of every principle of justice and humanity: respectfully submitted to the consideration of all who are interested in the welfare of British India; and soliciting the interference of the British Government, and of the Honorable the Court of Directors of the Honorable East India Company, to suppress this suicidal practice.* London 1827.

————, *The Suttee's cry to Britain; showing from essays published in India and official documents that the custom of burning Hindoo widows is not an integral part of Hindoism; and may be abolished with ease and safety.* 2nd ed., London n.d. [1828].

[Peggs, James ?], Meeting for the abolition of the burning of widows in India. In: *Oriental Herald* 20 (London 1829), 539–45.

Pelsaert, Francisco, *De Geschriften van Francisco Pelsaert over Mughal Indië, 1627. Kroniek en Remonstrantie.* Ed. D.H.A. Kolff/H.W. van Santen. Den Haag 1979.

————, *Jahangir's India. The Remonstrantie of Francisco Pelsaert.* Trans. W.H. Moreland. Cambridge 1925.

Pires, Tomé, *The Suma Oriental. An account of the East, from the Red Sea to Japan, written in Malacca and India in 1512–1515.* Ed. and Eng. trans. Armando Cortesão. Reprinted Nendeln 1967.

Plutarch, *Moralia.* Vol. 6, trans. by W.C. Helmbold, Cambridge, Mass. 1957.

————, Philopoemen. In: *Plutarch, Vitae Parallelae / Parallel Lives.* Vol. 10, trans. by Bernadotte Perrin, Cambridge, Mass. 1969, 255–319.

Postans, Marianne, *Cutch, or random sketches, taken during a residence in one of the northern provinces of western India; interspersed with legends and traditions.* London 1839.

Potts, E. Daniel, *British Baptist missionaries in India 1793–1837. The history of Serampore and its missions.* Cambridge 1967.

Poynder, John, *Human sacrifices in India. Substance of the speech of John Poynder, Esquire at the Courts of Proprietors of East Indian Stock, held on the 21st and 28th days of March 1827.* London 1827.

Prinsep, Henry T./Thornton, Thomas, *History of the Punjab, and of the rise, progress, and present condition of the sect and nation of the Sikhs.* 2 vols, London 1846.

Propertius, *Elegiae/Elegies.* Trans. by G.P. Goold, Cambridge, Mass. 1990.

Pyrard de Laval, François, *Voyage . . . contenant sa navigation aux Indes Orientales.* 2 parts, Paris 1619.

Qadeer, Imrana/Hasan, Zoya, Deadly politics of the state and its apologists. In: *EPW 22* (1987), 1946–1949.

Queen v. Mohit Pandey. In: *North Western Provinces High Court Reports* 3 (1871), 316.

Quigley, Declan, *The interpretation of caste.* Oxford 1993.

R., H., Immolation of widows. Letter to the editor of the Bengal Hurkaru, dated Jessore, 13.4.1826. In: *The Wesleyan-Methodist Magazine 50* (3rd series, vol. 6, 1827), 50–1.

Rahman, Muqaddesur, The custom of widow-burning in India. In: *Journal of the Bangladesh Itihas Samiti 2* (1973), 111–43.

Rajan, Rajeswari Sunder, *Real and imagined women. Gender, culture and postcolonialism.* London 1993.

————, The subject of Sati: pain and death in the contemporary discourse on Sati. In: *Yale Journal of Criticism 3/2* (1990), 1–27 (= chap. 2 of Rajan, *Women*).

Ram, Susan, Ram's Englishman. In: *EPW 27* (1992), 2172–4.

Rammohun Roy. In: *Calcutta Review 4* (1845), 355–93.

Ramusio, Giovanni Battista, *Navigazioni e viaggi.* Ed. Marica Milanesi. Vol. 1, Torino 1978.

Rao, Sakuntala, Suttee. In: *Annals of the Bhandarkar Research Institute 14* (Poona 1932/33), 219–40.

[Ravesteyn, Pieter Gielisz van,] Description of the country ruled by King Cotebipu, situated on the Coromandel Coast (ca. 1614). In: W.H. Moreland, ed., *Relations of Golconda in the early seventeenth century* (London 1931), 67–86.

Ray, Ajit Kumar, *Widows are not for burning. Actions and attitudes of the Christian Missionaries, the Native Hindus and Lord William Bentinck.* New Delhi 1985.

Ray, Rajat K., Introduction, in: V.C. Joshi, ed., 1–20.

Reïs, Sidi Ali, *The travels and adventures of the Turkish admiral Sidi Ali Reïs in India, Afghanistan, Central Asia and Persia, during the years 1553–1556.* Ed. and trans. Armin Vambéry. London 1899.

Remarks on the immolations in India; and particularly on the destruction of 1528 females burnt or buried alive in Bengal, in the years 1815, 1816, and 1817: as authenticated by a copy of the official returns now in England: with various arguments that these immolations may be safely and easily suppressed. London 1821.

Rennefort, Souchu de, Histoire des Indes orientales. Paris 1688.

Resende, Garcia de, *Miscellanea e variedade de historias, costumes, casos, e cousas que em seu tempo aconteceram.* Ed. Mendes dos Remedios. Coimbra 1917 (first published 1554).

Rig-Veda. Aus dem Sanskrit ins Deutsche übersetzt und mit einem laufenden Kommentar versehen von Karl Friedrich Geldner. 4 vols, Cambridge, Mass. 1951–1957.

Robinson, Edward Jewitt, *The daughters of India: their social condition, religion, literature, obligations, and prospects.* Glasgow 1860 (reprinted Ann Arbor 1980).

Rogerius, Abraham, *De open-deure tot het verborgen Heydendom.* Ed. W. Caland. Den Haag 1915.

Rosselli, John, *Lord William Bentinck. The making of a liberal imperialist 1774–1839.* London 1974.

Roth, Rudolf, Die Todtenbestattung im indischen Altertum. In: *Zeitschrift der Deutschen Morgenländischen Gesellschaft 8* (1854), 467–75.

Roy, Benoy Bhusan, *Socio-economic impact of sati in Bengal and the role of Raja Rammohun Roy.* Calcutta 1987.

Roy, Rammohun, *The English works.* Ed. Jogendra Chunder Ghose. 2 vols, Calcutta 1885–1887.

———, *The English works.* Ed. Kalidas Nag and Debajyoti Burman. Vol. 3, Calcutta 1947.

———, Some remarks in vindication of the resolution passed by the government of Bengal in 1829 abolishing the practice of female sacrifices in India. In: *Modern Review 55* (1934), 272–6.

Rüping, Klaus, Zur Askese in indischen Religionen. In: *Zeitschrift für Missionswissenschaft und Religionswissenschaft 61* (1977), 81–98.

Saar, Johann Jacob, *Reise nach Java, Banda, Ceylon und Persien 1644–1660.* Ed. S.P. L'Honoré Naber. Den Haag 1930 (first published 1662).

Sakala, Carol, *Women of South Asia. A guide to resources.* New York 1980.

Salahuddin Ahmed, A.F., *Social ideas and social change in Bengal 1818–1835.* Leiden 1965.

Saldanha, Mariano, O sati Hindu e o centenário da sua abolição. In: *Biblios 6* (1930), 360–80.

Sangari, Kumkum, Perpetuating of the myth. In: *Seminar* no. 342 (1988), 24–30 and in *Anand* 104–18.

Sangari, Kumkum/Vaid, Sudesh, Sati in modern India: A report. In: *EPW 16* (1981), 1284–8.

Santos, Joâo de, *Ethiopia Oriental e varia historia de cousas notaveis do Oriente.* 2 vols, Lisbon 1891–1892 (first published 1609).

Sarasvati, Ramabai, *The high-caste Hindu woman.* Philadelphia 1887.

Sarma, Suresh Chandra Deba, *The practice of 'suttee' in Ancient India.* N.p. 1935.

Sassetti, Filippo, *Lettere di vari paesi.* Ed. Vanni Bramanti. Milano 1970.

Sati and the State, in: *EPW* 22 (1987), 2233.

Sauvaget, Jean, ed. and trans., *'Aḫbār aṣ-Sin wa l-Hind. Relation de la Chine et de l'Inde rédigée en 851.* Paris 1948.

Saxena, R.K., *Education and social amelioration of women (a study of Rajasthan).* Jaipur 1978.

———, *Social reforms. Infanticide and sati.* New Delhi 1975.

Schouten, Wouter, *Oost-Indische Voyagie.* 2 parts, Amsterdam 1676.

Schroeder, Leopold von, *Indiens Literatur und Cultur in historischer Entwicklung.* Leipzig 1887.

Seed, Geoffrey, The abolition of Suttee in Bengal. In: *History, NS 40* (1955), 286–99.

Seminar, The Monthly Symposium: No. 342, February 1988: Sati. A symposium on widow immolation and its social context.

Sen, Dinesh Chandra, *Sati. A mythological story.* Calcutta n.d. [1916].

Sen, Surendra Nath, *Eighteen Fifty-Seven.* N.p. 1957.

Settar, S., *Inviting death. Indian attitude towards the ritual death.* Leiden 1989.

Settar, S./Sontheimer, Günther D., eds, *Memorial stones. A study of their origin, significance and variety.* Dharwad 1982 (also Wiesbaden 1982).

Sharma, Arvind, Emile Durkheim on Suttee as suicide. In: *International Journal of Contemporary Sociology 15* (1978), 283–91.

———, The scriptural sanction for Suttee in Hinduism. In: *Glory of India 2/3* (Sep. 1978), 11–16.

———, *Thresholds in Hindu-Buddhist studies.* Calcutta 1979.

Sharma, Arvind *et al.*, *Sati. Historical and phenomenological essays.* Delhi 1988.

Sharma, *Brijendra Nath: Social and cultural history of Northern India c. 1000–1200 AD.* New Delhi 1972.

Shastri, Shakuntala Rao, *Women in the sacred laws.* Bombay 1959.

Shee, Monika, *Tapas und tapasvin in den erzählenden Partien des Mahābhārata.* Reinbek 1986.

Shepherd, H., *Cursory remarks on the inefficiency of the ecclesiastical establishment of India, under the present system; and on the expediency of appointing a second bishop to the eastward of the Cape.* London 1827.

Shore, Frederick John, *Notes on Indian affairs.* 2 vols, London 1837

Singh, Indu/Prakash Renuka, Sati: The patri-politics. In: Sushma Sood, ed., *Violence against women.* Jaipur 1990, 363–72.

Singh, Iqbal, *Rammohun Roy. A biographical inquiry into the making of modern India*. Vol. 1, 2nd ed., Bombay 1983 (first published 1958).

Singh, Prabash P., *Women in India: a statistical panorama*. New Delhi 1991.

Singh, Santosh, *A passion for flames*. Jaipur 1989.

Singha, Radhika, The privilege of taking life: some 'anomalies' in the law of homicide in the Bengal Presidency. In: *Indian Economic and Social History Review 30* (1993), 181–214.

Sircar, D.C., *Studies in the society and administration of ancient and medieval India. Vol. 1: Society*. Calcutta 1967.

Sketch of popular ideas relative to the Burning of Widows, Shraddhas or Funeral Feasts, etc. taken from recent occurrences. In: *The Friend of India, Quarterly Series, Vol. 3* (Serampore 1825), 33–65.

Sleeman, William Henry, *Rambles and recollections of an Indian official*. Revised annotated edition by Vincent A. Smith. Reprinted Karachi 1973 (first published 1844).

Smith, George, *The life of William Carey, D.D., shoemaker and missionary*. London 1885.

Smith, Jane Idleman/Haddad, Yvonne Yazbeck, *The Islamic understanding of death and resurrection*. Albany 1981.

Smith, Vincent A., *The Oxford history of India*. Oxford 1919.

Solvyns, F. Baltazard, *A collection of two hundred and fifty coloured etchings descriptive of the manners, customs and dresses of the Hindoos*. 2 vols, Calcutta 1799.

Sonnerat, *Voyage aux Indes orientales et à la Chine, fait par ordre du Roi, depuis 1774 jusqu'en 1781*. 2 vols, Paris 1782.

Sontheimer, Günther-Dietz, *The joint Hindu family. Its evolution as a legal institution*. New Delhi 1977.

———, Some memorial monuments of western India. In: *German scholars on India. Contributions to Indian studies*. Vol. 2, Bombay 1976, 264–75.

Sousa, Esther Trigo de, A cremação das viúvas no Sul da Índia. In: *Actas do Congresso Internacional de Etnografia 1963*, vol. 4 (1965), 231–5.

Spivak, Gayatri Chakravorty, Can the Subaltern speak? In: Cary Nelson and Lawrence Grossberg, eds, *Marxism and the interpretation of culture*, Urbana, Illinois 1988, 271–313.

Sprockhoff, Joachim Friedrich, Die Alten im alten Indien. Ein Versuch nach brahmanischen Quellen. In: *Saeculum 30* (1979), 374–433.

———, *Saṃnyāsa. Quellenstudien zur Askese im Hinduismus. I. Untersuchung über die Saṃnyāsa-Upaniṣads*. Wiesbaden 1976.

Srinivas, M.N., A note on Sanskritization and Westernization. In: *Far Eastern Quarterly 15* (1955/56), 481–96.

Srivastava, Kanhaiya Lall, *The position of Hindus under the Delhi Sultanate 1206–1526*. New Delhi 1980.

Statham, John, *Indian recollections*. London 1832.

Stavorinus, John Splinter, *Voyages to the East-Indies*. Trans. from the Dutch by Samuel Hull Wilcocke. 3 vols, London 1798 (reprinted London 1969).

Stein, Dorothy, Burning widows, burning brides: the perils of daughterhood in India. In: *Pacific Affairs 61* (1988), 465–85.

——, Women to burn: suttee as a normative institution. In: Jagdish P. Sharma, ed., *Individualism and ideas in modern India*, Calcutta 1982, 41–75. (Abridged version in: *Signs. Journal of Women in Culture and Society 4*, 1978, 253–68, with a commentary by Vina Mazumdar, ibid., 269–73.)

Steinbach, Henry, *The Punjaub, being a brief account of the country of the Sikhs. With an introduction by W.H. McLeod*. Karachi 1976 (reprint of the 2nd ed., London 1846).

Sternbach, Ludwik, Indian tales and the smṛti-s: the tale of the clever magician (Vikramacarita). In: *Vishveshvaranand Indological Journal 10* (1972), 1–21.

Stietencron, H. von, Suicide as a religious institution. In: *Bharatiya Vidya 27* (1967), 7–24.

Stokes, Eric, *The English Utilitarians and India*. Oxford 1959.

Strabo, *Geographia/Geography*. 8 vols., trans. by Horace L. Jones, Cambridge, Mass. 1969.

Struys, Jan Janszoon, *Drie aanmerkelijke en seer rampspoedige Reysen door Italien, Griekenlandt, Lijflandt, Moscovien, Tartarijen, Meden, Persien, Oost-Indien, Japan, en verscheyden andere gewesten*. Amsterdam 1676.

[Stuart, Charles,] *Vindication of the Hindoos from the aspersions of the Reverend Claudius Buchanan, M.A. By a Bengal Officer*. London 1808.

Stutchbury, Elizabeth, Blood, fire and mediation: human sacrifice and widow burning in nineteenth century India. In: Michael Allen/S.N. Mukherjee, eds, *Women in India and Nepal*, Canberra 1982, 21–75.

Sutherland, Sally S., Suttee, Sati, and Sahagamana. An epic misunderstanding? In: *EPW 29* (1994), 1595–1605.

Suttee, The, A poem, with notes. London 1846.

Suttees. In: *Asiatic Journal 24* (1827), 277–84; 405–10.

Suttees. In: *Asiatic Journal NS 2/2* (1830), 205–6.

Swaminathan, A., Self immolation and human sacrifice in the history of South India. In: *Journal of Tamil Studies 16* (1979), 10–18.

Tafur, Pero, *Travels and adventures 1435–1439*. Ed. and trans. Malcolm Letts. London 1926.

Tavernier, Jean Baptiste, *Les six voyages . . . en Turquie, en Perse, et aux Indes, pendant l'espace de quarante ans*. 2 vols, Paris 1676.

Tawney, Charles Henry/ Penzer, N.M., eds, *The ocean of story*. Vol. 4 (London 1924, reprinted Delhi 1968), Appendix I, 255–72: Widow-Burning.

Tejsingh v. The State. In: *All India Reporter 1958 Rajasthan*, 169–72.

Temple, Richard Carnac, Panjab—Bashar—Song of a Sati—Himalayan dialect. In: *Indian Notes and Queries 4* (Oct. 1886), 17–18.

Terry, Edward, in: *Foster* 291–332.

Thackeray Ritchie, Anne/Evans, Richardson: *Lord Amherst and the British advance eastwards to Burma*. Oxford 1894.

Thakur, Upendra, *The history of suicide in India. An introduction*. Delhi 1963.

———, Self-immolation in India (1206–1765 AD) In: *Journal of the Bihar Research Society 52* (1966), 117–42.

Thapar, Romila, Death and the Hero. In: S.C. Humphreys/Helen King, eds, *Mortality and immortality: the anthropology and archaeology of death*, London 1981, 293–315.

Thevenot: *Voyages . . . en Europe, Asie et Afrique*. 3rd ed., 5 vols, Amsterdam 1727.

Thomas, Paul, *Women and marriage in India*. London 1939.

Thompson, Edward, The prohibition of widow-burning in British India. In: *London Quarterly Review 148* (1927), 57–66.

———, The suppression of suttee in native states. In: *Edinburgh Review 245* (1927), 274–86.

———, *Suttee. A historical and philosophical enquiry into the Hindu rite of widow-burning*. London 1928.

Thorburn, S.S., *The Punjab in war and peace*. Edinburgh 1904.

Tod, James, *Annals and antiquities of Rajasthan or the central and western Rajput states of India*. Ed. William Crooke. 3 vols, Oxford 1920 (first published 1829).

Townley, Henry, The Suttee. In: William Ellis, ed., *The missionary; or Christian's New Year's gift*. London n.d. [1833], 139–42.

Trial by fire. A report on Roop Kanwar's death. N.p., n.d. [1987]. Printed on behalf of the Women and Media Committee, Bombay Union of Journalist (sic), Bombay, n. pag.

Tully, Mark, *No full stops in India*. London 1991.

Tupper, Charles Lewis, *Our Indian protectorate. An introduction to the study of the relations between the British government and its Indian feudatories*. London 1893.

Twining, Thomas, *Travels in India a hundred years ago with a visit of the United States*. Ed. William H.G. Twining. London 1893.

[Twist, Johan van,] Generale Beschrijvinge van Indien. In: [Isaac Commelin,] ed., *Begin ende Voortgangh van de Vereenighde Nederlantsche Geoctroyeerde Oost-Indische Compagnie*. Vol. 2, n.p. 1646 (separately paginated).

Upadhyay, H.C., *Status of women in India*. 2 vols, New Delhi 1991.

Upadhyaya, Bhagwat Saran, *Women in Rgveda*. 3rd ed., New Delhi 1974.

Upreti, H.C./Upreti, Nandini, *The myth of Sati (some dimensions of widow burning)*. Bombay 1991.

Vaid, Sudesh/ Sangari, Kumkum, Institutions, beliefs, ideologies. Widow immolation in contemporary Rajasthan. In: *EPW 26* (1991), WS 2–18.

Valentyn, François, *Oud en Nieuw Oost-Indiën*. 5 vols, Dordrecht 1724–1726.

Valerius Maximus, *Memorable Doings and Sayings*. 2 vols., trans. by D.R. Shackleton, Cambridge, Mass. 2000.

Valle, Pietro della, *Viaggi*. 4 vols, Roma 1658–1663.

Van den Bosch, Lourens P., A burning question. Sati and sati temples as the focus of political interest. In: *Numen 37* (1990), 174–94.

Van den Broecke, Pieter, *Pieter van den Broecke in Azië*. Ed. W. Ph. Coolhaas. 2 vols, Den Haag 1962–1963.

Varthema, Ludovico de, *Itinerario*. Roma 1510.

Vigne, G.T., *Travels in Kashmir, Ladak, Iskardo, the countries adjoining the mountain-course of the Indus, and the Himalaya, north of the Punjab*. 2 vols, London 1842.

Vincenzo Maria di S. Caterina da Siena, *Il viaggio all'Indie orientali*. Venezia 1678.

Vishnoi, Savita, *Economic status of women in ancient India*. Meerut n.d. [*ca*. 1988].

Walker, Benjamin, *Hindu world. An encyclopedic survey of Hinduism*. 2 vols, London 1968.

Walsh, E.H.C., Virakal and sati memorial stones at Buddhpur and Buram. In: *Journal of the Bihar and Orissa Research Society 23* (1937), 429–43.

Ward, William, *Account of the writings, religion, and manners, of the*

Hindoos: including translations from their principal works. 4 vols, Serampore 1811.

——, *Farewell letters to a few friends in Britain and America, on returning to Bengal in 1821*. London 1821.

——, *A view of the history, literature, and mythology of the Hindoos: including a minute description of their manners and customs, and translations from their principal works*. 3 vols, London 1822.

Weinberger-Thomas, Catherine, Cendres d'immortalité. La crémation des veuves en Inde. In: *Archives de sciences sociales des religions 67* (1989), 9–51.

——, *Cendres d'immortalité. La crémation des veuves en Inde*. Paris 1996. Engl. trans. by Jeffrey Mehlman and David G. White, Chicago 2000.

Wilberforce, William, Substance of the speeches of William Wilberforce, Esq. on the clause in the East-India Bill for promoting the religious instruction and moral improvement of the natives of the British dominions in India, on the 22nd of June, and the 1st and 12th of July, 1813. In: *The Pamphleteer 3* (1814), 43–113.

Wilkins, W.J., *Modern Hinduism, being an account of the religion and life of the Hindus in northern India*. London 1887.

Wilson, Horace Hayman, On the supposed vaidik authority for the burning of Hindu widows and on the funeral ceremonies of the Hindus. In: H.H. Wilson: *Works*, vol. 2, London 1862, 270–92 (first published 1854).

Wintergerst, Martin, *Reisen auf dem mittelländischen Meere, der Nordsee, nach Ceylon und nach Java 1668–1710*. Ed. S.P. L'Honoré Naber. 2 vols, Den Haag 1932 (first published 1712).

Winternitz, Moritz, *Die Frau in den indischen Religionen. Part I: Die Frau im Brahmanismus*. Leipzig 1920.

——, *Geschichte der indischen Literatur*. 3 vols, Leipzig 1908–1920.

——, Die Witwe im Veda. In: *Wiener Zeitschrift für die Kunde des Morgenlandes 29* (1915), 172–203.

Withington, Nicholas, In: Foster 196–233.

Woodruff, Philip, *The men who ruled India*. 2 vols, London 1953–1954.

Wurffbain, Johann Sigmund, *Reise nach den Molukken und Vorder-Indien 1632–1646*. Ed. R. Posthumus Meyjes. 2 vols, Den Haag 1931 (first published 1686).

Yang, Anand A., Whose sati? Widow-burning in early nineteenth century India. In: Johnson-Odim, Cheryl/Strobel, Margaret, eds, *Expanding the boundaries of women's history*, Bloomington 1992, 74–98.

Yule, Henry, *Cathay and the way thither, being a collection of medieval notices of China*. 2nd ed., ed. Henri Cordier, 4 vols, reprinted Nendeln 1967 (first published 1913–1916).

Yule, Henry/ Burnell, A.C., *Hobson-Jobson. A glossary of colloquial Anglo-Indian words and phrases, and of kindred terms, etymological, historical, geographical and discursive*. 3rd ed., ed. William Crooke, London 1903 (reprinted Delhi 1979).

Zachariae, Theodor, Zur indischen Witwenverbrennung. In: *Zeitschrift des Vereins für Volkskunde 14* (1904), 198–210; 302–13; 395–407; 15 (1905) 74–90. Also in: Theodor Zachariae: *Opera Minora*, ed. Claus Vogel, vol. 2, Wiesbaden 1977, 545–99.

Zimmer, Heinrich, *Altindisches Leben. Die Cultur der vedischen Arier nach den Samhita dargestellt*. Berlin 1879.

Index

(Page numbers in *italics* refer to the footnotes)